Marko Bender

Spatial Proximity in Venture Capital Financing

GABLER RESEARCH

Entrepreneurial and Financial Studies

Herausgeber:

Professor Dr. Dr. Ann-Kristin Achleitner
und Professor Dr. Christoph Kaserer

Die Schriftenreihe präsentiert aktuelle Forschungsergebnisse aus dem Gebiet der Entrepreneurial und Corporate Finance. Sie greift an der Schnittstelle von Wissenschaft und Praxis innovative Fragestellungen der Unternehmensfinanzierung auf.

This series presents research results from the fields of entrepreneurial and corporate finance. Its focus lies on innovative research topics at the interface of science and practice.

Marko Bender

Spatial Proximity in Venture Capital Financing

A Theoretical and Empirical Analysis of Germany

GABLER

RESEARCH

Bibliographic information published by the Deutsche Nationalbibliothek
The Deutsche Nationalbibliothek lists this publication in the Deutsche Nationalbibliografie; detailed bibliographic data are available in the Internet at http://dnb.d-nb.de.

Dissertation Technische Universität München, 2010

This series was published from 2003 to 2007 by Verlag Wissenschaft & Praxis Dr. Brauner.

1st Edition 2011

Editorial Office: Stefanie Brich | Britta Göhrisch-Radmacher

Gabler Verlag is a brand of Springer Fachmedien.
Springer Fachmedien is part of Springer Science+Business Media.
www.gabler.de

Cover design: KünkelLopka Medienentwicklung, Heidelberg
Printed on acid-free paper
Printed in Germany

ISBN 978-3-8349-2684-5

Für meine Eltern,

ihre unendliche Liebe, unermüdliche Unterstützung

und grenzenloses Vertrauen.

Acknowledgments

This dissertation results from my work as a scientific assistant at the KfW Endowed Chair in Entrepreneurial Finance and the Center for Entrepreneurial and Financial Studies (CEFS) at the Technische Universität München (TUM). However, the completion of this dissertation would not have been possible without the support of many different individuals to whom I want to express my sincere appreciation and gratitude.

First of all, I am deeply indebted to Prof. Dr. Dr. Ann-Kristin Achleitner for taking over the supervision of my thesis and supporting me and my work in many different aspects. Throughout the early stages of my dissertation she inspired me with valuable ideas and gave me a lot of freedom to work on manifold topics in order to find the research questions for my thesis. In the course of my work she was always available for diverse discussions and finally she motivated me frequently. Furthermore, she is mainly responsible for the outstanding working environment at her chair and that I was able to conduct various interesting as well as challenging tasks with a high level of responsibility. The deep trust that she had into me and my work is a huge honor for me.

I am also grateful to Prof. Dr. Christoph Kaserer, the second referee of my thesis, for the initial support of my thesis, the help in acquiring the necessary data, and the fruitful discussions. Moreover, I would like to thank Prof. Dr. Isabell Welpe for taking over the chair of my doctoral examination committee.

Throughout my time at the KfW Endowed Chair in Entrepreneurial Finance and the CEFS I found a very kind working environment, had the opportunity to work together with many exceptional colleagues and found real friends. This combination facilitated very productive and critical scientific discussions without missing out a healthy portion of fun. In particular, I would like to express my sincere appreciation to Dr. Eva Lutz for her outstanding professional and personal support. She was always there for detailed discussions, gave profound feedback, and spent many hours for proofreading. Furthermore, I would like to thank Dr. Stephanie Schraml, Dr. Peter Heister, Dr. Markus Ampenberger, Dr. Oliver Klöckner, Dr. Annabell Geidner, Dr. Reiner Braun, Dr. Kay Müller, Nina Günther, Svenja Jarchow, Florian Tappeiner and Nico Engel for their unique team spirit, their adorable helpfulness, their invaluable input to my work in numerous discussions, and the many memorable moments that we enjoyed together. A special thank goes to Monika Paul, the heart of the chair having always a smile on her face, a story to tell, and who supported me in many aspects of my daily work.

Beyond the university I owe a special gratitude to my friends. They supported me emotionally and were allways there whenever I needed them, even though I did not have much time and they had to be satisfied with a telephone call many times. In particular, I would like to thank Danielle Lee for her selfless helpfulness in proofreading the whole dissertation from the viewpoint of a native speaker.

Throughout my dissertation my fiancée Daniela Meyer played a very special role and I want to express my warmest gratitude for all the love, care, and emotional support. Especially in the final phase of my dissertation she had to compromise a lot on spare time activities and supported me wherever she could, proofread the whole work and gave valuable feedback.

Last but not least I want to express my deepest gratitude to my family. Throughout all the years my beloved parents Karin and Hartmut Bender where always in place when I needed them, gave me the maximum emotional and active support possible, and trusted into me and my capabilities. My brother Stefan Bender was always there when I needed somebody to discuss or simply to chat and made sure that I got some diversion whenever I needed it.

Nuremberg, July, 2010
Dr. Marko Bender

Table of Contents

List of Figures XIII

List of Tables XV

List of Abbreviations XVII

List of Symbols XIX

1 Introduction 1

1.1 Problem and Aims of Analysis 1

1.2 Research Methodology 5

1.3 Outline of the Thesis 7

2 Fundamentals of Venture Capital Financing and Spatial Proximity 11

2.1 Venture Capital Financing 11

2.1.1 Definition of Venture Capital 11

2.1.2 Characteristics of Portfolio Companies 14

2.1.3 Characteristics of German Venture Capitalist Types 15

2.1.3.1 Private Venture Capitalists 17

2.1.3.2 (Quasi-)public Venture Capitalists 18

2.1.4 Venture Capital Investment Process 21

2.1.4.1 Deal Origination 22

2.1.4.2 Deal Screening 26

2.1.4.3 Deal Due Diligence 28

2.1.4.4 Deal Structuring 32

2.1.4.5 Investment Development 35

2.1.4.6 Investment Exit 38

2.2 Spatial Proximity 41

2.2.1 Definition of Spatial Proximity 41

2.2.2 Spatial Distribution of Venture Capitalists and Venture Capital Investments 42

2.2.3 First Implications Regarding the Role of Spatial Proximity in Venture Capital Financing 44

2.3 Overview of Relevant Literature 46

3 Relevant Theories for the Analysis of Spatial Proximity in Venture Capital Financing 61

3.1 Identification of Relevant Theories 61

3.2 Theories Relevant to the Venture Capitalist - Entrepreneur Dyad 66

3.2.1 New Institutional Economics as Starting Point 66

3.2.1.1 Property Rights Theory 68

3.2.1.2 Agency Theory 71

3.2.1.3 Transaction Cost Theory 88

3.2.2 Further Theories Explaining the Role of Spatial Proximity 94

3.2.2.1 Game Theory 94

3.2.2.2 Stewardship Theory 102

3.2.2.3 Social Exchange Theory 109

3.3 Theories Relevant beyond the Venture Capitalist - Entrepreneur Dyad: Network Approach 116

3.3.1 Theoretical Foundations 117

3.3.1.1 Approach of Inter-Organizational Networks 119

3.3.1.2 Formal Network Analysis 122

3.3.2 Relevant Networks 124

3.3.3 Implications of Spatial Proximity between Actors 130

3.4 Summary 131

4 Impact of Spatial Proximity throughout the Venture Capital Investment Process 133

4.1 Pre-Contractual Activities 135

4.1.1 Deal Origination 135

4.1.2 Deal Screening 141

4.1.3 Deal Due Diligence 145

4.1.4 Deal Structuring 153

4.2 Post-Contractual Activities 154

4.2.1 Investment Development 154

4.2.1.1 Monitoring 154

4.2.1.2 Support 159

4.2.2 Investment Exit 168

4.3 Summary and Testable Hypotheses 174

4.3.1 General Impact of Distance 175

4.3.2 New Venture Characteristics 178

4.3.3 Venture Capitalist Characteristics 181

4.3.4 Investment Round Characteristics 185

5 Empirical Analysis of Relationships between Spatial Proximity and the Type and Likelihood of Venture Capital Financing ... 187

5.1 Description of Dataset ... 188

5.1.1 Available Datasets for Analysis ... 188

5.1.2 Used Dataset ... 189

5.1.3 Measurement and Definition of Variables ... 195

5.1.3.1 Spatial Proximity ... 195

5.1.3.2 New Venture Characteristics ... 196

5.1.3.3 Venture Capitalist Characteristics ... 199

5.1.3.4 Investment Round Characteristics ... 202

5.1.3.5 Control Variables ... 204

5.1.4 Summary Statistics ... 206

5.1.5 Possible Selection Biases ... 208

5.2 Patterns in Spatial Proximity between Venture Capitalists and Investees ... 214

5.2.1 Empirical Strategy to Investigate Patterns in Spatial Proximity ... 214

5.2.2 First Bivariate Analyses ... 217

5.2.3 Ordered Logistic Regressions ... 222

5.2.4 Robustness Tests of Conducted Analyses ... 235

5.2.5 Limitations of Analyses ... 236

5.3 Impact of Spatial Proximity on the Likelihood of a Venture Capital Investment ... 238

5.3.1 Empirical Strategy to Investigate the Likelihood of a Venture Capital Investment ... 238

5.3.2 Rare Event Logistic Regressions ... 245

5.3.3 Robustness Tests of Conducted Analyses ... 272

5.3.4 Limitations of Analyses ... 273

5.4 Summary of Results and Discussion ... 274

6 Conclusion ... 285

6.1 Summary of Results ... 286

6.2 Implications of the Impact of Spatial Proximity on Venture Capital Financing ... 291

6.2.1 Implications for Entrepreneurs ... 291

6.2.2 Policy Implications ... 293

6.2.3 Implications for Venture Capitalists ... 296

6.3 Further Research and Outlook ... 297

Appendix **299**

A Definitions from VentureSource **299**

A.1 Venture Financing Round Types 299

A.2 Stages of Development 300

B Appendix – Description of Dataset **301**

C Appendix – Patterns in Spatial Proximity **302**

D Appendix – Likelihood of a Venture Capital Investment **315**

References **331**

List of Figures

Figure 1.1: Structure of the thesis ... 9

Figure 2.1: Differentiation of venture capital and private equity ... 11

Figure 2.2: Phases of the VC investment process ... 21

Figure 2.3: Initiation of contact between venture capitalist and entrepreneurial team ... 23

Figure 2.4: Exit channels of venture capitalists in Germany ... 39

Figure 2.5: Spatial distribution of venture capitalists and VC financing rounds across German districts ... 45

Figure 2.6: Embeddedness of this thesis in the relevant literature ... 47

Figure 3.1: Relevant theories to explain the role of spatial proximity between actors in the VC investment process ... 65

Figure 3.2: Classification of theories within new institutional economics ... 67

Figure 3.3: Classification of different measures to mitigate agency problems ... 74

Figure 3.4: Classification of different types of informational asymmetries ... 75

Figure 3.5: Prisoner's dilemma in choosing cooperation or defection ... 96

Figure 3.6: Factors influencing the VC financing relationship from a prisoner's dilemma perspective ... 100

Figure 3.7: Prisoner's dilemma in choosing among agency and stewardship behavior ... 104

Figure 3.8: Relationships relevant to a VC investment process, contents of relationships, and corresponding network types ... 130

Figure 4.1: Structure and role of chapter 4 throughout the thesis ... 134

Figure 5.1: Factors related with observed patterns in spatial proximity between venture capitalists and investees ... 214

Figure 5.2: Distribution of venture capitalist-investee dyads in regard to spatial proximity ... 216

Figure 5.3: Categorization of minimum travel time ... 217

Figure 5.4: Factors influencing the likelihood of a VC investment ... 238

Figure 5.5: Matrix of possible dyads ... 239

Figure 5.6: Comparison of original and matched sample regarding their spatial distribution ... 243

Figure 5.7: Impact of distance (min. travel time) on the likelihood of a VC financing relationship ... 252

Figure 5.8: Impact of distance (min. travel time) on the likelihood of a VC financing relationship for different venture and product development stages ... 257

Figure 5.9: Impact of distance (min. travel time) on the likelihood of a VC financing relationship for different levels of the entrepreneurial team's prior experience 260

Figure 5.10: Impact of distance (min. travel time) on the likelihood of a VC financing relationship for different characteristics of the new venture's industry 261

Figure 5.11: Impact of distance (min. travel time) on the likelihood of a VC financing relationship for new venture's located in urban and non-urban areas 262

Figure 5.12: Impact of distance (min. travel time) on the likelihood of a VC financing relationship for venture capitalists of different sizes 263

Figure 5.13: Impact of distance (min. travel time) on the likelihood of a VC financing relationship for different venture capitalists types 266

Figure 5.14: Impact of distance (min. travel time) on the likelihood of a VC financing relationship for different investment volumes 271

Figure 5.15: Impact of distance (min. travel time) on the likelihood of a VC financing relationship for different levels of syndication benefit 272

Figure B.1: Distribution of VC financing rounds in regard to the population density of the new venture's district 301

Figure D.1: Distribution of realized venture capitalist-investee dyads in regard to the syndication benefit 330

List of Tables

Table 2.1: Categorization of German venture capitalist types 16

Table 2.2: Origin of total deal flow and actual investments 25

Table 2.3: Importance of venture capitalist's investment criteria 31

Table 2.4: Overview of relevant literature 54

Table 3.1: Summary of informational asymmetries 89

Table 3.2: Characteristics of different organizational forms 120

Table 4.1: Summary of propositions and testable hypotheses 176

Table 5.1: Composition of the dataset over time and investment stages 191

Table 5.2: Composition of the dataset over industries 193

Table 5.3: Composition of the dataset over origin and type of venture capitalists 194

Table 5.4: Summary of variables 205

Table 5.5: Summary statistics for variables used in empirical analyses 206

Table 5.6: Summary statistics for original measures of spatial proximity 208

Table 5.7: Structural comparison of the sample and BVK data regarding time and investment stages 210

Table 5.8: Structural comparison of the sample and BVK data regarding venture capitalist type 212

Table 5.9: Correlation between the number of observations and distance 219

Table 5.10: Correlation coefficients 220

Table 5.11: Wilcoxon rank-sum tests on ln(1+min. travel time) 222

Table 5.12: Ordered logistic regressions – Base models 224

Table 5.13: Ordered logistic regressions – Details on venture and product development stage 226

Table 5.14: Ordered logistic regressions – Comparison of lead- and co-investors 232

Table 5.15: Definition of investment volume categories 241

Table 5.16: Rare event logistic regressions – Base models 246

Table 5.17: Rare event logistic regressions – Submodels leading to base models REL 2 and 3 248

Table 5.18: Characteristics of analyzed venture capitalist-investee dyads 251

Table 5.19: Rare event logistic regressions – Details on venture and product development stage 254

Table 5.20: Rare event logistic regressions – Details on the entrepreneurial team's prior experience 258

Table 5.21: Rare event logistic regressions – Details on the entrepreneurial team's prior experience 259
Table 5.22: Rare event logistic regressions – Structural differences between lead- and co-investors 268
Table 5.23: Summary of hypotheses and empirical results 275
Table 5.24: Partial effects on the relative likelihood of a VC financing relationship 279
Table B.1: Summary statistics of original metric variables 301
Table C.1: Correlation matrix of independent variables 302
Table C.2: Variance inflation factors – Base models 304
Table C.3: Ordered logistic regressions – Details on venture capitalists' experience and reputation 305
Table C.4: Ordered logistic regressions – Details on venture capitalists' type 306
Table C.5: Ordered logistic regressions – Details on the investment volume per venture capitalist 307
Table C.6: Ordered logistic regressions – Details on syndication 308
Table C.7: Brant test – Base models 309
Table C.8: Brant test – Details for Model OL 3 310
Table C.9: Ordinary least squares regressions – Base models 311
Table C.10: Tobit regressions– Base models 312
Table C.11: Ordered logistic regressions – Different measures of spatial proximity 313
Table C.12: Ordinary least squares regressions – Different measures of spatial proximity 314
Table D.1: Variance inflation factors – Base models of rare event logistic regressions 315
Table D.2: Rare event logistic regressions – Details on the venture capitalist's experience and reputation 316
Table D.3: Rare event logistic regressions – Details on the venture capitalist's specialization 318
Table D.4: Rare event logistic regressions – Details on the venture capitalist's type 320
Table D.5: Rare event logistic regressions – Details on lead- vs. co-investors 322
Table D.6: Rare event logistic regressions – Details on the investment volume 324
Table D.7: Rare event logistic regressions – Details on syndication 325
Table D.8: Logistic regressions – Base models 326
Table D.9: Rare event logistic regressions – Different measures of spatial proximity 328

List of Abbreviations

AIC	Akaike Information Criterion
Betw.	Between
Bus.	Business
BVK	Bundesverband deutscher Kapitalbeteiligungsgesellschaften
CEO	Chief executive officer
CFO	Chief financial officer
Coef.	Coefficient
COO	Chief operating officer
Coop.	Cooperative
CVC	Corporate venture capital
Dep.	Dependent
Dev.	Development
Df	Degrees of freedom
Diff.	Difference
Dist.	Distance
EVCA	European private equity and venture capital association
Exec.	Executive
Exp.	Expenses or experience depending on context
F.e.	Fixed effects
FRG	Federal Republic of Germany
Fundr.	Fundraising
GDR	German Democratic Republic
Ger.	Germany
GICS	Global Industry Classification Standard
HHI	Herfindahl-Hirschman Index
HTGF	High Tech Gründerfond
Indep.	Independent
Inst.	Institution
Inv.	Investment(s) or investor(s) depending on context
IPO	Initial public offering
KfW	Kreditanstalt für Wiederaufbau

Km	Kilometer
Ln	Natural logarithm
LR	Likelihood ratio
M&A	Mergers and acquisitions
Max.	Maximum
Min.	Minimum or minutes depending on context
MBG	Mittelständische Beteiligungsgesellschaft
Mgt.	Management
MSCI	Morgan Stanley Capital International
No.	Number
Obs.	Observations
OL	Ordered logistic
PE	Private equity
Prod.	Product
Prof.	Profitable
RAM	Reinforcement-Affect-Model
R&D	Research and development
REL	Rare event logistic
SC	Small cap
S.d.	Standard deviation
Shipp.prod.	Shipping product
Subs.	Subsidiary
Synd.	Syndication
UK	United Kingdom
US	United States
Var.	Variable
VC	Venture capital or venture capitalist depending on context
Vol.	Investment volume
ZEW	Zentrum für Europäische Wirtschaftsforschung

List of Symbols

C_{ET}	Entrepreneurial team cooperates
C_{VC}	Venture capitalist cooperates
D_{ET}	Entrepreneurial team defects
D_{VC}	Venture capitalist defects
i	Venture capitalist
I	Number of venture capitalists
j	Index of observation
k	industry segments / investment stages
K	Number industry segments / investment stages
N	Sample size
r	VC investment round
R	Number of VC investment rounds
r_i	VC investment round of venture capitalist i
R_i	Number of VC investment rounds of venture capitalist i
$\mathbf{W}$	Weighting matrix
w_1 / w_0	Fraction of ones (event) /zeros (no event) in the sample relative to the fraction of ones / zeros in the population
$\mathbf{X}$	Matrix of explanatory variables
$\mathbf{x_j}$	Vector of explanatory variables
Y_j	Observation j
$\hat{\beta}$	Estimator of regression coefficients
$\tilde{\beta}$	Estimator of regression coefficients that is corrected for rare events
$\hat{\pi}_j$	Estimator of the probability of a certain event Y_j=1

1 Introduction

1.1 Problem and Aims of Analysis

While venture capital (VC) is of paramount importance for the development of young high potential companies, and thus also economic growth, the supply of venture capital is highly concentrated in only a few clusters in many countries. In consequence, it is essential to understand the role of spatial proximity between venture capitalists and new ventures in VC financing relationships. However, especially for continental European countries, there is still a huge lack of knowledge in this regard. Hence, this thesis aims to contribute to fill this research gap.

Economies around the globe are characterized by a constant structural change. This change is driven by the human desire for innovation, progress and the resulting economic wealth. History shows that structural changes led to severe economical and societal upheavals and that employment and prosperity primarily emerged in those regions that were able to contribute to the structural change with their innovative capacity. Regions that were not able to participate in this process of structural change fell back dramatically.[1] Hence, a competition of regions emerges.

Research shows that innovations and economic growth are mainly driven by young, small and medium sized companies.[2] However, due to their young age and small size these companies usually do not have the necessary resources to unfold their full potential. Furthermore, innovation is inevitably associated with high levels of uncertainty. The early stage of development, the high uncertainty, and missing collaterals usually prevent the access to traditional forms of financing like debt capital or public capital markets. In consequence, venture capital is often the only alternative to fund young, innovative, high potential companies.[3]

Besides this necessity for venture capital many studies show that venture capital backed companies also outperform in many dimensions like innovation and patenting activity, employment growth, operational performance, or post-IPO performance. This is mainly due to the fact that most venture capitalists do not only provide financial resources but also offer a wide

---

1 Cf. Grossman/Helpman (1993), pp. 1-14; Porter (2000), pp. 19-21. Examples for economic development driven by innovations are the development of the automobile industry in Germany in the 19th and 20th century and the development of the information technology industry in the United States (cf. Flick (2001), p. 50; Castells (1991), pp. 33-125). In contrast, the German Ruhrgebiet is an example for a region that lags behind economically due to an insufficient participation in structural changes (cf. Faust (1999), pp. 11-13). These developments are also in line with Schumpeter's concept of creative destruction (cf. Schumpeter (1942), p. 83).

2 Cf. Schumpeter (1942), p. 106; Mellewigt/Witt (2002), p. 81; Audretsch (2002), pp. 14-35.

3 Cf. Gifford (1997), p. 459; Söderblom/Wiklund (2006), p. 12.

range of management and business support.[4] In addition to these direct effects, venture capital also has a positive indirect effect on economic renewal through spill-over effects of the R&D activities in the financed ventures.[5] As a result, venture capital is an important factor for regional economic development and federal governments, states, and municipalities have an increased interest in promoting the availability of venture capital in their regions.[6]

At the same time, the supply of venture capital is highly clustered in many countries. In the United States (US) venture capitalists concentrate in the Silicon Valley as well as Boston and New York, in the United Kingdom (UK) the venture capital industry is clustered in London, and in Germany the majority of venture capitalists locate in Munich, Frankfurt, Berlin, Hamburg, and Düsseldorf.[7] Furthermore, there are indications that spatial proximity between venture capitalists and their portfolio companies is of high relevance and that venture capitalists only have a limited spatial reach. As mentioned above, venture capitalists typically invest into young, innovative, and often technology oriented new ventures for which informational asymmetries are severe.[8] High uncertainties and permanent changes of the business environment require constant monitoring and a lack of experience of the entrepreneurial team calls for frequent support by the venture capitalist.[9] These facts may require regular interactions between venture capitalists and (potential) portfolio companies and are just some reasons for the prospective relevance of spatial proximity.[10] This argumentation is underlined by some, mainly US venture capitalists that state that they would only invest within a certain distance, while the stated maximum travel time from their office varies between 20 minutes and two hours.[11] But also German companies state that the regional presence of an equity investor is very important.[12] These two facts, a clustered venture capital supply and the importance of spatial proximity between venture capitalists and their (potential) portfolio companies, may lead to the existence of equity gaps or at least disadvantages to receive venture capital funding

---

4 Cf. Brav/Gompers (1997), pp. 1818-1820; Hellmann/Puri (2000), pp. 975-980; Kortum/Lerner (2000), pp. 691-692; Bottazzi/Da Rin/Hellmann (2008), pp. 503-507; Puri/Zarutskie (2009), pp. 27-28.

5 Cf. Jaffe (1986), p. 998; Audretsch/Feldman (1996), p. 639.

6 Cf. Sunley et al. (2005), pp. 259-262; Niefert et al. (2006), pp. 28-29.

7 Cf. Florida/Kenney (1988), p. 36; Mason/Harrison (1992), pp. 362-362; Sorenson/Stuart (2001), pp. 1570-1571; Mason/Harrison (2002), pp. 438-444; Powell et al. (2002), pp. 297-299; Martin et al. (2005), pp. 1215-1219; Butler/Goktan (2008), p. 33; Tian (2009), pp. 7-8. For the distribution of German venture capitalists see section 2.2.2.

8 See also Gompers/Lerner (2004), pp. 157-158.

9 Cf. Gorman/Sahlman (1989), pp. 234-237.

10 See e.g. Sorenson/Stuart (2001), pp. 1553-1555.

11 Cf. Zook, 2002, p. 163; Martin et al. (2005), p. 1213; The New York Times (2006).

12 Cf. Achleitner/Schraml/Tappeiner (2008), p. 35. This study analyzes German family firms. Nevertheless, it is likely that the respective result also applies to young, high potential companies.

in certain regions.[13] A first indication for the existence of such equity gaps is that venture capital investments also show regional imbalances and are mainly clustered in the same geographical regions as venture capitalists are.[14]

In contrast to the arguments above, German venture capitalists often state that the scarcity of promising investment opportunities prohibits being selective on a regional level and that they would invest everywhere.[15] Furthermore, we are living in a globalized world and especially financing relationships internationalize more and more.[16] Internet and modern telecommunication facilitate nearly costless communication over long distances and a dense network of flight connections is available at affordable prices. These facts oppose the potential importance of spatial proximity.

In consequence, there is a strong dissent regarding the importance of spatial proximity for venture capital financing. However, the existence of equity gaps would have important implications for entrepreneurial teams and public policy. First, entrepreneurial teams that wish to grow their new ventures could have an incentive to relocate their new ventures to one of the venture capital clusters. Second, municipalities that are located far off the existing venture capital clusters would need to focus on the establishment of venture capitalists in their regions in order to foster the development of young, innovative companies and thus to prevent to be left behind in economic development in the long run.[17]

The importance of spatial proximity between venture capitalists and new ventures for VC financing relationships would also have significant implications for venture capitalists in regard to their portfolio strategies and location decisions. Venture capitalists frequently specialize their operations in regard to dimensions like industries, investment stages, and/or regions.[18] These specialization strategies offer several benefits like improved deal selection and management support but also come at the cost of a reduced portfolio diversification.[19] However, if spatial proximity turns out to be an important factor for the emergence of successful VC financing relationships, it may pay-off for venture capitalists to increase the specialization of their operations on surrounding regions.[20] However, venture capitalists also depend on a strong deal flow in order to be able to be selective and to pick the most promising investment

---

13 Cf. Martin et al. (2005), pp. 1213-1214.

14 See section 2.2.2.

15 Cf. Fritsch/Schilder (2008), pp. 2127-2129.

16 Cf. Lothian (2002), pp. 722-723; Aizenman/Kendall (2008), pp. 5-9; Tykvová/Schertler (2008), p. 1.

17 See e.g. Zook (2002), p. 165; Martin et al. (2005), p. 1227.

18 Cf. Sahlman (1990), p. 489; Lossen (2007), pp. 57-61; Han (2009), pp. 15-17.

19 Cf. Gompers et al. (2009), pp. 818-821.

20 Cf. Christensen (2007), pp. 821-822.

opportunities.[21] In consequence, the growth of a venture capitalist or the specialization in certain industries or investment stages usually requires the expansion of the geographic scope in order to sustain a sufficient deal flow.[22] Hence, it may be necessary for venture capitalists to open branch offices in their more distant target areas if spatial proximity turns out to be an important factor.

Given the severe consequences of equity gaps for entrepreneurial teams and the regional economic development as well as the implications for venture capitalists it is important to fully understand: whether spatial proximity between venture capitalists and new ventures has an influence on VC financing relationships or not; how large this influence is; why the potential influence is in place and for which types of new ventures, venture capitalists, and investment rounds the impact of spatial proximity is especially severe.

Existing literature on the role of spatial proximity in venture capital financing mainly focuses on the US and only very little is known for continental European countries.[23] However, institutional theory and existing empirical evidence shows that there are large differences in entrepreneurial finance across countries and that country specific venture capital research is indispensable.[24] In addition, North American countries differ strongly in their spatial structure compared to continental European countries, which are spatially much more concentrated and have denser infrastructures. Hence, also the mean distance between venture capitalists and their investments differs substantially and the impact of distance on VC financing is likely to be different across countries.[25] Next to the necessity of country specific research, to the best knowledge of the author, no holistic theoretical framework regarding the impact of spatial proximity between venture capitalists and new ventures on the likelihood to successfully pass the different phases of the VC investment process exists so far. Furthermore, empirical evidence regarding the impact of spatial proximity on the likelihood of investment and for which types of new ventures, venture capitalists, and investment rounds spatial proximity is particularly important is very scarce and offers contradicting results.[26] In consequence, the contribution of this thesis to the existing literature is twofold. First, a holistic theoretical framework

---

21 Cf. Lockett/Wright (2001), p. 378.

22 Another reason which may require the expansion of a venture capitalist's target area is an increasing amount of assets under management and thus the need for a higher number of investments in order to invest the fund capital.

23 See section 2.3 for a detailed overview of relevant literature.

24 Regarding institutional theory see e.g. Busenitz/Gomez/Spencer (2000), pp. 995-996; Bruton/Fried/Manigart (2005), pp. 740-741. Regarding empirical evidence see e.g. Sapienza/Manigart/Vermeir (1996), pp. 456-462; Zacharakis (2007), pp. 699-705. See also section 2.3 for a detailed discussion.

25 Cf. Bruton/Fried/Manigart (2005), p. 753; Fritsch/Schilder (2008), pp. 2127-2129.

26 Cf. Sorenson/Stuart (2001), pp. 1571-1577; Cf. Engel (2003a), pp. 136-138; Fritsch/Schilder (2008), pp. 2127-2129.

will be developed that sheds light on the relationship between the spatial proximity of different types of venture capitalists and new ventures and the likelihood of a VC financing relationship throughout the investment process.

Second, based on the elaborated theoretical framework, the following two research questions will be answered both theoretically and empirically for German new ventures:

1 What kind of relationship exists between certain characteristics of ventures, venture capitalists and/or financing rounds and the observed spatial proximity between venture capitalists and new ventures?

2 What kind of impact has spatial proximity between different types of venture capitalists and new ventures on the likelihood of a specific venture capital financing to occur?

Hence, research question one requires an analysis of the observed patterns in spatial proximity between venture capitalists and their German investees in order to reveal, which types of new ventures, venture capitalists, and investment rounds are found to be closer to each other compared to others. One reason for these observed patterns in spatial proximity may be the likelihood of investment which is likely to depend on the distance between both parties. However, various other factors like Germany's spatial structure, the spatial distribution of venture capitalists, the spatial distribution of industry agglomerations, demographic issues, or the relocation of certain new ventures close to potential venture capitalists may also have an impact. Consequently, research question two asks more specifically to investigate the causal relationship between the spatial proximity of both parties and the likelihood of a VC investment.

Moreover, in order to set boundaries on the scope of this thesis it is important to mention that this work is mainly concerned with spatial aspects of venture capital financing within one country, particularly Germany. The internationalization of venture capital involves other aspects and a separate stream of literature exists.[27]

I would also like to note that usually the masculine gender is used within this thesis for convenience only. However, whenever the masculine gender is used, both men and women are meant equally.

1.2 Research Methodology

The research aims and questions, which were stated in section 1.1, are of high practical relevance for entrepreneurs, venture capitalists and policy makers. In consequence, this thesis also discusses practical implications and recommendations next to the theoretical and empiri-

[27] For a thorough overview see Wright/Pruthi/Lockett (2005), pp. 147-150.

cal analyses. Therefore, this research pursues an applied research approach in business administration.[28]

Furthermore, this research proceeds in accordance with critical rationalism, which was first recommended by Popper (1949).[29] Critical rationalism also became popular as "searchlight theory of science" because Popper used the metaphor of a searchlight to differentiate critical rationalism from traditional approaches.[30] The concept states that new theories or single hypotheses[31] should be developed by deduction and should then be tested empirically.[32] This implies that researchers develop profound expectations and subsequently illuminate specific aspects by empirical observation, similar to a searchlight in the dark. Aspects which are not considered in the expectations and the empirical testing remain in the dark. The developed hypotheses are not irrevocable, can be empirically rejected, and can be adapted for further research.[33] As a result empirically tested and reliable theories or hypotheses emerge.

The elaborated research aims and questions comprise various aspects and are complex in nature. Therefore, there is substantial doubt that a single established theory exists that explains all particularities of the main research object of this thesis, which is the role of spatial proximity throughout the VC investment process. In consequence, it seems reasonable to apply different "searchlight positions" and to apply multiple established theories in order to shed light on different aspects of the research object. This proceeding is especially adequate if the research object is not exclusively explained by a single theory and is proposed by several scholars.[34]

However, the application of multiple theories also has limitations. Basic assumptions of different theories are often contradicting, which leads to incommensurable theories.[35] Thus, different theories often cannot be compared even if they are applied to the same research object.

---

[28] For a differentiation of applied and fundamental research approaches in business administration see Heinen (1991), p. 12; Fülbier (2004), p. 267; Saunders/Lewis/Thornhill (2007a), pp. 7-8.

[29] Cf. Popper (1949), pp. 43-60; Popper (1973), p. 369. Critical rationalism constitutes a combination and advancement of classical rationalism and neopositivism (cf. Fülbier (2004), p. 268).

[30] Cf. Popper (1949), p. 48.

[31] In general, theories are defined as consistent systems of hypotheses (cf. Fülbier (2004), p. 270).

[32] In contrast, induction refers to the development of hypotheses as a result of the observation of empirical data (cf. Saunders/Lewis/Thornhill (2007b), pp. 118-119).

[33] Cf. Popper (1949), p. 48.

[34] See e.g. Eisenhardt (1989), pp. 71-72; Manigart/Sapienza (1998), pp. 240-241; Picot/Dietl/Franck (2005), p. 29.

[35] Cf. Scherer (2006), pp. 40-44.

Furthermore, the application of several theories could lead to a lacking focus on the actual research problem.[36]

Keeping these critical points in mind, the work at hand is going to apply several established theories in order to elaborate a holistic theoretical framework regarding the role of spatial proximity throughout the VC investment process. In regard to specific aspects carefully selected theories, which contribute most to the understanding of the problem, will be applied in order to find overall consistent explanations. Such an integration of different theories, which keeps the context specific aspects and limitations of different theories in mind, has already been applied by many scholars whose research cannot be allocated to a certain school of thought anymore.[37] Then, this theoretical framework will be used in order to develop testable hypotheses that answer research questions 1 and 2. Finally, the developed hypotheses are tested in the empirical analysis.

1.3 Outline of the Thesis

The thesis is structured into six chapters. After the introduction, the subsequent **chapter 2** discusses fundamental aspects of venture capital financing and spatial proximity. Hence, section 2.1 first defines venture capital financing and characterizes typical portfolio companies. Then, a categorization of venture capitalists for this thesis is developed. In addition, the section describes the general VC investment process, which is an important basis in order to develop a process oriented theoretical framework later on. Section 2.2 starts by introducing the concept of spatial proximity and continues with an analysis of the spatial distribution of venture capitalists and VC investments across Germany. Finally, first important implications for this research are derived. Section 2.3 categorizes the relevant literature regarding the role of spatial proximity in VC financing and identifies significant research gaps.

Chapter 3 provides an important theoretical fundament which will be used later on in order to elaborate a holistic, process oriented theoretical framework regarding the role of spatial proximity in VC financing. Therefore, section 3.1 identifies relevant theories that explain the impact of spatial proximity between the venture capitalist and new ventures in VC financing. Subsequently, sections 3.2 and 3.3 discuss the identified theories by providing their theoretical foundations, applying the theories to the context of venture capital, and deriving general theoretical implications of spatial proximity between actors. Section 3.4 provides a brief summary of the chapter.

---

[36] Cf. Picot/Dietl/Franck (2005), p. 29.

[37] See e.g. Neuss (2001), p. 9; Welpe (2004), pp. 49-52; Engel (2003b), pp. 165-166.

Chapter 4 draws on the description of the VC investment process of section 2.1 and the theoretical fundament of chapter 3 in order to elaborate a holistic theoretical frame work regarding the impact of spatial proximity between venture capitalists and new ventures throughout the VC investment process. Hence, multiple propositions regarding the impact of spatial proximity in each pre-contractual phase (section 4.1) and post-contractual phase (section 4.2) of the VC investment process are developed. According to the research aims and questions of this thesis the focus of the discussion lies on the impact of spatial proximity on the likelihood of a specific VC financing relationship to successfully pass each phase of the investment process. Finally, in section 4.3 the propositions of the different investment phases will be condensed to testable hypotheses regarding the patterns in spatial proximity between venture capitalists and investees (research question one) as well as the impact of spatial proximity on the likelihood of a specific VC financing relationship to occur (research question two).

In **Chapter 5** the hypotheses that were developed in section 4.3 are tested empirically in order to answer research questions one and two and thus also to verify important parts of the elaborated theoretical framework. Section 5.1 describes the used dataset in comparison to other existing data, defines necessary variables as well as their measurement, and provides informative summary statistics. The subsequent two sections analyze the data in regard to the two core research questions of this work. Section 5.2 investigates observed patterns in spatial proximity between venture capitalists and their German investees. Consequently, the analysis describes the status-quo and reveals which types of VC financing relationships are closer to each other compared to others. Then, section 5.3 continues to scrutinize the data regarding the causal relationship between the spatial proximity of both parties and the likelihood of a VC investment. Finally, section 5.4 summarizes and discusses the main results of the chapter.

Chapter 6 concludes the thesis by summarizing the main results, discussing important implications for entrepreneurs, venture capitalists and policy makers, and providing directions for future research. Figure 1.1 illustrates the structure of the thesis graphically.

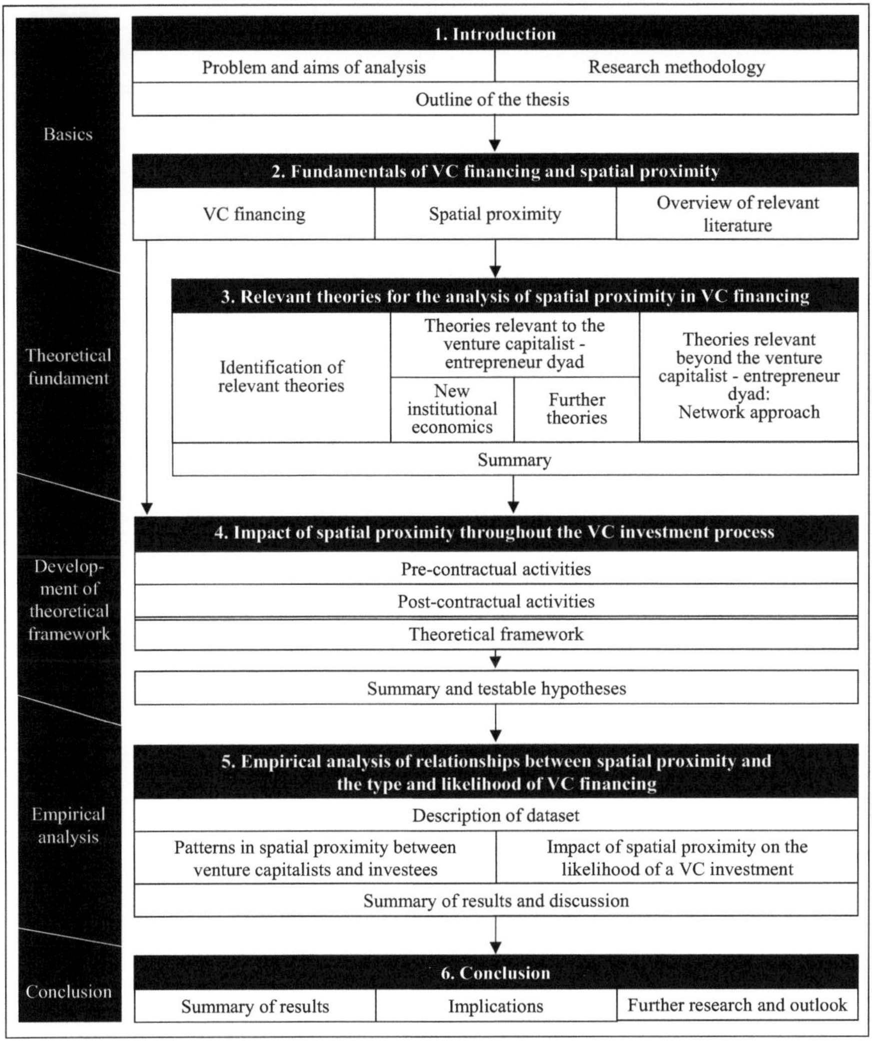

Figure 1.1: Structure of the thesis
Source: Own illustration.

2 Fundamentals of Venture Capital Financing and Spatial Proximity

2.1 Venture Capital Financing

2.1.1 Definition of Venture Capital

The term venture capital (VC) is not consistently used in the literature. Many European authors use the terms venture capital and private equity (PE) synonymously,[38] while most US authors use PE as a generic term and VC and PE in a narrow sense as subcategories.[39] Since the US definition is also more and more used in the literature as well as by practitioners in Europe, it is also used within this thesis.[40] Hence, VC and PE in a narrow sense are defined as subcategories of PE in a broad sense which refers to the provision of equity or mezzanine capital to companies that are not quoted on a stock market (Figure 2.1).[41] If not stated otherwise, PE refers to PE in a narrow sense within this thesis.

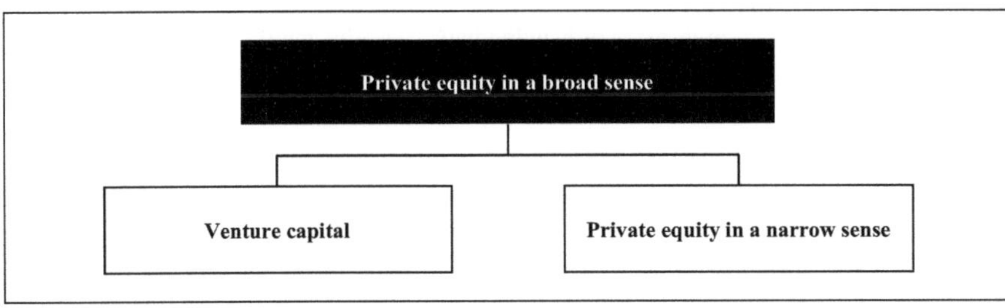

Figure 2.1: Differentiation of venture capital and private equity
Source: Based on Kaserer et al. (2007), p. 14.

VC refers to equity or mezzanine capital which is invested by institutional intermediaries (venture capitalists) into young, often technology related companies that are characterized by

---

38 Cf. Leopold (1993), p. 348; Leopold/Frommann (1998), pp. 7-8; Wöhe/Bilstein (2002), p. 169; Wright/Lockett (2002), pp. 76-77; Wright/Pruthi/Lockett (2005), p. 135.

39 Cf. Gompers (1995), p. 1462; Gompers/Lerner (2001), p. 146; Lerner/Schoar (2004), p. 17.

40 Cf. Nathusius (2001), p. 54; Kaserer et al. (2007), pp. 13-14; EVCA (2009).

41 Cf. Gompers/Lerner (2001), p. 146; Söderblom/Wiklund (2006), p. 12; Kaserer et al. (2007), p. 14; EVCA (2009). Mezzanine capital exhibits equity as well as debt characteristics. Thus, a broad range of financing instruments emerges and one can further differentiate between equity mezzanine capital (e.g. principal loans, silent partnerships) and debt mezzanine capital (e.g. subordinate loans) (cf. Achleitner/Fingerle (2004), pp. 24-25). For a detailed discussion of mezzanine instruments see also Wahl (2004), pp. 128-130. Furthermore, it is important to note that PE in a broad sense also includes transactions in which capital is raised in order to take a public company private (going private) (cf. Achleitner (2001), p. 514; Achleitner/Betzer/Hinterramskogler (2008), pp. 1-7).

a high growth and value generation potential but also high levels of uncertainty.[42] In accordance to the European private equity and venture capital association (EVCA), VC investments are defined to belong to the seed, start-up, or expansion stage.[43] Even though most VC investments are minority investments, the intention is to realize a capital gain by selling the whole company to a strategic investor (trade sale) or by taking the company public (IPO) after a holding period of three to seven years.[44] Venture capitalists usually do not receive interest payments or dividends throughout the holing period[45]. Furthermore, VC investments are characterized by a high degree of illiquidity since most companies mainly have intangible assets and need to maturate before they can be sold.[46] Due to the high level of uncertainty and the lack of collaterals other forms of financing are in most cases not available.[47] Venture capitalists are also often referred to as VC firms and the companies in which they invest are also called portfolio companies or investee companies.[48] The two actors together constitute a VC financing relationship.

Venture capitalists are intermediaries who raise capital for their VC funds predominantly from institutional fund investors (e.g. banks, insurance companies, pension funds) as well as from other investors (e.g. high net worth individuals, wealthy families, endowment funds, industry companies). This capital is then invested into new ventures and realized returns are subsequently distributed to the fund investors.[49] Fund investors are attracted by the potential for superior returns of VC investments but lack the resources and expertise to invest directly in new ventures by themselves.[50] In contrast, venture capitalists claim to have special knowledge in deal selection, deal structuring, and the investment development (monitoring and support). This knowledge is essential because VC investments are characterized by tremendous incentive and information problems.[51]

---

42 Cf. Sahlman (1990), p. 473; Gompers/Lerner (2001), p. 146; Kaplan/Strömberg (2003), p. 284; Kaserer et al. (2007), p. 14. Next to institutional venture capitalists also business angels exist which are private individuals that provide financial as well as non-financial support to companies that are in a very early stage of their development. Some authors refer to business angels as informal VC (cf. Brettel/Meier/Reissig-Thust (2004), p. 432; Mason (2007), p. 92). However, the work at hand focuses on institutional, or formal, VC.

43 Cf. EVCA (2009) and see section 2.1.2 for definitions of the investment stages.

44 Cf. Achleitner (2001), p. 514; Weitnauer (2001), p. 7; Kaserer et al. (2007), p. 14.

45 Cf. Achleitner/Nathusius (2004), p. 8.

46 Cf. Gompers/Lerner (2004), pp. 157-158.

47 Cf. Gifford (1997), p. 459; Grichnik/Schwärzel (2005), pp. 26-42; Söderblom/Wiklund (2006), p. 12.

48 Cf. Söderblom/Wiklund (2006), p. 12.

49 Cf. Achleitner (2003), p. 694, Gompers/Lerner (2004), p. 7; Mason (2007), p. 92; BVK (2009a), p. 11.

50 Cf. Mason (2007), p. 92.

51 Cf. Gompers/Lerner (2004), pp. 2-3.

Many venture capitalists also use their knowledge, management expertise, and network to support their investments and thus to enhance the development of their portfolio companies. This (hands-on) support is also referred to as value added and VC is consequently often called smart money.[52]

In order to manage the high risks and to improve inherent incentive structures, VC investments are mostly done in multiple financing rounds (staging) and portfolio companies have to achieve predefined milestones in order to receive further funding. This gives the venture capitalist the option to abandon an investment if it does not develop according to the investor's expectations. Furthermore, venture capitalists usually require additional rights to control and monitor the investment that go beyond the pure ownership rights.[53]

In addition, many VC investments are done by a syndicate of two or more venture capitalists. VC syndicates usually comprise one lead-investor, who is mainly responsible for the deal, and one or more co-investors.[54] Syndication offers various advantages to venture capitalists.[55] First, venture capitalists can participate in investment rounds with large investment volumes and are still able to diversify their portfolio sufficiently. Second, venture capitalists may profit from the reputation of one or more syndication partners or they get the opportunity to participate in a successful venture in a later financing round in order to improve their own reputation.[56] Third, venture capitalists may enhance their deal flow by inviting other investors in expectation to be invited in the future due to reciprocity. Finally, venture capitalists are able to divide the workload and transaction costs associated with an investment throughout the investment process. However, it is important to note that syndication also increases the costs of deal structuring and requires additional coordination among the syndication partners.[57]

In contrast to VC, PE in a narrow sense refers to the investment of equity or mezzanine capital into mature and established companies. As PE investments are not in the focus of this thesis, it is only discussed very briefly in order to set boundaries on the scope of this thesis. PE firms usually seek to acquire the majority of the company in order to gain full control and to be able to implement their investment strategy (buyout). Typical reasons for PE investments are the succession in family-owned companies, or the buyout and buyin of a business

52 Cf. Cumming/Fleming/Suchard (2005), p. 296; Fingerle (2005), pp. 141-168; Kaserer et al. (2007), p. 14.

53 Cf. Sahlman (1990), pp. 473-474; Gompers (1995), pp. 1461-1462.

54 Cf. Lerner (1994a), pp. 16-18, Nathusius (2005), pp. 36-37.

55 See Nathusius (2005), pp. 75-103 for a thorough discussion of potential reasons to syndicate VC investments.

56 This behavior is also called window dressing. See Nathusius (2005), pp. 85-87.

57 Cf. Nathusius (2005), p. 63.

by experienced managers.[58] Many PE transactions are also financed by a substantial fraction of debt and are thus highly leveraged. This is possible since mature companies usually have predictable cash flows and thus involve less risk compared to VC portfolio companies.[59]

2.1.2 Characteristics of Portfolio Companies

As stated in the previous section, venture capital is invested into young, often technology related companies that are characterized by a high growth and value generation potential but also high levels of uncertainty. This definition provides some information about the characteristics of (potential) portfolio companies which also imply demand as well as supply side factors of VC. On the demand side, the desire to raise VC implies the new venture's need for external capital, while the young age and high levels of uncertainty impede debt financing and the fundraising on public equity markets.[60] The young age further implies the potential lack of experience and the need for non-pecuniary resources like management support which could be provided by venture capitalists.[61] Contrary, the high growth and value generation potential of the venture is important for the supply side of VC and incentivizes venture capitalists to invest. It is also important to note that the mentioned characteristics are not independent from each other. A young age, high levels of uncertainty, and the potential for high growth and value generation are inevitably interconnected, cause and partly also depend on each other.[62]

The age of the new venture determines its development stage and depending on the development stage different VC investment stages can be defined. According to the EVCA seed stage financing is provided in order to research, assess and develop an initial concept before a company is set up. Start-up financing is provided by venture capitalists to companies that are in the process of being set up or may have been in business for a short time but have not sold their product commercially.[63] Finally, expansion stage financing is provided for the growth and expansion of a company. The raised capital may be used in order to finance the extension

---

58 Cf. Berg/Gottschalg (2005), p. 9; Kaserer et al. (2007), p. 15; EVCA (2009). For a detailed discussion of different types of buyouts see Geidner (2008), pp. 7-22.

59 Cf. Wright et al. (1995), p. 461; Berg/Gottschalg (2005), p. 9.

60 Cf. Gifford (1997), p. 459; Söderblom/Wiklund (2006), p. 12.

61 Cf. Cumming/Fleming/Suchard (2005), p. 296; Fingerle (2005), pp. 141-168.

62 E.g. a low company age leads to high levels of uncertainty and potentially high growth. At the same time venture capitalists also require a high growth and value generation potential and thus high potential returns in order to compensate for high uncertainty.

63 Seed as well as start-up financing is also called early stage financing.

of production capacity, market or product development, or to provide additional working capital. Hence, expansion capital is also called development capital.[64]

A high growth and value generation potential may be caused by different new venture characteristics. Nathusius (2005) elaborates that the growth potential of the industry of the new venture might be used as a proxy for the venture's growth potential. Industries with a high growth potential are trendsetting and often technology intensive industries like information technology, biotechnology, or renewable energies. Moreover, high growth industries are mostly characterized by a high importance of intangible assets like patents or a high research and development (R&D) intensity.[65] A high growth and value generation potential of a new venture may also be caused by innovative products, services, or business models, which allow the venture to increase its market share or even to create completely new markets.[66] As a result, portfolio companies are likely to belong to a high growth industry and/or are likely to have a high innovative capacity.

2.1.3 Characteristics of German Venture Capitalist Types

In an international context studies usually differentiate among (i) independent venture capitalists, who raise their capital mainly from third parties, (ii) captive/semi-captive venture capitalists, who raise all or most of their funds' capital from their main shareholder (shareholder of the management company; e.g. corporate venture capitalists), and (iii) venture capitalists that are largely influenced by the public sector.[67]

However, in Germany various, very specific venture capitalist types exist that might have important implications. Thus, scholars elaborated specific classifications of German venture capitalists.[68] Unfortunately, none of these classifications differentiates sufficiently among venture capitalists in regard to their shareholder structure, type of fund investors, and their investment strategy, which may have an impact on their spatial preferences. In consequence, a detailed classification of the German VC market accounting for the mentioned particularities was developed.

---

64 Cf. EVCA (2009). For a detailed description of the different financing stages see e.g. Schefczyk (2004), pp. 40-42.

65 Cf. Nathusius (2005), p. 19.

66 Hauschildt (1997) defines innovations as qualitatively new products, processes, services, business models, or the like which differ substantially from existing alternatives (cf. Hauschildt (1997), p. 6). Cf. Baum/Silverman (2004), pp. 416-417.

67 Cf. Sahlman (1990), p. 487; Gupta/Sapienza (1992), pp. 351-353; BVCA (2009), p. 20; EVCA (2008), p. 60.

68 See e.g. Schefczyk (1999), pp. 1123-1124; Schertler (2001), pp. 44-45; Bredeck (2002), p. 68; Engel (2003a), p. 212; Achleitner/Ehrhart/Zimmermann (2006), pp. 10-11; Achleitner et al. (2009), pp. 443-446.

For this purpose, data from Achleitner et al. (2009), which includes data regarding the shareholder structure, major fund investors, and regional preferences of all members of the Bundesverband deutscher Kapitalbeteiligungsgesellschaften (BVK) as of June 2007, and data from Achleitner/Ehrhart/Zimmermann (2006), which includes data of 79 BVK members concerning their characteristics and investment preferences in 2005, was reanalyzed.[69] In June 2007, the BVK had a total of 186 full members of which 152 stated that they would also invest in VC.[70] As a result, eight different types of venture capitalists were identified which can be further categorized into two classes of private venture capitalists and the class of (quasi-) public venture capitalists (Table 2.1).

Table 2.1: Categorization of German venture capitalist types
This table provides an overview of the number and regional focus of German venture capitalist types using data from Achleitner et al. (2009).

	BVK members in 06/2007			
	All venture capitalists		Venture capitalist with regional focus	
Type of venture capitalist	No.	% of total	No.	% of group
Private venture capitalists				
Venture capitalists with exclusively financial objectives				
Independent venture capitalists	81	53.3	2	2.5
Subs. of private financial corporations	6	3.9	0	0.0
Sub total	*87*	*57.2*	*2*	*2.3*
Corporate venture capitalists	10	6.6	0	0.0
Sub total	*10*	*6.6*	*0*	*0.0*
(Quasi-)public venture capitalists				
MBGs	15	9.9	15	100.0
Subs. of savings/coop. banks	16	10.5	13	81.3
Subs. of state banks or coop. central institutes	13	8.6	2	15.4
Subs. of inst. promoting economic development	9	5.9	9	100.0
Other German government	2	1.3	0	0.0
Sub total	*55*	*36.2*	*39*	*70.9*
Total	*152*	*100.0*	*41*	*27.0*

69 Cf. Achleitner/Ehrhart/Zimmermann (2006), pp. 102-104; Achleitner et al. (2009), pp. 443-446. From both datasets only venture capitalists were included.

70 Achleitner et al. (2009) reported a total of 185 full members because the public bank Kreditanstalt für Wiederaufbau (KfW) was not regarded as a venture capitalist as it does not have a separate VC subsidiary (cf. Achleitner et al. (2009), p. 444). However, the KfW is listed as a full member in the BVK directory and is frequently involved as a co-investor (BVK (2008a)). In consequence, the KfW is included here in order to analyze the German VC market. Furthermore, in accordance to the EVCA VC was defined as seed, start-up, and expansion stage financing (cf. EVCA (2009)). Expansion stage financing also includes later stage financing but no buyouts as defined by the BVK (cf. BVK (2009b)).

2.1.3.1 Private Venture Capitalists

Private venture capitalists can be categorized into the class of venture capitalists with exclusively financial objectives and corporate venture capitalists.

The class of venture capitalists with exclusively financial objectives includes (i) independent venture capitalists as well as (ii) captive venture capitalists that are subsidiaries of private financial corporations.[71] **Independent venture capitalists** make up the largest group of German venture capitalists (53%) and raise their capital from third parties (e.g. banks, insurance companies, pension funds, high net worth individuals, wealthy families, endowments funds, other fund of funds) which do not have a majority stake in the venture capitalist itself (management company).[72] Furthermore, venture capitalists of this class predominantly make equity investments but also use mezzanine instruments. Hands-on support is frequently provided.[73] Venture capitalists that are **subsidiaries of private financial corporations** usually raise most of their capital from their mother institutes.[74] However, it can be expected that both types of venture capitalists have a strong profit orientation. Furthermore, Table 2.1 shows that these venture capitalists usually do not have a specific regional focus.

Corporate venture capitalists are subsidiaries of non-financial corporations and most of their fund capital is raised from their holding company. Corporate venture capitalists usually also have some degree of profit orientation but differ from the above mentioned investors in regard to their strategic objectives. Corporations that maintain corporate venture capital (CVC) subsidiaries usually aim to build up long term strategic relationships with their investee companies and to monitor new technological developments. Hence, CVC can be regarded as a type of external R&D which leads to the fact that the overall profit orientation of these venture capitalists is lower compared to venture capitalists with exclusively financial objectives.[75] Corporate venture capitalists predominantly make equity investments and provide frequent hands-on support.[76] Due to the strategic objectives of corporate venture capitalists it is unlikely that these investors restrict their investments to specific areas. This is also sup-

[71] Private financial corporations exclude savings and cooperative banks as well as state banks and the central institutes of cooperative banks. These institutions will be discussed separately.

[72] Data from Achleitner et al. (2009).

[73] Data from Achleitner/Ehrhart/Zimmermann (2006). 70 of the 79 observations belong to investors that would also invest into VC. 32 observations are independent venture capitalists.

[74] Data from Achleitner et al. (2009). Data regarding the used financial instruments and the extent of hands-on support is not available for subsidiaries of private financial corporations (only two unrepresentative observations).

[75] Cf. Chesbrough (2002), pp. 4-11.

[76] Data from Achleitner/Ehrhart/Zimmermann (2006). Only three observations are corporate venture capitalists and the results have to be interpreted with caution.

ported by Table 2.1. The table further indicates that about 7% of German venture capitalists are of this type.

2.1.3.2 (Quasi-)public Venture Capitalists

The class of (quasi-)public venture capitalists includes (i) Mittelständische Beteiligungsgesellschaften (MBGs), (ii) subsidiaries of savings banks or cooperative banks, (iii) subsidiaries of state banks or cooperative central institutes, (iv) subsidiaries of institutions promoting economic development, and (v) other German government institutions. The main common characteristic of these venture capitalists is that they also intend to support the economic development of certain regions in addition to the generation of appropriate financial returns. In consequence, venture capitalists of this class are likely to pursue a 'double bottom line' and have a lower profit orientation compared to venture capitalists with exclusively financial objectives.[77] About 36% of the venture capitalists that are organized in the BVK belong to this class.

Mittelständische Beteiligungsgesellschaften are regional development agencies founded by private actors and public banks. Thus, these investors are strongly supported by the public sector and have diverse and often fragmented shareholders (e.g. chambers of commerce and industry (IHK), private banks, state banks, savings and cooperative banks, other public sector). MBGs predominantly invest in the form of silent partnerships[78] and most of their investments are underwritten by regional guarantee banks which in turn often receive guarantees from the federal states and the federal government. In addition, several refinancing programs of the Kreditanstalt für Wiederaufbau (KfW) exist.[79] Due to the strong influence of the public sector, these investors have several restrictions concerning their maximum investment volume and the portfolio company size. MBGs usually do not offer hands-on support.[80] Next to their focus on regional economic development these investors also have some degree of

---

[77] Venture capitalists are said to pursue a double bottom line if they aim to create financial returns for investors as well as social returns. For a detailed discussion see also Rubin (2001), p. 122.

[78] A silent partnership is a type of mezzanine capital in the form of a subordinated loan that carries no voting rights (cf. Achleitner/Fingerle (2004), pp. 24-25; Achleitner/Ehrhart/Zimmermann (2006), p. 65; BVK (2008c), p. 1).

[79] Cf. Sunley et al. (2005), p. 260; Achleitner/Ehrhart/Zimmermann (2006), pp. 90-94.

[80] Data from Achleitner/Ehrhart/Zimmermann (2006) (twelve observations). See also Achleitner/Ehrhart/Zimmermann (2006), p. 67.

profit orientation. Each German federal state runs one MBG[81] and each of them has a strong geographical focus on its respective federal state (Table 2.1).[82]

Subsidiaries of savings banks and, infrequently, cooperative banks are less influenced by the public sector but act similar to public institutions since many of them also have some regional development goals next to their financial goals. Their major shareholders as well as fund investors are regional savings banks (Sparkassen), whose shareholders are in turn mainly local public authorities, or cooperative banks (Raiffeisenbanken and Volksbanken).[83] These mother institutions usually have clearly defined regional business areas which also apply to their VC subsidiaries. In consequence, the venture capitalists' objective of regional economic development mainly accrues from the regional field of operation, the strong regional links, and the long term business relationship orientation of their mother institutions.[84] Only subsidiaries of independent savings banks, which do not have a municipal holder, also operate on a national level. This is also supported by Table 2.1 which shows that about 81% of these venture capitalists have a specific regional focus. Subsidiaries of savings banks and cooperative banks predominantly invest in the form of silent partnerships but also make frequent equity investments. Their level of hands-on management is usually limited to few investments.[85]

Similarly, **subsidiaries of state banks and cooperative central institutes** may act like public institutions because of their shareholder structure. State banks (Landesbanken) are mainly owned by public institutions and regional savings banks. Cooperative central institutes are mainly owned by regional cooperative banks.[86] Furthermore, state banks and cooperative central institutes are also the main fund investors of these venture capitalists. This leads to the fact that some of these venture capitalists have next to their financial goals also regional economic development as an objective. However, Achleitner et al. (2009) find that this group of venture capitalists are in transition and that more and more of them focus solely on financial returns. Furthermore, subsidiaries of state banks and cooperative central institutes predominantly make equity investments but also frequently use mezzanine financial instruments. The management of their portfolio companies is more hands-on compared to subsidiaries of sav-

---

[81] The states of Berlin and the surrounding Brandenburg have a joint MBG. Thus, 15 MBGs are existing (about 10% of German venture capitalists).

[82] For a detailed discussion of the characteristics of MBGs as well as the following venture capitalist types see also Achleitner et al. (2009), pp. 444-446.

[83] Cf. Achleitner et al. (2009), p. 444.

[84] Cf. DSGV (2005), pp. 1-6; DSGV (2009b); WGZ Bank (2009).

[85] Data from Achleitner/Ehrhart/Zimmermann (2006) (eleven observations).

[86] In Germany eleven state banks and two cooperative central institutes (DZ Bank and WGZ Bank) existed in 2007. Due to the financial crisis in 2008 and 2009 many state banks merged. In consequence, in September 2009 nine state banks belonged to 7 different conglomerates. Cf. DSGV (2009a) as well as the different company homepages.

ings banks or cooperative banks but less than the one of private venture capitalists.[87] Like their regional counterparts also state banks and cooperative central institutes have a clearly defined regional focus of one or several federal states. However, as can be seen in Table 2.1 only two of 13 venture capitalists of this group (15%) have a specific regional focus.

The major shareholders of **subsidiaries of institutions promoting economic development** are in many cases public promotional banks (Förderbanken) or non-profit associations. Nine venture capitalists of this type are organized in the BVK. Eight of them are subsidiaries of promotional banks or the federal state and are also mostly refinanced by these institutions. One is a subsidiary of a non-profit association and is mostly refinanced by public authorities.[88] As a result, all of these venture capitalists have financial as well as regional economic development objectives. Furthermore, subsidiaries of institutions promoting economic development predominantly make equity investments but also frequently invest in the form of silent partnerships. Hands-on management is also provided frequently.[89] All of the venture capitalists within this group have a regional focus which is mostly defined on the level of federal states (Table 2.1).

The group of **other German government** includes venture capitalists that are mainly influenced by the federal government and operate on a national level. Due to the strong influence of the public sector, all of these venture capitalists also have the objective of economic development next to the generation of appropriate financial returns. As can be seen in Table 2.1 only two of these investors are organized in the BVK which are the High-Tech Gründerfonds and the KfW.[90] These institutions usually invest in the form of equity combined with subordinated loans. As they usually assume the role of a co-investor within syndicated investments their hands-on support is limited.[91]

As a result, it became obvious that the different types of venture capitalists vary in regard to their objectives, the used financial instruments, the extent of provided hands-on support, and their regional focus. In contrast to private venture capitalists, which usually do not have a regional focus, about 71% of (quasi-)public venture capitalists limit their investments to certain regions. Especially MBGs and subsidiaries of institutions promoting economic development, as well as most subsidiaries of savings banks or cooperative central institutes state that they only invest in certain regions. These facts have important implications for the spatial structure

[87] Data from Achleitner/Ehrhart/Zimmermann (2006) (six observations).

[88] This venture capitalist is GENIUS Venture Capital and operates in Mecklenburg-Western Pomerania (cf. Genius Venture Capital (2007)).

[89] Data from Achleitner/Ehrhart/Zimmermann (2006) (four observations).

[90] The KfW also includes the former Deutsche Ausgleichsbank (DtA) and its former subsidiary Technologie-Beteiligungs-Gesellschaft (TBG) as both institutions merged in 2003 (cf. KfW Bankengruppe (2009)).

[91] Cf. Frank (2007), p. 30; BVK (2008a); HTGF (2009).

of a venture capitalist's investments as well as the importance of spatial proximity throughout the investment process.

2.1.4 Venture Capital Investment Process

The VC investment process is very similar in most cases. The identification and description of the critical phases of the investment process and the identification of the evaluation/selection criteria received a very high attention in the VC literature so far.[92] The probably most accepted model of the VC investment process was developed by Tyebjee/Bruno (1984a), who differentiate between deal origination, deal screening, deal evaluation, deal structuring, and post-investment activities, which include the investment development and exit (sale) of the portfolio company.[93] Another popular model was developed by Fried/Hisrich (1994) and focuses on pre-contractual activities. This model comprises origination, venture capital firm-specific screen, generic screen, first-phase evaluation, second-phase evaluation, and closing. Apart from the level of detail and the wording the overall structure of the VC investment process is well accepted in the literature for developed countries.[94] Thus, the work at hand largely follows Tyebjee/Bruno (1984a) and differentiates among six distinct phases: deal origination, deal screening, deal due diligence, deal structuring, investment development, and investment exit. The phases from deal origination to deal structuring are also referred to as pre-contractual phases. Investment development and investment exit constitute post-contractual phases.[95] Figure 2.2 illustrates the distinct phases of the VC investment process.

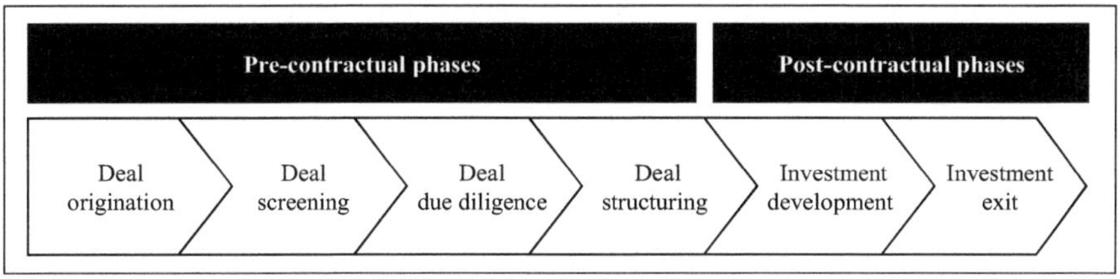

Figure 2.2: Phases of the VC investment process
Source: Based on Tyebjee/Bruno (1984a), pp. 1052-1054; Achleitner (2001), pp. 523-529.

92 See e.g. Wells (1974), pp. 31-191; Tyebjee/Bruno (1984a), pp. 1051-1066; Hall/Hofer (1993), pp. 25-42; Fried/Hisrich (1994), pp. 28-37; Boocock/Woods (1997), p. 37; Achleitner (2001), pp. 523-529.

93 Cf. Tyebjee/Bruno (1984a), pp. 1052-1054.

94 Cf. Wright/Robbie (1998), pp. 534-553 ; Achleitner (2001), pp. 523-529; Fingerle (2005), pp. 69-87. Modified models have been developed for transition economies (cf. Bliss (1999), pp. 241 - 257; Klonowski (2007), pp. 361-382).

95 The closing of the financing contract is the final action in the deal structuring phase and constitutes the transition to the phase of investment development.

The time period needed for pre-contractual phases of the VC investment process usually comprises several months and depends on the complexity of the business model, the urgency of the financing need of the entrepreneurial team, and the number of parties involved in the transaction.[96] Post contractual phases usually range over five to seven years.[97]

The following sections describe the different phases of the VC investment process in detail in order to give a thorough understanding of activities and circumstances of each phase. This understanding is necessary to develop comprehensive propositions and testable hypotheses later on in chapter 4.

2.1.4.1 Deal Origination

In order to be successful, venture capitalists depend on an adequate deal flow[98] which is high in quality and quantity.[99] High quality means to have access to investment opportunities into companies with a high potential for value generation. In addition, it must be possible to invest at reasonable financial terms and conditions in order to generate high capital gains.[100] High quantity refers to a high number of investment opportunities in order to be able to be more selective in the deal screening and due diligence phase, which in turn increases the average quality of investments.

Deal flow can be generated in multiple ways. In general, the contact between venture capitalists and entrepreneurial teams can be established directly or indirectly. Direct contacts are mainly established by cold contacts from venture capitalists or entrepreneurial teams, but they could also be based on prior contacts if both parties already know each other. Indirect contacts are established by referrals.[101] In the course of the initial contact venture capitalists usually directly receive or require a business plan.[102] Figure 2.3 illustrates different possibilities as well as supporting actions to initiate a contact between a venture capitalist and an entrepreneurial team.

---

96 Cf. Vogel (2001), p. 1053 cited in Fingerle (2005), p. 70. Furthermore, Fried/Hisrich (1994) empirically found that the pre-contractual phases span on average 97.1 days (s.d. = 45.0 days) and that a lead-investor spends on average 129.5 hours (s.d. = 99.8 hours) of their time (cf. Fried/Hisrich (1994), p. 31).

97 Cf. Gorman/Sahlman (1989), p. 233; Achleitner (2001), p. 523; Vater (2003), p. 137.

98 Cf. Lockett/Wright (2001), p. 378. Deal flow refers to a continuous stream of investment opportunities a venture capitalist has (cf. Söderblom/Wiklund (2006), p. 27).

99 Some authors also refer to deal origination as sourcing, search, or generation of deal flow (cf. Hall/Hofer (1993), p. 28; Achleitner (2001), p. 524).

100 Cf. Achleitner (2001), p. 524.

101 Cf. Fingerle (2005), p. 71.

102 Cf. Achleitner (2001), p. 524.

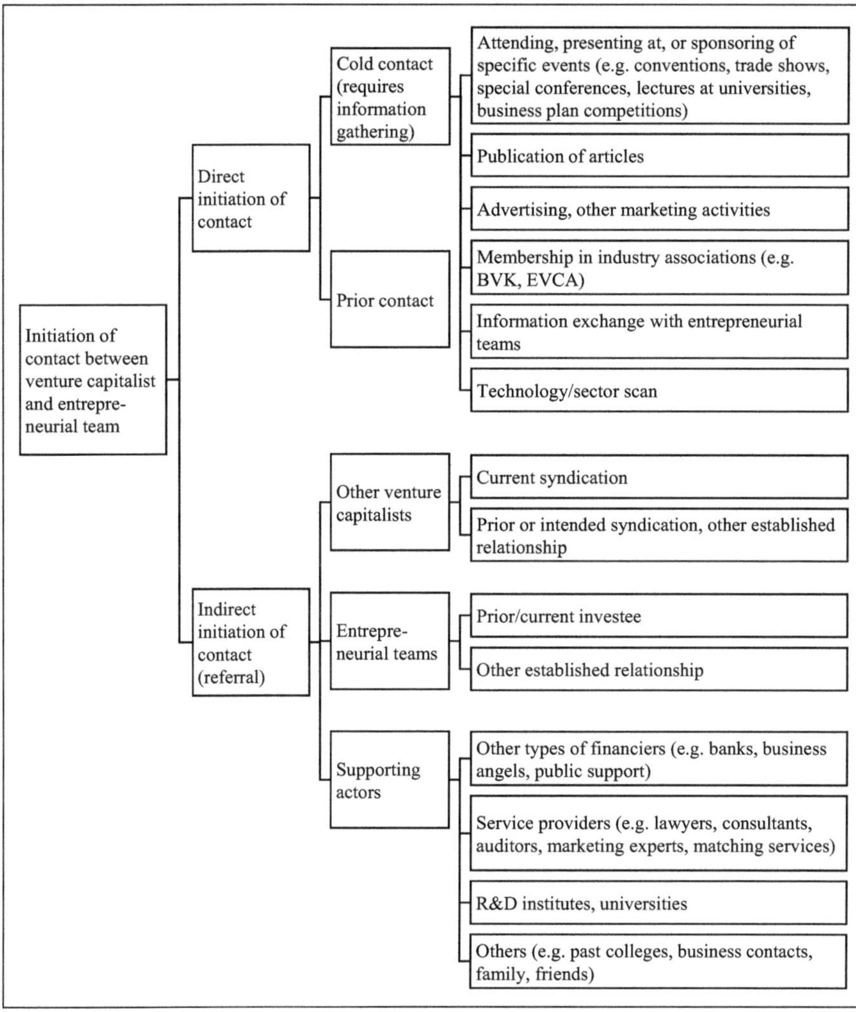

Figure 2.3: Initiation of contact between venture capitalist and entrepreneurial team
Source: Modified from Böhner (2007), p.52.

A cold contact refers to a contact between a venture capitalist and an entrepreneurial team which are formerly unknown to each other. In case of a cold contact either the venture capitalist or the entrepreneurial team has to gather information in order to get to know the other party. Therefore, the public visibility of both parties is crucial. The visibility of both parties can be enhanced by attending, presenting at, or sponsoring of specific events like conventions, trade shows, special conferences, lectures at universities, or business plan competitions. Also the publication of relevant articles as well as advertising and other marketing activities increases the visibility of the actors. Furthermore, the visibility of the venture capitalist can be enhanced by a membership in industry associations like the BVK or the EVCA.[103] To gather information, especially entrepreneurial teams could further communicate with more experienced other entrepreneurial teams.

A special form of cold contact, which is initiated by the venture capitalist, is the active search for investment opportunities by actively conducting technology[104] or sector scans in order to find promising investment opportunities.[105] Then the venture capitalist would systematically investigate specific technologies and industries and search for appropriate ventures and entrepreneurial teams.

Empirical studies analyzing the origin of deal flow usually differentiate between cold contacts initiated by the entrepreneurial team and the active search by venture capitalists.[106] As can be seen in Table 2.2 about one third of the deal flow is received by venture capitalists in the form of cold contacts initiated by the entrepreneurial team. In relation to the share of cold contacts venture capitalists invest relatively seldom into them.[107] The active search of investment opportunities by venture capitalists is rather unusual but is conducted more often the higher the competition among venture capitalists.[108]

Deal flow can also be originated by the indirect initiation of contact between venture capitalists and entrepreneurial teams. Then different types of third parties refer entrepreneurial teams to venture capitalists.[109] First, other venture capitalists, which invite others to syndicate, or venture capitalists, with whom a prior or current syndication relationship or another established relationship exists, could refer to investment opportunities.[110] Second, other entrepreneurial teams, with which an established relationship exists, could be a source of deal flow. Finally, other supporting actors like other types of financiers (e.g. banks, business angels, public support), service providers (e.g. lawyers, consultants, auditors, marketing experts,

---

[103] Cf. Tyebjee/Bruno (1984a), p. 1056; Dotzler (2001), pp. 6-7; Fingerle (2005), pp. 72-73; Böhner (2007), p. 52.

[104] Cf. Tyebjee/Bruno (1984a), p. 1056.

[105] Cf. Fingerle (2005), p. 71.

[106] Cf. Wells (1974), pp. 57-58; Tyebjee/Bruno (1984a), pp. 1055-1056; Sweeting (1991), p. 610.

[107] See Table 2.2 and Fried/Hisrich (1994), p. 31.

[108] See Table 2.2 and Sweeting (1991), p. 603, Fried/Hisrich (1994), p. 32; Wright/Robbie (1998), p. 536.

[109] Cf. Tyebjee/Bruno (1984a), p. 1056; Böhner (2007), p. 52.

[110] Cf. Wells (1974), pp. 57-58; Tyebjee/Bruno (1984a), pp. 1055-1056.

Table 2.2: Origin of total deal flow and actual investments
This table summarizes empirical studies regarding the origin of total VC deal flow and actual VC investments. In the study of Jugel (2001) six of the respondents were PE firms. Entr.: entrepreneurial, Inv.: investors (venture capitalist or PE firm), VCs: venture capitalists.

		Origin of total deal flow							Origin of actual investments		
	Study	Diebold Group (1974)	Wells (1974)	Sweeting (1991)	Jugel (2001)	Vater (2003)	Achleitner/ Ehrhart/ Zimmer-mann (2006)	Böhner (2007)	Wells (1974)	Tyebjee/ Bruno (1984a)	Böhner (2007)
	Time	NA	1972-1973	1988	2001	1998-1999	2002-2004	2006	1972-1973	1981-1984	2006
	Geographic location	US	US	UK	Germany	Germany	Germany	Germany	US	US	Germany
	Sample size	NA	68 deals	4 VCs	31 Inv.	7 VCs	16 VCs	125 VCs	76 deals	90 deals	125 VCs
direct	**Cold contact of entr. team**	**35.8%**	**35.3%**	**18.2%**	**24.0%**	**40.8%**	**32.8%**	**45.0%**	**17.1%**	**25.6%**	**15.0%**
direct	**Active search**	**NA**	**0.0%**	**27.3%**	**NA**	**12.5%**	**4.7%**	**NA**	**1.3%**	**9.4%**	**NA**
indirect	**Referral**	**51.5%**	**60.3%**	**54.5%**	**75.0%**	**46.7%**	**50.4%**	**55.0%**	**81.6%**	**65.0%**	**85.0%**
indirect	Other VC/PE firms, business angels	17.1%	29.4%	18.2%	NA	12.8%	15.9%	35.0%	47.4%	21.7%	42.0%
indirect	Proprietory network (prior investee, personal aquaintance, fund investors)	34.4%	20.6%	18.2%	NA	NA	22.4%	NA	17.1%	26.0%	NA
indirect	Other supporting actors		10.3%	18.2%	NA	33.9%	12.1%	NA	17.1%	17.3%	NA
	Others	**12.7%**	**4.4%**	**NA**	**NA**	**NA**	**12.3%**	**NA**	**0.0%**	**NA**	**NA**

deal broker), R&D institutes and universities, or others (e.g. potential employees, past colleagues, business contacts, family, friends) are an important source for potential investments.[111]

Table 2.2 indicates that about half to two thirds of the deal flow steams from referrals. In addition, referred deals seem to be of higher quality since a disproportionately high share of actual investments has been originated from this source. This is especially evident for investment opportunities which were referred by other VC/PE firms or business angels. A potential reason for this higher quality is a preselection process conducted by the referrers who better know the requirements of the specific venture capitalist than most entrepreneurial teams and who refer only deals of a certain quality in order to protect their own reputations.[112]

2.1.4.2 Deal Screening

One of the key tasks of venture capitalists is the selection of the most promising investment opportunities.[113] On average, a German venture capitalist receives about 320 to 440 investment proposals per year, but he invests only into 1% - 5 % of the total deal flow.[114] In order to secure certain aspects of the venture capitalist's investment strategy and to efficiently reduce the large number of investment opportunities, venture capitalists apply several venture capitalist specific (idiosyncratic) screens as well as a generic screen in the phase of deal screening.[115] The aim is to receive a reduced list of deal flow which is worth further investigation. This initial screening process takes usually only about 10 to 15 minutes.[116]

Typical venture capitalist specific screens include the venture capitalist's targeted investment volume, industries and technologies, the stage of financing, and the geographic location of the

---

[111] Cf. Bygrave (1988), p. 140; Fried/Hisrich (1994), p. 32; Mason/Harrison (1995), p. 157; Böhner (2007), p. 52.

[112] Cf. Fried/Hisrich (1994), p. 32.

[113] Diller/Kaserer (2009) find that superior performance of VC and PE investors is caused by superior selection abilities (cf. Diller/Kaserer (2009), pp. 667-674).

[114] Cf. Vater (2003), pp. 141 and 153; Achleitner/Ehrhart/Zimmermann (2006), pp. 42-44; Böhner (2007), p. 203.

[115] Originally, Tyebjee/Bruno (1984a) only identified a screen phase, which Fried/Hisrich (1994) refers to as a "venture capital firm-specific screen" (cf. Fried/Hisrich (1994), p. 35). However, Fried/Hisrich (1994) empirically found that venture capitalists also apply a generic screen, which is therefore included in the deal screening phase (cf. Fried/Hisrich (1994), p. 32).

[116] Cf. Sweeting (1991), p. 610.

investment.[117] Investment opportunities which do not meet these criteria are eliminated from the list.[118]

The investment volume a venture capitalist is willing to accept has to be in a certain range and highly depends on the targeted investment stage and industry.[119] In general, too small investment volumes are detrimental because venture capitalists face serious time constraints and the necessary time effort for selecting, monitoring, and supporting ventures is largely independent of the investment volume.[120] Too large investments are detrimental because they impede a sufficient diversification of a venture capitalist's portfolio. Therefore, the upper limit of the investment volume is determined by the size of the VC fund.[121] However, one possibility to still finance ventures with large capital requirements is the syndication with other venture capitalists.[122]

The majority of venture capitalists only invests into specific industries or technologies for two reasons. First, the pre- as well as post-contractual phases of the VC investment process require a certain familiarity with the specific industry or technology. Since venture capitalists have limited time and staff available, they can only build up expert knowledge and relevant networks in a limited number of industries and technologies. This results in specialization. Second, by investing into a specific venture with a specific product or service the venture capitalist does not only invest into the company but also into the future of the particular industry or technology. As different industries or technologies have particular growth perspectives, venture capitalists select their targeted industries and technologies carefully.[123]

Companies in different stages of their development have very distinct characteristics and face different problems. Therefore, capital, monitoring, as well as support requirements differ strongly among different investment stages which necessitate specific skills of the venture

---

[117] Cf. Tyebjee/Bruno (1984a), p. 1056; Fried/Hisrich (1994), p. 32. Further investment criteria might be not to invest into direct competitors of existing portfolio companies or to invest only into independent companies (cf. Fingerle (2005), p. 74).

[118] Riquelme/Rickards (1992) empirically find that, in contrast to the deal due diligence, in the deal screening phase venture capitalists evaluate in a non-compensatory manner. This means that an unacceptable value in one criterion cannot be compensated by another criterion (cf. Riquelme/Rickards (1992), pp. 505-506). For trade-off decisions in the due diligence phase see also Muzyka/Birley/Leleux (1996), pp. 273-274.

[119] Cf. Achleitner/Ehrhart/Zimmermann (2006), p. 35.

[120] Cf. Mason/Harrison (1995), p. 155; Manigart/Baeyens/van Hyfte (2002), p. 106.

[121] Cf. Tyebjee/Bruno (1984a), p. 1056.

[122] Cf. Tyebjee/Bruno (1984a), p. 1056; Nathusius (2005), pp. 87-89.

[123] Cf. Tyebjee/Bruno (1984a), p. 1057; Norton/Tenenbaum (1993), pp. 431-432; De Clercq et al. (2001), pp. 45-46, Vater (2003), pp. 130-131.

capitalist. In consequence, many venture capitalists limit their investments on certain investment stages.[124]

Finally, and most importantly for this thesis, some venture capitalists also limit their investments to a certain geographical region.[125] The rationale behind this is threefold. First, some venture capitalists target specific regions in order to induce regional development.[126] Second, venture capitalists may want to focus on certain emerging regions because they expect a higher chance of success for entrepreneurial teams in these regions.[127] Third, the limitation on certain geographical regions may result in an increased spatial proximity of the portfolio companies to the venture capitalist, which might lead to several benefits. These benefits and the role of spatial proximity between the venture and the venture capitalist are in the center of this thesis and will therefore not be explained in detail at this point.

Fried/Hisrich (1994) found that venture capitalists further apply a generic screen next to the criteria described above. Within this generic screen venture capitalists conduct a very quick evaluation of the investment opportunity, by using the business plan in combination with any existing knowledge a venture capitalist already has relevant to the proposal.[128] This comprehensive and more flexible evaluation leads to a further reduction of considered investment opportunities.

2.1.4.3 Deal Due Diligence

After the initial deal screening venture capitalists conduct an extensive deal due diligence on the remaining investment opportunities, which usually takes about three months.[129] In the course of the due diligence, venture capitalists assess the investment inherent risks as well as the required and potential return. Furthermore, an appropriate valuation method is chosen. Therefore, venture capitalists gather various information about the entrepreneurial team, the market potential, the product/service, the technology, financial needs, legal and tax concerns,

---

[124] Cf. Tyebjee/Bruno (1984a), p. 1057; Gupta/Sapienza (1992), p. 350; Norton/Tenenbaum (1993), pp. 435-436; De Clercq et al. (2001), p. 46; Shepherd/Zacharakis (2001), p. 144; Vater (2003), p. 129.

[125] Cf. Tyebjee/Bruno (1984a), p. 1057; Hall/Hofer (1993), p. 36; Fenn/Liang/Prowse (1995), p. 34; De Clercq et al. (2001), pp. 47-48.

[126] See also section 2.1.3.2.

[127] An example is the German venture capitalist smac partners GmbH, who focuses his investment activity on Europe and Israel.

[128] Cf. Fried/Hisrich (1994), p. 32.

[129] Fried/Hisrich (1994) state that it usually takes about 97.1 days to pass the pre-contractual phases. As the deal due diligence occupies the vast majority of the time, it can be assumed that the deal due diligence takes about three months. (cf. Fried/Hisrich (1994), p. 31; Fingerle (2005), p. 74).

as well as organizational and IT aspects of the venture.[130] If the venture does not have the potential to generate the required return, the investment process ends at this point.[131]

To gather the required information, venture capitalists conduct a deep analysis of the business plan, check the background and qualification of the entrepreneurial team, undertake personal meetings and talks with the entrepreneurial team, and visit the company's premises.[132] In addition, supporting actors, which have been introduced in section 2.1.4.1, play an important role in the due diligence process. Outside experts like technology experts from universities, technology consultants, patent advisors, and market research consultants are often hired in order to support the venture capitalist's assessment of the investment proposal.[133] Furthermore, actors from the direct environment of the venture are regularly involved since they continuously interact with the entrepreneurial team and therefore offer valuable information.[134]

However, for most ventures only little, if any, operating history or information about the track record of the entrepreneurial team is available. Therefore, the evaluation of an investment opportunity remains a subjective assessment, which is done on a multidimensional matrix.[135]

Numerous studies, which analyze the investment criteria of venture capitalists, exist in the literature.[136] These studies investigate various criteria, which could be relevant for the venture capitalist's evaluation. In general, these criteria can be classified into five major groups: entrepreneurial team/management, market, product/service, financials, and others.[137]

As can be seen in Table 2.3 there is a broad consensus in the literature that venture capitalists regard the entrepreneurial team to be of utmost importance for the success of the venture.[138]

---

130 Cf. Tyebjee/Bruno (1984a), p. 1053; Manigart et al. (1997), p. 29, Natusch (2002), pp. 543-549.

131 Moreover, Fried/Hisrich (1994) argue that the due diligence process is constituted by two phases, namely the first- and the second-phase evaluation. In the first-phase evaluation venture capitalists conduct an extensive due diligence in order to have a first rough understanding of the pricing and whether the deal is interesting. The second-phase evaluation is characterized by an "emotional" commitment of the venture capitalist. In this phase the venture capitalist basically made his choice and tries to determine potential obstacles and how they can be overcome (cf. Fried/Hisrich (1994), pp. 32-34).

132 Cf. Heyning (1999), pp. 157-159; Söderblom/Wiklund (2006), p. 28.

133 Cf. Heyning (1999), p. 160.

134 Cf. Natusch (2002), pp. 542-543.

135 Cf. Tyebjee/Bruno (1984a), p. 1053.

136 Cf. Wells (1974); Poindexter (1976); Tyebjee/Bruno (1984b); MacMillan/Siegel/Narasimha (1985); MacMillan/Zemann/Subbanarasimha (1987); Robinson (1987); Hall/Hofer (1993); Carter/van Auken (1994); Bacher/Guild (1996); Muzyka/Birley/Leleux (1996); Zutshi et al. (1999); Pries/Guild (2002); Zacharakis/Shepherd (2001); Brettel (2002).

137 Cf. MacMillan/Siegel/Narasimha (1985), p. 121; Brettel (2002), p. 308; Fingerle (2005), p. 76.

138 It is important to note that there is some discussion about the reliability of studies using retrospective self reported data since this data might be biased (cf. Shepherd/Zacharakis (1999), p. 198). For further discussion see also section 4.1.3.

Criteria indicating a high quality entrepreneurial team are the ability to evaluate and to react to risk well, familiarity with the target market and industry experience, capability of sustained intense effort, clear communication, attendance to detail, relevant track record, and leadership ability.[139]

The second most important group of investment criteria refers to the venture's target market. Important criteria include a significant growth rate, market size, whether the venture will stimulate an existing market, and existing entry barriers.[140]

Characteristics of the products and/or services the venture aims to offer are also important evaluation criteria. Here the empirical literature suggests that it is advantageous if a functioning prototype already exists, the products and/or services already demonstrated market acceptance, can be described as "high tech", and is proprietary or can otherwise be protected.[141] From a strategic point of view the products and/or services should offer a sustainable competitive advantage.[142]

The financials are the fourth most important set of investment criteria. Within this category it is beneficial if an investment only needs a short time to break even, offers a high rate of return, and can be easily exited (e.g., taken public or acquired).[143] The low evaluation of this category might be due to the fact that variables like return expectations result from many other factors and are thus highly aggregated and difficult to appraise at the time of investment.

Finally, various other investment criteria exist, which include e.g. the geographic location of the venture, the possibility of syndication, the familiarity of the venture capitalist with the target market, or the quality of the business plan.[144]

---

139 Cf. MacMillan/Siegel/Narasimha (1985), p. 121; Muzyka/Birley/Leleux (1996), p. 281; Brettel (2002), p. 311. Zutshi et al. (1999) state that about half of the empirical papers investigating venture capitalist's investment criteria used the set of investment criteria developed by MacMillan/Siegel/Narasimha (1985) (cf. Zutshi et al. (1999), p. 12).

140 Cf. MacMillan/Siegel/Narasimha (1985), p. 121; Carter/van Auken (1994), p. 66; Brettel (2002), p. 311.

141 Cf. MacMillan/Siegel/Narasimha (1985), p. 121; Brettel (2002), p. 311.

142 Cf. Muzyka/Birley/Leleux (1996), p. 281.

143 Cf. MacMillan/Siegel/Narasimha (1985), p. 121; Muzyka/Birley/Leleux (1996), p. 281; Brettel (2002), p. 311.

144 Cf. Brettel (2002), p. 308.The influence of the geographic location of the venture and especially the spatial proximity between the venture capitalist and the entrepreneurial team will be discussed in detail in section 4.1.3.

Table 2.3: Importance of venture capitalist's investment criteria
The meta ranking is based on and was derived in accordance to Fingerle (2005) by calculating the average rank across all studies (cf. Fingerle (2005), p. 76). Some studies did not feature ranks for all the given criteria.

Study (Geographic location, sample, method)	Entrepre-neurial team/ Management	Market	Product/ service	Financials
Tyebjee/Bruno (1984b) (US, 46 venture capitalists, interviews)	1	3	-	2
MacMillan/Siegel/Narasimha (1985) (US, 100 venture capitalists, questionnaires)	1	2	4	3
Hall/Hofer (1993) (US, 16 investments, verbal protocols)	1	2	3	3
Carter/van Auken (1994) (US, 69 venture capitalists, questionnaires)	1	2	3	4
Bacher/Guild (1996) (US, 40 venture capitalists, questionnaires)	1	2	3	4
Muzyka/Birley/Leleux (1996) (Europe, 73 venture capitalists, questionnaires)	1	4	2	3
Zutshi et al. (1999) (Singapore, 31 venture capitalists, questionnaires)	1	2	3	4
Brettel (2002) (Germany, 55 venture capitalists, questionnaires)	1	3	2	4
Kaplan/Strömberg (2004) (US, 67 investments, investment documentation)	2	1	3	4
Meta ranking	1	2	3	4

A point, which is often neglected in the literature, is that in the deal due diligence process not only the venture capitalist assesses the investment proposal, but also the entrepreneurial team gathers information about the venture capitalist. In the course of the venture capitalist's due diligence, the entrepreneurial team starts to frequently interact with the venture capitalist. This offers the entrepreneurial team the opportunity to get to know the venture capitalist and to gather information about his expected future behavior and contribution to the venture. This is important as a VC financing contract needs to be accepted by both parties and high potential ventures might have several financing options.

If the venture capitalist and the entrepreneurial team come to the conclusion that the respective VC investment or financing would be beneficial for them, they enter negotiations about the specific structure of the deal.

2.1.4.4 Deal Structuring

Within this phase details of the deal structure are finalized and several legal documents are negotiated.[145] In general, VC investments and thus also the specific terms are highly individual as the ventures and their circumstances are very heterogeneous and VC investments usually do not only include financing but also non-monetary support.[146] The specific terms of the deal are first reflected in a legally non-binding term sheet.[147] Finally, these terms are included in a range of legal documents like the shareholders' agreement, the articles of association, the by-laws of the management and supervisory board, and the employment contracts of the management.[148]

The outcome of the negotiations highly depends on the bargaining power of the entrepreneurial team and the venture capitalist.[149] However, deal structuring is a very critical stage for several reasons. First, a relatively high share of potential deals which passed the due diligence is still aborted in this stage. For the, US Fried/Hisrich (1994) found that venture capitalists estimate the share of aborted deals to be about 20%.[150] This is especially painful for both parties since the venture capitalist as well as the entrepreneurial team already incurred substantial sunk costs[151] by conducting the due diligence. One reason for this effect is that most entrepreneurial teams are very sensitive about what they perceive as fair or unfair.[152] Second, it has been found that an appropriate deal structure is crucial for the venture capitalist in order to earn his target rate of return.[153] Third, the negotiated terms represent the fundament of future cooperation between the venture capitalist and the entrepreneurial team.[154]

The aspects, which are subject for the negotiations in the deal structuring, can be classified into financial aspects as well as additional investor rights and agreements. The financial aspects characterizing the structure of a deal include topics like the valuation of the venture,[155]

---

145 Some authors also refer to this stage as closing (cf. Fried/Hisrich (1994), p. 34).

146 Cf. Achleitner (2001), p. 525.

147 Cf. Wilmerding (2003), p. 7.

148 Cf. Wilmerding (2003), p. 7; Fingerle (2005), p. 77.

149 Cf. Fingerle (2005), p. 77.

150 Cf. Fried/Hisrich (1994), p. 34.

151 Sunk costs are costs which have already been incurred and cannot be recovered anymore (cf. Arkes/Blumer (1985), pp. 124-125).

152 Cf. Boocock/Woods (1997), p. 40.

153 Cf. Wright/Robbie (1998), p. 541; Kaplan/Martel/Strömberg (2004), p. 3.

154 Cf. Sherling (1999), p. 181.

155 Some authors do also classify the valuation to the deal due diligence since the venture capitalist evaluates the venture in this phase (cf. Söderblom/Wiklund (2006), p. 29). However, the final price is subject to intense negotiations and also depends on further conditions like investor rights. Therefore, the valuation of the company is classified to deal structuring here.

funding requirements, or financial instruments. The negotiation of the value of the venture is of high importance but also turns out to be very difficult in most cases. The valuation of the venture determines the share of the venture which the venture capitalist gets for a certain amount of capital.[156] Thus, the valuation has a direct impact on the potential return the venture capitalist is going to realize. Moreover, the value of most ventures is very uncertain due to unsure potential risks and returns. Therefore, the information which is gathered in the due diligence is of utmost importance for the valuation of the venture. However, as has been stated in section 2.1.4.3, the evaluation of potential risks and returns is highly subjective, which regularly leads to high discrepancies in the valuation of the entrepreneurial team and the venture capitalist.

Next to the value of the venture also the specific funding requirements have to be determined. This includes the volume of financing required at a certain point of time and highly depends on the specific business plan. Here an important aspect is that most VC financings are staged.[157] This gives the venture capitalist the chance to react on current developments and thus reduces his risk. In consequence, less financial resources are wasted in case of a default and the ex-ante probability of liquidation is not affected.[158] However, extensive staging and thus short financing intervals might detract the entrepreneurial team from its core tasks since it frequently has to spend resources to negotiate further financing rounds. Hence, George/Nathusius (2007) found that top performing European venture capitalists apply extensive staging only in the case of poorly performing portfolio companies in order to reduce risks. In contrast, portfolio companies which have the potential to deliver outstanding returns are provided with enough capital to comfortably develop their business.[159]

VC financing contracts do also differ in regard to the financial instruments used. In general, venture capitalists use equity and mezzanine financial instruments in order to invest into their portfolio companies.[160] The specific financial instrument used depends on the stage of the venture and the regulatory framework. Early stage ventures are mostly equity financed, while mezzanine instruments are more likely in later financing stages.[161] This is mainly due to higher risk and return expectations for early stage compared to later stage ventures. Furthermore, in the case of equity financing US venture capitalists do more frequently use preferred stock,

---

156 Cf. Achleitner (2001), p. 526. See also Achleitner/Nathusius (2004) for a detailed discussion of valuation methods used in VC financing.

157 Cf. Gompers/Lerner (2004), pp. 171-172. See also section 2.1.1.

158 Cf. Sahlman (1990), pp. 506-507; Söderblom/Wiklund (2006), p. 29. Sahlman (1990) also argues that staging is the probably most important control mechanism a venture capitalist has (cf. Sahlman (1990), p. 506).

159 Cf. George/Nathusius (2007), p. 21.

160 Cf. Kaplan/Strömberg (2003), p. 284; BVK (2008b), p. 17.

161 Cf. Achleitner (2001), p. 526. See also section 2.1.1.

while German venture capitalists usually use common stock in combination with additional shareholder agreements.[162]

Besides the financial aspects, additional investor rights and agreements are of high importance for the financing relationship because these rights have an impact on the distribution of power and wealth between the venture capitalist and the entrepreneurial team.[163] These investor rights can be classified into seven categories: First, venture capitalists usually require extensive information rights, which allow them to monitor the entrepreneurial team in the post-investment phase.[164] Second, control rights include specific voting rights of the venture capitalist, veto rights of the venture capitalist for important decisions like mergers, acquisitions, or the creation of subsidiaries, and the distribution of board seats among different parties.[165] Third, management covenants might comprise vesting and non-compete clauses to impede the quitting of key employees.[166] Fourth, milestone agreements like earn-outs[167] or ratchets up/down[168] could be used to define specific measures in the case of predefined events. Thus, important performance incentives can be realized with the help of these agreements. Fifth, cash flow rights could be influenced by liquidation preferences, dividend preferences, and/or an antidilution protection.[169] Sixth, preemptive rights and rights of first refusal grant the participation of the venture capitalist in future financing rounds.[170] Seventh, disinvestment rights like tag-along,[171] drag-along,[172] redemption,[173] or registration rights[174] might be granted to the venture capitalist. These disinvestment rights are especially important since venture capitalists

---

162 Cf. Kaplan/Strömberg (2003), p. 284; Fingerle (2005), p. 78; Antonczyk/Brettel/Breuer (2007), p. 27; Bascha/Walz (2007), p. 222.

163 Cf. Antonczyk/Brettel/Breuer (2007), p. 27.

164 Cf: Sahlman (1990), p. 505.

165 Cf. Achleitner (2001), p. 526; Kaplan/Strömberg (2003), pp. 287-290.

166 Cf. Sahlman (1990), p. 505; Kaplan/Strömberg (2003), p. 292.

167 In case of an earn-out the venture capitalist pays an additional amount for its shares if the entrepreneurial team achieves certain milestones (Cf. Fiet et al. (1997), pp. 350-351).

168 In case of a ratchet up the entrepreneurial team's equity share increases if certain milestones are met and in case of a ratchet down the entrepreneurial team's equity share decreases if certain milestones are not met (cf. Manigart et al. (2002b), p. 18).

169 Cf. Kaplan/Strömberg (2003), pp. 290-292.

170 Cf. Sahlman (1990), p. 505.

171 Tag-along rights allow a shareholder to participate in any sale of shares by another shareholder (cf. Houben/ Nippel (2005), p. 331).

172 Drag-along rights force a shareholder to participate in any sale of shares by another shareholder (cf. Houben/ Nippel (2005), p. 331).

173 Redemption rights grant the venture capitalist the right to sell his shares to the entrepreneurial team (cf. Kaplan/Strömberg (2003), p. 291).

174 Registration rights entitle the venture capitalist to register their shares for public sale (cf. Sahlman (1990), p. 504).

invest their capital only for a limited period of time and therefore need to exit the venture at some point of time.[175]

Finally, VC financing contracts are designed such that if the venture performs poorly, the venture capitalists receive more control. Contrary, if the performance of the venture is very good, the venture capitalists keep their cash flow rights but relinquish most of their control rights.[176] Furthermore, venture capitalists try to strongly base the compensation of the entrepreneurial team on the value created.[177]

2.1.4.5 Investment Development

After the VC financing contract has been signed the phase of investment development[178] starts, in which venture capitalists monitor and frequently support their portfolio companies.[179] By conducting these activities venture capitalists aim on protecting and increasing the value of their portfolio companies. Thus, the aim is to reduce risks and maximize returns of the VC investments.[180]

Venture capitalists spend a considerable amount of time managing their investments. Gorman/ Sahlman (1989) found that US venture capitalists on average spend about 56% of their time in monitoring and supporting their portfolio companies.[181] However, there are huge differences in the intensity of the investment management which depends on the venture capitalist's portfolio management strategy, the role of the venture capitalist within a syndicated investment, the size of investment, the type of the venture, as well as the performance of the venture. In case of a passive portfolio management strategy (hands-off) the venture capitalist concentrates on his monitoring functions. In contrast, the venture capitalist conducts both monitoring and support in case of an active strategy (hands-on).[182] Furthermore, there are differences among lead- and co-investors within a syndicate, whereas lead-investors are far more active in sup-

---

175 Cf. Achleitner (2001), p. 526.

176 Cf. Kaplan/Strömberg (2003), p. 282.

177 Cf. Wright/Robbie (1998), p. 541.

178 Some authors also refer to this phase as venture management (cf. Nagtegaal (1999), pp. 183-185).

179 Cf. Gorman/Sahlman (1989), pp. 441-442; Barry et al. (1990), pp. 447-449, Baum/Silverman (2004), pp. 413-414.

180 Cf. Nagtegaal (1999), pp. 185-186; Manigart/Baeyens/van Hyfte (2002), p. 104; Jääskeläinen/Maula/Seppä (2006), p. 185.

181 Cf. Gorman/Sahlman (1989), p. 245. In general, Söderblom/Wiklund (2006) note that European venture capitalists are traditionally less active compared to US venture capitalists (cf. Söderblom/Wiklund (2006), p. 28).

182 Cf. Nagtegaal (1999), pp. 186-187; Achleitner (2001), p. 527.

porting their portfolio companies.[183] In regard to the volume of investment, it can be expected that venture capitalists dedicate more time to larger investments compared to smaller ones.[184] Previous studies also indicate that early stage investments or inexperienced entrepreneurial teams receive more support than later stage investments or experienced entrepreneurial teams respectively.[185] Moreover, venture capitalists are usually more involved in innovative ventures compared to less innovative ventures.[186] Finally, the actual performance of the portfolio company might impact the intensity of the venture capitalist's support. However, previous research delivers mixed results in regard to this aspect.[187]

By monitoring their portfolio companies venture capitalists primarily intend to protect the value of their investments and thus to reduce the investment risk.[188] Therefore, the development of the venture is tracked and the entrepreneurial team's actions are controlled. To accomplish these tasks, venture capitalists conduct a formal as well as informal monitoring and frequently serve as non-executives on the board of directors (one-tier model) or on the supervisory board (two-tier model).[189] The formal monitoring encompasses the periodic revision of budgets and business plans with the help of monthly, quarterly, and/or yearly reports. Therefore, the information rights, which have been granted to the venture capitalist in the financing contract, are of high importance.[190] Contrary, the informal monitoring is based on personal meetings, telephone calls, and the participation in management meetings.[191]

In addition to monitoring, venture capitalists frequently conduct additional supporting activities in order to enhance the value of their investments in the course of the holding period.[192] Fingerle (2005) conducted a thorough literature review of studies which examine venture

---

183 Cf. Gorman/Sahlman (1989), p. 245, Elango et al. (1995), p. 165; Wright/Lockett (2002), pp. 80-81.

184 Cf. Gifford (1997), p. 474.

185 Cf. Gorman/Sahlman (1989), p. 245; Sapienza/Timmons (1989), pp. 75-76; Sapienza/Amason/Manigart (1994), pp. 6 and 9; Sapienza/Gupta (1994), p. 1628; Elango et al. (1995), pp. 164-165; Achleitner/Ehrhart/Zimmermann (2006), p. 67; Bottazzi/Da Rin/Hellmann (2008), pp. 498-499.

186 Cf. Sapienza (1992), p. 19; Sapienza/Gupta (1994), p. 1628; Sapienza/Amason/Manigart (1994), pp. 9-10; Sapienza/De Clercq (2000), p. 64.

187 Prospect theory suggest that venture capitalists concentrate on only few "high-flyers" since these ventures have the greatest impact on the venture capitalists' portfolio performance (cf. Kahneman/Tversky (1979), pp. 274-288; Sapienza/Manigart/Vermeir (1996), p. 463). Contrary, other authors argue that venture capitalists' involvement increases the higher the need for oversight, which is mainly the case in poorly performing ventures (cf. Lerner (1995), p. 316).

188 Cf. Nagtegaal (1999), pp. 185-186; Manigart/Baeyens/van Hyfte (2002), p. 104.

189 Cf. Lerner (1995), p. 308; Sweeting/Wong (1997), pp. 136-141; Fingerle (2005), p. 270.

190 Cf. Sweeting/Wong (1997), p. 136; Nagtegaal (1999), pp. 193-195.

191 Cf. Sweeting/Wong (1997), pp. 137-138; Nagtegaal (1999), pp. 193-195.

192 Many authors refer to these activities also as value added and regard these activities as an integral part of the venture capitalist's activities (see e.g. Sapienza (1992), p. 10).

capitalists' supporting activities as well as their importance in the phase of investment development. He identified more than fifty different activities and clustered them into nine categories. Finally, Fingerle (2005) aggregated the individual rankings of activities of each study to fit the nine categories and elaborated an overall ranking of the categories across the different studies. The identified categories of activities are in the order of importance:[193]

- providing financial support,
- serving as a sounding board to the management,
- supporting in strategy development,
- providing feedback to the management,
- helping the management in operational aspects,
- providing contacts to third parties,
- recruiting management,
- providing ethical support to the management, and
- supporting in organizational planning.

The mentioned financial support goes beyond the initial financial support and also includes help to secure further financing from other sources. Furthermore, the type of support, which is needed by the portfolio company, highly depends on certain characteristic of the venture. For early stage ventures, for example, it is crucial to be able to elaborate a sound business plan, form a complementary team, or to detect the right target market. Contrary, in later stages specific financial and operative know-how is especially needed to manage the venture. Here, knowledge how to secure further financing, how to design the capital structure, how to prepare an IPO, situational experiences (e.g. turnaround situations), as well as industry specific support is highly important.[194]

Furthermore, portfolio companies also benefit from the reputation of their venture capitalists. The fact that a reputable venture capitalist invested into the focal venture serves as a valuable signal for third parties like customers, suppliers, investors, or potential personnel and thus reduces transaction barriers caused by asymmetric information.[195] The transmission of such a positive signal is called certification.[196]

---

[193] For further information on the studies included and the methodology see Fingerle (2005), pp. 141-143.

[194] Cf. Gorman/Sahlman (1989), p. 237; Achleitner (2001), pp. 517-518; Kaplan/Strömberg (2001), pp. 428-429.

[195] Cf. Sahlman (1990), p. 509; Fried/Hisrich (1995), p. 104.

[196] Cf. Megginson/Weiss (1991), p. 879.

Which specific kind of support is finally provided depends on the venture capitalist's type. Therefore, the fit between the venture's requirements and the venture capitalist's support is crucial for the success of the venture. This also leads to the frequent use of syndicated investments in order to complement the venture capitalists' support. Moreover, the composition of investment syndicates frequently change over subsequent financing rounds as the venture's requirements change in the course of development.[197]

2.1.4.6 Investment Exit

About five to seven years after their initial investment venture capitalists intend to sell the shares of their portfolio companies.[198] As venture capitalists generate most of their investment returns in the form of capital gains, the exit is vital for their return generation.[199]

First, the venture capitalist and the entrepreneurial team have to agree upon the point of time for an exit as well as the exit channel. Since both parties might have different interests, these decisions offer a high potential for conflicts.[200] Hence, it is important to consider the interests of all involved parties and to discuss potential exit strategies as early as possible.[201] In consequence, many aspects like tag-along or drag-along rights of potential exits have already been negotiated in the deal structuring phase.[202] Subsequently, the preparation of the portfolio company for the potential exit as well as the preparation of the exit itself starts. This includes activities like:[203]

- identifying potential purchasers,
- improving the venture's accounting and reporting systems,
- evaluation of the venture in order to determine a range for the sale price,
- assembling information to enable potential buyers to evaluate the venture,
- amending a firm's constitutional documents to enable the sale,
- changing the legal form or jurisdiction of incorporation,

---

197 Cf. Achleitner (2001), p. 518.

198 Cf. Tyebjee/Bruno (1984a), p. 1054; Gorman/Sahlman (1989), p. 233; Gompers (1996), p. 140.

199 Cf. Cumming/Macintosh (2003), p. 101. See also section 2.1.1.

200 Cf. Fried/Hisrich (1995), p. 110.

201 Cf. Wright/Robbie (1998), p. 549.

202 See section 2.1.4.4.

203 Cf. Cumming/Macintosh (2003), p. 128. This list of activities is of exemplary character and is not intended to be complete.

- negotiating contractual arrangements ancillary to a sale,
- board deliberations in respect of any or all of the above mentioned activities.

Finally, the transaction itself, which includes the transfer of shares to the new owners, is conducted.

Besides a write-off one has to differentiate between the repayment of mezzanine and debt instruments as well as regular exit channels to sell equity shares. Regarding regular exit channels actors may choose among four alternatives: initial public offering (IPO), trade sale, secondary sale, or company buyback.[204] Each exit channel has specific advantages and disadvantages and the choice of an optimal exit channel highly depends on the perspective (venture capitalist or entrepreneurial team), the actual situation of the venture as well as current market conditions.[205] Since portfolio companies which can be exited via an IPO or trade sale offer the highest returns, well established stock and IPO markets as well as an active mergers and acquisitions (M&A) market are particularly important.[206] Figure 2.4 depicts the observed exit channels for the German VC market from 2003 to 2008.

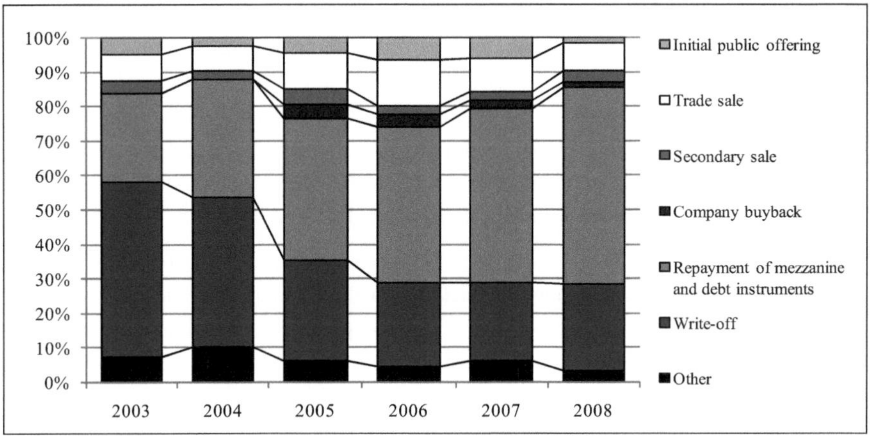

Figure 2.4: Exit channels of venture capitalists in Germany
For the years 2003 to 2007 the chart depicts the frequency of chosen exit channels of venture capitalists that are active in Germany. For 2008 the chart depicts the frequency of chosen exit channels for German VC investments. This transition results from a change in the reporting of the BVK. Mezzanine and debt instruments include silent partnerships and principal loans. Company buybacks were regarded as "other" before 2005. Multiple inclusions of ventures are possible in all cases. Source: BVK (various years); BVK (2009a), p. 19.

[204] Cf. Achleitner (2001), p. 527; Cumming/Macintosh (2003), p. 102.

[205] Cf. Achleitner (2001), p. 527.

[206] Cf. Amit/Brander/Zott (1998), p. 460.

In 2008, the most frequently observed exit channel was the **repayment of mezzanine and debt instruments** (59.7%). This category also gained importance since 2003 and within this category the repayment of silent partnerships accounts for the by far largest share.[207] This is mainly due to the activities of (quasi-)public venture capitalists like MBGs which make a high number of relatively small investments predominantly in the form of silent partnerships.[208]

The second most frequent exit channel was a **write-off** and accounted for 26.6% of all exits in 2008. Write-offs often involve the failure of a company and are thus also referred to as liquidation.[209] The share of write-offs decreased since 2003 which is mainly due to diminishing effects of the high-tech bubble from the late 1990s.[210] However, the high share of write-offs impressively illustrates the high risk of VC investments.

Regarding regular exit channels to sell equity shares the **trade sale** occurred most frequently (8.6%). In the course of a trade sale the portfolio company is acquired by another company. In most cases the acquirer is in an industry which is the same as, or similar to, the industry of the target company and thus the acquisition is motivated by strategic reasons. In consequence, the acquiring company may prefer a complete sale of the venture in order have full control over the ventures' assets and technology.[211]

Secondary sales took place in 3.3% of all exits in 2008. In the course of a secondary sale the venture capitalist sells his shares to another financial investor (e.g. another venture capitalist). This may be necessary if a portfolio company is not yet ready for an IPO or a trade sale, but a venture capitalist wants to sell his shares in order to restructure his portfolio or because his fund's term approaches the end of its lifetime. Since a secondary sale usually results in a relatively low price, venture capitalists usually want to avoid such scenarios.[212]

In 2008 in 2.0% of all exits the entrepreneurial team repurchased the shares of the venture capitalist in the course of a **company buyback**. In most cases a buyback indicates a poor performance of the venture and a lack of future growth opportunities, which prevents other exit channels like an IPO, a trade sale, or a secondary sale. The valuation of the venture is quite low in most cases, as the entrepreneurial team usually only has limited financial resources.[213]

---

[207] Cf. BVK (2009a), p. 19.

[208] Cf. Achleitner/Ehrhart/Zimmermann (2006), pp. 59 and 65.

[209] Cf. Achleitner (2001), p. 527.

[210] Cf. Fingerle (2005), p. 83.

[211] Cf. Cumming/Macintosh (2003), pp. 106-107 and 522.

[212] Cf. Achleitner (2001), p. 528; Cumming/Macintosh (2003), pp. 160-161.

[213] Cf. Achleitner (2001), pp. 528-529; Cumming/Macintosh (2003), p. 107.

In only 1.6% of all exits an **IPO** was feasible in 2008. However, previous years exhibited higher IPO rates and IPOs are much more important in terms of exit volume since they usually offer the highest exit proceedings. Hence, venture capitalists usually prefer an IPO in order to exit their investments.[214] In addition, the entrepreneurial team is not required to exit as well. A disadvantage of an IPO is that venture capitalists are not able to completely sell their shares immediately because they are usually required to hold their shares for a certain lock-up period.[215] In addition, an IPO is the most expensive exit channel and imposes the highest requirements on the portfolio company in terms of performance and all aspects of its organization in order to be able to deliver quarterly reports, to fulfill disclosure standards for public companies, and to work continually on its public and investor relations.[216]

2.2 Spatial Proximity

2.2.1 Definition of Spatial Proximity

In general, the proximity concept is an important concept in several fields of science like innovation studies, organizational science, regional science, or finance.[217] Besides spatial proximity, various other types of proximity like institutional, cultural, social, technological, cognitive, and organizational proximity exist in the literature.[218] However, the work at hand focuses on spatial proximity in the context of venture capital financing. More specifically, if not stated otherwise within this thesis, spatial proximity refers to the physical closeness of a venture capitalist and one of its current or potential portfolio companies. However, the spatial proximity between other dyads of actors like syndication partners or among entrepreneurial teams may also be important and will be indicated explicitly. Furthermore, distance is regarded as an antonym to spatial proximity. Various measures of spatial proximity, which is frequently also called geographical, local, territorial, or physical proximity,[219] have been proposed in the literature. First, many authors use a dichotomous measure and only discriminate between close

---

[214] Cf. Amit/Brander/Zott (1998), p. 460; Achleitner (2001), p. 527.

[215] Cf. Cumming/Macintosh (2003), p. 135. A lock-up is an agreement between the underwriter and existing shareholders not to sell any shares during a specified period of time (cf. Lin/Smith (1998), p. 245).

[216] Cf. Achleitner (2001), pp. 527-528; Fingerle (2005), p. 86.

[217] Cf. Coval/Moskowitz (1999), pp. 2045-2049; Knoben/Oerlemans (2006), p. 71.

[218] Cf. Knoben/Oerlemans (2006), pp. 73-74.

[219] Cf. Knoben/Oerlemans (2006), pp. 73-74. In social sciences authors also frequently refer to propinquity and the propinquity effect, which implies that physical proximity leads to a higher frequency of interactions and thus to higher interpersonal attraction (see section 3.2.2.3 and cf. Festinger/Schachter/Back (1950), pp. 36-45; Thibaut/Kelley (1959), pp. 39-42).

and distant actors or use a rough ordinal measure of spatial proximity.[220] Second, authors frequently measure spatial proximity between two actors as the air distance or car distance.[221] Finally, few studies also use the travel time between two actors as their primary measure.[222] In most cases spatial proximity is important because it facilitates frequent face-to-face interactions, and thus also the transfer of information, and reduces transaction costs like travel time and expenditures.[223] The description of the VC investment process in section 2.1.4 already showed that venture capitalists as well as entrepreneurial teams highly depend on reliable and timely information and frequent interactions. This could cause spatial proximity to be especially important in the context of venture capital. However, various theories imply the importance of spatial proximity in this context and these theories will be discussed in detail in chapter 3.

2.2.2 Spatial Distribution of Venture Capitalists and Venture Capital Investments

The spatial concentration of venture capitalists and their portfolio companies is well documented in the literature for many countries. For the US many authors report a high concentration of venture capitalists as well as VC investments especially in California, Boston, and New York.[224] For the UK various studies exist which document a high concentration of VC/PE firms and VC/PE investments in the South East and London area,[225] and in Israel venture capitalists and VC financed companies are clustered in the Tel Aviv area.[226] Furthermore, in France a high concentration of VC/PE firms and VC/PE investments exists in and around Paris.[227] Hence, it is not surprising that German venture capitalists and VC investments are also spatially clustered.[228] However, existing academic studies regarding the spatial distribution of German venture capitalists do not differentiate between PE firms, which only provide PE to mature companies e.g. in the course of buyouts, and venture capitalists as defined in

---

220 See e.g. Gupta/Sapienza (1992), p. 354; Cumming/Johan (2006), p. 371; Fritsch/Schilder (2008), p. 2121.

221 See e.g. Lerner (1995), p. 312; Sorenson/Stuart (2001), pp. 1563-1564; Engel (2003a), p. 212.

222 See e.g. Sapienza/Manigart/Vermeir (1996), p. 456; Fritsch/Schilder (2006), p. 5.

223 Cf. Knoben/Oerlemans (2006), p. 74. For a detailed discussion of transaction costs see section 3.2.1.3.

224 Cf. Florida/Kenney (1988), p. 36; Sorenson/Stuart (2001), pp. 1570-1571; Powell et al. (2002), pp. 297-299; Butler/Goktan (2008), p. 33; Tian (2009), pp. 7-8.

225 Cf. Mason/Harrison (1992), pp. 362-362; Mason/Harrison (2002), pp. 438-444; Martin et al. (2005), pp. 1215-1219. For the UK Mason/Harrison (2002) find that the spatial concentration of VC/PE investments decreased slightly from the 80s to the 90s. However, the authors also acknowledge that this effect is mainly driven by large PE deals (cf. Mason/Harrison (2002), pp. 444-447).

226 Cf. Schwartz/Bar-El (2007), pp. 634 and 640.

227 Cf. Martin/Sunley/Turner (2002), pp. 137-140.

228 Cf. Engel (2003a), p. 128; Martin et al. (2005), pp. 1215-1218; Fritsch/Schilder (2006), pp. 19-22; Fritsch/Schilder (2008), pp. 2117-2120.

section 2.1.1.[229] As PE investments differ from VC investments in regard to the investment volume as well as the value generation, it may be expected that PE firms tend to locate more in financial clusters (e.g. Frankfurt) compared to technology clusters (e.g. Munich).[230] Furthermore, existing studies only consider the headquarter of German VC/PE firms and discount their branches as well as most German branches of foreign investors.[231] In consequence, the spatial distribution of venture capitalists' offices in Germany was analyzed using data from VentureSource and Achleitner et al. (2009). For each German district, Panel A in Figure 2.5 maps the number of offices (headquarters and branches) of venture capitalists that invested into a German venture between January 2002 and March 2007 as reported by Venture-Source[232] as well as the number of offices of venture capitalists that are organized in the BVK and are not covered by Venture Source.[233] Furthermore, Panel A differentiates between private and (quasi-)public venture capitalists as defined in section 2.1.3.[234] It total, the dataset includes 293 German VC offices of which 69 (23.5%) are offices from (quasi-)public venture capitalists. As can be seen in Panel A in Figure 2.5 five major clusters of German VC offices exist. The by far largest cluster is Munich with 59 VC offices (20.1%). The second largest cluster, Frankfurt am Main, has 29 VC offices (9.9%) and is thus not even half as large as Munich. The other three clusters are Berlin (26 VC offices; 8.9%), Hamburg (23 VC offices; 7.8%), and Düsseldorf (21 VC offices; 7.2).[235] Hence, the supply of VC is clustered in Germany, even though the clustering is not as strong as in the UK or France. This finding is also in line with the results from Martin et al. (2005).[236] However, the above mentioned previous studies regarding the spatial distribution of German VC/PE firms found that no single cluster dominates the others and that Munich and Frankfurt have nearly the same size. This is definitely not the case and Munich dominates strongly if one only considers venture capitalists and also includes non BVK members as well as branches. Moreover, Panel A reveals that the fraction of VC offices from (quasi-)public venture capitalists is much higher in non-cluster

---

[229] Cf. Martin et al. (2005), pp. 1215-1218; Fritsch/Schilder (2006), pp. 19-22; Fritsch/Schilder (2008), pp. 2117-2120.

[230] Cf. Berg/Gottschalg (2005), pp. 11-25; BVK (2009a), p. 13.

[231] Existing studies only map the German main office of all members of the BVK (cf. Martin et al. (2005), pp. 1215-1218; Fritsch/Schilder (2006), pp. 19-22; Fritsch/Schilder (2008), pp. 2117-2120).

[232] See section 5.1.2 for a detailed description of the dataset.

[233] The data from Achleitner et al. (2009) includes all BVK members as of June 2007 and was originally collected from the BVK directory. Only full members of the BVK that stated that they would also invest in VC are considered. See also section 2.1.3 for a description of the data. Germany comprises 439 different districts.

[234] The grey circles represent the total number of venture capitalists for each German district. The white circles represent the fraction of (quasi-)public venture capitalists.

[235] Cologne has 8 VC offices. Thus, taking both districts together this region would be as large as Frankfurt am Main. However, this analysis is bassed on single districts.

[236] Cf. Martin et al. (2005), pp. 1215-1220.

locations (37.8%) compared to the five clusters (11.4%). This fact is especially pronounced in East German states.[237] 80% of the East German non-cluster VC offices are from (quasi-)public venture capitalists. Besides the differences between cluster and non-cluster locations there are also general differences between East and West Germany. The fraction of VC offices from (quasi-)public venture capitalists is considerably higher in East Germany (45.7%) compared to West Germany (19.4%). These facts demonstrate the effect of public policy to promote VC in German regions and explain, at least partly, the lower concentration of VC offices in Germany compared to other countries.

Panel B in Figure 2.5 illustrates the number of VC financing rounds that were raised by new ventures in the respective district between January 2002 and March 2007 as reported by VentureSource.[238] In total, the dataset includes 689 VC financing rounds. As can be seen in Panel B, two major regional clusters of VC financing rounds exist. The by far largest cluster is again Munich with 120 VC financing rounds (17.4%). The second cluster is Berlin and accounted for 83 VC financing rounds (12.0%). Next to these two clusters two smaller agglomerations of VC financing rounds exist in Hamburg (33; 4.8%) and Heidelberg (27; 3.9%). These findings largely correspond to the findings of prior studies regarding the spatial distribution of German VC investments.[239]

2.2.3 First Implications Regarding the Role of Spatial Proximity in Venture Capital Financing

In the previous section it became obvious that the location of venture capitalists' offices and the location of VC financing rounds are clustered and that these clusters largely overlap. Furthermore, Munich dominates all other areas in respect to both the number of venture capitalists' offices and the number of financing rounds. In addition, a comparison of these results with results from Fritsch/Schilder (2008) reveals that the number of VC financing rounds per district does not necessarily correspond to the number of R&D intensive start-ups, and thus potential investment opportunities, per district. In contrast, VC investments are concentrated

[237] Mecklenburg-Western Pomerania, Brandenburg, Saxony-Anhalt, Thuringia, Saxony, and parts of Berlin belonged to the former German Democratic Republic (GDR). For the sake of simplicity all parts of Berlin are considered to belong to East Germany.

[238] VC investments are mostly done in multiple financing rounds (staging) and each financing round represents a new investment decision (see also section 2.1.1). Hence, the number of financing rounds is more representative for the regional VC activity compared to the number of financed companies.

[239] Cf. Engel (2003a), p. 128; Fritsch/Schilder (2006), pp. 19-22.

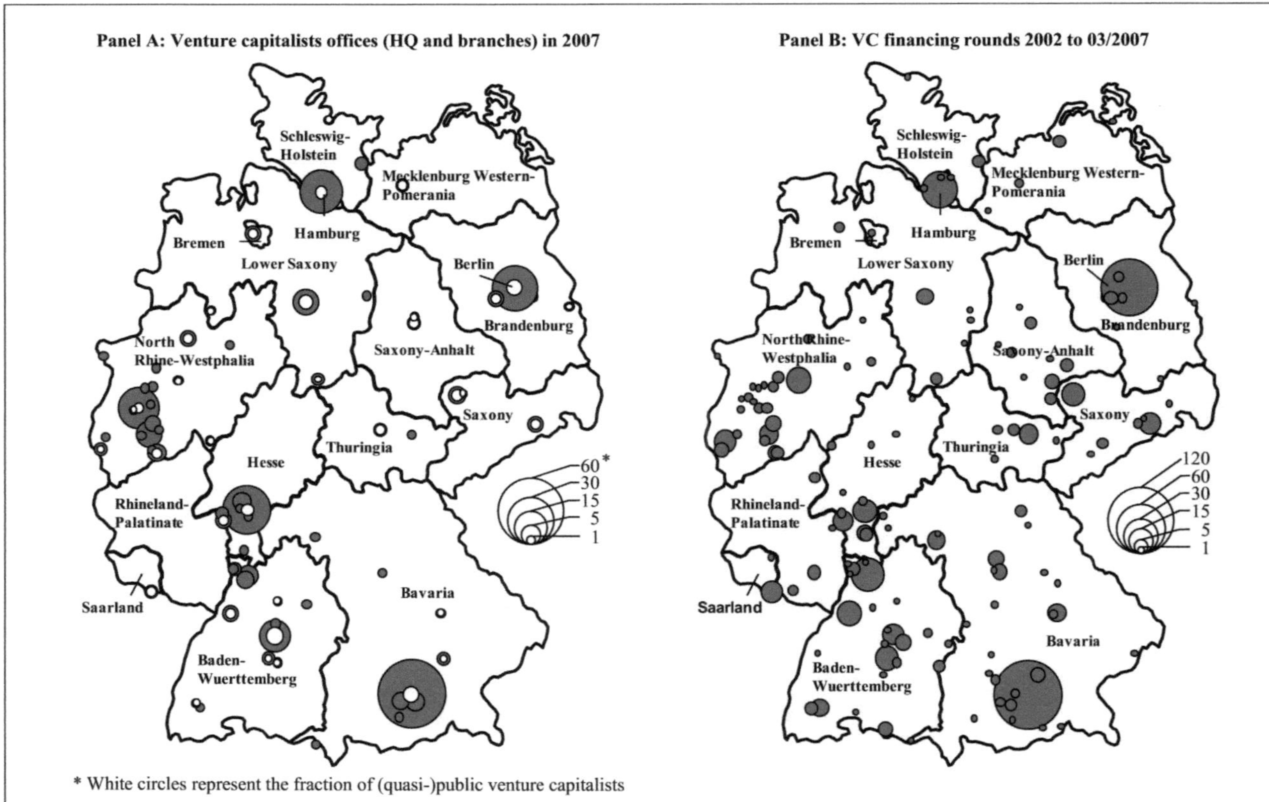

Figure 2.5: Spatial distribution of venture capitalists and VC financing rounds across German districts
Source: VentureSource; data from Achleitner et al. (2009); own illustration.

close to venture capitalists.[240] These facts might have several reasons. First, new ventures may be more likely to get VC funding if they are located close to venture capitalists and thus the identified VC clusters.[241] Second, entrepreneurial teams and/or venture capitalists might appreciate proximity to the other party which may lead to a relocation of the new venture close to potential venture capitalists.[242] Third, other reasons might exist which determine the spatial distribution of VC investment opportunities. Such reasons might be the clustering of relevant industries close to the venture capitalist clusters or demographic factors. In consequence, spatial proximity between venture capitalists and new ventures is or is perceived to be important for the emergence of a VC financing relationship if at least one of the first two reasonings applies. Thus, these facts give first hints for the importance of spatial proximity for German VC financing, which is the main topic of this thesis.

However, as has been mentioned in the introduction of this thesis the spatial clustering of the German VC supply in combination with a high relevance of spatial proximity would also have important implications for new ventures, venture capitalists, and public policy. Equity gaps in regard to the supply of venture capital may exist in regions in which no or only few venture capitalists are located. This may force entrepreneurial teams to relocate their ventures close to existing VC clusters and may hamper the regional economic development in those regions. Furthermore, it may be important for venture capitalists to open additional branch offices in distant target areas in order to successfully invest their capital. As a result, it is important to quantify the impact of spatial proximity on VC financing in order to judge the severity of the mentioned implications. This is one of the major aims of this thesis.

2.3 Overview of Relevant Literature

The role of spatial proximity in VC financing is discussed by practitioners and scholars in the US and the UK since the 1980s. However, in recent years there has been an increased interest in spatial aspects of VC financing which is demonstrated by a growing number of academic studies. Keeping the focus of this thesis in mind the literature regarding the role of spatial proximity in VC financing can be classified into four major categories. A classification of the

---

[240] See Fritsch/Schilder (2008), p. 2118 in comparison to Panel B in Figure 2.5. Fritsch/Schilder (2008) compare the location of R&D intensive start-ups and the location of venture capitalists and find only a small correspondence. In contrast to the argumentation above, they conclude that spatial proximity is not important for the emergence of a VC financing relationship since venture capialists locate themselves distant from investment opportunities (cf. Fritsch/Schilder (2008), pp. 2118-2120). However, the distribution of actual financing rounds shows another picture.

[241] Cf. Sorenson/Stuart (2001), p. 1550; Martin et al. (2005), p. 1218.

[242] Cf. Zook (2002), pp. 164-165.

relevant literature and the embeddedness of this thesis in that classification are shown in Figure 2.6.

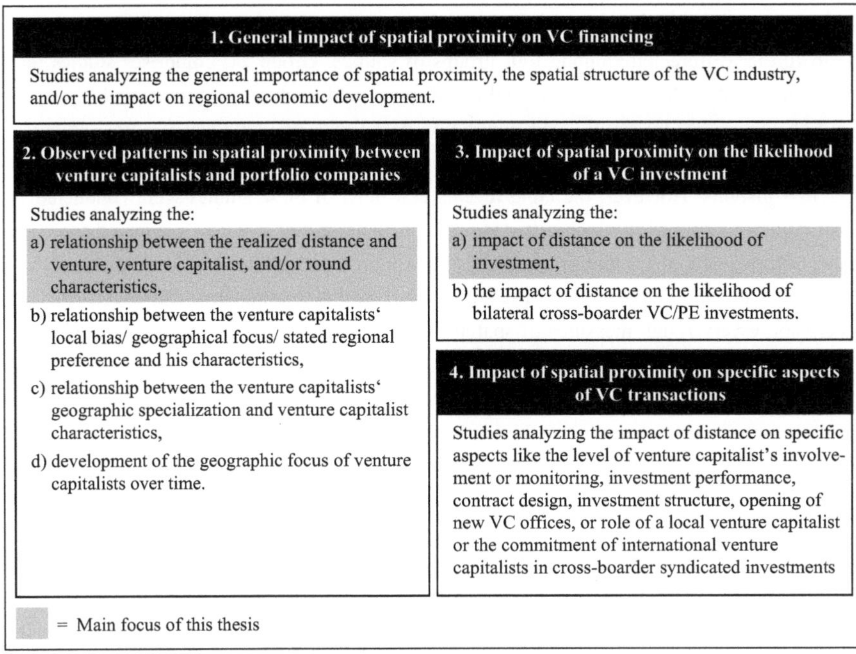

Figure 2.6: Embeddedness of this thesis in the relevant literature
Source: Own illustration.

The first category of studies comprises very **general studies** which analyze the importance of spatial proximity, the spatial structure of the VC industry, and/or the impact of the spatial structure on the regional economic development. Most of these studies have a theoretical or descriptive character. Multivariate methods are not applied. In general, it is found that the VC industry and investments are highly clustered within countries, that spatial proximity is important for VC investment activities, and as a result that regional equity gaps may exist which could hamper the regional economic development.[243] Only Fritsch/Schilder (2007) conclude that spatial proximity is not important for German VC investments and that syndication is

[243] Cf. Florida/Kenney (1988), p. 44; Mason/Harrison (1992), pp. 377-378, Mason/Harrison (2002), pp. 444-447; Martin/Sunley/Turner (2002), pp. 132-143; Zook (2004), p. 621; Martin et al. (2005), pp. 1213-1222; Patton/Kenney (2005), pp. 9-10; Fritsch/Schilder (2007), pp. 201-204.

used to overcome large distances.[244] Panel A in Table 2.4 provides a summary of these studies in regard to their focus, sample, methodology, and main results.[245]

The second category includes studies that are related to **observed patterns in spatial proximity between venture capitalists and portfolio companies.** Within this category it is possible to further differentiate among four groups of studies. Group 2a) comprises studies that analyze the relationship between the realized distance and venture, venture capitalist, and/or round characteristics by scrutinizing transaction based data of individual venture capitalist-investee dyads. Existing studies of this group are summarized in Panel B in Table 2.4 and offer first insights. However, the table reveals that most of these studies were conducted in North American countries which differ strongly in their spatial structure compared to continental European countries that are spatially much more concentrated and have denser infrastructures. Thus, the transferability of results to Germany is questionable. Moreover, existing studies apply very rough measures of spatial proximity and only differentiate between close and distant investments. Only Fritsch/Schilder (2006) analyze a German sample with a metric measure of spatial proximity. However, they analyze only a very limited set of venture and round characteristics and apply only bivariate methods. The study reveals that distance is positively related to the number of venture capitalists per round and the investment volume. The authors further argue that distance is not important for German VC investments and that syndication is used as an instrument to overcome large distances.[246] In contrast, the North American studies found strong spatial biases in the investments of their samples,[247] also for co-investors and thus syndicated deals.[248]

The second group of studies (2b) analyzes the relationship between the venture capitalists' local bias, geographical focus, or stated regional preference and his characteristics by scrutinizing data on the venture capitalist or fund level. A summary of studies belonging to this group as well as their main results is presented in Panel C in Table 2.4. Due to the research design of these studies only relationships with venture capitalist characteristics can be investigated. Furthermore, most of these studies apply very rough measures of spatial proximity. Only Cumming/Dai (2009) additionally analyze the role of a venture capitalist in a syndicated deal for a US sample by dividing the portfolio into lead- and co-investment portfolios and use a metric measure of spatial proximity. Fritsch/Schilder (2008) analyze a German sample of 75

---

[244] Cf. Fritsch/Schilder (2007), pp. 210-211.

[245] In order to provide an overwiew of the existing literature, Table 2.4 summarizes only the most important studies. The selection was made to the best knowledge of the author in regard to the relevance of the respective studies for this thesis.

[246] Cf. Fritsch/Schilder (2006), pp. 22-23.

[247] Cf. Powell et al. (2002), p. 303; Butler/Goktan (2008), p. 12.

[248] Cf. Cumming/Johan (2006), pp. 379-380.

venture capitalists but only consider a very limited set of venture capitalist characteristics. They find that a higher venture capitalist's share of distant syndication partners and a lower number of portfolio companies per investment manager lead to a higher share of distant portfolio companies. The authors argue again that due to a dense infrastructure and the limited number of investment opportunities distance is not important for German VC investments and that syndication is used as an instrument to overcome large distances.[249] International studies again find a strong local bias of lead- and co-investors.[250] Mayer/Schoors/Yafeh (2005) and Baumgärtner (2005) also scrutinize a German sample but do not reveal any relationships between the regional preferences or the geographical focus and the scrutinized venture capitalist characteristics.[251]

Group 2c) includes studies that analyze the relationship between the venture capitalists' geographic specialization and venture capitalist characteristics. Thus, these studies do not consider the spatial proximity between venture capitalists and investees but the level of diversification/specialization across different regions. The geographical specialization may be regarded as a rough measure of spatial proximity since most venture capitalists are located in their main focus area and additional investment regions are likely to be successively farther away. However, this does not have to be the case and results have to be interpreted very cautiously.[252] Furthermore, these studies also scrutinize data on the venture capitalist or fund level and have thus the same drawbacks as the studies of the second group. A summary of these studies as well as their main results is presented in Panel D in Table 2.4.

Studies analyzing the development of the geographic focus of venture capitalists over time constitute group 2d). Only the study from Christensen (2007) has its main focus in this segment and the most important facts are shown in Panel E in Table 2.4. However, also De Clercq et al. (2001), Cumming/Dai (2009), and Han (2009) report some results regarding the development of the average geographical specialization/local bias over time. Christensen (2007) finds for Denmark that the average distance between venture capitalists and ventures follows a v-shaped curve. With the development of the industry venture capitalists first diversify regionally to gather more deal flow. Then, as competition rises, venture capitalists start to specialize regionally.[253] These results might be supported by the other studies. De Clercq et al. (2001) find that Finish venture capitalists diversified geographically between 1994 and

---

[249] Cf. Fritsch/Schilder (2008), pp. 2128-2129.

[250] Cf. Cumming/Dai (2009), pp. 11, 15-16, and 37.

[251] Cf. Baumgärtner (2005), p. 105; Mayer/Schoors/Yafeh (2005), p. 603.

[252] An example would be a venture capitalist active in Germany and Isreal, and thus in two regions, versus a venture capitalist active in Germany, Swizerland, and Austria, and thus in three regions. The second one would be geographically more diversified according to the measures applied by the studies of the third group.

[253] Cf. Christensen (2007), pp. 824-827.

1997 which may represent a relatively early phase of the Finish VC industry.[254] In contrast, Cumming/Dai (2009) and Han (2009) find for US venture capitalists that the average geographical specialization/local bias increased since the 1980s which may represent the growing competition in this more mature market.[255]

Existing studies of the second category regarding observed patterns in spatial proximity provide first insights in respect to the magnitude of the impact of spatial proximity in VC financing and for which types of new ventures, venture capitalists, and/or financing rounds spatial proximity is likely to be particularly important. However, very little is known about the role of spatial proximity in VC financing of central European countries. Furthermore, it is not possible to make causal conclusions regarding the impact of spatial proximity on the likelihood of a single VC investment. The reason is that the observed patterns either refer to aggregated venture capitalist or fund characteristics, are based on preferences and not actual behavior, or that the patterns on the transaction level might also be determined by other omitted variables regarding the supply and demand of VC in certain regions/distances.[256]

The just mentioned drawbacks of the previous category lead to the third category of studies regarding the **impact of spatial proximity on the likelihood of a VC investment**. Group 3a) comprises studies that analyze the impact of distance on the likelihood of domestic VC investments. To the best knowledge of the author, there are only two studies within this group existing so far. A summary of the key facts of these studies is presented in Panel F in Table 2.4. Engel (2003a) analyzes the impact of spatial proximity between venture capitalists and investees on the likelihood of investment by scrutinizing the relationship between the regional presence of venture capitalists and the number of VC investments in that region. After controlling for various factors that might determine the potential VC demand within German districts he does not find a significant relationship between the number of venture capitalists in a specific district and the number of VC investments. This implies that spatial proximity has no impact on the likelihood of German VC investments.[257] Sorenson/Stuart (2001) analyze the likelihood of investment for US VC investments using a matched sample approach. They find that the likelihood of investment decreases dramatically with rising distance. Furthermore, Sorenson/Stuart (2001) prove that the effect of distance is less negative for venture capitalists with a well established network, for deals that are syndicated with trusted other venture capitalists, and/or for deals where a trusted syndication partner is close to the target.[258] However,

---

[254] Cf. De Clercq et al. (2001), p. 53.

[255] Cf. Cumming/Dai (2009), p. 30; Han (2009), p. 43.

[256] This aspect will be discussed in more detail in section 5.2.5.

[257] Cf. Engel (2003a), pp. 136-138.

[258] Cf. Sorenson/Stuart (2001), pp. 1571-1577.

the study only considers a very limited set of venture capitalist characteristics and control variables and does not investigate the impact of new venture characteristics.

Studies analyzing the impact of distance on the likelihood of bilateral cross-border VC/PE investments constitute group 3b). Even though these studies do not focus on the impact of spatial proximity within countries, they are listed here because of their relevance for the research in this thesis. Key facts as well as the main results of existing studies are presented in Panel G in Table 2.4. Using the air distance between the capital cities of two countries as a very rough measure of spatial proximity these studies find that distance reduces the volume and number of bilateral cross-border VC and PE investments. The effect is found to be stronger for smaller deals.[259]

In consequence, some empirical evidence for the impact of spatial proximity on the likelihood of investment exists for US VC investments and international cross-border VC/PE investments. However, first results from Engel (2003a) and the argumentation from Fritsch/Schilder (2006 and 2008) for Germany contradict the international findings. Thus, the impact of spatial proximity on the likelihood of German VC investments remains open. Furthermore, very little is known regarding the effect of venture, venture capitalist, and round characteristics on the impact of distance on the likelihood of investment.

The fourth category includes very specific studies that scrutinize the **impact of spatial proximity on specific aspects of VC transactions.** For the sake of brevity these studies are only briefly discussed here. Various mainly US studies analyze the impact of spatial proximity on the level of venture capitalists' involvement or monitoring in post-contractual investment phases. These studies find that distance has a negative impact on the frequency or likelihood of these activities.[260] Studies which investigate the impact of spatial proximity on the investment performance offer mixed results. For a US sample Chen et al. (2009) find that VC investments of venture capitalists that are located in one of the VC clusters into new ventures that are located outside the venture capitalist's Combined Statistical Area have a higher probability for a successful exist. Contrary, Tian (2009) finds for a US sample that proximate investments are more likely to be exited successfully. For a German sample, Engel (2003a) finds no impact of spatial proximity but a positive impact of regional specialization on employment growth and company survival.[261] Regarding the contract design Bengtsson/Ravid (2009) find for the US that contracts are more investor friendly for distant investments.[262] The

[259] Cf. Aizenman/Kendall (2008), p. 12; Tykvová/Schertler (2008), pp. 13-14.

[260] Cf. Sapienza/Timmons (1989), pp. 75-76; Gomez-Mejia/Balkin/Welbourne (1990), p. 113; Landström (1992), p. 215; Sapienza (1992), p. 19; Sapienza/Gupta (1994), p. 1628; Lerner (1995), pp. 315-316; Sapienza/Manigart/Vermeir (1996), p. 457.

[261] Cf. Engel (2003a), pp. 221-231; Chen et al. (2009), pp. 20-25; Tian (2009), pp. 26-27.

[262] Cf. Bengtsson/Ravid (2009), p. 12.

structure of VC financing also differs with respect to spatial proximity and Tian (2009) finds that distance increases the number and decreases the duration as well as the volume of financing rounds. However, the distance between venture capitalists and their portfolio companies has no impact on the total VC funding.[263] Furthermore, Chen et al. (2009) find that the decision to open new branch offices is influenced by the prior success of VC investments in a certain region. This indicates that venture capitalist want to be close to potentially successful investments.[264] Finally, Mäkelä/Maula (2006 and 2008) investigate cross-border VC. They find for Finland that local venture capitalists are crucial in order to attract cross-border VC and that the commitment of international venture capitalists in cross-border syndicated investments also depends on their distance to the portfolio company.[265]

Throughout this section it became obvious that the majority of existing studies focuses on the US. However, theory and existing empirical evidence shows that country specific research is indispensable. Institutional theory implies that the behavior of entrepreneurial teams and venture capitalists are strongly influenced by country specific institutions.[266] Empirical findings support that venture capital financing differs around the world in many dimensions like the assessment of information within the due diligence, the extent of venture capitalists general involvement, the role of the venture capitalist on the board of directors, or the importance of different management support activities and networks.[267] In addition, North American countries differ strongly in their general spatial structure compared to continental European countries which are spatially much more concentrated and have denser infrastructures. Hence, also the mean distance between venture capitalists and their investments differs substantially and the impact of distance on VC financing is likely to be different across countries.[268] In consequence, it is highly questionable whether international results are transferable to a continental European country like Germany and country specific research is indispensable.

As a result, it has to be concluded that for central European countries like Germany only little is known about the role of spatial proximity between venture capitalists and new ventures in VC financing. In particular, there is limited empirical evidence regarding the relationship between the observed spatial proximity and venture, venture capitalist, and round characteristics (patterns in spatial proximity; group 2a). Furthermore, there is a huge lack of knowledge re-

---

[263] Cf. Tian (2009), pp. 16-21.

[264] Cf. Chen et al. (2009), p. 13.

[265] Cf. Mäkelä/Maula (2006), p. 285; Mäkela/Maula (2008), pp. 249-252.

[266] Cf. Busenitz/Gomez/Spencer (2000), pp. 995-996; Wright/Lockett/Pruthi (2002), pp. 13-14; Bruton/Fried/Manigart (2005), pp. 740-741.

[267] Cf. Sapienza/Manigart/Vermeir (1996), pp. 456-462; Bruton/Fried/Manigart (2005), pp. 752-756; Zacharakis (2007), pp. 699-705.

[268] Cf. Bruton/Fried/Manigart (2005), p. 753; Fritsch/Schilder (2008), pp. 2127-2129.

garding the impact of spatial proximity on the likelihood of a VC investment and for which types of new ventures, venture capitalists, and investment rounds spatial proximity is particularly important (group 3a).

The analysis of the existing literature also revealed that, to the best knowledge of the author, no holistic theoretical framework regarding the impact of spatial proximity on the likelihood of investment throughout the VC investment process exists so far. Most studies only focus on very specific aspects of VC financing, e.g. venture capitalists' support activities, or derive very general hypothesis, e.g. that distance has a negative impact on the likelihood of investment. However, there is no academic literature that discusses the impact of spatial proximity for each phase of the VC investment process and that concludes for which types of new ventures, venture capitalists, or investment rounds spatial proximity is particularly important in order to successfully pass the respective investment phase.

As has been stated in the introduction, this thesis intends to fill these research gaps. First, a holistic theoretical framework regarding the impact of spatial proximity on the likelihood of investment throughout the VC investment process will be elaborated. Second, observed patterns in spatial proximity between venture capitalists and German new ventures will be scrutinized. Third, the impact of spatial proximity on the likelihood of investment will be analyzed for different types of new ventures, venture capitalists, and investment rounds.

Table 2.4: Overview of relevant literature

This table summarizes existing studies that are most important for the work at hand. Fin.: Finland; reg.: region.

Study	Reg.	Time	Analyzed aspect regarding spatial proximity	Main results regarding spatial proximity	Sample	Measure of spatial proximity	Methodology
Panel A: Studies analyzing the general importance of spatial proximity, the spatial structure of the VC industry, and/or the impact on regional economic development							
Fritsch/Schilder (2007)	DE	2004 - 2005	Importance of spatial proximity for VC investments	VC investments and venture capitalists are highly clustered but spatial proximity is not important	75 venture capitalists (interviews), aggregated BVK data	Share of portfolio companies at same site, with distance < 100 km, with distance > 100 km, abroad	Descriptive, bivariate, and qualitative analysis
Schwartz/Bar-El (2007)	Israel	1995 - 2004	Geographic distribution of VC investments in Israel	VC investments are highly clustered; regional equity gaps likely	1239 venture backed companies	-	Descriptive
Martin et al. (2005)	DE, UK	1999 - 2001	Importance of spatial proximity, spatial structure of VC investments, and existence of equity gap in certain regions	Spatial proximity to investee company is perceived to be important; venture capitalists and investments are highly concentrated in both countries, but especially in UK; indications for regional equity gaps	167 VC/PE firms (questionnaire), aggregated BVCA, EVCA, KfW, DtA, and DTI data	-	Theoretical, descriptive, and qualitative analysis
Patton/Kenney (2005)	US	1996 - 2000	Distance between the venture and the entrepreneurial support network (venture's legal counsel, investment bankers, venture capitalists, and independent directors)	54.88 % of venture capitalists are located within 50 miles of the venture; the mean distance is 494.04 miles and median distance is 15.5 miles.	44 semiconductor IPOs	Air distance in miles	Descriptive analysis

Table 2.4 cont.: Overview of relevant literature

Study	Reg.	Time	Analyzed aspect regarding spatial proximity	Main results regarding spatial proximity	Sample	Measure of spatial proximity	Methodology
Zook (2004)	US	1999-2000	Role of spatial proximity in the diffusion of knowledge, the construction of networks, and the resulting regional economic development.	Spatial proximity of actors is crucial for the diffusion of knowledge, the construction of social networks, and the regional economic development.	47 venture capitalists and business angels; 44 ETs (interviews)	-	Theoretical and qualitative analysis
Martin/Sunley/ Turner (2002)	EU	1999	Relevance of spatial proximity for the positive development of the VC industry, should public policy target clusters or dispersal	Spatial proximity between actors is important for a positive development of the VC industry and clusters may be most appropriate	Aggregated data from EVCA and national VC associations	-	Theoretical and descriptive analysis
Mason/Harrison (2002)	UK	1990s	Development of spatial structure of VC/PE industry and investments, existence of equity gap and implications for regional economic development	Concentration of VC/PE investments was reduced compared to the 80s but remains very high; reduction in concentration mainly due to increased number and volume of later stage deals	Aggregated BVCA and CMBOR data	-	Descriptive analysis
Mason/Harrison (1992)	UK	1980s	Spatial structure of VC/PE industry and investments, existence of equity gap and implications for regional economic development	High concentration of the VC/PE industry and investments; spatial proximity is important; equity gap for small volumes in peripheral regions likely which hampers regional economic development	Aggregated BVCA data	-	Descriptive analysis
Florida/Kenney (1988)	US	1980s	Importance of spatial proximity; spatial structure of VC industry, investments, capital flows, and syndication networks; implications for regional economic development	Spatial proximity is important; high concentration of the VC industry (financial and technology centers) and investments; capital flows from financial to technology centers; syndication used to overcome distance; VC is crucial for regional development and restructuring	Aggregated data from various sources	-	Descriptive analysis

Table 2.4 cont.: Overview of relevant literature

Study	Reg.	Time	Analyzed aspect regarding spatial proximity	Main results regarding spatial proximity	Sample	Measure of spatial proximity	Methodology
Panel B: Studies analyzing the relationship between the realized distance and venture, venture capitalist, and/or round characteristics							
Butler/Goktan (2008)	US	1983 - 2004	Relationship between distance and venture characteristics; impact of distance on under pricing and grandstanding in case of IPO	Close ventures are younger, smaller, and have lower asset tangibility; venture capitalists that invest in close ventures are less experienced; distance increases undervaluation at IPO and decreases likelihood for grandstanding	915 venture backed IPOs and their lead-investors	Dummy if distance < 25 miles	Multivariate analysis
Cumming/Johan (2006)	CA	1991 - 2003	Relationship between distance and venture, venture capitalist, and round characteristics	Companies that are publicly quoted, in a high-tech industry, or raising large volumes are more and turnaround companies are less likely to have a distant investor; government/labor sponsored venture capitalists as well as investors with offices in many provinces are likely to invest in proximity	10,450 VC/PE firm-investee dyads	Inter- or intra-provincial investment	Multivariate analysis
Fritsch/Schilder (2006)	DE	2004 - 2005	Relationship between distance and venture as well as round characteristics	Distance is positively related to the number of venture capitalists per round and the investment volume	563 venture capitalist-investee dyads	Travel time by car, distance in km	Bivariate analysis
			Relationship between distance and syndication	No direct relationship between the venture capitalist's distance and syndication, but the existence of a close syndication partner is positively related with the likelihood of syndication	420 venture capitalist-investee dyads	Travel time by car, distance in km	Multivariate analysis
Powell et al. (2002)	US	1988 - 1999	Relationship between distance and venture as well as venture capitalist characteristics	More than 50% of ventures received local funding; ventures with local funding are younger, smaller, and earlier in the research process; venture capitalists investing local are younger and smaller	213 venture backed biotech companies	Dummy if car travel time is < 1 hour	Descriptive analysis

Table 2.4 cont.: Overview of relevant literature

Study	Reg.	Time	Analyzed aspect regarding spatial proximity	Main results regarding spatial proximity	Sample	Measure of spatial proximity	Methodology
Panel C: Studies analyzing the relationship between the venture capitalists' local bias/ geographical focus/ stated regional preference and his characteristics							
Cumming/Dai (2009)	US	1980 - 2009	Relationship between venture capitalists' local bias and venture capitalist characteristics; development of local bias over time	More reputable venture capitalists and venture capitalists with broader networks exhibit less local bias; being lead-investor, staging and specialization in technology industries increase venture capitalists' local bias; venture capitalists' local bias increased over time	13,590 venture capitalist-year combinations	Local bias of portfolio relative to market benchmark portfolio (air distance)	Multivariate analysis
		1980 - 2004	Relationship of distance on investment performance	Proximity of closest syndication partner is positively related to the likelihood of IPO	41,250 VC financing rounds	Air distance in miles	Multivariate analysis
Fritsch/Schilder (2008)	DE	2004 - 2005	Relationship between venture capitalists' share of distant portfolio companies and venture capitalist characteristics	Higher share of distant syndication partners and lower number of portfolio companies per investment manager lead to a higher share of distant portfolio companies	75 venture capitalists (interviews)	Share of portfolio companies with distance >100 km	Multivariate analysis
Mayer/Schoors/ Yafeh (2005)	DE, Israel, JP, UK	2000	Relationship between regional preferences and sources of finance of VC funds	Neither financial systems nor sources of finance are the main explanations for the pronounced differences in specialization strategies	508 VC funds	Ordinal variable based on regional preference	Multivariate analysis
Baumgärtner (2005)	DE	2003	Relationship between venture capitalists' geographical focus and investment stage focus	No relationship between venture capitalists' investment stage focus and geographical specialization; all funds have a very high share of domestic investments	54 venture capitalists	Fraction of domestic, EU, and worldwide inv.	Descriptive and bivariate analysis
Hall/Tu (2003)	UK	2000	Relationship between the venture capitalists' regional preference and venture capitalist characteristics	Large and later stage venture capitalists are more likely to state that they would invest overseas; old venture capitalists are less likely to state to invest overseas	124 VC/PE firms	Dummy if VC firm would invest overseas	Multivariate analysis
Gupta Sapienza (1992)	US	1987	Relationship between the venture capitalists' regional preference and venture capitalist characteristics	Early stage and public venture capitalists prefer a more narrow geographic scope; corporate and larger venture capitalists prefer broader geographic scope	169 venture capitalists	Ordinal variable based on regional preference	Multivariate analysis

Table 2.4 cont.: Overview of relevant literature

Study	Reg.	Time	Analyzed aspect regarding spatial proximity	Main results regarding spatial proximity	Sample	Measure of spatial proximity	Methodology
Panel D: Studies analyzing the relationship between the venture capitalists' geographic specialization and venture capitalist characteristics							
Han (2009)	US	1978 - 2000	Determinants of specialization strategies, development over time, and impact on fund performance	Geographic specialization slightly increased over time and is negatively related to fund size, total capital under management, venture capitalist's age, number of prior successful investments, and the likelihood of IPO; geographic specialization is positively related to the number of prior successful investments in the focus region, and industry as well as stage specialization	1,586 VC funds	No spatial proximity but geographical specialization; HHI regarding the states in which the fund invested and self constructed concentration measure	Multivariate analysis
Knill (2009)	US	1998 - 2006	Impact of venture capitalists' specialization strategies on venture capitalists' growth	Geographic specialization in t-1 is negatively related to venture capitalists' growth in t	1,893 venture capitalist-year combinations	No spatial proximity but domestic/international geographical specialization based on the no. of regions/ countries with investments	Multivariate analysis
			Impact of venture capitalists' specialization strategies on investment performance	Geographic specialization is positively related to the likelihood of IPO or acquisition	43,677 venture capitalist-investee dyads		Multivariate analysis
Lossen (2007)	US, EU	1977 - 2000	Determinants of specialization strategies and impact on fund performance	Geographic specialization is negatively related to the fund size, funds raised in vintage year, seed/ early VC funds, and positively related to the return of the MSCI World Index in the vintage year; no relationship between geographic specialization and performance	174 VC/PE funds	No spatial proximity but geographical specialization; HHI regarding the countries in which the fund invested	Multivariate analysis

Table 2.4 cont.: Overview of relevant literature

Study	Reg.	Time	Analyzed aspect regarding spatial proximity	Main results regarding spatial proximity	Sample	Measure of spatial proximity	Methodology
De Clercq et al. (2001)	Fin.	1994 - 1997	Determinants of specialization strategies and development over time	Geographic specialization decreased over time and is negatively related to the number of portfolio companies, later investment stages, and stage diversification; geographic specialization is positively related to the average ownership in the portfolio companies	112 venture capitalist-year combinations	No spatial proximity but geographical specialization by self constructed index based on the no. of regions with inv.	Descriptive and bivariate analysis
Panel E: Studies analyzing the development of the geographic focus of venture capitalists over time							
Christensen (2007)	DK	1994 - 1999	Development of the geographic focus of venture capitalists over time	The average distance between venture capitalists and ventures follows a v-shaped curve; with the development of the industry venture capitalists first diversify regionally to gather more deal flow; then, as competition rises, venture capitalists start to specialize regionally	170 venture capitalist-investee dyads (only first time, lead-investor inv.)	Road distance in km	Descriptive analysis
Panel F: Studies analyzing the impact of distance on the likelihood of investment							
Engel (2003a)	DE	1996 - 2000	Relationship between the regional presence of venture capitalists and the number of VC investments in that region (controlling for potential VC demand)	No effect of the number of venture capitalists in region on the number of VC investments if one controls for potential VC demand	439 districts	No spatial proximity but presence of VC firms and investees in same district	Multivariate analysis
Sorenson/Stuart (2001)	US	1986 - 1998	Impact of distance on the likelihood of investment; impact of syndication and networks on importance of distance	Distance has a negative impact on the likelihood of investment; the effect of distance is less negative for venture capitalists with a well established network, for deals that are syndicated with trusted other venture capitalists, and/or for deals where a trusted syndication partner is close to the target	40,203 venture capitalist-investee dyads	Air distance in miles	Multivariate analysis

Table 2.4 cont.: Overview of relevant literature

Study	Reg.	Time	Analyzed aspect regarding spatial proximity	Main results regarding spatial proximity	Sample	Measure of spatial proximity	Methodology
Panel G: Studies analyzing the impact of distance on the likelihood of bilateral cross-boarder VC/PE investments							
Aizenman/ Kendall (2008)	World	1990 - 2007	Description of development, status-quo and determinants of bilateral cross-boarder VC/PE investments	Distance reduces the volume and number of bilateral cross-boarder VC and PE investments	1,760 country-pair-year combinations	Air distance in km between capital cities of countries	Multivariate analysis
Tykvová/ Schertler (2008)	World	2000 - 2006	Impact of distance on bilateral cross boarder VC/PE investments	Distance reduces the volume and number of bilateral cross-boarder VC and PE investments, small deals are more sensitive	5,220 country-pair-year observations	Air distance in km between capital cities of countries	Multivariate analysis
			Impact of syndication in investment decisions for distant investments	Syndication of foreign VC/PE firms with local and experienced veteran partners facilitates distant transactions	2,222 cross-border VC/PE firm-investee dyads	Air distance in km between capital cities of countries	Multivariate analysis

3 Relevant Theories for the Analysis of Spatial Proximity in Venture Capital Financing

To analyze the role of spatial proximity between the venture capitalist and the entrepreneurial team throughout the VC investment process, a plurality of theories will be used. The advantage of multiple theories is that critical relationships can be analyzed from different points of view, which are comparable to different searchlight positions to shed light on the research object.[269] This approach allows the generation of more refined insights compared to an analysis which is based only on one specific theory.

Therefore, this chapter outlines a theoretical fundament relevant to the research questions in focus. Subsequently, this theoretical fundament will be used in chapter 4 to elaborate a theoretical framework of the role of spatial proximity between actors in the different phases of the VC investment process by developing comprehensive propositions and testable hypotheses.

This chapter proceeds as follows. First, section 3.1 identifies several theories, which are expected to provide insights on the role of spatial proximity in the VC investment process. As a very broad range of theories might provide insights for the research at hand, this section does not claim to be complete and rather focuses on selected theories. Subsequently, the most promising theories are going to be discussed in more detail throughout sections 3.2 and 3.3. For each theory, theoretical fundamentals will be provided in order to recognize its full potential but also its limitations. Then, each theory will be applied to the VC context and general theoretical implications of spatial proximity between the venture capitalist and the entrepreneurial team will be elaborated. Section 3.4 provides a brief summary.

3.1 Identification of Relevant Theories

The major aim of this thesis is to analyze the role of spatial proximity between the venture capitalist and the entrepreneurial team throughout the VC investment process. As it has been discussed in section 2.1.4, in the course of VC financing not only financial resources are provided by the venture capitalist to the portfolio company but also non-financial support. Thus, next to financial theories also further theories, which offer insights into social relationships and organizational aspects between venture capitalists and the entrepreneurial teams, have to be considered. Furthermore, a specific VC financing relationship is embedded in a context of multiple relationships to other venture capitalists, other entrepreneurial teams as well as a multitude of supporting actors. Therefore, also theories which take interactions and relation-

---

[269] See section 1.2 for a detailed discussion of the research methodology.

ships beyond the venture capitalist-entrepreneurial team dyad into account have to be scrutinized in regard to their potential impact.

In the first place, financial theories are crucial in order to understand the financing relationship between venture capitalists and entrepreneurial teams and to be able to analyze the role of spatial proximity between actors in the VC investment process. The origin of modern financial theory is constituted by **neoclassical microeconomics** which puts perfect competitive capital markets into the center of analysis and postulates amongst others the independence of financing decisions and the market value of the company.[270] This theory is based on four main assumptions:[271]

- Perfect capital markets, on which no information and transaction costs exist and on which all market participants are able to act with equal efficiency.
- Equal access of all market participants to the capital market.
- Homogeneous expectations since any information is costlessly available to all market participants and all of them assess the implications of the information correctly.
- Given investment strategies, meaning that the rules which firms use to make current and future investment decisions are given.

Neoclassical microeconomics contributes strongly to the basic understanding of capital markets and each investment can be characterized by its risk-return properties.[272] However, since the assumptions of neoclassical microeconomics are very restrictive, the theory does not adequately model realistic capital markets. Especially VC markets, which can be characterized as having high information and transaction costs, strong informational asymmetries, a high level of illiquidity and an interdependency between financing and investment decisions, diverge in many aspects from the postulated perfect capital markets.[273] In addition, according to the theory institutions[274] and different financial instruments would not be necessary. Spatial proximity between actors would then have no influence at all since transactions could be conducted easily and without costs on perfect capital markets.[275] In consequence, neoclassical

[270] Cf. Schmidt/Terberger (1997), p. 55; Picot/Dietl/Franck (2005), pp. 35-45. Modigliani/Miller (1958) state that the capital structure of a company, and therefore also the differentiation between debt and equity, has no implications on the market value of the company (cf. Modigliani/Miller (1958), pp. 268-276).

[271] Cf. Fama (1978), pp. 273-274.

[272] Cf. Perridon/Steiner (2004), p. 538.

[273] Cf. Haarmann (2006), pp. 38-40.

[274] The term institution is not defined consistently in the literature (cf. Erlei/Leschke/Sauerland (1999), pp. 23-25). Within this work an institution is defined according to Richter/Furubotn (2003) as a system of related, formal and informal rules as well as all arrangements to enforce these rules (cf. Richter/Furubotn (2003), p. 7).

[275] Cf. Perridon/Steiner (2004), p. 538.

microeconomics is not an appropriate theory to analyze the role of spatial proximity in the VC investment process.

Subsequently, scholars started to explicitly address the shortcomings of neoclassical microeconomics and incorporated market frictions like transaction costs, informational asymmetries and resulting incentive problems. This led to the development of **new institutional economics**, which is based on neoclassical microeconomics. Important theories, which belong to the school of thought of new institutional economics, are property rights theory, agency theory as well as transaction cost theory.[276] Since new institutional economics is based on more realistic assumptions, it acknowledges the importance of institutions and offers important insights into VC financing relationships in general and the role of spatial proximity in particular. Therefore, the named theories of new institutional economics will be discussed in detail in section 3.2.1.

The theories of new institutional economics are also based on several assumptions like opportunistic behavior of actors or, in the case of agency theory, also hierarchical relationships. The appropriateness of these assumptions have been discussed controversially in the literature and led to the application of further theories in the VC context.[277]

Game theory attempts to explain the behavior of actors in strategic situations, in which conflicts of interest and information problems occur and in which the individual payoff or utility depends on the choice of strategy of the other actors. The theory does not assume a hierarchical relationship between actors and offers important insights about conditions promoting cooperative behavior of actors. Therefore, the theory has been applied to VC financing relationships by Cable/Shane (1997) and important insights in regard to the role of spatial proximity of actors in the VC investment process can be expected. Thus, section 3.2.2.1 discusses game theory in more detail.

Stewardship theory does not assume the opportunistic behavior of actors and postulates that the interests of actors are aligned under certain conditions. Thus, the theory contrasts agency theory and provides different implications in the case of VC financing, which also affect the role of spatial proximity of actors in the VC investment process. Therefore, stewardship theory is discussed in section 3.2.2.2.

The relationship between venture capitalists and their portfolio companies is usually very intense since the portfolio company does not only receive financial resources but also non-financial support. Furthermore, the implications of many theories mentioned above are influenced by factors like trust, reciprocity, or reputation. Therefore, social relationships between

---

[276] See section 3.2.1.

[277] See section 3.2.2 for further discussion.

the actors also play an important role in the VC investment process. **Social exchange theory** analyzes factors which influence the development and maintenance of social relationships and is strongly related to social capital and interpersonal attraction. It can be assumed that spatial proximity of actors influences social relationships and therefore also the VC investment process. Consequently, section 3.2.2.3 discusses social exchange theory in detail.

Next to these theories also **behavioral finance theories** could offer insights for the focused research questions. Behavioral finance encompasses a broad range of theories that "...drop[s] the traditional assumptions of expected utility maximization with rational investors in efficient markets".[278] Relevant examples are overconfidence[279] or the attention effect,[280] which could lead to the investor's preference for investments in spatial proximity. Since the field of behavioral finance is very broad and did not lead to substantial new insights in the context of VC within existing literature, these theories will not be discussed in detail for the sake of brevity and focus of the work at hand.[281]

The theories which have been mentioned so far mainly focus dyadic relationships between venture capitalists and entrepreneurial teams. Interactions and relationships beyond the venture capitalist-entrepreneurial team dyad are considered by the **network approach**. Networks are constituted by several actors and their relationships among each other. These relationships are likely to have an impact on informational problems or asymmetries and thus influence many of the implications made by the theories mentioned above. Furthermore, networks can be regarded as an additional organizational form next to markets and hierarchies and allow the analysis of VC financing relationships from an organizational point of view. Networks highly depend on the relationships between actors, which are likely to be influenced by spatial proximity. Therefore, the network approach might offer important implications for the work at hand and will be discussed in section 3.3.

In addition, the **resource-based theory** could be used in order to analyze certain aspects of the role of spatial proximity between actors in the VC investment process since the availability and provision of certain resources might be sensitive to spatial proximity.[282] However,

---

[278] Ritter (2003), p. 429.

[279] Overconfidence refers to behavior in which actors invest a relatively high proportion of their wealth into assets they are familiar with (e.g. local companies), even though this is bad for diversification (cf. Ritter (2003), p. 431).

[280] The attention effect refers to behavior in which actors do not process all information but invest in assets that have captured their attention, even though it might not be optimal (Gürtler/Hartmann (2005), pp. 381-382). This could lead to higher than optimal shares of local companies in the actor's portfolio.

[281] See Niederöcker (2002); Engel (2003b); Schefczyk (2004); Nathusius (2005) for similar approaches in considering behavioral finance. For further discussion of behavioral finance see Shefrin (2000) or Ritter (2003).

[282] For a thorough discussion of the resource-based theory in the case of VC investments see Fingerle (2005), pp. 141-168.

most of the relevant aspects can be subsumed under other theories. The impact of spatial proximity on the availability of venture capitalist's resources can be analyzed with the help of transaction cost theory[283] and the network approach[284] amongst others. Furthermore, the influence of spatial proximity on the provision of resources can be mainly analyzed by transaction cost theory and social exchange theory.[285] Therefore, the resource-based theory will not be discussed in detail within this chapter.

Figure 3.1 summarizes relevant theories to explain the role of spatial proximity between actors throughout the VC investment process which will be discussed in detail in subsequent sections.

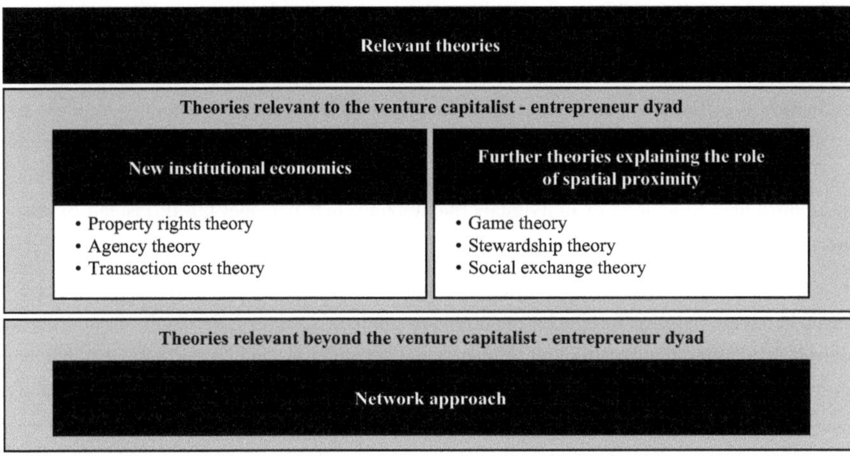

Figure 3.1: Relevant theories to explain the role of spatial proximity between actors in the VC investment process
Source: Own illustration.

283 See section 3.2.1.3.

284 See section 3.3.

285 See section 3.2.2.3.

3.2 Theories Relevant to the Venture Capitalist - Entrepreneur Dyad

3.2.1 New Institutional Economics as Starting Point

The term new institutional economics was first introduced by Oliver Williamson.[286] This generic term does not constitute a consistent theoretical framework, but it comprises different related theoretical approaches, which partly overlap, refer to, and complement each other.[287]

New institutional economics is based on neoclassical microeconomics.[288] It amplifies neoclassical theory by more realistic assumptions and therefore does not only explain market forces but also addresses certain market frictions. In addition, this school of thought account for the importance of institutions.[289] The theoretical approaches belonging to new institutional economics mainly discuss two forms of market frictions. First, the assumption that all market actors have access to perfect and costless information is dropped and the theories realize that information is difficult to obtain and to process. This leads to incomplete and asymmetric information of individuals. Second, the creation, enforcement, and monitoring of contracts imposes transaction costs.[290] Furthermore, new institutional economics assumes that everything can be attributed to actions of individuals maximizing their personal utility instead of maximizing profits.

These differences to neoclassical theory have important implications. On the one hand, opportunistic behavior and therefore incentive problems could arise since individuals act in order to maximize their individual utility and informational asymmetries and transaction costs hamper the enforcement of contracts.[291] On the other hand, individuals have a bounded rationality since they are limited in the access to and processing of information.[292] This could cause several inefficiencies like lower productivity, wrong division of labor or higher transaction costs.

---

[286] Cf. Williamson (1975), p. 1. Other important contributions to this school of thought are Coase (1937, 1960); Demsetz (1967); Alchian/Demsetz (1973); North/Thomas (1973); Ross (1973); Jensen/Meckling (1976); Williamson (1979); Fama (1980); Williamson (1988) to name a few.

[287] Cf. Picot/Dietl/Franck (2005), p. 46.

[288] See Coase (1960), pp. 1-44.

[289] Cf. Richter/Furubotn (2003), pp. 2-13.

[290] Cf. Williamson (1985), pp. 26-29.

[291] Cf. Picot/Dietl/Franck (2005), pp. 31-32. Opportunistic behavior is defined as a behavior, in which individual interests are pursued even though the actor is consciously aware of the potential damage of other individuals' interests (cf. Williamson (1975), pp. 26-27).

[292] For further discussion of the concept of bounded rationality see Picot/Dietl/Franck (2005), p. 33.

The theories of new institutional economics share the conviction that occurring inefficiencies can be mitigated by the definition of appropriate institutions.[293] These institutions become effective by influencing the motivation and coordination of individual actors.

The existing plurality of approaches belonging to new institutional economics can be classified within three major theories, which are shown in Figure 3.2.[294] Property rights theory as well as agency theory focus on informational asymmetries and necessary interest and incentive alignments. More specifically, property rights theory aims to reduce inefficiencies by aligning interests with the appropriate design of institutions and the definition of rights attached to certain resources. Agency theory analyzes the relationship between a principal and an agent and recommends measures to reduce prevailing information and incentive problems. In contrast, transaction cost theory focuses on costs arising due to the creation, use, and enforcement of institutions. In order to minimize transaction costs, the design of institutions and transaction structures are analyzed.

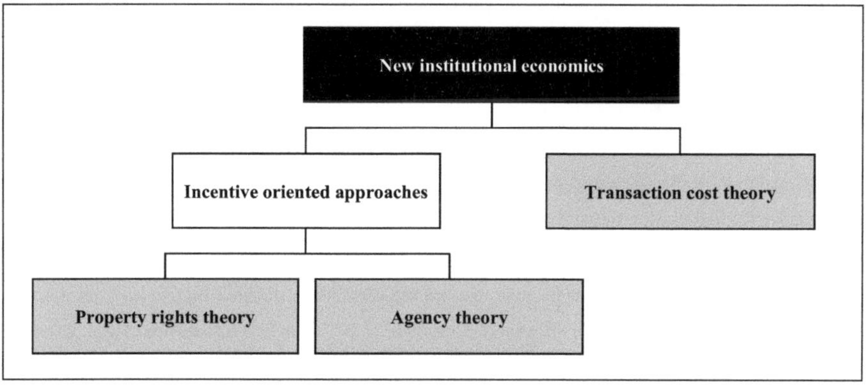

Figure 3.2: Classification of theories within new institutional economics
Source: Based on Williamson (1985), pp. 26-29; Perridon/Steiner (2004), p. 539.

New institutional economics applies a more realistic set of assumptions compared to the neoclassical theory. Therefore, it allows a more reasonable analysis of VC financing relationships. Consequently, the majority of recent articles dealing with entrepreneurial finance and more specifically with VC financing relationships applies concepts of new institutional economics.[295] Moreover, since spatial proximity between the venture capitalist and the venture

[293] Cf. Williamson (1985), pp. 26-29.

[294] Cf. Williamson (1985), pp. 26-29; Niederöcker (2002), pp. 35-37; Picot/Dietl/Franck (2005), p. 46. Other classifications can be also found in the literature. See e.g. Schefczyk (2004), p. 128.

[295] See Denis (2004), p. 303 for a review of recent literature.

would have no affect at all if one assumes perfect capital markets, new institutional economics provides a good starting point for the investigation of the role of spatial proximity in the VC investment process. Therefore, the theories classified in Figure 3.2 are discussed in more detail in the following sections.

3.2.1.1 Property Rights Theory

a) Theoretical Foundations

The theory of property rights[296] comprises a group of analytical concepts trying to explain the process and consequences of the creation, design, attribution, and transfer of rights.[297] The theory defines goods as a bundle of attached rights which are traded on markets. This is motivated by the fact that pure ownership of resources does not ultimately define the rights of action attached to these resources. "It is not the resource itself which is owned; it is a bundle, or a portion, of rights to use a resource that is owned."[298] The effective rights are ultimately defined by institutions made up by the prevailing law, contracts, conventions, or traditions. With the help of well defined property rights individuals are able to overcome conflicts about the use of scarce resources.[299]

Typically, four different types of property rights can be distinguished: the right to use resources, to change the form and/or substance of resources, to earn income from the resources, and to transfer the rights attached to the resources to others (e.g. sale or rent).[300]

Next to the basic assumptions of new institutionalism, which were discussed in the previous section, the theory assumes that property rights are ultimately defined by the institutional environment and are in the center of analysis instead of pure ownership. Furthermore, external effects as consequences of individual actions and their potential internalization are considered.[301]

---

[296] Important fundamental articles on property rights include Coase (1960); Demsetz (1967); Cheung (1970); Alchian/Demsetz (1973). A detailed overview of the theory of property rights gives Picot/Reichwald/Wigand (2001), pp. 46-50. Property rights are also referred to as entitlement rights or resource rights (cf. Schüller (1983), p. VII; Gerum (1992), col. 2119).

[297] Cf. Schefczyk (2004), p. 135.

[298] Alchian/Demsetz (1973), p. 17.

[299] Cf. Furubotn/Pejovich (1972), p. 1139; Nathusius (2005), p. 47. See also Alchian/Demsetz (1973), p. 17 for a basic introduction to the concept of property rights.

[300] Cf. Alchian/Demsetz (1972), p. 783; Picot/Reichwald/Wigand (2001), p. 47.

[301] Cf. Furubotn/Pejovich (1972), p. 1157; Picot (1991), p. 145; Schefczyk (2004), p. 136.

The central argument of the theory is that the definition of property rights determines the allocation and use of resources in a specific and predictable way and therefore has behavioral implications for relevant actors. This allows us to compare different organizational structures in terms of the optimal allocation of property rights.[302] For the evaluation of alternative property rights constellations negative external effects,[303] transaction costs, and in case of delegation, agency costs have to be considered.[304] An allocation of property rights is regarded as optimal if the inherent costs are minimized.[305]

Inefficiencies are generally assumed if property rights are allocated across different individuals because the economic consequences of specific actions affect individuals only partially (external effects). In consequence, individuals might not be rewarded sufficiently for their efforts or they do not have to bear full consequences of suboptimal behavior.[306] Furthermore, the enforcement of property rights in relation to third parties is more difficult the more individuals have a fraction of the specific right. This is due to increased costs of coordination and definition of responsibilities (transaction costs). In general, transaction costs emerge due to the creation, transfer, and enforcement of property rights.[307] Agency costs appear because of conflicts of interest and informational asymmetries.[308] In consequence, the efficiency of alternative allocations of property rights increases the more the economic consequences of certain actions are internalized.

b) Application to Venture Capital Financing

VC investments can be interpreted as the creation and/or transfer of property rights.[309] Therefore, the theory of property rights can be applied in a financial context and is able to give important insights into the VC financing relationship. For the work at hand the theory is of relevance for two reasons. First, it represents an important foundation of the related agency theory and transaction cost theory.[310] Second, the theory offers important insights for the de-

---

302 Cf. Furubotn/Pejovich (1972), p. 1139; Jensen/Meckling (1976), p. 308; Schefczyk (2004), pp. 136-137.

303 Cf. Coase (1960), pp. 1-44; Furubotn/Pejovich (1972), pp. 1142-1146.

304 See sections 3.2.1.2 and 3.2.1.3 for a discussion of agency cost and transaction costs.

305 Cf. Coase (1937), pp. 390-393; Picot/Reichwald/Wigand (2001), p. 48. The practical application of the concept is limited due to difficulties in measuring inherent costs (cf. Schefczyk (2004), pp. 136-137).

306 Cf. Coase (1960), pp. 1-44; Alchian/Demsetz (1972), pp. 779-783.

307 Cf. Alchian/Demsetz (1973), p. 26; Engel (2003b), p. 164. See also section 3.2.1.3.

308 See also section 3.2.1.2.

309 Cf. Schefczyk (2004), p. 135.

310 Cf. Schmidt (1988), pp. 248-262; Schmidt/Terberger (1997), p. 397. However, the role of property rights theory as basis for other neo-institutional theories is not universally accepted (cf. Perridon/Steiner (2004), pp. 538-539).

velopment of appropriate contracts between a venture capitalist and its portfolio companies as well as adequate monitoring structures for portfolio companies.[311]

One critical aspect of the theory of property rights is that the execution of property rights is not only restricted by explicit contracts but also by the actual behavior of actors. This leads to limitations of the predictability of the allocation and use of resources especially in the case of VC transactions. One example underlining this issue is that in the course of an exit, entrepreneurs regularly do not choose the buyer offering the highest price. The reason is that the entrepreneurs are not indifferent in regard to the person or type of their investors and partners. In consequence, this behavior restricts the right of the venture capitalist to sell his stake in the portfolio company.[312]

c) *Implications of Spatial Proximity between Actors*

Property rights theory and its role as a fundament of agency and transaction cost theory implies that spatial proximity between the venture capitalist and the entrepreneurial team influences several aspects of a VC financing relationship. In the course of a VC investment property rights are allocated across several actors, particularly the entrepreneurial team and the venture capitalist. The initiation, monitoring, and enforcement of these property rights impose transaction costs which might be sensitive to spatial proximity.[313] Furthermore, suboptimal structures of property rights and an inadequate design of contracts and monitoring structures might cause additional agency costs which may be higher in distance.[314] Due to these facts, agency and transaction costs and thus spatial proximity might impact whether property rights are allocated across several actors at all, which structure these rights may have, how contracts are designed, which monitoring structures are implemented, and thus if and how a VC transaction is accomplished.

---

311 Cf. Schefczyk (2004), p. 138, Baumgärtner (2005), p. 88.

312 Cf. Bindseil (1994), pp. 50-51; Schefczyk (2004), p. 137.

313 See section 3.2.1.3 for a detailed discussion of transaction cost theory and the impact of spatial proximity on transaction costs.

314 See section 3.2.1.2 for a discussion of agency theory and the impact of spatial proximity on agency costs.

3.2.1.2 Agency Theory

a) Theoretical Foundations

Agency theory[315] belongs to the school of thought of new institutionalism and analyzes the relationship between two economically acting parties – the principal and the agent. There are numerous definitions of an agency relationship.[316] These definitions range from relatively narrow ones which define an agency relationship as "… a contract under which one or more persons (the principal(s)) engage another person (the agent) to perform some service on their behalf which involves delegating some decision making authority to the agent …"[317] to very broad ones which state that an agency relationship is simply constituted by the dependency of one individual (principal) on the action of another individual (agent).[318] The major difference between these definitions is whether a hierarchical relationship between the two parties is needed or not. Therefore, it turns out to be useful to state a list of attributes characterizing an agency relationship. This list is not intended to be complete and not every agency relationship has to have all attributes. The intention is to provide a reference for the following analysis. Agency relationships are mainly characterized by:[319]

- Two acting parties, namely the agent and the principal.
- Delegation of property rights by the principal to the agent in order to perform certain tasks.
- Conflicting interests between both parties arising due to the maximization of their individual utility (assumption of opportunistic behavior).
- The choice of some action under uncertainty by the agent, which influences the utility of the principal.
- An informational asymmetry in the form that the agent has an information advantage in relation to the principal as well as incomplete information of the principal regarding the outcome of the agent's actions.

---

[315] Important fundamental articles include Ross (1973); Jensen/Meckling (1976); Fama (1980); Grossman/Hart (1983) as well as Eisenhardt (1989). An introduction to agency theory in the VC context provides Gompers/Lerner (2004), pp. 159-163.

[316] See for example Ross (1973), p. 134; Jensen/Meckling (1976), p. 308; Pratt/Zeckhauser (1985), p. 2, Arrow (1985), p. 37.

[317] Jensen/Meckling (1976), p. 308.

[318] Cf. Pratt/Zeckhauser (1985), p. 2.

[319] Cf. Ross (1973), pp. 134-135; Rees (1985), p. 3; Niederöcker (2002), pp. 45-46; Perridon/Steiner (2004), p. 539; Wolf (2005), p. 277.

- A contract[320] that states which compensation[321] the principal has to transfer to the agent is to be defined (definition of an incentive structure).
- The agent's utility depends both on the contractually defined compensation and the value of the action chosen by the agent.

Informational asymmetries and conflicts of interests are particularly important for the occurrence of agency problems. If one would have complete and costless information, no agency problems would occur because the principal would be able to fully observe and evaluate the actions of the agent. In consequence, he would be able to contractually define a compensation scheme for the agent which depends on his actions and outcomes and ensures that the agent acts in the best interest of the principal. Since this compensation scheme is known by the agent in advance, he would choose to act in accordance to the predefined contract. On the other hand, if there was no conflict of interests between the two parties, there would be no agency problems as well. However, following agency theory the agent seeks to opportunistically maximize his own utility and it is difficult or expensive for the principal to observe and assess the actions of the agent. Therefore, it can be assumed that the agent will not act in the best interest of the principal. In consequence, usually no pareto-efficient[322] solution (first-best solution) exists.[323] The focus of agency theory is now to characterize optimal forms of contracts between principals and agents in order to achieve an optimal solution under the constraints of imperfect markets (second-best solution).[324]

Jensen/Meckling (1976) describe two general solutions – namely monitoring[325] and bonding – to reduce the information and incentive problems described above.[326] Within this thesis, the term 'monitoring' used by Jensen/Meckling (1976) is going to be referred to as monitoring in a broad sense, which includes all measures initiated by the principal in order to establish appropriate incentives for and to monitor the agent. This results in an alignment of interests and a reduction of the inherent informational asymmetries.

---

[320] Rees (1985), p. 3 stresses that the term 'contract' has to be interpreted very broadly and could be of an explicit or implicit nature.

[321] This compensation can be pecuniary or non-pecuniary.

[322] The concept of pareto efficiency states that there is no other solution, which improves the utility of one party without decreasing the utility of another party (cf. Franke/Hax (1999), p. 416).

[323] Cf. Ross (1973), p. 138.

[324] Cf. Rees (1985), p. 3; Eisenhardt (1989), pp. 57-59.

[325] Jensen/Meckling (1976) use a very broad definition of 'monitoring'. To be more specific I am going to differentiate between monitoring in a broad sense and in a narrow sense. Monitoring in a broad sense refers to the term 'monitoring' used by Jensen/Meckling (1976) and includes monitoring in a narrow sense as well as screening, due diligence and self selection (see also Jensen/Meckling (1976), pp. 308-309; Picot/Dietl/Franck (2005), pp. 73, 77). Within this work and if not stated otherwise the term monitoring refers to monitoring in a narrow sense.

[326] Cf. Jensen/Meckling (1976), pp. 308-309.

Monitoring in a broad sense comprises measures like (i) monitoring in a narrow sense, (ii) screening, (iii) due diligence, and (iv) self selection. **Monitoring in a narrow sense** encompasses the measurement, observation, and control of the agent's behavior through budget restrictions, staged financing,[327] operating rules, and the like as well as rewarding appropriate or sanctioning inappropriate behavior of the agent with the help of compensation policies. Furthermore, one could think about consulting activities by the principal to educate the agent and therefore to mitigate informational asymmetries. **Screening and due diligence**[328] refers to activities by the principal to gather information in advance in order to better evaluate the qualification and motivation of the agent as well as the quality of a potentially proposed project. Finally, the principal could induce a **self selection**[329] process by offering different contracts to the agent. By choosing the contract which is most beneficial for the agent he implicitly admits certain information about his qualifications and motivation. The occurring monitoring costs (in a broad sense) have to be carried by the principal and reduce the specialization benefits obtained by delegation.

On the other hand, it could be advantageous for the agent to spend resources in order to demonstrate that he is going to act in the best interest of the principal (**bonding**). These activities include (i) signaling, (ii) building up a high reputation, (iii) high personal investments, and (iv) self bonding contracts.[330] **Signaling**[331] means that the agent intends to create a signal in order to mitigate informational asymmetries and therefore to create trust of the principal in the agent's qualification and future behavior. Examples are the acquisition of a certain degree of education, work certificates or the creation of very good sample work like a well elaborated business plan. For the effectiveness of signaling it is crucial that it is not cost efficient for the non qualified or non motivated agents to create false signals.[332] The agent could also invest to build up a high **reputation** which mitigates agency problems twofold. First, a high reputation of the agent serves as a signal for his qualification and motivation. Second, a high reputation

---

[327] Staged financing is defined as the progressive infusion of capital within different rounds of financing. For further discussion see Gompers/Lerner (2004), pp. 172-200.

[328] Some authors define screening and self selection synonymously (cf. Franke/Hax (1999), p. 414; Jost (2001), pp. 28-29). See sections 0 and 2.1.4.3 respectively for a detailed discussion and definition of screening and due diligence activities in the case of a VC investment.

[329] See Picot/Dietl/Franck (2005), pp. 85-88 for a detailed discussion of self selection processes.

[330] Building up a high reputation, high personal investments, and self bonding contracts could also be interpreted as signaling strategies, but in contrast to pure signaling strategies they also help to mitigate conflicts of interests and they are affected by spatial proximity in different ways. Consequently, they are discussed separately here.

[331] The concept of signaling goes back to Spence (1973), who analyzed the model in the context of labor markets. Important articles on signaling in the field of financial theory include Ross (1977) and Leland/Pyle (1977).

[332] Cf. Franke/Hax (1999), p. 414.

reduces conflicts of interest. Since it is very time consuming and costly for the agent to build up a high reputation, he has a very strong interest in preserving this reputation. In consequence, it is very important for him to obtain a positive feedback from the principal which leads to an alignment of interests between both parties.[333] High **personal investments** of the agent in the form of an equity stake in the relevant project lead to a high risk participation. **Self bonding contracts** include guarantees that the agent is not going to do certain actions as well as the assurance that he will compensate the principal if he behaves differently. Thus, personal investments and self bonding contracts affect agency problems similar to the creation of a high reputation and could also serve as signals to reduce informational asymmetries and contribute to the alignment of interests between principal and agent. Bonding costs are typically carried by the agent. The different types of measures to mitigate agency problems are classified in Figure 3.3.

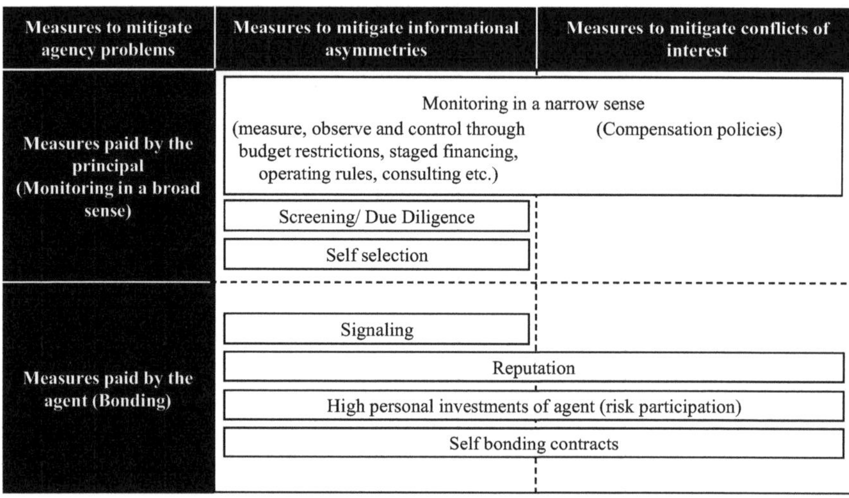

Figure 3.3: Classification of different measures to mitigate agency problems
Source: Own illustration.

The costs that occur because of agency problems are called agency costs and are an important factor to evaluate different incentive and monitoring structures. These agency costs can be defined as the difference between the first-best and second-best solution.[334] The principal and the agent usually incur some monitoring (in a broad sense) and bonding costs and there is

[333] Cf. Erlei/Leschke/Sauerland (1999), pp. 229-234.

[334] Cf. Picot/Dietl/Franck (2005), p. 73.

generally still some divergence between the behavior of the agent and the behavior which would maximize the welfare of the principal.[335] In consequence, Jensen/Meckling (1976) define agency costs as the sum of:

- the monitoring costs in a broad sense incurred by the principal,
- the bonding costs incurred by the agent, and
- the residual loss of economic welfare.[336]

These agency costs might be sensitive to the spatial proximity between the principal and the agent, which may cause agency theory to be highly relevant for this thesis.

As has been mentioned before, informational asymmetries are one of the main reasons for agency problems to occur. These asymmetries between the contracting parties may arise pre-contractual or post-contractual and cause different types of problems.[337] Consequently, three different types of informational asymmetries can be differentiated and are presented in Figure 3.4.

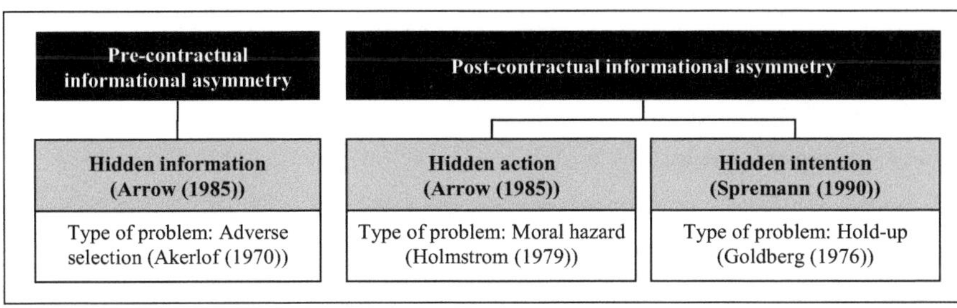

Figure 3.4: Classification of different types of informational asymmetries
Source: Based on Engel (2003b), pp. 142, 144; Nathusius (2005), p. 51; Picot/Dietl/Franck (2005), p. 77.

Hidden information

Hidden information refers to a pre-contractual information asymmetry in regard to the quality of goods, services or the like. This means that the information asymmetry exists before the principal chooses an agent and the contract is closed. Hidden characteristics are a special case

[335] Even though complete monitoring could be possible, it would not be economically viable. Cf. Ross (1973), p. 138.

[336] Cf. Jensen/Meckling (1976), p. 308.

[337] Cf. Picot/Dietl/Franck (2005), p. 77.

of hidden information and refer to information asymmetries in regard to the ability (talent, skill, experience, ingenuity, leadership, etc.) and motivation of the agent himself.[338]

The main problem, which could occur because of hidden information, is the problem of adverse selection.[339] The term 'adverse selection' has its origin within the theory of insurance and was first described by Akerlof (1970), who used the example of a second-hand car market (market for lemons).[340] Adverse selection might occur if principals are not able to differentiate between agents offering a low quality and those offering a high quality of goods or services. In consequence, principals expect an average quality and offer an average price for the good or service. As a result agents offering a low quality are paid too much and agents offering a high quality do not receive an appropriate compensation. This could lead to the result that those agents offering a high quality of goods and services leave the market which in turn leads to a further reduction of the average quality. This mechanism could lead to a breakdown of the whole market and therefore constitute a market failure.[341]

Hidden action

Hidden action[342] refers to a post-contractual informational asymmetry in regard to the agent's actions and effort. This means that the informational asymmetry exists after the principal has chosen an agent and the contract is closed. The main problem, which could occur because of hidden action, is the problem of moral hazard. The term 'moral hazard' also has its origin within the theory of insurance.[343]

The problem occurs because the behavior of the agent cannot be fully observed or evaluated by the principal. In addition, a conflict of interest could be prevalent since the agent's actions affect both his own utility and the utility of the principal. This could lead to an opportunistic behavior of the agent.[344] Hidden actions could lead to three different types of problems.

---

338 Cf. Arrow (1985), pp. 38-42; Niederöcker (2002), pp. 49-50.

339 For a fundamental discussion of adverse selection see Akerlof (1970). See also Leland/Pyle (1977), pp. 371-372 and specifically for VC Trester (1998), pp. 675-699. Some authors do not subordinate the problem of adverse selection to agency theory since there is no hierarchical relationship existing (cf. Schefczyk (2004), pp. 149-150; Schmidt/Terberger (1997), pp. 396-399). However, other authors argue that this type of problem is highly associated with agency theory and can also be subordinated here (cf. Richter/Furubotn (2003), pp. 218-219; Picot/Dietl/Franck (2005), pp. 74-75; Wolf (2005), p. 277). Moreover, Arrow (1985) state that adverse selection is part of the problem of hidden information which he subordinates to agency theory (cf. Arrow (1985), p. 38)

340 Cf. Arrow (1985), p. 38.

341 Cf. Akerlof (1970), pp. 489-490.

342 Cf. Arrow (1985), p. 38; Houben (2002), p. 2.

343 For a further discussion of the term moral hazard see Holmstrom (1979). Moral hazard in the case of insurances was discussed by Pauly (1968).

344 Cf. Spremann (1987), pp. 5-7.

The probably most common type of hidden action is shirking, which is sometimes also called effort incentive.[345] The problem occurs if after the contract is closed the agent does not fully participate in the marginal utility but has the complete burden of the effort, which is a disutility to the agent. This could lead to a less than optimal level of effort of the agent.[346]

Another type of hidden action is perk consumption, which is sometimes also called fringe benefits or consumption on the job. Here the agent increases his non pecuniary perk consumption and benefits to the full extent, while the costs have to be carried, at least partly, by the principal.[347]

Finally, the agent could choose an investment policy, which is not optimal for the principal. Three kinds of problems can be differentiated: the agent could invest into projects with a negative net present value (overinvestment), he could not invest in projects with a positive net present value (underinvestment) and he could initiate investments with a higher risk than desired by the principal (risk incentive).[348] The underinvestment and risk incentive problem are predominantly relevant in the debt capital context and are consequently not discussed here.[349] An overinvestment could be realized by an agent because of the existence of excess financial resources and the personal interest in certain projects or company growth. Similar to the problem of perk consumption the agent does not have to bear the full costs of these expenditures.[350]

Hidden intention

Hidden intention[351] refers to a post-contractual informational asymmetry in regard to the agent's actions. The main problem, which could occur because of hidden intention, is the problem of hold-up.[352] A hold-up is defined as the opportunistic exploitation of contractual loopholes by the agent and arises because most contracts are incomplete or difficult to verify.[353] The main informational asymmetry does not exist between the principal and the agent

---

345 Cf. Arrow (1985), p. 38.

346 Cf. Grossman/Hart (1983), pp. 10-18.

347 Cf. Jensen/Meckling (1976), pp. 312-319; Perridon/Steiner (2004), p. 542.

348 Cf. Niederöcker (2002), pp. 51-52.

349 An underinvestment emerges if entrepreneurs do not receive further debt capital to realize projects with positive net present values because they already have a high level of debt and informational asymmetries exist. The risk incentive emerges in the case of debt financing since entrepreneurs fully participate in the upside but only partially in the downside of the risky projects (cf. Perridon/Steiner (2004), pp. 542-543).

350 Cf. Jensen (1986), pp. 323-324.

351 Cf. Spremann (1990), pp. 566 and 568-570.

352 Cf. Goldberg (1976), pp. 439-441.

353 Cf. Spremann (1990), pp. 568-570; Milgrom/Roberts (1992), pp. 136-138. The concept of hold-up was first described by Marshall ([1890] 1959), pp. 453-54 and 626. Some authors do not classify the problem of hold-

but between the contracting parties (principal or agent) and third parties, mainly the court. This means that the principal is able to observe the opportunistic behavior of the agent, but he is unable to enforce his rights because of the described incomplete contracts and informational asymmetries regarding concluded agreements. Furthermore, the principal is not able to terminate the contract because of sunk costs caused by specific investments.[354] This leads to the situation that the agent could force the principal to renegotiate the contract.[355]

The general introduction to agency theory showed that agency relationships are ubiquitous in business life.[356] Financial agency theory constitutes a specialized stream of the theory and analyzes the financial policy of companies as well as financing contracts in regard to the incentive structure between investors and managers. The focus of this stream lies on the cooperation between equity/debt providers on the one hand and managers on the other hand as well as the relation of different capital providers with each other.[357]

b) Application to Venture Capital Financing

A great share of past research on the relationship between entrepreneurial teams and venture capitalists uses agency theory as its central theoretical framework.[358] In the course of a VC investment multiple agency relationships could be inherent.[359] First, the venture capitalist could be interpreted as a principal investing into a company and therefore engaging an entrepreneurial team as agents. Within this setup the entrepreneurial team is supposed to manage and grow the company and thus to create value for the venture capitalist which can be realized by an exit. Second, the entrepreneurial team could be interpreted as a principal engaging a venture capitalist as an agent. The venture capitalist is then supposed to support the entrepreneurial team financially as well as managerially and strategically in exchange for an equity stake. Third, an agency relationship between the venture capitalist and the fund investors, which provide the capital for the VC fund, could exist. Within this relationship the venture

up under agency theory but regard it as a fourth component of new institutional economics. These authors refer to the problem as theory of incomplete contracts (cf. Richter/Furubotn (2003), pp. 269-276; Schefczyk (2004), pp. 154- 156). As the problem of hold-up is caused by an informational asymmetry in the context of an agency relationship, the classification within agency theory is also valid (cf. Nathusius (2005), p. 59). Other authors applying the same classification are Engel (2003b), pp. 157-158; Nathusius (2005), pp. 59-60; Picot/Dietl/Franck (2005), pp. 74-77; Wolf (2005), pp. 277-278.

354 Cf. Arkes/Blumer (1985), pp. 124-126; Picot/Dietl/Franck (2005), p. 75.

355 Cf. Wolf (2005), pp. 277-278; Nathusius (2005), p. 59.

356 Possible agency relationships include: client and consultant, corporate executive and subordinate, shareholder and corporate executive. Cf. Pratt/Zeckhauser (1985), p. 2.

357 Cf. Decker (1994), p. 11, Nathusius (2005), p. 48.

358 Cf. e.g. Wright/Robbie (1998), pp. 521-563; Sapienza/De Clercq (2000), p. 59.

359 Cf. Cumming/Macintosh (2003), p. 4; Casamatta (2003), pp. 2059-2060; Gompers/Lerner (2004), pp. 159-163.

capitalist acts as an agent of the fund investors. Since this relationship is not in the focus of the work at hand, it will not be discussed in detail.[360]

In consequence, multiple agency relationships arise within the VC context. Moreover, various types of informational asymmetries and conflicts of interest, and thus agency problems, might be prevalent among venture capitalists and entrepreneurial teams. Since informational asymmetries are both essential for agency problems to occur and likely to be determined by the spatial proximity between venture capitalists and new ventures, potential agency problems are now discussed in regard to the type of informational asymmetry in more detail.

Hidden information

In case of a VC investment the problem of hidden information could occur in multiple ways.[361] If the venture capitalist is interpreted as the principal who has to choose an entrepreneurial team that applies for funding of their venture, the main informational asymmetry exists in regard to the price of the company. The price of the company has two components – (i) assets in place, which in most cases have a market price that is largely independent from future states of the world, and (ii) the opportunity, which constitutes the future potential of the venture.[362]

In regard to the valuation of **assets in place** the entrepreneurial team has an informational advantage compared to the venture capitalist since the team possesses complete insider information.[363]

In regard to the **opportunity** the situation is not that clear and highly depends on the specific company and the type and experience of the venture capitalist. The entrepreneurial team often is too optimistic, while the venture capitalist has more experience and market knowledge which allows him a better and more objective evaluation of the business model.[364] This could

---

360 A detailed discussion of the relationship between venture capitalists and their fund investors provide Robbie/Wright/Chiplin (1997).

361 Cf. Gompers/Lerner (2004), p. 159. Also see Amit/Glosten/Muller (1990), pp. 1233-1243 for a detailed discussion.

362 Cf. Engel (2003b), p. 145. The potential for future success, and therefore a huge part of the value of a company, is determined to a large extend by the current business plan and the knowledge of the entrepreneurs. This holds even though the future success of a company also depends on future actions and decisions of the management (cf. Engel (2003b), p. 145). For a general differentiation of assets in place and opportunity see Myers (1977), pp. 149-150.

363 For this and the following discussion cf. Engel (2003b), pp. 146-148.

364 Hamilton (2000) presents empirical evidence that after 10 years median entrepreneurial earnings are 35% less compared to the alternative earnings in a paid job of the same duration (Hamilton (2000), pp. 604-606). This is especially relevant for entrepreneurs with little entrepreneurial experience like boy groups and senior entrepreneurs in contrast to entrepreneurs with entrepreneurial experience like serial and experienced entrepreneurs (cf. Engel (2003b), p. 147; Casamatta/Haritchabalet (2006), p. 2). For a detailed discussion of different types of entrepreneurs cf. Engel (2003b), pp. 88-92.

lead to informational advantages of the venture capitalist. However, in case of very specific technologies or completely new business models or industries, for which no parallel markets exist and the venture capitalist has no experience yet, the entrepreneurial team could have a much better understanding due to its background and high involvement in its venture. This could lead to strong informational advantages for the entrepreneurial team.[365] Moreover, the entrepreneurial team has much more information about its own ability (talent, skill, experience, ingenuity, leadership, etc.)[366] and motivation. This is because young ventures usually do not have a track record and the personal track records of the founders are often only hardly informative.[367] Especially the development of young ventures is highly dependent on the entrepreneurial team. Their abilities have to be applied to the venture and determine the value of the opportunity fundamentally.[368]

Before the contract for the VC financing is closed the price of the company has to be determined in order to appoint the share price of the venture. In order to receive better financing conditions, the entrepreneurial team could have an incentive to represent the risk/return expectations as well as the feasibility of the venture as too positive and to understate the necessary resources to realize the project. This would lead to higher return expectations of the venture capitalist who overestimates the value of assets already in place and/or the ability and motivation of the team.[369] In contrast, the venture capitalist has an incentive to understate the chances for success of the venture in the market and the size of the opportunity.[370]

The reasons leading to informational asymmetries just mentioned are initiated by a conflict of interest in regard to the financing conditions. Further reasons for informational asymmetries also stem from the costs associated with information compilation and transfer, and the control of the distribution of confidential information.[371]

On the other hand, the entrepreneurial team could be interpreted as a principal looking for a venture capitalist in order to receive the necessary financial resources as well as high quality managerial and strategically support in exchange for an equity stake. Then an additional in-

---

365 For further discussion see also Houben (2002), p. 1.

366 Cf. Amit/Glosten/Muller (1990), p. 1233.

367 The existence and informative character of personal track records highly depend on the type and background of the entrepreneur.

368 The knowledge of the entrepreneurial team could be also seen as intangible resources belonging to assets in place. This view ignores that the knowledge itself is not contributing to the company value but the application of the knowledge to the venture. This application is highly interwoven with the business plan and therefore should be attributed to the opportunity (cf. Engel (2003b), p. 146).

369 Cf. Schefczyk (2004), p. 146.

370 Cf. Houben (2002), p. 1.

371 Cf. Schefczyk (2004), p. 150.

formational asymmetry in regard to the knowledge, quality, intentions, and the effort of the venture capitalist exists.[372]

Here the venture capitalist has an informational advantage since he has full information about his real experience, market knowledge, business know-how, networks, etc. Furthermore, he knows how much effort he intends to invest into the venture, whether he wants or is able to provide further financing later on, and when he intends to exit the venture.[373] The entrepreneurial team on the other hand could receive relevant information about the venture capitalist from his track record and reputation. This requires that the venture capitalist is already in business for some time or that there are other sources for the personal track record or reputation of the investment manager. In consequence, this information asymmetry is likely to diminish for well established venture capitalists. However, since the venture capitalist is interested in advantageous investment conditions he could have an incentive to overstate the impact of his support and/or his financial possibilities.

Schefczyk (2004) discusses the likelihood of adverse selection and a resulting potential market failure in the case of VC markets.[374] If the venture capitalist is assumed to be the principal, the general problem would be that he assumes an average quality of entrepreneurs and ventures because of lacking information. This would lead to the effect that above average entrepreneurial teams with an above average venture are driven out of the market by bad ones. Therefore, two assumptions have to be true. First, above average entrepreneurial teams must have other, alternative financing options. The access to debt capital is limited especially for early stage start-ups and personal resources as well as capital from family and friends are limited in volume. Business angel financing is likely to incur the same problems in regard to adverse selection as VC. In consequence, the only alternative would often be to either forego the venture or to pursue strategies to reduce prevalent informational asymmetries. Second, the venture capitalist must have alternative investment opportunities. Those could be below average entrepreneurial teams and ventures, other asset classes like bonds or real estate or later stage ventures for which informational asymmetries are less severe.[375] Investments in below average teams and ventures would result in poor performance and are therefore not an option. Also it is very unlikely that highly specialized venture capitalists switch to other asset classes since this is not in the interest of their fund investors as well. A stronger focus on later stage ventures can already be observed in the market.[376] An additional option for the venture capi-

[372] Cf. Casamatta (2003), pp. 2059-2060.

[373] Cf. Gompers (1996), pp. 135-138; Sapienza/De Clercq (2000), p. 60; Houben (2002), p. 2; Casamatta (2003), pp. 2059-2060; Schmidt (2003), p. 1140.

[374] Cf. Schefczyk (2004), p. 151.

[375] Cf. Engel (2003b), p. 150.

[376] Cf. Achleitner/Ehrhart/Zimmermann (2006), p. 60.

talist would be to recognize the problem of adverse selection and to employ measures to mitigate informational asymmetries. Hence, both parties have an interest to mitigate informational asymmetries in order to prevent the problem of hidden information.

This discussion can be extended to agency relationships in which the entrepreneurial team is the principal. Then the general problem would be that because of lacking information the entrepreneurial team assumes an average quality of the venture capitalist. Consequently, above average venture capitalists could be driven out of the market by bad ones. The assumptions for adverse selection to occur are similar to the ones discussed above. First, entrepreneurs would need alternative financing options, which now also include below average venture capitalists, or could invest in measures to mitigate informational asymmetries. Receiving financing from below average venture capitalists could lead to the result that the venture cannot develop its full potential, which is not in the interest of the entrepreneurial team. Second, above average venture capitalists would need investment opportunities in alternative asset classes or employ measures to reduce the informational asymmetries.[377]

As a result, if venture capitalists do not want to or cannot withdraw from certain market segments and if entrepreneurs do not want to be financed by below average venture capitalists, the problem of hidden information (and therefore also adverse selection) has to be addressed by certain measures reducing prevalent informational asymmetries. Possible measures to mitigate the problem of hidden information in case of VC investments are manifold. Screening and due diligence activities could be conducted to gather information about the entrepreneurial team and the venture or the venture capitalist respectively.[378] Contracts with different terms and conditions could be negotiated, which offers important insights about the other party and therefore constitutes a self selection process.[379] Signaling and the development of a high reputation could be employed by both parties in order to give signals in regard to the future behavior that can be expected. Finally, the entrepreneurial team could make high personal investments in the venture in order to signal their own confidence in themselves and their venture.[380]

---

[377] Hsu shows that venture capitalists with a high reputation are able to negotiate deals with inferior financing conditions for entrepreneurs (cf. Hsu (2004), pp. 1805-1844).

[378] Cf. Kaplan/Strömberg (2001), p. 428.

[379] This self selection process mainly reveals information about the entrepreneurial team, but the behavior of the venture capitalist in regard to certain terms could also offer information about the venture capitalist. Possible terms offering insights about the entrepreneurial team could be a disproportionate profit/loss participation of the team in the case of success/failure of the venture or a disproportionate participation of the entrepreneurial team if more capital is needed than expected in order to realize the project (cf. Schefczyk (2004), p. 146). For an empirical survey of components of VC financing contracts see e.g. Kaplan/Strömberg (2003), pp. 281-315.

[380] Cf. Schefczyk (2004), p. 146; Picot/Dietl/Franck (2005), p. 77.

Hidden action

Shirking might occur in the course of a VC investment because an equity stake is acquired by the venture capitalist. In consequence, neither the entrepreneurial team nor the venture capitalist fully participates in the marginal utility of his effort. Hence, shirking could occur in two different ways. First, if the entrepreneurial team is interpreted as the agent having the task to develop the venture, the entrepreneurs have to decide in a trade-off between additional effort and spare time. At the same time, it is difficult for the venture capitalist to fully observe the level of effort of the entrepreneurial team. Only the success of the venture can be observed ex-post in the form of profits or the value of the venture. In addition, it is not possible for the venture capitalist to differentiate completely whether the success of the venture is due to the entrepreneurs' effort or due to positive conditions (luck).[381] In consequence, the entrepreneurial team could choose to decrease its level of effort.

Especially in the case of a young venture the existence of shirking is not clear. On the one hand, the entrepreneur usually has invested a large share of his personal wealth in the venture and has relatively high profit participation. Furthermore, if the venture has been founded by an entrepreneurial team, the team members usually control each other or are personally related and do not want to betray each other. In consequence, shirking is not very likely to occur.[382] On the other hand, entrepreneurs could also aim at the creation or preservation of a certain standard of living instead of aiming at the success of the venture.[383] Then shirking is likely to occur. The likelihood of shirking usually also increases with the dilution of the equity share of the entrepreneurial team and therefore with the number of financing rounds.[384]

Second, the venture capitalist could be interpreted as the agent who is supposed to support the venture. Next to the decision of the venture capitalist how much time to spend at work he also is in charge of several investments and therefore has to decide how much effort he allocates to a certain investment. This depends on several aspects like the number of companies the investment manager is responsible for or the performance of the company.[385] Furthermore, it is difficult for the entrepreneurial team to observe and to evaluate the effort of the venture capi-

---

[381] Cf. Grossman/Hart (1983), p. 10.

[382] Cf. Erlei/Leschke/Sauerland (1999), pp. 98-99, Schulz (2000), p. 58.

[383] Several cases of this behavior occurred during the time of the new economy boom from 1998-2000. Some entrepreneurs focused very early financings by external investors but invested only little amounts of personal wealth. In consequence, these entrepreneurs could afford high standards of living for a certain period of time. (cf. Brettel/Thust/Witt (2001), p. 2; Engel (2003b), pp. 153-154; Metrick (2006), pp. 12-13; Inside CRM (2009)).

[384] Cf. Engel (2003b), p. 153.

[385] Cf. Lerner (1995), p. 316; Sapienza/Manigart/Vermeir (1996), p. 463; Kaplan/Strömberg (2001), p. 429; Kanniainen/Keuschnigg (2004), pp. 1942-1952; Jääskeläinen/Maula/Seppä (2006), pp. 185-206. See also section 2.1.4.5 regarding the impact of new venture performance on the involvement of venture capitalists.

talist. In consequence, the venture capitalist could choose to decrease his level of effort for a specific venture.[386]

Perk consumption is mainly conducted by the entrepreneurial team which then is in the role of an agent. In this case, examples for perk consumption are larger offices, bigger company cars, more business meals, or more business trips than necessary. Such expenditures usually lead to a reduction of the company value. The entrepreneurial team has an incentive for such perk consumption since it benefits to the full extent from the perks, but the costs have to be carried by all shareholders and therefore also by the venture capitalist.[387] This leads to a conflict of interest. The venture capitalist is able to observe almost all expenditures of the venture within the financial statements, but it is difficult to judge, whether these expenditures were really necessary or not. This results in an informational asymmetry and makes perk consumption likely in the VC context.

In regard to the investment policy the entrepreneurial team (agent) could "overinvest" since it has an interest in certain research projects or is emotionally attached to the venture. This could lead to an investment into a project or further investments into the venture even though the project or the whole company has a negative net present value and is therefore not profitable.[388] In the latter case the entrepreneurial team would delay the necessary liquidation of the venture. As in the case of perk consumption the venture capitalist might observe these investments, but it is difficult for him to scrutinize the profitability of the investments since he might not possess the required insider information. This could lead to an informational asymmetry.

Hidden actions lead to the reduction of the expected return of the principal. In an extreme case, hidden actions could also lead to the termination of the financing relationship or could deter the principal if he anticipates hidden actions. Different measures can be applied in order to mitigate problems of hidden action.

Monitoring in a narrow sense mainly reduces informational asymmetries and is especially used by the venture capitalist. The aim is to reduce decision possibilities of the entrepreneurial team by enforcing appropriate contracts with the help of suitable control mechanisms. Therefore, venture capitalists frequently sit as non-executives on the board of directors or the supervisory board, have broad control rights and impose frequent reporting obligations on the venture. But also the entrepreneurial team could engage in monitoring the venture capitalist's

---

386 Cf. Gifford (1997), p. 475; Houben (2002), p. 2; Schmidt (2003), pp. 1139-1142.

387 Cf. Gompers/Lerner (2004), p. 159.

388 These cases could also be regarded as perk consumptions. Thus, a perfect differentiation is not possible (cf. Schmidt (2003), p. 1148).

support by observing his actions. In addition, the venture capitalist and entrepreneurial team usually have regular meetings on site.[389]

A high reputation could deter both parties from hidden actions since they have to fear that potential misbehavior damages their reputation. This is important for both parties. Venture capitalists frequently conduct VC investments and therefore depend on their reputation. Entrepreneurial teams usually have to pass through several financing rounds in the course of the development of their venture. Consequently, both parties have an interest to behave appropriately and the reputation therefore contributes to an alignment of interests here. High personal investments in the venture and self bonding contracts by the team can be established at the time of the contract's closing to align interests of both parties and to make hidden actions less likely to occur.[390]

Hidden intention

In case of a VC investment the problem of hidden intention is likely to occur because most financing contracts are very complex and therefore often incomplete.[391] If the entrepreneurial team is interpreted as the agent, the venture capitalist incurs sunk costs after the entrepreneurial team invested the venture capitalist's capital in venture specific assets. Then the team could threaten not to act in the interest of the venture capitalist if the contract, and therefore also future cash flows, are not renegotiated. Possible threats of the team could be to reduce the effort or to withhold knowledge which is necessary for the venture's development.[392]

The venture capitalist could also be interpreted as an agent. Then the dependency of the entrepreneurial team could be threefold. First, the venture capitalist could force the entrepreneurial team to focus on a rather short-term performance, or the investor could aim an early exit (grandstanding) in order to build up his reputation.[393] Second, the venture capitalist could in theory withhold or reduce the promised support and could, for example, force the venture to pay additional fees for consulting services. Third, the dependency of the venture capitalist from the entrepreneurial team as described above usually changes in the course of the investment period. If the venture has to raise further funds in a new round, the entrepreneurial team

---

[389] Cf. Kaplan/Strömberg (2001), pp. 426-429; Gompers/Lerner (2004), pp. 159-163; Picot/Dietl/Franck (2005), p. 77.

[390] Cf. Spremann (1988), pp. 618-620; Barney et al. (1996b), pp. 91-105; Schefczyk (2004), p. 146; Gompers/Lerner (2004), pp. 159-163; Picot/Dietl/Franck (2005), p. 77.

[391] Cf. Kaplan/Strömberg (2003), pp. 281-282.

[392] Cf. Schulz (2000), pp. 71-72.

[393] Cf. Gompers (1996), pp. 135-138.

usually depends on the venture capitalist in order to receive additional funds at reasonable conditions or to receive good references.[394]

To mitigate problems of hidden intention, the venture capitalist could try to transform one sided dependencies into two sided ones. For this purpose he could engage in monitoring in a narrow sense and implement suitable contracts combined with appropriate compensation policies or negotiate staged financing. Furthermore, an alignment of interests could be achieved with the help of high personal investments or self bonding contracts of the entrepreneurial team.[395] Probably the most important measure to mitigate problems of hidden intention and the only one to prevent a venture capitalist's hold-up is a high reputation of the actors.[396] The reputation is very important for the entrepreneurial team as well as the venture capitalist as described above. In consequence, both parties have a strong interest in building and protecting their reputation.

As a result, various agency problems are likely to occur throughout a VC financing relationship in which the venture capitalist as well as the entrepreneurial team can be interpreted as the principal. Hence, the previously discussed measures to mitigate agency problems are of great importance for the success of VC financing.

Furthermore, it became obvious that agency theory offers a valuable application of the theory of property rights to many management problems. The theory also models agency relationships which are central for VC investments.[397] Nevertheless, agency theory also has several limitations and was criticized frequently.[398] First, agency theory assumes opportunistic behavior of the agent. Opportunistic behavior of economic actors might often be the case. However, agency theory neglects the possibility of altruistic behavior of agents, which certainly also can be observed in several situations.[399] Monitoring could also operate as a dysfunctional factor by lowering trust among the involved parties.[400] In addition, if one accepts opportunistic behavior as given, agency theory only offers a one sided view and it neglects the possibility of opportunistic behavior of the principal.[401] Second, agency theory assumes a short term

---

394 Cf. Engel (2003b), p. 159.

395 Cf. Picot/Dietl/Franck (2005), pp. 79-80. In regard to financing contracts Kaplan/Strömberg (2003) empirically confirm the widespread use of non-compete and vesting provisions. This indicates that venture capitalists care about the hold-up problem. (cf. Kaplan/Strömberg (2003), pp. 281-282).

396 Cf. Spremann (1988), pp. 618-620; Milgrom/Roberts (1992), pp. 139-140.

397 Cf. Sahlman (1990), pp. 473-521; Trester (1998), pp. 675-699; Wolf (2005), p. 280.

398 Cf. e.g. Bruton/Fried/Hisrich (1997), pp. 50-52; Cable/Shane (1997), pp. 146-147; Bruton/Fried/Hisrich (2000), pp. 73-75; Arthurs/Busenitz (2003), pp. 148-154.

399 Cf. Schefczyk (2004), p. 149.

400 Cf. Landström (1992), p. 218; Arthurs/Busenitz (2003), p. 156.

401 Cf. Wolf (2005), p. 280.

oriented maximization of the individual utility of the actors. In consequence, a more long term oriented maximization of the personal utility and multi-period learning processes of the principal are usually ignored.[402] Third, the probably most important critique is that it is very difficult to observe and to measure actual agency costs, which impedes the derivation of optimal business decisions.[403] Empirical evidence of agency theory in the VC context offers a heterogeneous picture. The majority of studies support agency theory as appropriate,[404] some reject it,[405] and others find mixed results.[406]

c) Implications of Spatial Proximity between Actors

As we have seen, many different measures can be applied in order to mitigate the different agency problems inherent in a VC transaction. The costs of these measures contribute directly to the agency costs which reduce the benefits and therefore the return expected from the relationship. This leads to a trade-off situation and could lead to the principal's or agent's decision not to establish or maintain a certain agency relationship.[407] In consequence, the efficiency of the applied measures is crucial. An agency relationship will only be established and maintained if for both parties the inherent (agency) costs are less or equal to the benefits expected from the relationship. Otherwise negotiations are aborted or existing relationships are terminated.

The costs of many measures, which could be applied to mitigate the agency problems discussed above, are sensitive to the spatial proximity between the venture capitalist and the venture. Monitoring in a narrow sense is easier and cheaper to conduct for both parties if the venture is spatially close to the investor. This is especially true for onsite meetings and personal contacts, and the acquisition of reliable information about the other party (e.g. through personal networks). This facilitates the observation of the other party's actions and makes it easier to intervene if necessary.[408]

Deal screening and due diligence are also easier and cheaper to accomplish for both parties if they are located close to each other. As with monitoring in a narrow sense this is especially true for onsite meetings and personal contacts, and the acquisition of reliable information

[402] An exception to this shortcoming constitutes the consideration of long term reputation effects of the actors.

[403] Cf. Schefczyk (2004), p. 149.

[404] See e.g. Gompers (1995), pp. 1461-1489; Kaplan/Strömberg (2001), pp. 426-430; Kaplan/Strömberg (2003), pp. 281-282; Kaplan/Strömberg (2004), pp. 2177-2181.

[405] See e.g. Landström (1992), pp. 199-223.

[406] See e.g. Arthurs/Busenitz (2003), pp. 145-162.

[407] Cf. Gompers/Lerner (2004), p. 159.

[408] Cf. Sorenson/Stuart (2001), pp. 1550-1553. See also section 3.3.3 for a discussion of the influence of spatial proximity of actors on various networks.

about the other party (e.g. through personal networks). In addition, the analysis of local markets is less difficult.

In addition, it is likely that the reputation of the other party is easier to be acknowledged and more effective in the case of spatial proximity. Furthermore, the reputation, especially of the venture capitalist, is more likely to be affected by the other party's statements.[409] This is true for mis- and well-behavior of the agent and can be negative and positive for him. The reasons are regional personal networks and a higher visibility of the actors.[410]

In consequence, it can be assumed that agency costs decrease, and therefore the establishment and continuation of successful agency relationships is more likely, the higher the spatial proximity between the venture capitalist and the venture.[411]

Table 3.1 summarizes the different types of informational asymmetries in the VC context as well as their implications for spatial proximity between the venture capitalist and the venture.

3.2.1.3 Transaction Cost Theory

a) Theoretical Foundations

Transaction cost theory[412] also belongs to the school of thought of new institutionalism and focuses on a single transaction which is defined as the transfer of property rights between specialized actors. Transaction costs occur in the course of a transaction and include all costs and disadvantages which are incurred by the contracting parties in order to realize a transaction.[413] Consequently, property rights are not in the focus of the transaction cost theory, but they constitute an important basic condition.[414] Furthermore, the theory does not except the

---

409 In regard to the entrepreneurial team's reputation it can be assumed that existing venture capitalists participate in further financing rounds or that new investors are going to conduct reference calls to previous venture capitalists. Therefore, spatial proximity between the venture capitalist and the venture is not that important. Spatial proximity could be relevant if an entrepreneurial team starts a new venture and tries to dissimulate the previous venture.

410 Cf. Sorenson/Stuart (2001), pp. 1550-1553.

411 This is also in line with Bengtsson/Ravid (2009), who find that VC contracts are much more investor friendly for distant investments, and Tian (2009), who finds that staging is more frequently applied for distant investments (cf. Bengtsson/Ravid (2009), pp. 12-13; Tian (2009), pp. 18-20). These findings imply that venture capitalists anticipate higher agency costs for distant investments.

412 Important fundamental articles include Coase (1937); Williamson (1975); Williamson (1979); Williamson (1988).

413 Cf. Picot/Dietl/Franck (2005), p. 57. Depending on the focus of the work many different definitions of transaction costs exit (see e.g. Ouchi (1980), p. 130; Williamson (1985), pp. 20-22; Richter/Furubotn (2003), pp. 57-58). Arrow (1969) defines transaction costs very broad as "cost[s] of running the economic system" and therefore focuses more on the institutional system (cf. Arrow (1969), p. 48 cited in Wolf (2005), p. 267).

414 Cf. Picot/Dietl/Franck (2005), pp. 56-57.

Table 3.1: Summary of informational asymmetries
Source: Cf. Schefczyk (2004), p. 146; Engel (2003b), pp. 142, 144 and 159; Picot/Dietl/Franck (2005), p. 77.

Type of informational asymmetry	Hidden information (Arrow (1985))	Hidden action (Arrow (1985))	Hidden intention (Spremann (1990))
Type of problem	• Adverse selection (Akerlof (1970))	• Moral hazard (Holmstrom (1979))	• Hold-up (Goldberg (1976))
Relevance in investment process	• Pre-contractual	• Post-contractual	• Post-contractual
General problem	• Insecurity regarding the quality of goods or services	• Insecurity regarding the agent's actions and effort	• Insecurity regarding the agent's actions • Contracts that are incomplete or difficult to verify
VC specific problems	• Misrepresentation of risk/return expectations as well as feasibility of the project • Misrepresentation of necessary resources • Misrepresentation of assets already in place • Misrepresentation of the qualification and motivation of the agent	• Misrepresentation of the motivation and effort of the agent (shirking) • Perk consumption, pursuit of interesting but not profitable projects • Suboptimal investment policy (overinvestment)	• Hold-up in regard to further resources (pecuniary and non-pecuniary) • Hold-up in regard to advantageous contracts
Measures to mitigate agency problem	Monitoring in a broad sense		
	• Screening/ Due diligence • Self selection	• Monitoring in a narrow sense	• Monitoring in a narrow sense
	Bonding		
	• Signaling • Reputation • High personal investments of agent (risk participation)	• Reputation • High personal investments of agent (risk participation) • Self bonding contracts	• Reputation • High personal investments of agent (risk participation) • Self bonding contracts
Role of spatial proximity between venture capitalist and venture	• Screening/ Due diligence easier to conduct • Reputation easier to acknowledge and more effective	• Monitoring in a narrow sense easier to conduct • Reputation easier to be affected	• Monitoring in a narrow sense easier to conduct • Reputation easier to be affected

existence of agency costs but explains possible market frictions by the more general concept of transaction costs.[415]

The theory goes back to Coase (1937), who analyzed whether certain transactions should be realized within a company versus over the market. Different alternatives are evaluated by comparing inherent transaction costs.[416] Williamson further developed Coase's concept and added the assumptions of bounded rationality and opportunistic behavior of the actors.

---

[415] Cf. Nathusius (2005), p. 60.

[416] Cf. Coase (1937), pp. 390-393.

Bounded rationality means that actors only have limited analytical and data processing capabilities. Opportunistic behavior is caused by the maximization of individual utility. These two behavioral assumptions are: a main difference to neoclassical theory, they imply that there is no costless and perfect information, and they are the main reasons for the occurrence of transaction costs. Important dimensions influencing the volume of transaction costs are uncertainty, the frequency of transactions, and the specificity of necessary investments. Uncertainty of transactions in combination with bounded rationality leads to incomplete contracting. The frequency determines how often transaction costs occur and the specificity of necessary investments lead to a higher dependency of the investing party as well as potential losses if the relationship is terminated.[417]

The sum of transaction costs can be used as criterion to evaluate different institutional structures or alternative transactions. In consequence, the minimization of transaction costs leads to an efficient solution.[418]

Richter/Furubotn (2003) differentiate between three different groups of transaction costs: market transaction costs which incur due to the usage of markets, company transaction cost which incur by transactions within a company, and political transaction costs which incur by establishing and changing institutional frameworks.[419] Since these groups are partly overlapping, an exact differentiation among these groups is not possible. Financing relationships between different companies constitute market transactions. In consequence, the work at hand concentrates on market transaction cost.

According to the occurrence in time one can differentiate between ex-ante and ex-post transaction costs.[420] Ex-ante transaction costs occur before the actual contract is closed and include search and information costs as well as negotiation and decision costs.[421] Ex-post transaction costs occur after the actual contract is closed and include monitoring and enforcement costs. In addition, Richter/Furubotn (2003) name a fourth group of transaction costs which arise in the whole course of the process and which they refer to as investments in social capital.[422]

417 Cf. Williamson (1981), pp. 553-556. See also Picot/Dietl/Franck (2005), pp. 58-62 for a more detailed discussion.

418 In this context an efficient solution is a second-best solution, which is the best solution under the assumption of positive transaction costs. Cf. Picot (1982), pp. 269-270 cited in Niederöcker (2002), p. 41.

419 Cf. Richter/Furubotn (2003), pp. 57-58.

420 Cf. Williamson (1985), pp. 20-22.

421 Cf. Richter/Furubotn (2003), pp. 58-61.

422 Cf. Richter/Furubotn (2003), pp. 58-61. Many different classifications of transaction costs exist (e.g. Coase (1960), p. 15; Picot/Dietl/Franck (2005), p. 57)

b) *Application to Venture Capital Financing*

In case of a VC investment numerous types of transaction costs occur and are of high relevance. Search and information costs arise for the entrepreneurial team as well as for the venture capitalist. Both first have to search for appropriate potential investors or entrepreneurial teams respectively and second have to gather information about the other party in order to evaluate the potential partner. The substantiated choice of a venture capitalist is of high importance for the entrepreneurial team because venture capitalists do not only provide financing but also add value by supporting, controlling, and monitoring their portfolio companies.[423] In consequence, the choice of the right venture capitalist is an important success factor for the venture. Similarly, for the venture capitalist the choice of an entrepreneurial team in combination with a good venture constitutes an elementary part of the investment decision and has strong implications for the venture capitalist's performance.[424] The identification of potential investors by the entrepreneurial team can be done through databases provided by associations like the German Private Equity and Venture Capital Association e.V. (BVK)[425], suitable mercantile directories, or personal references. Information about characteristics of the venture capitalist can be gathered by examining his track record, reputation, personal references and interviews. In order to find exceptional entrepreneurs with a good venture, the venture capitalist has to generate a high quality deal flow.[426] Information about characteristics of the entrepreneurial team and the venture are gathered in the course of the screening and due diligence process.[427] Transaction costs arising within this category for both parties are mainly time, labor effort, travel and communication expenses, costs for potential database access, as well as expenses for external consulting.[428]

Negotiation and decision costs also arise for both parties and occur in an iterative process. After both parties have identified potential contracting partners and gathered sufficient information, they have to evaluate the information and decide whether they start negotiations or continue searching for suitable partners. In the course of negotiations new information becomes available and both have to decide whether they continue negotiations or abort. This process continues until the parties agree on all open points and the contract is signed.[429] These

---

[423] See section 2.1.4.5.

[424] See section 2.1.4.3.

[425] See www.bvk-ev.de for further information.

[426] See section 2.1.4.1.

[427] See section 0 and 2.1.4.3.

[428] Agency costs arising in order to mitigate problems of hidden information (e.g. signaling) can also be regarded as transaction cost (see section 3.2.1.2 and cf. Richter/Furubotn (2003), pp. 59-60).

[429] See section 2.1.4.4.

processes are time consuming for the entrepreneurial team as well as the venture capitalist,[430] require high labor effort, travel and communication expenses, as well as external legal support. Furthermore, VC financing contracts are very complex and therefore difficult to negotiate and usually incomplete since VC investments have a high uncertainty and specificity.[431]

Monitoring and enforcement costs belong to ex-post transaction costs. They are mainly relevant for the venture capitalist, but they could also arise for the entrepreneurial team. After the financing contract is closed the venture capitalist has to monitor the entrepreneurs and the venture in order to observe whether the terms and conditions are met. If the entrepreneurial team does not perform as agreed upon, the venture capitalist has to enforce his rights which could also include legal steps. In addition, the entrepreneurial team might have to compile extensive reports in order to provide information for the venture capitalist. Likewise, the entrepreneurial team also has to monitor the venture capitalist to find out whether he provides the promised supporting activities or not. It is difficult for the entrepreneurial team to legally enforce its rights since most of the venture capitalist's support activities besides the financial support are not fixed in the financing contract. The only measure that the entrepreneurs could apply in order to put pressure on the investor is to harm the venture capitalist's reputation. Similar to the negotiation and decision costs within this group transaction costs mainly occur in the form of time, labor effort, travel and communication expenses as well as costs for legal support and law expenses.

The fourth group of transaction costs includes investments in social capital and arise pre- and post-contractual. This is necessary because the social structure of markets, and thus interpersonal relationships, has economic relevance. Entrepreneurial teams and venture capitalists are embedded in a complex network of social relationships. These relationships and contacts help to bear and to reduce the burden of uncertainty, to process complex information, and to decide under the restrictions of bounded rationality. Hence, these social networks help to reduce transaction costs of the other categories (e.g. search and information costs). Nonetheless, social networks have to be established and maintained which causes transaction costs mainly in the form of time, travel and communication expenses, as well as other expenses (e.g. business meals).[432]

Transaction costs arising for an individual venture capitalist could be reduced by syndication. Then, many costs can be divided among the syndication partners and individual costs highly

---

430 Costs of cognitive processing also belong to this group of transaction costs (cf. Loasby (1999), p. 33 cited in Richter/Furubotn (2003), p. 60).

431 Cf. Richter/Furubotn (2003), p. 60; Nathusius (2005), p. 61.

432 See Richter/Furubotn (2003), p. 61 for further discussion. The aspect of social networks is also discussed within other theories (see sections 3.2.2.3 and 3.3).

depend on the investor's role in the syndication. Namely, whether he is in the role of a lead- or co-investor. Nevertheless, additional transaction costs arise within a syndicate since additional contracting partners have to agree. This increases negotiation costs and makes contracts even more complex.[433]

Transaction cost theory analyzes important issues how to increase the efficiency of transactions and provides a criterion to compare alternatives. Especially economic dependencies and friction losses are discussed.[434] Therefore, the theory offers important insights into decisions of economic actors and thus also of venture capitalists and entrepreneurial teams.

However, the theory uses the sum of transaction costs as criterion for efficiency, which has to be minimized. It is therefore assumed implicitly that alternative transactions offer the same returns. Especially in VC financing this is usually not the case and therefore problematic. Furthermore, the sum of transaction costs are only a suitable criterion for efficiency if the identification of efficient VC transactions as well as the restructuring of existing transactions can be done without transaction costs. Since economic actors are assumed to have bounded rationality, these assumptions are not appropriate.[435] In addition, transaction costs are difficult to measure since they occur as direct or indirect costs as well as opportunity costs.[436] Moreover, uncertainty and the specificity of necessary investments influence the volume of transaction costs but are difficult to operationalize.[437]

c) Implications of Spatial Proximity between Actors

Many transaction costs inherent in a VC transaction are sensitive to the spatial proximity between the venture capitalist and the venture. Travel expenses usually increase with decreasing proximity due to transportation expenses and travel time. Furthermore, they are omnipresent in VC transactions and are part of search and information costs, negotiation and decision costs, monitoring and enforcement costs, as well as of the costs to build-up social capital. Information expenses are also likely to increase with decreasing proximity due to decreasing familiarity and experiences with markets, regional particularities or service providers. Social networks also tend to be regional[438] which also leads to higher transaction costs with decreasing proximity. These relationships are especially relevant since transaction cost theory implies

433 Cf. Nathusius (2005), pp. 62-64.

434 Cf. Wolf (2005), p. 272.

435 Cf. Wolf (2005), pp. 272-174.

436 Opportunity costs include costs like labor effort or time. Cf. Picot (1982), p. 271 cited in Nathusius (2005), p. 61.

437 Cf. Nathusius (2005), p. 61.

438 Cf. Blau (1977a), p. 268; Turner (1978), pp. 703-704; Sorenson/Stuart (2001), pp. 1547-1548. See also section 3.3.3 for a discussion of the influence of spatial proximity of actors on various networks.

that the sum of transaction costs is used as criterion to evaluate different institutional structures or alternative transactions. In consequence, if for a venture capitalist two alternative investment opportunities with an identical expected return exist, the venture capitalist will chose the one with lower transaction costs and thus the more proximate one. Similarly, if for an entrepreneurial team two alternative venture capitalists with identical characteristics exist, the team will also chose the one with lower transaction costs. Consequently, transaction costs are not only important in order to develop efficient institutions and contracts but also influence the decision which transactions will be realized and which ones are aborted.

It can be assumed that transaction costs decrease and that therefore the efficiency and likelihood of certain VC investments increases the higher the spatial proximity between the venture capitalist and the venture is.

3.2.2 Further Theories Explaining the Role of Spatial Proximity

As it has been discussed in the previous section, new institutional theories in general and especially agency theory are criticized by many scholars.[439] Major points of critique regard the assumptions of short term oriented, opportunistic behavior as well as hierarchical relationships between principals and agents in the VC context. Furthermore, it is argued that agency problems might be mitigated by the specific design of a VC financing contract and due to other measures like monitoring and bonding.[440] Therefore, the following sections discusses further theories which can be applied in the VC financing context and which might give additional insights on the relevance of spatial proximity between the venture capitalist and the entrepreneurial team.

3.2.2.1 Game Theory

a) Theoretical Foundations

Game theory has its origin in applied mathematics.[441] It originally attempts to mathematically capture the behavior of actors (players) in strategic situations in which conflicts of interest and information problems occur and in which the individual payoff or utility depends on the choice of strategy of the other actors.[442] Typical strategies could be cooperation or defection.

---

[439] Cf. e.g. Bruton/Fried/Hisrich (1997), pp. 50-52; Cable/Shane (1997), pp. 146-147; Bruton/Fried/Hisrich (2000), pp. 73-75; Arthurs/Busenitz (2003), pp. 148-154.

[440] Cf. Arthurs/Busenitz (2003), p. 153.

[441] Fundamental publications include von Neumann/Morgenstern (1944) and Axelrod (1984).

[442] Cf. Holler/Illing (2006), p. 1.

Cooperation refers to a behavior that "seek[s] mutual gains at the expense of short-term self-interest". [443] Defection refers to opportunistic, self-serving behavior that "seek[s] individual gains at the expense of long-term mutual benefit".[444] Therefore, the theory analyzes the behavior of opportunistic actors whereas a hierarchical relationship between actors must not exist.

Game theory usually attempts to find equilibria which are stable situations defined by some set of chosen strategies in which it is unlikely that the actors change their strategy.[445] Then, game theory can be applied to identify factors that lead to the choice and continuation of co-operative strategies.[446]

One of the most prominent games is the prisoner's dilemma. Here, the general setting is that two people are arrested for a crime. The police lack sufficient evidence to convict either one and consequently want them to give testimony against each other. Both suspects are not allowed to talk with each other. The police tell each suspect that if he testifies against the other (defection from the other suspect), he will be released and will receive a reward for testifying, provided the other suspect does not testify against him (payoff = 2). The other suspect would go to prison (payoff = -1). If both suspects testify against each other, both go to prison but still receive rewards for testifying (payoff = 0). If no one of the suspects testifies (cooperation), both will be released because of lacking evidence (payoff = 1). The resulting payoff structure is illustrated in Figure 3.5.[447]

---

[443] Cable/Shane (1997), p. 145.

[444] Cable/Shane (1997), p. 145.

[445] Cf. Holler/Illing (2006), p. 54. Probably the most famous equilibrium is the Nash equilibrium (cf. Nash (1950), pp. 48-49). See also Fudenberg/Tirole (2000) for a detailed discussion of the Nash equilibrium (Fudenberg/Tirole (2000), pp. 11-36).

[446] Cf. Axelrod/Dion (1988), pp. 1385-1389.

[447] Cf. Axelrod/Dion (1988), p. 1385; Fudenberg/Tirole (2000), pp. 9-10.

		Player 2	
		Cooperation	Defection
Player 1	Cooperation	1 , 1	-1 , 2
	Defection	2 ,-1	0 , 0

Figure 3.5: Prisoner's dilemma in choosing cooperation or defection
Source: Based on Fudenberg/Tirole (2000), p. 10.

The prisoner's dilemma is a metaphor to model situations of social conflict between two or more interdependent actors.[448] Both actors have to choose their strategy simultaneously and are not able to communicate with each other. Even though cooperation would maximize the collective payoff, the self-interest leads to an inefficient outcome (payoffs = 0). Each player receives a higher pay off if he defects, regardless the choice of the other player. If the game would be played repeatedly, there would be a higher likelihood of cooperation because the behavior within one round influences decisions in subsequent rounds. In that case other outcomes could be equilibria.[449]

Several factors are critical in order to achieve cooperation between actors in a repeated prisoner's dilemma. First, reliable information about past as well as planned behavior of other actors are central to build expectations about future behavior of other actors. Second, reciprocity and trust are important, which develop over several rounds of the game or, in other words, in the course of longer term relationships. Third, the actors' expectation about the number of future rounds, i.e. the duration of future relationship, must be high enough (long shadow of the future). Fourth, the number of actors should be as small as possible since cooperation becomes more difficult the larger the number of players is.[450]

The Prisoner's dilemma has been applied to various settings such as moral hazard in teams, business-government relationships, market pricing, and advertising.[451] For the analysis of the

[448] Cf. Pruitt (1967), pp. 21-27; Dawes (1980), pp. 182-183; Aram (1989), p. 268; Cable/Shane (1997), p. 145.

[449] Cf. Axelrod/Dion (1988), p. 1385; Fudenberg/Tirole (2000), pp. 9-10.

[450] Cf. Dawes (1980), pp. 185-188; Axelrod/Dion (1988), pp. 1385-1388; Komorita/Hilty/Parks (1991), pp. 511-515; Cable/Shane (1997), p. 146.

[451] Cf. Aram (1989), pp. 268-269; Corfman/Lehmann (1994), pp. 35-48; Fudenberg/Tirole (2000), p. 10.

relationship between venture capitalists and entrepreneurial teams recent literature also suggests the prisoner's dilemma to be a promising approach.[452]

b) Application to Venture Capital Financing

Cooperation between venture capitalists and entrepreneurial teams is essential for the success of ventures. E.g. Timmons/Bygrave (1986) found that an ongoing cooperative relationship between a venture capitalist and the entrepreneurial team is more important than the provision of VC itself.[453] Cable/Shane (1997) analyze the relationship theoretically and submit that cooperation between a venture capitalist and the entrepreneurial team constitutes a necessary but not a sufficient condition. This is due to a division of labor between both parties and inefficient markets to substitute either party in the relationship. Thus, cooperation of both parties leads to the highest mutual benefits.[454] However, cooperation between venture capitalists and entrepreneurial teams is not always the case since both parties could realize higher short term benefits from defection, unless both defect.[455] Repeated prisoner's dilemmas are also able to model social relationships that develop in the course of VC transactions.[456] Therefore, the prisoner's dilemma can be applied to analyze factors facilitating cooperation of both parties in VC financing relationships.

As discussed within other theories entrepreneurial teams and venture capitalists do have various temptations to act opportunistically and to defect in order to achieve higher short term benefits.[457] The main reason is that both parties have to make decisions under uncertainty and that they incur opportunity costs if they do not defect (conflict of interest) and that informational asymmetries exist which facilitate defection.[458] Thus, both parties could behave in a way that causes problems of hidden information,[459] hidden action or hidden intention as discussed in section 3.2.1.2. The entrepreneurial team could e.g. withhold or alter critical information, decrease their effort (shirking), misuse resources (perk consumption), or apply suboptimal investment policies. Venture capitalists could e.g. reduce their supporting activities

---

[452] Cf. Cable/Shane (1997), pp. 142-176; Sapienza/De Clercq (2000), pp. 60-69; Busenitz/Fiet/Moesel (2004), pp. 789-791; Welpe (2004), pp. 62-63; Welpe/Dowling (2005), pp. 291-292; Wijbenga/van Witteloostuijn (2006), pp. 91-114.

[453] Cf. Timmons/Bygrave (1986), pp. 161-162.

[454] See Cable/Shane (1997), pp. 143-145 for a detailed discussion.

[455] Cf. e.g. Sahlman (1990), p. 506; Cable/Shane (1997), p. 147; Casamatta (2003), pp. 2059-2062; Welpe (2004), pp. 74-77.

[456] Cf. Sapienza/Korsgaard (1996), pp. 544-547; Cable/Shane (1997), p. 147.

[457] See section 3.2.1.

[458] For this and the following paragraphs see Cable/Shane (1997), pp. 147-168 for a detailed discussion.

[459] Hidden information refers to pre-contractual problems per definition. However, these problems could also occur to a lesser extent after the contract has been closed in order to increase the probability of further financing.

(shirking), underinvest in the venture, force short-term performance, or aim an early exit (grandstanding).

Cable/Shane (1997) developed various propositions on factors which increase the likelihood of cooperation within a VC financing relationship. The different factors are illustrated in Figure 3.6. First, cooperation is assumed to be more likely if reliable information about the other party's cooperative behavior is easy to obtain.[460] Two factors impact the transfer of information: communication and social relationships. High quality and frequent communication increases the likelihood of cooperation since it makes the actions and strategies of the parties clearer, creates empathy for the other party, and allows a discussion of the dilemma.[461] Communication is supposed to be more important in early stages of the relationship and early stage ventures due to increased uncertainty. Positive social and business relationships promote cooperation by altering communication and trust as well as giving reasons to help each other.[462]

Second, personal similarity is also supposed to increase the likelihood of cooperation. Social psychology has found that individuals are more likely to be attracted to others which are perceived as similar to themselves. Thus, the probability of cooperation is enhanced due to reduced cognitive dissonance, improved communication, as well as increased predictability and trust in social interactions between actors perceiving themselves as similar.[463] In addition, stereotypes about dissimilar others could hamper cooperation. Cable/Shane (1997) focus on the comparison of specific characteristics and assume that relational demography similarity, work values congruence, and perceived power equality increase the likelihood of cooperation between entrepreneurial teams and venture capitalists. Thereby, relational demography refers to characteristics like age, gender, socio-economic status, or race. Work values mean the individual assessment of certain values like fairness over achievement or honesty over concern for others. Relative power refers to the ability of one party to force the other party to meet his or her demands. Hence, also aspects of social psychology are relevant for the likelihood of cooperation and will be discussed in more detail in section 3.2.2.3.

Third, different transaction procedures like bonding mechanisms, staging capital payouts, generosity, and penalties for defection might be used in order to induce cooperation.[464] Bonding mechanisms could be used to facilitate initial cooperation in the absence of trust between

---

[460] Cf. Abreu/Milgrom/Pearce (1991), pp. 1715-1716; Parkhe (1993), pp. 820-821.

[461] Cf. Blau (1977a), p. 259; Lindskold/Betz/Walters (1986), pp. 99-102; Zemel (1989), pp. 1-2; Dawes (1980), pp. 185-186; Gupta/Sapienza (1992), pp. 350-351.

[462] Cf. Chertkoff/Esser (1976), pp. 476-477; Sweeting (1991), p. 619.

[463] Cf. Turner (1978), p. 704; Jackson et al. (1991), pp. 685-687. See also section 3.2.2.3 for a discussion of interpersonal attraction.

[464] Cf. Keren/Raub (1993), pp. 444-447.

entrepreneurial teams and venture capitalists. Possible measures regarding the entrepreneurial team include antidilution provisions, forfeiture provisions, non-compete clauses, and vesting provisions.[465] The venture capitalist, on the other hand, could bond himself by investing resources upfront or granting employment contracts to the entrepreneurial team which prevents him from firing team members.[466] As mentioned above, cooperation is more likely if a prisoner's dilemma is repeated multiple times since present behavior has an impact on future decisions of the actors. Therefore, staging capital payments forces continued evaluation of a party's cooperation or defection strategy and increases the importance of reciprocity.[467] Generosity means not to defect immediately as soon as a defection of the other party is assumed. It therefore encourages the maintenance of and return to cooperative behavior.[468] Penalties for defection are especially relevant to venture capitalists who could penalize entrepreneurial teams' defection by diluting their equity share, firing team members and invoking non-compete clauses, or establishing appropriate compensation structures.[469] An effective penalty for non-cooperative venture capitalists which might be used by entrepreneurial teams is damaging a venture capitalist's reputation by distributing information about their (negative) experiences with the venture capitalist in the community.[470]

Further factors that could promote cooperation within a VC financing relationship include time pressure and appropriate payoff structures. Time pressure may induce cooperation by leading to less ambitious demands as well as larger and more frequent concessions of the actors.[471] Appropriate payoff structures allocate relatively high rewards to cooperative behavior and therefore make defection strategies relatively less attractive.[472]

---

[465] Antidilution provisions protect the venture capitalist's investment if the venture performs poorly and additional capital is required. Forfeiture provisions grant additional shares to the venture capitalist if the venture's performance is below a certain threshold. Non-compete clauses prohibit the entrepreneurial team to work in the same industry after leaving the venture. Vesting provisions aim on preventing the entrepreneurial team to leave the venture. Cf. Hoffman/Blakey (1987), pp. 17-18; Sahlman (1990), pp. 505 and 510.

[466] Cf. Hoffman/Blakey (1987), p. 18

[467] Cf. Axelrod/Dion (1988), pp. 1387-1388; Parkhe (1993), pp. 819-820.

[468] Generosity is particularly important if noise disturbs the perception of the other party's strategy (cf. Axelrod/Dion (1988), p. 1387).

[469] Cf. Hoffman/Blakey (1987), pp. 17-18; Sahlman (1990), pp. 505 and 510.

[470] Cf. Sahlman (1990), pp. 513-514.

[471] Cf. Chertkoff/Esser (1976), p. 471.

[472] Cf. Dawes (1980), pp. 174-175; Parkhe (1993), pp. 797-799 and 814.

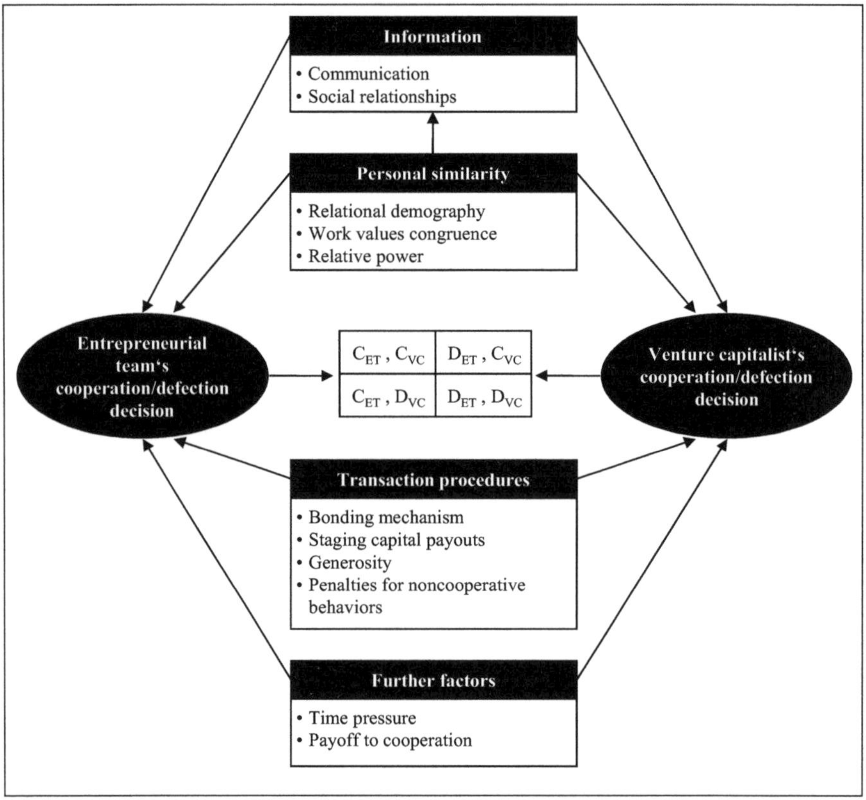

Figure 3.6: Factors influencing the VC financing relationship from a prisoner's dilemma perspective
C_{ET}: entrepreneurial team cooperates; C_{VC}: venture capitalist cooperates; D_{ET}: entrepreneurial team defects; D_{VC}: venture capitalist defects. Source: Based on Cable/Shane (1997), p. 153.

The conceptual model from Cable/Shane (1997) was developed exclusively to analyze relationships between venture capitalists and entrepreneurial teams in the post-contractual phases of the VC investment process. Thus, only two acting parties exist which already decided to collaborate.[473] However, some extensions of the prisoner's dilemma recognize the existence of more than two parties (several venture capitalists as well as several entrepreneurial teams) and include the possibility to choose whether a party enters the game with a specific party (i.e. the VC financing relationship) or not.[474] Then, also pre-contractual phases[475] could be ana-

[473] Cf. Cable/Shane (1997), p. 143.

[474] Cf. Gordon (1985), pp. 1075-1076.

lyzed with the help of the prisoner's dilemma. In these phases, the actors try to discover whether the other party is likely to cooperate in the future or not. Previous prisoner's dilemma research indicates that the reputation of actors and public communication is crucial within this process. Public communication is necessary in order to acknowledge the other's reputation. Then, all actors are likely to cooperate since no player is going to partner with somebody who defected in the past. An actor is only likely to defect if he is not planning to stay in business in the future.[476]

As a result, game theory and especially prisoner's dilemma research provides important insights for the analysis of the relationship between venture capitalists and entrepreneurial teams. Since this specific relationship is not hierarchical per definition and both parties could act opportunistically, prisoner's dilemma research offers important advantages in comparison to agency theory. Furthermore, the repeated prisoner's dilemma is able to model dynamic processes and social relationships better than the rather static agency theory.[477] This is true even though agency theory is also capable to incorporate the impact of dynamic processes and social relationships to a certain extent because reputation and social relationships are important means to mitigate informational asymmetries. A negative aspect of game theory is that most implications are based on the assumption of repeated interactions between the venture capitalist and the entrepreneurial team which is not necessarily the case.

c) Implications of Spatial Proximity between Actors

The efficiency and costs of most factors which increase the likelihood of the actors' cooperative behavior can be assumed to be sensitive to spatial proximity between the venture capitalist and the entrepreneurial team. First, information about the other party's behavior and reputation is easier and less costly to obtain in spatial proximity. Frequent personal interactions are more likely and less expensive the closer both parties are which enhances communication and the development of social relationships.[478] Moreover, regional personal networks increase the flow of information about past and present behavior of the other party from third parties.[479] Second, personal similarity can be assumed to increase if both parties are spatially proximate. This is because the relational demography in terms of socio-economic status, race, or work values, which are strongly influenced by culture, are likely to be more homogeneous

[475] Pre-contractual phases comprise deal origination, deal screening, due diligence, and deal structuring. See also section 2.1.4.

[476] Cf. Gordon (1985), pp. 1075-1076.

[477] Cf. Cable/Shane (1997), pp. 146-147. See section 3.2.1.2 for a discussion of agency theory.

[478] Cf. Blau (1977a), p. 268; Gupta/Sapienza (1992), p. 351; Lerner (1995), pp. 302-303. See also section 3.2.2.3 for further discussion.

[479] Cf. Blau (1977a), p. 268; Turner (1978), pp. 703-704; Sorenson/Stuart (2001), pp. 1547-1548. See also section 3.3.3 for a discussion of the influence of spatial proximity of actors on various networks.

within certain regions and thus in spatial proximity.[480] Third, certain transaction procedures are easier and less expensive to realize the closer both parties are. Bonding mechanisms and penalties for defection are only effective if misbehavior or defection can be observed by the other party which is more likely in spatial proximity as information is easier and less expensive to obtain.

Consequently, it can be assumed that cooperative behavior of both parties is easier and less expensive to obtain the higher the spatial proximity between the venture capitalist and the venture is. Thus, the probability of success[481] and in anticipation of this effect the likelihood of certain VC investments increases.

3.2.2.2 Stewardship Theory

a) Theoretical Foundations

Stewardship theory[482] is a relatively young theory and has its origin in sociological and psychological approaches.[483] In contrast to agency theory, stewardship theory analyzes the relationship between principals and stewards,[484] who are not motivated by individual goals, but whose interests are rather aligned with the interests of their principals.[485]

Therefore, stewardship theory can be seen as a modification of agency theory, which incorporates the critique of many scholars that not all agents act opportunistically.[486] In general, the existence of opportunistic agents is accepted by stewardship theory, but it is argued that human motives are much more diverse and also include intrinsic motives like opportunities for growth, achievement, affiliation, and self-actualization.[487] Therefore, another type of human being, for whom a pro-organizational, collectivistic behavior has higher utility than individua-

---

480 Cf. Thibaut/Kelley (1959), pp. 39-42; McPherson/Smith-Lovin/Cook (2001), pp. 429-430.

481 It is important to note that cooperation between venture capitalists and the entrepreneurial teams is no guarantee for success. Nevertheless, cooperation is a necessary (but not sufficient) condition for success (cf. Cable/Shane (1997), p. 143).

482 Important articles include Donaldson/Davis (1991); Fox/Hamilton (1994); Davis/Schoorman/Donaldson (1997b).

483 Cf. Davis/Schoorman/Donaldson (1997b), pp. 20-21.

484 The term steward is not explicitly defined. However, Donaldson/Davis (1991) describe a manager who acts according to stewardship theory as somebody who "wants to do a good job [and wants] to be a good steward of the corporate assets." (cf. Donaldson/Davis (1991), p. 51).

485 Cf. Davis/Schoorman/Donaldson (1997b), pp. 20-21. Agency theory assumes that agents opportunistically maximize their individual utility since informational asymmetries and conflicts of interests with their principals exist. See section 3.2.1.2 for a detailed discussion of agency theory.

486 See also Albanese/Dacin/Harris (1997), p. 609 for a discussion.

487 Cf. Donaldson/Davis (1991), p. 51; Davis/Schoorman/Donaldson (1997b), p. 28.

listic, self-serving behavior and who therefore acts in the best interest of the organization/principal, is assumed. Since cooperative behavior offers a relatively higher utility for the steward and since he acts accordingly, the steward can be considered as rational.[488] In consequence, a hierarchical relationship between principals and stewards exist, while the assumption of opportunism is disposed.

Stewardship theory comes to the conclusion that measures like monitoring and control, which are proposed by agency theory, damage the motivation of a steward and could thus lead to a loss in productivity and could provoke opportunistic, agent like behavior. As agency conflicts between principals and stewards do not exist, the theory suggests that stewards should be given autonomy and should be empowered by their principals in order to enhance their motivation and increase their creative productivity. This also includes measures to enable stewards to do their jobs and to create an environment in which stewards are able to act effectively.[489]

Empirical studies assuming that managers are either agents or stewards provide mixed support for agency and stewardship theory.[490] Wasserman (2006) suggests that both theories do not conflict each other but are rather complementary. As a result, each theory is more applicable in situations in which the other one is less applicable. In reality both agents as well as stewards might exist.[491]

This leads to a more differentiated analysis of economic relationships since the moral evaluation of actors is not per se negative. Davis/Schoorman/Donaldson (1997b) discuss psychological and situational factors and develop propositions under which conditions actors are likely to behave in accordance with a stewardship relationship.[492]

In order that a stewardship relationship is likely to occur and to be efficient, it is not sufficient that one party acts like a steward. Both parties have to act according to their respective role. The mentioned psychological and situational factors are antecedents of both parties' choice between agency and stewardship like behavior. Also, each party's expectation in regard to the choice of the other party influences its decision. In consequence, this choice is similar to the decision of a prisoner's dilemma, which is illustrated in Figure 3.7.[493] If both parties of the

---

[488] Cf. Davis/Schoorman/Donaldson (1997b), p. 24.

[489] Cf. Donaldson/Davis (1991), p. 60; Sapienza/Korsgaard (1996), p. 545; Davis/Schoorman/Donaldson (1997b), pp. 25-26.

[490] Cf. Donaldson/Davis (1991), p. 62; Donaldson/Davis (1994), pp. 151-159; Chrisman et al. (2007), pp. 1036-1037.

[491] Cf. Davis/Schoorman/Donaldson (1997a), p. 612; Wasserman (2006), p. 961.

[492] See Davis/Schoorman/Donaldson (1997b) for a detailed discussion of the psychological and situational factors (cf. Davis/Schoorman/Donaldson (1997b), pp. 27-38).

[493] See also section 3.2.2.1 for discussion of the prisoner's dilemma. For this and the following cf. Davis/Schoorman/Donaldson (1997b), pp. 38-40.

relationship choose to behave in accordance to or in expectation of an agency relationship, the result is a true agency relationship described in section 3.2.1.2. Then, the expectation of both parties is fulfilled and the aim of both is to minimize potential agency costs. If both parties choose to behave in accordance to or in expectation of a stewardship relationship, the result is a true stewardship relationship. In this case, the steward acts in the best interest of the principal and the principal tries to increase the involvement and empowerment of the steward. Since no agency costs occur, the mutual welfare of the relationship is maximized.

The dilemma occurs if both parties decide to act differently. If the principal acts according to an agency relationship and the other party like a steward, the steward will be frustrated and feel betrayed by the principal. Then it is very likely that the steward starts to develop agent like behavior and that the relationship converts to an agency relationship over time. In contrast, if the principal acts according to a stewardship relationship and the other party like an agent, the principal will feel angry and betrayed by the agent. Then it is likely that the principal either tries to remove the agent or starts to act according to an agency relationship. It can be assumed that this situation also is going to result in an agency relationship over time.

		Principal's choice	
		Agent	Steward
Manager's choice	Agent	Mutual agency relationship Minimize potential agency costs	Agent acts opportunistically Principal is angry and feels betrayed
	Steward	Principal acts opportunistically Steward is frustrated and feels betrayed	Mutual stewardship relationship Maximize potential performance

Figure 3.7: Prisoner's dilemma in choosing among agency and stewardship behavior
Source: Based on Davis/Schoorman/Donaldson (1997b), p. 39.

Since a stewardship relationship maximizes the welfare of both parties and both do not want to be betrayed, it is crucial for both parties to judge whether a stewardship relationship is likely to occur or not in a specific case.

Stewardship theory has been applied to a wide range of economic relations[494] like corporate governance in cooperative societies[495] or family firms,[496] contracting of and labor relations in non-profit organizations,[497] behavior of chief executive officers (CEOs) in CEO duality,[498] effectiveness of boards of directors,[499] and intercultural differences.[500]

Another application of the theory can be found in the analysis of the relationship between a venture capitalist and the entrepreneurial team[501] which is in the focus of the work at hand.

b) Application to Venture Capital Financing

In the case of VC financing the venture capitalist and the entrepreneurial team could, analogous to agency theory, be both interpreted as principal and steward. If the venture capitalist is interpreted as principal, the entrepreneurial team's interests would have to be fully aligned with the venture capitalist's interests. This is only true in certain situations and one has to apply a more differentiated analysis. Before the financing contract is structured, the interests of both parties are not aligned. This is because the entrepreneurial team already wants to promote the success of its venture, while the venture capitalist is only interested in good investment opportunities which could be any venture at this point of time. Within the financing process the phase of deal structuring constitutes kind of a transition period. After both parties decided that they would like to close a financing contract with each other, negotiations start. In the course of contract negotiations the fundament for the post-contractual relationship is built and both parties should be interested in the success of the venture now. It is important to recognize that it is unlikely, at least at the beginning of the relationship, that the entrepreneurial team will act in the interest of the venture capitalist just because it feels loyal or affiliated to the investor. In contrast, it is more likely that the interests of both parties are aligned because both have an interest in the success of the venture.[502]

---

494 See Klöckner (2008), pp. 47-49 for a short literature review.

495 Cf. Vargas Sánchez (2004), pp. 1-19.

496 Cf. Chrisman/Chua/Sharma (2005), pp. 555-575; Klöckner (2008), pp. 48-49.

497 Cf. Caers et al. (2006), pp. 25-47; van Slyke (2007), pp. 157-187.

498 Cf. Donaldson/Davis (1991), pp. 49-65; Fox/Hamilton (1994), pp. 69-81; Angwin/Stern/Bradley (2004), pp. 239-257.

499 Cf. Muth/Donaldson (1998), pp. 5-28; Roberts/McNulty/Stiles (2005), pp. 5-26.

500 Cf. Lee/O'Neill (2003), pp. 212-225.

501 Cf. Arthurs/Busenitz (2003), pp. 145-162. Wasserman (2006) analyses the executive compensation in new ventures and therefore investigates the relationship between executives and shareholders more generally.

502 Cf. Arthurs/Busenitz (2003), pp. 154-155. Further conflicts of interest between the venture capitalist and the entrepreneurial team could arise due to different time horizons for the investment. The general time horizon is usually known to the entrepreneurial team in advance, but it could be that especially young venture capitalists intend to exit an investment very early in order to quickly realize returns and obtain positive references. This behavior is usually referred to as grandstanding (cf. Gompers (1996), pp. 135-138).

In the course of a VC financing the entrepreneurial team sells part of its venture, but one could argue that the entrepreneurial team continues to feel and behave like an owner since it often invested large shares of its personal wealth, labor effort, and time and continues to own the majority of the new venture.[503] Therefore, one could expect the entrepreneurial team to behave like a steward.

The venture capitalist has a strong interest in a high portfolio return and therefore in the success of the portfolio company. In addition, the venture capitalist is responsible for the resources of his VC fund and has a high performance pressure. Therefore, the venture capitalist scrutinizes the entrepreneurial team and the venture carefully before an investment decision in the course of the deal screening and due diligence process. Thereafter the venture capitalist has to decide, consciously or subconsciously, whether he expects the entrepreneurial team to act like agents or like stewards and how he is going to behave. One could now argue that a venture capitalist would not invest into an entrepreneurial team and its venture if he expects the team to act opportunistically like an agent. However, the venture capitalist has a high responsibility for his funds and there are many more factors like market conditions, competitors or timing that impact the success of the venture and are not influenced by the intention of the team. In consequence, one could expect the venture capitalist to start the relationship by moderately monitoring and controlling the entrepreneurial team and the venture.[504]

If the venture develops according to the business plan, it is likely that the venture capitalist is going to further support the past actions and behavior of the entrepreneurial team and grants more autonomy and tries to further enhance the success of the team and the venture by empowering them. In this case, also the venture capitalist acts according to a stewardship relationship and a real stewardship relationship could develop.[505]

If, on the other hand, the venture constantly stays behind the business plan two possible reactions of the venture capitalist could emerge. First, the venture capitalist might suppose that the dissatisfying development of the venture is caused by a failure of the entrepreneurial team which did not act or does not have the ability as promised in advance. This would be interpreted as opportunistic, agent like behavior and the venture capitalist is likely to behave in accordance to an agency relationship by extending monitoring and controlling activities.[506] Then, an agency relationship will develop over time. Second, if the venture capitalist is solely

---

[503] Cf. Arthurs/Busenitz (2003), p. 155. See section 3.2.1.2 for an opposing argumentation.

[504] Cf. Sapienza/Amason/Manigart (1994), p. 3 and refer to section 2.1.4.5 for further discussion.

[505] However, George/Nathusius (2007) find that many of the most successful portfolio companies went through a crisis in the course of their development (cf. George/Nathusius (2007), p. 23).

[506] In an extreme case also the CEO of the venture might be replaced (cf. Bruton/Fried/Hisrich (2000), pp. 73-74). As a result, a new relationship between the venture capitalist and the new CEO would emerge as described above.

profit oriented and since the majority of VC portfolio returns is generated by high flyers, it is likely that the venture capitalist intends to exit the investment as soon as possible in order to get its money out.[507] In this case, the success of the venture is not in the focus of interest of the venture capitalist anymore and a stewardship relationship is unlikely to emerge. This reaction might also appear if the venture capitalist supposes other reasons than the entrepreneurial team, like market reactions, competitor activities or timing, for the dissatisfying development of the venture. In consequence, a mutual stewardship relationship in which the venture capitalist is the principal depends on multiple conditions and is not very likely to persist over the whole investment period because the venture capitalist might prefer to act according to agency theory in order to reduce his investment risk.

The entrepreneurial team could also be interpreted as principal starting at or after the financing contract is negotiated. In this case, the venture capitalist could act like a steward who supports the entrepreneurial team and the venture because he is also interested in the success of the venture. This behavior is most likely to continue if the venture develops according to the business plan as discussed above. Under these circumstances, the entrepreneurial team could act according to an agency or stewardship relationship. If the team acts according to a stewardship relationship, it would have to give autonomy to the venture capitalist and would have to empower him. This means that the entrepreneurial team would also have to provide the necessary information to the venture capitalist and would be willing to accept advice from the investor. As a result, a true stewardship relationship could emerge.

If the team does not act according to a stewardship relationship and just takes the financial resources from the investor without providing information and accepting advice, the venture capitalist may feel betrayed, stop the support and start to act like an opportunistic agent. However, this scenario is rather unrealistic since the support of the venture capitalist is one of the main advantages for entrepreneurial teams in choosing this financing source and since the provision of information by the team is usually contractually agreed on.[508]

A positive aspect of stewardship theory is that it offers recommended actions for relationships between non-opportunistic actors in which interests are aligned. Furthermore, it introduces a discussion whether the parties of an economic relationship act opportunistically or not. This provokes a reflection of agency theory and a more differentiated analysis.[509]

Nevertheless, stewardship theory also has several drawbacks. First, "[w]hile agency theory paints a gloomy picture of the agent, stewardship theory paints an excessively rosy picture of

---

[507] See section 2.1.4.5 regarding the impact of a portfolio company's performance on the extent of venture capitalist's support activities.

[508] Cf. Sahlman (1990), p. 505. See also section 2.1.4.4.

[509] Cf. Albanese/Dacin/Harris (1997), p. 609.

the steward."[510] In consequence, both theories assume a rather extreme behavior of actors, which probably is not the case in reality. Furthermore, the behavior of actors could change from situation to situation and it could change over time. In consequence, it is difficult to classify an actor as agent or steward. The true behavior of actors can probably be found somewhere in the middle.[511] In case of a VC investment this problem is especially severe since the entrepreneurial team usually does not act in the best interest of the principal but in the best interest of the venture. In consequence, interests are only aligned as long as the VC also wants to promote the venture. As soon as it turns out that the venture might not be profitable it could be that the team still wants to promote the venture, while the venture capitalist would prefer to liquidate it. Then interests diverge and venture capitalists have to be prepared in order to enforce their interests.

Second, there is a huge debate, whether stewardship theory is an own theory or part of agency theory and thus redundant.[512] There are many variations of agency theory existing and trust as well as long term relationships as means to reduce agency costs are also included in agency theory.[513] In addition, Picot/Dietl/Franck (2005) state that individual utility functions can be manifold and that opportunistic behavior could even include altruism if social appreciation and the wellbeing of others, e.g. the principal or the organization, are parts of the individual utility function.[514] Davis/Schoorman/Donaldson (1997a) reply that agency theory is based on agency conflicts and becomes obsolete if there are none.[515] However, a main difference between the theories can be identified in the point that agency theory provides recommendations about how to reduce the costs, while stewardship theory discusses strategies on how to enhance benefits of economic relationships.

Third, stewardship theory recommends not to monitor stewards but to give autonomy to the stewards and to empower them. This restricts the application of the theory to situations in which the principal can be absolutely sure that the other party is going to act like a steward because he doesn't want to be betrayed. Picot/Dietl/Franck (2005) provide an example of a bank which has to be protected even though the majority of people would not rob it. Nobody would come to the idea to leave the doors of the bank open.[516] Since there is no absolute security about the other party's characteristics, one has to be aware of opportunistic behavior and

[510] Arthurs/Busenitz (2003), p. 155.

[511] Cf. Albanese/Dacin/Harris (1997), p. 610; Arthurs/Busenitz (2003), p. 155. This critique was also anticipated by the authors (cf. Davis/Schoorman/Donaldson (1997a), p. 611).

[512] Cf. Albanese/Dacin/Harris (1997), pp. 609-610; Preston (1998), p. 9.

[513] Cf. Albanese/Dacin/Harris (1997), p. 609.

[514] Cf. Picot/Dietl/Franck (2005), p. 32.

[515] Cf. Davis/Schoorman/Donaldson (1997a), pp. 611-612.

[516] Cf. Picot/Dietl/Franck (2005), p. 32.

that is what professional economic actors, like venture capitalists and entrepreneurial teams, should do.

c) Implications of Spatial Proximity between Actors

Stewardship theory implies that spatial proximity between the venture capitalist and the venture could be relevant for three reasons. First, within the choice model of Davis/Schoorman/Donaldson (1997b) the principal has to decide whether he expects the other party to act according to stewardship theory or not.[517] Therefore, e.g. appropriate information, personal meetings and relationships are important which are easier to acquire or to arrange in spatial proximity. Second, the theory suggests that in case of a stewardship relationship the principal should give autonomy to the steward and should empower and enable him. This could also include the provision of contacts, access to networks as well as consulting which is also easier to accomplish in spatial proximity. Third, stewardship theory also implies that extensive monitoring damages the motivation of a steward and is thus contra productive. If monitoring activities are more intense in spatial proximity because they are easier and less costly to conduct, proximity might be detrimental for stewardship relationships. However, it is unlikely that venture capitalists conduct monitoring activities only because they are easy and cheap if they are not convinced that these activities are necessary. Hence, it is unlikely that spatial proximity contradicts stewardship relationships.

3.2.2.3 Social Exchange Theory

Besides the previously discussed theories which are mainly based on assumptions in regard to the individual behavior of actors, also social relationships between actors are important within the current research.[518]

a) Theoretical Foundations

In contrast to economic exchange theories which analyze the exchange of economic resources on markets, social exchange theory analyzes a much broader spectrum of exchange relationships. In general, social exchange theory considers interactions as an interdependent exchange of positive and negative stimuli which are referred to as rewards and costs.[519] Rewards can be as manifold as love, status, information, money, goods, or services.[520] Cost could include

---

[517] Cf. Davis/Schoorman/Donaldson (1997b), pp. 38-39.

[518] Cf. De Clercq/Sapienza (2001), pp. 108-109.

[519] Cf. Homans (1958), p. 606; Emerson (1976), pp. 335-337; Emerson (1987), p. 11.

[520] Foa/Foa (1976) developed these general categories of resources, which might have a utility to individuals (cf. Foa/Foa (1976), p. 101).

time, energy, investments, or opportunity costs.[521] In addition, fairness, dependencies, power, and satisfaction in relationships as well as the role of attractiveness and fit among actors are investigated.

The term social capital is tightly related to social exchange theory and has been established in order to refer to the beneficial effect of social relationships. Since social exchange refers to an exchange of rewards like access to information, support, and other resources, social relationships can be used to achieve personal goals and thus provide a utility to actors. Therefore, social relationships can be interpreted as a resource or "social capital".[522]

Specific personal attributes of actors which influence the personal fit among individuals and groups are analyzed by theories of interpersonal attraction.[523] Here, a clear systematization of theories is not possible. On the one hand, personal attributes can be seen as an essential part or facilitator of social exchanges.[524] On the other hand, social exchange theory can be seen as a part of interpersonal attraction theory since complementary needs and resources facilitate social exchanges and might lead to interpersonal attraction.[525]

Social exchange theory has its origins in psychology[526] and sociology[527]and has made valuable contributions to various fields of science.[528] An advantage of social exchange theory in comparison to agency theory, game theory, and stewardship theory is that it does not assume neither opportunism of the actors nor hierarchical relationships.

Social exchange theory can be considered as a system of theories which develop hypotheses about the behavior of actors in social relationships. The theory of interdependence was developed by Thibaut/Kelley (1959) and states that people evaluate relationships by comparing rewards and cost. In addition, a comparison level is introduced which represents the expectations of an actor. Therefore, the satisfaction of an actor in regard to a relationship can be de-

---

521 Cf. Welpe (2004), p. 56.

522 Cf. Coleman (1988), pp. 97-100; Holzer (2006), pp. 14-15. In general, social capital can be defined as "...the aggregate of the actual or potential resources which are linked to possession of a durable network of more or less institutionalized relationships of mutual acquaintance and recognition" (Bourdieu (1985), p. 248). Therefore, not only dyadic relationships are important but also social networks, which are discussed in section 3.3. For further discussion of the concept of social capital see also Portes (1998), pp. 1-24.

523 Cf. Hollingshead (1950), pp. 619-620; Hassebrauck/Küpper (2002), p. 156.

524 One example would be similar attitudes towards certain issues and a certain educational level, which facilitates intense discussions among actors with a productive output or just satisfaction. See also Thibaut/Kelley (1959), pp. 37-47 for a discussion of similarity, abilities, and complementary needs.

525 Cf. Hassebrauck/Küpper (2002), pp. 159-164.

526 Cf. Thibaut/Kelley (1959).

527 Cf. Homans (1961); Blau (1964).

528 Concepts of social exchange theory have been used e.g. in game theoretic approaches (cf. e.g. Colmann (2003)).

termined by rewards minus costs minus comparison level. Furthermore, a comparison level for alternative relationships exists which determines the commitment of an actor towards a certain relationship.[529] Rusbult (1980) further developed the theory of interdependence and included previous relation specific investments which increase the bond of a relationship.[530] Another theory is the equity theory which posits that the satisfaction and stability of a relationship is determined by the perceived fairness in regard to personal contributions and profits of the actors.[531]

Social exchange theory also states that the development of intense relationships is an evolutionary process in which actors interactively increase their commitments to the relationship.[532] In the course of this process actors put more and more of their resources at risk and norms emerge in regard to confidentiality, disclosure, fairness, and mutuality.[533] Since these interactions are usually not contractually agreed on or are difficult to enforce legally, this process is highly dependent on factors like trust, reciprocity, and reputation.[534] Trust generally means that an actor leaves himself vulnerable to trusted others[535] and includes various dimensions like confidence that the best effort will be made, confidence that proprietary information will be protected, or faith in the veracity and good intentions of exchange partners.[536] Reciprocity refers to the fact that each party puts incrementally more and more at risk[537] in expectation that the other party is going to do the same and does not defect. A good reputation of the actors provides important information about the partner if the actors are lacking own experiences. Therefore, reputation is likely to accelerate the relationship building process.

As mentioned above, theories of interpersonal attraction focus on specific personal attributes of actors which influence dyadic relationships and therefore also social exchanges.[538] Several factors and personal attributes, which increase the likelihood of interpersonal attraction, have been identified.

---

[529] Cf. Thibaut/Kelley (1959), pp. 12-24.

[530] Cf. Hassebrauck/Küpper (2002), pp. 160-161.

[531] Cf. Hatfield/Walster/Berscheid (1978) cited in Hassebrauck/Küpper (2002), pp. 161-164.

[532] Cf. Larson/Starr (1993), p. 9; Geyskens et al. (1996), pp. 314-315; De Clercq/Sapienza (2001), p. 118

[533] Cf. Larson/Starr (1993), p. 9.

[534] Cf. Blau (1964), pp. 91-97.

[535] Cf. Hosmer (1995), pp. 392-393; De Clercq/Sapienza (2001), p. 118.

[536] Cf. Sapienza/Korsgaard (1996), pp. 557-559. The development of trust and commitment can also be stimulated by procedural justice. This aspect is analyzed by procedural justice theory. Since procedural justice is unlikely to be affected by the spatial proximity between actors, it is not further discussed here. For a detailed discussion of procedural justice theory in the VC context see Sapienza/Korsgaard (1996); Busenitz et al. (1997); Arthurs/Busenitz (2003) among others.

[537] Cf. De Clercq/Sapienza (2001), p. 118.

[538] Cf. Hassebrauck/Küpper (2002), p. 156.

First, the Reinforcement-Affect-Model (RAM), which was developed by Clore/Byrne (1974), posits that interpersonal attraction to a specific person is caused by positive emotions which are generated by or linked to that specific person.[539] Second, the balance theory, which was developed by Heider (1958), posits that emotional and cognitive consistency increases the likelihood of interpersonal attraction. In consequence, people are attracted by people with similar attitudes towards other persons/groups, issues or objects.[540] Third, demographic similarity facilitates the development of social relationships and refers e.g. to similar age, gender, class, education, race, ethnicity, socioeconomic status, or religion.[541] The phenomenon that similar individuals are more likely to be attracted by each other is also called homophily.[542] Fourth, the propinquity effect implies that physical proximity leads to a higher frequency of interactions and thus to higher interpersonal attraction.[543] Fifth, complementary needs and resources imply that people are more likely to be attracted by each other if they have e.g. complementary talents or possessions. Then people are able to provide others with their resources at low costs and receive other resources in exchange.[544]

b) Application to Venture Capital Financing

Many empirical studies have used social exchange theory to build hypotheses[545] and important contributions to the analysis of the relationship between venture capitalists and entrepreneurial teams can be expected.[546] As mentioned earlier, contracts between venture capitalists and entrepreneurial teams are likely to be incomplete.[547] Next to measures like monitoring or incentive alignment, which are e.g. proposed by agency theory, also social relationships between venture capitalists and entrepreneurial teams are important for mutual gain.[548] As discussed earlier in the section, social relationships are based on trust and reciprocity and there-

---

539 Cf. Hassebrauck/Küpper (2002), p. 157.

540 Heider's balance theory was further developed by Newcomb (1961), who differentiated between attitudes towards persons and objects as well as the strength of attitudes. Cf. Hassebrauck/Küpper (2002), pp. 164-166.

541 Cf. Hollingshead (1950), p. 627; Thibaut/Kelley (1959), pp. 39-45; Jackson et al. (1991), pp. 685-687.

542 See also McPherson/Smith-Lovin/Cook (2001), pp. 415-444 for a thorough discussion of homophily and a review of literature.

543 Cf. Festinger/Schachter/Back (1950), pp. 36-45; Thibaut/Kelley (1959), pp. 39-42.

544 Cf. Thibaut/Kelley (1959), pp. 45-47.

545 Cf. Welpe (2004), p. 57.

546 See e.g. De Clercq/Sapienza (2001), pp. 107-127. In addition, relationships between venture capitalists and entrepreneurial teams are very intense such that even friendship emerges frequently (cf. Steier/Greenwood (1995), pp. 351-352).

547 Cf. Kaplan/Strömberg (2003), pp. 281-282.

548 Cf. De Clercq/Sapienza (2001), pp. 107-109.

fore reduce potential opportunism of entrepreneurial teams as well as venture capitalists.[549] Due to a more intense, free and possibly informal communication, asymmetric information among actors is reduced. Furthermore, trust diminishes the potential concern about the reliability of information.[550] In consequence, social relationships are likely to reduce contracting and monitoring costs and thus reduce transactions and agency costs.[551] Furthermore, the likelihood of cooperative behavior rises[552] and, besides information, social relationships also facilitate the access to a wide range of additional resources important for the development of a new venture.[553]

These effects are also well documented by past research. Sweeting (1991) found that venture capitalists actively tried to discover if they would get along with the entrepreneurial team and could trust them before the investment decision was made.[554] Sapienza/Korsgaard (1996) stressed the importance of trust between the venture capitalist and the entrepreneurial team for the success of the financing relationship.[555] Shane/Cable (2002) discovered that social relationships between venture capitalists and entrepreneurial teams are very important for the transfer of information.[556] Furthermore, Florin/Lubatkin/Schulze (2003) showed more generally that the entrepreneurial team's social relationships leverage the productivity of a venture and provide the venture with a durable source of competitive advantage.[557]

A further general implication of social exchange theory, which is relevant to VC financing relationships, is that relationships are built over time and that long term relationships are likely to be relatively strong. Two reasons can be identified for this effect. First, it is likely that more relation specific investments are made over time. Second, an intense relationship and trust between the actors needs time to develop since it is caused by an incremental and interactive increase of each party's commitment to the relationship.

Social exchange theory has contributed significantly to the understanding of interpersonal processes and relationships which are also relevant for VC financing relationships.[558] As stated above, social exchange theory is not a consistent theory but rather "...a frame of refer-

---

[549] Cf. Nahapiet/Ghoshal (1998), p. 249; Welpe (2008), pp. 1252-1254.

[550] Cf. Nahapiet/Ghoshal (1998), pp. 254-255; De Clercq/Sapienza (2001), p. 119.

[551] See sections 3.2.1.2 and 3.2.1.3.

[552] See section 3.2.2.1.

[553] Cf. Larson/Starr (1993), p. 6.

[554] Cf. Sweeting (1991), p. 619.

[555] Cf. Sapienza/Korsgaard (1996), pp. 544-545.

[556] Cf. Shane/Cable (2002), p. 377.

[557] Cf. Florin/Lubatkin/Schulze (2003), p. 374.

[558] Cf. Athenstaed/Freudenthaler/Mikula (2002), p. 86.

ence within which many theories ... can speak to one another...".[559] Therefore, the theory facilitates the integrative analysis of social phenomena which had to be analyzed separately before.[560] Furthermore, social exchange theory developed conceptual tools needed to analyze market imperfections that cannot be explained by economic theory and allow to integrate altruistic behavior of actors.[561] Finally, social exchange theory might be able to analyze aspects which go beyond rational self interest and to explore the affective aspects of decision making which could be associated to prejudices, convenience, or solidarity.[562]

But social exchange theory also has some potential drawbacks. Most of the concepts and theoretical research focus on individuals or small groups establishing friendship or marriage relationships.[563] It remains open, whether these results can be transferred to economic relationships or not. However, the work at hand uses social exchange theory in order to account for social relationships in business life. Furthermore, it is likely that in most cases the same processes also impact economic relationships.[564] Another potential drawback is that it is difficult to operationalize many theoretical constructs used by the theory like commitment, comparison levels, or dependency. Thus, it is difficult to confirm many hypotheses empirically.[565]

c) Implications of Spatial Proximity between Actors

The main impact of spatial proximity between actors which is implied by social exchange theory is that the likelihood of the development and maintenance of social relationships increases sharply if actors are located close to each other. This in turn facilitates the transfer of information and tacit knowledge.[566]

The increase of the likelihood of a relationship between actors in spatial proximity has first been investigated by sociologists, who studied the influence of spatial proximity on the likelihood of friendship and marriage.[567] However, it is likely that the same processes also impact economic relationships.[568] Several reasons for the importance of spatial proximity between

---

[559] Emerson (1976), p. 336.

[560] Cf. Athenstaed/Freudenthaler/Mikula (2002), p. 86.

[561] Cf. Emerson (1976), p. 359; Athenstaed/Freudenthaler/Mikula (2002), p. 86.

[562] Cf. Sapienza/Villanueva (2007), pp. 67 and 79-80.

[563] Cf. Emerson (1976), p. 336.

[564] Cf. Sorenson/Stuart (2001), p. 1547.

[565] Cf. Athenstaed/Freudenthaler/Mikula (2002), p. 87.

[566] Tacit knowledge refers to knowledge, which cannot be codified and which can only be transmitted by personal contact (cf. Polanyi (1967) cited in Nahapiet/Ghoshal (1998), p. 246). It includes e.g. "...theoretical and practical knowledge of people and the performance of different kinds of artistic, athletic, or technical skills." (Nahapiet/Ghoshal (1998), p. 247).

[567] Cf. e.g. Bossard (1932), pp. 220-222; Festinger/Schachter/Back (1950), pp. 36-45.

[568] Cf. Sorenson/Stuart (2001), p. 1547.

the venture capitalist and the entrepreneurial team can be identified. First, proximity between actors increases the likelihood of a social relationship because it leads to a higher frequency of interactions by raising the chance of random encounter and lowering the necessary effort to get in contact with each other.[569] In addition, the increased frequency of interactions leads to higher interpersonal attraction.[570]

Second, relationships are more likely to occur and to be maintained among actors which are similar to each other. As stated above, this similarity could occur in various dimensions and increases interpersonal attraction. This phenomenon of homophily is relevant in the current context since actors which are spatially close to each other are likely to be similar or to develop similarity in multiple dimensions like race, ethnicity, religion, culture, or work values. Furthermore, actors might personally identify themselves with a common region which could also lead to interpersonal attraction.[571]

Third, social exchange theory states that different relationships are evaluated against each other. Rewards, costs, and expectations as well as alternative relationships are important for the evaluation of existing or potential relationships and thus influence the decision which relationships are established or maintained.[572] The costs to establish or maintain a specific relationship are likely to be higher in distance. In addition, possible rewards of a relationship (e.g. transfer of tacit knowledge) might be higher in proximity. This might lead to a more intense and effective collaboration of the venture capitalist and the entrepreneurial team. In contrast, if actors decided to establish a certain relationship, relation specific investments are higher in distance and could therefore increase the bond.[573]

Fourth, the stability of a relationship is determined by the perceived fairness in regard to personal contributions and profits of the actors. If actors e.g. have to travel long distances in order to meet each other, they might perceive that they invested relatively more into the relationship and expect a higher profit. Otherwise the relationship might be seen as unfair.[574] This could lead to a higher conflict potential if the venture capitalist and the entrepreneurial team are located spatially distant from each other.

---

569 Cf. Thibaut/Kelley (1959), pp. 39-42; Blau (1977b), pp. 90-93; Turner (1978), pp. 703-704; McPherson/Smith-Lovin/Cook (2001), p. 429. These effects might have been weakened by the advent of new communication technologies, but they are still significant since most relationships are originally made and sustained through face-to-face interactions (cf. McPherson/Smith-Lovin/Cook (2001), p. 430).

570 Cf. Thibaut/Kelley (1959), pp. 39-42.

571 Cf. Thibaut/Kelley (1959), pp. 39-42. See also McPherson/Smith-Lovin/Cook (2001), pp. 415-444 for a thorough discussion of homophily and a review of literature.

572 Cf. Thibaut/Kelley (1959), pp. 12-24.

573 Cf. Hassebrauck/Küpper (2002), pp. 160-161.

574 Cf. Hatfield/Walster/Berscheid (1978) cited in Hassebrauck/Küpper (2002), pp. 161-164.

If social relationships exist between the venture capitalist and the entrepreneurial team, the transfer of information and tacit knowledge is easier and therefore more likely. This is because social relationships are based on trust and reciprocity, which promotes the transfer of information and decreases potential concerns about its reliability.[575] In addition, social relationships as well as spatial proximity lead to more frequent face-to-face interactions which facilitate the transfer of tacit knowledge.[576] These interactions also promote the development of informal relationships which are characterized by an even higher degree of trust.[577]

In conclusion, most of the effects imply that spatial proximity facilitates the development and maintenance of social relationships which alleviates the transfer of information and tacit knowledge.

3.3 Theories Relevant beyond the Venture Capitalist - Entrepreneur Dyad: Network Approach

For a thorough analysis of the impact of spatial proximity between a venture capitalist and an entrepreneurial team it is not sufficient to exclusively analyze the relationship of these two parties. The relationship between a venture capitalist and an entrepreneurial team is again embedded in multiple relationships to a multitude of supporting actors like other financiers (other venture capitalists, banks, business angels, public support), other entrepreneurs, service providers (lawyers, consultants, auditors, marketing experts, deal broker), R&D institutes and universities, or others (potential employees, past colleagues, business contacts, family, friends).[578] In addition, these supporting actors also have relationships with each other which results in a complex network of various actors. This complex network can be again divided in several sub networks of specific actors and relationships.[579]

As it has been discussed in previous sections, many potential problems inherent in the VC investment process are caused by informational problems or asymmetries between the actors.[580] The different networks mentioned above could serve as means to mitigate these informational problems or asymmetries. This is because information between two parties flows

---

575 Cf. Cf. Nahapiet/Ghoshal (1998), pp. 254-255; Uzzi/Gillespie (1999), p. 33 cited in Shane/Cable (2002), p. 366; Shane/Cable (2002), p. 377; Maula/Autio/Murray (2003), p. 131.

576 Cf. Sapienza/Manigart/Vermeir (1996), p. 457; Feldman (2000) cited in Patton/Kenney (2005), p. 3; Christensen/Drejer (2005), p. 808.

577 Cf. Birley (1985), p. 115.

578 Cf. Bygrave (1988), p. 140; Fried/Hisrich (1994), p. 32; Mason/Harrison (1995), p. 157; Böhner (2007), p. 52.

579 Cf. Barnes (1972) cited in Pappi (1987), p. 13.

580 See e.g. sections 3.2.1.2, 3.2.1.3 or 3.2.2.1.

more easily if a direct or indirect relationship exists or involved parties simply know who they have to approach if a problem occurs.[581] Thus, networks between different kinds of actors are crucially important within the VC investment process. Furthermore, these networks are likely to be influenced by spatial proximity between the actors. Therefore, this section theoretically discusses the influence of various networks on the VC investment process.

3.3.1 Theoretical Foundations

Although there have been various attempts to formulate a network theory, these are far from representing a consistent theory. In consequence, there is no real network theory existing so far. Instead several network approaches emerged which represent analytical frameworks with a methodological character or theoretical perspective.[582]

The work at hand focuses on the analysis of VC financing relationships. Therefore, the relationships between venture capitalists, entrepreneurial teams, as well as a multitude of supporting actors have to be analyzed. These actors represent individuals or organizations, which in turn are made up by multiple individuals. In consequence, for the work at hand social networks are in the focus of interest.[583]

Various definitions of social networks exist. A very popular definition of social networks describes them as "[…] a specific set of linkages among a defined set of persons, with the additional property that the characteristics of these linkages as a whole may be used to interpret the social behavior of the persons involved."[584] Thus, these networks are made up by actors (nodes) and specific relationships (ties) between these actors. In addition, social networks typically include coequal and autonomous but interdependent actors, which cooperate in order to better achieve their individual goals. Relationships are rather horizontal than vertical and actors' cooperation is based on trust.[585]

---

[581] See section 3.2.2.3 for a discussion of the influence of social relationships on information flows.

[582] Cf. Sydow (1992a), pp. 125-126; Jansen (2003), p. 11; Holzer (2006), p. 6.

[583] Other types of networks might be information networks, infrastructure networks, etc. (cf. Pappi (1987), pp. 12-13).

[584] Mitchell (1971), p. 2. Since social networks are very abstract constructs, it turns out to be helpful to consider various definitions in order to better understand social networks. Pappi (1987) defines social networks as a set of social actors like individuals, positions, organizations, etc., which are linked through a certain type of relationship (cf. Pappi (1987), p. 13). Fritsch (2001) provides another definition and states that "[A]ny set of social relationships may be called a 'network' if it consists of at least three individuals or institutions and is characterised [!] by some redundant vertical relationships that are only incompletely specified." (Fritsch (2001), p. 27).

[585] Cf. Weyer (2000), p. 11; Jansen (2003), p. 12.

The different network approaches also have their origin within sociology, where they first have been used to analyze social relationships and behaviors of individuals within groups.[586] Therefore, these approaches assume that individual actors socially interact with others, which leads to the development of social relationships and structures and thus influences their individual behaviors.[587]

Subsequently, these network approaches have been extended and organizations have been included next to individual actors. This led to network approaches analyzing social relationships of various economic actors as well as resulting social structures and behaviors. Today, the network approach is used within various scientific disciplines.[588]

Within the discussion of social networks two major approaches can be differentiated: the approach of inter-organizational networks and the formal network analysis.[589] The approach of inter-organizational networks considers networks as an additional independent type of coordinating actions among actors.[590] Therefore, it can be considered as a contribution to organizational theory which concentrates on a specific form of self-coordination between strategic actors.[591] A fundamental approach within this category is the network approach of new institutional economics.[592] In contrast, the formal network analysis considers social networks as structures of social relationships between actors which can be described by quantitative methods.[593] Thus, this approach represents a universal method to describe various structures of social relationships between actors.[594]

These two approaches do not compete against each other but are rather complementary perspectives which analyze social networks from different points of view and which could also be combined within an analysis.[595] Therefore, these two approaches will be discussed in the following sections.

---

586 Cf. Pappi (1987), p. 11; Jansen (2003), p. 37.

587 Cf. Granovetter (1985), pp. 481-510.

588 Cf. Jansen (2003), pp. 11 and 48-49.

589 Cf. Weyer (2000), p. 14; Jansen (2003), pp. 11-13. Other authors name additional approaches like the approach of political sciences, which analyzes regulation by and within networks (cf. Ahrens (2003), pp. 44-45; Hellmer et al. (1999), pp. 55-56). Since these approaches are not in the focus of the work at hand, they will not be further discussed.

590 Cf. Powell (1990), pp. 295-336; Sydow (1992b), pp. 239-311.

591 Cf. Weyer (2000), p. 17.

592 Cf. Powell (1990), pp. 295-336; Weyer (2000), p. 4.

593 Cf. Pappi (1987) 11-12; Scott (1988), pp. 109-127; Jansen (2000), pp. 35-62.

594 Cf. Weyer (2000), p. 17.

595 Cf. Weyer (2000), pp. 17-18.

3.3.1.1 Approach of Inter-Organizational Networks

Various types of inter-organizational networks exist, which are analyzed within different research streams.[596] All of them have in common that they consider networks as an additional independent type of organizational form to coordinate actions among actors. The most widely accepted theoretical network concept is the network approach of new institutional economics.[597] Therefore, this approach will be discussed before the different types of inter-organizational networks will be briefly introduced.

The network approach of new institutional economics has its origin within transaction cost theory.[598] Hence, networks are discussed from an economic perspective. This approach introduces the network as an additional organizational form next to the fundamental organizational forms of markets and hierarchies.[599] The different organizational forms particularly differ in the types of interactions among actors.[600] Markets are characterized as a form of interaction in which independent actors meet spontaneously without any perspective for future interactions and coordinate their actions exclusively with the help of a price mechanism.[601] A central coordinating authority is not needed. Consequently, the tone of communication is very precise and actors might mistrust each other. Furthermore, actors have a high flexibility in choosing their partners for interaction and have a low commitment towards them. Contracts constitute the normative basis of their interaction and potential conflicts are solved by haggling or by legal enforcement. In contrast, hierarchical organizational forms are based upon hierarchical structures and resulting dependencies. Interactions are governed by formal routines and decision making processes. Therefore, actors only have low flexibility in changing their interacting partners and display medium to high commitment towards them. The normative basis is constituted by employment relationships and potential conflicts are solved by administrative fiat or authority. Next to these organizational forms networks are characterized by interdependent forms of interaction for which the relation between the actors is crucial. Since relationships develop over time and are usually open ended, actors possess less flexibility in choosing their partners but have higher commitment towards them compared to markets. Contrary, actors have a higher degree of flexibility compared to hierarchies because no long term employment relationships exist. Instead, relationships are based on complementary strength of the actors which offer benefits for both parties in case of cooperation. In case of a conflict

[596] Cf. Weyer (2000), p. 15.

[597] Cf. Weyer (2000), p. 4.

[598] See section 3.2.1.3 for a discussion of transaction cost theory.

[599] Cf. Powell (1990), pp. 295-336. The concept of two fundamental organizational structures of markets and hierarchies goes back to Coase (1937) (cf. Coase (1937), pp. 388-391).

[600] Cf. Powell (1990), p. 301.

[601] Cf. Weyer (2000), pp. 6-7.

actors typically intend to solve those by mutual consent due to the importance of reciprocity and reputational concerns.[602] Table 3.2 summarizes the characteristics of the three organizational forms.

Table 3.2: Characteristics of different organizational forms
Source: Based on Powell (1990), p. 300.

	Organizational form		
Key characteristics	Market	Network	Hierarchy
Actor preferences or choices	• Independent	• Interdependent	• Dependent
Means of communication	• Prices	• Relational	• Routines
Tone or climate	• Precision and/or suspicion	• Open-ended, mutual benefits	• Formal, bureaucratic
Degree of flexibility	• High	• Medium	• Low
Amount of commitment among the parties	• Low	• Medium to high	• Medium to high
Normative basis	• Contract – property rights	• Complementary strengths	• Employment relationship
Methods of conflict resolution	• Haggling – resort to courts	• Norm of reciprocity – reputational concerns	• Administrative fiat – supervision

Based on the network approach of new institutional economics the term of an organizational network emerged.[603] Sydow (1992a) provided a well accepted definition of an organizational network. He defines an organizational network as an organizational form of economic activities to realize competitive advantages which are characterized by complex reciprocal, rather cooperative than competitive, and relatively stable relationships between legally independent but economically mostly dependent organizations.[604]

The discussed characteristics of the different organizational forms and the definition of an organizational network are important for the further analysis. Hence, it is possible to determine whether the focal relationships constitute an organizational network or not and to better understand specific phenomena.

---

[602] Cf. Powell (1990), pp. 300-305. Next to the view that networks constitute a different type of organizational form, which does not allow gradual transitions to the forms of markets and hierarchies, also other perceptions exist. Hence, some authors argue that markets and hierarchies constitute poles of a continuum and networks can be found in the middle of this continuum. See Weyer (2000), pp. 9-10 for further discussion.

[603] Cf. Nathusius (2005), p. 70.

[604] Sydow (1992a), p. 79 (“Ein Unternehmungsnetzwerk stellt eine auf die Realisierung von Wettbewerbsvorteilen zielende Organisationsform ökonomischer Aktivitäten dar, die sich durch komplex-reziproke, eher kooperative denn kompetitive und relativ stabile Beziehungen zwischen rechtlich selbständigen, wirtschaftlich jedoch zumeist abhängigen Unternehmungen auszeichnet.“).

Within the group of inter-organizational networks four different types can be differentiated: strategic networks, regional networks, innovation networks, and policy networks.[605] Strategic networks are characterized by the exclusive, strategically oriented cooperation of a limited number of organizations.[606] Here, the spatial proximity between actors is not necessarily required (even though it is supporting) because the cooperation between an end manufacturer and its suppliers is feasible as long as personal communication[607] is possible and transaction costs are maintainable. Regional networks are crucial for the success of organizations, especially for small and medium sized ones. Those networks facilitate a strong specialization of organizations and leads to a system of highly specialized actors which is not only connected by contractual relationships but also by personal informal contacts and relationships, a strong regional identification, as well as accompanying political measures. Personal, informal contacts are especially important because the actors use them to acquire information, contacts, and support in critical situations. Consequently, spatial proximity is crucial for the existence and efficiency of regional networks.[608] A third type of networks, which is in the focus of researchers, is the type of innovation networks. Two different approaches exist in order to explain the role of networks in the creation of innovations.[609] Some authors take reference to Granovetter (1973) and postulate that weak ties are especially important for the creation of innovations as it is not purposeful to always ask the same people with which an actor has strong ties.[610] Others postulate that only strong ties facilitate the emergence of innovations because intensive cooperation is necessary.[611] These two approaches can be also integrated since cooperating partners connected by strong ties also benefit from their own and their partners' weak ties. Policy networks constitute a new instrument of governmental control and are not in the focus of the work at hand.[612]

These different network types might be relevant in the VC context for several reasons. Therefore, the applicability and relevance of these different network types for venture capitalists, entrepreneurial teams and their common relationship will be discussed in section 3.3.2.

---

605 Cf. Weyer (2000), p. 15.

606 See Jarillo (1988), pp. 31-41 for a detailed discussion of strategic networks.

607 Interpersonal communication is essential for inter-organizational networks since trust facilitates information transfer and is strongly promoted by personal contacts (cf. Uzzi/Gillespie (1999), p. 33 cited in Shane/Cable (2002), p. 366; Weyer (2000), p. 21).

608 Cf. Weyer (2000), pp. 20-21.

609 Cf. Weyer (2000), p. 22; Fritsch (2001), pp. 30-31.

610 Cf. Granovetter (1983), p. 214; Fischer/Gensior (1995) cited in Weyer (2000), p. 22.

611 Cf. Elzen/Enserink/Smit (1996), pp. 109-110; Rammert (1997) cited in Weyer (2000), p. 22.

612 Cf. Weyer (2000), pp. 22-24.

3.3.1.2 Formal Network Analysis

The focus of formal network analysis[613] is to better understand and predict the behavior of actors by analyzing the structure of the actor's social relationships.[614] Therefore, one of the key assumptions is that individual actors are embedded in multiple social relationships which constitute social structures and influence their potential and actual individual behavior. For example, actors with a central position within a network could exert more influence than others in peripheral positions.[615]

A typical question of formal network analysis could be whether there are central actors from which many others depend or whether the actors are more or less coequal.[616]

Consequently, social relationships, which determine social structures, are in the focus of analysis and should be discussed in more detail. Social relationships are constituted by all types of communication, affects, evaluations, actions and potential contacts between two actors.[617] In regard to the intensity of these relationships one can differentiate between potential interactions (e.g. opportunities for contact due to common memberships in certain groups), actual interactions (e.g. exchange of goods), and durable social relationships (e.g. friendship).[618] Relationships can be further classified in regard to their content like transactions or transfer of material resources (e.g. capital), transfer of non-material resources (e.g. information, services), sentiment relations (e.g. friendship, liking, respect, hostility), kinship (e.g. marriage, descent), boundary penetration relationships (e.g. common personnel of organizations), instrumental relationships (e.g. as part of a job), or authority.[619] In regard to their content also multiple types of relationships could prevail between two actors. This leads to the differentiation between uniplex (one type of content) and multiplex (multiple types of contents) relationships.[620]

---

[613] Some authors also use the term social network analysis (cf. Pappi (1987), pp. 11-12; Wasserman/Faust (1994), p. 3; Jansen (2000), p. 36). However, Weyer (2000) uses the term 'formal network analysis' in order to better differentiate from other approaches and to stress the formal orientation of this approach (cf. Weyer (2000), p. 14).

[614] Cf. Pappi (1987), pp. 18-19.

[615] Cf. Granovetter (1985), pp. 483-487; Weyer (2000), p. 16. In contrast to the network approach of new institutional economics, the formal network analysis applies a broader definition of networks and does not make any assumptions in regard to hierarchies or dependencies among actors (cf. Jansen (2000), p. 36).

[616] Cf. Weyer (2000), p. 18.

[617] Cf. Pappi (1987), p. 17. Other authors like Weber (1976) use a very narrow definition of social relationships. As this very narrow definition is not appropriate within the context of social network analysis, Pappi (1987) uses a broader definition and simply refers to it as relationship (cf. Pappi (1987), p. 17).

[618] Cf. Pappi (1987), pp. 17-18. Granovetter (1973) also differentiates relationships in regard to their intensity (strength) and refers to strong and weak ties (cf. Granovetter (1973), p. 1361).

[619] Cf. Knoke/Kuklinski (1993), pp. 15-16; Wasserman/Faust (1994), p. 47.

[620] Cf. Pappi (1987), p. 14.

Formal characteristics of relationships within a network include their symmetry and transitivity. Symmetry refers to the reciprocity of a relationship. In case of reciprocity, both involved actors choose each other in order to establish a relationship. In contrast, asymmetric relationships are constituted by a one-sided decision. Reciprocity therefore requires both parties to perceive a utility from the relationship and a fair distribution of profits. Because most relationships require actions of both parties, reciprocity is critical for the constitution of many relationships. Some researchers also assume symmetry per definition if they are only interested in the pure existence of a relationship. Thus, symmetry per definition implies that relationships do not evolve without reciprocity.[621] Transitivity of a relationship means that relationships between A and B as well as B and C also imply a relationship between A and C.[622]

Social networks can be described in regard to several dimensions. As social networks consist of a specific set of linkages among a defined set of actors, one first has to define the subject of study in regard to actors and relationships.[623] Concerning the actors one has to differentiate whether all relationships among several actors in a defined population are in the focus of interest (whole/complete networks) or whether only relationships of one central person (ego) with others are to be analyzed (personal/egocentric networks).[624] The population can be defined in regard to various dimensions like geographic region, organizational type, or size. One-mode networks are made up by populations including only one type of actors. If two or more types of actors exist (e.g. venture capitalists and entrepreneurial teams), two-mode or even higher-mode networks emerge. A special type of two-mode networks is an affiliation network.[625] Here, only one type of actors exists. The second mode is constituted by a certain event, which links the actors (e.g. venture capitalists joining a syndicated investment).[626]

In respect to the type of relationships (intensity and/or content) one could analyze only a specific type of relationships (partial networks) or all kinds of relationships among actors (total networks).[627] After defining the network of interest, those can be illustrated by graphs or matrixes. Within graphs the actors (nodes) are depicted as points and the social relationships are represented as a line between the actors (edge).[628]

---

621 Cf. Sydow (1992a), p. 95; Pappi (1987), p. 16; Weyer (2000), p. 12.

622 Cf. Pappi (1987), p. 16; Jansen (2003), p. 63.

623 Cf. Mitchell (1971), p. 2.

624 Based on personal/egocentric networks one could also include the relationships among the actors, which are directly related to ego. This leads to the first-order zone (cf. Barnes (1972) cited in Pappi (1987), p. 13).

625 Other authors refer to this type of network as membership network or hypernetwork (cf. Breiger (1974), p. 183; McPherson (1982), pp. 225-249).

626 Cf. Wasserman/Faust (1994), pp. 29-30.

627 Cf. Barnes (1972) cited in Pappi (1987), p. 13.

628 See Wasserman/Faust (1994), pp. 92-166 for a detailed discussion of graphs and matrices.

One of the main tasks of formal network analysis is to explain and predict the behavior of actors by describing the form of a network and the position of specific actors within a network with the help of quantitative methods. Thus, social networks can be described by various quantitative measures like the centrality (degree, betweenness, closeness), density, and others. Due to the plurality of measures a detailed description is not purposeful here.[629] Furthermore, these measures have a descriptive character and therefore no explanatory power. In order to explain or to predict certain behaviors, additional assumptions about human behavior are necessary.[630] Then the formulation of hypotheses would be possible in a specific case. Moreover, formal network analysis considers social structures in a static manner and is therefore not able to provide any reasons for the development of certain positions of actors within a network.[631]

3.3.2 Relevant Networks

As mentioned above, the venture capitalist, the entrepreneurial team, and various supporting actors are embedded within numerous relationships constituting multiple potential networks. These different potential networks are of different types and play diverse roles in the VC investment process. Therefore, for a structured analysis, relevant relationships have to be identified in a first step. Second, it has to be investigated if these relationships constitute organizational networks. Third, the specific types of networks have to be determined. Subsequently, the implications of the identified networks on the impact of spatial proximity between the venture capitalist and the entrepreneurial team on the VC investment process will be discussed in section 3.3.3.

In general, three different types of actors are relevant to a VC investment process: venture capitalists, entrepreneurial teams, and supporting actors like other types of financiers (banks, business angels, public support), service providers (lawyers, consultants, auditors, marketing experts, deal broker), R&D institutes and universities, or others (potential employees, past colleagues, business contacts, family, friends).[632] In consequence, six different types of potential relationships emerge: relationships among venture capitalists, among entrepreneurial teams, among venture capitalists and entrepreneurial teams, among venture capitalists and

[629] See Wasserman/Faust (1994), pp. 167-344 for a detailed discussion of different descriptive network measures.

[630] Cf. Richter/Furubotn (2003), p. 333.

[631] Cf. Weyer (2000), p. 16.

[632] Cf. Bygrave (1988), p. 140; Fried/Hisrich (1994), p. 32; Mason/Harrison (1995), p. 157; Böhner (2007), p. 52.

supporting actors, among entrepreneurial teams and supporting actors, and among supporting actors.

The most widely discussed **relationship among venture capitalists** is a syndication relationship.[633] Syndication refers to the common investment of several venture capitalists into a venture within a specific financing round. A syndicated VC investment therefore comprises one or more syndication relationships among venture capitalists[634] and is limited in time to the period of investment. These syndication relationships are usually characterized by reciprocity because venture capitalists economically depend on the success of the current syndication relationships as well as on continuing relationships to other venture capitalists for future syndication. Furthermore, these are cooperative relationships which are accompanied by the transfer of information, deal flow, contacts, and other supporting activities (e.g. due diligence and management support).[635] Due to the financing contract these relationships are stable over the time of investment. The venture capitalists are legally independent and due to the common investment to a certain extent economically dependent on each other. In consequence, based on the definition from Sydow (1992a), syndicated investments constitute organizational networks.[636] Moreover, these networks constitute strategic networks since each of them is an exclusive, strategically oriented cooperation of a limited number of venture capitalists.

Outside a syndicated VC investment the character of the relationships among venture capitalists is not clear. On the one hand, venture capitalists are competitors for fund capital and the most promising investment opportunities. On the other hand, venture capitalists might cooperate for several reasons. The VC industry is still quite small in many countries.[637] Therefore, it is likely that venture capitalists personally know each other and that they might have realized syndicated investments together previously. Furthermore, venture capitalists expect reciprocity in the future if they helped each other in the past. Then venture capitalists might pass contacts and/or information about past experiences within certain industries or regions as well as with specific entrepreneurs or other actors. Furthermore, venture capitalists might also pass interesting deal flow if the proposed investment does not fit into one's own portfolio.[638] This two-sided relationship is also characterized as coopetition.[639] In consequence, existent rela-

---

633 See e.g. Bygrave (1988); Sorenson/Stuart (2001); Nathusius (2005) among others.

634 A venture capitalist either assumes a role as lead- or as co-investor (see section 2.1.1).

635 Cf. Nathusius (2005), pp. 109-115.

636 See Nathusius (2005), pp. 68-73 for a more detailed discussion of the character of syndicated investments.

637 Cf. EVCA (2008), p. 52; EVCA (various years-a).

638 Cf. Tyebjee/Bruno (1984a), p. 1055; Fried/Hisrich (1995), p. 104.

639 The term coopetition emerges from the terms cooperation and competition and means that two organizations could cooperate and compete at the same time. For a further discussion of coopetition see Dowling (1996); Nalebuff/Brandenburger (1996).

tionships among venture capitalists beyond syndicated investments are reciprocal[640] and venture capitalists are legally and economically independent. Since the relationship is characterized by coopetition, the relationship is rather instable and oscillates between cooperation and competition. As a result, an organizational network only exists among venture capitalists which have an established relationship (e.g. by prior syndication) and which are cooperative in regard to the content of the relationship. Depending on the roots and purposes of the relationships the type of the resulting networks could be a strategic or regional network.

The majority of entrepreneurs start a venture for the first time and therefore lack experiences, information, relevant contacts, and multiple other resources.[641] But also experienced entrepreneurs might lack information, relevant contacts and other resources. One reason is that new ventures, and especially the ones with high growth potential, often involve innovations and therefore new situations and problems. Hence, **relationships among entrepreneurial teams** are important within the entrepreneurial process. Platforms like the "Munich Network" try to link entrepreneurs with each other and with other actors like venture capitalists or other supporting actors.[642] Thus, experiences and information (e.g. in regard to venture capitalists and previous financing rounds) can be exchanged as well as partners for cooperation or human resources might be found. As many entrepreneurial teams have similar problems or follow comparable life styles, entrepreneurs identify themselves with their role and relationships to other entrepreneurs might be particularly intensive.[643] Another aspect is that some entrepreneurial teams might compete with each other in a certain industry. But also these relationships might be characterized rather by coopetition than by hostility, e.g. if a research consortium or licensing agreements exist.[644] However, most of the exchanged information and experiences, especially in the case of first-time entrepreneurs, are rather general and non-technical and therefore not critical for competitive entrepreneurial teams. Hence, most relationships among entrepreneurial teams are characterized by reciprocity and rather cooperative than competitive behavior. Moreover, entrepreneurial teams are legally and economically independent from each other. In consequence, even though entrepreneurial teams are economically independent and information about the stability of their relationships is scarce, entrepreneurial teams and the relationships among them show considerable parallels to an organizational network, which facilitates the application of corresponding network approaches. The type of these networks equals rather regional than strategic or innovation networks since it is not constituted by a

[640] An additional important reason for reciprocal relationships is that venture capitalists are very concerned about their reputation and that they therefore behave in a fair manner.

[641] Cf. Sternberg/Brixy/Hundt (2007), p. 32; Kohn/Spengler (2008), p. 34.

[642] Cf. Munich Network (2008).

[643] Cf. Turner (1978), p. 704; Jackson et al. (1991), pp. 685-687.

[644] Cf. Dowling (1996), pp. 157-158.

limited number of organizations and most platforms like the Munich Network have a regional character. Nevertheless, strategic or innovation networks may also be possible.

The **relationships among venture capitalists and entrepreneurial teams** have been theoretically discussed in detail in section 3.2 and are therefore not addressed in detail within this section. However, in order to discuss these relationships from a network perspective one has to differentiate between relationships among venture capitalists and entrepreneurial teams which already are in a VC financing relationship and actors which are not.

Nathusius (2005) thoroughly discussed these relationships in case of an existing VC financing relationship.[645] It can be assumed that both parties benefit from the relationship and that the relationship is characterized by reciprocity and a rather cooperative than competitive behavior.[646] The investment contract and the time horizon of a VC investment, which usually encompasses several years, lead to a fairly high stability of the relationship. Due to extensive contractual control rights of the venture capitalist, the entrepreneurial team is not legally independent from the venture capitalist even though mainly minority investments prevail. Furthermore, entrepreneurial teams highly depend on the financial and non-financial support of the venture capitalists and these in turn depend on the positive economic development of the venture. Therefore, both parties are economically dependent on each other.[647] Even though both parties are not legally independent from each other Nathusius (2005) concludes that sufficient analogies exist in order to apply network approaches based on the definition of organizational networks from Sydow (1992a). Moreover, these networks constitute strategic networks since each of them is an exclusive, strategically oriented cooperation of a limited number of venture capitalists and an entrepreneurial team.

If a financing relationship between venture capitalists and an entrepreneurial team does not exist (yet/anymore), venture capitalists are "only" a potential source of financial and non financial resources. This could lead to relationships. However, these relationships are a specific subgroup of and have similar properties like relationships among entrepreneurial teams and supporting actors. These relationships will be discussed later within this section.

Venture capitalists continuously search for new investment opportunities, invest into ventures, manage their existing investments by monitoring and supporting them, and exit their investments in order to realize the generated value. These activities lead to regular interactions with multiple actors and thus to various **relationships among venture capitalists and supporting**

---

[645] Cf. Nathusius (2005), pp. 68-73.

[646] Several situations exist in which it might be beneficial for one of the parties in the short term not to cooperate (see section 3.2.2.1 for a detailed discussion). However, in general, both parties should have an interest to cooperate in order to create value in the long run.

[647] Cf. Nathusius (2005), pp. 68-73.

actors.[648] These networks are critical for the venture capitalist in order to efficiently manage the VC investment process and are an integral component of the value added for their portfolio companies.[649] Bygrave (1988) underlines the importance of networks with others than venture capitalists and their impact on information flows and states that "…to ensure a supply of fresh information, members [of a specific venture capitalist network] should have as many links as possible to other organizations and individuals besides venture capitalists."[650] In consequence, the content of these relationships is mainly constituted by information, contacts, and/or direct or the opportunity for cooperation. Furthermore, these relationships are mostly beneficial for both parties because the supporting actors also depend on venture capitalists in their role as customers (e.g. lawyers, consultants) or in order to be contracted by one of their portfolio companies (e.g. consultants, potential employees, suppliers). Therefore, the relationships among venture capitalists and supporting actors are mostly reciprocal, cooperative, and stable. Besides, both parties are legally independent and some of the relationships are characterized by an economic dependency of one party to the other. In consequence, venture capitalists, supporting actors, and the relationships among these actors constitute organizational networks. These networks can have a strategic or regional character.

Already before the contact of an entrepreneurial team with a venture capitalist, the entrepreneurial team maintains various relationships in order to receive needed resources for the creation of the new venture. First, these are mainly prior business contacts, family, and friends in order to receive information, first physical and financial resources, as well as social support needed to start the venture. Over time the **relationships among entrepreneurial teams and supporting actors** increase in quantity and get more intense.[651] The supporting actors can be classified into informal (e.g. family, friends, business contacts) and formal contacts (e.g. banks, accountants, lawyers, government agencies).[652] The importance of these relationships was recognized by many authors.[653] Their main functions are the discovery of opportunities, securing resources, and obtaining legitimacy.[654] The main contents of these relationships are information, contacts, cooperation, as well as human and financial resources. As the relationships among venture capitalists and supporting actors also most of the relationships among

648 Cf. Mason/Harrison (1995), p. 157.

649 Cf. Tyebjee/Bruno (1984a), p. 1055; Fried/Hisrich (1995), pp. 103-104; Steier/Greenwood (1995), p. 348.

650 Bygrave (1988), p. 138.

651 Cf. Larson/Starr (1993), pp. 6-11.

652 Cf. Birley (1985), p. 107.

653 Cf. Birley (1985), p. 107; Jarillo (1988), pp. 31-32; Lorenzoni/Ornati (1988), p. 41; Jarillo (1989), pp. 133-134 and 144-146; Larson (1991), pp. 173-174; Larson (1992), pp. 98-101; Hansen (1995), p. 15; Steier/Greenwood (1995), p. 337.

654 Cf. Elfring/Hulsink (2003), p. 410.

entrepreneurial teams and supporting actors are characterized by reciprocity, cooperation and stability since they are beneficial for both parties and mostly endure over a certain period of time.[655] The actors are legally independent, but some of the actors are economically dependent on the other party. In consequence, entrepreneurial teams, supporting actors, and the relationships among these actors constitute organizational networks. Depending on their specific characteristics these networks could be strategic, regional or innovation networks.

Already Milgram (1967) recognized that actors around the world are connected by surprisingly short acquaintance chains.[656] In 1969 an experiment revealed that the average number of intermediary people between US citizens was 5.2.[657] Furthermore, it can be shown that acquaintance chains between people of a specific group are more likely to be used than between persons belonging to different groups.[658] Venture capitalists and entrepreneurial teams operate in similar "entrepreneurial spaces" and supporting actors of both parties are overlapping to a great extent. Both are likely to have contacts to other types of financiers (banks, business angels, public support), service providers (lawyers, consultants, marketing experts), and other entrepreneurs. Therefore, it can be assumed that also **relationships among the supporting actors** are likely to exist. Possible contents of these relationships could be manifold and include information, contacts, cooperation as well as human and financial resources. Since these actors are very heterogeneous, it is difficult to determine common characteristics of the relationships among them. However, most of these actors represent professional and/or economic individuals or organizations. Therefore, it can be assumed that existing relationships among them are characterized by reciprocity. Actors of different types are likely to cooperate with each other, while actors of equal types (e.g. lawyers) are likely to compete or behave in accordance to coopetition. Most of the actors are legally independent from each other. Contrary, a mixed picture is likely to exist in regard to economic dependency. Some might be economically independent and others might be dependent on each other due to business relationships. In consequence, due to the heterogeneity of relevant supporting actors and their relationships among each other, an overall conclusion whether organizational networks exist or not cannot be drawn. However, many of these actors and the relationships among them constitute networks which are likely to behave like organizational networks. Therefore, it is possible to apply network approaches based on the definition of organizational networks from Sydow

---

[655] Cf. Larson (1992), pp. 76-104. Some relationships especially to family and friends might not be motivated by reciprocity. Since it can be assumed that the importance of these kinds of relationships diminishes in the course of the company's development, this point is not further discussed.

[656] Cf. Milgram (1967), pp. 60-67.

[657] Cf. Travers/Milgram (1969), p. 436.

[658] Korte/Milgram (1970) conducted an experiment in which they identified acquaintance chains between black and white people as well as among white people. Acquaintance chains among white people had significantly greater likelihood of being used (cf. Korte/Milgram (1970), p. 103).

(1992a). Depending on their specific characteristics these networks could be strategic or regional networks.

The different relationships relevant to a VC investment process, their potential contents, and corresponding network types are illustrated in Figure 3.8.

	Venture capitalists	Entrepreneurial teams	Supporting actors
Venture capitalists	Syndication 1 ✓ • Information, deal flow, contacts, support • Type: strategic network No Syndication 2 (✓) • Information, deal flow, contacts • Type: strategic or regional network		
Entrepreneurial teams	Financing rel. 3 (✓) • Financial resources, information, contacts, support, monitoring • Type: strategic network No financing rel. 4 ✓ • Information, contacts • Type: strategic or regional network	5 (✓) • Information, contacts, cooperation, human resources • Type: strategic, regional, or innovation network	
Supporting actors	6 ✓ • Information, contacts, cooperation • Type: strategic or regional network	7 ✓ • Information, contacts, cooperation, human and financial resources • Type: strategic, regional, or innovation network	8 (✓) • Information, contacts, cooperation, human and financial resources • Type: strategic or regional network

Legend:
✓ = constitute organizational networks and network approach is applicable
(✓) = network approach based on organizational networks is applicable in this specific context
✗ = network approach based on organizational networks is not applicable

Figure 3.8: Relationships relevant to a VC investment process, contents of relationships, and corresponding network types
Source: Own illustration.

3.3.3 Implications of Spatial Proximity between Actors

The main impact of spatial proximity between actors (venture capitalists, entrepreneurial teams, and supporting actors) on the networks that have been described in the previous section is caused by effects implied by social exchange theory. The likelihood of existence of relationships and their intensity increases sharply if actors are located close to each other.

This in turn facilitates the transfer of information and tacit knowledge as well as the availability of specific resources.[659]

The increase of the likelihood of a relationship between actors in spatial proximity is mainly driven by an increased probability of random encounter and a reduced effort necessary to get in contact with others.[660] In addition, actors which are spatially close to each other are likely to be similar or to develop similarity in multiple dimensions like race, ethnicity, religion, culture, or work values. This similarity among actors promotes the development of relationships.[661] In consequence, the density of personal networks is likely to increase the smaller the geographic distance to the central person (ego) is.[662] This also leads to the fact that acquaintance chains between randomly selected actors tend to be shorter the closer the actors are located to each other.[663]

As discussed in section 3.2.2.3 the transfer of information and tacit knowledge is easier and therefore more likely if a relationship exists between the actors. In addition, if actors are located spatially close to each other, local networks emerge that facilitate the acquisition of local resources like local contacts or knowledge about local market particularities. Furthermore, Stuart/Sorenson (2003) argue that "...industries cluster because entrepreneurs find it difficult to leverage the social ties necessary to mobilize essential resources when they reside far from those resources".[664] This aspect is also intensively discussed within a broad literature on the development of economic clusters.[665] In consequence, spatial proximity leads to a higher density of networks, which facilitates the transfer of information and tacit knowledge as well as the acquisitions of local resources.

3.4 Summary

As discussed in section 1.2, the work at hand applies a plurality of theories to shed more light on various aspects of the research object. Therefore, chapter 3 identified and discussed several theories that offer insights about the role of spatial proximity between the venture capitalist

---

[659] See section 3.2.2.3 for further discussion.

[660] Cf. Thibaut/Kelley (1959), pp. 39-42.; Blau (1977b), pp. 90-93; Turner (1978), pp. 703-704; McPherson/Smith-Lovin/Cook (2001), p. 429.

[661] See section 3.2.2.3 and McPherson/Smith-Lovin/Cook (2001), pp. 415-444 for a thorough discussion and literature review.

[662] Cf. e.g. Carlsson (2002), p. 119.

[663] Cf. Travers/Milgram (1969), p. 436.

[664] Stuart/Sorenson (2003), p. 229.

[665] Cf. e.g. Porter (1998), p. 81.

and the entrepreneurial team throughout the VC investment process. For each theory, theoretical foundations have been provided and the theory has then been applied to the specific case of a VC investment. Finally, general theoretical implications on the relevance of spatial proximity between the actors have been discussed.

In summary, most of the theories imply that spatial proximity affects the VC investment process or the relationship between the venture capitalist and the entrepreneurial team in the form of a moderating factor by lowering costs (e.g. transaction costs), increasing the efficiency of specific instruments (e.g. to mitigate agency problems), or by facilitating certain actions (e.g. transfer of tacit knowledge). These theoretical implications will be discussed in detail for each phase of the VC investment process in chapter 4 in order to develop propositions and testable hypotheses about the influence of spatial proximity between actors on this process.

4 Impact of Spatial Proximity throughout the Venture Capital Investment Process

The VC investment process is fairly complex, and the venture capitalist, entrepreneurial team, as well as supporting actors conduct various but also very different activities in the particular phases of the process.[666] Furthermore, it became obvious in chapter 3 that various theories imply a high relevance of spatial proximity between the venture capitalist and the new venture in regard to specific aspects. Hence, it is not immediately obvious:

- whether spatial proximity between the venture capitalist and the new venture has an impact within particular phases of the investment process or not,
- what kind of impact spatial proximity potentially has in a particular phase,
- why the potential impact is in place, and
- for which kind of entrepreneurial teams, venture capitalists, and/or types of financing rounds the potential impact is particularly important.

In order to find answers to these questions, this chapter follows a process oriented approach. Based on the description of the VC investment process in section 2.1.4, relevant activities of involved actors as well as surrounding conditions are analyzed in regard to the impact of spatial proximity for each investment phase. In doing so, relevant theories which were identified and discussed in chapter 3 will be applied. This leads to the formulation of various propositions regarding the impact of spatial proximity in each phase of the investment process (sections 4.1 and 4.2). According to the research questions of this thesis, the focus of this discussion lies on the impact of spatial proximity on the likelihood of a potential VC financing relationship to successfully pass each phase of the investment process. Furthermore, it will be discussed for which kinds of ventures, venture capitalists, or financing rounds the impact of spatial proximity is particularly strong. This finally results in the likelihood of a VC financing relationship to occur and thus also influences the observed patterns in spatial proximity between venture capitalists and investees.

Finally, the propositions of the different investment phases will be condensed to testable hypotheses regarding the patterns in spatial proximity between venture capitalists and investees as well as the impact of spatial proximity on the likelihood of a specific VC financing relationship to occur (section 4.3). As a result, it will be possible to verify important parts of the elaborated theoretical framework empirically for German VC investments (chapter 5). Figure 4.1 illustrates the structure and role of this chapter throughout the thesis.

---

[666] Section 2.1.4 provides a detailed description of the different phases of the investment process.

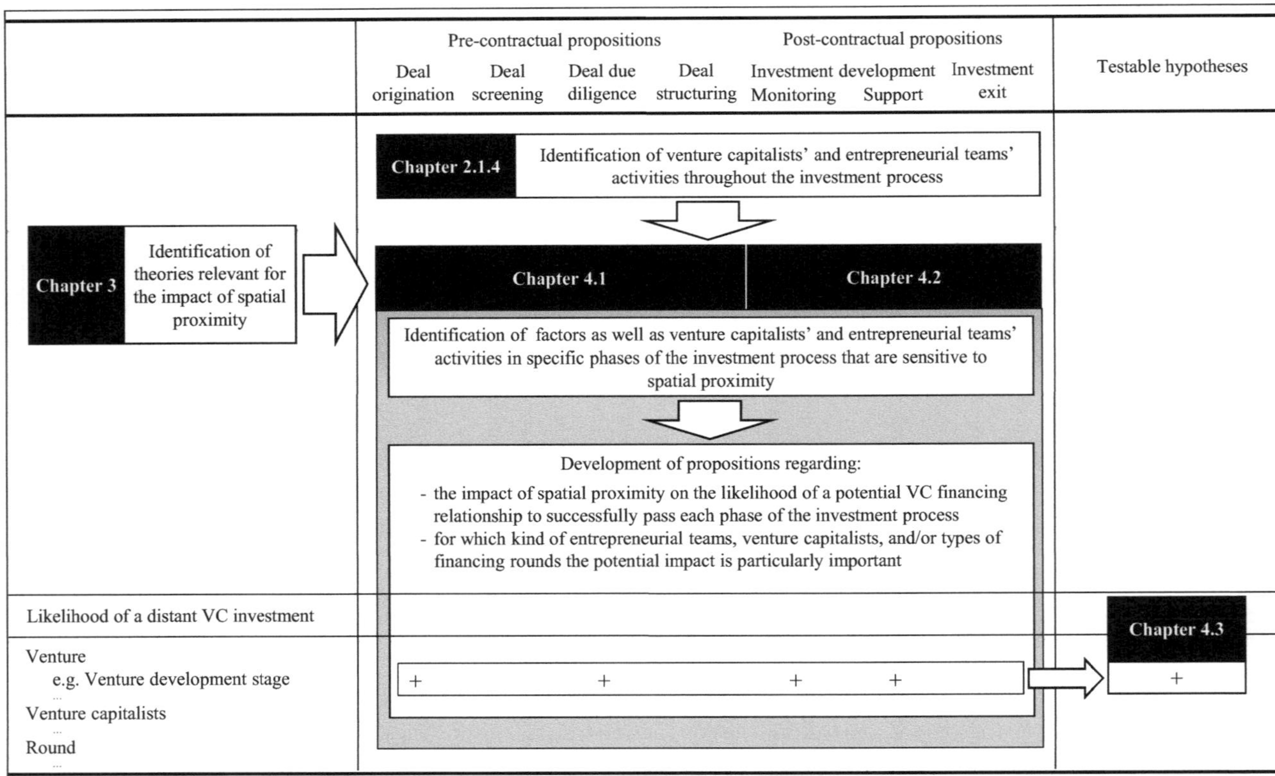

Figure 4.1: Structure and role of chapter 4 throughout the thesis
Source: Own illustration.

4.1 Pre-Contractual Activities

Pre-contractual activities start with the deal origination and continue throughout the deal screening and deal due diligence phase. Finally, the contract is negotiated in the deal structuring phase and the investment/financing decision is made effective by signing the contract.

4.1.1 Deal Origination

In order to invest VC, investors have to be aware of investment opportunities first. Therefore, the main purpose of deal origination is the generation of deal flow and thus to recognize investment opportunities. As it has been discussed in section 2.1.4.1, this deal flow can occur in different ways. The quantity and quality of the deal flow differs among the different sources and might also be sensitive to the spatial proximity between the venture capitalist and the entrepreneurial team.

Half to two thirds of the deal flow and the vast majority of investments are originated by **indirect contacts** through referrals.[667] Thus, the deal flow that stems from referrals is high in quantity and quality and the network approach as well as social exchange theory may offer important insights regarding the spatial structure of this deal flow. Referrals may come from various sources.

First, other venture capitalists with whom a current syndication relationship exists (network 1 in Figure 3.8) or other venture capitalists with whom another kind of relationship exists (network 2 in Figure 3.8) might refer investment opportunities or invite the focal venture capitalists to syndicate in an investment.[668] In general, these networks have a rather strategic character and it cannot be assumed that they have a specific spatial structure. An investment opportunity might be referred to a specific venture capitalist[669] or a specific venture capitalist might be invited to syndicate for several reasons.[670] One point is that the focal venture capitalist might be closer to the venture and could therefore conduct a better due diligence and provide

---

[667] See Table 2.2 in section 2.1.4.1. Furthermore, Figure 2.3 in section 2.1.4.1 provides an illustration of different possibilities as well as supporting actions to initiate a contact between a venture capitalist and an entrepreneurial team.

[668] Table 2.2 in section 2.1.4.1 indicates that the deal flow originated from other venture capitalists is of particularly high quality. In addition, Hochberg/Ljungqvist/Lu (2007) show that venture capitalists with central positions in the syndication network, and especially the regional syndication network, experience significantly better fund performance due to better deal flow and better value added (cf. Hochberg/Ljungqvist/Lu (2007), pp. 293 and 296).

[669] The venture capitalist would only receive a pure referral if the investment would not fit into the investment portfolio of the other venture capitalist. This possibility is rather unlikely in the case of prior syndication since both are likely to have a similar investment focus.

[670] In general, various reasons to syndicate exist (cf. Nathusius (2005), pp. 75-115). However, this analysis focuses on the selection of a specific syndication partner.

better hands-on support later on. In this case, syndication would be used to overcome large distances between other members of a potential syndicate and the venture.[671] This would imply a spatial bias of this deal flow. However, following the same reasoning a close venture capitalist might also invite other distant venture capitalists for other reasons than proximity since the close venture capitalist is able to conduct the due diligence and to provide hands-on support later on by himself. These reasons might be the venture capitalist's reputation or prior investment experiences in a specific industry sector or stage.[672] In consequence, the deal flow from other venture capitalists is not likely to have a spatial bias in general, but syndication might be used to overcome the distance between distant investors and the venture.

Second, entrepreneurial teams with whom a financing relationship exists (network 3 in Figure 3.8) or entrepreneurial teams with whom another established relationship exists (network 4 in Figure 3.8) might refer potential investment opportunities. As this thesis aims to explain spatial aspects of financing relationships between venture capitalists and entrepreneurial teams, no assumptions about the spatial distribution of entrepreneurial teams with whom a current or prior financing relationship exists or existed can be made here. However, if it turns out that venture capitalists mainly invest in spatial proximity and if the current and prior investees refer other entrepreneurial teams which they know through their local network, this could lead to an ever reinforcing circle of local investments. Furthermore, as discussed in section 3.3.2, venture capitalists are very active in the entrepreneurial community and also maintain various relationships to entrepreneurial teams with whom no financing relationship exists or existed. Social exchange theory and the network approach imply that this network is likely to be regional and therefore denser in spatial proximity. Social exchange theory also suggests that relationships in spatial proximity are likely to be characterized by a higher level of trust due to a higher frequency of interaction.[673] Moreover, it is easier for the venture capitalist to assess the reputation of the referring entrepreneurial team in spatial proximity. Both trust and reputation are crucial for the success of the referral process.[674] If it is assumed that the entrepreneurial teams are also embedded in rather regional networks, this could lead to a spatial bias of the referred investment opportunities. Thus, it can be expected that entrepreneurial teams with whom no financing relationship exists or existed are likely to refer investment opportunities in spatial proximity to the venture capitalist.

---

[671] Cf. Sorenson/Stuart (2001), pp. 1553-1555; Fritsch/Schilder (2006), pp. 10-18; Fritsch/Schilder (2008), pp. 2128-2129. See also sections 4.1.3 and 4.2.1.

[672] Cf. Lockett/Wright (2001), p. 378.

[673] Cf. Zook (2004), p. 632.

[674] Cf. Achleitner (2001), p. 524.

Third, supporting actors represent an important interface between venture capitalists and entrepreneurial teams (networks 6, 7, and 8 in Figure 3.8) and frequently refer entrepreneurial teams to venture capitalists (network 6 in Figure 3.8). As mentioned earlier also these networks are likely to be of a regional type and social exchange theory and the network approach imply that these networks are denser in spatial proximity.[675] Therefore, the same arguments as for the relationships between venture capitalists and entrepreneurial teams with whom no financing relationship exists or existed apply. In consequence, it is likely that supporting actors refer investment opportunities, which are located in spatial proximity to the venture capitalists.

The initial contact between the venture capitalist and the entrepreneurial team might also be established **directly** by a cold or prior contact.[676] In case of a cold contact one of the parties has to be aware of the other one. Thus, several activities can be conducted by the venture capitalist or the entrepreneurial team in order to either actively gather information about the other party or to facilitate the other party's acquisition of information by increasing one's own public visibility. The discussion in chapter 3 revealed that transaction cost theory, social exchange theory, and the network approach imply the importance of spatial proximity between venture capitalists and entrepreneurial teams for many of these activities.

First, transaction costs increase with rising distance.[677] Many activities, like attending, presenting at, or sponsoring specific events (e.g. conventions, trade shows, special conferences, lectures at universities, business plan competitions), or certain marketing activities only have limited spatial reach. At the same time travel expenses, time effort, and information expenses rise if a venture capitalist or an entrepreneurial team conducts these activities in distance. Therefore, it is likely that actors concentrate their activities at proximate regions which leads to a higher public visibility in spatial proximity. Furthermore, both parties might first search for the other party in spatial proximity since higher future transaction costs (e.g. travel expenses for a first personal meeting) are anticipated with rising distance.

Second, social exchange theory implies that social relationships are more likely and more intense in spatial proximity which also leads to a higher density of local networks compared to regionally wide spread networks. These local networks facilitate the acquisition of information of the actors and might lead to a contact between local actors.[678] Entrepreneurial teams

---

[675] Cf. Zook (2004), p. 632. This argument has also already been supported by Florida/Kenney (1988), who stated that venture capitalists rely on personalized, informal and therefore localized information networks with a variety of actors to identify investment opportunities (cf. Florida/Kenney (1988), p. 34).

[676] See Figure 2.3 in section 2.1.4.1 for an illustration of different possibilities as well as supporting actions to initiate a contact between a venture capitalist and an entrepreneurial team.

[677] See section 3.2.1.3 for a detailed discussion.

[678] See sections 3.2.2.3 and 3.3.3 for a detailed discussion.

might know each other (network 5 in Figure 3.8) and exchange e.g. information about past experiences with certain venture capitalists. Entrepreneurial teams also interrelate with supporting actors like other types of financiers, service providers, R&D institutes, or universities and receive recommendations whom to contact (network 7 in Figure 3.8). Furthermore, venture capitalists use their (local) networks to acquire timely and reliable information they need for their active search throughout technology and sector scans (network 6 in Figure 3.8).[679] Finally, supporting actors are also interconnected with each other which might lead to indirect information transfers about both parties (network 8 in Figure 3.8). As all of these networks are likely to be of the type of a regional network, spatial proximity between actors is especially important.[680] In consequence, spatial proximity between actors may increase the likelihood of a cold contact between a venture capitalist and an entrepreneurial team.

A prior contact between the venture capitalist and the entrepreneurial team might also lead to an investment opportunity for the venture capitalist (network 4 in Figure 3.8). These networks are also likely to be of a regional type and the same argumentation as for cold contacts applies. Therefore, it is assumed that spatial proximity between actors increases the likelihood of a direct contact that is based on a prior contact.

As a result of the above discussion, transaction cost theory, social exchange theory, and the network approach imply that venture capitalists' deal flow is regionally biased.

Proposition 1a: *The **likelihood of contact** between a venture capitalist and an entrepreneurial team, and thus that a specific investment finally takes place, decreases with rising distance.*

Many of the above mentioned arguments are based on the higher density of networks in spatial proximity. This effect may be especially strong and more important for young and small ventures in an early development stage as well as less experienced entrepreneurial teams. The discussion in sections 3.2.2.3 and 3.3 revealed that networks develop over time. Hence, ventures in an early development stage are likely to have small networks with a strong regional bias. This makes it even more difficult to gather information about or to be visible to distant venture capitalists. Furthermore, very small companies are highly dependent on existing networks since they are more difficult to identify and only very little public information is available.[681]

---

679 Cf. Mason/Harrison (1995), p. 157; Christensen (2007) points out that venture capitalists' local networks lead to a better deal flow and maybe better investment conditions (cf. Christensen (2007), p. 826).

680 E.g. Patton/Kenney (2005) found that the majority of supporting actors like a firm's legal counsel, investment bankers, or directors are located within a distance of 50 miles from the venture (cf. Patton/Kenney (2005), p. 10).

681 Cf. Sorenson/Stuart (2001), p. 1548.

In addition, the discussed effects of increasing transaction costs are especially strong for young and small ventures in an early development stage as they have limited resources and may therefore focus their activities regionally. In addition, these companies depend even more on the described activities to either actively gather information about venture capitalists or to facilitate the investors' acquisition of information since their public visibility is even smaller compared to older and larger ventures in later development stages.

Proposition 1b: ***Ventures in a late development stage*** *are more likely to get in contact with a distant venture capitalist compared to ventures in an earlier development stage.*

Proposition 1c: ***Entrepreneurial teams with profound prior experience*** *are more likely to get in contact with a distant venture capitalist compared to less experienced entrepreneurial teams.*

As it has been argued for entrepreneurial teams, also venture capitalist's networks develop over time. In the course of time venture capitalists deal with an increasing number of other venture capitalists, entrepreneurial teams as well as supporting actors. This effect is even more pronounced for large venture capitalists as they are likely to realize a higher number of deals within a certain time period.[682] Therefore, it can be assumed that more experienced and large venture capitalists possess networks which are less regionally biased.[683] Moreover, the effect that transactions costs are especially important for small ventures applies in a similar manner also to small venture capitalists. These investors have fewer resources available due to their smaller fund size[684] and also depend particularly strongly on the described activities to either actively gather information about new ventures or to increase their public visibility.

Furthermore, the previous discussion discovered that venture capitalists may invite other venture capitalists for several reasons. On the one hand, venture capitalists that are located quite distantly from the focal investment might invite other investors to syndicate because they are spatially more proximate to the focal investment. On the other hand, venture capitalists that are located close to the new venture might invite other investors independently from their location. Other reasons for an invitation might be their reputation or specific investment expe-

[682] Manigart et al. (2002c) empirically found that large venture capitalists syndicate more often and conclude that this effect prevails because large venture capitalists are more established, have more central network positions and are therefore invited more often to syndicate (cf. Manigart et al. (2002c), p. 4).

[683] Sorenson/Stuart (2001) provide empirical evidence that more experienced US venture capitalists invest in more distant targets due to more developed networks. However, they do no control for the venture capitalist's size (cf. Sorenson/Stuart (2001), pp. 1573-1577).

[684] Venture capitalists usually receive a fixed percentage (about 2.0 to 2.5% p.a.) of their fund volume in order to cover their operational expenses. These payments are referred to as management fees. Cf. Gompers/Lerner (1999), p. 25; Feinendegen/Schmidt/Wahrenburg (2003), p. 1176.

rience in an industry sector, stage, or market.[685] Therefore, it can be assumed that the deal flow of highly reputable or specialized venture capitalists is less spatially biased compared to other venture capitalists. The fact that syndication might be used to overcome the distance between distant investors and the venture induces that spatial proximity is less important for the members of a syndicate as long as at least one member is located close to the potential investment.

In consequence, it is likely that more experienced, large, highly reputable, or specialized venture capitalists receive more supra-regional deal flow compared to other venture capitalists and that syndication might be used to overcome large distances. As the experience and reputation of a venture capitalist is likely to be highly correlated with the age of the investor, common propositions will be formulated regarding these aspects.[686]

Proposition 1d: ***Large venture capitalists*** *are more likely to get in contact with a distant entrepreneurial team compared to smaller venture capitalists.*

Proposition 1e: ***Experienced or more reputable venture capitalists*** *are more likely to get in contact with a distant entrepreneurial team compared to less experienced or less reputable venture capitalists.*

Proposition 1f: ***Venture capitalists who are specialized in a specific industry or stage*** *are more likely to get in contact with a distant entrepreneurial team compared to less specialized venture capitalists.*

Proposition 1g: *Potential members of a* ***VC syndicate*** *are more likely to get in contact with a distant entrepreneurial team as long as other members are close to the entrepreneurial team.*

Finally, corporate venture capitalists may also be more likely to receive distant investment opportunities for several reasons. First, spatial proximity is likely to be less relevant for corporate venture capitalists because they enjoy a relatively high public visibility due to their holding company in most cases.[687] Second, corporate venture capitalists mostly focus their venture capital activities on industries related to the industry of their holding company and are thus specialized. In consequence, corporate venture capitalists are likely to be invited more frequently to syndicate due to strategic reasons, their experience as well as knowledge and not because of spatial proximity.

---

[685] Cf. Lockett/Wright (2001), p. 378; Mäkelä/Maula (2005), pp. 240-254; Lutz/George (2009), p. 19.

[686] Cf. Gorman/Sahlman (1989), p. 233; Sahlman (1990), p. 500; Gompers (1996), p. 136.

[687] Either the corporate venture capitalist is already known or the venture capital subsidiary may be referred by some representative of the corporation.

Proposition 1h: ***Corporate venture capitalists** are more likely to get in contact with a distant entrepreneurial team compared to other venture capitalist types.*

4.1.2 Deal Screening

Venture capitalists apply several venture capitalist specific (idiosyncratic) screens as well as a generic screen in order to secure certain aspects of the venture capitalist's investment strategy and to efficiently reduce the large number of investment opportunities.[688]

As discussed in section 0 typical idiosyncratic screens include the venture capitalist's targeted investment volume, industries and technologies, the stage of financing, and the geographic location of the investment.[689] The screens in regard to the venture capitalist's targeted investment volume, industries and technologies, as well as the stage of financing do not have a direct influence on the spatial proximity between the venture capitalist and the entrepreneurial team. In contrast, the geographical screen has an impact on the spatial proximity between actors in most cases. On the one hand, venture capitalists might apply a geographical screen in order to target a specific region. On the other hand, venture capitalists might want to increase the spatial proximity to their portfolio companies on purpose.

The reason for targeting a specific region might be twofold. Some, and mainly (quasi-)public, venture capitalists target specific regions in order to induce regional economic development.[690] Others focus specific emerging regions in order to increase the chance of success of their investments.[691] In the latter case venture capitalists might also restrict their investments to some distant regions. Then the geographical screen does not necessarily contribute to the spatial proximity between actors. However, it can be expected that in most cases the venture capitalist has a subsidiary in the targeted region[692] which leads to spatial proximity between the venture capitalist and the entrepreneurial team.

Proposition 2a: *Venture capitalists who apply a geographical screen and thus mainly **(quasi-)public venture capitalists** are likely to invest in more proximate ventures compared to other venture capitalist types.*

---

688 Cf. Tyebjee/Bruno (1984a), pp. 1056-1057; Fried/Hisrich (1994), p. 32. See also section 0 for further discussion.

689 Cf. Tyebjee/Bruno (1984a), pp. 1056-1057.

690 See section 2.1.3.2.

691 An example is the German venture capitalist smac partners GmbH, who focuses his investment activity on Europe and Israel.

692 E.g. all the MBGs are located in their focal region.

Some venture capitalists also apply a geographical screen in order to increase the spatial proximity to their portfolio companies intentionally.[693] Therefore, spatial proximity between actors is not a consequence which is caused by other effects but is directly intended. This differentiates the geographical screen from most other effects discussed in this chapter. There are multiple reasons which could lead to the venture capitalist's preference to invest in proximate ventures. These reasons may be explained by the theories discussed in chapter 3 and mainly become effective in subsequent phases of the VC investment process.[694] In consequence, multiple effects of spatial proximity might be anticipated by venture capitalists and lead to the application of a geographical screen. The analysis of these effects is one of the main research goals of this thesis. Furthermore, venture capitalists have to become aware of the effects of spatial proximity in VC finance. Thus, if there were positive effects of spatial proximity that lead to the application of a geographical screen, it can be expected that these screens are more frequently applied by experienced venture capitalists.

Another aspect which has to be considered is that a trade-off between the specialization in regard to different dimensions, which coincides with the application of venture capitalist specific screens, and the number of remaining investment opportunities exists. Vater (2003) found that venture capitalists only invest in about 5.4% of the investment opportunities which already passed the initial screens.[695] The remaining investment opportunities either do not have the required quality or do not get funded for other reasons.[696] Therefore, it is important for venture capitalists that their idiosyncratic screens are not too narrow in order to secure a sufficient number of investments. A limitation in some dimensions, e.g. industry and stage, might therefore prevent the limitation on a narrow geographical area. This also applies to corporate venture capitalists because these investors focus their activities on industries related to the industry of their holding company and are thus specialized. In addition, large venture capitalists, which need a relatively high number of investment opportunities in order to be able to invest into a sufficient number of ventures, may also not be able to apply a narrow geographical screen.[697] Consequently, venture capitalists that apply narrow idiosyncratic screens other

---

693 Cf. Tyebjee/Bruno (1984a), p. 1057; Hall/Hofer (1993), p. 36; De Clercq et al. (2001), pp. 47-48.

694 An obvious example of such an effect could be that expected travel expenses (transaction costs) rise with increasing distance. This could lead to a venture capitalist's preference of proximate investments.

695 Vater (2003) found that on average 39% of the investment opportunities remain after the initial screens and that venture capitalists finally invest into an average of 2.1% of the investment opportunities (cf. Vater (2003), p. 153). Hence, 5.4% of the investment opportunities which already passed the initial screens are financed.

696 Other reasons might be the failure of contract negotiations, a personal misfit between the venture capitalist and the entrepreneurial team, or the funding by another competing venture capitalist.

697 This is also in line with Hall/Tu (2003) who find that large UK venture capitalists state more frequently that they would also invest overseas and with Gupta/Sapienza (1992) who find for the US that large and corporate

than a geographical screen and very large venture capitalists are likely to invest into more distant ventures. This trade-off is likely to be less severe for experienced and reputable venture capitalists as these investors are expected to receive more and potentially better deal flow compared to other industry players. Hence, experienced and reputable venture capitalists are better able to apply a geographical screen if they decide to do so. As has been discussed above, there are also indications that experienced venture capitalists are more prone to apply a geographical screen. In contrast, less experienced and less reputable venture capitalists might be restricted by their deal flow which forces them to widen their geographical screen in order to build up their network and reputation.

Proposition 2b: ***Venture capitalists who are specialized in a specific industry or stage*** *are more likely to accept distant ventures in the deal screening phase compared to less specialized venture capitalists.*

Proposition 2c: ***Corporate venture capitalists*** *are more likely to accept distant ventures in the deal screening phase compared to other venture capitalists.*

Proposition 2d: ***Large venture capitalists*** *are more likely to accept distant ventures in the deal screening phase compared to smaller venture capitalists.*

Proposition 2e: ***Experienced and reputable venture capitalists*** *are less likely to accept distant ventures in the deal screening phase compared to less experienced and less reputable venture capitalists.*

Besides venture capitalist specific screens, venture capitalists also apply a generic screen. The generic screen is a very quick evaluation of the investment opportunity by using the business plan in combination with any existing knowledge relevant to the proposal.[698] For this first impression, the origin of the initial contact between venture capitalist and entrepreneurial team is very important. In comparison to a cold contact, the investment opportunity has a much higher chance to pass the generic screen if there has been a prior contact between both parties and if there is a personal relationship. As it has been discussed earlier, social exchange theory states that personal relationships evolve over time by repeated interactions and that these interactions are more likely in spatial proximity.[699]

Furthermore, the investment opportunity has a much higher chance of success if the investment opportunity has been referred by a third party which has a high reputation or whose rela-

venture capitalists are more prone to invest in distance (cf. Gupta/Sapienza (1992), p. 357; Hall/Tu (2003), p. 187).

[698] Cf. Fried/Hisrich (1994), p. 32.

[699] See section 3.2.2.3.

tionship to the venture capitalist is characterized by a high level of trust.[700] Again, a trustful relationship is more likely in spatial proximity. The reputation of a referrer might also be easier to recognize in spatial proximity due to an easier access to informal information. Thus, a trustful relationship to a reputable referrer is more likely if the referrer is located proximate to the venture capitalist. Furthermore, as it has been discussed in the previous section, the network approach implies that referrers are more likely to refer entrepreneurial teams located close to them.[701] In consequence, investment proposals from entrepreneurial teams which are located close to the venture capitalist, that have been referred by a third party, or to which a prior contact existed are more likely to pass the generic screen than others.

Further factors increasing the chance of success of investment proposals from proximate entrepreneurial teams are a higher likelihood of personal similarity, regional identification, and better information. Social exchange theory, or more specifically social attraction theory, states that actors are more likely to be attracted by similar others. This has also been recognized by Franke et al. (2006) for venture capitalists and entrepreneurial teams.[702] A similarity in certain dimensions is more likely if the actors are spatially close to each other.[703] Furthermore, venture capitalists may identify themselves with their region, which also leads to a higher personal attraction to regional entrepreneurial teams. Another factor is that the network approach implies that spatial proximity between actors contributes to a better transfer of information. Since social networks tend to be denser in spatial proximity, it is easier for venture capitalists to acquire, or they might even already have, information about regional particularities or characteristics of the entrepreneurial team itself.

These factors lead to a higher chance of proximate investment opportunities to pass the generic screen. In addition, the previous discussion discovered that there are at least some venture capitalists that apply a geographical screen which is likely to target proximate regions.

Proposition 2f: *The **likelihood that an investment opportunity passes the geographical screen as well as generic screen**, and thus that a specific investment finally takes place, decreases with rising distance.*

---

[700] Fried/Hisrich (1994) e.g. state that "[t]he generic screen will be less rigorously applied when the quality of the referrer is high" (Fried/Hisrich (1994), p. 32).

[701] Cf. Zook (2004), pp. 632-633.

[702] Cf. Franke et al. (2006), p. 803.

[703] See section 3.2.2.3.

4.1.3 Deal Due Diligence

In the course of the due diligence venture capitalists gather various information in order to assess the investment inherent risks as well as the potential for value generation.[704]

Various investment criteria are important for the venture capitalist's evaluation of an investment opportunity. As it has been discussed in section 2.1.4.3, these investment criteria can be classified into five major groups: entrepreneurial team/management, market, product/service, financials, and others.[705] Regarding the group of "other" investment criteria some studies investigated the importance of the geographic location of the venture for the investment decision of the venture capitalist.[706] In general, these studies find that venture capitalists regard the geographical location of the venture only to be of moderate or low importance. Furthermore, a detailed analysis of these studies recovers that the geographic location is rather a criterion in the deal screening phase and only has very low perceived importance in the deal due diligence. Tyebjee/Bruno (1984b), for example, classify the location of the venture as deal evaluation criterion and find that it has the same moderate importance like the financial history or growth potential of the venture.[707] In contrast, Tyebjee/Bruno (1984a) refer to the just mentioned study and regard the venture location as screening criterion.[708] Hall/Hofer (1993) differentiate between screening and assessment criteria and find that the venture location is a screening criterion but not an assessment criterion in the due diligence.[709] In addition, Muzyka/Birley/Leleux (1996) show that in general venture capitalists perceive that the location of the venture is only of minor importance, but that there is a significant minority for which the location of the venture is very important.[710] Unfortunately, the authors did not further describe the type of venture capitalists belonging to the mentioned minority and did not differentiate between screening criteria and criteria relevant to the deal due diligence.

In contrast, Kaplan/Strömberg (2004) find that some venture capitalists perceive it as a strength and reason to invest if a venture capitalist is strong in a particular geographic region, which means that he is located in that region and has prior regional investment experience.[711] Another point is that most of the above mentioned studies which investigate venture capital-

---

[704] See section 2.1.4.3.

[705] See also Table 2.3 for a ranking of the importance of these different groups of investment criteria.

[706] Cf. Tyebjee/Bruno (1984a), p. 1057; Tyebjee/Bruno (1984b), p. 198; Hall/Hofer (1993), pp. 36-37; Muzyka/Birley/Leleux (1996), pp. 281-284.

[707] Cf. Tyebjee/Bruno (1984b), p. 198.

[708] Cf. Tyebjee/Bruno (1984a), p. 1057.

[709] Cf. Hall/Hofer (1993), pp. 36-37.

[710] Cf. Muzyka/Birley/Leleux (1996), pp. 281-284.

[711] Cf. Kaplan/Strömberg (2004), p. 2186.

ist's investment criteria rely on self reported data about decisions made in the past.[712] Zacharakis/Meyer (1998) and Shepherd (1999) show that venture capitalists have only limited insight into their own decision making process.[713] Therefore, several scholars question the reliability of studies using retrospective self reported data.[714] In addition, already Svenson (1979) argued that it is not enough to study final decisions, but that "[t]he perceptual, emotional, and cognitive processes which ultimately lead to the choice of a decision alternative must also be studied if we want to gain an adequate understanding of human decision-making".[715] It is also important to note that even though specific investment criteria might be dictated, the extent to which that information is considered still highly depends on the specific investment manager and is therefore subjective.[716] For these reasons one can not preclude that the location of the entrepreneurial team or more precisely the spatial proximity between the venture capitalist and the entrepreneurial team has an impact on the due diligence process.

The deal due diligence is tremendously important for the mitigation of agency problems which are caused by informational asymmetries and conflicts of interests.[717] As the due diligence is a pre-contractual phase, the type of informational asymmetry most likely to occur is hidden information. This could also lead to the problem of adverse selection.[718] Within the due diligence the principal gathers various information which reduces informational asymmetries and therefore potential agency problems.

In addition, game theory implies that the venture capitalist and the entrepreneurial team have to decide, whether the other party is going to cooperate or not. As it has been discussed in section 3.2.2.1, various factors influence the likelihood of cooperation. One of these factors is reliable information about the other party's cooperative behavior, which also has to be gathered in the due diligence.

In a similar manner stewardship theory, especially the choice model of Davis/Schoorman/Donaldson (1997b), implies that the venture capitalist as well as the entrepreneurial team have to decide before the financing contract is closed, whether they expect the other party to act according to stewardship theory or not.[719] Thus, this implication is very sim-

---

712 See e.g. Brettel (2002), p. 309; Zutshi et al. (1999), p. 12 and cf. Shepherd/Zacharakis (1999), p. 198.

713 Cf. Zacharakis/Meyer (1998), p. 58; Shepherd (1999), p. 83.

714 Cf. Sandberg/Schweiger/Hofer (1988), p. 13; Shepherd/Zacharakis (1999), p. 198.

715 Svenson (1979), p. 86 cited in Bliss (1999), p. 244.

716 Cf. Zacharakis (2007), p. 704.

717 Cf. Manigart et al. (1997), p. 29.

718 See section 3.2.1.2.

719 See section 3.2.2.2 and especially Figure 3.7.

ilar to the implications of game theory since to act as a steward also means to cooperate. In order to be able to make this decision, both parties, again, need appropriate information.

In consequence, agency theory, game theory, and stewardship theory imply that information about the other party is crucial for a sound investment/financing decision and thus the success of the VC financing relationship. To gather the required information, venture capitalists conduct a deep analysis of the business plan, check the background and qualification of the entrepreneurial team, accomplish personal meetings and talks with the entrepreneurial team, and visit the company's premises.[720] Entrepreneurial teams might analyze previous investments of the venture capitalist, consult third parties about the venture capitalist's reputation, and try to get to know the venture capitalist in personal meetings and talks. As it has been discussed earlier in chapter 3, most of these activities are easier to conduct or cheaper the higher the spatial proximity between the actors is.

A deep **analysis of the business plan** by the venture capitalist also requires gathering information about the business model, market, and product or service. This might be easier in spatial proximity to the venture, due to a better knowledge of local conditions and markets.[721] In addition, social exchange theory and the network approach imply that local networks are particularly strong. This eases the access to local supporting actors like experts or consultants relevant to the venture.

In order to conduct a **background check on the entrepreneurial team** and to verify its track record, venture capitalists also heavily rely on their network, which is likely to be stronger in spatial proximity.[722] Therefore, it is easier to acquire information about the entrepreneurial team from supporting actors if the venture capitalist is located close to the team. Then it is more likely that the regional networks of both parties overlap and that the relevant information is transmitted.[723] The entrepreneurial team might also want to consult other entrepreneurs or supporting actors about the **reputation and past behavior of the venture capitalist**. As with the background check of the entrepreneurial team by the venture capitalist this is much easier if the venture capitalist and the team are located close to each other.

Personal meetings and talks between the venture capitalist and the entrepreneurial team as well as **visits of the company's premises** are also facilitated by spatial proximity due to re-

---

720 Cf. Heyning (1999), pp. 157-160.

721 Cf. Christensen (2007), p. 822; Mäkela/Maula (2008), pp. 249-251.

722 Cf. Banatao/Fong (2000), p. 302.

723 Tyebjee/Bruno (1984a) find that references of the entrepreneurial team are an important criterion indicating its quality (cf. Tyebjee/Bruno (1984a), p. 1058). Also Zook (2004), Harrison/Cooper/Mason (2004) and Mason (2007) state that the evaluation of the team is facilitated by local networks (cf. Harrison/Cooper/Mason (2004), p. 1064; Zook (2004), pp. 631-634; Mason (2007), p. 98).

duced transaction costs like travel expenses or travel time.[724] These transaction costs are relatively more important for investors if the investment volume is small as their amount does not increase proportionally to the investment volume.[725] This could lead to less personal meetings as well as visits and thus a lower decision quality or to the termination of the due diligence. Furthermore, social exchange theory implies that the likelihood of the development and maintenance of social relationships increases sharply if actors are located close to each other, which facilitates the development of trust and confidence as well as the transfer of information between the venture capitalist and the entrepreneurial team.[726] The increased trust and confidence also reduces skepticism towards the other party and thus increases the likelihood of investment/financing. Game theory also states that personal similarity of actors increases the likelihood of cooperative behavior.[727] This effect has its roots in social exchange theory or more precisely interpersonal attraction theory, which states that personal similarity promotes interpersonal attraction and therefore social relationships. This effect could also be relevant within the due diligence because the increased cooperation and interpersonal attraction might lead to the provision of sensitive or better information.[728]

In consequence, spatial proximity between actors facilitates the transfer of information and thus reduces informational asymmetries and agency costs, increases the likelihood of cooperation, and facilitates the decision whether the other party is going to act like a steward. Furthermore, spatial proximity reduces transaction costs and increases the likelihood of a social relationship. These facts increase the perceived quality of the investment/financing decision of the actors as well as the likelihood of a VC financing relationship, the higher the spatial proximity between the venture capitalist and the entrepreneurial team is.[729]

Proposition 3a: *The **likelihood to pass the due diligence**, and thus that an investment finally takes place, decreases with rising distance.*

Proposition 3b: *Distant investment/financing opportunities are more likely to pass the due diligence phase if the **investment volume is large** compared to smaller investment volumes.*

---

[724] See section 3.2.1.3.

[725] Cf. Elango et al. (1995), p. 170.

[726] See section 3.2.2.3.

[727] See section 3.2.2.1.

[728] See section 3.2.2.3.

[729] These results are in line with Chen et al. (2009), who find that US venture capitalists which are located in VC centers outperform with their distant investments. The authors conclude that venture capitalists apply higher hurdle rates for distant investments in order to compensate for higher transaction costs (cf. Chen et al. (2009), pp. 5-6).

The effects discussed above which emerge due to local networks might be weaker for more experienced venture capitalists and entrepreneurial teams since these actors are likely to have larger and more widespread networks. In addition, venture capitalists might require less information about experienced entrepreneurial teams as they are associated with less agency, defection, and business risks due to a higher reputation and higher managerial skills.[730]

Proposition 3c: ***Entrepreneurial teams with profound prior experience*** *are more likely to accept or to be accepted by distant venture capitalists in the deal due diligence phase compared to less experienced entrepreneurial teams.*

Proposition 3d: ***Experienced venture capitalists*** *are more likely to accept or to be accepted by distant ventures in the deal due diligence phase compared to less experienced venture capitalists.*

Furthermore, venture capitalists ultimately assess the risk-return ratio of an investment opportunity.[731] Therefore, the required return depends on the perceived risks whose evaluation is a highly complex and difficult task and requires additional information.

Relevant potential risks regarding the development stage of the venture and its products include (i) the liability of newness and smallness, (ii) the dependency on founders, (iii) the uncertainty of supply and demand, and (iv) the competitive uncertainty.[732] The liability of newness emerges as for most ventures only little, if any, operating history or information about the track record of the entrepreneurial team are available. New ventures are also usually very small and thus have a limited capital base and are very vulnerable by external shocks (liability of smallness). In addition, the venture highly depends on its founders who could break-up because of internal conflicts, illness of a key entrepreneur, or other reasons. Next to these points, it is uncertain if the venture will be able to finally develop its concepts to marketable products (uncertainty of supply) and whether customers are going to demand these products (uncertainty of demand). Finally, competitors might already develop or start to develop similar products (competitive uncertainty).[733] Since only little information about most entrepreneurial teams and their ventures is available and venture capitalists face serious time constraints, the assessment of these risks is very subjective. In consequence, trust and smooth information exchange, and therefore spatial proximity, between actors is particularly impor-

---

[730] Cf. Sapienza/Gupta (1994), p. 1628.

[731] Cf. Tyebjee/Bruno (1984a), pp. 1060-1061; Kaplan/Strömberg (2004), pp. 2184-2190.

[732] Cf. Fingerle (2005), pp. 44-48.

[733] Cf. Sorenson/Stuart (2001), p. 1548. For a detailed discussion of these risks see also Fingerle (2005), pp. 44-48.

tant for young and small ventures in an early development stage,[734] or ventures whose products are in an early development stage.[735]

Proposition 3e: ***Ventures in a late development stage*** *are more likely to pass the due diligence with a distant venture capitalist compared to ventures in an earlier development stage.*

Proposition 3f: ***Ventures whose products are in a late stage of development*** *are more likely to pass the due diligence with a distant venture capitalist compared to ventures whose products are in an earlier stage of development.*

Industry or business model specific characteristics of the new venture are likely to be further indicators for the level of risk and required information.[736] Intangible assets are more difficult to evaluate compared to tangible assets. Also, in the case of default the liquidation value of assets is positively related to the tangibility of assets since tangible assets are easier to sell and yield a price closer to their book value.[737] Hence, a greater fraction of intangible assets may be related to higher risks, potential agency costs and thus required information. A wrong valuation of intangible assets may lead to reduced returns in case of success or the venture capitalist's potential loss increases in case of the venture's default or inefficient continuation. Furthermore, a high R&D intensity may lead to a relatively high amount of firm specific assets which are more difficult to sell in case of the venture's default compared to less specialized assets.[738] Finally, entrepreneurs may be more prone to pursue personally beneficial investment strategies at the expense of their investors if the value of their venture largely depends on future growth options.[739] Thus, a high R&D intensity as well as a valuation primarily based on future growth options may indicate higher risks and, thus a need for additional information.[740] Because informational asymmetries are easier to mitigate in spatial proximity, it can be assumed that proximity is particularly important for ventures characterized by high asset intangibility, high R&D intensity, or substantial future growth options.

---

734 See also Gupta/Sapienza (1992), pp. 350-351.

735 Cf. Florida/Smith (1993), p. 434; Sweeting (1991), p. 604; Manigart et al. (1997), p. 30; . Sapienza/De Clercq (2000), pp. 58-60; Powell et al. (2002), pp. 303-304.

736 Cf. Gompers (1995), p. 1466; Cumming/Johan (2006), p. 374.

737 Cf. Williamson (1988), p. 586.

738 Cf. Gompers (1995), p. 1466; Shleifer/Vishny (1992), pp. 1364-1365.

739 Cf. Myers (1977), 170-171.

740 Cf. Gompers (1995), p. 1466.

Proposition 3g: ***Ventures characterized by high asset intangibility, high R&D intensity, or substantial future growth options*** *are less likely to be accepted by distant venture capitalists in the deal due diligence phase compared to other ventures.*

Another potentially important factor may be the region in which the new venture is located. Manigart et al. (1997) find for France that the perceived risk highly depends on the geographical region in which the venture is located. Unfortunately, the study sheds no light on the question whether the effect of the geographical location is caused by spatial proximity to or by characteristics of certain regions in France.[741] However, the perceived risk, the evaluation of future growth options, and therefore the importance of spatial proximity may differ among certain regions within a country or types of location.[742]

Since Germany was divided into the Federal Republic of Germany (FRG) and the German Democratic Republic (GDR) from 1949 to 1990, both states developed very differently. Thus, there were and there are still large economic differences between both parts.[743] This may cause venture capitalists to evaluate risks and potential returns differently in both areas. On the one hand, venture capitalists might evaluate risks to be higher in East Germany due to the lack of economic development that is still prevalent. On the other hand, investments in East Germany might offer exceptional returns due to governmental support and an economy which potentially catches up.

Therefore, it is unclear whether the importance of distance between a venture capitalist and a venture on the likelihood to pass the due diligence phase is higher or lower for ***East German ventures****. Thus, no proposition can be advanced. However, the geographic region could turn out to be an important variable for the impact of spatial proximity in the deal due diligence phase.*

Furthermore, venture capitalists may differ in their evaluation of risks and future growth options of investment opportunities located in urban and rural areas. Possible reasons are that new ventures located in urban areas (i) may profit from better infrastructures or (ii) that it may be easier to get in contact and to cooperate with other companies or (iii) to find additional human and other resources due to local networks within an urban area. In consequence, urban new ventures might have better perceived risk-return ratios compared to rural new ventures which make venture capitalists more confident and thus to require less information. In addi-

[741] Cf. Manigart et al. (1997), p. 38.

[742] See also Martin et al. (2005), p. 1221.

[743] Cf. Achleitner et al. (2009), pp. 439-440.

tion, venture capitalists may find it more convenient to travel to urban locations. Following these arguments, spatial proximity may be less relevant for urban new ventures.

Proposition 3h: ***Ventures located in urban areas*** *are more likely to be accepted by distant venture capitalists in the deal due diligence phase compared to ventures located in rural areas.*

In regard to different venture capitalist types corporate venture capitalists might behave differently compared to other venture capitalists. Next to the intention of profit generation corporate venture capitalists also follow strategic interests. These strategic interests may lead to additional synergies of an investment and the closing of a deal even though the perceived risk is relatively high due to a large distance to the venture.

Proposition 3i: **Corporate venture capitalists** are more likely to accept distant ventures in the deal due diligence phase compared to other venture capitalists.

If several venture capitalists intend to syndicate, in most cases the (potential) lead-investor conducts or is responsible for most tasks within the deal due diligence.[744] For the entrepreneurial team the lead-investor is the most important venture capitalist within a (potential) syndicate because he is the prime contact and is also expected to mainly attend the investment later on. In consequence, the effects mentioned above are expected to be stronger for lead-investors than for co-investors. However, independently from the potential role within a syndicate it can be expected that the members of a (potential) syndicate sensibly divide the workload of the due diligence and exchange information with each other. Hence, it is likely that the impact of spatial proximity between a venture capitalist and the venture is not that severe as long as at least one member of the (potential) syndicate is located close to the venture.[745]

Proposition 3j: *The effects of distance between a venture capitalist and a venture on the likelihood to pass the due diligence phase (P3a-k, excl. P3j) are stronger for* ***lead-investors*** *than for co-investors.*

Proposition 3k: *Distant investment/financing opportunities are more likely to pass the due diligence phase if at least one member of the potential* ***syndicate*** *is located close to the venture.*

[744] Cf. Weitnauer (2001), pp. 251-252; Wright/Lockett (2002), p. 74.

[745] Cf. Fritsch/Schilder (2006), pp. 10-11. This is also in line with Tykvová/Schertler (2008) who find that the syndication of foreign private equity investors with local and experienced veteran partners facilitates distant transactions (cf. Tykvová/Schertler (2008), p. 23).

4.1.4 Deal Structuring

Within the deal structuring phase the structure of a deal is finalized, several legal documents are negotiated and finally signed by both parties.[746] In general, property rights theory (section 3.2.1.1) and more specifically transaction cost theory (section 3.2.1.3) state that the initiation of contracts imposes costs, which tend to be higher if the contracting partners are located spatially distant from each other. Furthermore, contracts have to be more complete if the contracting partners are far away from each other because trustful social relationships are less likely to prevail and the impact of reputation might be weaker.[747] This leads to additional negotiations and also increases contracting costs. In addition, negotiations are not only less costly in spatial proximity but also might be easier since a social relationship and therefore also trust among the parties is more likely.[748] Finally, the network approach suggests that local networks might lead to a better and sometimes exclusive deal flow which could lead to less competition among venture capitalists and lower prices.[749] These facts might lead to a lower number of failing negotiations and thus to a higher likelihood of a VC investment the closer both parties are.

Proposition 4a: *The* ***likelihood to pass the deal structuring phase****, and thus that an investment finally takes place, decreases with rising distance.*

The costs to negotiate the VC investment contract are mostly insensitive to the investment volume and are therefore relatively more important for small investment volumes. Therefore, the variation of costs, which is induced by different distances, has a larger impact on small VC investments.

Proposition 4b: *Distant investment/financing opportunities are more likely to pass the deal structuring phase if the* ***investment volume*** *is large compared to smaller investment volumes.*

An integral part of the financial aspects of a VC investment contract is the valuation of the venture. In order to be able to determine an appropriate value of the venture, the venture capitalist needs various information which is mainly collected in the due diligence phase. Therefore, most of the aspects which were discussed in section 4.1.3 also have an impact on the ability of the venture capitalist to value the venture but will not be repeated here for the sake of brevity. Nonetheless, in general it can be stated that the valuation of a venture is likely to

---

[746] See section 2.1.4.4.

[747] See sections c), 3.2.2.3 and 3.3.3.

[748] See section 3.2.2.3.

[749] Cf. Christensen (2007), p. 826.

be easier and less costly to conduct if the venture is located in spatial proximity to the venture capitalist.

Besides the effects of spatial proximity on the likelihood to pass the deal structuring phase, further effects on the deal structure itself emerge. These effects include the harshness of VC contracts and thus how investor-friendly the contract is,[750] the extent of staging,[751] the usage of certain financial instruments,[752] and the remaining ownership share of the entrepreneurial team.[753] As these aspects are beyond the scope of this thesis, they are not discussed for the sake of brevity.

4.2 Post-Contractual Activities

After venture capitalists invested into a venture they engage in the investment development which comprises monitoring and in most cases support activities. As venture capitalists hold their portfolio companies only for a limited period of time, they start to prepare their exit about five to seven years after their initial investment and ultimately sell their shares.[754]

4.2.1 Investment Development

4.2.1.1 Monitoring

By monitoring their portfolio companies venture capitalists primarily intend to protect the value of their investments and thus to reduce the investment risk.[755] Similarly, the entrepreneurial team might monitor the activities of its venture capitalists to secure an adequate level of support. More specifically, the financing relationship between a venture capitalist and the entrepreneurial team is based on an investment contract that was closed in the deal structuring phase and which defines several property rights in regard to the new venture. These property rights have to be monitored and enforced in post-contractual phases.

Non-compliance with defined property rights may be caused by agency problems due to informational asymmetries and conflicts of interests. In post-contractual phases the types of

[750] Cf. Bengtsson/Ravid (2009), pp. 1-8.

[751] Cf. Tian (2009), pp. 1-5.

[752] One could argue that the extent to which equity or mezzanine capital is used depends on the risk structure of an investment and thus also on the spatial proximity between venture capitalists and investees.

[753] Cf. De Clercq et al. (2001), p. 55.

[754] Cf. Tyebjee/Bruno (1984a), p. 1054; Gorman/Sahlman (1989), p. 233; Gompers (1996), p. 140.

[755] See section 2.1.4.5.

informational asymmetries that are most likely to occur are hidden actions and hidden intentions. Monitoring in a narrow sense is one possibility to gather various information about the agent. This reduces informational asymmetries and therefore potential agency problems.[756]

In addition, also game theory implies that the venture capitalist and the entrepreneurial team have to monitor, whether the other party cooperates and is likely to cooperate in the future or not. Therefore, reliable information about the other party's behavior is crucial.[757]

In consequence, property rights theory, agency theory, and game theory imply that information and thus monitoring of the other party is crucial for a successful VC financing relationship. Hence, monitoring activities are conducted by venture capitalists applying an active as well as passive portfolio management strategy and comprise formal as well as informal monitoring. Furthermore, venture capitalists frequently serve as non-executives on the board of directors (one-tier model) or on the supervisory board (two-tier model).[758] Since the monitoring of the venture capitalist by the entrepreneurial team is not that common, it will not be further emphasized.

Within formal monitoring, budgets and business plans are periodically revised with the help of monthly, quarterly, and/or yearly reports. As these activities can also be conducted easily from a distance, their execution is not likely to be sensitive to spatial proximity between actors. Contrary, informal monitoring requires next to telephone calls also personal meetings and the participation in management meetings.[759] As these activities cause substantial transaction costs like travel expenses and time they are more difficult and expensive in distance.[760] Also, it is easier and more likely to receive relevant informal information about the behavior of the entrepreneurial team from third parties like other venture capitalists, entrepreneurial teams, or supporting actors in spatial proximity. This effect might be caused by local networks as implied by social exchange theory and the network approach.

Another effective method to monitor new ventures is to serve as non-executive on the board of directors (one-tier model) or on the supervisory board (two-tier model). This monitoring possibility is frequently used by venture capitalists.[761] However, the role as board member is associated with frequent visits, high involvement, and thus high transaction costs. In consequence, it is likely to be easier and cheaper to monitor new ventures as a board member in spatial proximity. Lerner (1995) finds empirical evidence for this assumption. He shows in his

---

[756] See section 3.2.1.2 and cf. Wright/Robbie (1998), p. 545.

[757] See section 3.2.2.1.

[758] See section 2.1.4.5.

[759] Cf. Sweeting/Wong (1997), pp. 137-138; Nagtegaal (1999), pp. 193-195.

[760] See section 3.2.1.3.

[761] Cf. Barry et al. (1990), pp. 467-469; Lerner (1995), p. 308; Fingerle (2005), p. 270.

study that spatial proximity is an important determinant for board membership. Furthermore, he finds that it is twice as likely for a venture capitalist to be a member of the board if the distance between the venture capitalist and the portfolio company is 5 miles compared to 500 miles.[762]

A further important point is that monitoring activities are not only easier and less costly to conduct but might also be less necessary in spatial proximity. As it has been discussed in section 3.2.2.3, social exchange theory suggests that trustful personal relationships are more likely to develop in spatial proximity. In case of such a relationship it is likely that investors require less monitoring and that the critical information is more effectively transmitted. In a similar vein, game theory implies that cooperative behavior is more likely if personal relationships exist among venture capitalists and entrepreneurial teams, which is more likely in spatial proximity. This line of reasoning is supported by different studies. Sweeting/Wong (1997) argue that trust between an investor and the investee reduces the required level of control.[763] In addition, Fried/Hisrich (1995) find that venture capitalists prefer personal relationships to exert power in the financing relationship over the power of their money and formal power.[764]

As a result, it can be assumed that many monitoring activities are more difficult, less effective and thus more costly in distance. Furthermore, it can be assumed that actors require more monitoring activities in distance. In anticipation of these effects actors might prefer proximate relationships compared to distant ones.[765]

Proposition 5a: *The required level of informal monitoring, the acceptance of board seats, and thus the reduction of investment risk is more costly in distance which leads to a* ***preference of actors for proximate relationships****.*

As discussed above, agency and game theory imply the need for adequate monitoring activities. Thus, monitoring of the entrepreneurial team's actions as well as of the development of the venture is especially important for ventures with high agency risks or high risks of entrepreneurial team's defection. In addition, Barney et al. (1989) find that the level of monitoring is correlated with the amount of business risks because venture capitalists desire to react appropriately to unexpected developments of the portfolio company.[766] Also, the positive effects of monitoring are especially high for ventures having high risks. In section 4.1.3 it has been discussed which kinds of ventures are likely to have high agency, defection, or business risks.

---

[762] Cf. Lerner (1995), p. 302.

[763] Cf. Sweeting/Wong (1997), p. 133.

[764] Cf. Fried/Hisrich (1995), pp. 105-108.

[765] Also Mason/Harrison (1995) recognized the importance of spatial proximity for effective monitoring activites (cf. Mason/Harrison (1995), p. 157).

[766] Cf. Barney et al. (1989), pp. 66-67.

In consequence, it is expected that monitoring activities, and thus spatial proximity, are especially relevant for young and small ventures in an early development stage, ventures whose products are in an early development stage, as well as ventures characterized by high asset intangibility, high R&D intensity, or substantial future growth options.

Proposition 5b: *Monitoring activities, and thus spatial proximity between actors, are more essential for* ***ventures in an early development stage*** *compared to ventures in a later development stage.*

Proposition 5c: *Monitoring activities, and thus spatial proximity between actors, are more essential for* ***ventures whose products are in an early stage of development*** *compared to ventures whose products are in a later stage of development.*

Proposition 5d: *Monitoring activities, and thus spatial proximity between actors, are more essential for* ***ventures characterized by high asset intangibility, high R&D intensity, or substantial future growth options*** *compared to other ventures.*

In addition to the types of ventures mentioned above, Sapienza/Gupta (1994) also find that the degree of monitoring diminishes for CEOs with high entrepreneurial experience. This might be due to lower risks implied by higher managerial skills and higher reputation of experienced entrepreneurs.[767]

Proposition 5e: *Monitoring activities, and thus spatial proximity between actors, are more essential for* ***less experienced entrepreneurial teams*** *compared to entrepreneurial teams with profound prior experience.*

Regarding the role of a venture capitalist within a syndicate a similar argumentation like in the due diligence phase applies. Within a syndicated VC investment lead-investors conduct or are responsible for most monitoring tasks.[768] For the entrepreneurial team the lead-investor is the most important venture capitalist within the syndicate because he conducts most monitoring and support activities. In consequence, the effects mentioned above are expected to be stronger for lead-investors than for co-investors. However, independently from the role within a syndicate it can be expected that the members of a syndicate sensibly divide the workload of monitoring activities and exchange information with each other. Hence, it is likely that the

[767] Cf. Sapienza/Gupta (1994), p. 1628.

[768] Cf. Wright/Lockett (2002), p. 74.

impact of spatial proximity between a venture capitalist and the venture is not that severe as long as at least one member of the syndicate is located close to the venture.[769]

Proposition 5f: *The effects of distance between a venture capitalist and a venture on the preference for proximate investments (P5a-h, excl. P5f) are stronger for* ***lead-investors*** *than for co-investors.*

Proposition 5g: *Spatial proximity between a venture capitalist and the portfolio company is less essential for the monitoring of the venture if at least one member of the* ***syndicate*** *is located close to the venture.*

The degree of monitoring activities is likely to increase with rising investment volumes for two reasons. First, the costs of monitoring relative to the investment volume, and thus expected absolute capital gains, diminishes with increasing investment volume. This might reduce cost constraints to monitor portfolio companies. Second, the higher the investment volume per deal the higher is the impact of that individual investment on the portfolio's performance and the smaller is the possibility to diversify the portfolio risk of a VC fund. This could lead to the desire of the venture capitalist to monitor large investments more frequently.[770] However, the volume of a VC investment might influence the desire for spatial proximity in order to conduct monitoring activities in two opposing directions. On the one hand, transaction costs associated with monitoring activities are relatively less important the higher the investment volume is. Consequently, venture capitalists might be less reluctant to overcome large geographical distances for their monitoring activities the higher the investment volume.[771] On the other hand, the increasing impact on the portfolio's return and the decreasing possibility to diversify the portfolio's risk could lead to the desire of the venture capitalist for more frequent monitoring and thus spatial proximity. Hence, the overall relationship between the preference for proximate investments due to required monitoring activities and the investment volume is not clear. However, the effect of a decreasing importance of transaction costs diminishes with an increasing investment volume, while the performance impact and the costs of not being able to appropriately diversify the portfolio increase. Therefore, the effect of the investment volume on the degree of monitoring might follow an inverted u-shaped pattern.

Proposition 5h: *Venture capitalists' preference for proximate investments decreases with rising* ***investment volumes*** *up to a certain threshold and increases thereafter.*

---

[769] Cf. Fritsch/Schilder (2006), pp. 10-11.

[770] Cf. Gifford (1997), p. 474; Vater (2003), p. 195. For the relative importance of a particular investment also the total fund size has to be considered. However, the direction of the effect remains the same.

[771] Cf. Fritsch/Schilder (2006), p. 9.

4.2.1.2 Support

By supporting their portfolio companies venture capitalists intend to increase the value of their investments and thus to maximize the investment return. However, there are great differences in the extent of active support which is only conducted by venture capitalists applying an active portfolio management strategy.[772] A description of different venture capitalist types and their portfolio management strategies was provided in section 2.1.3.

Due to their background, experience, knowledge, and networks venture capitalists are able to add significant value to their portfolio companies and thus increase their investment performance.[773] The activities to support their portfolio companies are manifold but can be categorized in the following nine classes:[774]

- providing financial support,
- serving as a sounding board to the management,
- supporting in strategy development,
- providing feedback to the management,
- helping the management in operational aspects,
- providing contacts to third parties,
- recruiting management,
- providing ethical support to the management, and
- supporting in organizational planning.

In order to be able to adequately support the new venture, venture capitalists need various pieces of information. In a first step, venture capitalists have to recognize the venture's need for support.[775] The recognition of the venture's need is hampered by several aspects. First, new ventures are characterized by high levels of uncertainty and dynamic environments. This leads to decisions under uncertainty, an unsecure management agenda, and consequently to difficulties in assessing the venture's need for support. Second, multiple informational asymmetries exist between the entrepreneurial team and the venture capitalist.[776] In consequence,

---

[772] See section 2.1.4.5.

[773] For a long time it was not clear whether venture capitalists' involvement leads to higher new venture performance or whether venture capitalists just select better new ventures. However, Bottazzi/Da Rin/Hellmann (2008) were able to account for this endogeneity problem. (cf. Sapienza (1992), pp. 20-21; Hellmann/Puri (2002), pp. 194-195; Bottazzi/Da Rin/Hellmann (2008), pp. 503-507).

[774] See section 2.1.4.5.

[775] Cf. Welpe/Dowling (2005), pp. 288-292.

[776] See section 3.2.1.2.

venture capitalists may lack important information like the true managerial skills of the entrepreneurial team, the quality of the business concept, or the potential of the venture's products. These informational asymmetries also lead to difficulties in assessing the venture's need for support. Finally, the venture capitalist might not realize the required level of support if he does not allocate sufficient time to a specific portfolio company.

The realization of the venture's need for support improves in the course of investment because informational asymmetries are reduced by observing the venture and its environment and since personal relationships and trust develop among the venture capitalist and the investee. These processes and thus the recognition of the required support are further facilitated by spatial proximity. Due to reduced transaction costs, spatial proximity permits more frequent face-to-face interaction of the venture capitalist and the entrepreneurial team and thus improves the transfer of information and tacit knowledge. In addition, social exchange theory suggests that personal relationships and trust evolves more easily in spatial proximity which reduces the venture's barrier to reveal critical information.[777]

In a second step, venture capitalists have to provide the support which is needed by the new venture. While some activities, like the provision of financial support, are mostly insensitive to spatial proximity others require frequent interaction or local networks and are thus easier to conduct in proximity.

In order to be able to act as a sounding board, to support in strategy development, operational aspects, or organizational planning as well as to provide feedback or ethical support, it is crucial for the venture capitalist to frequently interact with the entrepreneurial team and thus to secure a sufficient flow of information and tacit knowledge in both directions. This fact is acknowledged by many researchers. Hence, Knockaert et al. (2006) find that European venture capitalists rate frequent meetings with the entrepreneurial team as most important among value adding activities.[778] Also, Sapienza/De Clercq (2000) show that the value added by venture capitalists is positively related to the frequency of interaction between the investor and the CEO as well as the openness of communication.[779] Further, De Clercq/Sapienza (2005) state that it is essential for venture capitalists to interact intensively with their portfolio companies in order to gain critical expertise[780] and Jääskeläinen/Maula/Seppä (2006) find that venture capitalists add value primarily by a high involvement in their investee companies.[781] For the required interaction and involvement, telephone calls and emails are not sufficient and

---

[777] See sections 3.2.1.3 and 3.2.2.3.

[778] Cf. Knockaert et al. (2006), pp. 16-17.

[779] Cf. Sapienza/De Clercq (2000), p. 64.

[780] Cf. De Clercq/Sapienza (2005), p. 518.

[781] Cf. Jääskeläinen/Maula/Seppä (2006), p. 186.

frequent face-to-face contacts are needed.[782] As mentioned earlier, transaction costs like travel expenses and time are sensitive to the distance between the venture capitalist and the entrepreneurial team. In this context, it is also worth to note that venture capitalists have to allocate their time efficiently, as it is a scarce and expensive resource for them.[783] The more time they spend travelling, the less time they have to effectively support their portfolio companies. Thus, long travel times might deter venture capitalists to provide sufficient support.[784] This fact is also supported by empirical findings from Sapienza/Manigart/Vermeir (1996). They find that distance is significantly negatively correlated with the number of face-to-face interactions.[785] As has been mentioned earlier, more frequent personal interaction in spatial proximity leads to an improved transfer of information and tacit knowledge as well as the development of personal relationships and trust.[786] Another argument is that local networks, and thus proximity, might be beneficial to acquire information from third parties which is relevant for the above mentioned support activities. Hence, Bygrave (1988) states that venture capitalists should have as many links to other actors as possible in order to constantly obtain fresh information.[787] In addition, the provision of effective support requires manifold cooperation of the entrepreneurial team. As it has been discussed in section 3.2.2.1, game theory implies cooperation to be more likely in spatial proximity.

Venture capitalists also support their portfolio companies by providing contacts to third parties and recruiting management. To be able to fulfill these tasks, investors need a network which is relevant for the venture. Since networks tend to be local, spatial proximity to the venture is advantageous in most cases.[788]

As a result, spatial proximity between the venture capitalist and the entrepreneurial team facilitates the venture capitalist's recognition of the venture's need for support as well as the provision of the support itself. In anticipation of these effects, venture capitalists as well as entrepreneurial teams might prefer proximate relationships compared to distant ones.[789]

---

[782] Cf. Fritsch/Schilder (2008), p. 2125.

[783] Cf. Gorman/Sahlman (1989), p. 441.

[784] Cf. Manigart/Baeyens/van Hyfte (2002), p. 106; Jääskeläinen/Maula/Seppä (2006), p. 188.

[785] Cf. Sapienza/Manigart/Vermeir (1996), p. 457.

[786] See sections 3.2.1.3 and 3.2.2.3.

[787] Cf. Bygrave (1988), p. 138.

[788] Cf. Dixit/Jayaraman (2001), p. 43. An exception would be if a new venture intends to enter new and distant markets and thus wants to benefit from the network of venture capitalists who are located in or close to the new and distant markets (Cf. Mäkela/Maula (2008), pp. 249-252).

[789] This result is in line with previous empirical findings. Among others, Sapienza/Gupta (1994) found that the involvement of US venture capitalists decreased significantly with rising distance and Nagtegaal (1999) elaborates on a dutch study which found that in 40% of the cases the entrepreneurial team chose the venture ca-

Proposition 6a: *The recognition and provision of needed support activities is facilitated by spatial proximity which leads to a* ***preference of actors for proximate relationships****.*

As it has been discussed above, uncertainty, dynamic environments, and informational asymmetries are the main reasons that lead to difficulties in assessing the venture's need for support. Thus, spatial proximity might be especially relevant to new ventures which are characterized by high levels of these factors. In addition, support activities itself are facilitated by spatial proximity. In consequence, new ventures which need particularly high levels of support might benefit the most from short distances to their venture capitalists.

Section 4.1.3 discussed which kinds of ventures are characterized by high levels of uncertainty and relevant informational asymmetries. As a result, it might be especially difficult to recognize the need for support for young and small ventures in an early development stage and ventures whose products are in an early development stage. In addition, informational asymmetries and uncertainty might be more severe for entrepreneurial teams that gathered no profound experience prior to starting the new venture. These arguments were also acknowledged by Welpe/Dowling (2005) who state that the recognition of needed support is especially difficult for these types of ventures.[790]

Moreover, young and small ventures in an early development stage as well as entrepreneurial teams with no profound prior experience are likely to lack important resources like managerial, financial, organizational, reputational, and/or social resources as these resources are built-up over time. In consequence, the resource based theory implies that this lack of resources also leads to an increased level of venture capitalists' support activities.[791] This has also been shown by many empirical studies.[792] For German VC and PE investors Achleitner/Ehrhart/Zimmermann (2006) find that 73.3% of early stage investors and only 17.4% of later stage investors apply an active portfolio management strategy.[793] Bottazzi/Da Rin/Hellmann (2008) uncover for European venture capitalists that, compared to seed investments, start-up and later stage investments receive a significantly lower level of investor activism.[794] Similarly, Sa-

pitalist from whom the most value added could be expected (cf. Sapienza/Gupta (1994), p. 1628; Nagtegaal (1999), p. 189).

790 Cf. Welpe/Dowling (2005), pp. 289-290.

791 Cf. Sapienza (1992), p. 13; Lee/Lee/Pennings (2001), p. 634; Fingerle (2005), pp. 145-147 and 156.

792 Cf. Gorman/Sahlman (1989), p. 245; Sapienza/Timmons (1989), pp. 75-76; Sapienza/Amason/Manigart (1994), pp. 6 and 9; Sapienza/Gupta (1994), p. 1628; Elango et al. (1995), pp. 164-165; Achleitner/Ehrhart/Zimmermann (2006), p. 67; Bottazzi/Da Rin/Hellmann (2008), pp. 498-499.

793 Cf. Achleitner/Ehrhart/Zimmermann (2006), p. 67.

794 Cf. Bottazzi/Da Rin/Hellmann (2008), p. 499.

pienza/Amason/Manigart (1994) reveal that European venture capitalists spend on average about 47% more time on early stage ventures compared to late stage ventures.[795]

In regard to prior start-up experience, Sapienza/Amason/Manigart (1994) find that entrepreneurial teams with no start-up experience received 37% more attention in the Netherlands and France. Surprisingly, British venture capitalists spent 37% less time on inexperienced teams compared to experienced teams.[796] For the US, empirical evidence suggests that entrepreneurial teams with prior start-up experience tend to receive less attention from their venture capitalists.[797] Thus, the effect of the entrepreneurs' prior experience on the level of support seems to be country specific and empirical evidence for Germany is still missing.[798] However, as the resource based theory implies that entrepreneurial teams with no profound prior experience require a higher level of venture capitalists' support and since this fact is supported by the majority of studies it can be expected that also inexperienced German entrepreneurial teams receive a higher level of support compared to experienced teams.

To the best of the author's knowledge, no theoretical or empirical evidence exists for the impact of the product development stage on the level of venture capitalists' support so far.[799] However, as it has been discussed above, there are indications that it is more difficult for venture capitalists to recognize the need for support if the products of a new venture are in an early stage of development. Spatial proximity between the venture capitalist and the new venture might alleviate this problem.

Thus, it is expected that spatial proximity facilitates the recognition and provision of venture capitalists' support particularly strong for young and small ventures in an early development stage, ventures whose products are in an early development stage, as well as entrepreneurial teams without profound experience prior to starting the new venture.

Proposition 6b: *The recognition and provision of needed support activities, and thus spatial proximity between actors, are more essential for* ***ventures in an early development stage*** *compared to ventures in a later development stage.*

---

[795] Cf. Sapienza/Amason/Manigart (1994), p. 9.

[796] Cf. Sapienza/Amason/Manigart (1994), p. 9.

[797] Cf. Sapienza/Timmons (1989), pp. 75-76; Sapienza/Amason/Manigart (1994), p. 6; Sapienza/Gupta (1994), p. 1628.

[798] Haagen (2008) also analyses the impact of entrepreneurial team's experience on the level of venture capitalists' involvement for German and British biotechnology companies. Unfortunately he does not differentiate between these two countries due to very small sample sizes. Hence, no implications can be derived for Germany (Cf. Haagen (2008), pp. 407-414).

[799] One could argue that the venture and product development stage are highly correlated in most cases. However, both aspects are discussed separately in order to deduce independent and clear propositions.

Proposition 6c: *The recognition of needed support activities, and thus spatial proximity between actors, are more essential for* ***ventures whose products are in an early stage of development*** *compared to ventures whose products are in a later stage of development.*

Proposition 6d: *The recognition and provision of needed support activities, and thus spatial proximity between actors, are more essential for* ***less experienced entrepreneurial teams*** *compared to entrepreneurial teams with profound prior experience.*

Various researchers state that high levels of innovation also lead to technological and commercial risks and thus to high levels of uncertainty and informational asymmetries.[800] In consequence, it might be particularly difficult to recognize the need for support for ventures which are characterized by high levels of innovation.[801]

In addition, innovative new ventures may require a higher involvement and support of their venture capitalists for several reasons. First, innovation may lead to sustainable competitive advantages[802] for the venture but is especially challenging for new businesses because they lack most of the required resources.[803] Second, entrepreneurial teams of innovative new ventures might be scientifically or technologically strong but often lack managerial skills.[804] Third, dynamic environments which are typical for innovative new ventures require rapid shifts and quick decisions.[805] An increased level of venture capitalist's involvement in innovative new ventures as well as a higher added value is also supported by various empirical studies.[806]

Ventures with high levels of innovation are frequently characterized by high R&D intensities.[807] In addition, innovative ventures may also be characterized by substantial future growth options since innovation leads to sustainable competitive advantages in most cases. In consequence, it is expected that spatial proximity facilitates the recognition and provision of venture capitalists' support particularly strong for ventures characterized by high R&D intensity, or substantial future growth options.

---

800 Cf. Sapienza/Gupta (1994), p. 1628; Barney et al. (1996a), pp. 262-263; Sapienza/De Clercq (2000), p. 59.

801 Cf. Welpe/Dowling (2005), p. 289.

802 Cf. Porter (1998), p. 78.

803 Cf. Sapienza (1992), p. 13.

804 Cf. Gomez-Mejia/Balkin/Welbourne (1990), pp. 107-108; Fingerle (2005), pp. 31-33.

805 Cf. Barney et al. (1996a), pp. 262-263.

806 Cf. Sapienza (1992), p. 19; Sapienza/Gupta (1994), p. 1628; Sapienza/Amason/Manigart (1994), pp. 9-10; Sapienza/De Clercq (2000), p. 64.

807 Cf. Sapienza/Gupta (1994), p. 1625; Barney et al. (1996a), p. 265.

Proposition 6e: *The recognition and provision of needed support activities, and thus spatial proximity between actors, are more essential for* ***ventures characterized by high R&D intensity, or substantial future growth options*** *compared to other ventures.*

There are also large differences in regard to the intensity and type of post-investment support among different venture capitalists.[808] In regard to the experience of venture capitalists, Welpe/Dowling (2005) state that inexperienced venture capitalists might be less able to detect the actual need for support.[809] In addition, inexperienced venture capitalists might have smaller and more local networks as relevant networks develop over time. Empirical evidence regarding differences in the quantity and quality of support suggests that venture capitalists become more efficient over time. Experienced venture capitalists tend to interact less frequently with their portfolio companies but add more value compared to their less experienced counterparts.[810] Hence, it can be expected that spatial proximity between the venture capitalist and the venture is especially important for inexperienced venture capitalists in order to recognize and to provide the needed support.

Proposition 6f: *Spatial proximity between a* ***less experienced venture capitalist*** *and the portfolio company is more essential for the recognition and provision of needed support activities compared to more experienced venture capitalists.*

Concerning the degree of venture capitalists' specialization in regard to certain industries or stages, it may be easier for specialized venture capitalists to recognize the venture's actual need for support as these investors possess relevant industry or stage specific knowledge.[811] Hence, spatial proximity might not be that important for specialized venture capitalists to detect the need for support.

However, since specialized venture capitalists possess more relevant industry or stage specific knowledge they might also be able to provide better and more support to their portfolio companies. This hypothesis is supported by several researchers. For European venture capitalists, Knockaert et al. (2006) provide evidence that specialized actors are more involved in value

---

808 Cf. Rosenstein et al. (1993), p. 111; Elango et al. (1995), pp. 175-176; Sapienza/Manigart/Vermeir (1996), pp. 456-457.

809 Cf. Welpe/Dowling (2005), p. 290.

810 Cf. Rosenstein et al. (1993), p. 111; Sapienza/Manigart/Vermeir (1996), pp. 456-457. Sapienza/Manigart/Vermeir (1996) differentiate between "VC experience" and "new venture experience". While "VC experience" refers to general experience in the VC industry, "new venture experience" actually means experience within the focal industry. Thus, "new venture experience" will be discussed in more detail in regard to the venture capitalists industry specialization.

811 Cf. Welpe/Dowling (2005), p. 290.

adding activities.[812] Similarly, Sapienza/Manigart/Vermeir (1996) find that European and US venture capitalists with profound experience in the focal industry interact more frequently and provide far more value added to their portfolio companies.[813] Murray/Lott (1995) show that UK technology specialists apply a more active portfolio management strategy compared to other investors.[814] As spatial proximity eases the provision of venture capitalists' support, proximity might be more relevant for specialized venture capitalists.

In consequence, spatial proximity may be more relevant for less specialized venture capitalists to recognize the need for support and more relevant for specialized venture capitalists to finally provide the higher amount of supporting activities. For an investment/financing decision the ultimate provision of support activities might be more obvious and relevant to the actors. Thus, it is anticipated that spatial proximity is more relevant for specialized venture capitalists in order to provide support efficiently.

Proposition 6g: *Spatial proximity between a* ***specialized venture capitalist*** *and the portfolio company is more essential for the provision of needed support activities compared to less specialized venture capitalists.*

The degree of the venture capitalists' profit orientation might also influence the provision of support activities. Venture capitalists with exclusively financial objectives have incentive systems which have a stronger focus on the generation of financial returns. Thus, these investors might have a higher motivation to interact with their portfolio companies and to add value compared to (quasi-)public or corporate venture capitalists which also follow strategic interests.[815] Furthermore, German (quasi-)public venture capitalists frequently use mezzanine instruments to invest into new ventures and apply a less active portfolio management strategy.[816] For German venture capitalists, Achleitner/Ehrhart/Zimmermann (2006) find that 52.8% of independent venture capitalists and only 14.3% of the remaining venture capitalists are actively involved in the majority of their portfolio companies.[817] Similarly, Knockaert et al. (2006) find that European independent venture capitalists conduct more support activities compared to captive venture capitalists.[818]

[812] Cf. Knockaert et al. (2006), pp. 20-21.

[813] Cf. Sapienza/Manigart/Vermeir (1996), pp. 456-457.

[814] Cf. Murray/Lott (1995), p. 294.

[815] Cf. Knockaert et al. (2006), pp. 13 and 21.

[816] Cf. section 2.1.3; Achleitner/Ehrhart/Zimmermann (2006), pp. 65-67.

[817] Cf. Achleitner/Ehrhart/Zimmermann (2006), p. 67.

[818] Cf. Knockaert et al. (2006), p. 21.

In consequence, it can be expected that spatial proximity is more important for venture capitalists with exclusively financial objectives in order to effectively conduct their support activities.

Proposition 6h: *Spatial proximity between **corporate venture capitalists** and the portfolio company is less essential for the provision of support activities compared to venture capitalists with exclusively financial objectives.*

Proposition 6i: *Spatial proximity between **(quasi-)public venture capitalists** and the portfolio company is less essential for the provision of support activities compared to venture capitalists with exclusively financial objectives.*

As with monitoring activities, lead-investors conduct or are responsible for most support activities within a syndicated VC investment.[819] For the entrepreneurial team the lead-investor is the most important venture capitalist within the syndicate because he provides most of the support. Hence, Wright/Lockett (2003) uncover that UK lead-investors interact significantly more with their portfolio companies compared to co-investors.[820] Similarly, Elango et al. (1995) find that US lead-investors on average spend 19.6 hours a month to attend a specific portfolio company, while co-investors on average spend only 6.2 hours a month.[821] In consequence, the effects mentioned above are expected to be stronger for lead-investors than for co-investors. However, independent from the role within a syndicate it can be expected that the members of a syndicate sensibly divide the workload of supporting activities. Hence, it is likely that the impact of spatial proximity between a venture capitalist and the venture is not that severe as long as at least one member of the syndicate is located close to the venture.[822]

Proposition 6j: *The effects of distance between a venture capitalist and a venture on the preference for proximate investments (P6a-l, excl. P6j) are stronger for **lead-investors** than for co-investors.*

Proposition 6k: *Spatial proximity between a venture capitalist and the portfolio company is less essential for the provision of support activities if at least one member of the **syndicate** is located close to the venture.*

The argumentation in regard to the impact of the investment volume on support activities and the importance of spatial proximity is similar to the argumentation for monitoring activities. The degree of support activities is likely to increase with rising investment volumes. This is

---

819 Cf. Wright/Lockett (2002), p. 74.

820 Cf. Wright/Lockett (2003), p. 2094.

821 Cf. Elango et al. (1995), pp. 175-176.

822 Cf. Fritsch/Schilder (2006), pp. 10-11. In addition, Cumming/Dai (2009) provide empirical evidence for the US that spatial proximity of the closest syndication partner is positively related with the likelihood of the portfolio company to go public (cf. Cumming/Dai (2009), pp. 16-18).

due to decreasing relative costs of support activities as well as an increasing impact of that individual investment on the portfolio's performance the larger the investment volume. This could lead to the desire of the venture capitalist to increase the support for large investments.[823] However, the volume of a VC investment might influence the desire for spatial proximity in order to conduct support activities in two opposing directions. On the one hand, transaction costs associated with support activities and thus spatial proximity are relatively less important the higher the investment volume is.[824] On the other hand, the increasing impact on the portfolio's performance could lead to the desire of the venture capitalist for more support and thus spatial proximity. Hence, the overall relationship between the preference for proximate investments due to required support activities and the investment volume is not clear. However, the effect of a decreasing importance of transaction costs diminishes with an increasing investment volume, while the performance impact and the costs of not being able to appropriately diversify the portfolio increase. Therefore, the effect of the investment volume on the level of support might follow an inverted u-shaped pattern.

Proposition 6l: *Venture capitalists' preference for proximate investments decreases with rising* ***investment volumes*** *up to a certain threshold and increases thereafter.*

4.2.2 Investment Exit

Throughout the investment exit phase venture capitalists intend to sell the shares of their portfolio companies. Hence, after (i) the point of time for a potential exit of the venture capitalist and potentially the entrepreneurial team has been determined, both (ii) choose a potential exit channel, (iii) prepare the portfolio company for the exit, (iv) prepare the exit itself, and finally (v) conduct the transaction which includes the transfer of shares to the new owners.[825]

In order to generate high returns, the **timing of the exit** is particularly important. An optimal timing might be easier to realize if the venture capitalist and the venture are located close to each other. On the one hand, the venture has to be at the right stage of development and on the other hand the venture's markets as well as the exit markets have to be in the right condition to be able to realize an adequate price. Hence, the venture capitalist and the entrepreneurial team have to know the venture and the relevant markets well.[826] However, venture capitalists and the entrepreneurial team may have different interests regarding the point of

[823] Cf. Gifford (1997), p. 474; Vater (2003), p. 195.

[824] Cf. Fritsch/Schilder (2006), p. 9.

[825] See section 2.1.4.6.

[826] Cf. Lerner (1994b), pp. 313-315; Cumming/Macintosh (2003), p. 108.

time for an exit for several reasons. As a venture capitalist intends to achieve a high performance of its portfolio in terms of risk and return, it might be necessary to restructure the portfolio, and thus to sell certain portfolio companies, at some point of time. Also, the internal rate of return of a specific investment increases the shorter the holding period is. In addition, Gompers (1996) argues that venture capitalists improve their reputation the more successful exits (especially IPOs) they realize and shows that especially young venture capitalists try to exit early in order to increase their reputation and to be able to raise further funds.[827] Furthermore, most VC funds are closed end funds and thus only have a limited predetermined lifetime. Hence, a venture capitalist may be forced to exit an investment in order to repay funds to his investors. As a result, conflicts of interest regarding the point of time for an exit may emerge. Since the entrepreneurial team is much more involved in the venture due to its day to day activities, the entrepreneurial team usually has more information about the venture and its markets. However, the venture capitalist might have more information about the capital markets and potential buyers due to his experience and networks. Hence, conflicts of interest and informational asymmetries may lead to multiple agency conflicts in regard to the timing of an exit. As it has been discussed in section c), many measures to mitigate agency conflicts are easier and more efficient in spatial proximity. Especially the transfer of information is facilitated by proximity. Furthermore, social exchange theory implies that personal relationships are more likely to develop if the venture capitalist and the entrepreneurial team are close to each other. These relationships might help to reduce inherent conflicts of interest.

Cumming/Macintosh (2003) further argue that venture capitalists decide to exit as soon as their projected marginal value added is smaller or equal to their projected marginal costs in order to further support the specific portfolio company.[828] As it has been discussed in section 4.2.1.2, it is more costly to support portfolio companies in distance. This may lead to the desire of venture capitalists to exit distant investments earlier compared to closer ones which could lead to additional conflicts in the case of distant investments.

There are also differences among different **exit channels** in regard to the likelihood of agency problems. Cumming/Macintosh (2003) differentiate between common forms of exit as well as common exit strategies and other forms and strategies. In the terminology of Cumming/Macintosh a common form of exit is an exit in which both parties exit at the same time and on the same terms. A common exit strategy is a strategy which both parties regard as being worth pursuing at the time of investment. Thus, in most cases an IPO and a trade sale are both common forms of exit and common exit strategies. Contrary, a secondary sale and a buyback are usually neither a common form of exit nor a common exit strategy. Cum-

[827] This effect is also refered to as grandstanding (cf. Gompers (1996), pp. 154-155).

[828] Cf. Cumming/Macintosh (2003), pp. 109-111.

ming/Macintosh (2003) further argue that exit channels which are not common in one or the other form exhibit a higher potential for agency problems or opportunism. One example could be that the entrepreneurial team might depress the value of the venture if it expects a buyback in order to pay the venture capitalist as little as possible later on.[829] In consequence, secondary sales and buybacks are especially susceptible to potential agency conflicts and may require additional efforts to enforce property rights. As argued above, these conflicts might be easier to resolve and property rights may be easier to enforce in proximity.

The **preparation of the venture** for the potential exit might require some structural changes which could lead to further conflicts of interest. The entrepreneurial team is much stronger attached to its venture and it might feel responsible for the ventures' and its employees' future. This leads to a more long term oriented perspective of the entrepreneurial team. In contrast, the venture capitalist's primary interest is a high return on investment which might leads to a stronger focus on the exit, a high exit value, and thus a more short term oriented perspective.

In addition, the preparation of the venture for an exit, like the improvement of the venture's accounting and reporting systems, requires additional support of the venture capitalist.[830] As discussed in section 4.2.1.2, agency theory, transaction cost theory, game theory, social exchange theory and the network approach imply that it is more costly to support portfolio companies in distance.

In the course of the **preparation of the exit itself** agency problems mainly occur between the existing shareholders (entrepreneurial team and/or venture capitalist) and the new buyer due to a conflict of interest regarding the price of the venture and informational asymmetries regarding the quality and future potential of the company.[831] Hence, if shares are sold to a third party, it might be expected that spatial proximity between the venture capitalist and the entrepreneurial team has no or only a minor impact on these agency conflicts. However, in the case of a buyback, the entrepreneurial team repurchases shares from the venture capitalist and, as discussed above, agency conflicts may occur which are easier to mitigate in proximity. Moreover, multiple tasks that are necessary in order to prepare the exit might be easier or less costly in spatial proximity. If the shares are intended to be sold to an external buyer, the entrepreneurial team and the venture capitalist jointly have to: evaluate the venture in order to determine a range for the sales price, assemble information to enable potential buyers to evaluate the venture, amend the firm's constitutional documents to enable the sale, change the legal form or jurisdiction of incorporation, and/or negotiate contractual arrangements ancillary to a

[829] Cf. Cumming/Macintosh (2003), pp. 154-157.

[830] Cf. Cumming/Macintosh (2003), p. 128.

[831] Cf. Amit/Brander/Zott (1998), p. 453; Cumming/Macintosh (2003), p. 103; Bessler/Kurth (2007), pp. 29-31.

sale. Furthermore, board deliberations in respect of any or all of the mentioned activities are necessary.[832] Most of these activities require frequent interactions, joint efforts, and cooperation of the venture capitalist and the entrepreneurial team. As transaction cost theory, game theory, and social exchange theory imply, these are easier to accomplish in spatial proximity.[833]

Many of the above mentioned activities intend to reduce informational asymmetries between the seller and the new buyer of the venture. This reduces the risk of the new buyer and thus increases the exit valuation. Hence, the more the venture capitalist and the entrepreneurial team are able to reduce informational gaps of the buyer the higher will be the valuation of the venture.[834] As it has been argued above, many of the activities that intend to reduce informational gaps of the new buyer are easier or less costly to conduct in spatial proximity. Thus, it can be expected that exit valuations are higher if the venture capitalist and the entrepreneurial team are located in close proximity. This is also supported empirically by Butler/Goktan (2008) who found that venture backed IPOs with close venture capitalists have significantly lower underpricing.[835]

As a result, multiple agency conflicts and transaction costs may occur and cooperation of the venture capitalist and the entrepreneurial team is required in various aspects in the course of the investment exit phase. Various theories imply that agency conflicts are easier to mitigate, transaction costs are lower and cooperation more likely if the venture is located close to the venture capitalist. In addition, it is likely that exit valuations are higher if the venture capitalist and the entrepreneurial team are proximate to each other. These reasons might lead to a preference of actors for spatially proximate VC financing relationships.

Proposition 7a: *Spatial proximity between a venture capitalist and a portfolio company facilitates the exit process which leads to a* ***preference of actors for proximate relationships****.*

As it has been discussed in section 4.1.3, new ventures which are characterized by high asset intangibility, high R&D intensity, or substantial future growth options are associated with greater informational asymmetries between insiders and outsiders and thus a higher likelihood of agency conflicts between existing shareholders and potential buyers. In consequence, the above mentioned activities which intend to reduce informational asymmetries between the seller and the new buyer of the venture (e.g. the assembling of information to enable potential

---

832 See section 2.1.4.6.

833 See sections 3.2.1.3, 3.2.2.1, and 3.2.2.3.

834 Cf. Cumming/Macintosh (2003), pp. 103-104.

835 Cf. Butler/Goktan (2008), p. 27.

buyers to evaluate the venture) are especially important for these new ventures. This aspect is also acknowledged by Cumming/Macintosh (2003) who argue that technology ventures are likely to cause more informational asymmetries, have higher growth potential, and lead to more agency problems in the course of an exit.[836] In consequence, it can be expected that spatial proximity between the venture capitalist and the venture is especially important for ventures characterized by high asset intangibility, high R&D intensity, or substantial future growth options.

Proposition 7b: *Collaborative activities of the venture capitalist and the entrepreneurial team to reduce informational gaps of the new buyer, and thus spatial proximity between the venture capitalist and the entrepreneurial team, are more essential for ventures characterized by* ***high asset intangibility, high R&D intensity, or substantial future growth options compared to other ventures.***

In addition, venture capitalists vouch for the quality of the portfolio company and thus lend their reputations to the venture throughout the exit stage. Hence, the above mentioned activities which intend to reduce informational asymmetries between the seller and the new buyer of the venture, and thus spatial proximity between the venture capitalist and the entrepreneurial team, are less important for more reputable venture capitalists.[837]

Proposition 7c: *Collaborative activities of the venture capitalist and the entrepreneurial team to reduce informational gaps of the new buyer, and thus spatial proximity between the venture capitalist and the entrepreneurial team, are less essential for* ***more reputable venture capitalists*** *compared to less reputable venture capitalists.*

Venture capitalists that are specialized in a specific industry are likely to have a more profound knowledge of the ventures' technology and markets which reduces potential informational asymmetries and thus agency conflicts in regard to the timing and preparation of the exit. In addition, specialized venture capitalists are likely to have more and better contacts to potential strategic buyers. This increases the chance of a trade sale and thus reduces potential conflicts that might occur if a less preferred exit channel like a company buyback would have to be chosen. Finally, the venture capitalist may enjoy a certain reputation within an industry which decreases the necessity of activities to reduce informational asymmetries between the seller and the new buyer of the venture. In consequence, spatial proximity between the venture capitalist and the entrepreneurial team in order to mitigate agency conflicts, induce coop-

[836] Cf. Cumming/Macintosh (2003), p. 105.

[837] Cf. Cumming/Macintosh (2003), p. 108.

eration, or to reduce transaction costs is not that important for venture capitalists that are specialized into a specific industry.

Proposition 7d: *Spatial proximity between a venture capitalist* ***specialized in a certain industry*** *and the portfolio company is less essential for a successful exit compared to less specialized venture capitalists.*

Since corporate venture capitalists are mainly specialized into a certain industry, a similar argumentation as for specialized venture capitalists applies. In addition, it is likely that the holding company of the corporate venture capitalist is interested in acquiring the portfolio company. This would further reduce potential informational asymmetries between the seller and the new buyer of the venture. In consequence, spatial proximity between the venture capitalist and the entrepreneurial team in order to mitigate agency conflicts, induce cooperation, or to reduce transaction costs is not that important for corporate venture capitalists compared to other venture capitalists.

Proposition 7e: *Spatial proximity between a* ***corporate*** *venture capitalist and the portfolio company is less essential for a successful exit compared to other venture capitalists.*

Similar to monitoring and support activities, lead-investors are also likely to be responsible for the exit process within a syndicated VC investment.[838] In many cases the members of a syndicate exit jointly. In consequence, the effects mentioned above are expected to be stronger for lead-investors than for co-investors.[839] However, independently from the role within a syndicate it can be expected that the members of a syndicate sensibly divide the workload of the exit process. Hence, it is likely that the impact of spatial proximity between a venture capitalist and the venture is not that severe as long as at least one member of the syndicate is located close to the venture.[840]

Proposition 7f: *The effects of distance between a venture capitalist and a venture on the preference for proximate investments (P7a-g, excl. P7f) are stronger for* ***lead-investors*** *than for co-investors.*

Proposition 7g: *Spatial proximity between a venture capitalist and the portfolio company is less essential for a successful exit if at least one member of the* ***syndicate*** *is located close to the venture.*

---

[838] Cf. Wright/Lockett (2002), pp. 75-76.

[839] An exception is a secondary sale in which a venture capitalist sells his shares to another financial investor largely independently from other members of a VC syndicate. See also section 2.1.4.6.

[840] Cf. Fritsch/Schilder (2006), pp. 10-11.

4.3 Summary and Testable Hypotheses

In the previous sections various propositions regarding

- the general impact of spatial proximity on the respective investment phase

  as well as

- the kinds of new ventures, venture capitalists, or financing rounds for which the impact of spatial proximity is particularly strong

have been elaborated. These propositions represent the fundament of a consistent theoretical framework regarding the impact of spatial proximity on the likelihood of a VC investment throughout the investment process. The development of this theoretical framework is one of the major aims of this thesis. However, most of the elaborated propositions are not empirically testable as data regarding individual phases of the investment process is not freely available. In contrast, data regarding actual VC investments is available. Thus, one can observe which kind of potential financing relationships finally passed the deal structuring phase and entered post-contractual phases. If spatial proximity has an impact on the likelihood of a specific VC investment to occur, realized investments should exhibit specific patterns regarding the spatial proximity between venture capitalists and its investees. These patterns in spatial proximity between venture capitalists and investees are observable and thus empirically testable. However, other unobservable factors may also impact the observed patterns in spatial proximity which leads to problems in determining causal relationships. These issues will be discussed later on in section 5.2.5.

In addition, if it were possible to obtain a sample of potential VC financing relationships which were not realized, one could also empirically test the impact of spatial proximity on the likelihood of investment directly. Then also causal relationships regarding the impact of spatial proximity in VC financing would be possible. As will be discussed in section 5.3.1, the construction of such a sample is possible.

Hence, this section will develop testable hypotheses in regard to

a) the observed distance between the venture capitalist and investee of realized investments and thus the patterns in spatial proximity and

b) the underlying impact of spatial proximity on the likelihood of investment.

In order to develop testable hypotheses, the propositions of the previous sections will be condensed. As the likelihood of investment also influences the observed patterns in spatial proximity, the hypotheses largely overlap. In consequence, parallel hypotheses will be elaborated and particular differences will be discussed separately.

Strictly speaking, only propositions regarding pre-contractual phases of the investment process should influence the likelihood of investments. Propositions of post-contractual phases should primarily influence the performance of investments after the investment/financing decision has already been made.[841] However, venture capitalists are rational investors and frequently invest into new ventures.[842] Hence, it can be expected that they anticipate potential performance effects and consider these effects in their investment decisions. For entrepreneurial teams, the VC financing decision is one of the most fundamental decisions in the course of a company's development. Thus, one can expect that entrepreneurial teams will inform themselves thoroughly by consulting other entrepreneurs that received VC financing as well as other supporting actors. Hence, also entrepreneurial teams are expected to largely anticipate potential performance effects in their financing decisions. As a result, also post-contractual propositions will be considered to develop testable hypotheses.

Table 4.1 summarizes the propositions of previous sections as well as the resulting testable hypotheses. These hypotheses will be derived and discussed in the following sections.

4.3.1 General Impact of Distance

Table 4.1 indicates that all propositions of the different phases of the investment process imply a negative general impact of distance on the likelihood of a specific investment. These effects are implied by multiple theories, but the probably most important factors are that informational asymmetries and transaction costs increase with rising distance. Hence, it is hypothesized:

Hypothesis 1a: *The **number of observed VC investments** decreases with increasing distance.*

Hypothesis 1b: *The **likelihood of a specific VC investment** decreases with increasing distance between venture capitalist and investee.*

[841] The perfomance of a VC financing relationship primarily regards its risk-return-ratio. Thus, the performance is also determined by potential conflicts between the venture capitalist and the entrepreneurial team, the level of monitoring and support, as well as occurring transaction costs (cf. Timmons/Bygrave (1986), pp. 161-162; Cable/Shane (1997), pp. 143-145; Bottazzi/Da Rin/Hellmann (2008), pp. 503-507).

[842] Cf. Manigart et al. (2002a), pp. 306-309.

Table 4.1: Summary of propositions and testable hypotheses

This table summarizes the propositions which were developed throughout chapter 4 as well as resulting testable hypotheses. +/- indicates that distance has a positive/negative impact on the likelihood of a specific VC investment (panel A) or that a specific factor has a positive/negative impact on the likelihood of a distant VC investment. (+)/(-) indicates that the respective effect is not clear and that a judgment regarding the overall effect within this phase was made. {.} indicates that the respective effect emerges as a consequence of propositions regarding the general impact on the likelihood of a specific investment (panel A).

Summary of propositions and hypotheses	Pre-contractual propositions				Post-contractual propositions			Testable hypotheses	
	Deal origination	Deal screening	Deal due diligence	Deal structuring	Investment development: Monitoring	Investment development: Support	Investment exit	a) Observed patterns of SP	b) Likelihood of investment
Panel A: General impact on the likelihood of a specific investment									
Distance	-	-	-	-	-	-	-	-	
Panel B: Impact of various factors on the likelihood of a distant VC investment									
Venture									
Venture development stage (age, investment stage, size)	+		+		+	+		+	
Product development stage			+		+	(+)		+	
Prior experience of the team	+		+		+	+		+	
Knowledge intensity									
Asset intangibility			-		-		-	-	
R&D intensity			-		-	-	-	-	
Future growth options			-		-	-	-	-	
Region									
East German venture			open					+	open
Urban venture location			+					open	+

Table 4.1 cont.: Summary of propositions and testable hypotheses

Summary of propositions and hypotheses	Pre-contractual propositions				Post-contractual propositions			Testable hypotheses	
	Deal origination	Deal screening	Deal due diligence	Deal structuring	Investment development: Monitoring	Investment development: Support	Investment exit	a) Observed patterns of SP	b) Likelihood of investment
Venture capitalist									
Size	+	+						+	
Experience / reputation (age)	+	-	+			+	+	open	
Specialization									
Industry	+	+				-	+	open	
Stage	+	+				-		open	
Type									
Corporate investor	+	+	+			+	+	+	
(Quasi-)public venture capitalist		-				+		-	+
Lead-investor									
General effect (intercept)			-		-	-	-	-	
Impact on other propositions/hypotheses			more pronounce		more pronounced	more pronounced	more pronounced	more pronounced	
Round									
Investment volume			+	+	+ / -	+ / -		inverted u-shape	
Syndication	+		+		+	+	+	+	
Consecutive round			{-}	{-}	{-}	{-}		-	

4.3.2 New Venture Characteristics

Venture development stage

The developed propositions which are summarized in Table 4.1 suggest that the venture's development stage (age, investment stage, size) influences the impact of distance in the following phases: deal origination, deal due diligence, investment monitoring, and investment support. The propositions imply that the general negative impact of distance on the likelihood of investment is not that severe for ventures in a later development stage compared to ventures in an early development stage. Main reasons for these effects are lower levels of risk and opaqueness, higher availability of resources, and more developed and thus widespread networks of more mature ventures. Hence, the venture development stage has a positive impact on the likelihood of a distant investment and it is hypothesized:

Hypothesis 2.1a: ***Young*** *ventures are located closer to their venture capitalists compared to older ventures.*

Hypothesis 2.1b: *The impact of distance on the likelihood of investment becomes less negative the* ***older*** *the venture is.*

Hypothesis 2.2a: ***Seed stage*** *investment rounds are located closer to their venture capitalists compared to other investment rounds.*

Hypothesis 2.2b: *The impact of distance on the likelihood of investment is more negative for* ***seed stage*** *investment rounds compared to other investment rounds.*

Hypothesis 2.3a: ***Small*** *ventures are located closer to their venture capitalists compared to larger ventures.*

Hypothesis 2.3b: *The impact of distance on the likelihood of investment becomes less negative the* ***larger*** *the venture is.*

Product development stage

The theoretical analysis further uncovered that an advanced product development stage alleviates the negative impact of distance on the likelihood to successfully accomplish necessary activities throughout the deal due diligence, investment monitoring, and investment support phase (Table 4.1). These effects arise due to reduced levels of risk and opaqueness of ventures whose products are already well developed. As all propositions point into the same direction, the following hypotheses emerge:

Hypothesis 3a: *Ventures whose **products** are in an **early stage of development** are located closer to their venture capitalists compared to other ventures.*

Hypothesis 3b: *The impact of distance on the likelihood of investment is more negative for ventures whose **products** are in an **early stage of development** compared to other ventures.*

Prior experience of the entrepreneurial team

The summary in Table 4.1 shows that profound prior experience of the entrepreneurial team reduces the negative the impact of distance in the following phases: deal origination, deal due diligence, investment monitoring, and investment support. These effects are mainly caused by signaling managerial skills, a higher reputation, more developed and thus widespread networks, and a lower level of required support. This results in the following hypotheses:

Hypothesis 4a: *Entrepreneurial teams **lacking profound prior experience** are located closer to their venture capitalists compared to other teams.*

Hypothesis 4b: *The impact of distance on the likelihood of investment is less negative if the entrepreneurial team has **profound prior experience**.*

Knowledge intensity

A high knowledge intensity of the venture in the form of high asset intangibility, high R&D intensity, and substantial future growth options intensifies the negative impact of distance in several phases of the VC investment process. These phases are the deal due diligence, investment monitoring, investment support (only R&D intensity and future growth options), and investment exit (Table 4.1). The discussed effects for knowledge intensive ventures result primarily from higher levels of risk and opaqueness as well as a potentially increased need for management support. As all propositions point into the same direction, the following hypotheses emerge:

Hypothesis 5.1a: *Ventures characterized by **high asset intangibility** are located closer to their venture capitalists compared to other ventures.*

Hypothesis 5.1b: *The impact of distance on the likelihood of investment is more negative for ventures characterized by **high asset intangibility**.*

Hypothesis 5.2a: *Ventures characterized by **high R&D intensity** are located closer to their venture capitalists compared to other ventures.*

Hypothesis 5.2b: *The impact of distance on the likelihood of investment is more negative for ventures characterized by* ***high R&D intensity****.*

Hypothesis 5.3a: *Ventures characterized by* ***substantial future growth options*** *are located closer to their venture capitalists compared to other ventures.*

Hypothesis 5.3b: *The impact of distance on the likelihood of investment is more negative for ventures characterized by* ***substantial future growth options****.*

Region

The theoretical analysis, which is summarized in Table 4.1, indicates that the location of the new venture in East or West Germany may affect the importance of spatial proximity for the likelihood of investment in the due diligence phase. East German new ventures may be regarded to possess higher risks but may also offer a higher potential. Thus, the direction of the effect remains open. However, regarding the patterns in spatial proximity additional, mostly structural, facts have to be considered. Due to the different development of the Federal Republic of Germany and the German Democratic Republic from 1949 to 1990, large economic differences between both parts still exist.[843] In consequence, apart from Berlin, only relatively few venture capitalists are located in the former GDR which may lead to larger distances between venture capitalists and new ventures in general. Hence, it is hypothesized:

Hypothesis 6.1a: *Ventures located in* ***West Germany*** *are located closer to their venture capitalists compared to East German ventures.*

As mentioned above, it remains open how the new venture's location in East or West Germany may affect the impact of spatial proximity in regard to the likelihood of investment.

In consequence, no hypothesis regarding the new venture's location in East or West Germany on the likelihood of investment can be formulated. Nonetheless, the new venture's location could turn out to be a relevant variable for the importance of spatial proximity in VC investing.

The summary in Table 4.1 further shows that the likelihood of a distant VC investment is higher for new ventures located in urban areas. This is mainly caused by a different risk-return perception of venture capitalists for ventures in different locations throughout the deal due diligence. Besides this effect on the likelihood of investment, various structural differ-

[843] Cf. Achleitner et al. (2009), pp. 439-440.

ences among urban and rural areas exist and may influence the patterns in spatial proximity between venture capitalists and investees. Urban areas are e.g. more likely to be located close to a highway (Autobahn) or airport compared to rural areas. Moreover, most venture capitalists are also located in, potentially the same, urban areas. In consequence, urban new ventures are likely to be closer or to need less travel time to their venture capitalists in general.

As the discussed effects contradict each other, the overall relationship between the observed distance between venture capitalists and investees and the new ventures' location in urban or non-urban areas is not clear. Thus, no hypothesis can be advanced. Nonetheless, the new ventures' location in urban or non-urban areas could turn out to be a relevant variable for observed patterns in spatial proximity between venture capitalists and investees.

In regard to the likelihood of investment it is hypothesized:

Hypothesis 6.2b: *The impact of distance on the likelihood of investment is less negative for ventures* ***located in urban areas.***

4.3.3 Venture Capitalist Characteristics

Size

The size of the venture capitalist alleviates the negative impact of distance on the likelihood of investment throughout the deal origination and the deal screening phase (Table 4.1). This is primarily due to a higher availability of resources, the pressure to invest larger amounts of fund capital, a higher public visibility, and more widespread networks. Since both propositions point into the same direction, the following hypotheses emerge:

Hypothesis 7a: *New ventures are located closer to* ***small venture capitalists*** *compared to larger venture capitalists.*

Hypothesis 7b: *The impact of distance on the likelihood of investment becomes less negative the* ***larger*** *the venture capitalist.*

Experience and reputation

As the experience and reputation of a venture capitalist is likely to be highly correlated with the age of the investor, common hypotheses will be formulated regarding these aspects.[844] The theoretical analysis revealed contradicting propositions regarding the experience and reputation of a venture capitalist (Table 4.1). On the one hand, the propositions that emerge from

[844] Cf. Gorman/Sahlman (1989), p. 233; Sahlman (1990), p. 500; Gompers (1996), p. 136.

activities in the deal origination, deal due diligence, investment support, and investment exit imply that the general negative impact of distance on the likelihood of investment is not that severe for highly experienced and reputable venture capitalists compared to other investors. This is mainly due to the development of larger and more widespread networks as well as specific investment experience and reputation which lead to the generation of more supra-regional deal flow. These aspects also facilitate gathering information about distant investment opportunities in the due diligence. Furthermore, experienced venture capitalists are more efficient in supporting their portfolio companies as well as their networks and reputation might help to find a new buyer in the exit phase.[845]

On the other hand, experienced venture capitalists may prefer to concentrate their activities on proximate investments and might be more able to apply a geographic screen in the deal screening phase. This is caused by the fact that besides the spatial structure of the venture capitalist's network, and thus deal flow, also the quantity and quality of deal flow has to be considered. As discussed, more experienced venture capitalists are expected to have tighter and larger networks, a higher reputation, and thus are likely to receive more and potentially better deal flow compared to younger industry players. Hence, if older venture capitalists have the choice, they may focus their efforts on more proximate investment opportunities because these are easier to assess and to manage in the future. In contrast, less experienced venture capitalists might be restricted by their deal flow which forces them to also accept more distant investment opportunities in order to build up their network and reputation.[846]

In consequence, the overall relationship between the likelihood of a distant investment and the age of a venture capitalist is not clear. Furthermore, no additional implications regarding the observed patterns in spatial proximity can be derived. Thus, no hypothesis can be advanced. Nonetheless, the experience of the venture capitalist could turn out to be a relevant variable for the importance of spatial proximity in VC investing.

Specialization

Regarding the venture capitalist's specialization in certain industries or investment stages the theoretical analysis of the different phases of the investment process offers mixed results. On the one hand, the propositions that emerge from activities in the deal origination, deal screening, and for an industry specialization also investment exit imply that the general negative impact of distance on the likelihood of investment is not that severe for specialized venture

---

[845] See sections 4.1.1, 4.1.3, 4.2.1.2, and 4.2.2.

[846] See section 4.1.2. In addition to these arguments, Cumming/Dai (2009) argue that experienced and reputable venture capitalists are more frequently chosen by local new ventures. However, this argument does not seem very reasonable (cf. Cumming/Dai (2009), p. 16).

capitalists. These effects are caused by three main reasons. First, specialized venture capitalists may be contacted by supra-regional entrepreneurial teams or other venture capitalists because of their specific experiences and skills within a certain industry or stage. Second, specialized venture capitalists might not be able to apply a narrow geographical screen in addition to their stage or industry screen because of restrictions in the quantity of deal flow. Third, venture capitalists specialized in a certain industry might be better able to also support distant portfolio companies in the exit phase due to their specific knowledge and networks.

On the other hand, specialized venture capitalists are likely to be more active in supporting their portfolio companies. In consequence, it would be beneficial for specialized venture capitalists to be located close to their portfolio companies. An indication which of the contradicting effects dominates does not exist.

Therefore, it is unclear whether the likelihood of a distant investment is higher for more or less specialized venture capitalists. Thus, no hypothesis can be formulated. Nonetheless, the specialization of the venture capitalist could turn out to be a relevant variable for the impact of spatial proximity in VC investing.

Type

For corporate venture capitalists the negative impact of spatial proximity is less severe throughout the deal origination, deal screening, deal due diligence, investment support, and investment exit phase (Table 4.1). Main reasons for these effects are a higher public visibility, their industry specialization, specific knowledge and networks, but also their strategic interests and reduced profit orientation. As all propositions point into the same direction, the following hypotheses emerge:

Hypothesis 8.1a: *The distance between **corporate venture capitalists** and their investees is higher compared to other types of venture capitalists.*

Hypothesis 8.1b: *The impact of distance on the likelihood of investment is less negative for **corporate venture capitalists** compared to other types of venture capitalists.*

For (quasi-)public venture capitalists, the implications of the developed propositions are not clear. Most (quasi-)public venture capitalists apply a geographical screen which leads to the fact that very distant investments are almost impossible. Contrary, (quasi-)public venture capitalists are likely to be less profit oriented due to additional, non-financial goals and different incentive systems. Furthermore, many of these investors prefer to use mezzanine financial instruments to invest into their portfolio companies and are likely to apply a less active portfolio management strategy. Hence, if an investment opportunity passed the geographical screen, it is likely that spatial proximity is less important for the likelihood of investment compared to other types of venture capitalists.[847] Hence, it is hypothesized:

Hypothesis 8.2a: ***(Quasi-)public venture capitalists*** *are located closer to their portfolio companies compared to other types of venture capitalists.*

Hypothesis 8.2b: *The impact of distance on the likelihood of investment is less negative for* ***(quasi-)public venture capitalists*** *compared to other types of venture capitalists if one controls for the defined geographical screen of these investors.*

Lead-investor

Table 4.1 offers a homogeneous picture regarding the impact of the venture capitalist's role within a syndicated investment on the effect of spatial proximity across different phases of the VC investment process. Thus, it is proposed that the negative impact of distance is more severe for lead-investors throughout the deal due diligence, investment monitoring and support, as well as investment exit phase. Furthermore, in these phases the effects of venture, venture capitalist, and round characteristics on the importance of spatial proximity are more pronounced for lead-investors compared to co-investors.[848] These effects are primarily caused by the fact that lead-investors are usually responsible for most tasks in the mentioned investment phases. Since the proposition that the mentioned effects are more pronounced for lead-investors only refers to some investment phases, one can only conclude that the overall effects of venture, venture capitalist, and round characteristics on the importance of spatial proximity differ among lead- and co-investors. A general hypothesis regarding the direction of the difference in the overall effects between lead- and co-investors is not possible. However, a thorough discussion of these issues follows in sections 5.2.3 and 5.3.2. The following hypotheses emerge:

Hypothesis 9.1a: ***Lead-investors*** *are located closer to their portfolio companies compared to co-investors.*

Hypothesis 9.1b: *The impact of distance on the likelihood of investment is more negative for* ***lead-investors*** *compared to co-investors.*

---

[847] See sections 4.1.2 and 4.2.1.2.

[848] See also sections 4.1.3, 4.2.1, and 4.2.2.

Furthermore, it is hypothesized:

Hypothesis 9.2a/b: *Some of the effects of the elaborated hypotheses differ between* ***lead- and co-investors****.*

4.3.4 Investment Round Characteristics

Investment volume

The investment volume influences the impact of distance in the following phases: deal due diligence, deal structuring, investment monitoring, and investment support. Even though the propositions imply linear as well as non-linear effects, the propositions of the different phases of the investment process do not contradict each other (Table 4.1). In general it is proposed that increasing investment volumes alleviate the negative impact of distance due to a decreasing relative importance of transaction costs. However, in the case of very high investment volumes with a high impact on the portfolio risk and return, venture capitalists may have the desire for more frequent monitoring, support, and thus spatial proximity. Hence, an overall inverted u-shaped effect emerges and it is hypothesized:

Hypothesis 10a: *The distance between a venture capitalist and investee increases with rising* ***investment volume*** *of the venture capitalist up to a certain threshold and decreases thereafter.*

Hypothesis 10b: *The impact of distance on the likelihood of investment becomes less negative with rising* ***investment volume*** *of the venture capitalist up to a certain threshold and more negative thereafter.*

Syndication

The theoretical analysis revealed that the existence of a syndication partner located close to the target mitigates the negative impact of distance throughout the deal origination, deal due diligence, investment monitoring and support, as well as investment exit (Table 4.1). The rationales behind these effects are supra-regional invitations to join a syndicate and that the members of a syndicate sensibly divide the workload throughout the investment process and exchange information with each other. As all propositions point into the same direction, the following hypotheses emerge:

Hypothesis 11a: *The distance between venture capitalists and their investees is higher if at least one member of the (potential)* ***syndicate*** *is located close to the venture.*

Hypothesis 11b: *The impact of distance on the likelihood of investment is less negative if at least one member of the (potential)* ***syndicate*** *is located close to the venture.*

Consecutive financing rounds

Hypothesis 1a states that the likelihood of a specific VC investment (financing round) decreases with increasing distance between a venture capitalist and the venture. If hypothesis 1a is valid and if the validity of this hypothesis is not only driven by activities and circumstances in the deal origination, deal screening, and/or investment exit phase, then the hypothesis should also have an impact on the spatial structure of consecutive financing rounds. In this context, consecutive financing rounds refer to follow-on investments of a venture capitalist in a specific venture.

The phases of deal origination, deal screening, and investment exit are not relevant for the investment/financing decision of a consecutive financing round. The reason is that both parties already know each other and that an exit has to be conducted in any case at some point in time. However, the propositions regarding the general impact of spatial proximity on the respective investment phases also state that distance is detrimental for many activities in the deal due diligence, deal structuring, and investment development phases. These points should lead to a lower likelihood of consecutive financing rounds for distant portfolio companies compared to close ones. Furthermore, next to the anticipation of a more difficult investment support for distant ventures, it is also likely that financing rounds which include regionally dispersed actors already incurred more problems compared to financing rounds with close actors. In addition, venture capitalists could be more willing to finance consecutive financing rounds of ventures close to them as they have built up a closer personal relationship. Underlining these arguments, Sapienza/Gupta (1994) find first empirical evidence that geographic distance and the venture's performance are negatively correlated. In consequence, the likelihood of receiving consecutive financing rounds is expected to be higher for deals with closer spatial proximity between the venture capitalist and the investee and it is hypothesized:

Hypothesis 12a: *The observed distance between venture capitalists and their investees decreases the more financing rounds both parties already realized with each other.*

5 Empirical Analysis of Relationships between Spatial Proximity and the Type and Likelihood of Venture Capital Financing

This chapter aims to shed further light on the impact of spatial proximity on VC financing relationships in Germany by empirically testing hypotheses regarding observable patterns in spatial proximity and the impact of spatial proximity on the likelihood of investment. These hypotheses have been developed in chapter 4 and were derived from a comprehensive theoretical framework regarding the impact of spatial proximity between venture capitalists and investees throughout the investment process. In consequence, this chapter intends to verify important parts of the elaborated theoretical framework for German VC investments.

A comprehensive empirical study of the impact of spatial proximity on German VC transactions is highly required for at least two reasons. First, there are great differences in the spatial structure of different countries. Especially North American countries differ largely from continental European countries which are spatially much more concentrated and have denser infrastructures. Strictly speaking, the spatial structure, infrastructures, institutional frameworks, and the development stage of the VC industry are unique like a finger print for each country which causes country specific analyses to be necessary.[849] Second, existing empirical studies analyze only single and very specific effects of spatial proximity between venture capitalists and investees. A comprehensive empirical study is still missing.[850]

The chapter is organized as follows: section 5.1 describes the dataset used in this chapter. In section 5.2, relationships between characteristics of ventures, venture capitalists and/or financing rounds and the observed spatial proximity between venture capitalists and investees (patterns in spatial proximity) are analyzed. Section 5.3 investigates the impact of spatial proximity on the likelihood of a specific venture capital financing to occur. Finally, section 5.4 summarizes the empirical results and discusses whether the likelihood of investment is causal for the observed patterns in spatial proximity.

---

[849] The importance of country specific research is also underpinned by Bruton/Fried/Manigart (2005) and Zacharakis (2007) among others (cf. Bruton/Fried/Manigart (2005), p. 750; Zacharakis (2007), p. 704). Furthermore, multiple studies find strong differences in regard to important aspects of VC among countries (cf. e.g. Sapienza/Manigart/Vermeir (1996), pp. 439-441; Lerner/Schoar (2003), pp. 29-31).

[850] See section 2.3.

5.1 Description of Dataset

5.1.1 Available Datasets for Analysis

Various different data sources can be used to study the impact of spatial proximity on German VC transactions. The data sources which are frequently used for scientific VC research are Thomson Venture Economics and VentureSource from DowJones-VentureOne.[851] These databases contain information about VC and PE transactions as well as the financed companies and the participating VC/PE firms and their respective funds. The data are largely self-reported, but several plausibility checks are conducted by the database providers. Kaplan/Sensoy/Strömberg (2002) provide a detailed overview on these databases and compare both in regard to several dimensions. Overall, they "find that the VentureOne data are generally more reliable, more complete, and less biased than the Venture Economics data."[852]

Another potential database is provided by the Center of Private Equity Research (CEPRES).[853] The database contains detailed information on a large number of VC and PE funds as well as its portfolio companies. However, the data is not suitable for the research at hand as the anonymous data does not include detailed information about the location of the portfolio companies.

Some scholars also chose to use hand collected unique datasets. These datasets are mostly created by indentifying venture capitalists in a first step[854] and collecting additional data on the respective investors and their portfolio companies with the help of questionnaires and/or interviews in a second step.[855] This approach offers the advantage that the data collection can be harmonized with the research design. However, the collection of unique datasets is also very labor, time, and cost intensive and therefore not suitable for most large sample studies.

---

[851] Cf. Kaplan/Sensoy/Strömberg (2002), p. 1. VentureXpert from Thomson Financial is part of Thomson Venture Economics. Studies using Thomson Venture Economics are e.g. Lerner (1995), Sorenson/Stuart (2001), Butler/Goktan (2008), or Tian (2009). Studies using VentureSource are e.g. Davila/Foster/Gupta (2003), Gompers et al. (2009), or Cumming/Dai (2009).

[852] Kaplan/Sensoy/Strömberg (2002), p. 2. It is important to note that the study is based on US VC transactions only.

[853] CEPRES is a joint research initiative between VCM Capital Management GmbH, today Sal. Oppenheim Banking Group, a German PE fund of funds and the chair of banking and finance at the Johann Wolfgang Goethe-University of Frankfurt am Main.

[854] Venture capitalists might be identified with the help of VC associations like the EVCA or databases like Pratt's Guide to Venture Capital Sources.

[855] Studies using this method are e.g. Tyebjee/Bruno (1984a), Sapienza/Manigart/Vermeir (1996), or Brettel (2002).

Additional data sources that are used by some researchers include databases from the Zentrum für Europäische Wirtschaftsforschung (ZEW) or VC facts.[856] These data sources are either proprietary or cover only a small fraction of VC transactions and are thus not available or desirable for most scientific studies. Furthermore, VC associations like the BVK or the EVCA provide a wide range of aggregated data. However, these data only offer information about the regional distribution of investment on a high level. Deal based data is not available due to non-disclosure agreements.

As a result, data from VentureSource and/or Thomson Venture Economics seem to be most appropriate in order to study the impact of spatial proximity on German VC financing relationships, while there are some indications that VentureSource data is more reliable, more complete, and less biased than the Venture Economics data.

5.1.2 Used Dataset

The research at hand is based on data from VentureSource which is a database from Dow-Jones-VentureOne and provides various data on investors and venture-backed companies.[857] The sample includes all VC transactions of German new ventures that received funding between January 2002 and March 2007.[858] VC transactions were defined according to VentureSource and include seed, first, second, and later stage rounds. These VentureSource financing round classes correspond to seed, start-up, and expansion stage financing rounds as defined by the EVCA.[859] Restart financing rounds, which represent turnaround situations, were excluded from the analysis.[860]

In total, the sample comprises 1402 dyads of venture capitalists and portfolio companies which emerge from 498 portfolio companies that were financed by 309 venture capitalists in the course of 689 financing rounds.[861] In case of syndicated investments a dyad is defined for each participating investor and the respective new venture. This is necessary in order to be able to exactly measure spatial proximity between a specific venture capitalist and a portfolio

---

[856] Studies using these databases are e.g. Engel (2003a) or Fritsch/Schilder (2006).

[857] The author thanks DowJones-VentureOne for granting access to their VentureSource database and thus making this research project possible.

[858] The data was retrieved from VentureSource on March 21st, 2007.

[859] Cf. EVCA (2009) and see section 2.1.2 for definitions of the investment stages.

[860] A definition of the VentureSource financing round classes can be found in appendix A. VentureSource only lists four ventures that received restart financing in the respective time period. Hence, the data regarding restart investments seems not to be representative and has been excluded from the analysis.

[861] Dyads with business angels and undisclosed venture capitalists had to be excluded due to missing values in respect to most variables. Dyads with venture capitalists for which the address was not available were also excluded.

company. To account for the different roles of venture capitalists within a syndicate, the empirical analyses control for lead- and co-investors. If a new venture received several financing rounds, separate dyads for each financing round are included in the sample. This is reasonable since each financing round represents a new investment/financing decision and the venture capitalist could refuse to inject additional resources. The data that was collected from VentureSource includes the location of all branches of both parties, the portfolio companies' age, size, product development stage, entrepreneurial team's background, and industry, the venture capitalists' size, age, and role as co- or lead-investor, as well as the type, total amount raised, and number of investors in the financing round.

Table 5.1 and Table 5.2 display the distribution of financing rounds and venture capitalist-investee dyads by number and investment volume over time, investment stages and industries. For some financing rounds VentureSource did not report the investment volume. Hence, the statistics have been split into the full sample and a subsample for which the investment volume was available.

The development of financing rounds by number and volume over time largely corresponds to the development of the German VC market as reported by the BVK.[862] The small fractions of financing rounds and dyads in 2007 are due to the fact that the data was collected until March 2007. The reported investment volume over the whole period totals 2.16 billion Euro. On average about 3.90 million Euro were invested per financing round, while the average volume seems to increase from 2002 to 2006. The large investment volume per financing round in 2007 is due to one large biotechnology financing round of 40 million Euro. Since most of the financing rounds are syndicated, also the investment volume per venture capitalist is reported in Table 5.1. On average each venture capitalist invested 1.65 million Euro per financing round.[863] This average volume per venture capitalist also seems to increase from 2002 to 2006.

About 4.4% of the sample are seed financing rounds, while the rest of the sample is distributed fairly equally over first, second and later stage rounds. In terms of venture capitalist-investee dyads, only about 3.0% of the sample correspond to seed rounds, 27.0% to first rounds, 29.9% to second rounds, and 40.1% to later stage rounds. The financing volume per round increases from seed rounds over first/second rounds to later stage rounds. However, this trend is less pronounced for the average investment volume per venture capitalist. These

---

[862] For further comparisons of the sample and the universe of VC transactions reported by the BVK see section 5.1.5.

[863] For the calculation of the investment volume per venture capitalist also business angels, undisclosed investors, and investors without address information have been considered. As previously discussed, no dyads were constructed for these investors.

Table 5.1: Composition of the dataset over time and investment stages

This table illustrates the composition of the used dataset regarding different time periods and investment stages. Therefore, the number of financing rounds and dyads, the investment volume, the average volume per financing round, and the average volume per investor was analyzed. In case of syndicated investments a dyad is defined for each participating investor and the respective new venture. To calculate the investment volume per investor, it was assumed that each investor participating in a financing round contributes equally to the total amount raised and also business angels, undisclosed investors, and investors without address information were considered. The used investment stages correspond to the round class reported by VentureSource.

	Full sample				Sample with reported investment volume (m€)							
	Financing rounds		Dyads		Financing rounds					Dyads		
	Obs.	%	Obs.	%	Obs.	%	Volume	%	Vol./Round	Obs.	%	Vol./Investor
Total	689	100.0	1402	100.0	553	100.0	2157.5	100.0	3.90	1200	100.0	1.65
Year												
2002	218	31.6	406	29.0	175	31.6	511.8	23.7	2.92	350	29.2	1.38
2003	137	19.9	272	19.4	108	19.5	398.0	18.4	3.69	225	18.8	1.63
2004	124	18.0	262	18.7	104	18.8	429.7	19.9	4.13	234	19.5	1.65
2005	115	16.7	270	19.3	95	17.2	454.3	21.1	4.78	236	19.7	1.77
2006	90	13.1	175	12.5	68	12.3	316.2	14.7	4.65	144	12.0	1.98
2007	5	0.7	17	1.2	3	0.5	47.5	2.2	15.83	11	0.9	4.32
Stage												
Seed	30	4.4	42	3.0	27	4.9	16.8	0.8	0.62	39	3.3	0.41
First	220	31.9	379	27.0	164	29.7	576.2	26.7	3.51	301	25.1	1.76
Second	210	30.5	419	29.9	182	32.9	630.4	29.2	3.46	385	32.1	1.51
Later Stage	229	33.2	562	40.1	180	32.5	934.1	43.3	5.19	475	39.6	1.81

facts indicate that the number of investors per round increases the later the investment stage is.

Table 5.2 reports that the majority of financing rounds corresponds to new ventures in healthcare (38.0%) and information technology (47.5%) industries. In 7.8% of the rounds new ventures in the business/consumer/retail group and in 6.7% of the rounds new ventures in other industries were financed. Regarding venture capitalist-investee dyads, healthcare (44.7%) and information technology (43.3%) dyads are almost equally weighted. The investment volume per financing round varies substantially from 0.65 million Euro for healthcare service companies to 8.85 million Euro for energy companies. However, the investment volume per investor does not vary in the same magnitude which again suggests that the number of investors per financing round increases the larger the financing round is.

Table 5.3 shows the distribution of venture capitalist-investee dyads by origin and type of the venture capitalist. The German new ventures of the sample were financed by venture capitalists from 15 different countries. 83.7% of all dyads include a domestic venture capitalist or an investor that has at least one office in Germany. This already gives a first hint on the importance of spatial proximity in VC financing. Further 10.8% of the dyads include venture capitalists from other continental European countries. Within this group, Swiss venture capitalists account for the largest share (4.7%). In 2.9% of the dyads a UK venture capitalist and in 0.6% a Scandinavian investor was involved. Finally, 2.0% of the dyads include a US venture capitalist.

Regarding the type of the venture capitalist, most dyads include a venture capitalist with exclusively financial objectives (71.8%). In 21.3% of the dyads, a (quasi-)public venture capitalist and in 7.0% a corporate venture capitalist was involved. The average investment volume per investor varies substantially with the type of the investor. Venture capitalists with exclusively financial objectives invest on average about 60% more per investment round compared to (quasi-)public venture capitalists.[864]

[864] This is a very conservative estimation of the difference in the investment volume per investor since it has been assumed that all venture capitalists contribute equally to the investment amount of an investment round (see section 5.1.3.4 for further details). In consequence, the difference among the groups might be blurred due to investment rounds with different types of investors.

Table 5.2: Composition of the dataset over industries

This table illustrates the composition of the used dataset regarding different industries. The first level corresponds to the VentureSource industry group and the second level to the industry segment. IS: Information systems, Adv. spec. mat. & chem.: Advanced specialty materials & chemicals. For further explanations see also Table 5.1.

	Full sample				Sample with reported investment volume (m€)							
	Financing rounds		Dyads		Financing rounds					Dyads		
	Obs.	%	Obs.	%	Obs.	%	Volume	%	Vol./Round	Obs.	%	Vol./Investor
Total	689	100.0	1402	100.0	553	100.0	2157.5	100.0	3.90	1200	100.0	1.65
Industry												
Business/consumer/retail												
Consumer/business products	17	2.5	22	1.6	10	1.8	16.5	0.8	1.65	15	1.3	1.09
Consumer/business services	24	3.5	33	2.4	20	3.6	33.8	1.6	1.69	29	2.4	1.01
Media/content/information	6	0.9	6	0.4	4	0.7	6.5	0.3	1.62	4	0.3	1.47
Retailers	7	1.0	9	0.6	6	1.1	16.8	0.8	2.79	8	0.7	2.10
Sub total	*54*	*7.8*	*70*	*5.0*	*40*	*7.2*	*73.5*	*3.4*	*1.84*	*56*	*4.7*	*1.22*
Healthcare												
Biopharmaceuticals	174	25.3	483	34.5	152	27.5	911.0	42.2	5.99	441	36.8	1.90
Healthcare services	4	0.6	4	0.3	3	0.5	2.0	0.1	0.65	3	0.3	0.36
Medical devices/equipment	67	9.7	119	8.5	56	10.1	215.5	10.0	3.85	103	8.6	1.86
Medical software & IS	17	2.5	21	1.5	14	2.5	25.9	1.2	1.85	17	1.4	1.47
Sub total	*262*	*38.0*	*627*	*44.7*	*225*	*40.7*	*1154.4*	*53.5*	*5.13*	*564*	*47.0*	*1.87*
Information technology												
Communications & networks	49	7.1	116	8.3	41	7.4	213.0	9.9	5.19	103	8.6	2.03
Electronics & computers	48	7.0	86	6.1	41	7.4	97.6	4.5	2.38	77	6.4	1.17
Information services	37	5.4	54	3.9	16	2.9	40.9	1.9	2.56	23	1.9	1.55
Semiconductors	20	2.9	46	3.3	17	3.1	73.5	3.4	4.32	43	3.6	1.51
Software	173	25.1	305	21.8	139	25.1	320.1	14.8	2.30	257	21.4	1.18
Sub total	*327*	*47.5*	*607*	*43.3*	*254*	*45.9*	*745.0*	*34.5*	*2.93*	*503*	*41.9*	*1.40*
Other												
Adv. spec. mat. & chem.	19	2.8	30	2.1	14	2.5	34.5	1.6	2.47	22	1.8	1.44
Energy	21	3.0	59	4.2	16	2.9	141.6	6.6	8.85	48	4.0	2.50
Other companies	6	0.9	9	0.6	4	0.7	8.4	0.4	2.10	7	0.6	1.20
Sub total	*46*	*6.7*	*98*	*7.0*	*34*	*6.1*	*184.5*	*8.6*	*5.43*	*77*	*6.4*	*2.08*

Table 5.3: Composition of the dataset over origin and type of venture capitalists
This table illustrates the composition of the used dataset regarding the origin and type of involved venture capitalists. Therefore, the number of dyads and the average volume per investor was analyzed. In case of syndicated investments a dyad is defined for each participating investor and the respective new venture. To calculate the investment volume per investor, it was assumed that each investor participating in a financing round contributes equally to the total amount raised and also business angels, undisclosed investors, and investors without address information were considered.

	Full sample (dyads)		Sample with reported inv. vol. in m€ (dyads)		
	Obs.	%	Obs.	%	Vol./Investor
Total	1402	100.0	1200	100.0	1.65
Origin of venture capitalist					
Germany	1173	83.7	997	83.1	1.55
Switzerland	66	4.7	61	5.1	2.10
United Kingdom	41	2.9	31	2.6	2.66
France	30	2.1	28	2.3	2.04
United States	28	2.0	27	2.3	2.58
Netherlands	15	1.1	14	1.2	1.68
Denmark	14	1.0	13	1.1	1.97
Belgium	10	0.7	8	0.7	2.18
Austria	9	0.6	8	0.7	1.45
Sweden	6	0.4	4	0.3	3.17
Luxembourg	3	0.2	2	0.2	3.20
Spain	3	0.2	3	0.3	1.54
Norway	2	0.1	2	0.2	1.17
Italy	1	0.1	1	0.1	1.95
Poland	1	0.1	1	0.1	0.71
Type of venture capitalist					
Venture capitalists with exclusively financial objectives					
Independent venture capitalists	932	66.5	798	66.5	1.82
Subs. of a financial corporation	72	5.1	64	5.3	1.86
Other	2	0.1	2	0.2	1.58
Sub total	*1006*	*71.8*	*864*	*72.0*	*1.82*
Corporate venture capitalists	98	7.0	87	7.3	1.46
Sub total	*98*	*7.0*	*87*	*7.3*	*1.46*
(Quasi-)public venture capitalists					
MBG	7	0.5	7	0.6	0.71
Subs. of savings/coop. banks	54	3.9	45	3.8	0.94
Subs. of state banks or coop. central institutes	52	3.7	48	4.0	1.38
Subs. of inst. promoting economic development	137	9.8	107	8.9	1.16
Other German government	48	3.4	42	3.5	1.08
Sub total	*298*	*21.3*	*249*	*20.8*	*1.14*

5.1.3 Measurement and Definition of Variables

5.1.3.1 Spatial Proximity

As discussed in section 2.2.1, various measures of spatial proximity like spherical air distance, car distance, or car travel time exist and have been previously proposed in the literature.[865] However, these measures have the common weakness of providing very large values for longer distances, especially for intercontinental relationships. These long distances do not represent actual travel times if good flight connections exist. In order to represent spatial proximity more realistically, one has to estimate the shortest travel time which can be achieved with different means of transport including car or air plane. In consequence, this dataset is the first that includes a flight option and investigates the minimum travel time for each dyad as the primary measure of spatial proximity between the venture capitalist and the new venture.

By including a flight option, this study adequately accounts for long distances between the venture capitalist and the new venture. As a result it is also possible to realistically include international and especially intercontinental relationships in the analysis.

The minimum travel time between the two parties of a specific dyad was determined as follows: First, Google Maps was used in order to collect the average travel time by car between the two parties' ZIP codes for all dyads.[866] Second, an additional flight option was investigated if the travel time by car was equal or greater than three hours.[867] For this purpose, each party of the respective dyads was assigned to an appropriate airport and the average flight time between the venture capitalist's and the new venture's airport was determined.[868] In addition, car travel times between the actors and their airports were collected using Google Maps. Then, the travel time was assumed to be the sum of the car travel time from the venture capitalist to its airport, a check-in time of 60 minutes, the average flight time to the venture's airport, a check-out time of 30 minutes and the car travel time from the airport to the venture. Finally, the smaller value of car or flight option was used as minimum travel time. In 33.2% of the dyads the flight option was finally used.

---

[865] Cf. Lerner (1995), p. 312; Sorenson/Stuart (2001), pp. 1563-1564; Fritsch/Schilder (2006), p. 5.

[866] Cf. Google (2009).

[867] For travel times by car less than three hours, the flight option was not considered because the total travel time using an air plane, which includes journeys to/from the airport, check-in and check-out times, as well as an average flight time of approximately one hour within Germany, is normally greater than three hours.

[868] The appropriate airport was assigned to each venture capitalist and portfolio company as follows: First, Germany was divided into 97 areas according to the first two digits of the five digit ZIP code (three of the potentially 100 areas are not assigned in Germany). Second, each of the areas was assigned to the closest of the 13 largest German airports. If there was no flight connection between two airports or if a foreign venture capitalist was involved, the optimal flight connection was investigated manually.

The travel time by car and the car distance was also collected as additional measures of spatial proximity in order to compare empirical results and to check their robustness. For American venture capitalists, the ground distance to their portfolio companies was calculated using http://www.indo.com/cgi-bin/dist. As the calculation of a minimum travel time by car is not meaningful for transatlantic dyads, those dyads were coded as missing values and not included in the dataset.

In case a venture capitalist runs several offices, it was assumed that the office located the closest to the new venture is in charge of the deal. This assumption is necessary as no information regarding the responsible office for a specific deal is available. This approach is also accepted by other authors and is likely to be valid in the vast majority of cases.[869] However, in some cases and especially for large investors it may be that investors concentrate their activities regarding certain investment stages or industries in different offices. Then, the assumption would not be valid. Since no information about the activities of each single VC office is available, the assumption is necessary. Moreover, the described scenario in which the assumption is not valid is expected to occur only in few cases and should thus only have minor impacts on empirical results.

Furthermore, it can be assumed that actors do not perceive and evaluate distance in a linear fashion. It is likely that a one hour increase in travel time from one hour to two hours does not have the same effect as a one hour increase from five to six hours. Hence, if the distance is included as an independent variable in the empirical models, it is included in the form of its natural logarithm.[870] In cases where the distance represents the dependent variable further transformations are necessary. These transformations will be discussed later in the respective section.

5.1.3.2 New Venture Characteristics

Venture development stage

The development stage of the new venture is measured by the new venture's age at the respective financing round's closing date and the round's investment stage as provided by VentureSource. Some companies had missing values regarding their founding dates and thus their age. These missing values were investigated using the LexisNexis database.[871]

---

[869] Cf. Lerner (1995), p. 312; Butler/Goktan (2007), p. 8.

[870] The inclusion of distance in the form of its natural logarithm is well accepted in the literature (cf. Sorenson/Stuart (2001), pp. 1564-1565; Butler/Goktan (2008), p. 42; Tian (2009), p. 31)

[871] Cf. LexisNexis (2008).

In the empirical models, the new venture's age is included in the form of its natural logarithm to account for the fact that the impact of growing experiences, networks, and the like does not increase linearly with rising age. At the beginning of a company's lifetime various new projects like the development of products, a company's strategy, and an appropriate organizational structure have to be conducted. Furthermore, numerous new relationships to suppliers, customers, employees, lawyers, banks, etc. have to be established. These activities lead to a strong relative growth of a company's experiences, networks, etc. in the first months and years. This growth is likely to diminish over time due to a saturation effect.

Regarding the round's investment stage three dummy variables for (i) seed, (ii) first, as well as (iii) second and later stage rounds according to the VentureSource round class definition have been established.[872]

Unfortunately, VentureSource only provides limited information regarding the size of the new venture. A good proxy for the new venture's size would be its number of employees at the time of the financing round. However, only the most recent available number of employees is provided by VentureSource. As many new ventures exhibit a strong growth over the time of a venture capitalists' involvement, this number is not appropriate. Hence, the size of the venture in the form of its number of employees is not included in the main empirical models. Another measure of a new venture's size would be its revenues at the time of investment. Unfortunately, this information is not available for most ventures.

Product development stage

The product development stage is measured by three dummy variables: "Business concept only" adopts the value of one if the stage of development according to VentureSource is start-up which means that the venture is in a conceptual phase and product development has not begun. "Product development / tests" is one for ventures that are currently developing one or more products but have not yet begun shipping. This corresponds to the VentureSource stages of development of product development as well as product in beta test or in clinical trials. "Shipping product / profitable" is one for ventures that ship at least one revenue-generating product or if the venture has reported that it is profitable. The VentureSource stages of development included in this group have the same name.

[872] See appendix A for a list of VentureSource round class definitions.

Prior experience of the entrepreneurial team

An entrepreneurial team is said to have profound prior experience if at least one member of the team had a high executive position in another company before he joined the entrepreneurial team of the respective venture. An executive position is regarded as high if the respective person had a position as chief executive officer (CEO), chief financial officer (CFO), chief operating officer (COO), managing director, director, president, or a position of a comparable level. Prior experience of the entrepreneurial team is measured by a dummy variable that adopts the value of one in the described cases.

Knowledge intensity

To measure different aspects of a new venture's knowledge intensity like asset intangibility, R&D intensity, or the level of future growth options, a similar approach to Gompers (1995) was chosen.[873] Because individual accounting data of portfolio companies is not available, generic industry variables for each new venture were constructed. Annual industry averages for each GICS code (Global Industry Classification Standard) were calculated by using all German companies listed in the Thomson ONE Banker database. The six digit GICS group was used if the eight digit GICS group had fewer than four companies. In case there were still not enough companies in one group, the level was further reduced until at least four companies were in the group. Following this procedure, annual industry variables for the asset intangibility (intangibles to total assets), R&D intensity (R&D expenses to total assets), and growth options (book to market ratio) were calculated.[874] In addition, each new venture of the sample was assigned to an eight digit GICS code according to its VentureSource industry code. Finally, the data were matched by date and industry to each financing round. To differentiate between ventures that are likely to be characterized by high asset intangibility, high R&D intensity, or substantial future growth options, three dummy variables were constructed. These variables indicate whether a venture's industry is in the top percentile of asset intangibility or R&D intensity or whether it is in the bottom percentile in terms of book to market ratios.[875]

---

[873] Cf. Gompers (1995), p. 1469.

[874] Other authors frequently use the market to book ratio to measure a company's future growth options (cf. Myers (1977), 150; Gompers (1995), pp. 1466-1467). However, some benchmark companies have very small or even negative book values as reported by Thomson ONE Banker. This leads to very high or even negative market to book ratios and makes an interpretation impossible. Hence, the book to market ratio has been used.

[875] To determine the top, respectively bottom, percentile the distribution of the industry variables over the whole sample of financing rounds was used.

Region

To differentiate between East and West German new ventures, a dummy variable was collected that adopts the value of one if the new venture is located in the former GDR according to its ZIP code.

Furthermore, a new venture is defined to be located in an urban area if the population density was greater or equal to 3000 inhabitants per square kilometer at the time of the financing round. To calculate the annual population density of each German district, the yearly number of each district's inhabitants and the size of its area was collected from the GENESIS database of the federal statistical office.[876] Finally, a dummy variable that adopts the value of one if a venture was located in an urban area at the time of the financing round was constructed. Figure B.1 in the appendix shows the distribution of VC financing rounds in regard to the population density of the new venture's district.

5.1.3.3 Venture Capitalist Characteristics

Size

The size of a venture capitalist was measured by its assets under management in million Euro as provided by VentureSource. Unfortunately, VentureSource only provides the last available amount of a venture capitalist's assets under management. However, several plausibility checks revealed that the information which was provided in March 2007 does not deviate much from a venture capitalist's assets under management in 2004, which represents the middle of the analyzed time period. Hence, it can be expected that a venture capitalist's assets under management do not fundamentally change from year to year and that the provided information can be used as a proxy for a venture capitalist's size.

For several venture capitalists information about its assets under management was missing. Hence, the missing data was investigated for the year 2004 using the Directory of EVCA Members, the Financial Yearbook Germany, the Thomson ONE Banker database, or an extensive web research in this order. If the data was not available for the year 2004, the data which was available and closest to this year was chosen.[877]

The effects of an absolute increase in a venture capitalist's size are expected to diminish with increasing size. It is rather likely that the relative change of the venture capitalist's size impacts the importance of spatial proximity in VC financing. Thus, venture capitalist's size in

[876] Cf. Statistisches Bundesamt Deutschland (2009).

[877] Cf. EVCA (various years-a); Anderer (various years).

terms of assets under management is included in the form of its natural logarithm in the empirical models. However, the linear form will also be tested for the sake of robustness.

Experience and reputation

As previously mentioned in section 4.3.3, the experience and reputation of a venture capitalist is likely to be highly correlated with the age of the investor.[878] Hence, the venture capitalist's age at the time of the financing round was used as a proxy for these variables. The respective age was calculated as the time difference of the closing date and July 1st of the venture capitalist's founding year. However, some venture capitalists report very early founding years. In most cases these are captive venture capitalists that report the founding year of their holding company.[879] Since considerable VC activities did not start before the mid-1970s in the US and the 1980s in Germany, the venture capitalist's founding year was set to 1970 if he had reported an earlier one.[880] For some venture capitalists information regarding their founding dates and thus their age was not available from VentureSource. These missing values were investigated using the database of BVK Members on the BVK website, the Thomson ONE Banker database, or an extensive web research in this order.[881]

Similar to the argumentation for the new venture's age it is expected that the impact of growing experience, networks, and reputation does not increase linearly with rising age of a venture capitalist. It is likely that an incremental increase of experience and reputation has a greater impact for newly founded venture capitalists that have no track-record compared to venture capitalists that are well established in the industry. Thus, the venture capitalist's age is included in the form of its natural logarithm in the empirical models. However, it was not possible to formulate a clear hypothesis regarding the impact of the venture capitalist's age on the importance of spatial proximity. In consequence, also alternative functional forms of the impact of the venture capitalist's age will be tested in the empirical models.

Specialization

To measure the specialization across different industries and investment stages, and thus to characterize the portfolio strategy of a venture capitalist, Herfindahl-Hirschman Indices (HHI)

---

[878] Cf. Gorman/Sahlman (1989), p. 233; Sahlman (1990), p. 500; Gompers (1996), p. 136.

[879] Examples are Sal. Oppenheim & Cie KGaA who reports 1789 or the Credit Suisse First Boston who reports 1856 as their respective founding years.

[880] Cf. BVK (1995), p. 14; Nathusius (2001), p. 53; Gompers/Lerner (2004), pp. 1 and 8-9.

[881] Cf. BVK (2008a).

were calculated.[882] The HHI goes back to Herfindahl (1950) and Hirschman (1945) and is a standard measure for all kinds of economic concentration.[883] The main advantages of the HHI are that it is a one-dimensional measure and thus unambiguous, that it is independent of underlying scales and varies between zero and one, and that it reflects changes in the number of different classes as well as in the distribution of shares across classes.[884]

In order to measure the industry specialization of each venture capitalist, the distribution of his realized investment rounds across the VentureSource industry segments in the whole sample time period was analyzed. VentureSource classifies each venture into one of 16 different industry segments. Table 5.2 in section 5.1.2 gives an overview about the distribution of investment rounds across the different industry segments. To measure the stage specialization of a venture capitalist, the distribution of his realized investment rounds across the VentureSource round classes in the whole sample period was analyzed. VentureSource classifies each investment round as either seed, first, second or later stage round. Table 5.1 in section 5.1.2 gives an overview about the distribution of investment rounds across the different investment stages. An HHI was only calculated for those venture capitalists which participated in at least three investment rounds throughout the sample period.[885]

To calculate the industry or stage HHI for a specific investor *i*, the fraction of investment rounds per industry / stage *k* was determined for each of the *K* industries / stages over all investment rounds R_i of the investor. The respective fractions were then squared and summed up:

$$Industry\ or\ stage\ HHI_i = \sum_{k=1}^{K} \left(\frac{\sum_{r_i=1}^{R_i} f_{kr_i}}{R_i} \right)^2$$

with k = $1,2,\ldots,K$ industry segments / investment stages

r_i = $1,2,\ldots,R_i$ investment rounds of venture capitalist *i*

$$f_{kri} = \begin{cases} 1 & \text{if the investment round } r_i \text{ belongs to industry segment / stage } k \\ 0 & \text{otherwise} \end{cases}$$

---

[882] Cf. Lossen (2007), pp. 44-45.

[883] Cf. Hirschman (1945) and Herfindahl (1950) cited in Lossen (2007), p. 44.

[884] Cf. Hall/Tideman (1967), pp. 163-165.

[885] Different thresholds regarding the minimum number of investment rounds in order to calculate a HHI have been tested. The results turned out to be robust in respect to these different thresholds.

In consequence, a HHI of 1 indicates a very high specialization (i.e. a venture capitalist investing in only one industry or stage) and a HHI close to 0 indicates a very high diversification.

Type

The type of a venture capitalist was determined by an analysis of his shareholder structure. Most of the venture capitalists report their shareholder structure to the BVK which publishes them on their website.[886] In case a venture capitalist was not included, a web research was conducted or the venture capitalist was contacted directly. Thus, it was possible to classify each venture capitalist into one of the following groups: venture capitalists with exclusively financial objectives (i.e. independent venture capitalists, subsidiaries of private financial corporations, and others), corporate venture capitalists (i.e. subsidiaries of non-financial corporations), and (quasi-)public venture capitalists (MBGs, subsidiaries of savings or cooperative banks, state banks, promotional banks, and other institutions linked to the German government).[887] In the empirical models, a dummy variable was included for each of these groups.

Lead-investor

To differentiate between lead- and co-investors, a dummy variable that adopts the value of one for lead-investors was created based on the data provided by VentureSource.

5.1.3.4 Investment Round Characteristics

Investment volume

To test the impact of the investment volume on the patterns in spatial proximity and the likelihood of distant investments, it is assumed that each venture capitalist contributes equally to the total amount raised in a financing round. Thus, the investment volume per venture capitalist is determined by dividing the total amount raised as provided by VentureSource by the number of participating investors in a financing round.[888]

---

[886] Cf. BVK (2008a).

[887] See also section 2.1.3 and Achleitner et al. (2009), p. 444.

[888] For the calculation of the investment volume per venture capitalist also business angels, undisclosed investors, and investors without address information have been considered. As previously discussed, no dyads were constructed for these investors.

Hypothesis 11a and 11b suggest an inverted u-shaped effect in regard to the impact of the investment volume on the importance of spatial proximity. In consequence, the investment volume will be included in its linear form in combination with a quadratic form in order to test the proposed inverted u-shaped effect.

Syndication

The benefit of syndication to overcome the distance between a venture capitalist and his investee was measured by the ratio of the venture capitalist's distance to the portfolio company and the distance of the closest syndication partner to the portfolio company.

$$Syndication\ benefit = \frac{VC\ investor's\ distance + 1}{Distance\ of\ closest\ syndication\ partner + 1} - 1$$

The numerator as well as the denominator were increased by one in order to avoid a division by zero and to cause the syndication benefit to be zero if the venture capitalist's distance is equal to the distance of the closest syndication partner.[889] In order to test the robustness of this construct, also further variables were constructed: The first variable is a count variable of the number of syndication partners in an investment round. The second variable is a dummy variable that indicates if the venture capitalist is located far away from the venture, but a close syndication partner exists. This variable equals one if the closest syndication partner is located within 30 minutes and if the focal venture capitalist is located further than three hours from the investee. Finally, the impact of the difference between a venture capitalist's distance to the portfolio company and the distance of the syndication partner located closest to the respective portfolio company as suggested by Fritsch/Schilder (2006) is tested.[890]

Consecutive financing rounds

A discrete variable indicating the count number of the follow on financing round of an investor was generated. The variable has a value of zero for a first time investment of a specific venture capitalist into a new venture, one for the first follow on investment of this investor into the same new venture, two for the second, and so forth.

---

[889] The distance might refer to the minimum travel time, the car travel time, or the car distance depending on the respective model.

[890] Cf. Fritsch/Schilder (2006), p. 12.

5.1.3.5 Control Variables

To control for further effects influencing spatial proximity between venture capitalists and portfolio companies, several control variables were collected.

VC market condition

To control for changes in the general VC market condition, the total German VC fundraising in the previous calendar year and the total German VC investments in the calendar year of the respective financing round were collected from the EVCA.[891] These variables were included in the form of their natural logarithm in the empirical models because it is expected that relative rather than absolute changes impact the importance of spatial proximity.

Economic environment for new ventures

The economic environment for new ventures is measured by the discrete return of the Morgan Stanley Capital International (MSCI) Germany Small Cap (SC) Index over the last twelve months before the respective financing round. The variables MSCI Germany Small Cap Index was collected from DataStream.

Number of venture capitalist's offices

The venture capitalist's total number of offices as provided by VentureSource was included to control for effects in the patterns in spatial proximity between both parties which are simply induced by multiple offices.

Table 5.4 summarizes all variables as well as their measures, scales, and units.

[891] Data of the EVCA industry statistic which refers to the fundraising and investments by German venture capitalists has been collected. Cf. EVCA (various years-b).

Table 5.4: Summary of variables

This table provides a summary of analyzed variables. Econ. dev.: economic development; excl.: exclusively; inh.: inhabitants; ind. av.: industry average; prof.: profitable; pop. dens.: population density; pos.: position.

Variable	Measure	Scale	Unit
Proximity / distance	Minimum travel time (car/plane)	Metric	Ln(minutes)
	Travel time (car)	Metric	Ln(minutes)
	Distance (car)	Metric	Ln(km)
Venture			
Venture development stage			
Age	Age of venture	Metric	Ln(years)
Investment stage	Seed round	Dummy	Seed (1)
	First round	Dummy	First (1)
	Second or later stage round	Dummy	Later (1)
Size	Number of employees	Metric	Ln(employees)
Product development stage	Business concept only	Dummy	Concept only (1)
	Product development/tests	Dummy	Prod.dev./tests (1)
	Shipping product/profitable	Dummy	Shipping/prof. (1)
Prior experience of the entrepreneurial team	Previous high executive position	Dummy	Prior exec. pos. (1)
Industry's knowledge intensity			
Asset intangibility	Top 10% of ind. av. of intangible assets/ total assets	Dummy	High (1)
R&D intensity	Top 10% ind. av. of R&D exp./total assets	Dummy	High (1)
Future growth options	Bottom 10% ind. av. of book to market ratio	Dummy	Low (1)
Region			
East / West	Venture located in east Germany	Dummy	East (1)
Urban Area	Venture located in urban area (pop. dens. of district >= 3000 Inh./km²)	Dummy	Urban (1)
Venture capitalist			
Size	Assets under management	Metric	Ln(million Euro)
Experience / reputation	Age of venture capitalist	Metric	Ln(years)
Specialization			
Industry	HHI of industry concentration among inv.	Metric	
Stage	HHI of stage concentration among inv.	Metric	
Type			
Venture capitalists with excl. financial objectives	Venture capitalist is indep. venture capitalist, subs. of a private financial corporation, or another venture capitalist	Dummy	Indep. VC (1)
Corporate investor	Venture capitalist is corporate investor	Dummy	CVC (1)
(Quasi-)public venture capitalists	Venture capitalist is MBG, subs. of savings/ coop. bank, subs. of state bank or coop. central inst., subs. of inst. promoting econ. dev., or other government	Dummy	(Quasi-)public (1)
Lead-investor	Investor is lead-investor	Dummy	Lead-inv. (1)
Round			
Investment volume	Investment volume per venture capitalist	Metric	Million Euro
Syndication	Ratio of venture capitalist's distance and distance of the closest syndication partner	Metric	
Consecutive round	Number of previous rounds in which investor was involved	Ordinal	1 (2nd) to X

Table 5.4 cont.: Summary of variables

Variable	Measure	Scale	Unit
Control variables			
VC market condition			
VC fundraising	German VC fundraising in previous year	Metric	Euro (m)
VC investments	German VC investments in calendar year	Metric	Euro
Economic environment			
Market return	Discrete return of MSCI Germany Small Cap Index in 12 months before closing	Metric	
Venture capitalist's offices	Number of venture capitalist's offices	Metric	Offices
Calendar year	Year of closing	Dummy	Year (1)

5.1.4 Summary Statistics

Summary statistics for the variables used in the empirical analyses are shown in Table 5.5. These statistics are based on venture capitalist-investee dyads. The mean natural logarithm (ln) of the minimum travel time and the car travel time between venture capitalists and their investees is equivalent to 71.2 minutes and 78.0 minutes respectively. The mean ln of the car distance in equivalent to 107.9 km.

The average ln of financed new ventures corresponds to 3.2 years and the average ln of the number of employees corresponds to 30.3. This fairly high average number of employees already indicates possible problems due to the drawbacks of the measurement of this variable discussed in section 5.1.3.2. Regarding the venture capitalist, the mean ln of its size in terms of assets under management is equivalent to 157.6 million Euro. Furthermore, the average venture capitalist is 9.0 years in business and has an industry and stage specialization of 0.43. On average, each venture capitalist invests about 1.65 million Euro per financing round. The mean ln of the German VC fundraising in the previous calendar year and the German VC investments of the current calendar year corresponds to 1.15 and 1.05 billion Euro respectively.

Table 5.5: Summary statistics for variables used in empirical analyses
This table provides summary statistics for the dependent and independent variables. Variables are defined in Table 5.4. For dummy variables the mean column reports the frequency of observations. Ger.: Germany; ltm: last twelve months; tr.: travel.

Variable	Mean	Median	S.D.	Min.	Max.	Obs.
Proximity / Distance						
Ln(1+min. travel time in min.)	4.28	4.78	1.40	0.00	7.06	1402
Ln(1+car travel time in min.)	4.37	4.73	1.51	0.00	6.91	1374
Ln(1+car distance in km)	4.69	5.28	1.97	0.00	9.18	1402

Table 5.5 cont.: Summary statistics for variables used in empirical analyses

Variable	Mean	Median	S.D.	Min.	Max.	Obs.
Venture						
Venture development stage						
Ln(age in years)	1.15	1.38	1.14	-4.51	3.16	1402
Dummy seed stage round	0.03	0.00	0.17	0.00	1.00	1402
Dummy first round	0.27	0.00	0.44	0.00	1.00	1402
Dummy later stage round	0.70	1.00	0.46	0.00	1.00	1402
Ln(number of employees)	3.41	3.43	0.86	0.00	6.50	1355
Product development stage						
Dummy business concept only	0.02	0.00	0.14	0.00	1.00	1402
Dummy product development/tests	0.35	0.00	0.48	0.00	1.00	1402
Dummy shipp.prod./profitable	0.63	1.00	0.48	0.00	1.00	1402
Dummy prior exec. experience	0.41	0.00	0.49	0.00	1.00	1402
Industry's knowledge intensity						
Dummy high asset intangibility	0.11	0.00	0.31	0.00	1.00	1402
Dummy high R&D intensity	0.13	0.00	0.34	0.00	1.00	1402
Dummy low book/market	0.11	0.00	0.31	0.00	1.00	1402
Region						
Dummy East German venture	0.25	0.00	0.43	0.00	1.00	1402
Dummy urban venture location	0.25	0.00	0.43	0.00	1.00	1402
Venture capitalist						
Ln(assets under management in m€)	5.06	4.83	1.94	0.69	10.57	1256
Ln(age in years)	1.79	1.76	0.99	-3.13	3.60	1375
Specialization						
HHI industry	0.43	0.34	0.23	0.19	1.00	1200
HHI stage	0.43	0.40	0.14	0.25	1.00	1200
Type						
Dummy VC with excl. fin. objectives	0.72	1.00	0.45	0.00	1.00	1402
Dummy corporate VC	0.07	0.00	0.26	0.00	1.00	1402
Dummy (quasi-)public VC	0.21	0.00	0.41	0.00	1.00	1402
Dummy lead-investor	0.36	0.00	0.48	0.00	1.00	1402
Round						
Investment volume per VC (m€)	1.65	1.20	1.46	0.01	14.97	1200
Syndication						
Syndication benefit (min. tr. time)	12.74	0.00	52.09	0.00	816.00	1402
Syndication benefit (car tr. time)	16.24	0.00	72.03	0.00	996.00	1374
Syndication benefit (car distance)	61.90	0.00	428.71	0.00	9463.00	1402
No. of consecutive round	0.78	0.00	1.01	0.00	7.00	1402
Control variables						
VC market condition						
Ln(Ger. VC fundraising in m€ (t-1))	7.05	6.92	0.58	6.41	7.81	1402
Ln(Ger. VC investments in m€)	6.96	6.87	0.24	6.56	7.20	1402
Return of MSCI SC Germany (ltm)	0.08	0.16	0.32	-0.46	0.83	1402
Venture capitalist's no. of offices	3.64	1.00	8.08	1.00	37.00	1402

To complement the understanding of the different measures of spatial proximity between venture capitalists and their portfolio companies, Table 5.6 displays summary statistics of the untransformed original measures for the whole sample and for lead- and co-investors separately. Table B.1 in appendix 0 shows further summary statistics of the untransformed original measures of the other metric variables. The average minimum travel time and the average car travel time of venture capitalists to their portfolio companies is 135.3 minutes and 167.1 minutes respectively. The average car distance is 437.1 km. As can be seen in Table 5.6, lead-investors are on average closer to their portfolio companies, while the median does not differ much. This is caused by the fact that the maximum distance of co-investors is larger than for lead-investors. A more differentiated analysis of patterns in spatial proximity between venture capitalists and investees and the impact of a venture capitalist's role within syndicated investment follows in subsequent sections.

Table 5.6: Summary statistics for original measures of spatial proximity
This table provides summary statistics for different measures of spatial proximity and different subsamples.

Variable	Mean	Median	S.D.	Min.	Max.	Obs.
Min. travel time (min.)						
Total	135.31	118.00	133.45	0	1166	1402
Lead-investors	124.87	116.00	109.60	0	974	504
Co-investors	141.16	118.50	144.87	0	1166	898
Car travel time (min.)						
Total	167.11	112.00	171.00	0	997	1374
Lead-investors	161.27	113.50	162.66	0	723	500
Co-investors	170.45	112.00	175.60	0	997	874
Car distance (km)						
Total	437.11	195.00	1106.08	0	9672	1402
Lead-investors	331.63	195.50	680.23	0	9189	504
Co-investors	496.30	195.00	1281.24	0	9672	898

5.1.5 Possible Selection Biases

To be able to generalize empirical findings, it is important to analyze to which extent the sample represents the population of German VC investments. The representativeness would be highest if one had a perfect random sample of the population. However, the used sample was collected from VentureSource which contains mainly self-reported data from venture capitalists.[892] Hence, there might be a selection bias regarding the type of venture capitalists that report data to VentureSource and the type of investments which these venture capitalists report to the database. For the US, Kaplan/Sensoy/Strömberg (2002) find that VentureSource reports a largely unbiased sample in terms of the amount of financing as well as the industry

[892] Cf. Kaplan/Sensoy/Strömberg (2002), p. 1.

structure and performance of portfolio companies.[893] However, the coverage of the database might differ across countries due to their particularities. In consequence, the aim of this section is to compare the structure of the sample with the population of German VC investments in order to evaluate the representativeness of the sample.

One of the most comprehensive data sources regarding the German VC market is the BVK. The BVK cooperates with the EVCA in compiling national and European VC statistics but offers more detailed statistics regarding particular investment stages (VC vs. PE) and specific German industry players (e.g. MBGs).

Table 5.7 depicts the composition of the used sample and BVK data over time and investment stages in terms of financed companies and investment volume.[894] Regarding the number of financed companies about 36.7% of the sample was financed in early investment stages (seed or first rounds). The BVK reported that 43.5% of the companies were in early investment stages. The remaining companies were financed in second or later stages (expansion stage). Hence, the sample seems to slightly under-represent early investment stages.[895] This leads to the fact that the sample represents about 11.7% of the early stage companies and 15.6% of the expansion stage companies covered by the BVK. The sum over all investment stages simply adds-up the financed companies of the different stages, while the total corrects for double counting if a company received two financing rounds in one year. The BVK does not correct for double counting of financed companies across different investment stages. Thus, the sum is used to compare the coverage over all investment stages. Overall, the sample represents about 13.9% of the companies covered by the BVK. Furthermore, the used sample represents a higher fraction of companies in 2003 and a slightly lower share in 2006.

Regarding the investment volume about 27.9% of the sample volume and 34.9% of the volume reported by the BVK was invested in early investment stages. The remaining volume was invested in second or later stages (expansion stage). Hence, the sample also seems to slightly under-represent early investment stages in terms of volume. Concerning quantity, the sample covers a much higher fraction of the BVK data in terms of volume compared to number of companies. The sample represents about 33.2% of the early stage volume and 45.9% of the expansion stage volume covered by the BVK. Overall, the sample represents about 41.5% of the investment volume covered by the BVK. Again, the sample represents a higher fraction of the BVK volume in 2003 and a lower share in 2006.

---

[893] Cf. Kaplan/Sensoy/Strömberg (2002), pp. 1-2 and 21.

[894] The BVK does not report statistics regarding the number of financing rounds. Hence, comparisons were made in terms of financed companies. This leads to slightly different numbers compared to Table 5.1.

[895] Unfortunately, VentureSource and BVK definitions of the different investment stages do not perfectly match. In consequence, the results of this analysis only have an indicative character and it is not possible to go into more detail.

Table 5.7: Structural comparison of the sample and BVK data regarding time and investment stages
This table compares the used sample and BVK data over time and investment stages in terms of financed companies and investment volume. The sum simply adds-up the financed companies of the different stages, while the total corrects for double counting if a company received two financing rounds in one year. The BVK does not correct for double counting across different investment stages. Thus, the sum is used to compare the coverage over all investment stages.

	Number of companies							Investment volume (m€)						
Stage	2002	2003	2004	2005	2006	Total	%	2002	2003	2004	2005	2006	Total	%
	Full sample							Sample with reported investment volume						
Seed Round	14	5	2	4	5	30	4.4	6.5	2.1	1.2	1.8	5.3	16.8	0.8
First Round	73	41	40	36	29	219	32.3	150.7	101.2	154.9	101.4	64.1	572.2	27.1
Early stage	*87*	*46*	*42*	*40*	*34*	*249*	*36.7*	*157.1*	*103.3*	*156.1*	*103.2*	*69.4*	*589.0*	*27.9*
Second/later stage	*129*	*89*	*81*	*75*	*56*	*430*	*63.3*	*354.6*	*294.8*	*273.6*	*351.1*	*246.9*	*1520.9*	*72.1*
Sum	*216*	*135*	*123*	*115*	*90*	*679*	*100.0*	*511.8*	*398.0*	*429.7*	*454.3*	*316.2*	*2110.0*	*100.0*
Total	*210*	*133*	*118*	*113*	*90*	*664*								
	BVK							BVK						
Seed	95	28	26	20	68	237	4.8	76.8	27.0	21.9	6.6	31.2	163.5	3.2
Start-up	639	324	330	325	269	1887	38.6	484.0	265.5	331.6	298.3	233.1	1612.5	31.7
Early stage	*734*	*352*	*356*	*345*	*337*	*2124*	*43.5*	*560.8*	*292.5*	*353.5*	*304.9*	*264.3*	*1776.0*	*34.9*
Expansion stage	*805*	*441*	*490*	*521*	*507*	*2764*	*56.5*	*704.5*	*373.8*	*611.9*	*949.7*	*670.1*	*3310.0*	*65.1*
Sum/total	*1539*	*793*	*846*	*866*	*844*	*4888*	*100.0*	*1265.3*	*666.3*	*965.4*	*1254.6*	*934.4*	*5086.0*	*100.0*
	Sample / BVK (%)							Sample / BVK (%)						
Seed	14.7	17.9	7.7	20.0	7.4	12.7		8.4	7.6	5.6	27.3	17.0	10.3	
Start-up	11.4	12.7	12.1	11.1	10.8	11.6		31.1	38.1	46.7	34.0	27.5	35.5	
Early stage	*11.9*	*13.1*	*11.8*	*11.6*	*10.1*	*11.7*		*28.0*	*35.3*	*44.2*	*33.9*	*26.2*	*33.2*	
Expansion stage	*16.0*	*20.2*	*16.5*	*14.4*	*11.0*	*15.6*		*50.3*	*78.9*	*44.7*	*37.0*	*36.8*	*45.9*	
Sum	*14.0*	*17.0*	*14.5*	*13.3*	*10.7*	*13.9*		*40.4*	*59.7*	*44.5*	*36.2*	*33.8*	*41.5*	
Total	*13.6*	*16.8*	*13.9*	*13.0*	*10.7*	*13.6*								

The fact that the sample represents a much higher fraction of the BVK data in terms of volume compared to the number of companies implies that the average investment volume of the sample is higher compared to the BVK data. As mentioned above, this might be due to two reasons. First, specific types of venture capitalists might not report their investments to VentureSource to the same extent as other types of investors. Second, certain types of investments may not be reported to VentureSource to the same extent as other types of investments.

Unfortunately, the availability of statistics regarding the investment activities of different venture capitalist types is fairly limited. However, the BVK provides at least separate statistics for MBGs and provided separate statistics for corporate venture capitalists until 2003. Table 5.8 shows the composition of the used sample and BVK data over time and venture capitalist types in terms of financed companies and investment volume. Due to the high frequency of syndicated investments it is necessary to correct for double counting in calculating the total. Hence, the fractions of MBGs and other investors do not add-up to 100 percent. Furthermore, it is not possible to calculate the number of companies financed by other venture capitalists as a residual value. In the used sample MBGs are involved as investors in only about 1.1% of the financed companies. In contrast, BVK data suggests that MBGs are involved as investors in about 42.8%. However, one could also argue that investments of MBGs are likely to be over-represented in the BVK data because the analysis in section 2.1.3 uncovered that all MBGs are organized in the BVK but by far not all private venture capitalists. Nevertheless, the used sample is not representative regarding investments of MBGs. In terms of investment volume Table 5.8 offers a similar picture. Only 0.3% of the volume was invested by MBGs within the used sample, while 14.6% of the volume was invested by MBGs according to the BVK data.[896] This underlines the fact that the used sample is not representative regarding investments of MBGs. The statistics for corporate venture capitalists from 2002 and 2003 (not reported in Table 5.8) suggest that corporate venture capitalists are well represented by the sample in terms of financed companies and investment volume.

Furthermore, Table 5.8 and Table 5.3 suggest that MBGs on average invest smaller amounts compared to other investors. According to BVK data, MBGs are involved as investors in 42.8% of the financed companies but contribute only 14.6% of the total investment volume. In addition, the average investment volume per investor and round is 0.71 million Euro for MBGs compared to 1.82 million Euro for venture capitalists with exclusively financial objectives. These facts explain, at least partly, the difference in the sample's coverage in terms of financed companies and investment volume.

---

[896] To calculate to investment volume of specific investors it was assumed that all members of a syndicated investment contribute equally to the total amount raised of the financing round. See also section 5.1.3.4.

Table 5.8: Structural comparison of the sample and BVK data regarding venture capitalist type
This table compares the used sample and BVK data regarding the venture capitalist type in terms of financed companies and investment volume. The total is corrected for double counting across different venture capitalist types.

	Number of companies							Investment volume (m€)						
Venture capitalist type	2002	2003	2004	2005	2006	Total	%	2002	2003	2004	2005	2006	Total	%
	Full sample							Sample with reported investment volume						
MBGs	1		2	3	1	7	1.1	0.4		2.1	1.2	1.3	5.0	0.3
Other venture capitalists	210	133	118	113	90	664	100.0	483.1	366.9	382.8	416.0	283.4	1932.2	99.7
Total	*210*	*133*	*118*	*113*	*90*	*664*	*100.0*	*483.5*	*366.9*	*385.0*	*417.2*	*284.6*	*1937.2*	*100.0*
	BVK							BVK						
MBGs	491	414	346	423	416	2090	42.8	191.2	143.0	149.8	124.1	134.8	742.9	14.6
Other venture capitalists	na	na	na	na	na	na	na	1074.1	523.3	815.6	1130.5	799.6	4343.1	85.4
Total	*1539*	*793*	*846*	*866*	*844*	*4888*	*100.0*	*1265.3*	*666.3*	*965.4*	*1254.6*	*934.4*	*5086.0*	*100.0*
	Sample / BVK (%)							Sample / BVK (%)						
MBGs	0.2	0.0	0.6	0.7	0.2	0.3		0.2	0.0	1.4	1.0	0.9	0.7	
Other venture capitalists	na	na	na	na	na	na		45.0	70.1	46.9	36.8	35.4	44.5	
Total	*13.6*	*16.8*	*13.9*	*13.0*	*10.7*	*13.6*		*38.2*	*55.1*	*39.9*	*33.3*	*30.5*	*38.1*	

Regarding the types of investments reported by VentureSource it was further revealed that early stage investments are not that well covered by VentureSource compared to second or later stage (expansion stage) investments. Since early stage financing rounds are likely to be smaller compared to later stage financing rounds, this might also explain parts of the difference in the sample's coverage in terms of financed companies and investment volume.[897]

Unfortunately, the BVK and VentureSource use very different industry definitions which prevent a reliable comparison of the used sample with BVK data in regard to the industry structure. Furthermore, other non-observable investment characteristics might exist which determine the likelihood that an investment is reported to VentureSource.

As a result, the used sample slightly under-represents early stage investments compared to BVK data and is not representative for MBG investments. However, this also leads to the fact that the used sample better represents equity investments and thus "pure venture capital" investments as MBGs primarily use mezzanine financial instruments to invest in their portfolio companies.[898] The sample might also differ from the population of German VC investments in regard to other investment characteristics for which an analysis is not possible. However, these biases are not problematic if the empirical analysis controls for the respective characteristics. Most of the empirical models presented in later sections include variables for the investment stage, the venture capitalist type as well as various additional new venture, venture capitalist, and round characteristics.

---

[897] See Table 5.1 in section 5.1.2.

[898] Cf. Achleitner/Ehrhart/Zimmermann (2006), p. 65.

5.2 Patterns in Spatial Proximity between Venture Capitalists and Investees

This section investigates relationships between characteristics of ventures, venture capitalists and/or financing rounds and the actually observed spatial proximity/distance between venture capitalists and investees as presented in Figure 5.1. Thus, this section addresses research question one which was stated in section 1.1. The aim is to extend the understanding of the status quo of observable patterns in spatial proximity between the actors. In consequence, the analysis reveals which kinds of venture capitalist-investee dyads are likely to have smaller or larger distances between each other.

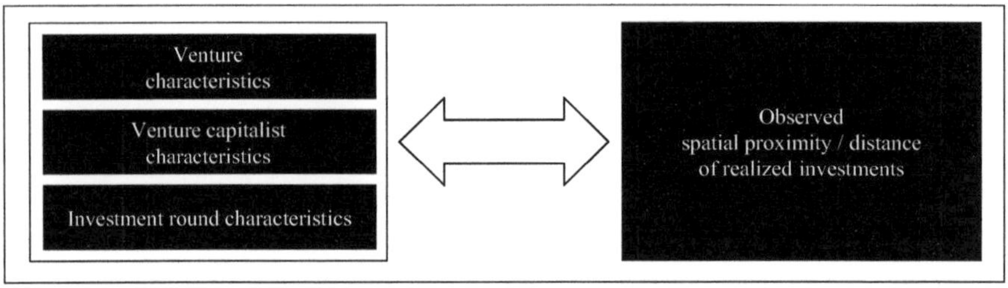

Figure 5.1: Factors related with observed patterns in spatial proximity between venture capitalists and investees
Source: Own illustration.

5.2.1 Empirical Strategy to Investigate Patterns in Spatial Proximity

To investigate the observed patterns in spatial proximity between venture capitalists and their German investees, and thus to test the hypotheses elaborated in section 4.3, bivariate as well as multivariate methods will be applied. To gain a first understanding of prevailing relationships, correlation analyses and Wilcoxon rank-sum tests will be conducted in the course of the bivariate analysis. However, with these methods it is not possible to test most hypotheses rigorously since bivariate analyses are not able to extract the effect of single variables under the ceteris-paribus assumption.[899] In consequence, also multivariate regressions of the distance between venture capitalists and investees on relevant variables will be conducted. Then, spatial proximity is regarded as dependent variable. However, it is important to note that this does not imply a causal relationship. Some new ventures and venture capitalists might intentionally choose their location and thus determine the spatial proximity to the other party. Nevertheless, in most cases it is likely that new ventures and venture capitalists have a given location and thus spatial proximity between each other. In this case, the spatial proximity might

[899] Cf. Wooldridge (2008), p. 68.

influence the likelihood of investment and thus the composition of the observed sample of realized investments. In consequence, the proposed multivariate regressions are able to reveal relationships under the ceteris paribus assumption, but it is not possible to detect causal effects. Further limitations of the analyses will be discussed in section 5.2.5.

Figure 5.2 shows the distribution of venture capitalist-investee dyads in regard to spatial proximity. All three measures reveal a high concentration of dyads with travel times below 30 minutes or a distance smaller than 40 km.[900] About 28.5% of all dyads have travel times smaller than 30 minutes between each other and for about 31.2% of all dyads the distance between both parties is less than 40 km. These facts might indicate a strong spatial bias of venture capitalists and/or investees in choosing their partners. The existence and magnitude of this potential spatial bias will be tested in subsequent sections. Furthermore, Figure 5.2 reveals that the different measures of spatial proximity and especially the minimum travel time, which is the primary measure of proximity of this thesis, are not normally distributed. All measures of spatial proximity are restricted to positive values. In addition, the distributions of the minimum travel time, and to a lesser extent also of the car travel time, exhibit multiple maxima. In the case of the minimum travel time this is due to the inclusion of the flight option which leads to many observations with a minimum travel time between three and four and a half hours. In consequence, ordinary least squares (OLS) and in case of multiple maxima even Tobit models are not appropriate to analyze the observed spatial proximity since the assumption of normally distributed error terms is likely to be violated. This might lead to false conclusions regarding the sampling distribution of the coefficient estimates.[901]

Despite these distributional problems, the travel times and distances can sensibly be divided in ordinal categories, which are easy to interpret and robust in regard to the distribution of the variable and potential outliers. Thus, ordered logistic (OL) regressions are used to test most of the hypotheses.

Each dyad was assigned to a certain category depending on its minimum travel time. The used categories are depicted in Figure 5.3. The first category contains all dyads with a minimum travel time from zero to half an hour which represents a very short distance and means that the venture is a taxi ride away. The second category (greater than half an hour to one and a half hours) represent relatively short car distances, while the third category (greater than one and a half hours to three hours) already contains quite substantial car distances. The forth category (greater than three to four hours) mainly contains national and European flight connections as well as longer car distances. Finally, the fifth category (greater than four hours) con-

---

[900] The first bar of all figures represents a travel time/distance of zero, which means that both parties are located in the same ZIP code area. The second bar represents a travel time/distance greater than 0 but smaller or equal than 15 min./20 km.

[901] Cf. Wooldridge (2008), pp. 117-119.

tains flight connections and very long car distances. Hence, an ordinal measure of minimum travel time was developed.

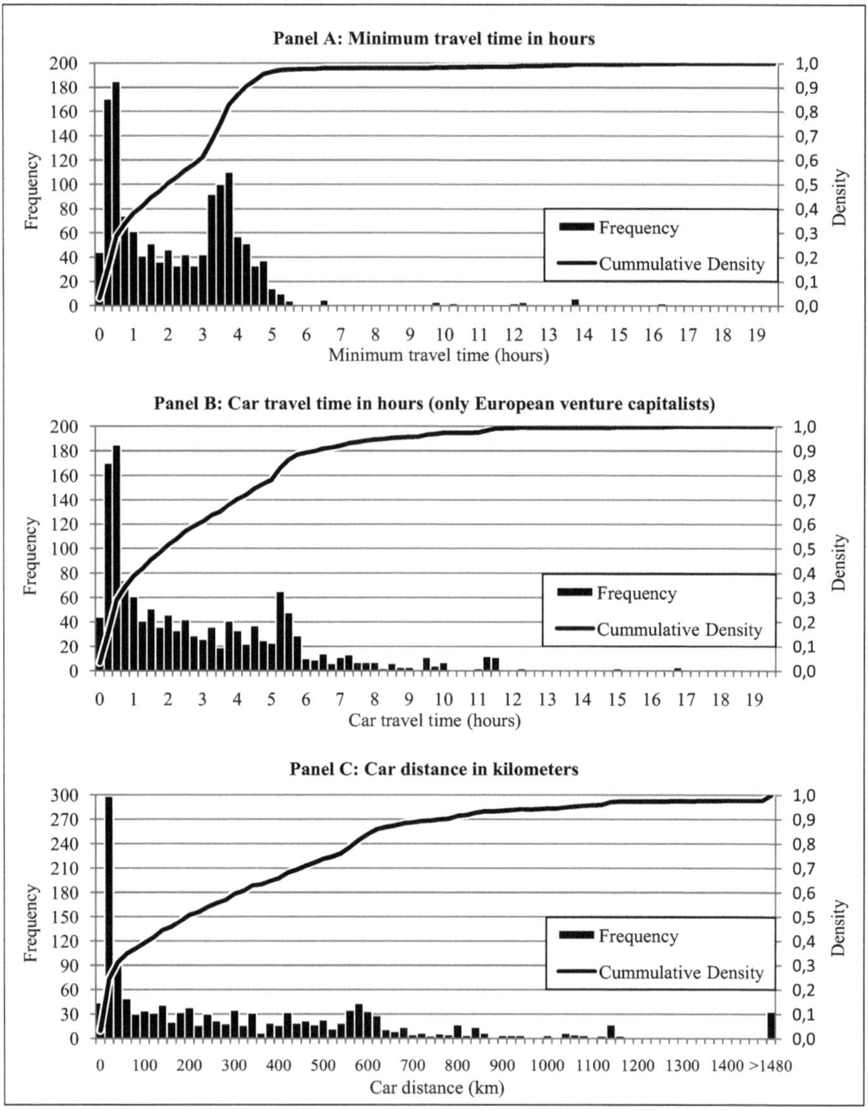

Figure 5.2: Distribution of venture capitalist-investee dyads in regard to spatial proximity

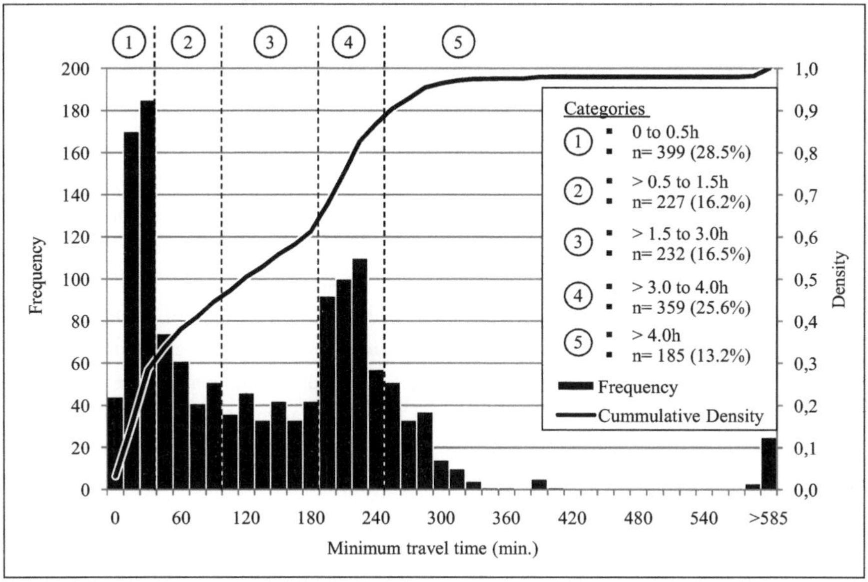

Figure 5.3: Categorization of minimum travel time

The car travel time and car distance will be mainly used to test the robustness of the proposed empirical models and are also classified into sensible categories.[902] Furthermore, OLS models which use the natural logarithm of one plus a specific measure of spatial proximity and Tobit models which use the original measures of spatial proximity as dependent variables will be used to evaluate the robustness of the results.[903]

5.2.2 First Bivariate Analyses

In this section, correlation analyses and Wilcoxon rank-sum tests[904] are conducted to explore bivariate relationships between the observed spatial proximity/distance and the corresponding

[902] For all measures of spatial proximity also alternative classifications were used to test the robustness of the models. Car travel time was classified into the following five groups: 0 to 0.5h, >0.5 to 1.5h, >1.5 to 3.0h, >3.0 to 5.0h, and >5h. Car distance was classified into the following five groups: 0 to 20km, >20 to 100km, >100 to 300km, >300 to 600km, and >600km.

[903] Including the dependent variable in the form of its natural logarithm mitigates the problem of having a strictly positive dependent variable and results are more robust in regard to outliers (cf. Wooldridge (2008), p. 191).

[904] The Wilcoxon rank-sum test is also known as the Mann-Whitney two-sample statistic (cf. Wilcoxon (1945), pp. 80-83; Mann/Whitney (1947), pp. 50-60).

number of realized investments as well as the spatial proximity/distance and the independent variables (certain characteristics of the venture, venture capitalist, and investment round and control variables).

Hypothesis 1a states that the number of observed VC investments decreases with increasing distance. Figure 5.2 graphically illustrates the distribution of venture capitalist-investee dyads in regard to different measures of distance and gives first indications that this relationship might be true. However, especially for the minimum travel time the relationship is not that clear since the distribution has multiple maxima. To rigorously test hypothesis 1a, variables were constructed that contain the frequency of observations within intervals of 15 minutes or 20 kilometers respectively.[905] Then, a correlation analysis for the number of observations and the mean distance of each interval was conducted. Table 5.9 depicts the results of this analysis. The Pearson product-moment correlation coefficients for the number of observations per interval and the mean distance of each interval are all negative and significantly different from zero at least at the 5% level. In addition, the absolute value of the correlation coefficients is fairly large for the mean minimum and car travel time. The relatively low absolute value of the coefficient for the mean car distance is due to the inclusion of very large values for transatlantic dyads.[906] In consequence, the null hypothesis that there is no linear relationship between the number of observed VC investments and distance is rejected. However, Figure 5.2 indicates that the relationship is likely to be non-linear. Hence, also Kendall's tau rank correlation coefficients were calculated since Kendall's tau does not imply strictly linear relationships and does not require the variables to be normally distributed. All coefficients are negative, economically significant and statistically significant different from zero at the level of 1%. In addition, correlation coefficients between the number of observations and the natural logarithm of the mean distance of each interval were calculated. The Pearson product-moment correlation coefficients have a higher absolute value compared to the coefficients of the original linear form and are all significant at the 1% level. This suggests that the natural logarithm of distance is an appropriate form to include distance in linear empirical models.[907]

As a result, Hypothesis 1a is supported in general. However, if distance is measured by the minimum travel time, an exception has to be made. As mentioned above, the distribution of dyads in regard to the minimum travel time has multiple maxima and is thus not strictly monotonic decreasing. This is due to the inclusion of the flight option which leads to many ob-

---

[905] The first interval contains all observations with travel times/distances below or equal to 15 min./20 km, the second interval contains all observations with travel times/distances greater than 15 min./20 km and below or equal to 30 min./40 km and so on.

[906] If the analysis is restricted to pure European dyads a Pearson product-moment correlation coefficient for the car distance of -0.4111 which is significant at the 1% level emerges.

[907] In addition, different sizes of the intervals were tested. All results remained unchanged.

servations with a minimum travel time between three and four and a half hours. In consequence, Hypothesis 1a does not hold for this time interval if distance is measured by the minimum travel time.

Table 5.9: Correlation between the number of observations and distance
This table presents Pearson product-moment correlation coefficients and Kendall's tau rank correlation coefficients between the interval mean of different measures for spatial proximity and the number of observations in that interval. The sample consists of 1402 dyads of venture capitalists and German portfolio companies which have closed a financing round between January 2002 and March 2007. Intervals have a size of 15 minutes or 20 kilometers respectively. Analyses with the car travel time exclude dyads with US investors.

		Pearson product-moment correlation coefficient with number of obs. in interval		Kendall's tau rank correlation coefficient with number of obs. in interval	
Variable	Number of intervals	ρ	p-value	τ	p-value
Mean min. travel time of interval	78	-0.6188	0.0000	-0.5481	0.0000
Mean car travel time of interval	85	-0.6170	0.0000	-0.7661	0.0000
Mean car distance of interval	124	-0.2111	0.0186	-0.6159	0.0000
Ln(mean min. travel time of interval)	78	-0.8427	0.0000	-0.5481	0.0000
Ln(mean car travel time of interval)	85	-0.8715	0.0000	-0.7661	0.0000
Ln(mean car distance of interval)	124	-0.5947	0.0000	-0.6159	0.0000

To analyze bivariate relationships between the spatial proximity/distance and the independent variables, further correlation analyses were conducted. As many of the variables are dichotomous or categorical and not normally distributed Table 5.10 depicts Kendall's tau rank correlation coefficients. The correlations are fairly small in most cases but reveal several significant bivariate relationships. Most of these relationships have the expected sign as stated in the respective hypotheses developed in section 4.3. In consequence, only some particularities will be discussed here.

The dummy variable indicating seed stage rounds has a negative correlation with distance which is significant at least at the 5% level. In addition, the dummy variable for later stage rounds has a positive correlation with distance which is significant at the 5% level for the ln of the minimum travel time and at the 10% level for the other measures. However, to test differences between seed stage and first rounds as well as first and later stage rounds additional Wilcoxon rank-sum tests were conducted. To rank the different observations, the ln of the minimum travel time was used. Results of these tests are shown in Table 5.11 and indicate that first rounds have a higher mean rank (distance) compared to seed stage rounds and later stage rounds have a higher mean rank compared to first rounds. Nevertheless, only the first relationship is significant (p-value < 1%).

The dummy variable indicating a moderate product development stage (product development/tests) has a positive correlation with distance which is significant at the 1% level for the ordinal measure and at the 5% level for the ln of the minimum travel time and the ln of the car distance. Surprisingly, the dummy variable indicating the highest product development stage (shipping product/profitable) is negatively correlated with the different measures of distance and this correlation is significant at the 5% level for the ordinal measure of minimum travel time and the ln of the minimum travel time. This would lead to an inverse relationship as has been expected. Again, Wilcoxon rank-sum tests were conducted. The results of these tests indicate that new ventures in a moderate product development stage have a higher mean rank (distance) compared to ventures in an early product development stage (business concept only). This difference is significant at the 10% level. Furthermore, new ventures in a late product development stage have a lower mean rank compared to new ventures in a moderate product development stage. This difference is significant at the 5% level. In consequence, a linear relationship between distance and the product development stage is not likely at this point of analysis.

The dummy variable indicating a high R&D intensity has a positive correlation with distance which is significant at the 5% level for the ordinal measure and the ln of minimum travel time. A negative relationship was expected. Regarding the industry and stage specialization of venture capitalists it was not possible to develop clear hypotheses. However, positive correlations between all measures of distance and both types of specialization exist and are significant at the 1% level. The investment volume per venture capitalist has a positive correlation with all types of measures of distance which is significant at the 1% level. Following the hypothesis, an inverted u-shaped effect and no linear effect has been expected.

Comparing the different measures of distance, the ln of the minimum travel time offers more clear correlation results in terms of absolute value of the correlation coefficients compared to the ln of the minimum car travel time or car distance in the majority of cases. This may indicate the superiority of this measure. A full correlation matrix of the independent variables can be found in Table C.1 in the appendix.

Table 5.10: Correlation coefficients

This table presents the correlation coefficients based on Kendall's tau between different measures for spatial proximity and the independent variables. The sample consists of 1402 dyads of venture capitalists and German portfolio companies which have closed a financing round between January 2002 and March 2007. The number of observations might vary due to missing values. Excl. fin.: exclusively financial; tr.: travel.

	Kendall's tau rank correlation coefficient			
Variable	1	2	3	4
Proximity / Distance				
1 Ordinal min. travel time	1.0000			
2 Ln(1+min. travel time in min.)	0.8876***	1.0000		
3 Ln(1+car travel time in min.)	0.8495***	0.9128***	1.0000	
4 Ln(1+car distance in km)	0.8493***	0.8927***	0.9698***	1.0000

Table 5.10 cont.: Correlation coefficients

Variable	Kendall's tau rank correlation coefficient 1	2	3	4
Venture				
Venture development stage				
Ln(age in years)	0.0356*	0.0418**	0.0308*	0.0325*
Dummy seed stage round	-0.0607**	-0.0688***	-0.0634***	-0.0652***
Dummy first round	-0.0207	-0.0232	-0.0150	-0.0132
Dummy later stage round	0.0426*	0.0481**	0.0383*	0.0371*
Ln(number of employees)	0.1256***	0.1266***	0.1142***	0.1193***
Product development stage				
Dummy business concept only	-0.0286	-0.0306	-0.0260	-0.0310
Dummy product development/tests	0.0649***	0.0563**	0.0232	0.0490**
Dummy shipp.prod./profitable	-0.0558**	-0.0467**	-0.0152	-0.0394*
Dummy prior exec. experience	0.0323	0.0279	0.0150	0.0320
Industry's knowledge intensity				
Dummy high asset intangibility	-0.0683***	-0.0643***	-0.0588***	-0.0592***
Dummy high R&D intensity	0.0593**	0.0546**	0.0233	0.0386*
Dummy low book/market	0.0068	0.0065	-0.0034	0.0050
Region				
Dummy East German venture	0.0122	0.0183	0.0495**	0.0408*
Dummy urban venture location	-0.0381	-0.0403*	0.0024	0.0024
Venture capitalist				
Ln(assets under management in m€)	0.1167***	0.1229***	0.1053***	0.1092***
Ln(age in years)	-0.0024	0.0053	-0.0035	0.0018
Specialization				
HHI industry	0.1410***	0.1161***	0.0961***	0.1055***
HHI stage	0.1135***	0.1050***	0.0922***	0.0999***
Type				
Dummy VC with excl. fin. objectives	0.1841***	0.1576***	0.1642***	0.1645***
Dummy corporate VC	0.0659***	0.0668***	0.0524**	0.0615***
Dummy (quasi-)public VC	-0.2437***	-0.2150***	-0.2117***	-0.2194***
Dummy lead-investor	-0.0320	-0.0305	-0.0181	-0.0305
Round				
Investment volume per VC (m€)	0.1585***	0.1500***	0.1290***	0.1407***
Syndication				
Syndication benefit (min. tr. time)	0.3739***	0.3540***	0.3241***	0.3421***
Syndication benefit (car tr. time)	0.3702***	0.3486***	0.3478***	0.3451***
Syndication benefit (car distance)	0.3926***	0.3709***	0.3460***	0.3687***
No. of consecutive round	-0.0507**	-0.0460**	-0.0496**	-0.0415**
Control variables				
VC market condition				
Ln(German VC fundraising in m€ (t-1))	-0.0193	-0.0184	-0.0206	-0.0181
Ln(German VC investments in m€)	-0.0217	-0.0114	-0.0247	-0.0219
Return of MSCI SC Germany (ltm)	0.0192	0.0252	0.0219	0.0199
Venture capitalist's no. of offices	-0.0641***	-0.0477**	-0.0525**	-0.0517**

* significant at 10%; ** significant at 5%; *** significant at 1% (two-sided)

Table 5.11: Wilcoxon rank-sum tests on ln(1+min. travel time)
This table presents Wilcoxon rank-sum tests to reveal differences in the distribution of the natural logarithm of (1+min. travel time) across different subsamples. The sample consists of 1402 dyads of venture capitalists and German portfolio companies which have closed a financing round between January 2002 and March 2007.

Variable	Value	Obs.	Mean rank	z	p-value
Investment stage					
Seed stage vs. first round	Seed stage round	42	162.98	-2.6960	0.0070
	First round	379	216.32		
First vs. later stage round	First round	379	656.32	-1.4110	0.1582
	Later stage round	981	689.84		
Product development stage					
Concept only vs. prod. dev.	Business concept only	28	210.21	-1.7330	0.0832
	Product dev./tests	486	260.22		
Prod. dev. vs. shipp.prod.	Product dev./tests	486	722.97	2.4520	0.0142
	Shipp.prod./profitable	888	668.09		

5.2.3 Ordered Logistic Regressions

The bivariate analyses delivered some information about the relationships between the observed spatial proximity/distance of venture capitalists and investees and exogenous factors. However, it was not possible to test most hypotheses rigorously. In consequence, this section continues to explore patterns in spatial proximity with multivariate regressions. As the distribution of the minimum travel time, as the primary measure of distance, has multiple maxima and is not normal, ordered logistic (OL) regressions of the minimum travel time between venture capitalists and investees on relevant variables will be conducted.[908] These models will be estimated with the maximum likelihood method, account for potential heteroskedasticity by estimating Huber-White robust standard errors,[909] and correct the standard errors for nonindependence across observations on the same venture capitalist.[910]

Table 5.12 shows the results of OL regressions with ordinal categories of the minimum travel time as dependent variable and the basic set of independent variables according to the hypotheses developed in section 4.3. The dependent, ordinal variable contains five categories which were built based on the minimum travel time as described in section 5.1.3.1. A higher category number indicates a larger minimum travel time between the venture capitalist and the new venture. Model OL 1 includes all variables except variables regarding the specialization of the venture capitalist and control variables. Model OL 2 additionally includes the con-

---

908 See section 5.2.1.

909 Cf. White (1980), pp. 817-838.

910 Stata only allows the correction of standard errors for nonindependence in regard to one dimension. As the multiple inclusion of venture capitalists is more severe than the one for new ventures, the correction is made for venture capitalists.

trol variables described in section 5.1.3.5 and Model OL 3 also includes variables measuring the specialization of the venture capitalist. The sample size reduces to 950 venture capitalist-investee dyads for this model since the HHI regarding industries and investment stages was only calculated for those venture capitalists which participated in at least three investment rounds throughout the sample period.[911] Model OL 4 additionally controls for year fixed effects.[912] The likelihood ratio (LR) test on joint significance of all variables is significant at the 1% level for all models. Furthermore, the models explain the data relatively well, which is indicated by fairly high values of the Nagelkerke's R^2 and results are robust across the different model specifications. Although Model OL 4 provides a slightly better fit compared to Model OL 3 as indicated by the Akaike Information Criterion (AIC) and Nagelkerke's R^2, Models OL 2 and 3 are more parsimonious. In consequence, the following analyses are mainly based on Models OL 2 and 3. Variance inflation factors (VIF) for all models are reported in Table C.2 in the appendix.

Venture and product development stage

Model OL 2 in Table 5.12 shows that on average younger portfolio companies exhibit more spatial proximity to their investors and thus supports Hypothesis 2.1a.[913] Hypothesis 2.2a, seed stage investment rounds are usually financed by proximate investors, is not supported ceteris paribus as the coefficient is not significant. The correlation matrix in Table C.1 reveals that the seed round dummy is negatively correlated to the portfolio companies' age as well as the investment volume per venture capitalist and positively correlated with the product development stage dummy indicating that the venture has a business concept only. The coefficients of these variables are significant in most models which indicates that these variables overlay the effect of the seed round dummy on the minimum travel time. VIFs (Table C.2) do not indicate problems of multicollinearity for these variables.[914] However, to disentangle the single effects of variables regarding the venture development stage and the product development stage Table 5.13 presents further models which include the respective variables separately. In addition, the size of the new venture in terms of its number of employees is included in

---

[911] Unreported tests show that the composition of the reduced sample is nearly the same as the full sample and that no selection bias is introduced.

[912] The variables for German VC fundraising in the previous calendar year and German VC investments in the current calendar year were excluded due to multicollinearity with year fixed effects.

[913] The coefficients of ln(age) are not significant in Models OL 3 and 4 (p-values of 0.119 and 0.101 respectively). However, it is likely that this is only because of the reduced sample size in these models.

[914] Wooldridge (2008) suggests that a VIF above 10 might indicate a problem of multicollinearity. He further elaborates on the fact that a high VIF of some variables does not mean that the whole model is misspecified but that the significance tests of the coefficients of these variables have to be interpreted with caution (cf. Wooldridge (2008)).

Table 5.12: Ordered logistic regressions – Base models
This table presents the results of ordered logistic regressions with ordinal categories of the minimum travel time as dependent variable. The sample consists of venture capitalists and German portfolio companies which have closed a financing round between January 2002 and March 2007. Varying sample sizes are due to missing values. Standard errors are adjusted for serial correlation, heteroskedasticity, and nonindependence across observations of the same venture capitalist.

Variable	OL 1	OL 2	OL 3	OL 4
Dep. var.: Ordinal min. travel time				
Venture				
Ln(age)	0.1505**	0.1887**	0.1236	0.1305
Dummy seed stage round	-0.2473	-0.0841	-0.1158	-0.2746
Dummy later stage round	0.1748	0.1627	0.1579	0.1834
Dummy business concept only	0.9140*	0.9595**	1.1116**	1.3562***
Dummy shipp.prod./profitable	-0.1258	-0.0919	0.0548	0.0793
Dummy prior exec. experience	-0.2281	-0.2895*	-0.3855**	-0.3513*
Dummy high asset intangibility	-0.5360**	-0.4609*	-0.5213*	-0.4316
Dummy high R&D intensity	0.1304	0.2265	0.1019	0.2258
Dummy low book/market	-0.0946	-0.0806	0.0311	-0.1698
Dummy East German venture	0.5110**	0.5626**	0.6026**	0.6151**
Dummy urban venture location	-0.4298	-0.4843	-0.5387	-0.5260
Venture capitalist				
Ln(assets under management)	0.1031	0.3490***	0.3870***	0.3957***
Ln(age)	-0.2655*	-0.1006	-0.1214	-0.1819
HHI industry			0.3995	0.3721
HHI stage			1.8219***	1.7834***
Dummy corporate VC	0.2830	0.2452	0.2209	0.2205
Dummy (quasi-)public VC	-1.0320***	-1.4454***	-1.3499***	-1.4122***
Dummy lead-investor	-0.0646	-0.0988	-0.0696	-0.0736
Round				
Investment volume per VC	0.3432***	0.2683***	0.2525***	0.2153**
(Investment volume per VC)^2	-0.0319***	-0.0278***	-0.0259***	-0.0237***
Syndication benefit	0.0108***	0.0101***	0.0094***	0.0097***
No. of consecutive round	-0.1559	-0.2507***	-0.2554**	-0.2706***
Control variables				
Ln(German VC fundraising (t-1))		0.1789	0.1543	
Ln(German VC investments)		0.0470	-0.1043	
Return of MSCI SC Germany (ltm)		0.4651*	0.4845*	0.0270
VC's no. of offices		-0.0985***	-0.0966***	-0.0942***
Year f.e.	No	No	No	Yes
cut1	-0.7236	1.7528	1.6181	0.5639
cut2	0.0665	2.6072	2.5022	1.4545**
cut3	0.8735	3.4902*	3.3979*	2.3569***
cut4	2.6046***	5.3277***	5.5270***	4.4919***
N	1075	1075	950	950
LR Chi^2	228.27***	345.03***	305.07***	313.88***
Nagelkerke's R^2	0.200	0.287	0.288	0.295
Log. Likelihood	-1563.11	-1504.73	-1300.23	-1295.83
AIC	3174.21	3065.46	2660.46	2655.66

* significant at 10%; ** significant at 5%; *** significant at 1% (two-sided)

Models OL 2.4 and 2.5.[915] Model OL 2.2 reveals that the minimum travel time between venture capitalists and investees is significantly longer for later stage rounds compared to earlier rounds (seed stage and first round) if one does not control for other variables regarding the venture or product development stage. Unreported regressions which only include the seed stage dummy do not reveal a significant relationship. Hence, there is still no evidence for Hypothesis 2.2a although the general direction of the relationship between the investment stage and the observed spatial proximity is supported.

Hypothesis 2.3a, new ventures with large numbers of employees are financed by more distant venture capitalists, is also not supported ceteris paribus. Although the point estimate of the coefficient is positive it is not significant in Model OL 2.4. Nonetheless, the coefficient becomes significant in Model OL 2.5 if one does not control for other variables regarding the venture or product development stage. In consequence, there is some evidence for Hypothesis 2.3a under the just mentioned restrictions.

Most models in Table 5.12 indicate that new ventures whose products are in a very early product development stage (business concept only) are financed by significantly more distant venture capitalists compared to other new ventures. This contradicts Hypothesis 3a. If one does not control for variables regarding the venture development stage, this effect becomes insignificant (Model OL 2.3). Furthermore, conducted robustness tests reveal some problems regarding the product development stage and suggest that the results have to be interpreted with caution. Robustness tests will be discussed in detail in section 5.2.4.

The variables regarding the venture and product development stage can also be interpreted as measures for the general maturity of a new venture. Hence, it is tested if a factor analysis is appropriate and whether the inclusion of a maturity factor offers additional insights. The Cronbach's alpha of the new venture's age, the investment stage, and the product development stage has a value of 0.71, the Kaiser-Meyer-Olkin-Criteria has a value of 0.69, and the anti-image covariance is sufficiently close to a diagonal matrix according to Backhaus et al. (2006).[916] In consequence, a factor analysis is applicable in general. However, unreported regressions which include a maturity factor that was derived by a factor analysis do not lead to additional insights.

---

[915] The size of the new venture in terms of its number of employees is likely to entail significant measurement errors. In consequence, this variable is not included in the main models and results have to be interpreted with caution. See section 5.1.3.2 for further discussion.

[916] Cf. Cronbach (1951), p. 299; Backhaus et al. (2006), pp. 275-276.

Table 5.13: Ordered logistic regressions – Details on venture and product development stage
This table presents the results of ordered logistic regressions with ordinal categories of the minimum travel time as dependent variable. The models are based on Model OL 2 and scrutinize further details regarding the venture and product development stage. The sample consists of venture capitalists and German portfolio companies which have closed a financing round between January 2002 and March 2007. Varying sample sizes are due to missing values. Standard errors are adjusted for serial correlation, heteroskedasticity, and nonindependence across observations of the same venture capitalist.

Variable	OL 2	OL 2.1	OL 2.2	OL 2.3	OL 2.4	OL 2.5
Dep. var.: Ordinal min. travel time						
Venture						
Ln(age)	0.1887**	0.1761***			0.1844**	
Dummy seed stage round	-0.0841		0.0006		0.0946	
Dummy later stage round	0.1627		0.3370**		0.1628	
Ln(number of employees)					0.1323	0.1955**
Dummy business concept only	0.9595**			0.4974	1.0133*	
Dummy shipp.prod./profitable	-0.0919			0.0834	-0.1289	
Dummy prior exec. experience	-0.2895*	-0.2694	-0.3286*	-0.2889*	-0.3368*	-0.3505**
Dummy high asset intangibility	-0.4609*	-0.4028	-0.3892	-0.4318*	-0.5352**	-0.4789*
Dummy high R&D intensity	0.2265	0.2563	0.2747	0.3104*	0.2460	0.3056*
Dummy low book/market	-0.0806	-0.0479	-0.0177	0.0365	-0.0452	0.0696
Dummy East German venture	0.5626**	0.5599**	0.6046**	0.6151**	0.5780**	0.5903**
Dummy urban venture location	-0.4843	-0.4845	-0.5018	-0.4676	-0.4818	-0.4539
Venture capitalist						
Ln(assets under management)	0.3490***	0.3502***	0.3398***	0.3543***	0.3478***	0.3460***
Ln(age)	-0.1006	-0.0952	-0.0925	-0.0935	-0.0874	-0.0868
Dummy corporate VC	0.2452	0.2482	0.2264	0.2040	0.2604	0.2199
Dummy (quasi-)public VC	-1.4454***	-1.4285***	-1.4446***	-1.4843***	-1.4781***	-1.4756***
Dummy lead-investor	-0.0988	-0.1153	-0.0794	-0.1213	-0.1013	-0.1014
Round						
Investment volume per VC	0.2683***	0.2558***	0.2790***	0.2720***	0.2416***	0.2122**
(Investment volume per VC)^2	-0.0278***	-0.0264***	-0.0291***	-0.0282***	-0.0255***	-0.0234***
Syndication benefit	0.0101***	0.0102***	0.0100***	0.0100***	0.0099***	0.0100***
No. of consecutive round	-0.2507***	-0.2355***	-0.2357***	-0.1786**	-0.2513***	-0.1909**

Table 5.13 cont.: Ordered logistic regressions – Details on venture and product development stage

Variable	OL 2	OL 2.1	OL 2.2	OL 2.3	OL 2.4	OL 2.5
Control variables						
Ln(German VC fundraising (t-1))	0.1789	0.1737	0.0891	0.0768	0.2207	0.1450
Ln(German VC investments)	0.0470	0.0566	0.0693	0.0842	0.0721	0.1150
Return of MSCI SC Germany (ltm)	0.4651*	0.4464*	0.3648	0.3486	0.5084**	0.4286*
VC's no. of offices	-0.0985***	-0.0982***	-0.0970***	-0.0970***	-0.1005***	-0.0989***
cut1	1.7528	1.7331	1.2353	1.1969	2.6025	2.3527
cut2	2.6072	2.5837	2.0820	2.0413	3.4606*	3.2017
cut3	3.4902*	3.4646*	2.9621*	2.9176	4.3735**	4.1074**
cut4	5.3277***	5.2949***	4.7892***	4.7409**	6.2087***	5.9267***
N	1075	1075	1075	1075	1047	1047
LR Chi^2	345.03***	339.23***	334.18***	330.04***	355.26***	341.27***
Nagelkerke's R^2	0.287	0.283	0.280	0.277	0.301	0.291
Log. Likelihood	-1504.73	-1507.63	-1510.15	-1512.22	-1456.43	-1463.42
AIC	3065.46	3063.26	3070.31	3074.45	2970.86	2974.85

* significant at 10%; ** significant at 5%; *** significant at 1% (two-sided)

Prior experience of the entrepreneurial team

Models OL 2 to 4 reveal that new ventures which have at least one team member with profound prior experience are located significantly closer to their venture capitalists than other ventures. This contradicts hypothesis 4a. One reason might be that experienced entrepreneurs gained their experience mainly in entrepreneurial clusters like Munich or Berlin and are thus located closer to their venture capitalists.[917] However, further research is required in order to reveal the roots of this effect.

Industries' knowledge intensity

Regarding the portfolio companies' industry, the results indicate that the observed minimum travel time between venture capitalists and portfolio companies with high asset intangibility is significantly lower compared to others. This supports hypothesis 5.1a. The effects of high research intensity (hypothesis 5.2a: high R&D expenses to total assets) and high future growth perspectives (hypothesis 5.3a: low book/market value) are not significant.

Region of the venture

All models in Table 5.12 prove that East German ventures are located significantly more distant to their venture capitalists compared to West German ventures. This implies that there are still structural differences among these parts of Germany and supports hypothesis 6.1a. The results do not reveal significant differences in the spatial proximity among new ventures located in urban areas and other ventures.[918]

Size of the venture capitalist

The results show that larger venture capitalists in terms of assets under management have a larger investment radius because they are under pressure to invest their assets (Table 5.12). Thus, hypothesis 7a is supported.

---

[917] See also section 2.2.2.

[918] In Model OL 3 the coefficient of the urban venture location dummy is negative and has a p-value of 0.119. Thus, the coefficient is quite close to being significant. This would indicate that the effects of a superior infrastructure and co-location with venture capitalists outweighs the lower importance of spatial proximity for urban new ventures and leads to smaller observed distances.

Experience and reputation of the of the venture capitalist

The point estimates of the coefficients of the venture capitalist's age are negative in all models in Table 5.12 and the coefficient is significantly different from zero in Model OL 1. This would imply that the distance between venture capitalists and investees is likely to decrease with rising age of the venture capitalist. However, if one controls for the venture capitalists' number of offices, the effect diminishes (Model OL 2 to 4). As it was not possible to formulate a clear hypothesis for the effect of the venture capitalists' age on the observed spatial proximity between actors, alternative functional forms were also tested (Table C.3 in the appendix). Neither a pure linear nor a u-shaped effect turned out to be significant. Hence, it is not possible to prove an overall effect of the venture capitalist's age on the observed spatial proximity which might be due to the contradicting effects that were discussed in section 4.3.3.

Specialization of the venture capitalist

Models OL 3 and 4 further indicate that the minimum travel time is likely to increase significantly the higher the venture capitalist's stage specialization. In consequence, venture capitalists are willing or forced to give up the advantages of spatial proximity in order to generate a higher quantity of deal flow and to be able to follow their stage specialization strategy. However, the coefficient of the venture capitalist's industry specialization is not significantly different from zero in both models. This may have two reasons. First, Table 4.1 in section 4.3 shows that spatial proximity is particularly important for specialized venture capitalists (industry or stage) in order to support their portfolio companies. In consequence, the empirical results may indicate that spatial proximity is more important in order to provide the required level of support activities for venture capitalists which are specialized in certain industries compared to investors which are specialized in certain stages. Second, the empirical results may be caused by the spatial structure of investment opportunities. New ventures of certain industries (e.g. biotech) are regionally clustered,[919] while clusters of specific investment stages do not exist to the same extent. In consequence, venture capitalists that are specialized in a certain industry may locate close to a corresponding industry cluster and are thus still able to generate sufficient deal flow. In contrast, venture capitalists that are specialized in certain investment stages have to broaden their investment radius in order to find a sufficient number of investment opportunities.

---

[919] E.g. the Munich Biotech Cluster in Martinsried, the Biotech Cluster Rhine-Neckar (BioRN), or the optical industry cluster in Jena.

Type of the venture capitalist

Hypothesis 8.1a, corporate venture capitalists are willing to invest in more distant ventures due to their primarily strategic interests, is not supported by the empirical results. This is also true if the variable regarding the industry specialization of venture capitalists is excluded from the models. However, the point estimates of the coefficients of the corporate venture capitalist dummy in Table 5.12 point in the hypothesized direction.

The results support hypothesis 8.2a which states that (quasi-)public venture capitalists invest in more proximate ventures. As stated in section 4.3.3, these venture capitalists are mainly influenced by public policy or other restrictions which leads to a limitation of their target area on specific regions. Additional regressions reveal that this is true for all types of (quasi-)public venture capitalists (Table C.4 in the appendix).

Lead-investor

Even though the point estimates of the lead-investor dummy in Table 5.12 point in the hypothesized direction, the estimated coefficients are not significantly different from zero. Hence, hypothesis 9.1a, which states that lead-investors are expected to be located more proximate to the new ventures compared to co-investors, is not supported by the data (Models OL 1 to 4). However, there are indications that structural differences among lead- and co-investors other than the general intercept exist.

Table 5.14 displays regressions on different subsamples which are based on Model OL 3. Models OL 3.2 and 3.3 (Lead-inv.) include only those dyads in which the respective venture capitalist served as lead-investor and Models OL 3.2 and 3.3 (Co-inv.) include the remaining dyads.[920] The variables regarding the investment and product development stage were included separately since they are correlated and may lead to unstable coefficient estimates in small subsamples. As can be seen in Table 4.1, the role of a venture capitalist as lead- or co-investor is likely to have an impact on the importance of spatial proximity in certain phases of the investment process. These phases are deal due diligence as well as investment monitoring, support and exit. In consequence, the empirical models should have different coefficients for the two subsamples. These expected differences of the coefficients are also summarized in Table 5.14. Most of these expectations are straight forward. The effect of an increasing venture development stage in terms of the new venture's age on the likelihood of a distant investment is positive in the relevant investment phases. Since these effects are assumed to be stronger for lead-investors, the coefficient of the new venture's age is also assumed to be

[920] Different subsamples were used because the inclusion of interaction terms with the lead-investor dummy would have led to a very high number of variables in the model.

higher. The other expectations are developed in an analogous manner. One exception is the venture capitalist's size which has no effect in the relevant investment phases.[921] However, the main effect of size is that venture capitalists are forced to increase their investment radius in order to find a sufficient number of investment opportunities. If venture capitalists are aware of the benefits of spatial proximity for the investment management, it can be assumed that venture capitalists chose to participate as co-investors in distant investments. In consequence, it is likely that the effect of size on observed minimum travel times is larger for co-investors compared to lead-investors.

To test whether the coefficients differ significantly across the two subsamples, various Chi^2-tests (Wald tests) have been conducted using the estimates from Model OL 3.2. Table 5.14 reports the results of two-sided tests as well as one-sided tests if applicable. The age of the new venture has a significant effect on the expected minimum travel time for lead-investors. This effect is also significantly larger for lead-investors compared to co-investors (significant at the 10% level (one-sided)).

Furthermore, venture capitalists that are specialized in regard to a certain industry tend to invest in distant ventures in the role of a co-investor. The coefficient of industry specialization is positive for co-investors, while it is negative for lead-investors. The difference of the coefficients has a p-value of 0.1018 in Model OL 3.2 and is significant at the 10% level (two-sided) in Model 3.3. This difference between lead- and co-investors is in line with propositions 2d and 6g. Proposition 2d states that specialized venture capitalists may be forced to broaden their investment radius in order to receive a sufficient number of investment opportunities and applies to lead- and co-investors. In addition, proposition 6g states that specialized venture capitalists benefit more from spatial proximity in order to support their portfolio companies compared to non-specialized venture capitalists and explains why only co-investors extend their investment radii. There are indications that this effect also applies to venture capitalists that are specialized in certain investment stages. But this effect is statistically not significant. As a result, hypothesis 9.2a, some of the effects of the elaborated hypotheses differ between lead- and co-investors, is supported by the data.

[921] See Table 4.1 in section 4.3.

Table 5.14: Ordered logistic regressions – Comparison of lead- and co-investors

This table presents the results of ordered logistic regressions with ordinal categories of the minimum travel time as dependent variable. The models are based on Model OL 3 and are estimated for lead- and co-investors separately. The sample consists of venture capitalists and German portfolio companies which have closed a financing round between January 2002 and March 2007. Standard errors are adjusted for serial correlation, heteroskedasticity, and nonindependence across observations of the same venture capitalist. Furthermore, the table displays expected differences between the lead- and co-investor coefficients as well as corresponding chi²-difference-tests. Appl.: applicable, exp.: expected.

Variable	OL 3	OL 3.2		OL 3.3		Exp. diff. betw. lead- and co-inv. coef.	Differ-ence	Chi²	df	p-value (two-sided)	p-value (one-sided, if appl.)
		Lead-inv.	Co-inv.	Lead-inv.	Co-inv.						
Dep. var.: Ordinal min. travel time											
Venture											
Ln(age)	0.1236	0.2167**	0.0181	0.2523**	0.0618	+	0.1986	2.07	1	0.1507	0.0754*
Dummy seed stage round	-0.1158	0.2963	0.4064			-	-0.1101	0.02	1	0.8866	0.4433
Dummy later stage round	0.1579	0.1441	0.2853			+	-0.1412	0.16	1	0.6896	
Dummy business concept only	1.1116**			1.0013	1.0062*	-	-0.0049		1	0.9956	0.4978
Dummy shipp.prod./profitable	0.0548			-0.0556	0.1728	+	-0.2284	0.57	1	0.4507	
Dummy prior exec. experience	-0.3855**	-0.2399	-0.5495**	-0.2107	-0.5081**	+	0.3096	1.06	1	0.3033	0.1517
Dummy high asset intangibility	-0.5213*	-0.5367*	-0.4095	-0.5694*	-0.4575	-	-0.1272	0.07	1	0.7941	0.3971
Dummy high R&D intensity	0.1019	0.0323	0.0591	0.0111	0.1370	-	-0.0268	0.01	1	0.9409	0.4705
Dummy low book/market	0.0311	0.2508	-0.1579	0.2687	-0.0668	-	0.4087	0.79	1	0.3752	
Dummy East German venture	0.6026**	0.9583**	0.4048	0.9542**	0.3836	open	0.5535	2.36	1	0.1244	
Dummy urban venture location	-0.5387	-0.4432	-0.5069	-0.4224	-0.4771	+	0.0637	0.02	1	0.8848	0.4424
Venture capitalist											
Ln(assets under management)	0.3870***	0.3179***	0.3933***	0.3289***	0.4001***	-	-0.0754	0.47	1	0.4917	0.2459
Ln(age)	-0.1214	-0.2553*	-0.0455	-0.2635*	-0.0582	+	-0.2098	1.29	1	0.2558	
HHI industry	0.3995	-0.2509	0.8136	-0.3276	0.8291	open	-1.0645	2.68	1	0.1018	
HHI stage	1.8219***	1.2639	2.0134**	1.3568	2.1403**	-	-0.7495	0.64	1	0.4249	0.2125
Dummy corporate VC	0.2209	1.2325	-0.0459	1.1491	-0.0869	+	1.2784	1.42	1	0.2332	0.1166
Dummy (quasi-)public VC	-1.3499***	-1.3917***	-1.3200***	-1.4103***	-1.3322***	+	-0.0717	0.04	1	0.8388	
Dummy lead-investor	-0.0696										
Round											
Investment volume per VC	0.2525***	0.3151**	0.4614*	0.2939**	0.4722**	+	-0.1463	2.43	2	0.2969	
(Investment volume per VC)²	-0.0259***	-0.0298***	-0.0720*	-0.0282***	-0.0722*	-	0.0422				
Syndication benefit	0.0094***	0.0070**	0.0104***	0.0072**	0.0105***	+	-0.0034	1.17	1	0.2798	
No. of consecutive round	-0.2554**	-0.2162	-0.2146*	-0.1936	-0.1961*	-	-0.0016		1	0.9922	0.4961

Table 5.14 cont.: Ordered logistic regressions – Comparison of lead- and co-investors

Variable	OL 3	OL 3.2		OL 3.3		Exp. diff. betw. lead- and co-inv. coef.	Differ-ence	Chi²	df	p-value (two-sided)	p-value (one-sided, if appl.)
		Lead-inv.	Co-inv.	Lead-inv.	Co-inv.						
Control variables											
Ln(German VC fundr. (t-1))	0.1543	0.2092	0.1064	0.2233	0.1068						
Ln(German VC investments)	-0.1043	0.2876	-0.2956	0.2683	-0.2464						
Return of MSCI SC Germany (ltm)	0.4845*	0.9925*	0.1533	0.9888*	0.1753						
VC's no. of offices	-0.0966***	-0.0828***	-0.1002***	-0.0835***	-0.0999***						
cut1	1.6181	4.2355	0.2352	4.1597	0.6681						
cut2	2.5022	5.0906	1.1516	5.0177	1.5865						
cut3	3.3979	5.8741	2.1395	5.8013	2.5722						
cut4	5.5270***	8.0273**	4.3185**	7.9585**	4.7560*						
N	950	342	608	342	608						
LR Chi²	305.07***	106.05***	218.26***	107.40***	219.43***						
Nagelkerke's R²	0.288	0.280	0.316	0.283	0.318						
Log. Likelihood	-1300.23	-467.46	-822.09	-466.79	-821.51						
AIC	2660.46	988.93	1698.19	987.57	1697.01						

* significant at 10%; ** significant at 5%; *** significant at 1% (two-sided)

Investment volume

The empirical analyses further support hypothesis 10a, the distance between a venture capitalist and investee increases with rising investment volume of the venture capitalist up to a certain threshold and decreases thereafter. Models OL 1 to 4 in Table 5.12 reveal that the linear and quadratic effect of the investment volume are both significantly different from zero. Hence, with increasing investment volume the positive linear effect is more and more offset by the negative quadratic effect. This results in an inverted u-shaped relationship. Models OL 2 and 3 imply that the likelihood of a distant investment increases up to an investment volume of about 4.8 to 4.9 m€ and decreases thereafter. This is an intriguing result as it implies that for small investments transaction costs outweigh the desire to monitor investments more intensively. In contrast, for large investments the need for closer monitoring outweighs the relatively lower transaction costs. To further validate the robustness of this result, additional regressions were conducted. Separate regressions on two subsamples were calculated in order to test the inverted u-shaped effect as implied by hypothesis 10a. The first subsample includes all dyads with investment volumes per venture capitalist up to 4.85 m€ and the second subsample includes all dyads with investment volumes of at least 4.85 m€. The results of these regressions can be found in Table C.5 in the appendix and support an inverted u-shaped effect of the VC investment volume (Models OL 2.10 and 2.11). An overall monotonic linear effect of the investment volume is not supported by Model OL 2.09.

Syndication

The data shows that observed minimum travel times are significantly higher if the deal is syndicated and at least one syndication partner resides closer to the portfolio company than the venture capitalist of the focal dyad. Thus, hypothesis 11a is supported (Table 5.12). This also indicates that syndication is likely to be an instrument to overcome large distances between venture capitalists and investees. Alternative measures of syndication and its spatial benefits also offer significant results. The tested measures include: the number of syndication partners in an investment round; a dummy variable that indicates if the venture capitalist is located far away from the venture, but a close syndication partner exists; and the difference between a venture capitalist's distance to the portfolio company and the distance of the syndication partner located closest to the respective portfolio company. The results of these alternative model specifications can be found in Table C.6 in the appendix. Hence, the impact of syndication on the likelihood of a distant investment is robust.

Consecutive investment round

Consecutive investment rounds by the same venture capitalist are likely to be closer to the investor in terms of minimum travel time which supports hypothesis 12a. This result indicates that the spatial proximity between both parties is important for the continuation of the relationship. The observed closer proximity of consecutive investment rounds may have two rationales. Either the involved parties decide not to continue distant relationships more often because closer relationships have more advantages. Or portfolio companies decide to move their venture closer to typical locations of venture capitalists after initial investment rounds because proximity is regarded as success factor. As the second rationale seems to be less realistic, the effect may prove the importance of spatial proximity for venture capital investment decisions.

5.2.4 Robustness Tests of Conducted Analyses

Various robustness checks were conducted to verify the empirical results presented above. In unreported regressions, multiple alternative category definitions for the different measures of spatial proximity were tested. Furthermore, alternative model definitions including smaller sub-models were tested. The main results remained unchanged which supports the reported results.

Moreover, all model specifications were tested for multicollinearity. A summary of VIFs of the base models can be found in Table C.2. The maximum VIF is 5.30 and thus problems of multicollinearity are unlikely.[922]

It is also important to note that ordered logistic regressions incorporate a parallel lines assumption. Thus, it is assumed that the coefficients are equal across different response categories since only one equation over all response categories is estimated.[923] The Brant test of the parallel lines assumption with null hypothesis that all coefficients are equal across different response categories is rejected for the Models OL 1 to 4.[924] However, a detailed analysis reveals that this is caused only by single variables and that the results regarding the tested hypotheses are not influenced. For most variables, the sign of the coefficient does not change across different response categories even though the test of exact equality is rejected. Regard-

---

[922] Wooldridge (2008) suggests that a VIF above 10 might indicate a problem of multicollinearity (cf. Wooldridge (2008)). Furthermore, this moderate VIF of 5.30 for the linear term of the investment volume is caused by a correlation with the quadratic term of the investment volume. The VIFs of the other variables are equal or below 2.49.

[923] Some authors also refer to this assumption as proportional-odds assumption (cf. Hardin/Hilbe (2007), p. 254).

[924] Cf. Brant (1990), pp. 1171-1178.

ing the coefficients which have been significant in Models OL 1 to 4 the sign only changes significantly for the dummy variable indicating an early product development stage (business concept only). Hence, the results regarding this variable, which also contradict hypothesis 3a, have to be interpreted with caution. The results of the Brant tests for Models OL 1 to 4 are summarized in Table C.7. Table C.8 displays exemplary results of a more detailed analysis of Model OL 3.

A detailed outlier analysis also did not reveal that the results depend only on a few observations. Therefore, potential outliers were identified using leverage-versus-squared-residual plots, Cook's D influence statistics, and a DfBeta statistics after corresponding OLS regressions.[925] Then, the potential outliers were excluded from the OL regressions. The OL results did not change substantially after the exclusion of potential outliers.

In addition, OLS and Tobit regressions as well as OLS and OL regressions using different measures of spatial proximity were conducted and support the robustness of results as most results remain unchanged with minor differences in the significance of the coefficients. OLS regressions which use ln(1 + minimum travel time) and Tobit regressions which use the original untransformed minimum travel time as dependent variables are reported in Table C.9 and Table C.10 in the appendix. These regressions use the same sets of independent variables like Models OL 1 to 4. OL and OLS regressions using different measures of spatial proximity and the same sets of independent variables like Models OL 2 and 3 can be found in Table C.11 and Table C.12 in the appendix. As the car travel time is only available for European venture capitalists, the sample has been restricted to European investors for these regressions. This ensures the comparability of the different models.

5.2.5 Limitations of Analyses

The aim of this first block of analyses was to extend the understanding of prevalent patterns in the observed spatial proximity in VC finance in Germany. Therefore, ordered logistic regressions of distance on various relevant variables were conducted.

However, an important limitation of these analyses is the problem of causality. Spatial proximity between actors is not a pure endogenous variable that is determined by the location decision of venture capitalists and new ventures. It is rather likely that venture capitalists and/or new ventures base their decision to close a deal also on the (given) geographical distance between them. This effect then determines the composition of the used sample of VC financing rounds and causes the relationships that were detected above. Furthermore, it is likely that the observed spatial proximity is also determined by other omitted variables which may cause

[925] Cf. Rousseeuw/Leroy (2003), pp. 216-245.

problems of endogeneity.[926] One constructed example is that young entrepreneurs, who might be likely to found an internet startup, prefer to live in vibrant entrepreneurial centers like Munich or Berlin and older entrepreneurs, who might be more likely to found an old economy venture, prefer to live in other areas. Then, the analysis of patterns in spatial proximity would suggest that internet startups are located closer to their investors compared to old economy ventures. However, this fact does not mean that spatial proximity is especially important for internet startups in order to receive VC financing. In consequence, the results regarding patterns in spatial proximity cannot be interpreted as causal relationships but have to be interpreted as correlations.

One exception to the just mentioned problem of causality is the result that new ventures which are located close to their venture capitalists are more likely to remain in the sample and to receive consecutive financing rounds. This result gives a first hint on the general relevance of spatial proximity for the likelihood of (consecutive) VC financing. In order to investigate causal relationships of specific characteristics of new ventures, venture capitalists, and investment rounds on the importance of spatial proximity for the likelihood of a VC investment, another research design is necessary which will be discussed in section 5.3.

In addition, the availability of data was restricted to the discussed sample of German VC transactions. It was not possible to retrieve additional data. In consequence, the sample size is limited and it was not possible to calculate additional variables regarding network positions of single venture capitalists or their previous investment experience.[927] Furthermore, this fact leads to a considerable number of missing values regarding the specialization of venture capitalists because the specialization variables were calculated only for investors with at least three financing rounds in the sample.

---

[926] Cf. Wooldridge (2008), pp. 506-517.

[927] See e.g. Sorenson/Stuart (2001), pp. 1566-1569.

5.3 Impact of Spatial Proximity on the Likelihood of a Venture Capital Investment

This section investigates the impact of spatial proximity on the likelihood of a specific venture capital financing relationship to occur. In consequence, this section explores for which kinds of new ventures, venture capitalists, and investment rounds spatial proximity is particularly important (Figure 5.4) and addresses research question two, which was stated in section 1.1.

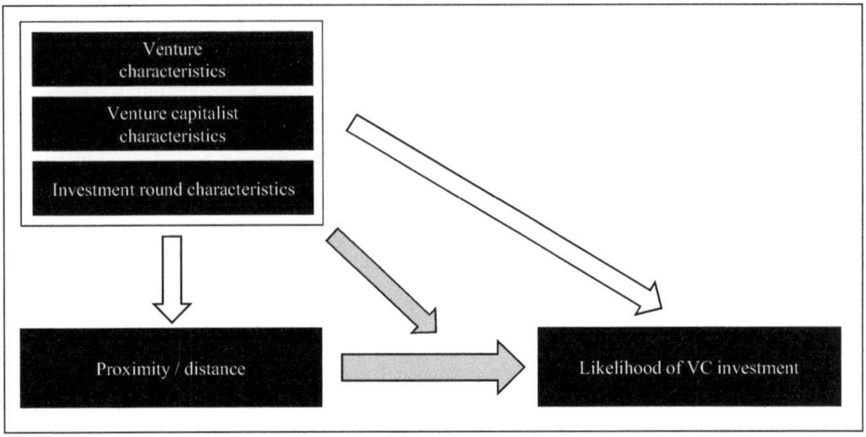

Figure 5.4: Factors influencing the likelihood of a VC investment
Source: Own illustration.

5.3.1 Empirical Strategy to Investigate the Likelihood of a Venture Capital Investment

To investigate the impact of spatial proximity on the likelihood of a specific VC financing relationship to occur, and thus to test the hypotheses elaborated in section 4.3, it is necessary to retrieve a control sample of unrealized but comparable relationships. Then, it is possible to model the likelihood that a particular venture capitalist invests in a given target company with multivariate methods.

Many studies like Stuart (1998) or Gulati (1995) analyze every possible dyad between venture capitalists and new ventures in order to scrutinize the effects of various covariates on the probability of tie formation between two actors.[928] As discussed by Sorenson/Stuart (2001), this approach creates two problems.[929] First, this approach does not correctly account for the

[928] Cf. Stuart (1998), p. 681; Gulati (1995), p. 30.

[929] Cf. Sorenson/Stuart (2001), p. 1561.

fact of nonindependence across cases since each venture capitalist would be used R=689 times and each VC investment round would be used I=309 times in order to construct the sample.[930] Here R is the total number of VC investment rounds in the sample and I is the total number of venture capitalists as illustrated in Figure 5.5. This large number of repeated inclusions of venture capitalists and VC investment rounds may lead to a systematic underestimation of standard errors for variables that do not change from dyad to dyad.[931]

	VC investment rounds (*r*)						
Venture capitalists (*i*)	1	2	3	...	687	688	689
1	0	0	1	...	0	0	0
2	0	1	0	...	0	1	0
3	0	0	0	...	0	0	0
...	...	...	...	...	...	...	...
307	0	0	0	...	0	0	0
308	0	0	1	...	0	0	0
309	0	0	0	...	0	0	1

Figure 5.5: Matrix of possible dyads
Source: Own illustration.

Second, this method would require extensive data collection efforts. The different measures of spatial proximity would have to be collected for each combination of a venture capitalist and an investee as described in section 5.1.3.1. As some components of this process, like the identification of a feasible flight connection, require manual data collection, this process would be very burdensome for the 153.882 possible combinations.[932]

Following Sorenson/Stuart (2001), one possible solution to these problems would be to retrieve a random sample from the total number of possible dyads. However, the realized dyads and thus the "ones" in Figure 5.5 provide most information about the factors which influence the likelihood of a VC investment.[933] In consequence, King/Zeng (2001) propose to apply choice-based sampling by including all realized observations and a random selection of unrea-

930 For a thorough discussion of the nonindependence problem and possible solutions see Lincoln (1984), pp. 56-61; Krackhardt (1988), pp. 359-381; Mizruchi (1989), p. 412.

931 Separate venture capitalist-investee dyads would be constructed for each investment round since each investment round represents a new investment decision.

932 To calculate the total number of possible travel connections the total number of new ventures and not the number of investment rounds has to be used.

933 Cf. Cosslett (1981), pp. 1289-1290; Imbens (1992), pp. 1187-1188; Imbens/Lancaster (1996), p. 289; King/Zeng (2001), p. 141.

lized observations.[934] This approach was also applied by Sorenson/Stuart (2001) who include all realized VC financing relationships in their analysis and construct a matching sample of unrealized VC financing relationships by "pairing each VC firm that funded a startup in a given quarter of a calendar year with a [random] startup funded by a different venture capitalist in that same quarter".[935] Hence, Sorenson/Stuart (2001) only control for temporal variations of VC market conditions and assume that each venture capitalist would potentially invest in each new venture of the database. This is a rather unrealistic assumption and leads to an inflation of the number of alternative investment opportunities and consequently to an underestimation of investment probabilities. The reason is that most venture capitalists specialize in specific market segments (investment stages, investment volumes, industries, and/or regions) in order to gain competitive advantages.[936] For the German market, this effect might be especially severe due to the higher share of (quasi-)public venture capitalists that are only allowed to invest in certain regions.[937]

In consequence, this study uses a more exact and realistic approach to construct a matched sample of potential VC financing relationships that did not occur. Each venture capitalist that participated in a VC financing round is matched with another financing round that:

- was raised by another new venture in which the venture capitalist did not invest,
- was closed in the same calendar year,
- was in the same investment stage,
- had a similar investment volume per venture capitalist,
- was raised by a new venture in the same VentureSource industry segment, and
- was raised by a new venture that was located in the target region of the respective venture capitalist.

A similar investment volume per venture capitalist was defined as stated in Table 5.15. Thus, a venture capitalist that invested up to 0.5 m€ was matched to an alternative financing round with an average investment volume per venture capitalist of up to 0.75 m€. If an investment volume was not provided for a certain financing round, no restrictions were made regarding the investment volume for the matching sample.

---

934 Choice based sampling is also often called endogenous stratified sampling. Cf. King/Zeng (2001), pp. 141-143.

935 Sorenson/Stuart (2001), p. 1561.

936 Cf. Gupta/Sapienza (1992), pp. 347-349; Gompers et al. (2009), pp. 825-827.

937 See section 2.1.3. Examples are MBGs, subsidiaries of savings banks, subsidiaries of institutions promoting economic development, and subsidiaries of state banks whose investment areas are mostly restricted to their state or region.

Table 5.15: Definition of investment volume categories
This table provides a summary of the definition of categories for the investment volume per venture capitalist that were used in order to generate the matched sample.

Investment volume per venture capitalist (m€) of original investment round	Range of investment volumes per venture capitalist (m€) for potential matches
> 0 to 0.50	> 0 to 0.75
> 0.50 to 0.75	> 0.25 to 1.00
> 0.75 to 1.50	> 0.50 to 2.00
> 1.50 to 2.00	> 1.00 to 4.00
> 2.00 to 5.00	> 1.50 to 6.00
> 5.00	> 4.00

The target regions of venture capitalists were defined according to the information provided by the database of BVK Members on the BVK website or the venture capitalist's website.[938] Hence, the whole of Germany was assigned as a target region for most venture capitalists with exclusively financial objectives, corporate venture capitalists, governmental institutions like the KfW or the High Tech Gründerfond (HTGF), and foreign venture capitalists. The respective or certain federal states were assigned as target regions for MBGs, most subsidiaries of institutions promoting economic development, and most subsidiaries of state banks and cooperative central institutes. Finally, the target region was defined according to the stated region on the level of districts for subsidiaries of savings and cooperative banks.

If it was not possible to identify an alternative financing round, the above mentioned criteria were relaxed in the following order: First, the restrictions on the investment volume were relaxed (necessary for 414 rounds). Then the industry criterion was relaxed from the VentureSource industry segment to the industry group (necessary for 262 rounds).[939] Next the time frame for the closing date was stepwise relaxed (necessary for 126 rounds, 51 rounds were matched using the whole sample). If there was still no match, the industry group criteria was removed (necessary for 51 rounds) and, finally, the investment stage criteria was abandoned (necessary for 14 rounds). For three investment rounds, it was not possible to find an alternative round. The described procedure is reasonable as it is likely that also venture capitalists relax their investment criteria if they are not able to find a sufficient number of investment opportunities. For each financing round existed on average about 9.36 alternative rounds that met all selection criteria.[940] If more than one possible match existed, the match was chosen according to an equally distributed random number.

---

[938] Cf. BVK (2008a).

[939] See also Table 5.2 for an overview of VentureSource industry segments and groups.

[940] The actual number of alternative investments is likely to be higher since the VentureSource database only represents a fraction of the German VC market.

The alternative financing round retained all its characteristics like the investment stage or the financing volume. Regarding the lead- or co-investor characteristic, the venture capitalist retained his status from the original round in order to make an analysis of the venture capitalist's role within syndicated deals possible.

As a result, a control sample of unrealized but comparable VC financing relationships was constructed. This sample has the additional advantage that the alternative new ventures actually received VC funding from another investor and thus passed a certain quality threshold in order to receive VC funding. In consequence, the issue of potential quality differences between realized VC financing relationships and those that never happen is eliminated.[941] Furthermore, and most importantly for this study, the described sample construction ensures that the spatial structure of actual portfolio companies (sample of realized investments) and potential investment targets (matched sample) is the same. This means e.g. that biotech companies of the realized and matched sample have the same probabilities of being located in a biotech cluster and thus have the same likelihood of spatial proximity. Thus, the effect of potentially omitted variables and thus endogeneity is eliminated if one compares the realized sample with the matched sample. Figure 5.6 illustrates the spatial distribution of the original and the matched sample by comparing the fraction of the respective subsample for different levels of the ln(1+min. travel time). As expected, the original sample has a much stronger spatial bias towards short distances between venture capitalists and their investees compared to the matched sample.

In order to test the hypotheses, the likelihood that a particular VC financing relationship occurs is modeled with the help of logistic regressions. In these multivariate analyses a dummy variable indicating whether a deal actually took place or not will be regressed on the spatial proximity / distance between the venture capitalist and the venture, interaction terms of distance and characteristics of the new venture, venture capitalist, and investment round, as well as various control variables. Since the total sample of realized and unrealized VC financing relationships is perfectly balanced regarding the characteristics of the venture capitalist, these variables do not have an impact on the likelihood of a specific dyad per definition.[942] Furthermore, the sample is nearly balanced regarding most characteristics of the new venture and

---

[941] Cf. Sorenson/Stuart (2001), p. 1561.

[942] Balanced in regard to a certain characteristic means that for each realized dyad another unrealized dyad exists which has exactly the same properties in regard to that characteristic. The three dyads for which it was not possible to find a suitable match are excluded from the analysis.

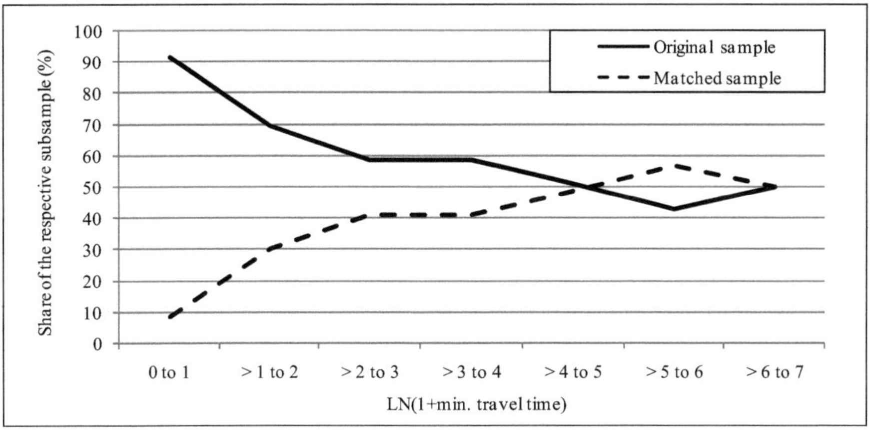

Figure 5.6: Comparison of original and matched sample regarding their spatial distribution
This figure gives an overview of the share of original and matched dyads for different levels of the ln(1+minimum travel time).

the investment round. However, for each variable for which the sample is not perfectly balanced additional control variables will be included in the empirical models. In consequence, the effects of new venture, venture capitalist, and investment round characteristics on the likelihood of a VC investment are neutralized or controlled. Figure 5.4 also indicates that the aforementioned characteristics might impact the spatial proximity between venture capitalists and ventures due to their choice of location.[943] This has no effect on the results regarding the impact of spatial proximity on the likelihood of investment for two reasons. First, location decisions that are made before a VC investment contract is closed have the same effects on realized as well as unrealized dyads because the final contracting partners are not fixed yet. Second, if a new venture moves closer to a venture capitalist after or shortly before the VC financing contract is closed, this change of location can be interpreted as a precondition of the VC financing relationship and thus underlines the impact of spatial proximity. As a result, the described research design only leaves the direct effect of spatial proximity on the likelihood of investment in the model.[944] According to the hypotheses elaborated in section 4.3 the effect of spatial proximity might be more or less intense for certain ventures, venture capitalists, and/or investment rounds. These effects are modeled by the previously mentioned interaction terms to rigorously test the hypotheses.

---

943 The analysis of patterns of spatial proximity in section 5.2 revealed correlations between these characteristics and the spatial proximity. However, these correlations might be also due to omitted variables or the fact that proximate ventures might have a higher likelihood to be financed which has an impact on the spatial patterns of the sample. See section 5.2 for further discussion.

944 See Figure 5.4.

By applying choice-based sampling in the current context and subsequently analyzing the data with the help of logistic regressions introduces two more methodological problems. King/Zeng (2001) show that logit coefficients are biased even for large samples if the fraction of ones is substantially smaller than the fraction of zeros in the population, i.e. in the case of rare events. This is the case in the current setting. As has been mentioned above for each VC financing relationship on average about 9.36 alternative relationships existed within one calendar year. This leads to a fraction of ones of only about 9.65%.[945] Furthermore, logit coefficients are biased if the fraction of ones in the sample does not correspond to the fraction of ones in the population. This is also the case since the sample is constructed by choice-based sampling and each realized VC financing dyad (ones) is matched by only one alternative dyad (zeros).[946] It is possible to account for the fact that the fraction of ones differs between the sample and the population by the methods of weighting and prior correction.[947] However, the problem of rare events remains.

Therefore, King/Zeng (2001) developed a method in order to correct logit coefficient estimates in the case of rare events and choice-based sampling. The standard logistic regression model assumes that the probability $\hat{\pi}_0$ of a certain event $Y_0=1$, given the values of the explanatory variables $\mathbf{x_0}$, is a function of the likelihood estimate $\hat{\beta}$.

$$\Pr(Y_0 = 1|\hat{\beta}) = \hat{\pi}_0 = \frac{1}{1 + e^{-x_0\hat{\beta}}}$$

King/Zeng (2001) prove that the bias in $\hat{\beta}$ can be estimated by the following weighted least-squares expression:

$$bias(\hat{\beta}) = (\mathbf{X'WX})^{-1}\mathbf{X'W}\xi$$

were $\xi_j = 0.5Q_{jj}[(1 + w_1)\hat{\pi}_j - w_1]$, Q_{jj} are the diagonal elements of $\mathbf{X(X'WX)^{-1}X'}$, $\mathbf{W} = diag\{\hat{\pi}_j(1 - \hat{\pi}_j)w_j\}$, w_1 is the fraction of ones in the sample relative to the fraction of ones in the population, $w_j = w_1 Y_j + w_0(1 - Y_j)$, and w_0 is the fraction of zeros in the sample relative to the fraction of zeros in the population. The estimation of this expression is basically a weighted least-squares regression of ξ on $\mathbf{X}$ using $\mathbf{W}$ as weight. Then the bias corrected estimate is $\tilde{\beta} = \hat{\beta} - bias(\hat{\beta})$.[948] Tomz/King/Zeng (1999) implemented this method in Stata.[949]

---

945 Cf. King/Zeng (2001), pp. 150-157.

946 Cf. Manski/Lerman (1977)

947 Cf. King/Zeng (2001), pp. 143-145.

948 Cf. King/Zeng (2001), pp. 146-148.

949 See Tomz/King/Zeng (1999) to download the relogit.ado file.

Finally, each venture capitalist and new venture enters the analysis more than once due to the described sample construction. Even though this issue is much less severe in the proposed empirical strategy as if one would analyze each potential dyad as illustrated in Figure 5.5 there might still be issues of nonindependence across observations. In consequence, hypothesis tests will be based on robust standard errors that are estimated without the assumption of independence across observations on the same venture capitalist.[950]

5.3.2 Rare Event Logistic Regressions

This section presents the results of logistic regressions which test the hypotheses regarding the impact of spatial proximity between the venture capitalist and the investee on the likelihood of a VC financing relationship. The coefficient estimates are adjusted for rare events and choice-based sampling as proposed by King/Zeng (2001) using a weighting procedure. The share of VC financing relationships that actually occurred on the total number of potential relationships is set to 9.65% since this is the fraction that is implied by the sample matching procedure as described in section 5.3.1.[951] Various interaction terms are used in order to test whether spatial proximity is especially important for certain groups or characteristics. The original variables were mean centered before calculating the product term in order to prevent unnecessary correlations and thus multicollinearity between the interaction terms and the original variables.[952]

Table 5.16 displays the results of the base models including all variables according to the hypotheses elaborated in section 4.3.[953] Model REL 1 (rare event logistic regression) was used in order to conduct an outlier analysis using Pregibon's Delta-Beta influence statistic, a coun-

[950] Stata only allows the correction of standard errors for nonindependence in regard to one dimension. As the multiple inclusion of venture capitalists is more severe than the one for new ventures, the correction is made for venture capitalists.

[951] The share of VC financing relationships that actually occurred on the total number of potential relationships has been varied in unreported regressions. The reported results are robust in regard to alternative specifications.

[952] Cf. Jaccard/Turrisi (1990), p. 28.

[953] Since these models also include interaction terms regarding the impact of the investment stage, 14 observations have been excluded for which no match in the same stage existed. Hence, the original variables regarding the investment stage do not have to be included next to the interaction terms and the models are more parsimonious. Additional 325 dyads and their matches had to be excluded due to missing values.

Table 5.16: Rare event logistic regressions – Base models
This table presents the results of rare event logistic regressions with a dummy variable indicating whether a VC financing relationship actually occurred (1) or not (0) as dependent variable. The sample consists of realized dyads of venture capitalists and German portfolio companies which have closed a financing round between January 2002 and March 2007 and a matching sample. Financing rounds with missing values or for which no match existed are excluded pairwise. Models REL 2 to 5 exclude five outliers pairwise. Model REL 5 additionally restricts the sample to German venture capitalists. Coefficients and standard errors are adjusted for rare events, choice-based sampling, serial correlation, heteroskedasticity, and nonindependence across venture capitalists. V.: venture.

Variable	REL 1	REL 2	REL 3	REL 4	REL 5
Dep. var.: realized dyad (yes/no)					
Distance (ln[1+min. travel time])	-0.2827***	-0.3530***	-0.3634***	-0.3627***	-0.4764***
Venture					
Ln(age) × dist.	0.0082	-0.0081	-0.0207	-0.0204	-0.0429
_Intercept	-0.0600	-0.0782*	-0.1028**	-0.1013**	-0.1140**
Dummy seed stage round × dist.	0.0341	-0.5402	-0.6122	-0.5989	-0.3782
Dummy later stage round × dist.	-0.0450	0.0504	0.0226	0.0237	0.0507
Dummy bus. concept only × dist.	0.1664	-0.8878	-0.9438	-0.9507	-0.6771
_Intercept	-0.5578	-0.1389	-0.1803	-0.1879	-0.0137
Dummy shipp.prod./prof. × dist.	0.0155	-0.0151	-0.0069	-0.0099	0.0446
_Intercept	-0.0138	0.0019	0.0084	0.0044	0.0808
Dummy prior exec. exp. × dist.	0.1515*	0.1451	0.1625	0.1609	0.2084*
_Intercept	0.0070	-0.0081	-0.0297	-0.0281	-0.0295
Dummy high asset intang. × dist.	-0.2671**	-0.2954**	-0.2979**	-0.2969**	-0.2732*
_Intercept	0.0258	0.0313	0.1477	0.1411	0.2632*
Dummy high R&D intensity × dist.	0.0539	-0.2575*	-0.3720**	-0.3727**	-0.4119**
_Intercept	0.0073	0.1258	0.0726	0.0590	0.1243
Dummy low book/market × dist.	-0.1696	-0.2059	-0.1114	-0.1103	-0.0625
_Intercept	0.2120	0.2280	0.3017**	0.2919*	0.3364**
Dummy East Ger. venture × dist.	-0.1327	-0.1119	-0.0850	-0.0838	0.0494
_Intercept	-0.2638**	-0.2510**	-0.2570**	-0.2561**	-0.1337
Dummy urban v. location × dist.	0.1458	0.1789*	0.2259**	0.2249**	0.1166
_Intercept	-0.2466**	-0.2580**	-0.1857	-0.1901	-0.3075**
Venture capitalist					
Ln(assets under mgt.) × dist.	0.0442**	0.0566***	0.0484*	0.0488*	0.0351
Ln(age) × dist.	0.0255	0.0058	0.0236	0.0235	0.0328
_Intercept	-0.0029	-0.0067	-0.0155	-0.0144	-0.0323
HHI industry × dist.			-0.1998	-0.2024	-0.4325
HHI stage × dist.			0.4225	0.4252	0.3039
Dummy corporate VC × dist.	0.0567	0.0425	0.0529	0.0522	0.0851
Dummy (quasi-)public VC × dist.	0.1946*	0.2638**	0.2497**	0.2492**	0.2110*
Dummy lead-investor × dist.	-0.0736	-0.0807	-0.0774	-0.0769	-0.1059
Round					
Inv. volume per VC × dist.	0.2106***	0.2174***	0.2256**	0.2242**	0.1745*
_Intercept	0.0349	0.0315	0.0411	0.0418	-0.0276
(Inv. volume per VC)² × dist.	-0.0268**	-0.0271**	-0.0298**	-0.0295**	-0.0207*
_Intercept	0.0062	0.0060	0.0035	0.0034	0.0118
Syndication benefit × dist.	0.0020**	0.0019*	0.0026**	0.0026**	-0.0063
_Intercept	-0.0037**	-0.0034**	-0.0053**	-0.0053**	0.0024
Control variables					
Ln(Ger. VC fundraising (t-1))	-0.1019	-0.1045	-0.0575		-0.0860
Ln(Ger. VC investments)	0.0568	0.0417	0.0399		0.1423
Return of MSCI SC Ger. (ltm)	-0.2247	-0.2352	-0.1441	-0.1416	-0.2056
Constant	-0.4288	0.0484	-0.2086	-0.3557	-0.2458
Year f.e.	No	No	No	Yes	No

Table 5.16 cont.: Rare event logistic regressions – Base models

Variable	REL 1	REL 2	REL 3	REL 4	REL 5
N	2126	2116	1866	1866	1650
LR Chi²	60.73***	70.87***	70.01***	69.97***	70.17***
Log. Likelihood	-644.27	-636.02	-557.12	-557.14	-488.50

* significant at 10%; ** significant at 5%; *** significant at 1% (two-sided)

terpart to Cook's distance, which is commonly used in linear regression models.[954] Five outliers were successively identified that had a Delta-Beta much greater than all other observations (>0.5 whereas the average Delta-Beta was 0.0150). In consequence, these outliers as well as their corresponding matching/original dyads were excluded from the analysis in order to obtain more robust results (Model REL 2). Model REL 3 additionally includes the variables regarding the venture capitalist's specialization and Model REL 4 controls for year fixed effects.[955] Finally, the analysis is restricted to German venture capitalists in Model REL 5. These base models offer important insights regarding the size and direction of the ceteris paribus impact of different variables. Models REL 2 and 3 will be used as reference models for the analyses in this section since these models are more parsimonious compared to the fixed effects Model REL 4. An analysis of the VIFs revealed a low to moderate probability of multicollinearity problems for Models REL 1 to 4. Most VIFs are below 3.75. Only the variables regarding the investment volume and the syndication benefit have moderately high VIFs of 5.24 to 7.21. Hence, further robustness checks are conducted for these variables throughout this section. Model REL 5 offers a similar picture regarding the VIFs, but there is a very high probability of multicollinearity problems for the variables regarding the syndication benefit (VIF of 17.06 and 17.93). Hence, the coefficients of these variables are not reliable in this specific model. A detailed overview of VIFs for all base models can be found in Table D.1 in the appendix.

Furthermore, it has to be noted that the large number of variables in the base models might inflate the estimated standard errors and thus impede the detection of significant relationships. In consequence, also smaller, more focused models will be analyzed throughout the section in order to obtain a detailed understanding of the impact of various variables. Table 5.17 gives a first impression by showing the results of various submodels which lead to Models REL 2 and 3 by a stepwise inclusion of variables. Most coefficients are fairly robust across different model specifications.

---

[954] Cf. Long/Freese (2001), pp. 151-152.

[955] Unreported tests show that the composition of the reduced sample is nearly the same as the full sample and that no selection bias is introduced.

Table 5.17: Rare event logistic regressions – Submodels leading to base models REL 2 and 3
This table presents the results of rare event logistic regressions with a dummy variable indicating whether a VC financing relationship actually occurred (1) or not (0) as dependent variable. The sample consists of realized dyads of venture capitalists and German portfolio companies which have closed a financing round between January 2002 and March 2007 and a matching sample. Financing rounds with missing values or for which no match existed as well as five outliers are excluded pairwise. Coefficients and standard errors are adjusted for rare events, choice-based sampling, serial correlation, heteroskedasticity, and nonindependence across venture capitalists. V.: venture.

Variable	REL 2.1	REL 2.2	REL 2.3	REL 2.4	REL 2.5	REL 2.6	REL 2.7	REL 2.8	REL 2	REL 3
Dep. var.: realized dyad (yes/no)										
Distance (ln[1+min. travel time])	-0.3178***	-0.3276***	-0.3313***	-0.3273***	-0.3375***	-0.3609***	-0.3909***	-0.3482***	-0.3530***	-0.3634***
Venture										
Ln(age) × dist.				-0.0163	-0.0125	-0.0086	0.0068	0.0055	-0.0081	-0.0207
_Intercept				-0.0686**	-0.0661*	-0.0739**	-0.0566	-0.0615	-0.0782*	-0.1028**
Dummy seed stage round × dist.				-0.4115	-0.3686	-0.7306**	-0.6611*	-0.6481*	-0.5402	-0.6122
Dummy later stage round × dist.				0.1619*	0.1286	0.0610	0.0438	0.0476	0.0504	0.0226
Dummy bus. concept only × dist.									-0.8878	-0.9438
_Intercept									-0.1389	-0.1803
Dummy shipp.prod./prof. × dist.									-0.0151	-0.0069
_Intercept									0.0019	0.0084
Dummy prior exec. exp. × dist.					0.0930	0.1361	0.1353	0.1476	0.1451	0.1625
_Intercept					-0.1372	-0.0664	-0.0306	-0.0108	-0.0081	-0.0297
Dummy high asset intang. × dist.					-0.2030*	-0.2403**	-0.3040**	-0.3014**	-0.2954**	-0.2979**
_Intercept					-0.0627	-0.0395	0.0298	0.0286	0.0313	0.1477
Dummy high R&D intensity × dist.					-0.1397	-0.2436*	-0.2374*	-0.2406*	-0.2575*	-0.3720**
_Intercept					0.1365	0.1687	0.1428	0.1372	0.1258	0.0726
Dummy low book/market × dist.					-0.1377	-0.1903	-0.2126*	-0.2092	-0.2059	-0.1114
_Intercept					0.1241	0.1688	0.1861	0.2240*	0.2280	0.3017**
Dummy East Ger. venture × dist.							-0.1190	-0.1239	-0.1119	-0.0850
_Intercept							-0.2536**	-0.2639**	-0.2510**	-0.2570**
Dummy urban v. location × dist.							0.1878**	0.1878**	0.1789*	0.2259**
_Intercept							-0.2378*	-0.2473**	-0.2580**	-0.1857

Table 5.17 cont.: Rare event logistic regressions – Submodels leading to base models REL 2 and 3

Variable	REL 2.1	REL 2.2	REL 2.3	REL 2.4	REL 2.5	REL 2.6	REL 2.7	REL 2.8	REL 2	REL 3
Venture capitalist										
Ln(assets under mgt.) × dist.						0.0669***	0.0565***	0.0565***	0.0566***	0.0484*
Ln(age) × dist.						0.0246	0.0090	0.0057	0.0058	0.0236
_Intercept						-0.0103	-0.0080	-0.0057	-0.0067	-0.0155
HHI industry × dist.										-0.1998
HHI stage × dist.										0.4225
Dummy corporate VC × dist.			0.0596	0.1162	0.1083	0.0686	0.0404	0.0456	0.0425	0.0529
Dummy (quasi-)public VC × dist.			0.2400**	0.2331**	0.2300**	0.3186***	0.2659**	0.2655**	0.2638**	0.2497**
Dummy lead-investor × dist.						-0.1175	-0.0861	-0.0782	-0.0807	-0.0774
Round										
Inv. volume per VC × dist.		0.2502***	0.2649***	0.2459***	0.2234***	0.2116***	0.2218***	0.2200***	0.2174***	0.2256**
_Intercept		0.0377	0.0305	0.0262	0.0498	0.0186	0.0312	0.0317	0.0315	0.0411
(Inv. volume per VC)² × dist.		-0.0324***	-0.0331***	-0.0307***	-0.0287***	-0.0261**	-0.0274**	-0.0272**	-0.0271**	-0.0298**
_Intercept		0.0056	0.0060	0.0062	0.0043	0.0075	0.0063	0.0063	0.0060	0.0035
Syndication benefit × dist.								0.0018*	0.0019*	0.0026**
_Intercept								-0.0033*	-0.0034**	-0.0053**
Control variables										
Ln(Ger. VC fundraising (t-1))	-0.0713	-0.0552	-0.0554	-0.0847	-0.1003	-0.0972	-0.1056	-0.0985	-0.1045	-0.0575
Ln(Ger. VC investments)	0.0999	0.0358	0.0328	0.0173	0.0465	0.0866	0.0975	0.0618	0.0417	0.0399
Return of MSCI SC Ger. (ltm)	-0.2145*	-0.1923	-0.1682	-0.1952	-0.2211	-0.2388	-0.2158	-0.2325	-0.2352	-0.1441
Constant	-0.9732	-0.6951	-0.6205	-0.2299	-0.2656	-0.4191	-0.2147	-0.1854	0.0484	-0.2086
N	2788	2384	2384	2364	2364	2116	2116	2116	2116	1866
LR Chi²	36.50***	41.12***	44.23***	48.98***	52.50***	60.60***	68.77***	69.77***	70.87***	70.01***
Log. Likelihood	-866.45	-735.94	-734.38	-725.67	-723.90	-641.16	-637.07	-636.57	-636.02	-557.12

* significant at 10%; ** significant at 5%; *** significant at 1% (two-sided)

Spatial proximity / distance

The results in Table 5.16 and Table 5.17 prove that the distance in terms of minimum travel time between a venture capitalist and a new venture has a robust and significant negative effect on the likelihood of a VC financing relationship. Thus, hypothesis 1b is supported. Furthermore, the magnitude of the effect of distance is considerable. To illustrate the impact of distance on the likelihood of a VC financing relationship, the probability of a relationship was estimated for different types of venture capitalist-investee dyads and varying distances. The first type of dyad is the mean venture capitalist-investee dyad of the sample of Model REL 2.1. Hence, the respective mean was set for all venture, venture capitalist, and investment round variables using the sample of Model REL 2.1. As such a dyad does not exist in reality, it rather has a hypothetical character.[956] In consequence, four additional median dyads are used to illustrate the impact of distance. These median dyads are: (i) the median venture capitalist-investee dyad regarding all realized dyads as well as a median (ii) seed, (iii) first, and (iv) later round venture capitalist-investee dyad regarding all realized dyads of the respective group. The control variables are held constant at the median of realized dyads for all relationships. Model REL 2.1 was used to estimate the probability of a VC financing relationship for the mean dyad and Model REL 3 was used for the median dyads. Table 5.18 summarizes the values of the different variables that were used to estimate the probabilities.[957]

The absolute magnitude of the probability of a specific VC financing relationship highly depends on the number of alternative dyads. The higher the number of alternative dyads is the lower the absolute probability of a specific relationship. The number of alternative dyads for a specific type of dyad, in turn, depends on the narrowness of the criteria used to construct the matching sample as described in section 5.3.1. Hence, it is not possible to estimate the absolute probability of a specific dyad and to compare this probability to the probability of alternative types of dyads. However, it is possible to estimate the development of the probability of a specific VC financing relationship with varying distance. In consequence, Figure 5.7 illustrates the impact of distance on the relative likelihood of the different types of VC financing

[956] E.g. a venture capitalist which is 21.1% (quasi-)public and 78.9% private does not exist. Either the venture capitalist is (quasi-)public or not.

[957] As Model REL 2.1 only includes the distance and control variables, the values regarding venture, venture capitalist and round characteristics, which are shown in Table 5.18, are not set but implied by the model.

Table 5.18: Characteristics of analyzed venture capitalist-investee dyads
This table presents the new venture, venture capitalist, and round characteristics of the mean venture capitalist-investee dyad of the sample of Model REL 2.1, a median venture capitalist-investee dyad regarding all realized dyads, as well as a median seed, first, and later round venture capitalist-investee dyad regarding all realized dyads of the respective group.

Variable	Mean dyad (sample of REL 2.1)	Median dyad (of all realized dyads)	Median seed round dyad (of all realized dyads)	Median first round dyad (of all realized dyads)	Median later round dyad (of all realized dyads)
Venture					
Venture development stage					
Age in years	3.3532	3.9877	0.1192	2.2493	4.6219
Dummy seed stage round	0.0269	0	1	0	0
Dummy first round	0.2715	0	0	1	0
Dummy later stage round	0.7016	1	0	0	1
Product development stage					
Dummy business concept only	0.0197	0	0	0	0
Dummy product development/tests	0.3382	0	1	0	0
Dummy shipp.prod./profitable	0.6420	1	0	1	1
Dummy prior exec. experience	0.4268	0	0	0	0
Industry's knowledge intensity					
Dummy high asset intangibility	0.0997	0	0	0	0
Dummy high R&D intensity	0.1291	0	0	0	0
Dummy low book/market	0.1044	0	0	0	0
Region					
Dummy East German venture	0.2905	0	0	0	0
Dummy urban venture location	0.2733	0	0	0	0
Venture capitalist					
Assets under management in m€	158.2945	124.9000	51.3000	100.0000	125.0000
Age (years)	5.9794	5.8192	4.3397	4.9712	6.2521
Specialization					
HHI industry	0.4293	0.3438	0.3249	0.3333	0.3580
HHI stage	0.4321	0.3964	0.3422	0.3776	0.4074
Type					
Dummy VC with excl. fin. objectives	0.7195	1	1	1	1
Dummy corporate VC	0.0696	0	0	0	0
Dummy (quasi-)public VC	0.2109	0	0	0	0
Dummy lead-investor	0.3572	0	1	0	0
Round					
Investment volume per VC (m€)	1.6217	1.2000	0.2500	1.4000	1.1440
Syndication benefit (min. tr. time)	15.7074	0.0000	0.0000	0.0000	0.0526
Control variables					
VC market condition					
Ger. VC fundraising in m€ (t-1)	1012.4200	1012.4200	1012.4200	1012.4200	1012.4200
Ger. VC investments in m€	965.3800	965.3800	965.3800	965.3800	965.3800
Return of MSCI SC Germany (ltm)	0.1587	0.1587	0.1587	0.1587	0.1587

relationships (dyads). The relative likelihood of a VC financing relationship is defined as the probability of a VC financing relationship with a certain distance *d* divided by the probability of the same relationship with a distance of zero.[958]

$$Relative\ likelihood\ of\ VC\ financing\ relationship = \frac{\Pr(Y_0 = 1|\hat{\beta}, d)}{\Pr(Y_0 = 1|\hat{\beta}, d = 0)}$$

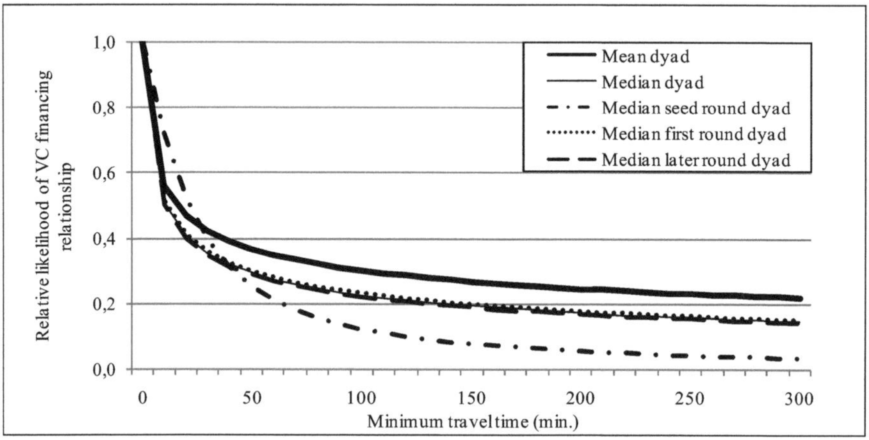

Figure 5.7: Impact of distance (min. travel time) on the likelihood of a VC financing relationship
Model REL 2.1 was used to estimate the probability of a VC financing relationship for the mean dyad and Model REL 3 was used for the median dyads.

For the mean dyad, the likelihood of a VC financing relationship decreases by about 25% with each triplication of the minimum travel time. The likelihood that a specific VC financing relationship occurs is about 56.0% if the minimum travel time between both parties is 10 min. compared to a minimum travel time of zero.[959] The relative likelihood further decreases by 24.6% to 42.2% for a minimum travel time of 30 min. and decreases by additional 26.1% to 31.2% for a minimum travel time of 90 min. This illustrates the economic relevance of distance which might be underestimated by many venture capitalists and entrepreneurial teams. Distance has an even larger impact on the likelihood of a specific VC investment for the median dyads and especially for the median seed round dyad.[960] Probabilities of the overall me-

[958] A distance of zero indicates that both parties are located in the same ZIP code area.

[959] Probabilities for distances close to zero have to be interpreted with caution due to the logarithmic functional form of distance in the empirical models.

[960] In order to check the robustness of the results of Model REL 3 for the median dyads Model REL 3 was also used to estimate probabilities for a mean dyad. The results were almost identical to Model REL 2.1 which indicates that the results of the larger Model REL 3 are reliable.

dian dyad, the median first round dyad, and the median later round dyad are very similar. Thus, results will be discussed only for the overall median dyad in the following analyses. For the overall median dyad, the likelihood of a VC financing relationship decreases by about 33% with each triplication of the minimum travel time. For the median seed round dyad it is not possible to generalize the impact of distance that easily. The relative likelihood decreases by 45.5% for a triplication of the minimum travel time from 10 to 30 min. and further decreases by 65.2% if the minimum travel time changes from 30 to 90 min.

These cases impressively illustrate the impact of spatial proximity on the likelihood of investment and the high sensitivity to different types of dyads like e.g. seed round dyads. To disentangle the different effects and to test the remaining hypotheses, this section continues to discuss single effects under the ceteris paribus assumption.

Venture and product development stage

Model REL 2 and 3 in Table 5.17 do not reveal any significant relationships regarding the venture as well as product development stage × distance interaction terms. However, as has been mentioned in section 5.2.3 and as can be seen in Table C.1 in the appendix, these variables correlate with each other and might measure similar aspects concerning the maturity of a new venture. This is also implied by significant coefficients regarding the investment stage in Models REL 2.4 and 2.6 to 2.8 in Table 5.17. To disentangle the single effects of the venture and product development stage variables, Table 5.19 presents further models which include the respective variables separately. In addition, the size of the new venture in terms of its number of employees is tested in Models REL 2.12 and 2.13.[961] Model REL 2.9 shows that the point estimate of the new venture's age × distance interaction term is positive but not significant at the 10% level. Hence, Hypothesis, 2.1b is finally not supported. The coefficients of the investment stage × distance interaction terms in Model REL 2.10 suggest that distance reduces the likelihood of a VC financing relationship significantly more if the target company is in the seed investment stage. Hence, this reduced model provides some evidence for Hypothesis 2.2b.[962] Regarding the effect of the new venture's size on the impact of distance on the likelihood of a VC investment, Models REL 2.12 and 2.13 do not reveal a significant relationship and Hypothesis 2.3b is not supported. This might be due to potential measurement errors

---

[961] The size of the new venture in terms of its number of employees is likely to entail significant measurement errors. In consequence, this variable is not included in the main models and results have to be interpreted with caution. See section 5.1.3.2 for further discussion.

[962] Model 2.8 in Table 5.17 shows that this effect is also significant if one controls for the new venture's age. In addition, the point estimates of the coefficients suggest that the size of the effect is quite stable.

Table 5.19: Rare event logistic regressions – Details on venture and product development stage

This table presents the results of rare event logistic regressions with a dummy variable indicating whether a VC financing relationship actually occurred (1) or not (0) as dependent variable. The models are based on Model REL 2 and scrutinize further details regarding the venture and product development stage. The sample consists of realized dyads of venture capitalists and German portfolio companies which have closed a financing round between January 2002 and March 2007 and a matching sample. Financing rounds with missing values or for which no match existed as well as five outliers are excluded pairwise. Coefficients and standard errors are adjusted for rare events, choice-based sampling, serial correlation, heteroskedasticity, and nonindependence across venture capitalists. V.: venture.

Variable	REL 2	REL 2.9	REL 2.10	REL 2.11	REL 2.12	REL 2.13
Dep. var.: realized dyad (yes/no)						
Distance (ln[1+min. travel time])	-0.3530***	-0.3434***	-0.3543***	-0.3587***	-0.3866***	-0.3795***
Venture						
Ln(age) × dist.	-0.0081	0.0391			0.0107	
_Intercept	-0.0782*	-0.0495			-0.1483***	
Dummy seed stage round × dist.	-0.5402		-0.6280*		-0.4184	
Dummy later stage round × dist.	0.0504		0.0626		0.0404	
Ln(number of employees) × dist.					-0.0987	-0.0578
_Intercept					0.1987***	0.1227**
Dummy bus. concept only × dist.	-0.8878			-0.9186*	-0.8175	
_Intercept	-0.1389			-0.0038	-0.2644	
Dummy shipp.prod./prof. × dist.	-0.0151			0.0225	0.0855	
_Intercept	0.0019			-0.0277	-0.0753	
Dummy prior exec. exp. × dist.	0.1451	0.1618*	0.1490	0.1714*	0.1593	0.1609*
_Intercept	-0.0081	0.0122	-0.0112	0.0057	-0.0410	-0.0117
Dummy high asset intang. × dist.	-0.2954**	-0.3115**	-0.3002**	-0.3022**	-0.3276**	-0.3289**
_Intercept	0.0313	0.0264	0.0175	0.0112	0.0984	0.0615
Dummy high R&D intensity × dist.	-0.2575*	-0.2314*	-0.2392*	-0.2291	-0.2374	-0.2623*
_Intercept	0.1258	0.1620	0.1407	0.1396	0.1313	0.2058*
Dummy low book/market × dist.	-0.2059	-0.2407**	-0.2191*	-0.2309*	-0.2094	-0.2362*
_Intercept	0.2280	0.2474*	0.1820	0.2078	0.2608*	0.2200*
Dummy East Ger. venture × dist.	-0.1119	-0.1375*	-0.1171	-0.1136	-0.0953	-0.0937
_Intercept	-0.2510**	-0.2692**	-0.2822**	-0.2838**	-0.2572**	-0.2842**
Dummy urban v. location × dist.	0.1789*	0.1930**	0.1859**	0.1806*	0.1935**	0.1999**
_Intercept	-0.2580**	-0.2627**	-0.2493**	-0.2634**	-0.2572*	-0.2645**

Table 5.19 cont.: Rare event logistic regressions – Details on venture and product development stage

Variable	REL 2	REL 2.9	REL 2.10	REL 2.11	REL 2.12	REL 2.13
Venture capitalist						
Ln(assets under mgt.) × dist.	0.0566***	0.0576***	0.0562***	0.0561***	0.0618***	0.0632***
Ln(age) × dist.	0.0058	0.0109	0.0073	0.0143	0.0085	0.0207
_Intercept	-0.0067	-0.0029	-0.0148	-0.0130	-0.0066	-0.0241
Dummy corporate VC × dist.	0.0425	0.0533	0.0296	0.0353	0.0725	0.0385
Dummy (quasi-)public VC × dist.	0.2638**	0.2493**	0.2682**	0.2489**	0.2553**	0.2709**
Dummy lead-investor × dist.	-0.0807	-0.0967	-0.0821	-0.1084	-0.1139	-0.1499*
Round						
Inv. volume per VC × dist.	0.2174***	0.2244***	0.2217***	0.2269***	0.2798***	0.2542***
_Intercept	0.0315	0.0312	0.0372	0.0338	-0.0301	0.0047
(Inv. volume per VC)² × dist.	-0.0271**	-0.0272**	-0.0275**	-0.0282**	-0.0328**	-0.0297**
_Intercept	0.0060	0.0063	0.0058	0.0060	0.0091	0.0071
Syndication benefit × dist.	0.0019*	0.0020**	0.0018*	0.0019**	0.0020**	0.0019**
_Intercept	-0.0034**	-0.0035**	-0.0031*	-0.0034**	-0.0035**	-0.0033*
Control variables						
Ln(Ger. VC fundraising (t-1))	-0.1045	-0.0767	-0.0761	-0.0656	-0.1221*	-0.0654
Ln(Ger. VC investments)	0.0417	0.0614	0.0706	0.0595	0.0787	0.0912
Return of MSCI SC Ger. (ltm)	-0.2352	-0.2011	-0.1971	-0.1770	-0.2004	-0.1475
Constant	0.0484	-0.3972	-0.4368	-0.3995	-0.3698	-0.9083
Year f.e.	#NV	#NV	#NV	#NV	#NV	#NV
N	2116	2134	2116	2134	2008	2024
LR Chi²	70.87***	68.82***	68.95***	69.03***	75.07***	69.16***
Log. Likelihood	-636.02	-642.76	-636.98	-642.65	-599.65	-607.68

* significant at 10%; ** significant at 5%; *** significant at 1% (two-sided)

of this variable as discussed in section 5.1.3.2. Finally, the coefficients of the product development × distance interaction terms in Model REL 2.11 imply that distance has a significantly more negative effect on the likelihood of investment if the new venture has nothing more than a business concept. Thus, there is some evidence for Hypothesis 3b. For the interpretation of the results regarding the investment and product development stage it is important to note that these results are not ceteris paribus with regard to the excluded variables. However, the point estimates of the coefficients change only slightly compared to Model REL 2 which suggests that an economic effect exists.

To further illustrate the magnitude of the identified significant relationships, Figure 5.8 depicts the estimated relative likelihood of a VC financing relationship for the median venture capitalist-investee dyad and varying investment and product development stages.[963] Model REL 2 was used to calculate the probabilities of investment in order to retrieve a conservative estimate of the ceteris paribus effects. As can be seen in Table 5.19 the effects are larger in Models REL 2.10 and 2.11. The decrease of the likelihood of investment with rising minimum travel time is much stronger for seed stage rounds compared to first and later stage rounds. Seed stage dyads with a minimum travel time of three hours only have 6.5% of the likelihood of investment which would emerge if both parties would reside in the same ZIP code area. Later stage dyads still have 20.4% of the reference likelihood of investment. A similar picture emerges for a comparison of different product development stages.[964] The decrease of the likelihood of investment is much more severe for new ventures that have a business concept only. After a minimum travel time of three hours only 4.4% of the reference likelihood remains, while new ventures that are already in the product development stage still have 21.4% of the reference likelihood.

Prior experience of the entrepreneurial team

The results in Table 5.16 offer mixed results regarding the effect of the entrepreneurial team's prior experience on the importance of distance. The coefficient of the entrepreneurial team's prior experience dummy × distance interaction term is positive in all models but only significant if one restricts the sample to German venture capitalists (Model REL 5). In the main reference Models REL 2 and 3, the coefficient is not significant (p-values of 0.134 and 0.115 respectively). The results in Table 5.20 show that the coefficient of the entrepreneurial team's

[963] This approach basically adapts the calculation of partial effects as suggested by Wooldridge (2008) to the current research setting (cf. Wooldridge (2008), p. 583).

[964] Figure 5.8 does not include the product development stage "shipping product/profitable" since the coefficient of the interaction term with distance changes its sign from Model REL 2 to 2.11. Hence, the stage "product development/tests" was chosen for comparison.

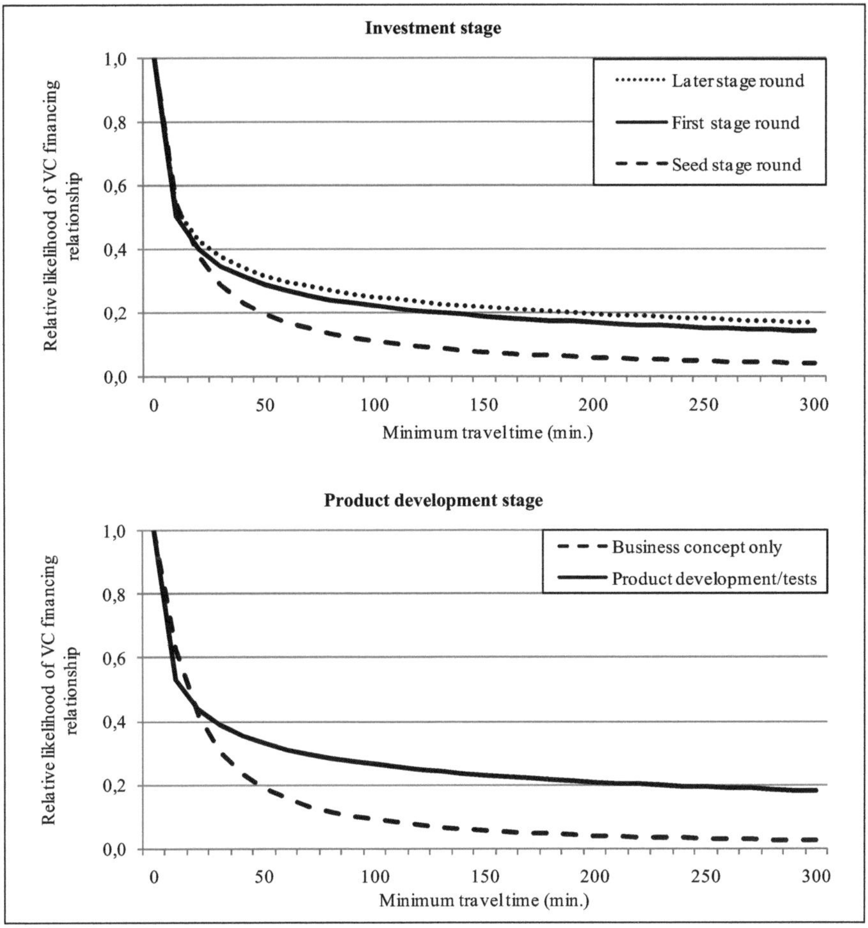

Figure 5.8: Impact of distance (min. travel time) on the likelihood of a VC financing relationship for different venture and product development stages
Model REL 2 and characteristics of the median venture capitalist-investee dyad were used to calculate the probabilities.

prior experience dummy × distance interaction term is positive and significant at least at a 5% level in Models REL 2.14 to 2.17. If one controls for the investment volume (Model REL 2.18), the coefficient of the prior experience interaction term drops quite substantially but is still significant at a 10% level. Table C.1 reveals that the entrepreneurial team's prior experience is positively correlated with the investment volume. One reason might be that entrepreneurs with profound prior experience pursue higher profile business concepts which also have

Table 5.20: Rare event logistic regressions – Details on the entrepreneurial team's prior experience
This table presents the results of rare event logistic regressions with a dummy variable indicating whether a VC financing relationship actually occurred (1) or not (0) as dependent variable. The models scrutinize further details regarding the entrepreneurial team's prior experience and include variables stepwise. The sample consists of realized dyads of venture capitalists and German portfolio companies which have closed a financing round between January 2002 and March 2007 and a matching sample. Financing rounds with missing values or for which no match existed as well as five outliers are excluded pairwise. Coefficients and standard errors are adjusted for rare events, choice-based sampling, serial correlation, heteroskedasticity, and nonindependence across venture capitalists. V.: venture.

Variable	REL 2.14	REL 2.15	REL 2.16	REL 2.17	REL 2.18	REL 2.19	REL 2	REL 3
Dep. var.: realized dyad (yes/no)								
Distance (ln[1+min. travel time])	-0.3339***	-0.3408***	-0.3424***	-0.2990***	-0.3267***	-0.3330***	-0.3530***	-0.3634***
Venture								
Ln(age) × dist.						-0.0286	-0.0081	-0.0207
_Intercept						-0.1009**	-0.0782*	-0.1028**
Dummy seed stage round × dist.						-0.5785*	-0.5402	-0.6122
Dummy later stage round × dist.						0.0616	0.0504	0.0226
Dummy bus. concept only × dist.						-1.0373	-0.8878	-0.9438
_Intercept						-0.1361	-0.1389	-0.1803
Dummy shipp.prod./prof. × dist.						0.0275	-0.0151	-0.0069
_Intercept						0.0108	0.0019	0.0084
Dummy prior exec. exp. × dist.	0.1935**	0.2041***	0.2298***	0.2511***	0.1682*	0.1521*	0.1451	0.1625
_Intercept	-0.1586*	-0.1626*	-0.1931**	-0.1302	-0.0351	-0.0476	-0.0081	-0.0297
Dummy high asset intang. × dist.			-0.1504	-0.1529	-0.2499**	-0.2340**	-0.2954**	-0.2979**
_Intercept			0.0878	0.0765	-0.0596	-0.0350	0.0313	0.1477
Dummy high R&D intensity × dist.			-0.1428	-0.2326*	-0.2470*	-0.2423	-0.2575*	-0.3720**
_Intercept			0.1926*	0.2386**	0.2019*	0.1528	0.1258	0.0726
Dummy low book/market × dist.			-0.1187	-0.1860	-0.2248*	-0.1741	-0.2059	-0.1114
_Intercept			0.1617	0.1989*	0.1758	0.2033	0.2280	0.3017**
Dummy East Ger. venture × dist.							-0.1119	-0.0850
_Intercept							-0.2510**	-0.2570**
Dummy urban v. location × dist.							0.1789*	0.2259**
_Intercept							-0.2580**	-0.1857

Table 5.21: Rare event logistic regressions – Details on the entrepreneurial team's prior experience

Variable	REL 2.14	REL 2.15	REL 2.16	REL 2.17	REL 2.18	REL 2.19	REL 2	REL 3
Venture capitalist								
Ln(assets under mgt.) × dist.				0.0827***	0.0687***	0.0659***	0.0566***	0.0484*
Ln(age) × dist.				0.0231	0.0330	0.0229	0.0058	0.0236
_Intercept				-0.0011	-0.0156	-0.0091	-0.0067	-0.0155
HHI industry × dist.								-0.1998
HHI stage × dist.								0.4225
Dummy corporate VC × dist.		0.0628	0.0471	0.0408	0.0641	0.0718	0.0425	0.0529
Dummy (quasi-)public VC × dist.		0.2376**	0.2231**	0.2999***	0.3181***	0.3146***	0.2638**	0.2497**
Dummy lead-investor × dist.				-0.1166*	-0.1456*	-0.1160	-0.0807	-0.0774
Round								
Inv. volume per VC × dist.					0.2124***	0.2128***	0.2174***	0.2256**
_Intercept					0.0242	0.0198	0.0315	0.0411
(Inv. volume per VC)^2 × dist.					-0.0262**	-0.0267**	-0.0271**	-0.0298**
_Intercept					0.0071	0.0071	0.0060	0.0035
Syndication benefit × dist.				0.0024**	0.0015	0.0015	0.0019*	0.0026**
_Intercept				-0.0041**	-0.0025	-0.0027	-0.0034**	-0.0053**
Control variables								
Ln(Ger. VC fundraising (t-1))	-0.0911	-0.0888	-0.1119*	-0.0835	-0.0456	-0.1040	-0.1045	-0.0575
Ln(Ger. VC investments)	0.0698	0.0603	0.1108	0.0852	0.0760	0.0478	0.0417	0.0399
Return of MSCI SC Ger. (ltm)	-0.1960	-0.1797	-0.2138*	-0.2280	-0.1863	-0.2612*	-0.2352	-0.1441
Constant	-0.4819	-0.3692	-0.5838	-0.7926	-0.9595	-0.1804	0.0484	-0.2086
N	2788	2788	2788	2496	2134	2116	2116	1866
LR Chi^2	42.05***	45.68***	48.82***	60.07***	58.03***	62.70***	70.87***	70.01***
Log. Likelihood	-863.68	-861.86	-860.29	-762.00	-648.16	-640.11	-636.02	-557.12

* significant at 10%; ** significant at 5%; *** significant at 1% (two-sided)

higher funding requirements. The inclusion of variables regarding the venture development stage leads to an additional drop of the coefficient of the prior experience interaction, but the coefficient still remains significant (Model REL 2.19). The coefficient becomes insignificant after the inclusion of the variables concerning the new venture's region (Model REL 2). As the coefficient is relatively stable in its magnitude it is likely that the coefficient loses its significance due to the large number of variables in the model. In consequence, there is weak statistical evidence for hypothesis 4b; the impact of distance on the likelihood of investment is less negative if the entrepreneurial team has profound prior experience. Figure 5.9 illustrates the size of the effect. The impact of distance (min. travel time) on the likelihood of a VC financing relationship is more severe if the entrepreneurial team has no profound prior experience. Then, dyads with a minimum travel time of three hours only have 20.4% of the likelihood of investment which would emerge if both parties would reside in the same ZIP code area. Dyads with entrepreneurial teams that have profound prior experience still have 34.3% of the reference likelihood of investment.

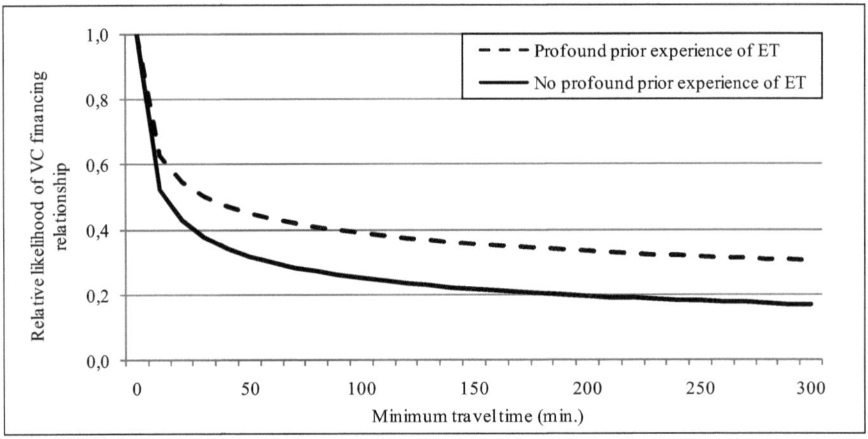

Figure 5.9: Impact of distance (min. travel time) on the likelihood of a VC financing relationship for different levels of the entrepreneurial team's prior experience
Model REL 2 and characteristics of the median venture capitalist-investee dyad were used to calculate the probabilities.

Industries' knowledge intensity

The results in Table 5.17 clearly show that distance reduces the likelihood of investment more precipitously if the new venture acts in a knowledge intensive industry. The coefficients of the high asset intangibility dummy × distance interaction term and the high R&D intensity dummy × distance interaction term are negative and significant (Models REL 2 and 3).

Hence, hypotheses 5.1a and 5.2a are supported. In addition, there is some empirical evidence for hypothesis 5.3b, spatial proximity is more important for new ventures with high future growth perspectives (i.e. low book/market ratio) (Model REL 2.7). However, the coefficient of the low book/market ratio dummy × distance interaction term slumps if one controls for the venture capitalist's specialization (Model REL 3) and the effect is not significant in most models. In consequence, hypothesis 5.3b is not supported.

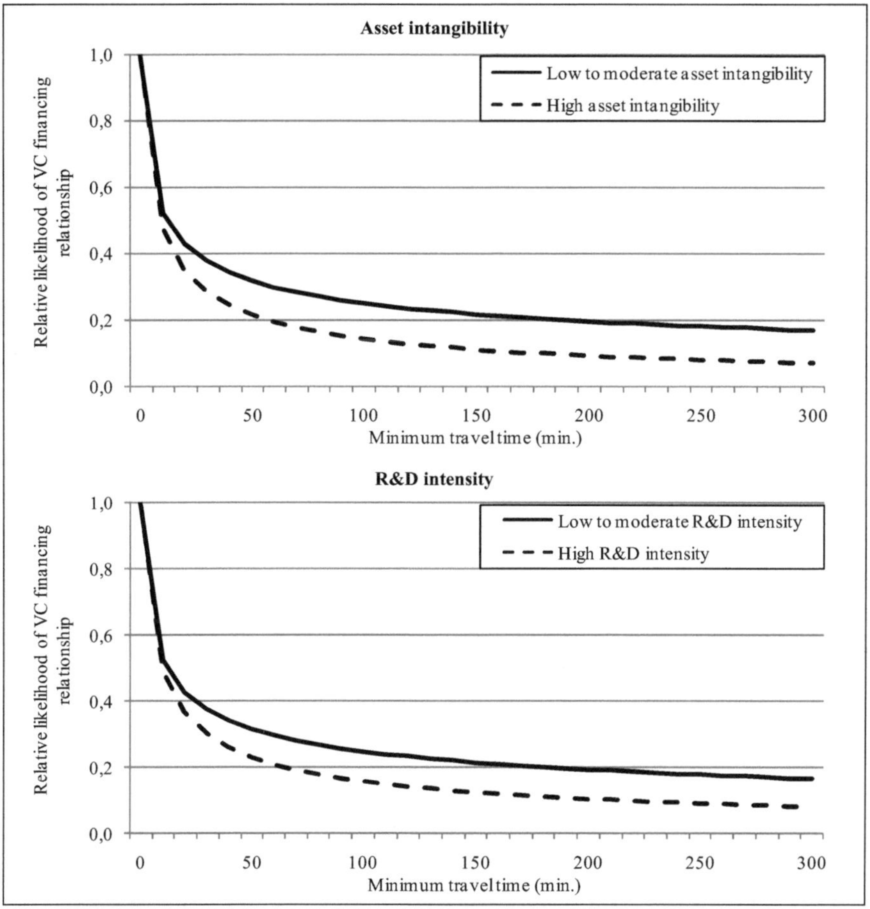

Figure 5.10: Impact of distance (min. travel time) on the likelihood of a VC financing relationship for different characteristics of the new venture's industry

Model REL 2 and characteristics of the median venture capitalist-investee dyad were used to calculate the probabilities.

Figure 5.10 illustrates the size of the significant effects which have nearly the same magnitude. New ventures that conduct their business in an industry with low or moderate asset intangibility/R&D intensity and are located three hours from the focal venture capitalist still have 20.4% of the likelihood of investment which would emerge if both parties would reside in the same ZIP code area. In contrast, new ventures that conduct their business in an industry with high asset intangibility/R&D intensity only have 9.9%/11.3% of the reference likelihood of investment.

Region of the venture

The data reveals no differences for the impact of spatial proximity on the likelihood of investment among East and West German ventures (Table 5.17) as the East German venture dummy × distance interaction term is not significant in all models.[965] In contrast, Models REL 2 and 3 prove that distance reduces the likelihood of investment less if the new venture is located in an urban area. Hence, hypothesis 6.2b is supported. Figure 5.11 illustrates that the effect of the new venture's location is quite substantial. New ventures located in urban areas still have 37.9% of the reference likelihood of investment if they are located three hours from their investor, while other new ventures are left with 20.4%.

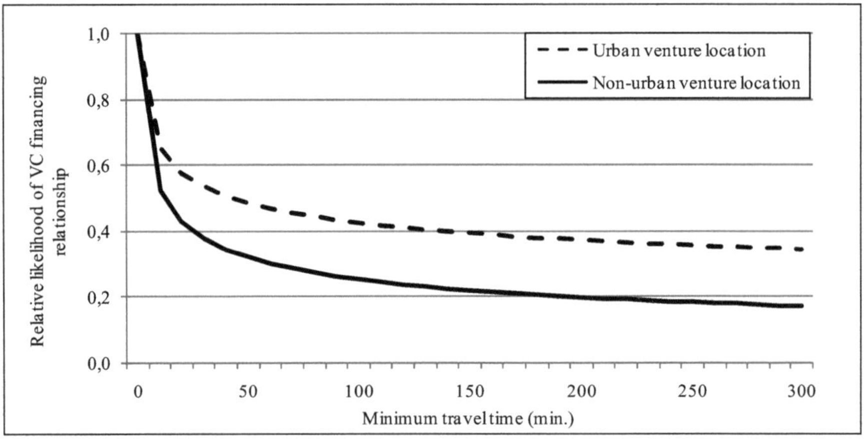

Figure 5.11: Impact of distance (min. travel time) on the likelihood of a VC financing relationship for new venture's located in urban and non-urban areas
Model REL 2 and characteristics of the median venture capitalist-investee dyad were used to calculate the probabilities.

---

965 The significant coefficient of the East German venture dummy (intercept term) only corrects for differences between the original and the matched sample and has no relevant implications for the hypothesis test.

Size of the venture capitalist

The results in Table 5.17 also clearly show that larger venture capitalists in terms of assets under management are less sensitive to distance and are thus more likely to invest in distant new ventures. Hence, hypothesis 7b is supported. Figure 5.12 illustrates the size of the effect. Large venture capitalists which have about 1.1 bn€ under management invest with a probability of 31.7% into new ventures located three hours away compared to new ventures located in their ZIP code area. Small venture capitalists that have about 22.6 m€ under management invest with a probability of only 15.3% into new ventures located three hours away.

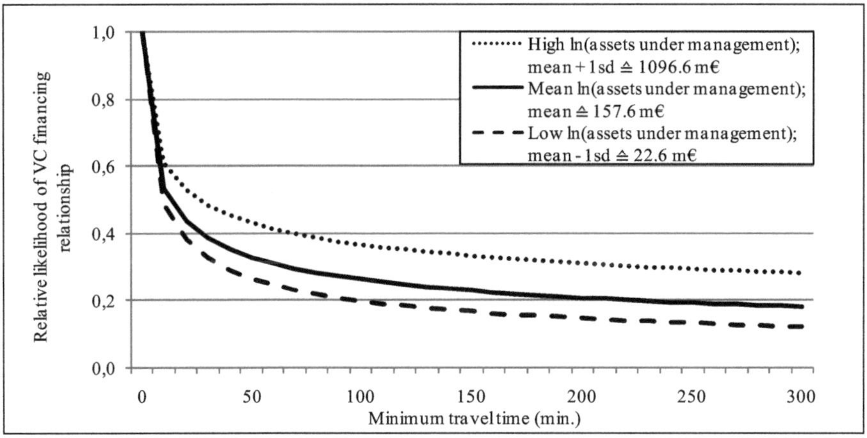

Figure 5.12: Impact of distance (min. travel time) on the likelihood of a VC financing relationship for venture capitalists of different sizes
Model REL 2 and characteristics of the median venture capitalist-investee dyad were used to calculate the probabilities.

Experience and reputation of the venture capitalist

The empirical models in Table 5.17 imply that the venture capitalist's age has no effect on the importance of distance. Even though an analysis of multicollinearity did not reveal any problems (Table D.1 in the appendix), Table C.1 shows that the venture capitalist's age is correlated with the venture capitalist's size. Hence, further regressions are conducted to disentangle the effects of these variables. Table D.2 in the appendix displays the results and discovers that the coefficient of the venture capitalist age × distance interaction term is positive and significant in Models 2.20 and 2.22 to 2.25. This would imply that the impact of distance on the likelihood of investment becomes less negative with rising age of the venture capitalist. Consequently, the effects of larger and more widespread networks, specific investment experience and reputation, as well as higher efficiency in supporting distant portfolio companies would outweigh the effect of being able to pick proximate investments due to a higher quantity and quality of deal flow for experienced investors.[966] However, if one controls for the venture capitalist's size, the coefficient of the venture capitalist age × distance interaction term slumps and becomes insignificant (Model 2.26). This implies that the venture capitalist's size captures most of the underlying effects that lead to a reduced importance of spatial proximity. In consequence, an effect of the venture capitalist's age is not supported by the data.[967] However, it is important to mention that the venture capitalist's size may also capture a large extent of a venture capitalist's cumulated experience and reputation. Hence, there might be effects of experience and reputation which are just difficult to isolate.

Specialization of the venture capitalist

Model REL 3 in Table 5.17 suggests that there is no significant difference in the impact of distance on the likelihood of investment between specialized and unspecialized venture capitalists. In order to check the reliability of this result, further regressions were conducted. The results of these additional regressions in Table D.3 reveal that the specialization of the venture capitalist in regard to certain industries or investment stages has a significant effect on the importance of spatial proximity if one does not control for urban venture locations and the size of the venture capitalist (Models REL 3.1 to 3.7). Then the coefficient of the industry HHI × distance interaction term is negative and significant which implies that the likelihood of investment decreases more precipitously for venture capitalists that are highly specialized in a certain industry. In contrast, the coefficient of the stage HHI × distance interaction term is positive and significant which implies that the likelihood of investment decreases less precipitously for venture capitalists that are highly specialized in a certain stage. As can be seen in Table 4.1 in section 4.3, spatial proximity is particularly important for specialized venture capitalists in order to support their portfolio companies. Contrary, spatial proximity may be less important for the likelihood of investment because these investors are also likely to have supra-regional networks and might be forced to broaden their investment radius in order to generate a sufficient number of deal flow. Hence, the results in Models REL 3.1 to 3.7 may indicate that the effect which results from the support activities preponderates for venture capitalists which are specialized in certain industries, while the deal flow effect preponderates for investors which are specialized in certain stages. However, the effect of industry specialization drops in magnitude and becomes insignificant if one controls for urban venture locations (Model REL 3.8). This is quite surprising as Table C.1 in the appendix shows only a

[966] See section 4.3.3 for a thorough discussion.

[967] In unreported regressions additional functional forms for the effect of the venture capitalist's age, like a pure linear or a u-shaped relationship, were tested but did not reveal further insights.

relatively small correlation between the dummy for urban venture locations and the industry specialization of the venture capitalist. A possible explanation is that the observed effect results from the fact that industry specialists invest into new ventures that are likely to be R&D intensive, need laboratories, or require other facilities and are thus not likely to reside in the center of urban areas. It is rather likely that these ventures have their offices in science parks which are located in peripheral areas of economic centers or midsized cities.[968] This fact is supported by the negative correlation between the R&D intensity dummy and the dummy for urban venture locations (Table C.1). Hence, part of the increased importance of distance is caused by the non-urban or rural location of the new venture and not by the industry specialization of the venture capitalist. The effect of the venture capitalist's stage specialization becomes insignificant if one additionally controls for the venture capitalist's size (Model REL 3). This supports the hypothesis that the effect of stage specialization which is observed in Models REL 3.1 to 3.8 is mainly driven by the need for deal flow generation which is also captured by the size of the venture capitalist. In consequence, even though the previous analysis revealed some interesting relationships and tendencies no significant effects can be proved under the ceteris paribus assumption.

Type of the venture capitalist

Hypothesis 8.1b, the impact of distance on the likelihood of investment is less negative for corporate venture capitalists compared to other types of venture capitalists, is not supported by the empirical results in Table 5.17. This is also true if the variable regarding the industry specialization of venture capitalists is not included in the models. Nevertheless, although the coefficients of the corporate venture capitalist dummy × distance interaction term are insignificant in Table 5.17 they point into the hypothesized direction.

Contrary, the results clearly support hypothesis 8.2b which states that (quasi-)public venture capitalists are more likely to invest in distant ventures compared to other types of venture capitalists if one controls for the defined geographical screen of these investors.[969] To investigate for which types of (quasi-)public venture capitalists this effect is particularly important, additional regressions are shown in Table D.4. Models REL 2.27 and 3.9 reveal that the effect is mainly driven by MBGs and subsidiaries of institutions promoting economic develop-

---

[968] E.g. the Munich Biotech Cluster, which is located close to Munich but does not belong to the same urban district, the Biotech Cluster Rhine-Neckar (BioRN) with its center in Heidelberg or the optical industry cluster in Jena.

[969] The matching sample procedure controls for the geographical screen of venture capitalists. See section 5.2.1 for further discussion.

ment.[970] Furthermore, Model REL 2.28 illustrates that the coefficient of the other German government institutions dummy × distance interaction term becomes significant if one only controls for the most important characteristics of a dyad. These results are quite plausible as these types of venture capitalists have a clear public mandate to promote economic development. Subsidiaries of savings and cooperative banks as well as subsidiaries of state banks and cooperative central institutes seem to behave more like venture capitalists with exclusively financial objectives. Figure 5.13 illustrates the impact of distance on the likelihood of investment for (quasi-)public venture capitalists and for other types of venture capitalists. The difference is quite large compared to other effects. (Quasi-)public venture capitalists invest with a probability of 55.6% into new ventures located three hours away compared to new ventures located in their ZIP code area. Venture capitalists with exclusively financial objectives invest with a probability of only 20.4% into new ventures located three hours away.

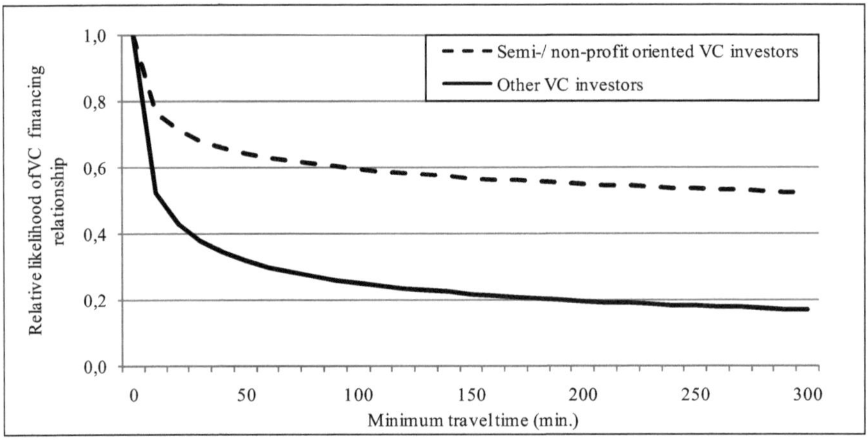

Figure 5.13: Impact of distance (min. travel time) on the likelihood of a VC financing relationship for different venture capitalists types
Model REL 2 and characteristics of the median venture capitalist-investee dyad were used to calculate the probabilities.

Lead-investor

Even though the coefficients of the lead-investor dummy × distance interaction term in Table 5.17 point in the hypothesized direction, the estimated coefficients are not significantly different from zero. Additional regressions in Table D.5 reveal that the coefficient of the lead-

970 The coefficient of the MBG dummy × distance interaction term has to be interpreted with caution due to a very small sample size within this category.

investor dummy × distance interaction term is negative and significant if one controls only for those variables that are most commonly scrutinized in venture capital research. These variables are the investment stage, new venture's industry, venture capitalist's size, age, and type, investment volume, as well as control variables (Model REL 2.32). The coefficient further remains negative and significant if one controls for East German venture locations but drops in absolute size and becomes insignificant if one controls for urban venture locations (Models REL 2.33 and 2.34). Hence, hypothesis 9.1b, which states that distance reduces the likelihood of investment more precipitously for lead-investors compared to co-investors, is finally not supported under the ceteris paribus assumption. However, there are indications for structural differences among lead- and co-investors other than the general impact of distance.

Table 5.22 displays regressions on different subsamples which are based on Model REL 3. Models REL 3.11 and 3.12 (Lead-inv.) include only those dyads in which the respective venture capitalist served as lead-investor. The variables regarding the investment and product development stage were included separately because they are correlated and lead to unstable coefficient estimates in small subsamples. Models REL 3.11 and 3.12 (Co-inv.) include the remaining co-investor dyads. Expected differences between lead- and co-investors are derived analogous to section 5.2.3. The role of a venture capitalist as lead- or co-investor is likely to have an impact on the effect of distance on the likelihood of investment in certain phases of the investment process. These phases are deal due diligence as well as investment monitoring, support and exit (Table 4.1 in section 4.3). In consequence, the empirical models should have different coefficients for the two subsamples. These expected differences of the coefficients are also summarized in Table 5.22. Most of these expectations are straight forward.[971] One exception is the venture capitalist's size which has no effect on the importance of spatial proximity in the relevant investment phases.[972] However, the main effect of size is that venture capitalists are forced to increase their investment radius in order to find a sufficient number of investment opportunities. If venture capitalists are aware of the benefits of spatial proximity for the investment management, it can be assumed that venture capitalists chose to participate as co-investors in distant investments. In consequence, it is likely that the effect of size on the importance of spatial proximity for the likelihood of investment is larger for co-investors compared to lead-investors. To test whether the coefficients differ significantly across the two subsamples, various Chi^2–tests (Wald tests) have been conducted using the estimates from Model REL 3.11. Only for the variables regarding the product development

[971] E.g. the effect of an increasing venture development stage in terms of the new venture's age on the likelihood of a distant investment is positive in the relevant investment phases. As these effects are assumed to be stronger for lead-investors, the coefficient of the new venture's age × distance interaction term is also assumed to be higher. The other expectations are developed in an analogous manner.

[972] See Table 4.1 in section 4.3.

Table 5.22: Rare event logistic regressions – Structural differences between lead- and co-investors

This table presents the results of rare event logistic regressions with a dummy variable indicating whether a VC financing relationship actually occurred (1) or not (0) as dependent variable. The models are based on Model REL 3 and are estimated for lead- and co-investors separately. The sample consists of realized dyads of venture capitalists and German portfolio companies which have closed a financing round between January 2002 and March 2007 and a matching sample. Financing rounds with missing values or for which no match existed as well as five outliers are excluded pairwise. Coefficients and standard errors are adjusted for rare events, choice-based sampling, serial correlation, heteroskedasticity, and nonindependence across venture capitalists. Furthermore, the table displays expected differences between the lead- and co-investor coefficients as well as corresponding chi²-difference-tests. Appl.: applicable, exp.: expected; V.: venture.

		REL 3.11		REL 3.12		Exp. diff.					
Variable	REL 3	Lead-inv.	Co-inv.	Lead-inv.	Co-inv.	betw. lead- and co-inv. coef.	Differ-ence	Chi²	df	p-value (two-sided)	p-value (one-sided, if appl.)
Dep. var.: realized dyad (yes/no)											
Distance (ln[1+min. travel time])	-0.3634***	-0.5614***	-0.3484***	-0.5564***	-0.3435***	-	-0.2130	1.25	1	0.2634	0.1317
Venture											
Ln(age) × dist.	-0.0207	0.0860	-0.0654	0.0935	-0.0514	+	0.1514	1.76	1	0.1850	0.0925*
_Intercept	-0.1028**	0.0271	-0.0966**	0.0419	-0.1252**						
Dummy seed stage round × dist.	-0.6122	-0.4349	-0.4424			-	0.0075	0.00	1	0.9920	
Dummy later stage round × dist.	0.0226	-0.0957	0.2138			+	-0.3095	1.89	1	0.1687	
Dummy bus. concept only × dist.	-0.9438			-0.6777	-1.0045*	-	0.3268	0.05	1	0.8223	
_Intercept	-0.1803			0.0461	-0.3276						
Dummy shipp.prod./prof. × dist.	-0.0069			-0.1826	0.0838	+	-0.2664	1.00	1	0.3163	
_Intercept	0.0084			-0.0781	0.0586						
Dummy prior exec. exp. × dist.	0.1625	0.2242	0.1232	0.1913	0.1870	+	0.1010	0.18	1	0.6697	0.3348
_Intercept	-0.0297	-0.2950	0.0696	-0.2830	0.1031						
Dummy high asset intang. × dist.	-0.2979**	-0.2097	-0.3737*	-0.1941	-0.4230**	-	0.1640	0.25	1	0.6200	
_Intercept	0.1477	0.3129	0.0349	0.3179	0.0218						
Dummy high R&D intensity × dist.	-0.3720**	-0.2138	-0.3909**	-0.3006	-0.3824**	-	0.1771	0.35	1	0.5527	
_Intercept	0.0726	-0.1856	0.1857	-0.2068	0.2113						
Dummy low book/market × dist.	-0.1114	0.3149	-0.2897*	0.3307	-0.2785*	-	0.6046	2.44	1	0.1180	
_Intercept	0.3017**	0.6065**	0.1582	0.6171**	0.2033						
Dummy East Ger. venture × dist.	-0.0850	0.0348	-0.1734	0.0255	-0.1465	open	0.2082	0.87	1	0.3503	
_Intercept	-0.2570**	-0.4509**	-0.2699*	-0.4710**	-0.2285						
Dummy urban v. location × dist.	0.2259**	0.1591	0.3228***	0.1664	0.3102**	+	-0.1637	0.51	1	0.4731	
_Intercept	-0.1857	0.0325	-0.2185	0.0162	-0.2657						

Table 5.22 cont.: Rare event logistic regressions – Structural differences between lead- and co-investors.

Variable	REL 3	REL 3.11 Lead-inv.	REL 3.11 Co-inv.	REL 3.12 Lead-inv.	REL 3.12 Co-inv.	Exp. diff. betw. lead- and co-inv. coef.	Difference	Chi²	df	p-value (two-sided)	p-value (one-sided, if appl.)
Venture capitalist											
Ln(assets under mgt.) × dist.	0.0484*	0.0288	0.0713**	0.0335	0.0650**	-	-0.0425	0.49	1	0.4844	0.2422
Ln(age) × dist.	0.0236	-0.0204	-0.0007	-0.0108	0.0100	+	-0.0197	0.02	1	0.8912	
_Intercept	-0.0155	-0.0843*	-0.0070	-0.0762	-0.0160						
HHI industry × dist.	-0.1998	-1.2139**	0.1602	-1.3413**	0.1725	open	-1.3741	5.16	1	0.0232**	
HHI stage × dist.	0.4225	1.0154*	0.1836	1.0618*	0.2608	-	0.8318	1.57	1	0.2099	
Dummy corporate VC × dist.	0.0529	0.3382	0.0106	0.3348	0.0036	+	0.3276	0.35	1	0.5547	0.2774
Dummy (quasi-)public VC × dist.	0.2497**	0.1820	0.2819**	0.2196	0.2416*	+	-0.0999	0.15	1	0.7022	
Dummy lead-investor × dist.	-0.0774										
Round											
Inv. volume per VC × dist.	0.2256**	0.3391**	0.2743**	0.3438**	0.2878**	+	0.0648				
_Intercept	0.0411	0.1108	0.0923	0.0979	0.1127			0.37	2	0.8297	0.4149
(Inv. volume per VC)² × dist.	-0.0298**	-0.0476*	-0.0417**	-0.0473*	-0.0454**	-	-0.0059				
_Intercept	0.0035	0.0187	-0.0215	0.0182	-0.0240						
Syndication benefit × dist.	0.0026**	-0.0050	0.0005	-0.0042	0.0010	+	-0.0055	0.16	1	0.6887	
_Intercept	-0.0053**	-0.0058	-0.0011	-0.0068	-0.0019						
Control variables											
Ln(Ger. VC fundraising (t-1))	-0.0575	0.1719	-0.1935**	0.1972	-0.1998*						
Ln(Ger. VC investments)	0.0399	0.0028	0.1251	-0.1458	0.1571						
Return of MSCI SC Ger. (ltm)	-0.1441	0.2959	-0.3697	0.3097	-0.3485						
Constant	-0.2086	-0.8066	0.0510	0.0782	-0.1731						
N	1866	664	1202	672	1212						
LR Chi²	70.01***	46.92*	41.30	47.04*	42.40						
Log. Likelihood	-557.12	-187.25	-360.78	-189.72	-363.40						

* significant at 10%; ** significant at 5%; *** significant at 1% (two-sided)

stage Model REL 3.12 is used. Table 5.22 reports the results of two-sided tests as well as one-sided tests if applicable. The coefficient of the new venture's age × distance interaction term points into the hypothesized direction (hypothesis 2.1.b) for lead-investors and the coefficient's difference between lead- and co-investors is significant at the 10% level (one-sided)). Furthermore, distance reduces the likelihood of investment significantly more precipitously for lead-investors that are specialized in a certain industry compared to other lead-investors. This effect also differs significantly between lead- and co-investors (significant at the 5% level (two-sided)). As a result, hypothesis 9.2b, some of the effects of the elaborated hypotheses differ between lead- and co-investors, is supported by the data.

Investment volume

The empirical analyses further support hypothesis 10b, the impact of distance on the likelihood of investment becomes less negative with rising investment volume of the venture capitalist up to a certain threshold and again more negative thereafter. All models in Table 5.17 reveal that the coefficients of the interaction terms with the linear and quadratic effects of the investment volume are both significantly different from zero and point into the hypothesized direction. Hence, with increasing investment volume the positive linear effect, which reduces the negative impact of distance, is more and more offset by the negative quadratic effect. This results in an inverted u-shaped relationship. Models REL 2 and 3 imply that the negative impact of distance diminishes in magnitude up to an investment volume of about 3.8 to 4.0 m€ and becomes again more negative thereafter.[973] In consequence, transaction costs outweigh the desire to monitor investments more intensively for smaller investments. In contrast, for very large investments the need for closer monitoring outweighs the relatively lower transaction costs.

To further validate the robustness of this result, additional regressions were conducted. The results of these regressions can be found in Table D.6 in the appendix. To test the inverted u-shaped effect as implied by hypothesis 10b, separate regressions on two subsamples were calculated. The first subsample includes all dyads with investment volumes per venture capitalist up to 3.9 m€ and the second subsample includes all dyads with investment volumes of at least 3.9 m€. Models REL 2.37 and 2.38 support an inverted u-shaped effect of the VC investment volume. An overall monotonic linear effect of the investment volume is not supported by Model REL 2.36. Figure 5.14 illustrates the size of the effect. Venture capitalists invest with a probability of 42.0% into new ventures that raise about 3.1 m€ per investor and

[973] The determined threshold for the likelihood of investment is lower compared to the threeshold that was identified for the patterns in spatial proximity. This difference is likely to be caused by omitted variables in the first analysis regarding observed patterns in spatial proximity.

are located three hours away compared to new ventures located in their ZIP code area. The relative likelihood of investment is reduced to 12.1% if the venture raises only about 0.2 m€ and is located three hours away compared to new ventures located in the same ZIP code area.

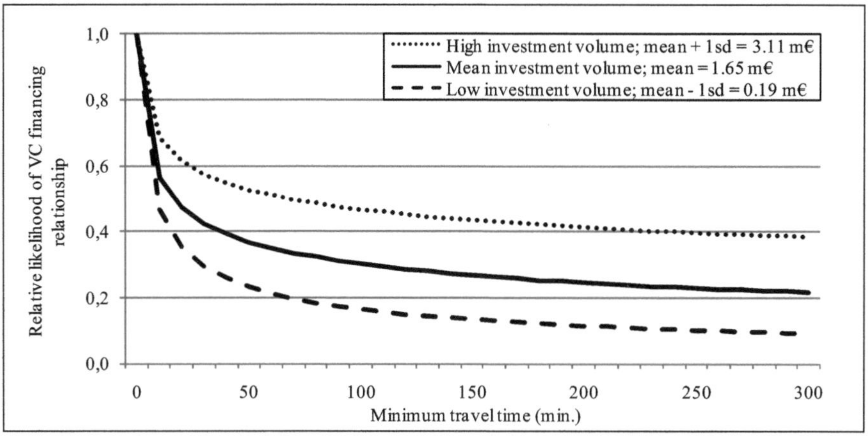

Figure 5.14: Impact of distance (min. travel time) on the likelihood of a VC financing relationship for different investment volumes
Model REL 2 and characteristics of the median venture capitalist-investee dyad were used to calculate the probabilities.

Syndication

The data reveals that distance reduces the likelihood of investment significantly less if the deal is syndicated and at least one syndication partner resides closer to the portfolio company than the venture capitalist of the focal dyad. This is implied by the positive and significant coefficients of the syndication benefit × distance interaction terms in Models REL 2 and 3 in Table 5.17. Thus, hypothesis 11b is supported by the data. This result also implies that it is likely that syndication is used as an instrument to overcome large distances between venture capitalists and investees. Alternative measures of syndication and its spatial benefits also offer significant results. These measures are: a dummy variable that indicates if the venture capitalist is located far away from the venture but a close syndication partner exists; and the difference between a venture capitalist's distance to the portfolio company and the distance of the syndication partner located closest to the respective portfolio company. Contrary, solely a higher number of syndication partners in an investment round does not reduce the negative effect of distance. The results of these alternative model specifications can be found in Table D.7 in the appendix. Hence, the effect of syndication on the importance of distance is robust for the complete sample. Nonetheless, it has to be noted that the effect diminishes if the sample is restricted to German venture capitalists (Model REL 5 in Table 5.16). This would imply that the positive effect of syndication is mainly driven by foreign venture capitalists. However, as mentioned above, Table D.1 reveals potential problems of multicollinearity for the variables regarding the syndication benefit in the restricted model. In unreported regressions, the alternative measures of syndication and its spatial benefits suffer the same problems. In consequence, it remains open whether the effect of the syndication benefit also applies to domestic venture capitalists or not. Figure 5.15 illustrates the size of the effect for the complete sample. If the new venture is located three hours from the venture capitalist and the investor has a high syndication benefit, 30.2% of the reference likelihood of investment remain. If no syndication partner exists that is closer to the target, only 20.4% of the reference likelihood of investment remains if the venture resides three hours away.

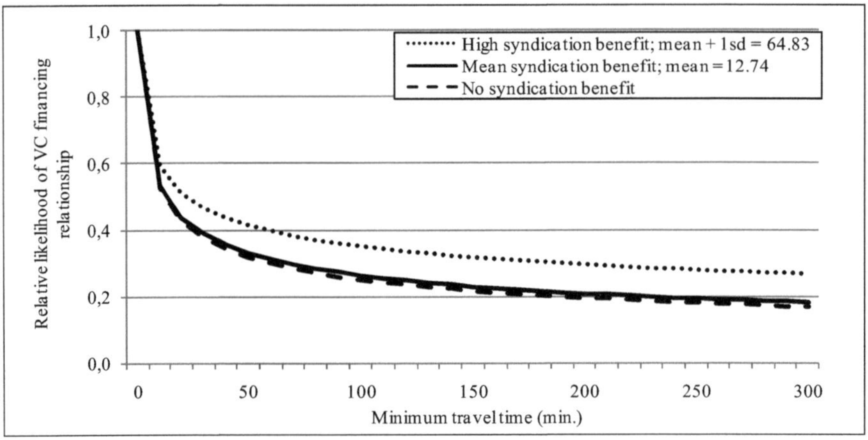

Figure 5.15: Impact of distance (min. travel time) on the likelihood of a VC financing relationship for different levels of syndication benefit
Model REL 2 and characteristics of the median venture capitalist-investee dyad were used to calculate the probabilities.

5.3.3 Robustness Tests of Conducted Analyses

In order to verify the robustness of results, multiple alternative model specifications as well as alternative variable definitions were tested. The results were found to be robust as discussed above. The hypothesis of model specification errors is also rejected for all base models using the Stata command linktest.

Moreover, all model specifications were tested for multicollinearity. A summary of VIFs of the base models can be found in Table D.1 in the appendix. Only the variables regarding the investment volume and the syndication benefit have moderately high VIFs of 5.24 to 7.21.

Hence, further robustness checks were conducted for these variables throughout the section and results were found to be robust. The coefficients of the variables regarding the syndication benefit in Model REL 5 are not reliable due to potential multicollinearity. Thus, the results regarding these variables in this specific model have to be interpreted with caution.

Based on Model REL 1, a detailed outlier analysis was conducted using Pregibon's Delta-Beta influence statistic, a counterpart to Cook's distance, which is commonly used in linear regression models.[974] As discussed above, five outliers were successively identified and excluded from the analysis together with their corresponding matching/original dyads. In consequence, it is not likely that the results are driven by only few observations.

In addition, standard weighted logistic regressions as well as rare event logistic regressions using different measures of spatial proximity were conducted and support the robustness of results. Most results remain unchanged with minor differences in the significance of the coefficients. The standard weighted logistic regressions which assume a fraction of ones of 9.65% and the same sets of independent variables like Models REL 1 to 5 are reported in Table D.8 in the appendix. Rare event logistic regressions which are based on Models REL 2 and 3 but use different measures of spatial proximity to construct the variables can be found in Table D.9 in the appendix. As the car travel time is only available for European venture capitalists, the sample has been restricted to European investors for these regressions. This ensures the comparability of the different models.

Finally, Model REL 5 in Table 5.16 shows that most coefficients remain stable if one restricts the sample to German venture capitalists. This implies that most relationships apply to German as well as foreign venture capitalists. Only the effect of the syndication benefit on the importance of spatial proximity drops significantly in Model REL 5. Unfortunately, no conclusions can be drawn as these variables suffer from potential problems of multicollinearity in Model REL 5.

5.3.4 Limitations of Analyses

The main limitation of the presented analyses lies in the limited sample size and the large number of covariates. This makes it difficult to detect significant relationships under the ceteris paribus assumption. In addition, restrictions in the data availability prevented the calculation of additional variables regarding network positions of single venture capitalists or their previous investment experience.[975] Moreover, the mentioned restrictions led to a considerable

---

[974] Cf. Long/Freese (2001), pp. 151-152.

[975] See e.g. Sorenson/Stuart (2001), pp. 1566-1569.

number of missing values regarding the specialization of venture capitalists because the specialization variables were calculated only for investors with at least three financing rounds in the sample. This fact leads to an underrepresentation of venture capitalists with only few investments in Germany and thus mainly foreign venture capitalists. Hence, the variables regarding the venture capitalist's specialization were excluded in the majority of the analyses.

For the interpretation of results, it is important to keep in mind that it was not possible to estimate absolute values of the investment probability. Hence, it is not possible to compare different types of dyads in regard to their absolute investment probability. However, it is possible to compare different types of dyads in regard to their sensitivity to spatial proximity.

5.4 Summary of Results and Discussion

This chapter aims to extend the understanding of the impact of spatial proximity on VC financing relationships in Germany. Therefore, the hypotheses, which were developed in chapter 4, were tested empirically and important aspects of the theoretical framework regarding the role of spatial proximity throughout the investment process were verified. In order to test the hypotheses, first, observed patterns in spatial proximity between venture capitalists and investees were analyzed and it was investigated how different characteristics of the new venture, the venture capitalist and the financing round relate to the spatial proximity between actors. This first part scrutinizes relationships that are observable in the market and reveals which kinds of venture capitalist-investee dyads are likely to have smaller or larger distances between each other. Since the likelihood of investment has a strong impact on the observed patterns in spatial proximity, most effects should coincide with the non-observable likelihood of investment which was scrutinized in a second step. Here, the impact of spatial proximity on the likelihood of a VC financing relationship was analyzed using a matched sample approach.

The discussion in chapter 4 illustrated that most hypotheses emerge from multiple theories. This is because the impact of spatial proximity on the VC investment process is highly complex and has multiple facets. In consequence, it is not possible to relate the empirical results of this chapter to single theories in most cases. However, the most important effects and theories will be highlighted throughout this section if possible. Table 5.23 summarizes the hypotheses as well as the empirical results of the regression analyses conducted in this chapter.

Table 5.23: Summary of hypotheses and empirical results
This table summarizes the hypotheses as well as the empirical results of the regression analyses conducted in this chapter. +/- indicates that distance is expected to have a positive/negative impact on the likelihood of a specific VC investment (panel A) or that a specific factor has a positive/negative impact on the likelihood of a distant VC investment (Panel B). Results in parenthesis indicate that the respective result was confirmed in a reduced model but was found to be valid in general. N.s.: not significant at a 10% level.

Summary of hypotheses and empirical results	Testable hypotheses: a) Observed patterns of SP	Testable hypotheses: b) Likelihood of investment	Empirical results: a) Observed patterns of SP	Empirical results: b) Likelihood of investment
Panel A: General impact on the likelihood of a specific investment				
H1: Distance	-		supported	supported
Panel B: Impact of various factors on the likelihood of a distant VC investment				
Venture				
Venture development stage				
H2.1: Age	+		supported	n.s.
H2.2: Investment stage	+		n.s.	(supported)
H2.3: Size	+		(supported)	n.s.
H3: Product development stage	+		opposite	(supported)
H4: Prior experience of the entrepreneurial team	+		opposite	(supported)
Industry's knowledge intensity				
H5.1: High asset intangibility	-		supported	supported
H5.2: High R&D intensity	-		n.s.	supported
H5.3: Low book to market ratio	-		n.s.	n.s.
Region				
H6.1: East German venture	+	open	supported	n.s.
H6.2: Urban venture location	open	+	n.s.	supported
Venture capitalist				
H7: Size	+		supported	supported
Effect of age	open		n.s.	n.s.
Specialization				
Effect of industry specialization	open		n.s.	n.s.
Effect of stage specialization	open		pos. effect	n.s.
Type				
H8.1: Corporate investor	+		n.s.	n.s.
H8.2: (Quasi-)public venture capitalist	-	+	supported	supported
Lead-investor				
H9.1: General effect (intercept)	-		n.s.	n.s.
H9.2: Impact on other propositions/hypotheses	more pronounced		supported	supported

Table 5.23 cont.: Summary of hypotheses and empirical results

Summary of hypotheses and empirical results	Testable hypotheses a) Observed patterns of SP	Testable hypotheses b) Likelihood of investment	Empirical results a) Observed patterns of SP	Empirical results b) Likelihood of investment
Round				
H10: Investment volume	inverted u-shape		supported	supported
H11: Syndication	+		supported	supported
H12: Consecutive round	-		supported	

Table 5.23 shows that many results of the two empirical analyses coincide, but that there are also numerous differences. As a main result, both analyses prove that **spatial proximity** has an impact on VC financing in Germany. The bivariate analysis of patterns in spatial proximity proves that the number of VC financing relationships diminishes significantly with increasing distance between both parties of a dyad. Furthermore, the multivariate analysis uncovers that consecutive financing rounds are more likely to happen for close dyads. The second analysis further substantiates these findings and reveals that the likelihood of investment decreases dramatically with rising distance between both parties. This result is in line with the findings from Sorenson/Stuart (2001) and Cumming/Johan (2006) for the US and Canada respectively.[976]

Keeping in mind that Germany is a highly populated country with a dense infrastructure in central Europe the size of this effect is overwhelming and might has been underestimated by practitioners and scholars so far. Fritsch/Schilder (2008) conducted 75 interviews with German venture capitalists in 2004 and 2005 and found that German venture capitalists do not perceive spatial proximity to be an important factor. According to the interviewed venture capitalists the reasons are that Germany is fairly small, has a well-developed travel infrastructure, and that a lack of promising investment opportunities prohibits being selective.[977] This discrepancy might have two reasons. First, the analysis in chapter 4 revealed that a plurality of theories may explain the importance of spatial proximity throughout the VC investment process.[978] Thus, if venture capitalists do not intentionally reject distant investment opportunities due to reasons like increased travel times and expenses, it might be rather informational problems that prevent the initial contact and a successful investment process for distant in-

[976] Cf. Sorenson/Stuart (2001), pp. 1571-1577; Cumming/Johan (2006), p. 372. The study of Cumming/Johan (2006) includes VC as well as PE investments.

[977] Cf. Fritsch/Schilder (2008), pp. 2127-2129.

[978] These theories are: transaction cost theory, agency theory, social exchange theory, the network approach, property rights theory, game theory, and finally stewardship theory.

vestments.[979] Second, venture capitalists might be prone to unconscious behavior and might not be fully aware of their decision making processes. This fact was already shown by Zacharakis/Meyer (1998) and Shepherd (1999) who criticized studies that fully rely on ex-post self reported data.[980] However, another key finding of the empirical studies is that the **investment volume** per venture capitalist has a strong relationship with the spatial pattern of VC investments and has a large and very robust impact on the importance of spatial proximity for the likelihood of investment. Both relationships have an inverted u-shaped form. In the case of the second study the effect implies that the negative impact of distance on the likelihood of investment is more and more reduced up to an investment volume of about 3.9 m€. For investment volumes above this threshold, the negative impact of distance becomes more severe again. Nevertheless, the majority of VC transactions has an investment volume for which an increased volume leads to a decreased importance of spatial proximity.[981] The main reason for this effect is the decreased importance of transaction costs, and thus also travel time and expenses, relative to the investment volume. In consequence, the effect of the investment volume shows that not only informational problems lead to the detected importance of spatial proximity. It is likely that venture capitalists are selective and that also unconscious behaviors of venture capitalists, who are not fully aware of their decision processes, contribute to the relevance of spatial proximity in VC transactions. The inverted u-shaped effect of the investment volume has a second important implication as it proves that agency and/or game theoretical problems are prevalent and become dominant for very high investment volumes.

In order to compare the size of the impact of different variables, partial effects on the relative likelihood of a VC financing relationship were calculated for the median dyad at a min. travel time of 180 minutes. Table 5.24 presents the results for the significant effects of the likelihood of investment analysis as presented in Table 5.23. To calculate the partial effects, all variables were held constant at their median and only the focal variable was varied. In case of non discrete variables the partial effect was calculated for the mean +/- one standard deviation. Another exception is the effect of the new venture's product development stage. For this variable the value "product development/tests", and thus the middle category, was chosen as the reference category. The reason is to obtain more robust results since the coefficients for the "shipping product/profitable" variables are varying around zero and are not significant. The further discussion of the results which are presented in Table 5.23 follows in the order that is implied by the size of the effects. However, for the interpretation of the results and the

---

[979] The existence of informational problems was already mentioned by Fritsch/Schilder (2008) as a reason for spatial proximity to be potentially relevant (cf. Fritsch/Schilder (2008), pp. 2129).

[980] Cf. Zacharakis/Meyer (1998), p. 58; Shepherd (1999), p. 83.

[981] About 91.6% of all realized dyads have an investment volume per investor that is smaller than 3.9 m€. The analysis of patterns in spatial proximity leads to a maximum of the effect at about 4.8 m€.

ranking one has to keep in mind that many variables have different scales. This may limit the comparability of results.

Table 5.24 reveals that the discussed effect of the investment volume on the importance of spatial proximity is the second largest in magnitude. The largest effect is caused by the **type of the venture capitalist**. One of the German particularities is the large number of (quasi-) public venture capitalists. The analysis of the observed patterns of spatial proximity reveals that these investors invest in significantly more proximate targets compared to other venture capitalists. This is mainly due to their investment policies in terms of geographical screens.[982] However, controlling for the geographical screen the analysis of the likelihood of investment shows that spatial proximity is far less important for (quasi-)public venture capitalists compared to others. This is mainly caused by their public mandate to promote the economy, differences in the venture capitalists' compensation schemes, and the application of different financial instruments. Corporate venture capitalists do not behave differently compared to investors with exclusively financial objectives. Thus, the findings from Gupta/Sapienza (1992) that US corporate venture capitalists have a broader investment radius are not confirmed for the more recent German sample used in this study.[983]

The third largest effect regarding the likelihood of investment is caused by the type of the **new venture location**, namely whether the new venture is located in an urban or a non-urban area. The analysis of the observed patterns does not reveal a significant relationship, but the second analysis shows that distance reduces the likelihood of investment less if the new venture is located in an urban area. This indicates that venture capitalists evaluate the risk-return ratio differently in urban and non-urban locations throughout their investment due diligence. The empirical analyses further showed that East German ventures are financed by more distant venture capitalists which implies that there are still structural differences regarding the existence of venture capitalists. Besides the larger average distance between venture capitalists and East German ventures, the fact that a new venture is located in East Germany has no additional effect on the likelihood of investment.

Moreover, the **product development stage** also turns out to have strong effects on the importance of spatial proximity for the likelihood of investment. Spatial proximity is much more important for new ventures in a very early product development stage (business concept only).[984] However, the analysis of patterns in spatial proximity implies the opposite, new ven-

---

[982] Cumming/Johan (2006) found a similar effect for Canadian government or labor-sponsored VC and PE investors (cf. Cumming/Johan (2006), pp. 387-389).

[983] Cf. Gupta/Sapienza (1992), pp. 357-358.

[984] The effect is only significant if one does not control for the venture development stage. However, the size of the effect is stable across different model specifications.

Table 5.24: Partial effects on the relative likelihood of a VC financing relationship

This table presents the relative likelihood of a VC financing relationship at a minimum travel time of 180 minutes for the median dyad and varying new venture, venture capitalist, and round characteristics. The table only presents significant effects of the likelihood of investment analysis as shown in Table 5.23.

Hypothesis	Value of respective variable		Relative likelihood of VC relationship at a minimum travel time of 180 min.			
	Reference value/category	Alternative value/category	Reference value/category (Ref)	Alternative value/cat. (Alt)	Partial effect (Alt - Ref)	Rank
Venture						
H2.2b: Investment stage	Later stage round	Seed stage round	20.40%	6.46%	-13.94%	6
H3b: Product development stage	Product development/tests	Business concept only	21.41%	4.42%	-16.99%	4
H4b: Prior experience of the ET	No profound prior experience	Profound prior experience	20.40%	34.28%	13.88%	7
H5.1b: High asset intangibility	Low or moderate asset intangiblity	High asset intangibility	20.40%	9.91%	-10.49%	8
H5.2b: High R&D intensity	Low or moderate R&D intensity	High R&D intensity	20.40%	11.32%	-9.08%	10
H6.2b: Urban venture location	Non-urban venture location	Urban venture location	20.40%	37.92%	17.52%	3
VC investor						
H7b: Size	Low ln(assets under mgt.); mean - 1sd ≙ 22.6 m€	High ln(assets under mgt.); mean + 1sd ≙ 1096.6 m€	15.29%	31.67%	16.38%	5
H8.2b: Semi-/non-profit VC investor	Other VC investor	Semi-/non-profit oriented VC investor	20.40%	55.57%	35.17%	1
Round						
H10b: Investment volume	Low investment volume; mean - 1sd = 0.19 m€	High investment volume; mean + 1sd = 3.11 m€	12.05%	41.95%	29.90%	2
H11b: Syndication	No syndication benefit	High syndication benefit; mean + 1sd = 64.83	20.40%	30.22%	9.82%	9

tures that have only a business concept are financed by venture capitalists that are on average further away. As this relationship diminishes if one excludes the investment stage from the regressions and since bivariate analyses also suggest that early product development stages are financed by close venture capitalists, it is likely that the effect is only significant because of spurious correlations or omitted variables.[985] These results prove the importance of comprehensive statistical analyses with different research approaches.

The fifth largest effect is caused by the venture capitalists' **size**. It is shown that large venture capitalists invest into more distant targets and the second analysis uncovers that this relationship is caused by a reduced importance of spatial proximity for these investors. This suggests that large venture capitalists receive more supra-regional deal flow due to larger networks, a higher visibility, and less resource restrictions and/or that large venture capitalists are less restrictive with their geographical screens in order to find a sufficient number of investment opportunities. This finding is in line with the preliminary findings of Cumming/Dai (2009) that larger US venture capitalists exhibit less spatial bias. Unfortunately, Cumming/Dai (2009) do not test their hypothesis ceteris paribus with other important variables like the age of the venture capitalist.[986]

The **venture development stage** is also related to the observed patterns in spatial proximity and has effects on the likelihood of investment. Ventures in an early development stage are financed by more proximate venture capitalists compared to more mature ventures. This relationship is significant for the new venture's age, but there is also some empirical evidence that larger ventures are financed by more distant venture capitalists.[987] However, these two relationships seem not to be caused by a lower importance of spatial proximity for older and larger ventures as both effects are far from being significant in the second analysis. The relationship might rather be caused by omitted variables like the age of the entrepreneurs which could cause young ventures to be located in thriving entrepreneurial centers and thus closer to venture capitalists or office space and prices which could cause large ventures to locate in more peripheral areas. Contrary, the investment stage has a substantial and robust impact on the importance of spatial proximity for the likelihood of investment. Distance reduces the likeli-

---

985 The average minimum travel time for new ventures that have a business concept only is 100.96 min. and for other new ventures the minimum travel time is 136.01 min.

986 Cf. Cumming/Dai (2009), p. 15.

987 These empirical findings coincide with descriptive results from Powell et al. (2002) for US ventures (cf. Powell et al. (2002), p. 300). In addition, Butler/Goktan (2008) find that ventures within close proximity to their venture capitalists are younger and smaller at the time of their IPO. However, as they measure the age and size of the venture at the time of the IPO the results are not comparable (cf. Butler/Goktan (2008), pp. 15-16).

hood of investment much more for seed stage rounds compared to other investment rounds.[988] The discussion in chapter 4 reveals that this effect may be caused by a broad range of theories.

An effect of comparable size is caused by the prior **experience of the entrepreneurial team**. Spatial proximity is less important for the likelihood of investment if at least one member of the team had a high executive position in another company before he joined the entrepreneurial team of the focal venture. This effect is mainly caused by larger networks of the experienced team member and reduced agency costs due to signaling. Nevertheless, the analyses of the observed patterns in spatial proximity show that new ventures with an experienced entrepreneurial team are financed by more proximate venture capitalists. This relationship must be caused by some omitted variable as the relationship is not caused by differences in the impact of distance on the likelihood of investment. As was mentioned in 5.2.3 one potentially omitted variable might be the spatial distribution of experienced entrepreneurs. If these entrepreneurs gained their experience predominantly in entrepreneurial clusters like Munich or Berlin and also started their business in these clusters, they would also be located closer to their venture capitalists.

The empirical analyses further prove that the **industry's knowledge intensity** of the new venture is related to the observed patterns in spatial proximity. Furthermore, this relationship is caused by an increased importance of spatial proximity for knowledge intensive industries. Hence, new ventures whose industry is characterized by high asset intangibility are financed by more proximate venture capitalists. A similar effect is found by Butler/Goktan (2008). Their results show for the US that venture backed IPOs that are close to their venture capitalists have higher asset intangibility than others.[989] In addition, high asset intangibility and/or high R&D intensity increase the negative impact of distance on the likelihood of investment. These effects are mainly caused by increased uncertainty and resulting agency costs as well as transaction costs in order to evaluate, monitor, support, and to exit the investment.

The existence of a close **syndication** partner is related to more distant investments which are caused by a reduced negative impact of distance on the likelihood of investment. For the majority of VC financing relationships the effect on the likelihood of investment is relatively small. Thus, Table 5.24 reports a relatively small effect of the syndication benefit. However,

---

988 The effect is only significant if one does not control for the venture product development stage. However, the size of the effect is stable across different model specifications. See section 5.3.2 for a detailed discussion.

989 Cf. Butler/Goktan (2008), pp. 15-16. In contrast, Cumming/Johan (2006) find for a Canadian sample that life science or high-tech ventures are less likely to be located in the same province. They explain their unexpected results with country specific circumstances and the fact that life science or high-tech ventures may offer higher expected returns and are thus also considered by distant venture capitalists (cf. Cumming/Johan (2006), pp. 387-391).

the distribution of the syndication benefit variable reveals that the effect can be substantial for some VC investments. A more detailed analysis reveals that the negative effect of distance on the likelihood of investment is neutralized if the syndication benefit is equal or greater to 207.3. This means that the minimum travel time of the focal venture capitalst is about 207 times as large as for the closest syndication partner.[990] This is the case for only about 2.0% of the realized dyads and 0.7% of the realized dyads involving a German venture capitalist. Figure D.1 in the appendix shows the distribution of realized venture capitalist-investee dyads in regard to the syndication benefit. In consequence, the negative impact of distance on the likelihood of investment remains substantial also for most syndicated investments. However, it is likely that venture capitalists use syndication with venture capitalists that are close to the target in order to reduce the negative impact of large distances. This result is in line with the findings from Sorenson/Stuart (2001) and Cumming/Dai (2009) for the US. However, the conclusion of Fritsch/Schilder (2006 and 2008) that syndication is used to offset the negative impact of distance and that spatial proximity is not important for German VC investments is not supported.[991]

Table 5.23 also reports a significant positive relationship between a venture capitalist's **stage specialization** and the observed distance to his portfolio companies. However, the analyses of the likelihood of investment only find week evidence for the impact of the venture capitalist's specialization on the importance of distance. In consequence, it is likely that the observed effect is, at least partially, caused by other non-observable effects.

Finally, although the distance between venture capitalists and investees is not significantly lower and spatial proximity does not seem to be more important for **lead-investors,** there are some indications for structural differences between lead- and co-investors. The venture development stage in terms of the venture's age has a more pronounced positive relationship with the observed distance between the actors. This relationship is further underpinned by the fact that distance is significantly less important for the likelihood of investment the older the venture is. In addition, venture capitalists that are specialized into a certain industry invest into more proximate targets if they are in the role of a lead-investor compared to their co-investments. This relationship is caused by a higher importance of spatial proximity for lead-investors in order to better support their portfolio companies.

The analyses presented in this chapter do not support the hypothesis that older, more experienced venture capitalists behave different compared to younger investors. The significant effects diminish as soon as one controls for the venture capitalist's size in terms of assets un-

---

[990] See section 5.1.3.4 for details on the calculation of the syndication benefit.

[991] Cf. Sorenson/Stuart (2001), p. 1577; Fritsch/Schilder (2006), pp. 22-23; Fritsch/Schilder (2008), pp. 2126-2129; Cumming/Dai (2009), pp. 15-16 and 37.

der management. In consequence, this study does not support one of the main results from Sorenson/Stuart (2001) who find that spatial proximity is less important for older venture capitalists due to the development of networks. Since Sorenson/Stuart (2001) do not control for the size of the venture capitalist in their regressions, it would be interesting to test whether their results change if they include the venture capitalist's size or not.[992] Furthermore, the results do not support the preliminary findings of Cumming/Dai (2009) that older (more reputable) US venture capitalists exhibit less spatial bias. One reason may be again that these scholars also do not test their hypothesis ceteris paribus with respect to the size of the venture capitalist.[993] In consequence, it remains open whether the decreased spatial bias of older venture capitalists is caused by a higher experience, reputation, and/or networks or if the effect is caused by the pure necessity to increase the investment radius in order to find more investment opportunities.

As a result, this chapter provided important empirical support for the relevance of spatial proximity to VC financing in Germany and comparable continental European countries. Furthermore, the impact of spatial proximity on the VC investment process is effected by various new venture, venture capitalist, and investment round characteristics. Thus, important aspects of the theoretical framework that was elaborated in chapter 4 are verified.

---

[992] Cf. Sorenson/Stuart (2001), pp. 1573-1576.

[993] Cf. Cumming/Dai (2009), p. 15.

6 Conclusion

This thesis dealt with the role of spatial proximity between venture capitalists and new ventures throughout the VC investment process and is of high practical and scientific relevance. Young and innovative high potential companies are central for the prosperous economic development of regions. At the same time, venture capital is often one of the few financing options for these companies and it is widely accepted that venture capitalists play a key role in their development.[994] Hence, it is of utmost importance to secure an appropriate availability of venture capital for new ventures. However, it became clear throughout this thesis that the supply of venture capital is highly clustered in many countries and that Germany is no exception in this regard. Furthermore, it was revealed that spatial proximity between venture capitalists and new ventures represents an important factor in VC financing relationships. The clustering of venture capital supply and the importance of spatial proximity for the emergence of VC financing relationships leads to important implications for entrepreneurs, venture capitalist, and policy makers.

Despite the high practical relevance of this topic, to the best knowledge of the author no holistic theoretical framework regarding the impact of spatial proximity on the likelihood to successfully pass the different phases of the VC investment process existed prior to this thesis. Moreover, for continental European countries very little was known about (i) the relationship between certain characteristics of ventures, venture capitalists and/or financing rounds and the observed spatial proximity between both parties and (ii) the impact of spatial proximity on the likelihood of investment. In consequence, this thesis aimed to close these research gaps. Thereby, this thesis may also be seen in the light of two, broader streams of research. The first stream relates to the role of spatial proximity in various financial phenomena like venture capital financing, mutual or hedge fund management, debt financing, or M&A.[995] The second stream of research aims to understand determinants of the emergence of business relationships in the field of new venture financing, especially venture capital.[996] This concluding chapter presents the most important findings of the preceding analyses, discusses important implications, and provides directions for future research.

---

994 Cf. Achleitner (2001); Sahlman (1990); Audretsch (2002), pp. 14-35; section 1.1. Gifford (1997), p. 459; Söderblom/Wiklund (2006), p. 12.

995 See e.g. Gupta/Sapienza (1992); Lerner (1995); Coval/Moskowitz (1999); Petersen/Rajan (2002); Kang/Kim (2008); Uysal/Kedia/Panchapagesan (2008).

996 See e.g. Sapienza/Amason (1993); Barney et al. (1994); Fried/Hisrich (1995); Sapienza/De Clercq (2000); De Clercq/Sapienza (2001); Welpe (2004); Welpe (2008).

6.1 Summary of Results

The first aim of this thesis was to provide a **holistic theoretical framework** regarding the relationship between spatial proximity of different types of venture capitalists and new ventures and the likelihood of a VC investment throughout the investment process. In order to elaborate this theoretical framework, Popper's "searchlight theory of science" was applied and multiple theories, and thus different "searchlight positions", were considered. Hence, it was possible to shed light on various aspects of the role of spatial proximity in VC financing.

The theoretical framework was developed in three steps. First, different theories that explain the role of spatial proximity throughout the VC investment process were identified. These theories are: theories that belong to the school of thought of new institutionalism (property rights theory, agency theory, and transaction cost theory), game theory, stewardship theory, social exchange theory, and the network approach. Second, a theoretical fundament was built and the different theories were each described in general and in the context of venture capital. Furthermore, theoretical implications of spatial proximity between actors for VC financing relationships were derived for each theory. Third, for each phase to the VC investment process relevant activities of the entrepreneurial team, the venture capitalist and third parties were identified and the mentioned theories were used to scrutinize the role of spatial proximity between new ventures and venture capitalists. As a result, multiple propositions were elaborated regarding the general impact of spatial proximity within the respective investment phase as well as for which kinds of new ventures, venture capitalists, or financing rounds the impact of spatial proximity is particularly strong. These propositions constitute the fundament of the theoretical framework.

The analysis revealed that large distances between venture capitalists and new ventures have a negative impact on the likelihood to successfully pass an investment phase for all phases of the process. However, it was also found that large differences regarding the impact of spatial proximity within single investment phases among different types of new ventures, venture capitalists, and financing rounds have to be expected. In respect to the applied theories it became clear that all theories contribute to the understanding of spatial proximity in VC financing in a particular way, but the most important aspects are transaction costs and informational asymmetries. Transaction costs are relevant in all phases of the VC investment process except the deal screening phase. Furthermore, they are highly sensitive to spatial proximity as transaction costs like travel time, travel expenses, as well as search and information costs are likely to increase significantly with rising distance between two parties. Informational asymmetries occur in each phase of the VC investment process, are found to be relevant for most theories, are expensive to reduce, and are likely to increase with rising distance. They are one of the core reasons for agency problems (agency theory), hinder the enforcement of property rights (property rights theory), hamper cooperation (game theory), and influence the decision of the contracting parties to expect opportunistic behavior (stewardship theory). In addition, informational asymmetries are likely to be smaller within close proximity, as they are efficiently reduced by interpersonal relationships, trust, as well as social networks (social exchange theory and network approach) and because many activities which aim to reduce informational asymmetries again incur transaction costs.

Furthermore, this thesis aimed to answer two research questions both theoretically and empirically. Therefore, testable hypotheses concerning the research questions were elaborated by condensing the propositions regarding the individual investment phases. Then, a large dataset of 1402 dyads of venture capitalists and German new ventures which closed a financing round between January 2002 and March 2007 was used to empirically test the hypotheses. In respect to the measure of spatial proximity, this is the first dataset that uses the minimum travel time including travel by car and/or plane as a realistic measure.[997] Thus, it was possible to include intercontinental deals in the analyses.

The **first research question** to be answered was: What kind of relationship exists between certain characteristics of ventures, venture capitalists and/or financing rounds and the observed spatial proximity between venture capitalists and German new ventures? As a result, pronounced patterns in the observed spatial proximity between venture capitalists and their investees were revealed. A bivariate analysis supports the general hypothesis that the number of VC financing relationships diminishes significantly with increasing distance between both parties of a dyad. This gives a first hint on the general importance of spatial proximity in German VC financing. Furthermore, ordinal logistic regressions were used to depict patterns in the geographic dispersion of the VC financing dyads. Therefore, an ordinal measure of spatial proximity that is based on the minimum travel time between VC financing dyads was used as dependent variable.

Key findings are that new ventures in an early stage of development in terms of their age and size as well as ventures in knowledge-intensive industries that are characterized by high asset intangibility are likely to be located close to their venture capitalists. The most important reason for these relationships is that informational asymmetries are likely to be particularly severe for these ventures. Furthermore, it was uncovered that East German ventures are likely to be financed by more distant venture capitalists. This is mainly due to a lower number of venture capitalists' offices in East German states and proves that there are still structural differences between East and West Germany.

[997] Cf. Bender/Nathusius (2009), pp. 11-12.

In addition, it was found that larger venture capitalists are forced to increase their investment radius in order to find a sufficient number of investment opportunities and seem to have a larger network from which to benefit as they are found to realize more geographically dispersed deals. Similarly venture capitalists with a high degree of stage specialization were found to realize deals with less spatial proximity. This effect is also likely to be caused by the need to generate deal flow. As expected, (quasi-) public venture capitalists are focused on local new ventures in their investment strategies. Lead-investors were not found to be located closer to their portfolio companies in general, but it was found that there are structural differences in the effects between lead- and co-investors.

In regard to the investment volume, an inverted u-shaped relationship exists. Up to an investment volume of about 4.8 m€ investors are willing to increase their investment radius as the relative importance of transaction costs declines. However, for investment volumes larger than about 4.8 m€ the desire to monitor larger investments more intensively outweighs the advantage of a reduced relative impact of transaction costs. The analyses also show that the existence of a syndication partner in close proximity to the target is positively related to more distant VC financing relationships. Finally, venture capitalists and new ventures are likely to be closer in the case of consecutive financing rounds. This result indicates that new ventures which are located close to their venture capitalists are more likely to remain in the sample and to receive consecutive financing.

An important limitation of these first analyses is the problem of causality. Spatial proximity between actors is not a pure endogenous variable but is also likely to impact the investment decision. This effect then determines the composition of the used sample of VC financing rounds and causes the detected relationships. Furthermore, it is likely that the observed spatial proximity is also determined by other omitted variables, which may cause problems of endogeneity. In consequence, the results regarding the patterns in spatial proximity cannot be interpreted as causal relationships but have to be interpreted as correlations. One exception to the just mentioned problem of causality is the result that new ventures which are located close to their venture capitalists are more likely to remain in the sample and to receive consecutive financing rounds. This result is an additional indication that spatial proximity has an impact on the likelihood of (consecutive) VC financing.

These limitations lead to **research question two**: What kind of impact has spatial proximity between different types of venture capitalists and new ventures on the likelihood of a specific venture capital financing to occur? Consequently, research question two asks more specifically to investigate the causal relationship between the spatial proximity of both parties and the likelihood of a VC investment. In order to answer this research question, a matched sample approach was used. Therefore, a matched sample of potential VC financing relationships that did not occur was constructed. Each venture capitalist that participated in a VC financing round was matched with another financing round that:

- was raised by another new venture in which the venture capitalist did not invest,
- was closed in the same calendar year,
- was in the same investment stage,
- had a similar investment volume per venture capitalist,
- was raised by a new venture in the same industry segment, and
- was raised by a new venture that was located in the target region of the respective venture capitalist.[998]

This sample construction ensures that the spatial structure of actual portfolio companies (sample of realized investments) and potential investment targets (matched sample) is the same. Thus, the effect of potentially omitted variables and thus endogeneity is eliminated if one compares the realized sample with the matched sample. In consequence, it was possible to detect causal effects of spatial proximity by using rare event logistic regressions on a dummy variable that indicates whether a deal actually occurred or not. The method of rare event logistic regressions was developed by King/Zeng (2001) and corrects logit coefficient estimates for rare events and choice-based sampling.

As the likelihood of investment has a strong impact on the observed patterns in spatial proximity and thus the results of the first analysis, it was expected that most effects coincide with the non-observable likelihood of investment. However, the analysis of the likelihood of investment also uncovered numerous interesting differences.

One of the main results is that it was possible to quantify the effect of spatial proximity on the likelihood of a VC investment. It was found that the likelihood of investment decreases dramatically with rising distance between both parties. For the overall median dyad the likelihood of a VC financing relationship decreases by about 33% with each triplication of the minimum travel time. Keeping in mind that Germany is a highly populated country with a dense infrastructure in central Europe the size of this effect is overwhelming and might have been underestimated by practitioners and scholars so far. This underestimation might have two reasons. First, if venture capitalists do not intentionally reject distant investment opportunities, it might be rather informational problems that prevent the initial contact and a successful investment process for distant investments. Second, venture capitalists may be prone to unconscious behavior and may not be fully aware of their decision making processes. This

998 For some VC financing dyads it was not possible to finde an appropriate match and for some dyads selected restrictions had to be widened. See section 5.3.1 for a detailed description of the costruction of the matched sample.

would support the argumentation from Zacharakis/Meyer (1998) and Shepherd (1999) who criticized studies that fully rely on ex-post self reported data.[999]

Moreover, large differences exist in the impact of spatial proximity on the likelihood of investment for different types of new ventures, venture capitalists, and financing rounds. The largest difference in the importance of spatial proximity exists between private and (quasi-) public venture capitalists. After controlling for different geographical screens, it was found that the negative effect of distance is much less severe for (quasi-)public venture capitalists. This effect is mainly caused by their public mandate to promote the regional economic development. The second largest effect is caused by the investment volume. The inverted u-shaped effect that was found by the first analysis was supported. It was uncovered that the negative impact of distance on the likelihood of investment is more and more reduced up to an investment volume of about 3.9 m€ due to the decreased importance of transaction costs relative to the investment volume. For investment volumes above this threshold, the negative impact of distance becomes more severe again due to agency and/or game theoretical problems. The difference in the determined threshold is most likely caused by omitted variables in the patterns analysis.

Further results are that distance reduces the likelihood of investment particularly strong for new ventures in an early investment or product development stage, for entrepreneurial teams that lack profound prior experience, and/or for ventures in knowledge-intensive industries that are characterized by high asset intangibility or R&D intensity. The most important reason for these effects is that informational asymmetries are likely to be especially severe for these ventures. In addition, some of these findings differ substantially from the findings of the first analysis and show that an analysis of observable patterns in spatial proximity is not sufficient to fully understand the underlying effects. It was also uncovered that distance hinders the emergence of VC financing relationships significantly less for urban ventures compared to ventures located in non-urban areas. This effect was not observable in the patterns analysis and proves that venture capitalists evaluate the risk-return ratio differently depending of the venture's location.

In respect to the venture capitalist it was found that spatial proximity is less an issue for large investors in terms of assets under management. This indicates that the observed patterns in spatial proximity regarding the venture capitalist's size are mainly driven by differences in the likelihood of investment. As in the first analysis, no general difference was discovered between lead- and co-investors. Nevertheless, it was found that there are some structural differences in the effects mentioned above between lead- and co-investors.

[999] Cf. Zacharakis/Meyer (1998), p. 58; Shepherd (1999), p. 83.

Finally, the data indicates that the existence of a syndication partner in close proximity to the target reduces the negative impact of distance on the likelihood of investment. Hence, it is likely that venture capitalists use syndication in order to overcome large distances. However, the size of the effect is not large enough in order to compensate the general negative impact of distance. In consequence, the conclusion of Fritsch/Schilder (2006 and 2008) that syndication is used to offset the negative impact of distance and that spatial proximity is not important for German VC investments is not supported.[1000]

Overall, this study proves that local and regional aspects retain their importance even though the economy globalizes, although modern telecommunication and the internet facilitate a nearly costless transmission of information over long distances, and even though the travel infrastructure improves more and more.[1001] The results indicate that spatial proximity plays an important role in venture capital financing and has a strong impact on the likelihood of a VC investment and thus also on the observed patterns in spatial proximity. Thus, these findings contradict the results of Fritsch/Schilder (2008). In addition, it was shown that the patterns in spatial proximity are shaped by a broad combination of characteristics of the new venture, the venture capitalist and the financing round. These patterns are strongly, but not exclusively, influenced by significant variations of the importance of spatial proximity for the likelihood of investment among different VC financing relationships. Moreover, this is the first study that uses the minimum travel time including travel by car and/or plane as a realistic measure of spatial proximity. To the best knowledge of the author, this is also the first study that scrutinizes the impact of the new venture's location in urban and non-urban areas, the product development stage, the experience of the entrepreneurial team, and the venture capitalist's specialization in this specific context.

6.2 Implications of the Impact of Spatial Proximity on Venture Capital Financing

6.2.1 Implications for Entrepreneurs

The analyses within this thesis indicate that regional equity gaps are likely to exist in Germany. Martin et al. (2005) define regional equity gaps as situations in which in specific regions "the quantity of capital supplied is for one reason or another insufficient or rationed relative to demand."[1002] Hence, regional equity gaps may imply severe disadvantages in raising venture

[1000] Cf. Fritsch/Schilder (2006), pp. 22-23; Fritsch/Schilder (2008), pp. 2126-2129.

[1001] Studies that come to similar results are e.g.: Porter (1998), pp. 77-78; Audretsch (2000), pp. 342-343.

[1002] Martin et al. (2005), p. 1210. For a thourough discussion of regional equity gaps from a theroretical point of view see Martin et al. (2005), pp. 1210-1214.

capital for entrepreneurs which are located in these regions. These disadvantages are twofold. First, new ventures may have a lower likelihood of being funded. Second, in case of receiving venture capital funding the financing conditions are likely to be worse due to a lack of competition among venture capitalists.[1003] As it has been discussed in sections 2.1.1 and 2.1.2, venture capital is often one of the few or even the only option to finance young and innovative high potential companies. In consequence, regional equity gaps are of paramount importance for the location decision of new ventures. Entrepreneurial teams that wish to grow their new ventures could have a strong incentive or may even be forced to relocate their ventures close to one of the venture capital clusters.

In consequence, it is essential to discuss in which regions and for which types of new ventures equity gaps are likely to exist. In section 2.2.2 the uneven spatial distribution of venture capitalists' offices in many countries and especially Germany has been discussed. It was uncovered that venture capitalists concentrate in five German main clusters and that Munich is by far the largest of these agglomerations. The other clusters are Frankfurt am Main, Berlin, Hamburg and Düsseldorf. In addition, the previous section clarified the strong negative impact of distance on the likelihood of VC investment. The information about the spatial clustering of venture capital supply and the impact of spatial proximity on the likelihood of investment facilitates the identification of regions for which the likelihood of investment is particularly low relative to other regions. This is possible since the underlying likelihood of investment, or more precisely the relative likelihood of a VC financing relationship as discussed in section 5.3.2, is independent of the actual demand in a specific region. In contrast, it expresses the likelihood of investment into a (potentially existing) venture with a certain distance relative to the likelihood of investment that would exist if the same venture would reside in the same ZIP code area as the venture capitalist.

The spatial distribution of venture capitalists in Panel A in Figure 2.5 uncovers that there are two regions in which only very few venture capitalist offices exist and which are particularly far from the existing venture capital clusters. The first region covers the east of Thuringia, south of Saxony-Anhalt, and south-west of Saxony and the second region covers the north-east of Mecklenburg Western-Pomerania. Consequently, new ventures located in these regions are disadvantaged in raising venture capital compared to new ventures located in other regions that are closer to the VC clusters. Following the preceding analyses, these disadvantages are especially strong for new ventures in an early venture or product development stage, in a knowledge intensive industry, with an inexperienced entrepreneurial team, which are located in non-urban areas, and/or which raise only small investment volumes.

[1003] Cf. Lerner (1995), p. 303.

The disadvantage in raising venture capital in the named regions may also be enforced by the additional fact that the few venture capitalists in these regions have a limited capacity and are not able to cover each potential deal. This in turn may restrain supra-regional venture capitalists to invest as they become skeptical if local venture capitalists with alleged superior information do not have the intention to invest is a specific deal. Furthermore, the analyses in this thesis showed that syndication with local partners is used by venture capitalists to mitigate the negative effects of large distances. This may be also more difficult in regions with only few venture capitalists.[1004]

6.2.2 Policy Implications

Districts and municipalities in which only few venture capitalists reside and which are located far off the existing venture capital clusters should engage in the establishment of venture capitalists in their regions.

The analyses in this thesis showed that the regional presence of venture capitalists is crucial for young and innovative high potential companies in order to obtain venture capital funding. Furthermore, prior research uncovered that venture capital is essential for these companies in order to unfold their full potential.[1005] In consequence, a strong local venture capital community is likely to promote the development and settlement of high potential companies,[1006] to spur innovation within regions,[1007] and thus also to enhance the regional economic development.[1008]

In this context, it is important to note that a local venture capital community and the entrepreneurial environment, and thus also the number of high potential companies in a region, cross-fertilize each other.[1009] This has two important implications. First, it is not sufficient only to promote regional venture capital if the entrepreneurial environment is weak. Thus, also the general entrepreneurial environment, which is influenced by factors like the local presence of capable human resources, R&D institutes and universities, specialized service providers like

---

[1004] Cf. Florida/Kenney (1988), pp. 42-43; Mason/Harrison (2002), p. 446; Zook (2004), pp. 632-634.

[1005] Cf. Brav/Gompers (1997), pp. 1818-1820; Gifford (1997), p. 459; Hellmann/Puri (2000), pp. 975-980; Kortum/Lerner (2000), pp. 691-692; Shane (2004), pp. 94-95; Söderblom/Wiklund (2006), p. 12; Bottazzi/Da Rin/Hellmann (2008), pp. 503-507; Puri/Zarutskie (2009), pp. 27-28.

[1006] See also section 6.2.1 and cf. Zook (2002), p. 165.

[1007] Cf. Kortum/Lerner (2000), pp. 691-692; Kaserer et al. (2007), pp. 30-33; EFI (2009), pp. 24-25.

[1008] Cf. Schumpeter (1942), p. 106; Mellewigt/Witt (2002), p. 81; Audretsch (2002), pp. 14-35; Martin et al. (2005), p. 1227; Sunley et al. (2005), pp. 259-262; Niefert et al. (2006), pp. 28-29.

[1009] Cf. Shane (2004), pp. 94-95; Martin et al. (2005), pp. 1209-1210; Mason (2007), pp. 102-105 and 108-109; Samila/Sorenson (2008), pp. 6-35.

lawyers, consultants, or deal brokers, but also an adequate number of new ventures, should be promoted.[1010]

Second, regions with a weak local presence of venture capital may be trapped in a vicious circle of low supply and demand of venture capital.[1011] As discussed in the previous section, entrepreneurial teams may have incentives to relocate their ventures if they have or perceive disadvantages in raising venture capital in their region. This leads to the fact that regional role models of successful high potential companies are missing which would be strong motivators for other entrepreneurial teams. Furthermore, the development of specialized service providers like lawyers, consultants, or deal brokers within these regions is hampered. As a result, although the local presence of venture capitalists is by itself not sufficient, it is a necessary factor for the development of regional high potential companies and thus regional economic growth. Hence, public policy should promote the establishment of a local venture capital community.

Public venture capital support may be originated by different authorities like the European Union, the federal government, governments of federal states, or local authorities. Furthermore, various types of public venture capital support exist which also have different spatial implications. In general, public venture capital support may be classified into four categories: (i) the establishment of (quasi-)public venture capitalists which are under public influence, (ii) the public funding of private venture capitalists, (iii) co-investing with venture capitalists, and (iv) refinancing of venture capital investments.[1012]

The establishment of (quasi-)public venture capitalists like MBGs, subsidiaries of savings banks, subsidiaries of state banks, or subsidiaries of promotional banks has the advantage that policy makers have an impact on the location of these venture capitalists in order to strengthen the presence of investors in specific regions. The analysis of the spatial structure of venture capitalists in section 2.1.3 shows that already a relatively high number of (quasi-)public venture capitalists exists in Germany and that these investors are less spatially clustered compared to private venture capitalists. However, recent research and the discussion in section 2.1.3 uncovered that there are large differences in the investment behavior and effectiveness between (quasi-)public and private venture capitalists. The main difference is that (quasi-) public venture capitalists mostly lack value adding competencies and are thus less effective

---

[1010] Cf. Fogel (2001), p. 103; Venkataraman (2004), pp. 162-166; Zook (2005), pp. 66-67.

[1011] Cf. Martin et al. (2005), p. 1211.

[1012] Cf. Sunley et al. (2005), pp. 259-262; Niefert et al. (2006), pp. 28-29.

compared to other investors.[1013] Hence, there are considerable doubts whether (quasi-)public venture capitalists are able to compensate for a lack of private venture capitalists.

The public funding of private venture capitalists offers the advantage that the provided capital is likely to be used effectively and efficiently. However, if these initiatives do not focus on specific regions, a high share of this public support is likely to be allocated to existing venture capital clusters because most venture capitalists are located there. In consequence, this kind of public venture capital support reinforces the existing, clustered spatial structure of venture capital supply if public authorities do not limit their funding to venture capitalists in specific regions.

In contrast to the first two alternatives, the public co-investment with venture capitalists and the refinancing of venture capital investments on a deal by deal basis offers the opportunity to stimulate venture capital activities in specific regions. However, similar to the second alternative it is likely that also these types of public support reinforce existing venture capital clusters if public authorities do not limit their support to investments in specific regions.

An additional alternative to promote the economic development of deprived regions is the public support of private community development venture capital (CDVC) initiatives. CDVC refers to the use of venture capital to finance businesses in order to create financial returns for investors as well as social returns. Therefore, CDVC firms pursue a double bottom line approach.[1014] The aimed social returns can be manifold, but many CDVC firms intend to foster regional economic development by creating high value jobs, entrepreneurial capability, and wealth.[1015] Achleitner et al. (2009) provide a thorough discussion of the CDVC concept and its status quo in Germany.

On a national perspective, this thesis does not intent to conclude whether public policy should foster the dispersion of venture capital supply or the development of sizable venture capital clusters.[1016] This thesis rather intends to scrutinize the impact of spatial proximity in venture capital financing and its implications for different actors in order to better understand the effect of alternative public policies.

[1013] Cf. Venkataraman (2004), pp. 154, Mason (2007), p. 109. Section 2.1.3 revealed that subsidiaries of institutions promoting economic development, and thus also promotional banks, seem to mirror private venture capitalists best by frequently providing hands-on management.

[1014] Cf. Rubin (2001), p. 122.

[1015] Cf. Jegen (1998), pp. 188-189; Achleitner et al. (2009), p. 442.

[1016] Another stream of literature exists which discusses the advantages and disadvantages of clustering vs. dispersion. See e.g.: Porter (1998), pp. 77-90; Martin/Sunley/Turner (2002) p. 136.

6.2.3 Implications for Venture Capitalists

The strong impact of spatial proximity between venture capitalists and new ventures on the emergence of VC financing relationships has significant implications for venture capitalists regarding their applied portfolio strategy, their location decisions, but also regarding their used selection criteria. Many German venture capitalists state that spatial proximity to (potential) portfolio companies is beneficial but is not an important selection criterion.[1017] Nevertheless, empirical evidence confirms a considerable relevance of spatial proximity. This indicates that venture capitalists may underestimate the importance of spatial proximity for their operations.

The theoretical analysis revealed multiple rational reasons but also, at least partly, irrational reasons for the observed effects. Rational reasons such as transaction costs or informational asymmetries and potential irrational reasons such as different risk-return perceptions or unconscious behavior of the venture capitalist. The rational reasons for the impact of spatial proximity imply that proximity is an important factor for the emergence of successful VC financing relationships. This should be considered for the definition of portfolio strategies and venture capitalists may focus their operations on surrounding regions in order to fully benefit from the positive proximity effects. Furthermore, venture capitalists have to realize that, despite their frequently cited networks, they only have a limited spatial reach. Hence, venture capitalists should reconsider their general location decisions. The strong clustering of venture capitalists certainly has important rational reasons like the development of syndication networks or the local presence of specialized service providers like lawyers or deal brokers. Nevertheless, this effect may also be caused by a 'herd effect' and the OECD (1996) argues that the difficulties of venture capitalists to find good investment opportunities may be partly caused by geographical mismatches between the supply of, and demand for, venture capital.[1018] Moreover, the limited spatial reach may hamper the expansion of a venture capitalist's operations. Consequently, venture capitalists should consider opening new branch offices in distant target areas. In contrast, the irrational reasons for the impact of spatial proximity imply that it may be necessary for venture capitalists to critically reconsider their decision making processes and selection criteria in order to judge whether the detected magnitude of the impact of spatial proximity is justified or not.

Finally, the discussed implications are especially severe for venture capitalists specialized in early investment stages or knowledge intensive industries as well as for small venture capitalists because spatial proximity is particularly important for these investors.

[1017] Cf. Fritsch/Schilder (2008), pp. 2126-2129.

[1018] Cf. OECD (1996), p. 17; Martin et al. (2005), p. 1225.

6.3 Further Research and Outlook

Despite the thorough theoretical and empirical analyses of spatial proximity in VC financing that were conducted, this thesis may also be used as a starting point for additional future research. In order to empirically test parts of the theoretical framework, this thesis used a large sample of German venture capital transactions reported by VentureSource. As a result, important insights were gained. Nevertheless, it was not possible to test hypotheses regarding the different phases of the VC investment process. Hence, it would be interesting to use e.g. questionnaires in order to collect more detailed data in respect to the different phases of the VC investment process. This would lead to further and more differentiated insights in respect to the origin of the effects that were discovered within this thesis. In order to differentiate between effects that are caused by the venture capitalists' investment criteria and other effects, future research could also use experimental designs. Venture capitalists could be asked whether they would invest in different investment opportunities, which also differ in respect to their location and their distance to the investor, or not. Subsequently, this data could be used to conduct a conjoint analysis.

In addition, further research is required in respect to potential measures that alleviate the disadvantages of large distances between venture capitalists and new ventures. Tian (2009) provides first insights regarding the relationship of spatial proximity between the venture capitalist and the portfolio company and the extend of staging and Bengtsson/Ravid (2009) analyze the relationship between spatial proximity and the harshness of VC financing contracts.[1019] However, only little is known about the usage of different financial instruments in order to face the disadvantages of large distances as well as the effectiveness of the different measures.

Another important aspect is the fact that the venture capital industry is still developing in most countries and that venture capital conditions change constantly.[1020] Hence, future studies could investigate the development of the impact of spatial proximity, and thus also the impact of informational asymmetries and transaction costs, over time or within different market cycles. In consequence, important insights regarding the moderating effects of macroeconomic factors or the competition among venture capitalists could be gained.[1021] Moreover, it may be fruitful to extend the analysis to different countries in order to further investigate the impact of institutional and cultural factors on the importance of spatial proximity between ac-

[1019] Cf. Bengtsson/Ravid (2009), pp. 12-13; Tian (2009), pp. 16-22.

[1020] Cf. Böhner (2007), p. 46.

[1021] First results regarding the development of the geographic focus of venture capitalists over time are provided by Christensen (2007) for Denmark. However, there is still a huge lack of knowledge regarding the impact of different market cycles and other makroeconomic factors.

tors. This may also offer additional insights regarding potential measures to face the negative impact of distance on the likelihood of a VC investment.

Finally, it is crucial to further investigate the impact of spatial proximity between venture capitalists and their portfolio companies on the VC investment performance. Existing studies only use very rough measures of the investment performance like the employment growth, the company survival, or the likelihood that a portfolio company is acquired or goes public and offer contradicting results.[1022] Hence, further research in this area may reveal additional, important implications in respect to promising portfolio strategies of venture capitalists.

In conclusion, the discussed field of study still offers promising avenues for future research which is particularly important in the light of an ongoing globalization of the economy. In order to gain further insights, this thesis offers an important fundament by providing a holistic theoretical framework and comprehensive empirical evidence for Germany and comparable continental European countries. In consequence, this thesis demonstrates and quantifies the importance of spatial proximity in venture capital financing and uncovers which types of new ventures, ventures capitalists, and investment rounds are particularly affected. Finally, important implications for entrepreneurs, venture capitalists, and public policy were derived.

[1022] Cf. Engel (2003a), pp. 221-231; Chen et al. (2009), pp. 20-25; Tian (2009), pp. 26-27.

Appendix

A Definitions from VentureSource

The following definitions are derived from the online help of VentureSource.[1023]

A.1 Venture Financing Round Types

Seed Round: Seed rounds are initial rounds invested in companies at very early stages of development, typically with the founders and product developers such as engineers or molecular biologists on board, but without a complete management team in place. Most seed rounds do not exceed $2.5 million in amount raised.

First Round, Second Round: This ordinal nomenclature is used to describe most venture rounds. Companies often refer to financing rounds as “first,” “second,” “third,” etc. even though the legal term for the transaction as stated in closing documents and amendments to the documents of incorporation may refer to them as series A preferred, series B common, etc.

Later Stage: VentureSource classifies all equity rounds subsequent to the second round as later rounds.

Restart: A restart round requires a judgment by the Research team unless the company itself characterizes the financing round as restart funding. Generally, a restart round is characterized by a significantly reduced valuation causing significant dilution, which serves to "wash out" existing investors who do not participate in the restart round. Often a restart is accompanied by a change in business direction or a dramatic shift in marketing strategy. The business status of a company that has completed a restart round is also “Restart.”

Note: If, following a restart, a company raises subsequent rounds that it refers to as “First,” “Second,” “Third,” etc., the round type for those rounds will be r1st, r2nd, r3rd, etc.

[1023] Cf. VentureSource (2007).

A.2 Stages of Development

Startup: A startup is a business that is in a purely conceptual phase--product development has not begun. This business stage corresponds to the seed round of venture capital financing.

Product Development: Companies in product development are currently developing one or more products, but have not yet begun shipping. At the development stage and beyond, a company can have received any number of venture capital rounds, from an initial venture round through the final financing round before a liquidity event.

Product in Beta Test or Clinical Trials: For information technology companies, this is an intermediate period when the company is technically still in product development, but a prototype is being tested by select customers prior to market introduction. For medical therapeutics companies (e.g., medical compounds or drugs) and medical device companies, this stage signifies that the product is out of development and has progressed to human clinical trials.

Shipping Product: The shipping stage indicates that at least one revenue-generating product is being shipped, although other products may still be in development or beta test. For service companies, this stage indicates that the company is providing services to a customer base and receiving revenues for those services.

Profitable: The profitable stage indicates that the company is shipping products or providing services from which it derives revenues, and the company has reported that it is profitable.

B Appendix – Description of Dataset

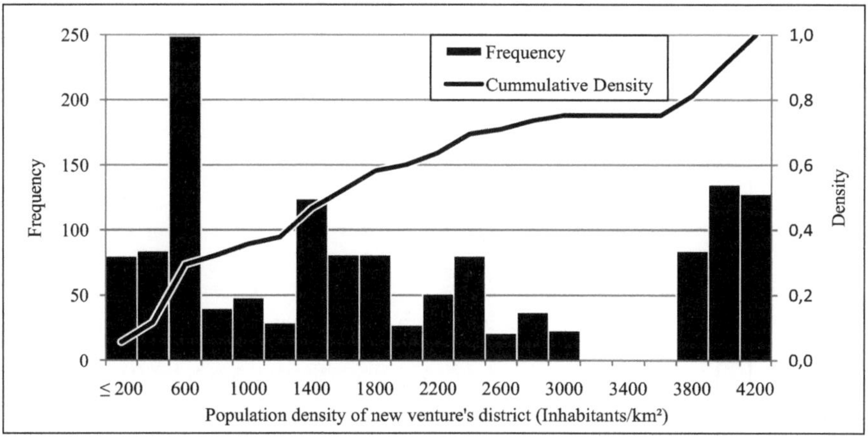

Figure B.1: Distribution of VC financing rounds in regard to the population density of the new venture's district
Source: Own illustration.

Table B.1: Summary statistics of original metric variables
This table provides summary statistics for independent metric variables in their original untransformed form.

Variable	Mean	Median	S.D.	Min.	Max.	Obs.
Venture						
Venture development stage						
Age in years	4.66	3.99	3.58	0.01	23.56	1402
Number of employees	44.15	31.00	56.70	1.00	668.00	1355
Industry's knowledge intensity						
Asset intangibility	0.17	0.15	0.06	0.00	0.34	1402
R&D intensity	0.12	0.11	0.09	0.00	0.33	1402
Book/market	0.88	0.73	0.43	-1.19	2.13	1402
Venture capitalist						
Assets under management in m€	1303.76	124.90	3704.26	2.00	38766.54	1256
Age in years	9.03	5.82	8.59	0.04	36.63	1375
Control variables						
VC market condition						
German VC fundraising (t-1) in m€	1357.56	1012.42	775.13	609.49	2464.31	1402
German VC investments in m€	1080.00	965.38	243.36	703.59	13 3.77	1402

C Appendix – Patterns in Spatial Proximity

Table C.1: Correlation matrix of independent variables

This table presents the correlation coefficients based on Kendall's tau between the independent variables. The sample consists of 1402 dyads of venture capitalists and German portfolio companies which have closed a financing round between January 2002 and March 2007. The number of observations might vary due to missing values.

Variable	1	2	3	4	5	6	7	8	9	10	11	12	13	14	15
1 Ln(venture age in years)	1.000														
2 Dummy seed stage round	-0.208 *	1.000													
3 Dummy first round	-0.335 *	-0.107 *	1.000												
4 Dummy later stage round	0.402 *	-0.268 *	-0.929 *	1.000											
5 Ln(number of venture employees)	0.216 *	-0.176 *	-0.107 *	0.166 *	1.000										
6 Dummy business concept only	-0.161 *	0.573 *	0.005	-0.218 *	-0.097 *	1.000									
7 Dummy product development/tests	-0.148 *	0.065 *	0.124 *	-0.144 *	-0.094 *	-0.104 *	1.000								
8 Dummy shipp.prod./profitable	0.193 *	-0.231 *	-0.124 *	0.206 *	0.120 *	-0.188 *	-0.957 *	1.000							
9 Dummy prior exec. experience	0.000	-0.045	-0.161 *	0.173 *	0.197 *	-0.057 *	0.188 *	-0.169 *	1.000						
10 Dummy high asset intangibility	-0.083 *	0.076 *	0.042	-0.069 *	-0.037	0.100 *	-0.036	0.006	0.039	1.000					
11 Dummy high R&D intensity	-0.034	-0.044	0.022	-0.005	-0.010	-0.041	0.382 *	-0.366 *	0.123 *	-0.134 *	1.000				
12 Dummy low book/market	0.147 *	0.021	-0.131 *	0.119 *	-0.013	-0.049	0.155 *	-0.138 *	0.082 *	-0.050	-0.134 *	1.000			
13 Dummy East German venture	0.110 *	-0.063 *	-0.001	0.024	0.071 *	-0.047	-0.017	0.031	-0.035	-0.012	-0.028	0.042	1.000		
14 Dummy urban venture location	0.045 *	-0.058 *	-0.102 *	0.120 *	0.004	-0.043	-0.159 *	0.169 *	0.136 *	0.133 *	-0.155 *	0.005	0.150 *	1.000	
15 Ln(VC assets under management in m€)	0.036	-0.094 *	-0.079 *	0.112 *	0.182 *	-0.060 *	0.063 *	-0.045	0.198 *	-0.060 *	0.028	0.044	-0.057 *	0.047 *	1.000
16 Ln(VC age in years)	0.106 *	-0.086 *	-0.105 *	0.133 *	0.119 *	-0.062 *	0.033	-0.015	0.129 *	-0.065 *	0.007	0.101 *	-0.017	0.044 *	0.365 *
17 HHI industry	-0.003	0.029	-0.044	0.031	-0.023	0.019	0.179 *	-0.183 *	0.062 *	0.026	0.119 *	0.078 *	-0.080 *	-0.031	-0.085 *
18 HHI stage	0.122 *	-0.095 *	-0.097 *	0.130 *	0.153 *	-0.108 *	0.007	0.025	0.051 *	-0.042	0.001	0.000	0.011	0.066 *	0.116 *
19 Dummy VC with excl. fin. objectives	0.028	-0.057 *	-0.032	0.052	0.119 *	-0.080 *	0.064 *	-0.040	0.075 *	0.004	0.049	-0.022	-0.203 *	0.004	0.044
20 Dummy corporate VC	-0.051 *	-0.015	0.022	-0.016	0.027	0.021	-0.041	0.034	-0.001	0.033	-0.058 *	-0.040	-0.004	0.024	0.013
21 Dummy (quasi-)public VC	0.001	0.072 *	0.021	-0.048	-0.148 *	0.075 *	-0.045	0.023	-0.082 *	-0.025	-0.018	0.049	0.226 *	-0.019	-0.055 *
22 Dummy lead-investor	-0.056 *	0.069 *	0.167 *	-0.187 *	-0.096 *	0.052 *	-0.062 *	0.046	-0.117 *	0.047	-0.056 *	-0.040	0.002	-0.030	-0.045
23 Investment volume per VC (m€)	0.060 *	-0.188 *	0.068 *	0.009	0.315 *	-0.128 *	0.227 *	-0.189 *	0.248 *	-0.056 *	0.072 *	0.090 *	0.005	0.034	0.247 *
24 Syndication benefit (min. tr. time)	0.032	-0.043	-0.116 *	0.128 *	0.123 *	-0.050 *	0.191 *	-0.175 *	0.177 *	-0.043	0.126 *	0.099 *	-0.029	0.041 *	0.155 *
25 Syndication benefit (car tr. time)	0.025	-0.041	-0.111 *	0.123 *	0.118 *	-0.049 *	0.169 *	-0.153 *	0.162 *	-0.042	0.114 *	0.087 *	-0.023	0.042 *	0.147 *
26 Syndication benefit (car distance)	0.030	-0.045	-0.110 *	0.123 *	0.121 *	-0.052 *	0.187 *	-0.169 *	0.167 *	-0.048 *	0.127 *	0.096 *	-0.024	0.048 *	0.140 *
27 No. of consecutive round	0.227 *	-0.151 *	-0.398 *	0.442 *	0.005	-0.122 *	-0.088 *	0.122 *	0.077 *	-0.048	-0.014	0.110 *	0.039	0.056 *	-0.069 *
28 Ln(German VC fundraising in m€ (t-1))	-0.168 *	0.067 *	0.026	-0.050 *	-0.080 *	0.063 *	-0.004	-0.015	-0.093 *	0.121 *	0.022	-0.096 *	-0.046	-0.080 *	-0.087 *
29 Ln(German VC investments in m€)	-0.081 *	0.029	0.007	-0.017	-0.042 *	0.069 *	-0.001	-0.020	-0.110 *	0.010	0.014	-0.148 *	-0.016	-0.020	-0.050 *
30 Return of MSCI SC Germany (ltm)	0.117 *	-0.029	-0.036	0.045 *	0.007	-0.036	0.005	0.005	0.046 *	-0.119 *	-0.061 *	0.182 *	0.009	0.041 *	0.076 *
31 VC's no. of offices	0.000	-0.064 *	-0.041	0.063 *	0.154 *	-0.027	-0.030	0.037	0.127 *	0.013	-0.010	0.000	-0.092 *	0.038	0.407 *

Table C.1 cont.: Correlation matrix of independent variables

Variable	16	17	18	19	20	21	22	23	24	25	26	27	28	29	30	31
16 Ln(VC age in years)	1.000															
17 HHI industry	-0.097 *	1.000														
18 HHI stage	0.047 *	0.099 *	1.000													
19 Dummy VC with excl. fin. objectives	0.096 *	0.107 *	0.082 *	1.000												
20 Dummy corporate VC	-0.108 *	0.136 *	0.029	-0.437 *	1.000											
21 Dummy (quasi-)public VC	-0.041	-0.187 *	-0.103 *	-0.828 *	-0.142 *	1.000										
22 Dummy lead-investor	-0.038	-0.029	0.020	0.170 *	-0.112 *	-0.117 *	1.000									
23 Investment volume per VC (m€)	0.119 *	0.013	0.075 *	0.165 *	-0.006	-0.179 *	0.007	1.000								
24 Syndication benefit (min. tr. time)	0.036	0.135 *	0.053 *	0.026	0.069 *	-0.071 *	-0.270 *	0.104 *	1.000							
25 Syndication benefit (car tr. time)	0.035	0.124 *	0.040	0.039	0.047 *	-0.071 *	-0.265 *	0.095 *	0.957 *	1.000						
26 Syndication benefit (car distance)	0.031	0.133 *	0.051 *	0.040	0.056 *	-0.078 *	-0.275 *	0.107 *	0.920 *	0.941 *	1.000					
27 No. of consecutive round	0.079 *	0.058 *	-0.014	0.016	-0.009	-0.012	-0.174 *	-0.089 *	-0.053 *	-0.062 *	-0.051 *	1.000				
28 Ln(German VC fundraising in m€ (t-1))	-0.142 *	0.002	-0.030	0.015	0.008	-0.022	0.044	-0.040	-0.053 *	-0.052 *	-0.058 *	-0.089 *	1.000			
29 Ln(German VC investments in m€)	-0.084 *	-0.008	-0.033	0.012	-0.019	-0.002	0.015	-0.069 *	-0.012	-0.013	-0.014	-0.067 *	0.369 *	1.000		
30 Return of MSCI SC Germany (ltm)	0.145 *	-0.006	0.017	0.014	-0.054 *	0.019	0.013	0.019	0.027	0.025	0.026	0.075 *	-0.485 *	-0.219 *	1.000	
31 VC's no. of offices	0.333 *	-0.174 *	0.023	0.106 *	0.052 *	-0.149 *	-0.006	0.136 *	-0.006	-0.013	-0.021	-0.065 *	-0.045 *	-0.035	0.033	1.000

* significant at 5%; τ > 0.500 ; 0.300 < τ ≤ 0.500

Table C.2: Variance inflation factors – Base models
This table presents variance inflation factors for the base models presented in Table 5.12.

	Variance inflation factor (VIF)			
Variable	OL 1	OL 2	OL 3	OL 4
Venture				
Ln(age)	1,8667	1,9434	1,9554	1,9659
Dummy seed stage round	1,7187	1,7236	1,6819	1,7062
Dummy later stage round	1,7819	1,7986	1,8342	1,8579
Dummy business concept only	1,4579	1,4597	1,4190	1,4513
Dummy shipp.prod./profitable	1,5249	1,5320	1,5334	1,5329
Dummy prior exec. experience	1,3154	1,3335	1,3294	1,3337
Dummy high asset intangibility	1,1033	1,1387	1,1378	1,1640
Dummy high R&D intensity	1,3072	1,3342	1,2983	1,3955
Dummy low book/market	1,2258	1,2847	1,2975	1,4218
Dummy East German venture	1,3289	1,3312	1,3596	1,3630
Dummy urban venture location	1,3051	1,3081	1,3275	1,3445
Venture capitalist				
Ln(assets under management)	1,7249	2,2612	2,4875	2,4921
Ln(age)	1,5504	1,6759	1,8347	1,9162
HHI industry			1,3618	1,3689
HHI stage			1,1606	1,1623
Dummy corporate VC	1,0718	1,0760	1,0892	1,0923
Dummy (quasi-)public VC	1,2067	1,2504	1,3303	1,3418
Dummy lead-investor	1,1204	1,1298	1,1331	1,1322
Round				
Investment volume per VC	5,1805	5,2966	5,2029	5,2966
(Investment volume per VC)^2	4,4435	4,4889	4,3887	4,4145
Syndication benefit	1,0757	1,0929	1,0944	1,0980
No. of consecutive round	1,3414	1,3713	1,4145	1,4264
Control variables				
Ln(German VC fundraising (t-1))		2,1529	2,0897	
Ln(German VC investments)		1,1818	1,1685	
Return of MSCI SC Germany (ltm)		1,9850	1,9490	2,8178
VC's no. of offices		1,8322	2,0279	2,0570
Year f.e.	No	No	No	Yes
Max. VIF	5,1805	5,2966	5,2029	5,2966
Mean VIF	1,7325	1,7909	1,7656	1,9956

Table C.3: Ordered logistic regressions – Details on venture capitalists' experience and reputation
This table presents the results of ordered logistic regressions with ordinal categories of the minimum travel time as dependent variable. The models are based on Model OL 2 and scrutinize further details regarding the venture capitalists' age. The sample consists of venture capitalists and German portfolio companies which have closed a financing round between January 2002 and March 2007. Varying sample sizes are due to missing values. Standard errors are adjusted for serial correlation, heteroskedasticity, and nonindependence across observations of the same venture capitalist.

Variable	OL 1	OL 2	OL 2.6	OL 2.7
Dep. var.: Ordinal min. travel time				
Venture				
Ln(age)	0.1505**	0.1887**	0.1887**	0.1897**
Dummy seed stage round	-0.2473	-0.0841	-0.0475	-0.0628
Dummy later stage round	0.1748	0.1627	0.1633	0.1693
Dummy business concept only	0.9140*	0.9595**	0.9259*	0.9516*
Dummy shipp.prod./profitable	-0.1258	-0.0919	-0.0939	-0.0891
Dummy prior exec. experience	-0.2281	-0.2895*	-0.2900*	-0.2911*
Dummy high asset intangibility	-0.5360**	-0.4609*	-0.4607*	-0.4624*
Dummy high R&D intensity	0.1304	0.2265	0.2297	0.2296
Dummy low book/market	-0.0946	-0.0806	-0.0872	-0.0799
Dummy East German venture	0.5110**	0.5626**	0.5670**	0.5633**
Dummy urban venture location	-0.4298	-0.4843	-0.4829	-0.4879
Venture capitalist				
Ln(assets under management)	0.1031	0.3490***	0.3377***	0.3439***
Ln(age)	-0.2655*	-0.1006		
Age			-0.0048	-0.0321
$(\text{Age})^2$				0.0009
Dummy corporate VC	0.2830	0.2452	0.2664	0.2607
Dummy (quasi-)public VC	-1.0320***	-1.4454***	-1.4385***	-1.4368***
Dummy lead-investor	-0.0646	-0.0988	-0.0972	-0.0992
Round				
Investment volume per VC	0.3432***	0.2683***	0.2665***	0.2687***
$(\text{Investment volume per VC})^2$	-0.0319***	-0.0278***	-0.0274***	-0.0280***
Syndication benefit	0.0108***	0.0101***	0.0100***	0.0101***
No. of consecutive round	-0.1559	-0.2507***	-0.2589***	-0.2510***
Control variables				
Ln(German VC fundraising (t-1))		0.1789	0.1894	0.1821
Ln(German VC investments)		0.0470	0.0425	0.0565
Return of MSCI SC Germany (ltm)		0.4651*	0.4528*	0.4542*
VC's no. of offices		-0.0985***	-0.0986***	-0.1065***
cut1	-0.7236	1.7528	1.8755	1.8341
cut2	0.0665	2.6072	2.7291	2.6885
cut3	0.8735	3.4902*	3.6114*	3.5716*
cut4	2.6046***	5.3277***	5.4482***	5.4099***
N	1075	1075	1075	1075
LR Chi^2	228.27***	345.03***	343.62***	344.79***
Nagelkerke's R^2	0.200	0.287	0.286	0.287
Log. Likelihood	-1563.11	-1504.73	-1505.43	-1504.85
AIC	3174.21	3065.46	3066.87	3067.69

* significant at 10%; ** significant at 5%; *** significant at 1% (two-sided)

Table C.4: Ordered logistic regressions – Details on venture capitalists' type
This table presents the results of ordered logistic regressions with ordinal categories of the minimum travel time as dependent variable. The models scrutinize further details regarding the venture capitalists' type. Standard errors are adjusted for serial correlation, heteroskedasticity, and nonindependence across observations of the same venture capitalist. B.: bank; centr.: central; econ. dev.: economic development; sav. savings.

Variable	OL 2	OL 2.8	OL 3	OL 3.1
Dep. var.: Ordinal min. travel time				
Venture				
Ln(age)	0.1887**	0.1872**	0.1236	0.1259
Dummy seed stage round	-0.0841	-0.2810	-0.1158	-0.3033
Dummy later stage round	0.1627	0.1648	0.1579	0.1630
Dummy business concept only	0.9595**	1.1362**	1.1116**	1.2573**
Dummy shipp.prod./profitable	-0.0919	-0.0826	0.0548	0.0680
Dummy prior exec. experience	-0.2895*	-0.2720	-0.3855**	-0.3539*
Dummy high asset intangibility	-0.4609*	-0.4417*	-0.5213*	-0.5192*
Dummy high R&D intensity	0.2265	0.2541	0.1019	0.1370
Dummy low book/market	-0.0806	-0.0826	0.0311	0.0156
Dummy East German venture	0.5626**	0.6046**	0.6026**	0.6572**
Dummy urban venture location	-0.4843	-0.4797	-0.5387	-0.5372
Venture capitalist				
Ln(assets under management)	0.3490***	0.3065***	0.3870***	0.3438***
Ln(age)	-0.1006	-0.1239	-0.1214	-0.1511
HHI industry			0.3995	0.4764
HHI stage			1.8219***	1.7471**
Dummy corporate VC	0.2452	0.2524	0.2209	0.2403
Dummy (quasi-)public VC	-1.4454***		-1.3499***	
Dummy MBG		-0.9282*		-0.9049*
Dummy subs. of sav./coop. banks		-1.6625***		-1.4740***
Dummy subs. of state b./coop. centr. inst.		-1.6784***		-1.8883***
Dummy subs. of inst. promoting econ. dev.		-1.5884***		-1.4315***
Other German government		-0.7838**		-0.7083**
Dummy lead-investor	-0.0988	-0.0770	-0.0696	-0.0424
Round				
Investment volume per VC	0.2683***	0.2934***	0.2525***	0.2808***
(Investment volume per VC)²	-0.0278***	-0.0293***	-0.0259***	-0.0277***
Syndication benefit	0.0101***	0.0100***	0.0094***	0.0092***
No. of consecutive round	-0.2507***	-0.2390***	-0.2554**	-0.2448**
Control variables				
Ln(German VC fundraising (t-1))	0.1789	0.1841	0.1543	0.1664
Ln(German VC investments)	0.0470	0.0168	-0.1043	-0.1372
Return of MSCI SC Germany (ltm)	0.4651*	0.4567*	0.4845*	0.4798*
VC's no. of offices	-0.0985***	-0.0914***	-0.0966***	-0.0888***
cut1	1.7528	1.4220	1.6181	1.3286
cut2	2.6072	2.2844	2.5022	2.2218
cut3	3.4902*	3.1746	3.3979	3.1242
cut4	5.3277***	5.0086***	5.5270***	5.2509**
N	1075	1075	950	950
LR Chi²	345.03***	351.56***	305.07***	311.82***
Nagelkerke's R²	0.287	0.292	0.288	0.294
Log. Likelihood	-1504.73	-1501.46	-1300.23	-1296.86
AIC	3065.46	3066.92	2660.46	2661.72

* significant at 10%; ** significant at 5%; *** significant at 1% (two-sided)

Table C.5: Ordered logistic regressions – Details on the investment volume per venture capitalist
This table presents the results of ordered logistic regressions with ordinal categories of the minimum travel time as dependent variable. The models are based on Model OL 2 and scrutinize further details regarding the investment volume per venture capitalist. The sample consists of venture capitalists and German portfolio companies which have closed a financing round between January 2002 and March 2007. Model OL2.10 only includes dyads with investment volumes per venture capitalist up to 4.85 m€ and Model OL2.11 includes all dyads with investment volumes of at least 4.85 m€. Standard errors are adjusted for serial correlation, heteroskedasticity, and nonindependence across observations of the same venture capitalist.

Variable	OL 2	OL 2.9	OL 2.10	OL 2.11
Dep. var.: Ord nal min. travel time				
Venture				
Ln(age)	0.1887**	0.1976***	0.1784**	-0.6091
Dummy seed stage round	-0.0841	-0.2101	-0.0807	-
Dummy later stage round	0.1627	0.1125	0.1744	5.0418
Dummy business concept only	0.9595**	0.9525**	0.9589**	-
Dummy shipp.prod./profitable	-0.0919	-0.1220	-0.0366	3.8515**
Dummy prior exec. experience	-0.2895*	-0.2292	-0.2780	-7.2535*
Dummy high asset intangibility	-0.4609*	-0.4838*	-0.4146	0.0941
Dummy high R&D intensity	0.2265	0.2301	0.2714	16.7665**
Dummy low book/market	-0.0806	-0.0462	-0.0160	8.3424**
Dummy East German venture	0.5626**	0.5669**	0.5010*	13.3237*
Dummy urban venture location	-0.4843	-0.4718	-0.4953	-1.2171
Venture capitalist				
Ln(assets under management)	0.3490***	0.3625***	0.3480***	-0.5280
Ln(age)	-0.1006	-0.0939	-0.0929	2.9144
Dummy corporate VC	0.2452	0.2257	0.2745	-30.2320***
Dummy (quasi-)public VC	-1.4454***	-1.4889***	-1.4219***	-1.9051**
Dummy lead-investor	-0.0988	-0.1250	-0.0867	1.4046
Round				
Investment volume per VC	0.2683***	0.0587	0.1919***	-0.1316
(Investment volume per VC)²	-0.0278***			
Syndication benefit	0.0101***	0.0099***	0.0103***	0.0225
No. of consecutive round	-0.2507***	-0.2573***	-0.2283**	-6.0495
Control variables				
Ln(German VC fundraising (t-1))	0.1789	0.2031	0.1426	11.0013**
Ln(German VC investments)	0.0470	-0.0075	0.0523	5.1699
Return of MSCI SC Germany (ltm)	0.4651*	0.4645*	0.4092*	14.8844*
VC's no. of offices	-0.0985***	-0.0998***	-0.1007***	-0.1256*
cut1	1.7528	1.3739	1.5871	112.5648*
cut2	2.6072	2.2247	2.4221	117.0786*
cut3	3.4902*	3.1023	3.2940	120.6423*
cut4	5.3277***	4.9287***	5.1106***	132.8930
N	1075	1075	1037	38
LR Chi²	345.03***	336.55***	333.59***	70.01***
Nagelkerke's R²	0.287	0.281	0.288	0.886
Log. Likelihood	-1504.73	-1508.97	-1450.60	-21.99
AIC	3065.46	3071.94	2955.20	87.97

* significant at 10%; ** significant at 5%; *** significant at 1% (two-sided)

Table C.6: Ordered logistic regressions – Details on syndication
This table presents the results of ordered logistic regressions with ordinal categories of the minimum travel time as dependent variable. The models are based on Model OL 2 and scrutinize further details regarding the syndication of VC transactions. The sample consists of venture capitalists and German portfolio companies which have closed a financing round between January 2002 and March 2007. Varying sample sizes are due to missing values. Standard errors are adjusted for serial correlation, heteroskedasticity, and nonindependence across observations of the same venture capitalist.

Variable	OL 2	OL 2.12	OL 2.13	OL 2.14
Dep. var.: Ordinal min. travel time				
Venture				
Ln(age)	0.1887**	0.1859**	0.1542**	0.1783**
Dummy seed stage round	-0.0841	0.1032	-0.1922	-0.1153
Dummy later stage round	0.1627	0.1489	0.0656	-0.1143
Dummy business concept only	0.9595**	0.9733*	1.1808**	1.3765***
Dummy shipp.prod./profitable	-0.0919	-0.0791	0.0518	0.1781
Dummy prior exec. experience	-0.2895*	-0.2149	-0.4407***	-0.4775***
Dummy high asset intangibility	-0.4609*	-0.3962	-0.4204*	-0.3999
Dummy high R&D intensity	0.2265	0.1501	0.1368	-0.2338
Dummy low book/market	-0.0806	0.0594	-0.3423*	-0.5776***
Dummy East German venture	0.5626**	0.5354**	0.6565***	0.6462***
Dummy urban venture location	-0.4843	-0.5630*	-0.8942***	-0.6202**
Venture capitalist				
Ln(assets under management)	0.3490***	0.3674***	0.3213***	0.2095***
Ln(age)	-0.1006	-0.1128	-0.0679	-0.0612
Dummy corporate VC	0.2452	0.2617	0.3533	0.4966
Dummy (quasi-)public VC	-1.4454***	-1.4816***	-1.1928***	-0.9890***
Dummy lead-investor	-0.0988	-0.1110	0.0562	0.4399***
Round				
Investment volume per VC	0.2683***	0.2217**	0.3277***	0.3465***
(Investment volume per VC)^2	-0.0278***	-0.0232***	-0.0289***	-0.0256***
Syndication benefit	0.0101***			
No. of synd. partners		0.0658*		
Dummy close synd. partner			2.9526***	
Difference betw. VC' distance and distance of closest synd. partner				0.0209***
No. of consecutive round	-0.2507***	-0.2621***	-0.1766**	-0.0664
Control variables				
Ln(German VC fundraising (t-1))	0.1789	0.2264	0.2993**	0.4958***
Ln(German VC investments)	0.0470	-0.1688	-0.1551	-0.3807
Return of MSCI SC Germany (ltm)	0.4651*	0.5071**	0.5994**	0.8074***
VC's no. of offices	-0.0985***	-0.1029***	-0.0835***	-0.0564***
cut1	1.7528	0.7250	1.4103	1.5317
cut2	2.6072	1.5646	2.3316	2.6043
cut3	3.4902*	2.4202	3.3565	3.8501*
cut4	5.3277***	4.1636**	5.6342**	6.7311***
N	1075	1075	1075	1075
LR Chi^2	345.03***	288.73***	547.11***	842.82***
Nagelkerke's R^2	0.287	0.246	0.417	0.569
Log. Likelihood	-1504.73	-1532.88	-1403.69	-1255.83
AIC	3065.46	3121.76	2863.38	2567.66

* significant at 10%; ** significant at 5%; *** significant at 1% (two-sided)

Table C.7: Brant test – Base models

This table summarizes the results of the Brant test of the parallel lines assumption for Models OL 1 to 4. The null hypothesis is that all coefficients/the respective coefficient are/is equal across the different response categories. A significant chi² statistic rejects this null hypothesis.

	Chi²			
Variable	OL 1	OL 2	OL 3	OL 4
Venture				
Ln(age)	5.64	4.48	4.78	4.72
Dummy seed stage round	7.16*	7.59*	11.00**	8.67**
Dummy later stage round	3.25	3.11	2.85	2.49
Dummy business concept only	7.60*	7.76*	7.23*	6.28*
Dummy shipp.prod./profitable	1.78	1.66	1.38	1.26
Dummy prior exec. experience	3.24	1.97	1.19	1.09
Dummy high asset intangibility	1.59	1.57	2.26	2.69
Dummy high R&D intensity	13.12***	13.95***	4.03	4.75
Dummy low book/market	5.34	6.62*	2.90	2.23
Dummy East German venture	8.98**	11.62***	5.86	6.40*
Dummy urban venture location	116.44***	111.34***	96.92***	105.27***
Venture capitalist				
Ln(assets under management)	8.61**	4.05	6.68*	7.38*
Ln(age)	7.63*	6.32*	3.81	4.09
HHI industry			18.31***	17.92***
HHI stage			12.61***	12.73***
Dummy corporate VC	3.90	4.97	3.31	3.27
Dummy (quasi-)public VC	39.82***	48.30***	43.93***	45.85***
Dummy lead-investor	3.41	3.62	3.56	3.51
Round				
Investment volume per VC	4.74	3.70	8.89**	9.55**
(Investment volume per VC)²	4.41	3.16	8.43**	8.95**
Syndication benefit	36.24***	29.62***	27.02***	27.51***
No. of consecutive round	1.86	1.33	0.19	0.26
Control variables				
Ln(German VC fundraising (t-1))		9.00**	6.99*	
Ln(German VC investments)		4.37	1.64	
Return of MSCI SC Germany (ltm)		3.83	2.21	0.93
VC's no. of offices		13.26***	12.31***	11.74***
Year f.e.	No	No	No	Yes
Joint test for all variables	375.61***	425.67***	379.93***	386.96***

* significant at 10%; ** significant at 5%; *** significant at 1% (two-sided)

Table C.8: Brant test – Details for Model OL 3

This table presents the estimated coefficients of the binary logistic regressions that were used in order to conduct the Brant test of the parallel lines assumption for Model OL 3. The first column (y>1) tests category 1 versus 2, 3, 4, and 5; the second (y>2) tests 1 and 2 versus 3, 4, and 5; etc.

	Coefficient			
Variable	y>1	y>2	y>3	y>4
Venture				
Ln(age)	0.2272	0.0622	0.0508	0.1094
Dummy seed stage round	-0.5476	-0.2332	0.7811	0.9211
Dummy later stage round	-0.0696	0.2745	0.2791	0.3583
Dummy business concept only	2.3078	1.2814	-0.2215	0.5635
Dummy shipp.prod./profitable	0.0907	0.1661	0.0829	0.4081
Dummy prior exec. experience	-0.4842	-0.3390	-0.3207	-0.4129
Dummy high asset intangibility	-0.6843	-0.6430	-0.3698	-0.6365
Dummy high R&D intensity	-0.0855	-0.2272	0.0899	0.5060
Dummy low book/market	-0.0105	-0.3140	-0.0526	-0.4215
Dummy East German venture	0.7956	0.7557	0.7886	-0.0610
Dummy urban venture location	-1.5077	-0.5544	0.2470	-0.2328
Venture capitalist				
Ln(assets under management)	0.3738	0.3451	0.4918	0.3523
Ln(age)	-0.2085	-0.1480	-0.2292	0.1596
HHI industry	0.2723	-0.3587	0.7922	1.4404
HHI stage	1.3882	2.4579	0.5631	1.8462
Dummy corporate VC	0.4888	-0.0252	0.2780	0.1571
Dummy (quasi-)public VC	-0.6549	-1.9491	-2.3692	-1.6191
Dummy lead-investor	-0.0664	-0.1998	0.0466	0.0430
Round				
Investment volume per VC	0.1657	0.1990	0.2994	1.4300
(Investment volume per VC)^2	-0.0106	-0.0270	-0.0360	-0.2368
Syndication benefit	0.0839	0.0299	0.0187	0.0038
No. of consecutive round	-0.2258	-0.2330	-0.2189	-0.1656
Control variables				
Ln(German VC fundraising (t-1))	0.4213	0.3579	0.0751	-0.4199
Ln(German VC investments)	-0.3007	-0.3097	0.0801	-0.0370
Return of MSCI SC Germany (ltm)	0.8128	0.5202	0.2944	0.1999
VC's no. of offices	-0.0749	-0.1077	-0.1799	-0.1966
Constant	-1.8055	-2.0571	-4.2072	-3.9855

Table C.9: Ordinary least squares regressions – Base models

This table presents the results of ordinary least squares regressions with ln(1+minimum travel time) as dependent variable. The sample consists of venture capitalists and German portfolio companies which have closed a financing round between January 2002 and March 2007. Varying sample sizes are due to missing values. Standard errors are adjusted for serial correlation, heteroskedasticity, and nonindependence across observations of the same venture capitalist.

Variable	OLS 1	OLS 2	OLS 3	OLS 4
Dep. var.: ln(1+min. travel time)				
Venture				
Ln(age)	0.1341**	0.1561***	0.1272**	0.1279**
Dummy seed stage round	-0.6347	-0.5354	-0.5508	-0.6357
Dummy later stage round	0.1070	0.1003	0.0752	0.1032
Dummy business concept only	0.8306**	0.8392**	0.8502***	0.9566***
Dummy shipp.prod./profitable	-0.0619	-0.0470	-0.0070	-0.0043
Dummy prior exec. experience	-0.1401	-0.1552	-0.1744	-0.1558
Dummy high asset intangibility	-0.3718**	-0.3099*	-0.3172*	-0.2566
Dummy high R&D intensity	-0.0432	-0.0087	-0.0616	-0.0180
Dummy low book/market	-0.1504	-0.1543	-0.0555	-0.1887
Dummy East German venture	0.3323*	0.3669**	0.3855**	0.3956**
Dummy urban venture location	-0.3533*	-0.3794**	-0.4129**	-0.4130**
Venture capitalist				
Ln(assets under management)	0.1168	0.2591***	0.2755***	0.2789***
Ln(age)	-0.2060*	-0.0935	-0.1410	-0.1701*
HHI industry			-0.3303	-0.3249
HHI stage			1.1017**	1.0665**
Dummy corporate VC	0.2505	0.2115	0.1728	0.1615
Dummy (quasi-)public VC	-0.5283**	-0.7164***	-0.7090***	-0.7371***
Dummy lead-investor	-0.0406	-0.0668	-0.0435	-0.0429
Round				
Investment volume per VC	0.1726**	0.1043	0.0744	0.0518
(Investment volume per VC)^2	-0.0158**	-0.0113**	-0.0089*	-0.0074
Syndication benefit	0.0050***	0.0043***	0.0041***	0.0043***
No. of consecutive round	-0.1162	-0.1706**	-0.1566**	-0.1690**
Control variables				
Ln(German VC fundraising (t-1))		0.1760*	0.1571	
Ln(German VC investments)		0.0932	0.0387	
Return of MSCI SC Germany (ltm)		0.3427**	0.3698**	0.0299
VC's no. of offices		-0.0624***	-0.0615***	-0.0602***
Constant	3.9238***	1.4688	1.6683	3.4863***
Year f.e.	No	No	No	Yes
N	1075	1075	950	950
F-value	6.089***	22.047***	16.596***	15.842***
R^2	0.163	0.241	0.249	0.257
Adj. R^2	0.148	0.224	0.228	0.234

* significant at 10%; ** significant at 5%; *** significant at 1% (two-sided)

Table C.10: Tobit regressions– Base models

This table presents the results of left-censored tobit regressions with the minimum travel time as dependent variable. The sample consists of venture capitalists and German portfolio companies which have closed a financing round between January 2002 and March 2007. Varying sample sizes are due to missing values. Standard errors are bootstrapped and the censoring value is 0.

Variable	Tobit 1	Tobit 2	Tobit 3	Tobit 4
Dep. var.: min. travel time				
Venture				
Ln(age)	11.6999***	13.4581***	6.6374**	6.5149*
Dummy seed stage round	-26.4998	-16.8934	-14.6949	-20.3568
Dummy later stage round	3.9447	3.4097	4.6608	7.0480
Dummy business concept only	41.7184	41.1421	42.0567*	48.5263*
Dummy shipp.prod./profitable	-15.4050	-13.6898	2.0969	2.2785
Dummy prior exec. experience	-9.1167	-10.0037	-15.5810***	-14.3029**
Dummy high asset intangibility	-20.4762	-14.8752	-18.4998**	-14.2403
Dummy high R&D intensity	17.0680	20.4332	5.6959	7.7895
Dummy low book/market	-6.3577	-4.5730	-4.9104	-14.1960
Dummy East German venture	27.7781***	31.0559***	33.2149***	34.0080***
Dummy urban venture location	-7.8716	-10.4592	-8.4394	-8.8671
Venture capitalist				
Ln(assets under management)	8.1742***	21.0998***	20.5701***	20.7818***
Ln(age)	-19.2439**	-8.8653	-7.6741	-9.4907*
HHI industry			37.2000*	37.9380*
HHI stage			81.9801***	79.4034***
Dummy corporate VC	11.9440	8.1896	-2.7049	-3.8741
Dummy (quasi-)public VC	-65.6269***	-82.8174***	-68.3935***	-70.2423***
Dummy lead-investor	-7.3600	-9.3172	-2.5455	-2.4670
Round				
Investment volume per VC	19.9671***	13.7874***	9.3352	7.8901
(Investment volume per VC)^2	-1.9622**	-1.5608***	-1.1159	-1.0156
Syndication benefit	0.7292***	0.6713***	0.6617***	0.6732***
No. of consecutive round	-5.1154	-9.8024**	-7.5917**	-8.4698**
Control variables				
Ln(German VC fundraising (t-1))		11.8755	5.9238	
Ln(German VC investments)		17.7324	-0.5419	
Return of MSCI SC Germany (ltm)		21.2221	17.8580	-7.7492
VC's no. of offices		-5.6648***	-4.8773***	-4.8081***
Constant	104.1854***	-154.6426	-47.1790	18.6708
Year f.e.	No	No	No	Yes
N	1075	1075	950	950
LR Chi^2	800.860***	1391.550***	2261.390***	1363.750***
McFadden's R^2	0.019	0.026	0.032	0.033
Log. Likelihood	-6491.65	-6444.38	-5498.62	-5494.54
AIC	13027.31	12940.76	11053.25	11049.07

* significant at 10%; ** significant at 5%; *** significant at 1% (two-sided)

Table C.11: Ordered logistic regressions – Different measures of spatial proximity
This table presents the results of ordered logistic regressions with ordinal categories of different measures of spatial proximity as dependent variable. The models are based on Models OL 2 and OL 3. The sample is restricted to European investors and consists of venture capitalists and German portfolio companies which have closed a financing round between January 2002 and March 2007. Varying sample sizes are due to missing values. Standard errors are adjusted for serial correlation, heteroskedasticity, and nonindependence across observations of the same venture capitalist. Intang.: intangible; v.: venture.

Variable	OL 2.14	OL 2.15	OL 2.16	OL 3.4	OL 3.5	OL 3.6
Dep. var.: Ordinal ...	min. travel time	car time	car distance	min. travel time	car time	car distance
Venture						
Ln(age)	0.166**	0.138*	0.147*	0.120	0.096	0.110
Dummy seed stage round	-0.070	-0.100	-0.315	-0.108	-0.125	-0.337
Dummy later stage round	0.217	0.201	0.147	0.194	0.211	0.173
Dummy bus. concept only	0.968**	0.943*	1.294***	1.118**	1.085**	1.425***
Dummy shipp.prod./prof.	-0.027	0.013	0.024	0.060	0.068	0.086
Dummy prior exec. exp.	-0.313*	-0.364**	-0.369**	-0.391**	-0.436**	-0.439**
Dummy high asset intang.	-0.495*	-0.611**	-0.570**	-0.539*	-0.681**	-0.659**
Dummy high R&D intensity	0.148	-0.012	-0.033	0.066	-0.023	-0.067
Dummy low book/market	-0.113	-0.203	-0.321*	0.024	-0.048	-0.207
Dummy East German venture	0.600**	0.710***	0.593**	0.615**	0.685**	0.554*
Dummy urban v. location	-0.527*	-0.115	-0.329	-0.609*	-0.196	-0.394
Venture capitalist						
Ln(assets under mgt.)	0.328***	0.345***	0.313***	0.371***	0.376***	0.329***
Ln(age)	-0.097	-0.142	-0.090	-0.121	-0.166	-0.087
HHI industry				0.207	-0.116	0.114
HHI stage				1.793**	1.647**	1.575**
Dummy corporate VC	0.272	0.199	0.249	0.285	0.132	0.176
Dummy (quasi-)public VC	-1.395***	-1.392***	-1.375***	-1.342***	-1.369***	-1.335***
Dummy lead-investor	-0.060	-0.040	0.044	-0.061	-0.036	0.066
Round						
Investment volume per VC	0.267***	0.220***	0.196**	0.263***	0.212**	0.201**
(Investment volume per VC)²	-0.027***	-0.023***	-0.018***	-0.027***	-0.022***	-0.017***
Syndication benefit	0.010***	0.010***	0.006***	0.009***	0.011***	0.006***
No. of consecutive round	-0.270***	-0.234**	-0.212**	-0.276***	-0.239**	-0.224**
Control variables						
Ln(German VC fundr. (t-1))	0.153	0.287*	0.243	0.159	0.249	0.229
Ln(German VC inv.)	0.015	-0.102	0.020	-0.102	-0.207	-0.087
Return of MSCI SC Germany (ltm)	0.448*	0.589**	0.567**	0.481*	0.544*	0.527*
VC's no. of offices	-0.094***	-0.093***	-0.091***	-0.095***	-0.095***	-0.090***
cut1	1.324	1.496	1.696	1.505	1.190	1.641
cut2	2.183	2.348	2.542	2.393	2.069	2.501
cut3	3.075	3.178	3.605	3.291	2.912	3.577
cut4	5.021***	4.242**	5.424**	5.467**	4.002*	5.485**
N	1053	1053	1053	942	942	942
LR Chi²	311.5***	328.8***	363.8***	286.4***	296.3***	319.7***
Nagelkerke's R²	0.268	0.280	0.305	0.275	0.282	0.301
Log. Likelihood	-1473.6	-1499.0	-1478.0	-1289.7	-1334.8	-1313.7
AIC	3003.3	3054.0	3012.0	2639.4	2729.7	2687.4

* significant at 10%; ** significant at 5%; *** significant at 1% (two-sided)

Table C.12: Ordinary least squares regressions – Different measures of spatial proximity
This table presents the results of ordinary least squares regressions with different measures of spatial proximity as dependent variable. The models are based on Models OLS 2 and OLS 3. The sample is restricted to European investors and consists of venture capitalists and German portfolio companies which have closed a financing round between January 2002 and March 2007. Varying sample sizes are due to missing values. Standard errors are adjusted for serial correlation, heteroskedasticity, and nonindependence across observations of the same venture capitalist. . Intang.: intangible; v.: venture.

Variable	OLS 2.1	OLS 2.2	OLS 2.3	OLS 3.1	OLS 3.2	OLS 3.3
Dep. var.:	Ln(1+min. tr. time)	Ln(1+car time)	Ln(1+car distance)	Ln(1+min. tr. time)	Ln(1+car time)	Ln(1+car distance)
Venture						
Ln(age)	0.141**	0.144**	0.180**	0.123**	0.119*	0.151*
Dummy seed stage round	-0.557	-0.503	-0.497	-0.582	-0.551	-0.533
Dummy later stage round	0.119	0.123	0.114	0.099	0.102	0.098
Dummy bus. concept only	0.847**	0.867**	1.129***	0.860***	0.898***	1.180***
Dummy shipp.prod./prof.	-0.004	0.005	0.017	-0.005	0.018	0.047
Dummy prior exec. exp.	-0.183*	-0.183	-0.230	-0.191*	-0.208*	-0.264*
Dummy high asset intang.	-0.345**	-0.377*	-0.450*	-0.347**	-0.386**	-0.487**
Dummy high R&D intensity	-0.085	-0.086	-0.092	-0.100	-0.104	-0.105
Dummy low book/market	-0.193	-0.198	-0.218	-0.087	-0.107	-0.111
Dummy East German venture	0.375**	0.444**	0.543**	0.380**	0.442**	0.518*
Dummy urban v. location	-0.390**	-0.304	-0.565**	-0.444**	-0.363*	-0.622**
Venture capitalist						
Ln(assets under mgt.)	0.246***	0.275***	0.318***	0.258***	0.279***	0.319***
Ln(age)	-0.094	-0.103	-0.124	-0.135	-0.134	-0.159
HHI industry				-0.451	-0.410	-0.474
HHI stage				1.066**	1.309***	1.444***
Dummy corporate VC	0.202	0.215	0.296	0.200	0.159	0.273
Dummy (quasi-)public VC	-0.663***	-0.813***	-0.999***	-0.687***	-0.808***	-0.991***
Dummy lead-investor	-0.026	-0.040	-0.063	-0.023	-0.021	-0.039
Round						
Investment volume per VC	0.100	0.121	0.137	0.085	0.106	0.130
(Investment volume per VC)^2	-0.011**	-0.013**	-0.014*	-0.010*	-0.011*	-0.013*
Syndication benefit	0.006***	0.004***	0.003***	0.006***	0.005***	0.004***
No. of consecutive round	-0.165**	-0.178**	-0.209**	-0.160**	-0.167**	-0.197**
Control variables						
Ln(German VC fundr. (t-1))	0.166	0.173	0.268*	0.164	0.168	0.255*
Ln(German VC inv.)	0.058	0.015	-0.026	0.031	-0.024	-0.066
Return of MSCI SC Germany (ltm)	0.337*	0.357*	0.525**	0.364**	0.367*	0.518**
VC's no. of offices	-0.059***	-0.067***	-0.081***	-0.059***	-0.066***	-0.079***
Constant	1.775	2.040	1.778	1.777	2.008	1.782
N	1053	1053	1053	942	942	942
F-value	27.17***	20.06***	21.94***	19.20***	18.05***	21.88***
R^2	0.231	0.244	0.246	0.247	0.259	0.259
Adj. R^2	0.213	0.226	0.228	0.226	0.238	0.238

* significant at 10%; ** significant at 5%; *** significant at 1% (two-sided)

D Appendix – Likelihood of a Venture Capital Investment

Table D.1: Variance inflation factors – Base models of rare event logistic regressions
This table presents variance inflation factors for the base models presented in Table 5.16.

	Variance inflation factor (VIF)				
Variable	REL 1	REL 2	REL 3	REL 4	REL 5
Distance (ln[1+min. travel time])	1.5669	1.5927	1.5958	1.5971	2.2954
Venture					
Ln(age) × dist.	2.3562	2.1970	2.2754	2.2781	2.3053
_Intercept	1.5272	1.4973	1.5526	1.5529	1.5606
Dummy seed stage round × dist.	1.6632	1.4954	1.5297	1.5437	1.7562
Dummy later stage round × dist.	1.8813	1.8125	1.9043	1.9048	1.9094
Dummy bus. concept only × dist.	1.7257	1.9588	2.2393	2.2441	2.1665
_Intercept	1.5740	1.8844	2.2003	2.2074	2.0632
Dummy shipp.prod./prof. × dist.	1.7231	1.6310	1.7480	1.7486	1.7665
_Intercept	1.6708	1.6569	1.6741	1.6764	1.6696
Dummy prior exec. exp. × dist.	1.4849	1.4926	1.5143	1.5182	1.4986
_Intercept	1.3526	1.3644	1.3774	1.3785	1.3941
Dummy high asset intang. × dist.	1.2011	1.1817	1.1461	1.1477	1.1344
_Intercept	1.2123	1.2028	1.1664	1.2065	1.1687
Dummy high R&D intensity × dist.	1.5250	1.4754	1.5019	1.5023	1.5066
_Intercept	1.4670	1.5041	1.4775	1.5841	1.4820
Dummy low book/market × dist.	1.3046	1.2970	1.2797	1.2807	1.2289
_Intercept	1.3641	1.3614	1.3278	1.4225	1.3140
Dummy East Ger. venture × dist.	1.4728	1.4788	1.5156	1.5195	1.5753
_Intercept	1.4017	1.3991	1.4194	1.4196	1.4460
Dummy urban v. location × dist.	1.4746	1.4612	1.5004	1.5060	1.6073
_Intercept	1.3441	1.3452	1.3775	1.4083	1.4485
Venture capitalist					
Ln(assets under mgt.) × dist.	1.6945	1.7141	2.0710	2.0736	2.1557
Ln(age) × dist.	1.7438	1.7561	1.9979	2.0010	2.1108
_Intercept	1.2213	1.2210	1.2402	1.2665	1.3106
HHI industry × dist.			1.5513	1.5532	1.4344
HHI stage × dist.			1.2107	1.2109	1.2258
Dummy corporate VC × dist.	1.0852	1.0837	1.0812	1.0816	1.1277
Dummy (quasi-)public VC × dist.	1.3167	1.3295	1.4649	1.4679	1.3846
Dummy lead-investor × dist.	1.1579	1.1383	1.1630	1.1636	1.1567
Round					
Inv. volume per VC × dist.	5.9711	5.9091	5.9468	5.9542	5.4543
_Intercept	5.2760	5.2529	5.5717	5.5958	5.7938
(Inv. volume per VC)² × dist.	6.8016	6.7433	7.1589	7.1802	7.5086
_Intercept	6.2382	6.1998	6.9182	6.9390	7.9909
Syndication benefit × dist.	6.4951	6.4660	6.8172	6.8491	17.0844
_Intercept	6.7458	6.7185	6.9559	6.9618	17.9598
Control variables					
Ln(Ger. VC fundraising (t-1))	2.1170	2.1158	2.0342		2.0698
Ln(Ger. VC investments)	1.1903	1.1871	1.1759		1.2007
Return of MSCI SC Ger. (ltm)	2.0491	2.0511	1.9836	2.6940	1.9852
Year f.e.	No	No	No	Yes	No
Max. VIF	6.8016	6.7433	7.1589	7.1802	17.9598
Mean VIF	2.3166	2.3104	2.3596	2.4670	2.9803

Table D.2: Rare event logistic regressions – Details on the venture capitalist's experience and reputation

This table presents the results of rare event logistic regressions with a dummy variable indicating whether a VC financing relationship actually occurred (1) or not (0) as dependent variable. The models scrutinize further details regarding the venture capitalist's age and include variables stepwise. The sample consists of realized dyads of venture capitalists and German portfolio companies which have closed a financing round between January 2002 and March 2007 and a matching sample. Financing rounds with missing values or for which no match existed as well as five outliers are excluded pairwise. Coefficients and standard errors are adjusted for rare events, choice-based sampling, serial correlation, heteroskedasticity, and nonindependence across venture capitalists. V.: venture.

Variable	REL 2.20	REL 2.21	REL 2.22	REL 2.23	REL 2.24	REL 2.25	REL 2.26	REL 2	REL 3
Dep. var.: realized dyad (yes/no)									
Distance (ln[1+min. travel time])	-0.3232***	-0.3346***	-0.3418***	-0.3706***	-0.3708***	-0.3416***	-0.3330***	-0.3530***	-0.3634***
Venture									
Ln(age) × dist.				-0.0346	-0.0306	-0.0299	-0.0286	-0.0081	-0.0207
_Intercept				-0.0860**	-0.0932**	-0.0961**	-0.1009**	-0.0782*	-0.1028**
Dummy seed stage round × dist.				-0.5903*	-0.6283*	-0.6060*	-0.5785*	-0.5402	-0.6122
Dummy later stage round × dist.				0.1084	0.1016	0.0770	0.0616	0.0504	0.0226
Dummy bus. concept only × dist.				-1.0375*	-1.0683*	-1.0894*	-1.0373	-0.8878	-0.9438
_Intercept				-0.1497	-0.1224	-0.1274	-0.1361	-0.1389	-0.1803
Dummy shipp.prod./prof. × dist.				0.0968	0.0498	0.0620	0.0275	-0.0151	-0.0069
_Intercept				-0.0939	-0.0567	-0.0519	0.0108	0.0019	0.0084
Dummy prior exec. exp. × dist.				0.1212	0.1446*	0.1497*	0.1521*	0.1451	0.1625
_Intercept				-0.1141	-0.1230	-0.1055	-0.0476	-0.0081	-0.0297
Dummy high asset intang. × dist.					-0.2240**	-0.2183*	-0.2340**	-0.2954**	-0.2979**
_Intercept					-0.0241	-0.0344	-0.0350	0.0313	0.1477
Dummy high R&D intensity × dist.					-0.1524	-0.1484	-0.2423	-0.2575*	-0.3720**
_Intercept					0.1107	0.1076	0.1528	0.1258	0.0726
Dummy low book/market × dist.					-0.1172	-0.1301	-0.1741	-0.2059	-0.1114
_Intercept					0.1434	0.1561	0.2033	0.2280	0.3017**
Dummy East Ger. venture × dist.								-0.1119	-0.0850
_Intercept								-0.2510**	-0.2570**
Dummy urban v. location × dist.								0.1789*	0.2259**
_Intercept								-0.2580**	-0.1857

Table D.2 cont.: Rare event logistic regressions – Details on the venture capitalist's experience and reputation

Variable	REL 2.20	REL 2.21	REL 2.22	REL 2.23	REL 2.24	REL 2.25	REL 2.26	REL 2	REL 3
Venture capitalist									
Ln(assets under mgt.) × dist.							0.0659***	0.0566***	0.0484*
Ln(age) × dist.	0.0837**	0.0600	0.0862**	0.0770**	0.0790**	0.0785**	0.0229	0.0058	0.0236
_Intercept	0.0109	0.0047	-0.0116	-0.0058	-0.0079	-0.0091	-0.0091	-0.0067	-0.0155
HHI industry × dist.									-0.1998
HHI stage × dist.									0.4225
Dummy corporate VC × dist.			0.1533	0.1768	0.1496	0.1270	0.0718	0.0425	0.0529
Dummy (quasi-)public VC × dist.			0.3034***	0.2800***	0.2782***	0.2659**	0.3146***	0.2638**	0.2497**
Dummy lead-investor × dist.						-0.0828	-0.1160	-0.0807	-0.0774
Round									
Inv. volume per VC × dist.		0.2446***	0.2587***	0.2332***	0.2195***	0.2126***	0.2128***	0.2174***	0.2256**
_Intercept		0.0375	0.0310	0.0365	0.0363	0.0361	0.0198	0.0315	0.0411
(Inv. volume per VC)² × dist.		-0.0319***	-0.0321***	-0.0305***	-0.0294**	-0.0285**	-0.0267**	-0.0271**	-0.0298**
_Intercept		0.0058	0.0062	0.0058	0.0054	0.0056	0.0071	0.0060	0.0035
Syndication benefit × dist.						0.0016	0.0015	0.0019*	0.0026**
_Intercept						-0.0024	-0.0027	-0.0034**	-0.0053**
Control variables									
Ln(Ger. VC fundraising (t-1))	-0.0667	-0.0528	-0.0552	-0.0994*	-0.1112*	-0.1002	-0.1040	-0.1045	-0.0575
Ln(Ger. VC investments)	0.1104	0.0554	0.0512	0.0273	0.0628	0.0490	0.0478	0.0417	0.0399
Return of MSCI SC Ger. (ltm)	-0.2170*	-0.1960	-0.1604	-0.1858	-0.2264	-0.2261	-0.2612*	-0.2352	-0.1441
Constant	-1.0716	-0.8243	-0.6760	0.1569	-0.0336	-0.1357	-0.1804	0.0484	-0.2086
N	2734	2338	2338	2318	2318	2318	2116	2116	1866
LR Chi²	38.64***	42.45***	47.07***	56.97***	59.40***	60.41***	62.70***	70.87***	70.01***
Log. Likelihood	-848.24	-720.68	-718.37	-707.07	-705.86	-705.35	-640.11	-636.02	-557.12

* significant at 10%; ** significant at 5%; *** significant at 1% (two-sided)

Table D.3: Rare event logistic regressions – Details on the venture capitalist's specialization

This table presents the results of rare event logistic regressions with a dummy variable indicating whether a VC financing relationship actually occurred (1) or not (0) as dependent variable. The models scrutinize further details regarding the venture capitalist's industry and stage specialization and include variables stepwise. The sample consists of realized dyads of venture capitalists and German portfolio companies which have closed a financing round between January 2002 and March 2007 and a matching sample. Financing rounds with missing values or for which no match existed as well as five outliers are excluded pairwise. Coefficients and standard errors are adjusted for rare events, choice-based sampling, serial correlation, heteroskedasticity, and nonindependence across venture capitalists. V.: venture.

Variable	REL 3.1	REL 3.2	REL 3.3	REL 3.4	REL 3.5	REL 3.6	REL 3.7	REL 3.8	REL 3
Dep. var.: realized dyad (yes/no)									
Distance (ln[1+min. travel time])	-0.3255***	-0.3396***	-0.3427***	-0.3504***	-0.3477***	-0.3440***	-0.3376***	-0.3654***	-0.3634***
Venture									
Ln(age) × dist.				-0.0257	-0.0239	-0.0291	-0.0304	-0.0162	-0.0207
_Intercept				-0.1072**	-0.1171**	-0.1274***	-0.0989**	-0.1006**	-0.1028**
Dummy seed stage round × dist.				-0.4491	-0.4801*	-0.7345*	-0.6773*	-0.7035*	-0.6122
Dummy later stage round × dist.				0.0975	0.0667	0.0157	0.0311	0.0184	0.0226
Dummy bus. concept only × dist.				0.2564	0.3705	-1.2411*	-1.1865*	-1.0989	-0.9438
_Intercept				-0.9541**	-1.0930**	-0.1666	-0.1224	-0.1473	-0.1803
Dummy shipp.prod./prof. × dist.				0.1435	0.1036	0.0907	0.0825	0.0439	-0.0069
_Intercept				-0.0406	-0.0199	-0.0120	-0.0538	-0.0355	0.0084
Dummy prior exec. exp. × dist.				0.1185	0.1527*	0.1690*	0.2003**	0.1509	0.1625
_Intercept				-0.1180	-0.1367	-0.0961	-0.1193	-0.0898	-0.0297
Dummy high asset intang. × dist.					-0.2111*	-0.2245*	-0.2580**	-0.3236**	-0.2979**
_Intercept					0.1180	0.1466	0.1650	0.1855	0.1477
Dummy high R&D intensity × dist.					-0.1874	-0.2392	-0.2554	-0.2805*	-0.3720**
_Intercept					0.0407	0.0652	0.0331	0.0418	0.0726
Dummy low book/market × dist.					-0.0115	-0.0300	-0.0325	-0.0559	-0.1114
_Intercept					0.1804	0.2325*	0.2278*	0.2472*	0.3017**
Dummy East Ger. venture × dist.							0.0239	-0.0617	-0.0850
_Intercept							-0.3667***	-0.3083**	-0.2570**
Dummy urban v. location × dist.								0.2612***	0.2259**
_Intercept								-0.1557	-0.1857

Table D.3 cont.: Rare event logistic regressions – Details on the venture capitalist's specialization

Variable	REL 3.1	REL 3.2	REL 3.3	REL 3.4	REL 3.5	REL 3.6	REL 3.7	REL 3.8	REL 3
Venture capitalist									
Ln(assets under mgt.) × dist.									0.0484*
Ln(age) × dist.						0.0824**	0.0607	0.0407	0.0236
_Intercept						-0.0138	-0.0089	-0.0004	-0.0155
HHI industry × dist.	-0.4829***	-0.5191***	-0.4511***	-0.3686**	-0.3892**	-0.3505**	-0.3639*	-0.2571	-0.1998
HHI stage × dist.	0.6583***	0.5524**	0.5380**	0.4672**	0.4555**	0.5198**	0.5335**	0.4708*	0.4225
Dummy corporate VC × dist.			0.1775	0.1951	0.1927	0.1562	0.1591	0.0922	0.0529
Dummy (quasi-)public VC × dist.			0.2275**	0.2196*	0.2060*	0.2549**	0.1624	0.1969	0.2497**
Dummy lead-investor × dist.						-0.1015	-0.0930	-0.0595	-0.0774
Round									
Inv. volume per VC × dist.		0.2363***	0.2551***	0.2413***	0.2177**	0.2022**	0.2126**	0.2086**	0.2256**
_Intercept		0.0331	0.0266	0.0335	0.0332	0.0412	0.0489	0.0570	0.0411
(Inv. volume per VC)² × dist.		-0.0306**	-0.0317***	-0.0314**	-0.0293**	-0.0279**	-0.0286**	-0.0283**	-0.0298**
_Intercept		0.0060	0.0063	0.0056	0.0055	0.0044	0.0039	0.0030	0.0035
Syndication benefit × dist.						0.0024*	0.0025**	0.0027**	0.0026**
_Intercept						-0.0044**	-0.0048**	-0.0050**	-0.0053**
Control variables									
Ln(Ger. VC fundraising (t-1))	-0.0355	-0.0098	-0.0088	-0.0636	-0.0850	-0.0790	-0.0808	-0.0642	-0.0575
Ln(Ger. VC investments)	0.0827	0.0150	0.0161	0.0101	0.0535	0.0589	0.0255	0.0523	0.0399
Return of MSCI SC Ger. (ltm)	-0.1218	-0.0771	-0.0590	-0.0867	-0.1277	-0.1329	-0.1097	-0.1078	-0.1441
Constant	-1.1010	-0.8331	-0.8058	-0.1085	-0.2933	-0.3505	-0.0517	-0.2386	-0.2086
N	2384	2048	2048	2028	2028	2006	2006	2006	1866
LR Chi²	40.80***	43.37***	45.94***	52.53***	54.95***	61.58***	65.62***	70.04***	70.01***
Log. Likelihood	-736.10	-628.19	-626.91	-617.27	-616.06	-605.76	-603.74	-601.53	-557.12

* significant at 10%; ** significant at 5%; *** significant at 1% (two-sided)

Table D.4: Rare event logistic regressions – Details on the venture capitalist's type
This table presents the results of rare event logistic regressions with a dummy variable indicating whether a VC financing relationship actually occurred (1) or not (0) as dependent variable. The models scrutinize further details regarding the venture capitalist's type. The sample consists of realized dyads of venture capitalists and German portfolio companies which have closed a financing round between January 2002 and March 2007 and a matching sample. Financing rounds with missing values or for which no match existed as well as five outliers are excluded pairwise. Coefficients and standard errors are adjusted for rare events, choice-based sampling, serial correlation, heteroskedasticity, and nonindependence across venture capitalists. B.: bank; centr.: central; econ. dev.: economic development; sav. savings; v.: venture.

Variable	REL 2	REL 2.27	REL 2.28	REL 3	REL 3.9	REL 3.10
Dep. var.: realized dyad (yes/no)						
Distance (ln[1+min. travel time])	-0.3530***	-0.3421***	-0.3397***	-0.3634***	-0.3451***	-0.3466***
Venture						
Ln(age) × dist.	-0.0081	-0.0119		-0.0207	-0.0210	
_Intercept	-0.0782*	-0.0827*		-0.1028**	-0.1001**	
Dummy seed stage round × dist.	-0.5402	-0.5282	-0.6212*	-0.6122	-0.5651	-0.6341
Dummy later stage round × dist.	0.0504	0.0952	0.1375*	0.0226	0.0637	0.1220
Dummy bus. concept only × dist.	-0.8878	-0.9113		-0.9438	-0.9655	
_Intercept	-0.1389	-0.1547		-0.1803	-0.1699	
Dummy shipp.prod./prof. × dist.	-0.0151	-0.0197		-0.0069	-0.0073	
_Intercept	0.0019	-0.0035		0.0084	0.0040	
Dummy prior exec. exp. × dist.	0.1451	0.1517		0.1625	0.1690	
_Intercept	-0.0081	-0.0135		-0.0297	-0.0294	
Dummy high asset intang. × dist.	-0.2954**	-0.2986**	-0.2253*	-0.2979**	-0.2986**	-0.2007
_Intercept	0.0313	0.0270	-0.0725	0.1477	0.1382	0.0453
Dummy high R&D intensity × dist.	-0.2575*	-0.2418	-0.1644	-0.3720**	-0.3383*	-0.2454*
_Intercept	0.1258	0.1136	0.1366	0.0726	0.0541	0.0575
Dummy low book/market × dist.	-0.2059	-0.1720	-0.1739	-0.1114	-0.0841	-0.1071
_Intercept	0.2280	0.2087	0.0841	0.3017**	0.2797*	0.1128
Dummy East Ger. venture × dist.	-0.1119	-0.1139		-0.0850	-0.1011	
_Intercept	-0.2510**	-0.2387*		-0.2570**	-0.2370*	
Dummy urban v. location × dist.	0.1789*	0.1664*		0.2259**	0.2130**	
_Intercept	-0.2580**	-0.2484*		-0.1857	-0.1757	

Table D.4 cont.: Rare event logistic regressions – Details on the venture capitalist's type

Variable	REL 2	REL 2.27	REL 2.28	REL 3	REL 3.9	REL 3.10
Venture capitalist						
Ln(assets under mgt.) × dist.	0.0566***	0.0691***	0.0781***	0.0484*	0.0651**	0.0798***
Ln(age) × dist.	0.0058	-0.0209		0.0236	-0.0030	
_Intercept	-0.0067	0.0003		-0.0155	-0.0179	
HHI industry × dist.				-0.1998	-0.1011	-0.1693
HHI stage × dist.				0.4225	0.3693	0.2614
Dummy corporate VC × dist.	0.0425	0.0326	0.0142	0.0529	0.0338	0.0175
Dummy (quasi-)public VC × dist.	0.2638**			0.2497**		
Dummy MBG × dist.		1.7053**	1.6038*		2.1895**	2.4753***
Dummy subs. of sav./coop. b. × dist.		0.2022	0.1108		0.2002	0.0945
Dummy subs. of state b./coop. centr. inst. × dist.		-0.0237	-0.0038		-0.0216	0.0291
Dummy subs. of inst. promoting econ. dev. × dist.		0.4577***	0.5679***		0.4760***	0.5808***
Other German government × dist.		0.0834	0.1681*		0.1114	0.1723
Dummy lead-investor × dist.	-0.0807	-0.0658	-0.1122	-0.0774	-0.0518	-0.1073
Round						
Inv. volume per VC × dist.	0.2174***	0.2156***	0.2350***	0.2256**	0.2175**	0.2282**
_Intercept	0.0315	0.0221	0.0052	0.0411	0.0375	0.0099
(Inv. volume per VC)² × dist.	-0.0271**	-0.0274**	-0.0283**	-0.0298**	-0.0294**	-0.0283**
_Intercept	0.0060	0.0069	0.0086	0.0035	0.0037	0.0068
Syndication benefit × dist.	0.0019*	0.0017*		0.0026**	0.0024*	
_Intercept	-0.0034**	-0.0032*		-0.0053**	-0.0052**	
Control variables						
Ln(Ger. VC fundraising (t-1))	-0.1045	-0.1016	-0.0483	-0.0575	-0.0501	0.0038
Ln(Ger. VC investments)	0.0417	-0.0051	0.0409	0.0399	-0.0024	0.0550
Return of MSCI SC Ger. (ltm)	-0.2352	-0.2275	-0.1969	-0.1441	-0.1365	-0.0942
Constant	0.0484	0.3259	-0.6452	-0.2086	-0.0268	-1.1041
N	2116	2116	2116	1866	1866	1866
LR Chi²	70.87***	75.15***	63.15***	70.01***	74.40***	62.30***
Log. Likelihood	-636.02	-633.88	-639.89	-557.12	-554.93	-560.98

* significant at 10%; ** significant at 5%; *** significant at 1% (two-sided)

Table D.5: Rare event logistic regressions – Details on lead- vs. co-investors

This table presents the results of rare event logistic regressions with a dummy variable indicating whether a VC financing relationship actually occurred (1) or not (0) as dependent variable. The models scrutinize further details regarding the venture capitalist's role within syndicates and include variables stepwise. The sample consists of realized dyads of venture capitalists and German portfolio companies which have closed a financing round between January 2002 and March 2007 and a matching sample. Financing rounds with missing values or for which no match existed as well as five outliers are excluded pairwise. Coefficients and standard errors are adjusted for rare events, choice-based sampling, serial correlation, heteroskedasticity, and nonindependence across venture capitalists. V.: venture.

Variable	REL 2.29	REL 2.30	REL 2.31	REL 2.32	REL 2.33	REL 2.34	REL 2.35	REL 2	REL 3
Dep. var.: realized dyad (yes/no)									
Distance (ln[1+min. travel time])	-0.3230***	-0.3326***	-0.3429***	-0.3544***	-0.3466***	-0.3880***	-0.3970***	-0.3530 ***	-0.3634***
Venture									
Ln(age) × dist.							-0.0058	-0.0081	-0.0207
_Intercept							-0.0722*	-0.0782 *	-0.1028**
Dummy seed stage round × dist.				-0.6340*	-0.6300*	-0.6169*	-0.5532	-0.5402	-0.6122
Dummy later stage round × dist.				0.1003	0.1088	0.0982	0.0471	0.0504	0.0226
Dummy bus. concept only × dist.							-0.8840	-0.8878	-0.9438
_Intercept							-0.1081	-0.1389	-0.1803
Dummy shipp.prod./prof. × dist.							-0.0215	-0.0151	-0.0069
_Intercept							0.0065	0.0019	0.0084
Dummy prior exec. exp. × dist.							0.1309	0.1451	0.1625
_Intercept							-0.0284	-0.0081	-0.0297
Dummy high asset intang. × dist.				-0.2120*	-0.2146*	-0.2754**	-0.2984**	-0.2954 **	-0.2979**
_Intercept				-0.0717	-0.0493	0.0109	0.0321	0.0313	0.1477
Dummy high R&D intensity × dist.				-0.1977	-0.1956	-0.1991	-0.2573*	-0.2575 *	-0.3720**
_Intercept				0.1535	0.1267	0.1328	0.1361	0.1258	0.0726
Dummy low book/market × dist.				-0.1966	-0.2079*	-0.2178*	-0.2132	-0.2059	-0.1114
_Intercept				0.1020	0.0995	0.1399	0.1885	0.2280	0.3017**
Dummy East Ger. venture × dist.					-0.0868	-0.1374*	-0.1076	-0.1119	-0.0850
_Intercept					-0.3341***	-0.2515**	-0.2408**	-0.2510 **	-0.2570**
Dummy urban v. location × dist.						0.2054**	0.1810**	0.1789 *	0.2259**
_Intercept						-0.2444**	-0.2479*	-0.2580 **	-0.1857

Table D.5 cont.: Rare event logistic regressions – Details on lead- vs. co-investors

Variable	REL 2.29	REL 2.30	REL 2.31	REL 2.32	REL 2.33	REL 2.34	REL 2.35	REL 2	REL 3
Venture capitalist									
Ln(assets under mgt.) × dist.			0.0636***	0.0644***	0.0651***	0.0539***	0.0565***	0.0566***	0.0484*
Ln(age) × dist.			0.0443	0.0340	0.0269	0.0176	0.0094	0.0058	0.0236
_Intercept			-0.0201	-0.0257	-0.0262	-0.0194	-0.0091	-0.0067	-0.0155
HHI industry × dist.									-0.1998
HHI stage × dist.									0.4225
Dummy corporate VC × dist.			0.0702	0.0338	0.0493	0.0072	0.0366	0.0425	0.0529
Dummy (quasi-)public VC × dist.			0.3049***	0.3249***	0.2870**	0.2783**	0.2654**	0.2638**	0.2497**
Dummy lead-investor × dist.	-0.1703***	-0.1523**	-0.1605**	-0.1380*	-0.1321*	-0.0977	-0.0880	-0.0807	-0.0774
Round									
Inv. volume per VC × dist.		0.2429***	0.2399***	0.2387***	0.2502***	0.2503***	0.2180***	0.2174***	0.2256**
_Intercept		0.0371	0.0237	0.0135	0.0203	0.0304	0.0319	0.0315	0.0411
(Inv. volume per VC)² × dist.		-0.0314***	-0.0285**	-0.0284**	-0.0293**	-0.0300**	-0.0271**	-0.0271**	-0.0298**
_Intercept		0.0058	0.0073	0.0079	0.0075	0.0064	0.0059	0.0060	0.0035
Syndication benefit × dist.								0.0019*	0.0026**
_Intercept								-0.0034**	-0.0053**
Control variables									
Ln(Ger. VC fundraising (t-1))	-0.0665	-0.0489	-0.0389	-0.0615	-0.0833	-0.0790	-0.1109*	-0.1045	-0.0575
Ln(Ger. VC investments)	0.1013	0.0440	0.0313	0.0858	0.0630	0.0994	0.0802	0.0417	0.0399
Return of MSCI SC Ger. (ltm)	-0.1998	-0.1730	-0.1361	-0.2035	-0.2006	-0.1879	-0.2174	-0.2352	-0.1441
Constant	-0.9943	-0.7744	-0.6265	-0.7777	-0.4159	-0.4855	-0.0056	0.0484	-0.2086
N	2788	2384	2134	2116	2116	2116	2116	2116	1866
LR Chi²	38.98***	42.77***	52.04***	58.15***	62.27***	67.13***	69.80***	70.87***	70.01***
Log. Likelihood	-865.21	-735.11	-651.15	-642.38	-640.32	-637.89	-636.56	-636.02	-557.12

* significant at 10%; ** significant at 5%; *** significant at 1% (two-sided)

Table D.6: Rare event logistic regressions – Details on the investment volume

This table presents the results of rare event logistic regressions with a dummy variable indicating whether a VC financing relationship actually occurred (1) or not (0) as dependent variable. The models scrutinize further details regarding the effect of the investment volume. The sample consists of realized dyads of venture capitalists and German portfolio companies which have closed a financing round between January 2002 and March 2007 and a matching sample. Financing rounds with missing values or for which no match existed as well as five outliers are excluded pairwise. Model REL 2.37 only includes dyads with investment volumes per venture capitalist up to 3.9 m€ and Model REL 2.38 includes all dyads with investment volumes of at least 3.9 m€. Coefficients and standard errors are adjusted for rare events, choice-based sampling, serial correlation, heteroskedasticity, and nonindependence across venture capitalists. V.: venture.

Variable	REL 2	REL 2.36	REL 2.37	REL 2.38
Dep. var.: realized dyad (yes/no)				
Distance (ln[1+min. travel time])	-0.3530***	-0.3492***	-0.3605***	-0.0495
Venture				
Ln(age) × dist.	-0.0081	-0.0014	-0.0234	0.3785*
_Intercept	-0.0782*	-0.0818*	-0.0748	-0.4469**
Dummy seed stage round × dist.	-0.5402	-0.5988*	-0.5391	-
Dummy later stage round × dist.	0.0504	0.0176	0.1388	-1.4488**
Dummy bus. concept only × dist.	-0.8878	-0.8987	-1.0238	-
_Intercept	-0.1389	-0.1319	-0.1050	-
Dummy shipp.prod./prof. × dist.	-0.0151	-0.0474	-0.0856	0.6359
_Intercept	0.0019	0.0216	0.0380	-0.4974
Dummy prior exec. exp. × dist.	0.1451	0.1742*	0.1247	1.3585***
_Intercept	-0.0081	0.0024	0.0499	-1.0047
Dummy high asset intang. × dist.	-0.2954**	-0.2888**	-0.2913**	0.8405
_Intercept	0.0313	0.0281	0.0488	0.5103
Dummy high R&D intensity × dist.	-0.2575*	-0.2791*	-0.2879*	-0.5595
_Intercept	0.1258	0.1431	0.0885	0.0371
Dummy low book/market × dist.	-0.2059	-0.2114	-0.2926**	-0.7998
_Intercept	0.2280	0.2450*	0.1977	1.2122
Dummy East Ger. venture × dist.	-0.1119	-0.1118	-0.0593	-0.7585
_Intercept	-0.2510**	-0.2393**	-0.2475*	1.2492
Dummy urban v. location × dist.	0.1789*	0.1855**	0.0702	1.3460**
_Intercept	-0.2580**	-0.2597**	-0.3250**	-0.1089
Venture capitalist				
Ln(assets under mgt.) × dist.	0.0566***	0.0560***	0.0563**	0.1142
Ln(age) × dist.	0.0058	0.0120	-0.0019	0.2601
_Intercept	-0.0067	-0.0060	-0.0585**	0.3966**
Dummy corporate VC × dist.	0.0425	0.0297	0.0651	-1.0792
Dummy (quasi-)public VC × dist.	0.2638**	0.2489**	0.2830**	0.4782
Dummy lead-investor × dist.	-0.0807	-0.0961	-0.1085	0.1741
Round				
Inv. volume per VC × dist.	0.2174***	0.0561	0.1916***	-0.2254
_Intercept	0.0315	0.0535*	0.0778	0.2522**
(Inv. volume per VC)² × dist.	-0.0271**			
_Intercept	0.0060			
Syndication benefit × dist.	0.0019*	0.0019**	0.0009	0.0160
_Intercept	-0.0034**	-0.0034**	-0.0023	-0.0096
Control variables				
Ln(Ger. VC fundraising (t-1))	-0.1045	-0.0965	-0.1625**	0.3117
Ln(Ger. VC investments)	0.0417	0.0310	0.1575	0.3769
Return of MSCI SC Ger. (ltm)	-0.2352	-0.2334	-0.2160	-1.8121*
Constant	0.0484	0.0239	-0.2927	-7.7752

Table D.6 cont.: Rare event logistic regressions – Details on the investment volume

Variable	REL 2	REL 2.36	REL 2.37	REL 2.38
N	2116	2116	1945	171
LR Chi²	70.87***	67.44***	67.53***	32.15
Log. Likelihood	-636.02	-637.74	-583.43	-38.19

* significant at 10%; ** significant at 5%; *** significant at 1% (two-sided)

Table D.7: Rare event logistic regressions – Details on syndication

This table presents the results of rare event logistic regressions with a dummy variable indicating whether a VC financing relationship actually occurred (1) or not (0) as dependent variable. The models scrutinize further details regarding the role of syndication to overcome distance. The sample consists of realized dyads of venture capitalists and German portfolio companies which have closed a financing round between January 2002 and March 2007 and a matching sample. Financing rounds with missing values or for which no match existed as well as five outliers are excluded pairwise. Coefficients and standard errors are adjusted for rare events, choice-based sampling, serial correlation, heteroskedasticity, and nonindependence across venture capitalists. V.: venture.

Variable	REL 2	REL 2.39	REL 2.40	REL 2.41
Dep. var.: realized dyad (yes/no)				
Distance (ln[1+min. travel time])	-0.3530***	-0.4069***	-0.1597**	-0.2162***
Venture				
Ln(age) × dist.	-0.0081	-0.0155	-0.0058	-0.0064
_Intercept	-0.0782*	-0.1135**	-0.0757*	-0.0783*
Dummy seed stage round × dist.	-0.5402	-0.5313	-0.5416	-0.5801
Dummy later stage round × dist.	0.0504	0.0659	0.0449	0.0446
Dummy bus. concept only × dist.	-0.8878	-0.8886	-0.8932	-0.7392
_Intercept	-0.1389	-0.0484	-0.1666	-0.4010
Dummy shipp.prod./prof. × dist.	-0.0151	-0.0100	-0.0156	-0.0456
_Intercept	0.0019	0.1222	-0.0039	-0.0700
Dummy prior exec. exp. × dist.	0.1451	0.1281	0.1650*	0.1800*
_Intercept	-0.0081	-0.0720	0.0086	0.0521
Dummy high asset intang. × dist.	-0.2954**	-0.3014**	-0.3024**	-0.3069**
_Intercept	0.0313	0.0668	0.0326	0.0108
Dummy high R&D intensity × dist.	-0.2575*	-0.2629*	-0.2574*	-0.2338
_Intercept	0.1258	0.0192	0.1373	0.1789
Dummy low book/market × dist.	-0.2059	-0.2184*	-0.2194*	-0.1902
_Intercept	0.2280	0.1724	0.1927	0.2817**
Dummy East Ger. venture × dist.	-0.1119	-0.1007	-0.1127	-0.1492
_Intercept	-0.2510**	-0.2075*	-0.2439**	-0.2892**
Dummy urban v. location × dist.	0.1789*	0.1763*	0.1890**	0.1632*
_Intercept	-0.2580**	-0.2445*	-0.2157*	-0.2308*
Venture capitalist				
Ln(assets under mgt.) × dist.	0.0566***	0.0528***	0.0546***	0.0612***
Ln(age) × dist.	0.0058	0.0130	0.0042	-0.0004
_Intercept	-0.0067	-0.0187	-0.0183	-0.0158
Dummy corporate VC × dist.	0.0425	0.0173	0.0569	0.0847
Dummy (quasi-)public VC × dist.	0.2638**	0.2388**	0.2835**	0.2794**
Dummy lead-investor × dist.	-0.0807	-0.1192	-0.0621	-0.0371

Table D.7 cont.: Rare event logistic regressions – Details on syndication

Variable	REL 2	REL 2.39	REL 2.40	REL 2.41
Round				
Inv. volume per VC × dist.	0.2174***	0.2332***	0.1987**	0.1903**
_Intercept	0.0315	-0.0258	0.0199	0.0009
(Inv. volume per VC)² × dist.	-0.0271**	-0.0300**	-0.0249**	-0.0242**
_Intercept	0.0060	0.0136	0.0066	0.0073
Syndication benefit × dist.	0.0019*			
_Intercept	-0.0034**			
No. of synd. partners × dist.		-0.0095		
_Intercept		0.0931***		
Dummy close synd. partner × dist.			1.0112***	
_Intercept			-1.2075***	
Distance - distance of closest synd. partner × dist.				0.0031***
_Intercept				-0.0209***
Control variables				
Ln(Ger. VC fundraising (t-1))	-0.1045	-0.1030	-0.1227*	-0.1516**
Ln(Ger. VC investments)	0.0417	-0.0448	0.0861	0.0713
Return of MSCI SC Ger. (ltm)	-0.2352	-0.1914	-0.2321	-0.3116*
Constant	0.0484	0.6098	-0.9599	-0.0607
N	2116	2116	2116	2116
LR Chi²	70.87***	75.84***	74.00***	83.38***
Log. Likelihood	-636.02	-633.54	-634.46	-629.77

* significant at 10%; ** significant at 5%; *** significant at 1% (two-sided)

Table D.8: Logistic regressions – Base models

This table presents the results of logistic regressions with a dummy variable indicating whether a VC financing relationship actually occurred (1) or not (0) as dependent variable. The sample consists of realized dyads of venture capitalists and German portfolio companies which have closed a financing round between January 2002 and March 2007 and a matching sample. Financing rounds with missing values or for which no match existed are excluded pairwise. Models Logit 2 to 5 exclude five outliers pairwise. Model Logit 5 additionally restricts the sample to German venture capitalists. Coefficients and standard errors are adjusted for choice-based sampling, serial correlation, heteroskedasticity, and nonindependence across venture capitalists.

Variable	Logit 1	Logit 2	Logit 3	Logit 4	Logit 5
Dep. var.: realized dyad (yes/no)					
Distance (ln[1+min. travel time])	-0.3003***	-0.3733***	-0.3870***	-0.3868***	-0.5035***
Venture					
Ln(age) × dist.	0.0110	-0.0070	-0.0183	-0.0181	-0.0397
_Intercept	-0.0595	-0.0802*	-0.1060**	-0.1045**	-0.1181**
Dummy seed stage round × dist.	-0.0651	-0.7348**	-0.7970**	-0.7887**	-0.5583
Dummy later stage round × dist.	-0.0442	0.0550	0.0221	0.0235	0.0511
Dummy bus. concept only × dist.	-0.0278	-1.0104	-1.1158	-1.1206	-0.9565
_Intercept	-0.5383	-0.1399	-0.1609	-0.1653	0.0803
Dummy shipp.prod./prof. × dist.	0.0171	-0.0090	0.0011	-0.0017	0.0537
_Intercept	-0.0228	-0.0077	-0.0040	-0.0074	0.0664
Dummy prior exec. exp. × dist.	0.1572*	0.1483	0.1681	0.1669	0.2134*
_Intercept	0.0028	-0.0129	-0.0354	-0.0340	-0.0364

Table D.8 cont.: Logistic regressions – Base models

Variable	Logit 1	Logit 2	Logit 3	Logit 4	Logit 5
Venture					
Dummy high asset intang. × dist.	-0.2908**	-0.3180**	-0.3231**	-0.3224**	-0.3012*
_Intercept	0.0174	0.0374	0.1575	0.1528	0.2770*
Dummy high R&D intensity × dist.	0.0432	-0.2671*	-0.3857**	-0.3864**	-0.4306**
_Intercept	0.0043	0.1259	0.0739	0.0645	0.1267
Dummy low book/market × dist.	-0.1973	-0.2246*	-0.1288	-0.1284	-0.0842
_Intercept	0.2105	0.2281	0.3047**	0.2947*	0.3420**
Dummy East Ger. venture × dist.	-0.1402	-0.1176	-0.0883	-0.0874	0.0472
_Intercept	-0.2631**	-0.2526**	-0.2610**	-0.2605**	-0.1392
Dummy urban v. location × dist.	0.1595*	0.1914**	0.2420**	0.2417**	0.1327
_Intercept	-0.2517**	-0.2620**	-0.1918	-0.1946	-0.3159**
Venture capitalist					
Ln(assets under mgt.) × dist.	0.0493**	0.0605***	0.0532*	0.0536*	0.0395
Ln(age) × dist.	0.0215	0.0040	0.0186	0.0184	0.0286
_Intercept	-0.0046	-0.0089	-0.0173	-0.0168	-0.0334
HHI industry × dist.			-0.2248	-0.2275	-0.4779
HHI stage × dist.			0.4609	0.4635	0.3526
Dummy corporate VC × dist.	0.0620	0.0471	0.0516	0.0508	0.0814
Dummy (quasi-)public VC × dist.	0.2175*	0.2831**	0.2633**	0.2630**	0.2217*
Dummy lead-investor × dist.	-0.0700	-0.0800	-0.0759	-0.0757	-0.1042
Round					
Inv. volume per VC × dist.	0.2445***	0.2511***	0.2571***	0.2562***	0.2114**
_Intercept	0.0198	0.0137	0.0190	0.0193	-0.0529
(Inv. volume per VC)² × dist.	-0.0333***	-0.0336***	-0.0361**	-0.0359**	-0.0282**
_Intercept	0.0093	0.0094	0.0078	0.0078	0.0166
Syndication benefit × dist.	0.0021**	0.0019*	0.0026**	0.0026*	-0.0060
_Intercept	-0.0038**	-0.0034*	-0.0053**	-0.0054**	0.0020
Control variables					
Ln(Ger. VC fundraising (t-1))	-0.1017	-0.1089	-0.0607		-0.0886
Ln(Ger. VC investments)	0.0513	0.0400	0.0364		0.1385
Return of MSCI SC Ger. (ltm)	-0.2184	-0.2362	-0.1448	-0.1429	-0.2041
Constant	-0.2901	0.2116	-0.0213	-0.2075	-0.0427
Year f.e.	No	No	No	Yes	No
N	2126	2116	1866	1866	1650
LR Chi²	60.73***	70.87***	70.01***	69.97***	70.17***
Nagelkerke's R²	0.060	0.070	0.078	0.078	0.089
Log. Likelihood	-644.27	-636.02	-557.12	-557.14	-488.50
AIC	1362.53	1346.05	1192.25	1196.28	1055.00

* significant at 10%; ** significant at 5%; *** significant at 1% (two-sided)

Table D.9: Rare event logistic regressions – Different measures of spatial proximity

This table presents the results of rare event logistic regressions with a dummy variable indicating whether a VC financing relationship actually occurred (1) or not (0) as dependent variable. The sample consists of realized dyads of venture capitalists and German portfolio companies which have closed a financing round between January 2002 and March 2007 and a matching sample. Financing rounds with missing values or for which no match existed as well as five outliers are excluded pairwise. Different measures of spatial proximity were used to calculate the variables. The sample is restricted to European investors. Coefficients and standard errors are adjusted for rare events, choice-based sampling, serial correlation, heteroskedasticity, and nonindependence across venture capitalists. V.: venture.

Variable	REL 2.42 min. travel time	REL 2.43 car time	REL 2.44 car distance	REL 3.13 min. travel time	REL 3.14 car time	REL 3.15 car distance
Dep. var.: realized dyad (yes/no)						
Distance (ln[1+min. travel time])	-0.3853***	-0.3232***	-0.2251***	-0.4401***	-0.3434***	-0.2221***
Venture						
Ln(age) × dist.	-0.0265	-0.0288	-0.0138	-0.0252	-0.0295	-0.0155
_Intercept	-0.0897**	-0.0937**	-0.0999**	-0.1011**	-0.1113**	-0.1167**
Dummy seed stage round × dist.	-0.5403	-0.5117	-0.3726	-0.5307	-0.5246	-0.3597
Dummy later stage round × dist.	0.0642	0.0614	0.0337	0.0283	0.0258	0.0086
Dummy bus. concept only × dist.	-0.9095	-0.7066	-0.7040	-0.9832	-0.7187	-0.7111
_Intercept	-0.0930	-0.2728	-0.1248	-0.1365	-0.3430	-0.1909
Dummy shipp.prod./prof. × dist.	0.0260	0.0201	0.0254	0.0035	0.0165	0.0191
_Intercept	0.0411	0.0515	0.0395	0.0250	0.0444	0.0193
Dummy prior exec. exp. × dist.	0.1207	0.0934	0.0813	0.1582	0.1225	0.0967
_Intercept	-0.0437	-0.0387	-0.0310	-0.0446	-0.0361	-0.0240
Dummy high asset intang. × dist.	-0.2918**	-0.2730**	-0.1928**	-0.2985**	-0.2760**	-0.1889**
_Intercept	0.0620	0.0692	0.0720	0.1593	0.1606	0.1538
Dummy high R&D intensity × dist.	-0.3070*	-0.2523*	-0.1937*	-0.3851**	-0.3390**	-0.2467*
_Intercept	0.1242	0.1152	0.1102	0.0739	0.0620	0.0544
Dummy low book/market × dist.	-0.2079	-0.2050*	-0.1446	-0.0900	-0.0865	-0.0542
_Intercept	0.2367	0.2436*	0.2598*	0.2873*	0.3134**	0.3342**
Dummy East Ger. venture × dist.	-0.0672	-0.0523	-0.0557	-0.0632	-0.0435	-0.0512
_Intercept	-0.2087*	-0.2083*	-0.2071*	-0.2423*	-0.2302*	-0.2251*
Dummy urban v. location × dist.	0.1743*	0.1730**	0.1430**	0.1771*	0.1798*	0.1458**
_Intercept	-0.2751**	-0.2434*	-0.2596**	-0.2151	-0.1980	-0.2068

Table D.9 cont.: Rare event logistic regressions – Different measures of spatial proximity

Variable	REL 2.42 min. travel time	REL 2.43 car time	REL 2.44 car distance	REL 3.13 min. travel time	REL 3.14 car time	REL 3.15 car distance
Venture capitalist						
Ln(assets under mgt.) × dist.	0.0509**	0.0498***	0.0388***	0.0446	0.0409*	0.0332*
Ln(age) × dist.	0.0228	0.0117	0.0125	0.0283	0.0212	0.0101
_Intercept	-0.0102	-0.0006	-0.0053	-0.0245	-0.0130	-0.0134
HHI industry × dist.				-0.2652	-0.2506	-0.2347
HHI stage × dist.				0.4527	0.4772*	0.4245**
Dummy corporate VC × dist.	0.0496	0.0218	0.0172	0.0948	0.0239	0.0149
Dummy (quasi-)public VC × dist.	0.2669**	0.2308**	0.1800**	0.2438*	0.2096*	0.1572*
Dummy lead-investor × dist.	-0.0746	-0.0625	-0.0443	-0.0733	-0.0581	-0.0398
Round						
Inv. volume per VC × dist.	0.2076**	0.1936***	0.1350**	0.2331**	0.2188**	0.1407**
_Intercept	0.0197	0.0281	0.0174	0.0411	0.0507	0.0293
(Inv. volume per VC)² × dist.	-0.0261**	-0.0232**	-0.0168**	-0.0311**	-0.0283**	-0.0183**
_Intercept	0.0073	0.0057	0.0077	0.0032	0.0012	0.0055
Syndication benefit × dist.	0.0012	0.0012*	0.0009**	-0.0033	0.0008	0.0011
_Intercept	-0.0024	-0.0025	-0.0021**	0.0000	-0.0030	-0.0032**
Control variables						
Ln(Ger. VC fundraising (t-1))	-0.1189*	-0.1320**	-0.1236*	-0.0795	-0.0797	-0.0709
Ln(Ger. VC investments)	0.0578	0.0454	0.0541	0.0707	0.0508	0.0550
Return of MSCI SC Ger. (ltm)	-0.2470	-0.2660	-0.2493	-0.1607	-0.1765	-0.1605
Constant	0.1832	0.0896	-0.3606	0.0728	-0.2148	-0.7312
N	2072	2072	2072	1852	1852	1852
LR Chi²	69.87***	67.82***	67.31***	70.24***	68.39***	68.44***
Log. Likelihood	-622.56	-623.59	-623.84	-552.56	-553.49	-553.46

* significant at 10%; ** significant at 5%; *** significant at 1% (two-sided)

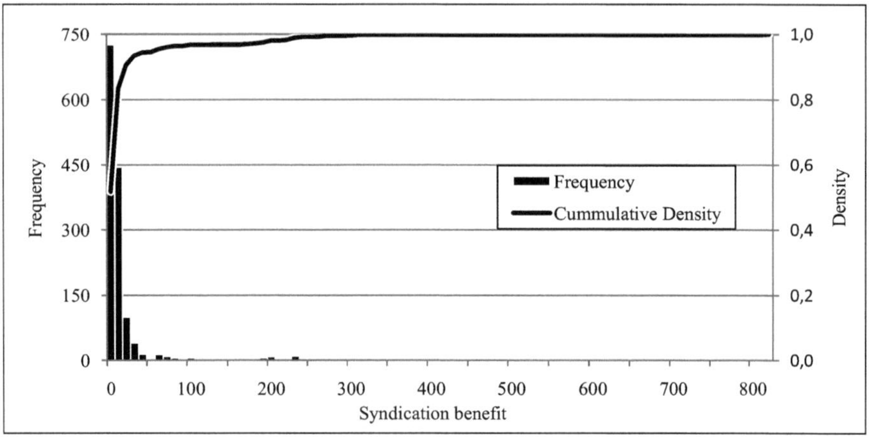

Figure D.1: Distribution of realized venture capitalist-investee dyads in regard to the syndication benefit
Source: Own illustration.

References

Abreu, D. / Milgrom, P. / Pearce, D. (1991): Information and Timing in Repeated Partnerships, in: Econometrica, 59 (6), pp. 1713-1733.

Achleitner, A.-K. (2001): Venture Capital, in: R.-E. Breuer (Ed.): Handbuch Finanzierung, Ed. 3, Gabler, Wiesbaden, pp. 513-529.

Achleitner, A.-K. (2003): Venture Capital, in: W. Lück (Ed.): Lexikon der Betriebswirtschaft, Ed. 6, Oldenbourg, Munich, pp. 694.

Achleitner, A.-K. / Bender, M. / Braun, R. / Geidner, A. (2009): Community Development Venture Capital: Concept and Status Quo in Germany, in: International Journal of Entrepreneurship and Innovation Management, 9 (4), pp. 437-452.

Achleitner, A.-K. / Betzer, A. / Hinterramskogler, B. (2008): Private Equity Investors as Corporate Governance Mechanism in Continental Europe – Evidence from Blockholder-based Governance Regimes, CEFS Working Paper No. 2008-15, 10/2008, Center for Entrepreneurial and Financial Studies.

Achleitner, A.-K. / Ehrhart, N. / Zimmermann, V. (2006): Beteiligungsfinanzierung nach der Marktkonsolidierung – Anhaltende Defizite in der Frühphase, KfW Bankengruppe, Frankfurt a.M.

Achleitner, A.-K. / Fingerle, C. (2004): Finanzierungssituation des deutschen Mittelstandes, in: A.-K. Achleitner / C. von Einem / B. von Schröder (Ed.): Private Debt – alternative Finanzierung für den Mittelstand, Schäffer-Poeschel, Stuttgart, pp. 5-40.

Achleitner, A.-K. / Nathusius, E. (2004): Venture Valuation – Bewertung von Wachstumsunternehmen, Schäffer-Poeschel, Stuttgart.

Achleitner, A.-K. / Schraml, S. / Tappeiner, F. (2008): Private Equity in Familienunternehmen – Erfahrungen mit Minderheitsbeteiligungen, Stiftung Familienunternehmen, Munich.

Ahrens, D. (2003): Was sind Netzwerke?, in: K. Henning / R. Oertel / I. Isenhardt (Ed.): Wissen – Innovation – Netzwerke. Wege zur Zukunftsfähigkeit, Springer, Berlin, pp. 44-48.

Aizenman, J. / Kendall, J. (2008): The Internationalization of Venture Capital and Private Equity, Working Paper Series, 09/2008, University of California.

Akerlof, G.A. (1970): The Market of Lemons: Quality and the Market Mechanism, in: Quarterly Journal of Economics, 84 (3), pp. 488-500.

Albanese, R. / Dacin, M.T. / Harris, I.C. (1997): Dialogue: Agents as Stewards, in: Academy of Management Review, 22 (3), pp. 609-611.

Alchian, A.A. / Demsetz, H. (1972): Production, Information Costs and Economic Organization, in: American Economic Review, 62 (5), pp. 777-795.

Alchian, A.A. / Demsetz, H. (1973): The Property Right Paradigm, in: Journal of Economic History, 33 (1), pp. 16-27.

Amit, R. / Brander, J. / Zott, C. (1998): Why do venture capital firms exist? Theory and Canadian evidence, in: Journal of Business Venturing, 13 (6), pp. 441-466.

Amit, R. / Glosten, L. / Muller, E. (1990): Entrepreneurial ability, venture investments, and risk sharing, in: Management Science, 36 (10), pp. 1232-1245.

Anderer, T. (various years): FYB Financial Yearbook Germany, Munich.

Angwin, D. / Stern, P. / Bradley, S. (2004): Agent or Steward: The Target CEO in a Hostile Takeover Can a Condemned Agent be Redeemed?, in: Long Range Planning, 37 (3), pp. 239-257.

Antonczyk, R.C. / Brettel, M. / Breuer, W. (2007): Venture Capital Financing in Germany – The Role of Contractual Arrangements in Mitigating Incentive Conflicts, Working Paper, 02/2007, Lerhstuhl für Wirtschaftswissenschaften für Ingenieure und Naturwissenschaftler, RWTH Aachen.

Aram, J.D. (1989): The Paradox of Interdependent Relations in the Field of Social Issues in Management, in: Academy of Management Review, 14 (2), pp. 266-283.

Arkes, H.R. / Blumer, C. (1985): The Psychology of Sunk Cost, in: Organizational Behavior and Human Decision Processes, 35 (1), pp. 124-140.

Arrow, K.J. (1969): The Organization of Economic Activity: Issues Pertinent to the Choice of Market versus Non-Market Allocation, in: The Analysis and Evaluation of Public Expenditures: The PPB System, Joint Economic Committee Print, U.S. Government Printing Office, Washington, D.C., 1, pp. 47-64.

Arrow, K.J. (1985): The Economics of Agency, in: J.W. Pratt / R.J. Zeckhauser (Ed.): Principals and Agents: The Structure of Business, Harvard Business School, Boston, pp. 37-51.

Arthurs, J.D. / Busenitz, L.W. (2003): The Boundaries and Limitations of Agency Theory and Stewardship Theory in the Venture Capitalist/Entrepreneur Relationship, in: Entrepreneurship Theory and Practice, 28 (2), pp. 145-162.

Athenstaed, U. / Freudenthaler, H.H. / Mikula, G. (2002): Die Theorie sozialer Interdependenz, in: D. Frey / M. Irle (Ed.): Theorien der Sozialpsychologie – Band II Gruppen-, Interaktions- und Lerntheorien, Ed. 2, Hans Huber, Bern, pp. 62-91.

Audretsch, D.B. (2000): Corporate form and spatial form, in: G.L. Clark / M.P. Feldman / M.S. Gertler (Ed.): The Oxford Handbook of Economic Geography, Oxford University Press, New York, pp. 333-347.

Audretsch, D.B. (2002): The dynamic role of small firms: Evidence from the U.S., in: Small Business Economics, 18 (1-3), pp. 13-40.

Audretsch, D.B. / Feldman, M.P. (1996): R&D Spillovers and the Geography of Innovation and Production, in: The American Economic Review, 86 (3), pp. 630-640.

Axelrod, R. / Dion, D. (1988): The further evolution of cooperation, in: Science, 242 (4884), pp. 1385-1390.

Axelrod, R.M. (1984): The Evolution of Cooperation, Basic Books, New York.

Bacher, J. / Guild, P. (1996): Financing early stage technology based companies: investment criteria used by investors, in: Frontiers of Entrepreneurship Research, 21, pp. 363-376.

Backhaus, K. / Erichson, B. / Plinke, W. / Weiber, R. (2006): Multivariate Analysemethoden – Eine anwendungsorientierte Einführung, Ed. 11, Springer, Berlin.

Banatao, D.P. / Fong, K.A. (2000): The Valley of Deals: How Venture Capital Helped Shape the Region, in: C.-M. Lee / W.F. Miller (Ed.): Silicon Valley Edge: A Habitat for Innovation and Entrepreneurship, Stanford University Press, Stanford, pp. 295-313.

Barnes, J.A. (1972): Social networks, Addison-Wesley Pub. Co, Massachusetts.

Barney, J. / Busenitz, L. / Fiet, J. / Moesel, D. (1989): The structure of venture capital governance: an organizational economic analysis of relations between venture capital firms and new ventures, in: Academy of Management Proceedings, pp. 64-68.

Barney, J. / Busenitz, L. / Fiet, J. / Moesel, D. (1994): The relationship between venture capitalists and managers in new firms: determinants of contractual covenants, in: Managerial Finance, 20 (1), pp. 19-30.

Barney, J. / Busenitz, L. / Fiet, J. / Moesel, D. (1996a): New venture teams' assessment of learning assistance from venture capital firms, in: Journal of Business Venturing, 11 (4), pp. 257-272.

Barney, J. / Fiet, J. / Busenitz, L. / Moesel, D. (1996b): The substitution of bonding for monitoring in venture capitalist relations with high technology enterprises, in: Journal of High Technology Management Research, 7 (1), pp. 91-105.

Barry, C. / Muscarella, C. / Peavy III, J. / Vetsuypens, M. (1990): The role of venture capital in the creation of public companies, in: Journal of Financial Economics, 27 (2), pp. 447-471.

Bascha, A. / Walz, U. (2007): Financing practices in the German venture capital industry: An empirical study, in: G.N. Gregoriou / M. Kooli / R. Kraeussl (Ed.): Venture Capital in Europe, Elsevier, Oxford, pp. 217-231.

Baum, J.A.C. / Silverman, B.S. (2004): Picking winners or building them? Alliance, intellectual, and human capital as selection criteria in venture financing and performance of biotechnology startups, in: Journal of Business Venturing, 19 (3), pp. 411–436.

Baumgärtner, C. (2005): Die Portfoliosteuerung von Venture Capital-Gesellschaften: Eine theoretische und empirische Analyse, Universität Hohenheim, Hohenheim.

Bender, M. / Nathusius, E. (2009): Patterns in Spatial Proximity between Venture Capital Investors and Investees in Germany – An Empirical Analysis, CEFS Working Paper No. 2009-06, 05/2009, Center for Entrepreneurial and Financial Studies.

Bengtsson, O. / Ravid, S.A. (2009): The Importance of Geographical Location and Distance on Venture Capital Contracts, Working Paper, 01/2009, Cornell University, University of Pennsylvania.

Berg, A. / Gottschalg, O.F. (2005): Understanding Value Generation in Buyouts, in: Journal of Restructuring Finance, 2 (1), pp. 9-37.

Bessler, W. / Kurth, A. (2007): Agency Problems and the Performance of Venture-backed IPOs in Germany: Exit Strategies, Lock-up Periods, and Bank Ownership, in: European Journal of Finance, 13 (1), pp. 29-63.

Bindseil, U. (1994): Verfügungsrechte an organisierten Wertpapiermärkten untersucht auf der Grundlage der Theorie unvollständiger Verträge, Universität des Saarlandes, Saarbrücken.

Birley, S. (1985): The role of networks in the entrepreneurial process, in: Journal of Business Venturing, 1 (1), pp. 107-117.

Blau, P.M. (1964): Exchange and power in social life, Wiley, New York.

Blau, P.M. (1977a): Inequality and heterogeneity - A primitive theory of social structure, Free Press, New York.

Blau, P.M. (1977b): Inequality and heterogeneity – A primitive theory of social structure, Free Press, New York.

Bliss, R.T. (1999): A venture capital model for transitioning economies: The case of Poland, in: Venture Capital, 1 (3), pp. 241 - 257.

Böhner, I. (2007): Network, Network Position and the Deal Flow of Venture Capital Firms, RWTH Aachen, published online: http://darwin.bth.rwth-aachen.de/opus3/volltexte/2007/2018/, Aachen.

Boocock, G. / Woods, M. (1997): The Evaluation Criteria used by Venture Capitalists: Evidence from a UK Venture Fund, in: International Small Business Journal, 16 (1), pp. 36.

Bossard, J.H.S. (1932): Residential Propinquity as a Factor in Marriage Selection, in: American Journal of Sociology, 38 (2), pp. 219-224.

Bottazzi, L. / Da Rin, M. / Hellmann, T. (2008): Who are the active investors?: Evidence from venture capital, in: Journal of Financial Economics, 89 (3), pp. 488-512.

Bourdieu, P. (1985): The forms of capital, in: J.G. Richardson (Ed.): Handbook of Theory and Research for the Sociology of Education, Greenwood Press, New York, pp. 241-258.

Brant, R. (1990): Assessing proportionality in the proportional odds model for ordinal logistic regression, in: Biometrics, 46 (4), pp. 1171-1178.

Brav, A. / Gompers, P. (1997): Myth or reality? The long-run underperformance of initial public offerings: evidence from venture and nonventure capital-backed companies, in: Journal of Finance, 52 (5), pp. 1791-1821.

Bredeck, T. (2002): Private Equity im Firmenkundengeschäft regionaler Kreditinstitute: Eine geschäftspolitische Analyse, Universität Basel, Münster.

Breiger, R.L. (1974): The Duality of Persons and Groups, in: Social Forces, 53 (2), pp. 181-189.

Brettel, M. (2002): Entscheidungskriterien von Venture Capitalists, in: Die Betriebswirtschaft, 62 (3), pp. 305-325.

Brettel, M. / Meier, D. / Reissig-Thust, S. (2004): Vetragsgestaltung von Venture Capitalists und Business Angels im Vergleich, in: Die Betriebswirtschaft, 64 (4), pp. 431-447.

Brettel, M. / Thust, S. / Witt, P. (2001): Die Beziehung zwischen VC-Gesellschaften und Start-Up-Unternehmen, WHU Working Paper No. 81, 09/2001, WHU.

Bruton, G. / Fried, V. / Hisrich, R.D. (1997): Venture Capitalist and CEO Dismissal, in: Entrepreneurship Theory and Practice, 21 (3), pp. 41-54.

Bruton, G.D. / Fried, V.H. / Hisrich, R.D. (2000): CEO Dismissal in Venture Capital-Backed Firms: Further Evidence From an Agency Perspective, in: Entrepreneurship Theory and Practice, 24 (4), pp. 69.

Bruton, G.D. / Fried, V.H. / Manigart, S. (2005): Institutional Influences on the Worldwide Expansion of Venture Capital, in: Entrepreneurship Theory and Practice, 29 (6), pp. 737-760.

Busenitz, L.W. / Fiet, J.O. / Moesel, D.D. (2004): Reconsidering the venture capitalists' "value added" proposition: An interorganizational learning perspective, in: Journal of Business Venturing, 19 (6), pp. 787-807.

Busenitz, L.W. / Gomez, C. / Spencer, J.W. (2000): Country institutional profiles: Unlocking entrepreneurial phenomena, in: Academy of Management Journal, 43 (5), pp. 994-1003.

Busenitz, L.W. / Moesel, D.D. / Fiet, J.O. / Barney, J.B. (1997): The Framing of Perceptions of Fairness in the Relationship Between Venture Capitalists and New Venture Teams, in: Entrepreneurship Theory and Practice, 21 (3), pp. 5-21.

Butler, A.W. / Goktan, S. (2007): Does Distance Still Matter? Evidence from the Venture Capital Market, Working Paper, 09/2007, University of Texas.

Butler, A.W. / Goktan, S. (2008): On the Matching of Companies and Their Financial Intermediaries: Evidence from Venture Capital, Working Paper, 09/2008, University of Texas, California State University.

BVCA (2009): BVCA Private Equity and Venture Capital Report on Investment Activity 2008, British Private Equity and Venture Capital Association, London.

BVK (1995): BVK Statistik – Das Jahr 1994 in Zahlen, Bundesverband Deutscher Kapitalbeteiligungsgesellschaften – German Private Equity and Venture Capital Association e.V., Berlin.

BVK (2008a): BVK Mitgliederverzeichnis, www.bvkap.de/privateequity.php/cat/81/title/Ordentliche_Mitglieder_(Investoren, Bundesverband Deutscher Kapitalbeteiligungsgesellschaften – German Private Equity and Venture Capital Association e.V., [Access: 30/08/2008].

BVK (2008b): BVK Statistik – Das Jahr 2007 in Zahlen, Bundesverband Deutscher Kapitalbeteiligungsgesellschaften – German Private Equity and Venture Capital Association e.V., Berlin.

BVK (2008c): Teilstatistik – Aktivitäten der Mittelständischen Beteiligungsgesellschaften 2007, Bundesverband Deutscher Kapitalbeteiligungsgesellschaften – German Private Equity and Venture Capital Association e.V., Berlin.

BVK (2009a): BVK Statistik – Das Jahr 2008 in Zahlen, Bundesverband Deutscher Kapitalbeteiligungsgesellschaften – German Private Equity and Venture Capital Association e.V., Berlin.

BVK (2009b): Glossar, http://www.bvkap.de/privateequity.php/cat/31/title/Glossar, Bundesverband Deutscher Kapitalbeteiligungsgesellschaften – German Private Equity and Venture Capital Association e.V., [Access: 09/09/2009].

BVK (various years): BVK Statistik – Teilstatistik Venture Capital 2003-2007, Bundesverband Deutscher Kapitalbeteiligungsgesellschaften – German Private Equity and Venture Capital Association e.V., Berlin.

Bygrave, W. (1988): The structure of the investment networks of venture capital firms, in: Journal of Business Venturing, 3 (2), pp. 137-158.

Cable, D. / Shane, S. (1997): A prisoner's dilemma approach to entrepreneur-venture capitalist relationships, in: Academy of Management Review, 22 (1), pp. 142-176.

Caers, R. / Du Bois, C. / Jegers, M. / De Gieter, S. / Schepers, C. / Pepermans, R. (2006): Principal-agent relationships on the stewardship-agency axis, in: Nonprofit Management and Leadership, 17 (1), pp. 25-47.

Carlsson, B. (2002): Institutions, Entrepreneurship, and Growth: Biomedicine and Polymers in Sweden and Ohio, in: Small Business Economics, 19 (2), pp. 105-121.

Carter, R. / van Auken, H. (1994): Venture capital firms' preferences for projects in particular stages of development, in: Journal of Small Business Management, 32 (1), pp. 60-73.

Casamatta, C. (2003): Financing and Advising: Optimal Financial Contracts with Venture Capitalists, in: Journal of Finance, 58 (5), pp. 2059-2086.

Casamatta, C. / Haritchabalet, C. (2006): Competition between Informed Venture Capitalists for the Financing of Entrepreneurs, IDEI Working Paper, no. 444, 11/2006, University of Toulouse.

Castells, M. (1991): The informational city: Information technology, economic restructuring, and the urban-regional process, Blackwell, Oxford.

Chen, H. / Gompers, P.A. / Kovner, A. / Lerner, J. (2009): Buy Local? The Geography of Successful and Unsuccessful Venture Capital Expansion, Working Paper, 06/2009, Harvard University.

Chertkoff, J.M. / Esser, J.K. (1976): A review of experiments in explicit bargaining, in: Journal of Experimental Social Psychology, 12 (5), pp. 464-486.

Chesbrough, H. (2002): Making sense of corporate venture capital, in: Harvard Business Review, 80 (3), pp. 4-11.

Cheung, S.N.S. (1970): The Structure of a Contract and the Theory of a Non-Exclusive Resource, in: Journal of Law and Economics, 13 (1), pp. 49-70.

Chrisman, J.J. / Chua, J.H. / Kellermanns, F.W. / Chang, E.P.C. (2007): Are family managers agents or stewards? An exploratory study in privately held family firms, in: Journal of Business Research, 60 (10), pp. 1030-1038.

Chrisman, J.J. / Chua, J.H. / Sharma, P. (2005): Trends and Directions in the Development of a Strategic Management Theory of the Family Firm, in: Entrepreneurship Theory and Practice, 29 (5), pp. 555-575.

Christensen, J.L. (2007): The Development of Geographical Specialization of Venture Capital, in: European Planning Studies, 15 (6), pp. 817-833.

Christensen, J.L. / Drejer, I. (2005): The strategic importance of location: Location decisions and the effects of firm location on innovation and knowledge acquisition, in: European Planning Studies, 13 (6), pp. 807-814.

Clore, G.L. / Byrne, D. (1974): A reinforcement-affect-model of attraction, in: T.L. Huston (Ed.): Foundations of interpersonal attraction, Academic Press, New York, pp. 143-170.

Coase, R.H. (1937): The nature of the firm, in: Economica, 4 (16), pp. 386-405.

Coase, R.H. (1960): The Problem of Social Cost, in: Journal of Law and Economics, 3, pp. 1-44.

Coleman, J.S. (1988): Social Capital in the Creation of Human Capital, in: American Journal of Sociology, 94 (Supplement: Organizations and Institutions: Sociological and Economic Approaches to the Analysis of Social Structure), pp. 95-120.

Colmann, A.M. (2003): Cooperation, psychological game theory, and limitations of rationality in social interaction, in: Behavioral and Brain Sciences, 26 (2), pp. 139-198.

Corfman, K.P. / Lehmann, D.R. (1994): The Prisoner's Dilemma and the Role of Information in Setting Advertising Budgets, in: Journal of Advertising, 23 (2), pp. 35-48.

Cosslett, S.R. (1981): Maximum Likelihood Estimator for Choice-Based Samples, in: Econometrica, 49 (5), pp. 1289-1316.

Coval, J.D. / Moskowitz, T.J. (1999): Home Bias at Home: Local Equity Preference in Domestic Portfolios, in: Journal of Finance, 54 (6), pp. 2045-2073.

Cronbach, L.J. (1951): Coefficient alpha and the internal structure of tests, in: Psychometrika, 16 (3), pp. 297-334.

Cumming, D.J. / Dai, N. (2009): Local Bias in Venture Capital Investments, Working Paper, 07/2009, York University, University of New Mexico.

Cumming, D.J. / Fleming, G. / Suchard, J.-A. (2005): Venture Capitalist Value-added activities, fundraising and drawdowns, in: Journal of Banking and Finance, 29 (2), pp. 295-331.

Cumming, D.J. / Johan, S.A. (2006): Provincial Preferences in Private Equity, in: Financial Market Research, 20 (4), pp. 369–398.

Cumming, D.J. / Macintosh, J.G. (2003): Venture Capital Exits in Canada and the United States, in: University of Toronto Law Journal, 53 (2), pp. 101-199.

Davila, A. / Foster, G. / Gupta, M. (2003): Venture capital financing and the growth of startup firms, in: Journal of Business Venturing, 18 (6), pp. 689-708.

Davis, J.H. / Schoorman, F.D. / Donaldson, L. (1997a): Reply: The Distinctiveness of Agency Theory and Stewardship Theory, in: Academy of Management Review, 22 (3), pp. 611-613.

Davis, J.H. / Schoorman, F.D. / Donaldson, L. (1997b): Toward a stewardship theory of management, in: Academy of Management Review, 22 (1), pp. 20-47.

Dawes, R.M. (1980): Social Dilemmas, in: Annual Review of Psychology, 31, pp. 169-193.

De Clercq, D. / Goulet, P.K. / Kumpulainen, M. / Mäkelä, M. (2001): Portfolio investment strategies in the Finnish venture capital industry: A longitudinal study, in: Venture Capital, 3 (1), pp. 41-62.

De Clercq, D. / Sapienza, H. (2001): The creation of relational rents in venture capitalist-entrepreneur dyads, in: Venture Capital: An International Journal of Entrepreneurial Finance, 3 (2), pp. 107-127.

De Clercq, D. / Sapienza, H.J. (2005): When Do Venture Capital Firms Learn from Their Portfolio Companies?, in: Entrepreneurship Theory and Practice, 29 (4), pp. 517-535.

Decker, R.O.A. (1994): Eine Prinzipal-Agent-theoretische Betrachtung von Eigner-Manager-Konflikten in der Kommanditgesellschaft auf Aktien und der Aktiengesellschaft, Köln.

Demsetz, H. (1967): Toward a theory of property rights, in: American Economic Review, 57 (2), pp. 347-359.

Denis, D.J. (2004): Entrepreneurial finance: an overview of the issues and evidence, in: Journal of Corporate Finance, 10 (2), pp. 301-326.

Diebold Group (1974): Venture Capital Investment Guarantee Study, NTIS Report PB-252867, National Science Foundation, Washington D.C.

Diller, C. / Kaserer, C. (2009): What Drives Private Equity Returns? – Fund Inflows, Skilled GPs, and/or Risk?, in: European Financial Management, 15 (3), pp. 643-675.

Dixit, A. / Jayaraman, N. (2001): Internationalization strategies of private equity firms, in: Journal of Private Equity, 5 (1), pp. 40-54.

Donaldson, L. / Davis, J.H. (1991): Stewardship Theory or Agency Theory: CEO Governance and Shareholder Returns, in: Australian Journal of Management, 16 (1), pp. 49-65.

Donaldson, L. / Davis, J.H. (1994): Boards and Company Performance – Research Challenges the Conventional Wisdom, in: Corporate Governance, 2 (3), pp. 151-160.

Dotzler, F. (2001): What do venture capitalists really do, and where do they learn to do it?, in: Journal of Private Equity, 5 (1), pp. 6-12.

Dowling, M. (1996): Multifaceted Relationships Under Coopetition – Description and Theory, in: Journal of Management Inquiry, 5 (2), pp. 155-167.

DSGV (2005): Sparkassen – Institute aller Bürgerinnen und Bürger – Fakten, Analysen, Positionen | 14, Deutscher Sparkassen- und Giroverband, Berlin.

DSGV (2009a): Landesbanken, http://www.dsgv.de/de/sparkassen-finanzgruppe/organisation/landesbanken/index.html, Deutscher Sparkassen- und Giroverband, [Access: 11.09.2009].

DSGV (2009b): Sparkassen, http://www.dsgv.de/de/sparkassen-finanzgruppe/organisation/sparkassen/index.html, Deutscher Sparkassen- und Giroverband, [Access: 11.09.2009].

EFI (Ed.) (2009): Gutachten zu Forschung, Innovation und technologischer Leistungsfähigkeit 2009, Expertenkommission Forschung und Innovation, Berlin.

Eisenhardt, K.M. (1989): Agency Theory: An Assessment and Review, in: Academy of Management Review, 14 (1), pp. 57-74.

Elango, B. / Fried, V.H. / Hisrich, R.D. / Polonchek, A. (1995): How venture capital firms differ, in: Journal of Business Venturing, 10 (2), pp. 157-179.

Elfring, T. / Hulsink, W. (2003): Networks in Entrepreneurship: The Case of High-technology Firms, in: Small Business Economics, 21 (4), pp. 409-422.

Elzen, B. / Enserink, B. / Smit, W.A. (1996): Socio-Technical Networks: How a Technology Studies Approach May Help to Solve Problems Related to Technical Change, in: Social Studies of Science, 26 (1), pp. 95-141.

Emerson, R.M. (1976): Social Exchange Theory, in: Annual Review of Sociology, 2, pp. 335-362.

Emerson, R.M. (1987): Toward a Theory of Value in Social Exchange, in: K.S. Cook (Ed.): Social Exchange Theory, Sage, Newbury Park, pp. 11-46.

Engel, D. (2003a): Venture Capital für junge Unternehmen, Europa Universität Viadrina Frankfurt (Oder), Mannheim.

Engel, R. (2003b): Seed-Finanzierung wachstumsorientierter Unternehmensgründungen, Technische Universität München, Sternenfels.

Erlei, M. / Leschke, M. / Sauerland, D. (1999): Neue Institutionenökonomik, Schäffer-Poeschel, Stuttgart.

EVCA (2008): EVCA Yearbook 2007, European Private Equity and Venture Capital Association, Zaventem.

EVCA (2009): Glossary, http://www.evca.eu/toolbox/glossary.aspx?id=982, European Private Equity and Venture Capital Association, [Access: 08.09.2009].

EVCA (various years-a): Directory of EVCA Members, European Private Equity and Venture Capital Association, Zaventem.

EVCA (various years-b): EVCA Yearbook, European Private Equity and Venture Capital Association, Zaventem.

Fama, E.F. (1978): The Effects of a Firm's Investment and Financing on the Welfare of its Security Holders, in: American Economic Review, 68 (3), pp. 272.

Fama, E.F. (1980): Agency Problems and the Theory of the Firm, in: Journal of Political Economy, 88 (2), pp. 288-307.

Faust, H. (1999): Das RUHRGEBIET–Erneuerung einer europäischen Industrieregion, in: Europa Regional, 7 (2), pp. 10-18.

Feinendegen, S. / Schmidt, D. / Wahrenburg, M. (2003): Die Vertragsbeziehungen zwischen Investoren und europäischen Venture Capital-Fonds: Eine empirische Untersuchung und Klassifizierung unterschiedlicher Vertragsmuster, in: Zeitschrift für Betriebswirtschaft, 73 (11), pp. 1167-1195.

Feldman, M.P. (2000): Location and innovation: the new economic geography of innovation, spillovers, and agglomeration, in: G.L. Clark / M.P. Feldman / M.S. Gertler (Ed.): The Oxford Handbook of Economic Geography, Oxford University Press, New York, pp. 373-394.

Fenn, G. / Liang, N. / Prowse, S. (1995): The economics of the private equity market, Board of Governors of the Federal Reserve System (U.S.), Staff Studies 168, Washington, D.C.

Festinger, L. / Schachter, S. / Back, K.W. (1950): Social Pressures in Informal Groups: A Study of Human Factors in Housing, Harper, New York.

Fiet, J. / Busenitz, L. / Moesel, D. / Barney, J. (1997): Complementary Theoretical Perspectives on the Dismissal of New Venture Team Members, in: Journal of Business Venturing, 12 (5), pp. 347-366.

Fingerle, C.H. (2005): Smart Money – Influence of Venture Capitalists on High Potential Companies, Technische Universität München, Sternenfels.

Fischer, J. / Gensior, S. (1995): Einleitung: Netz-Spannungen, in: J. Fischer / S. Gensior (Ed.): Netz-Spannungen – Trends in der sozialen und technischen Vernetzung von Arbeit, Edition sigma, Berlin, pp. 11-48.

Flick, R. (2001): Automobilindustrie und Motorisierung in Deutschland bis 1939, in: R. Boch (Ed.): Geschichte und Zukunft der deutschen Automobilindustrie, Franz Steiner, Stuttgart, pp. 49-84.

Florida, R.L. / Kenney, M. (1988): Venture Capital, High Technology and Regional Development, in: Regional Studies, 22 (1), pp. 3-48.

Florida, R.L. / Smith, D.F. (1993): Venture Capital Formation, Investment, and Regional Industrialization, in: Annals of the Association of American Geographers, 83 (3), pp. 434-451.

Florin, J. / Lubatkin, M. / Schulze, W. (2003): A social capital model of high-growth-ventures, in: Academy of Management Journal, 46 (3), pp. 374-384.

Foa, U.G. / Foa, E.B. (1976): Resource theory of social exchange, in: J.W. Thibaut / J.T. Spence / R.C. Carson (Ed.): Contemporary topics in Social Psychology, General Learning Press, Morristown, pp. 99-131.

Fogel, G. (2001): An analysis of entrepreneurial environment and enterprise development in Hungary, in: Journal of Small Business Management, 39 (1), pp. 103-109.

Fox, M.A. / Hamilton, R.T. (1994): Ownership and diversification: agency theory or stewardship theory, in: Journal of Management Studies, 31 (1), pp. 69-81.

Frank, B. (2007): Geld für junge, innovative Unternehmen – High-Tech Gründerfonds zieht positive Zwischenbilanz, in: VentureCapital Magazin, 2007 (6), pp. 30-31.

Franke, G. / Hax, H. (1999): Finanzwirtschaft des Unternehmens und Kapitalmarkt, Ed. 4, Berlin.

Franke, N. / Gruber, M. / Harhoff, D. / Henkel, J. (2006): What you are is what you like – similarity biases in venture capitalists' evaluations of start-up teams, in: Journal of Business Venturing, 21 (6), pp. 802-826.

Fried, V.H. / Hisrich, R.D. (1994): Toward a model of venture capital investment decision making, in: Financial Management, 23 (3), pp. 28-37.

Fried, V.H. / Hisrich, R.D. (1995): The Venture Capitalist: A Relationship Investor, in: California Management Review, 37 (2), pp. 101-113.

Fritsch, M. (2001): Innovation by Networking: An Economic Perspective, in: K. Koschatzky / M. Kulicke / A. Zenker (Ed.): Innovation Networks – Concepts and Challenges in the European Perspective, Physica, Heidelberg, pp. 25-34.

Fritsch, M. / Schilder, D. (2006): Is Venture Capital a Regional Business? – The Role of Syndication, Freiberg Working Papers 09-2006, 09/2006, TU Freiberg.

Fritsch, M. / Schilder, D. (2007): Is there a regional equity gap for innovative start-ups? The case of Germany, in: M. Dowling / J. Schmude (Ed.): Empirical Entrepreneurship in Europe: New Perspectives, Edward Elgar, Cheltenham, pp. 200-213.

Fritsch, M. / Schilder, D. (2008): Does Venture Capital investment really require spatial proximity? An empirical investigation, in: Environment and Planning A, 40 (9), pp. 2114-2131.

Fudenberg, D. / Tirole, J. (2000): Game theory, MIT Press, Cambridge.

Fülbier, U. (2004): Wissenschaftstheorie und Betriebswirtschaftslehre, in: Wirtschaftswissenschaftliches Studium, 33 (5), pp. 266-271.

Furubotn, E.G. / Pejovich, S. (1972): Property Rights and Economic Theory: A Survey of Recent Literature, in: Journal of Economic Literature, 10 (4), pp. 1137-1162.

Geidner, A. (2008): Der Wandel der Unternehmensführung in Buyouts – Eine Untersuchung Private-Equity-finanzierter Desinvestitionen, Technische Universität München, Munich.

Genius Venture Capital (2007): Wir, www.genius-vc.de, [Access: 06.08.2007].

George, G. / Nathusius, E. (2007): The European Venture Capital Market: Scaling Beyond Current Boundaries, European Private Equity and Venture Capital Association, London.

Gerum, E. (1992): Property Rights, in: E. Frese (Ed.): Handwörterbuch der Organisation, Ed. 3, Schäffer-Poeschel, Stuttgart, pp. 2116-2128.

Geyskens, I. / Steenkamp, J.-B.E.M. / Scheer, L.K. / Kumar, N. (1996): The effects of trust and interdependence on relationship commitment: A trans-Atlantic study, in: International Journal of Research in Marketing, 13 (4), pp. 303-317.

Gifford, S. (1997): Limited attention and the role of the venture capitalist, in: Journal of Business Venturing, 12 (6), pp. 459-482.

Goldberg, V.P. (1976): Regulation and Administered Contracts, in: The Bell Journal of Economics, 7 (2), pp. 426-448.

Gomez-Mejia / Balkin / Welbourne, T. (1990): Influence of venture capitalists on high technology management, in: Journal of High Technology Management, 1 (1), pp. 103-118.

Gompers, P.A. (1995): Optimal Investment, Monitoring, and the Staging of Venture Capital, in: Journal of Finance, 50 (5), pp. 1461-1489.

Gompers, P.A. (1996): Grandstanding in the venture capital industry, in: Journal of Financial Economics, 42 (1), pp. 133-156.

Gompers, P.A. / Kovner, A. / Lerner, J. / Scharfstein, D. (2009): Specialization and Success: Evidence from Venture Capital, in: Journal of Economics and Management Strategy, 18 (3), pp. 817-844.

Gompers, P.A. / Lerner, J. (1999): An analysis of compensation in the U.S. venture capital partnership, in: Journal of Financial Economics, 51 (1), pp. 3-44.

Gompers, P.A. / Lerner, J. (2001): The Venture Capital Revolution, in: Journal of Economic Perspectives, 15 (2), pp. 145-168.

Gompers, P.A. / Lerner, J. (2004): The Venture Capital Cycle, Ed. 2, MIT Press, Cambridge/MA.

Google (2009): Google Maps, http://maps.google.de, [Access: 25/01/2009].

Gordon, T. (1985): Adam Smith and the Prisoners' Dilemma, in: Quarterly Journal of Economics, 100 (Supplement), pp. 1073-1081.

Gorman, M. / Sahlman, W. (1989): What do venture capitalists do?, in: Journal of Business Venturing, 4 (4), pp. 231-248.

Granovetter, M. (1983): The Strength of Weak Ties: A Network Theory Revisited, in: Sociological Theory, 1, pp. 201-233.

Granovetter, M. (1985): Economic Action and Social Structure: The Problem of Embeddedness, in: American Journal of Sociology, 91 (3), pp. 481-510.

Granovetter, M.S. (1973): The Strength of Weak Ties, in: American Journal of Sociology, 78 (6), pp. 1360-1380.

Grichnik, D. / Schwärzel, F. (2005): Chancen und Risiken der Gründungsfinanzierung aus informationsökonomischer Sicht, in: C.J. Börner / D. Grichnik (Ed.): Entrepreneurial Finance: Kompendium der Gründungs- und Wachstumsfinanzierung, Physica, Heidelberg, pp. 25-45.

Grossman, G.M. / Helpman, E. (1993): Innovation and growth in the global economy, The MIT Press, Boston.

Grossman, S. / Hart, O. (1983): An Analysis of the Principal-Agent-Problem, in: Econometrica, 51 (1), pp. 7-45.

Gürtler, M. / Hartmann, N. (2005): Gründungsfinanzierung und beschränkte Rationalität, in: C.J. Börner / D. Grichnik (Ed.): Entrepreneurial Finance: Kompendium der Gründungs- und Wachstumsfinanzierung, Physica, Heidelberg, pp. 369-389.

Gulati, R. (1995): Social structure and alliance formation patterns: A longitudinal analysis, in: Administrative Science Quarterly, 40 (4), pp. 619-652.

Gupta, A.K. / Sapienza, H.J. (1992): Determinants of Venture Capital Firms' Preferences Regarding the Industry Diversity and Geographic Scope of their Investments, in: Journal of Business Venturing, 7 (5), pp. 347-362.

Haagen, F. (2008): The role of smart money: What drives venture capital support and interference within biotechnology ventures?, in: Zeitschrift für Betriebswirtschaft, 78 (4), pp. 397-422.

Haarmann (2006): Economic Determinants of Private Equity Investments in Switzerland – A Survey of the Medical Technology Industry, University of Zürich, Bern.

Hall, G. / Tu, C. (2003): Venture capitalists and the decision to invest overseas, in: Venture Capital, 5 (2), pp. 181.

Hall, J. / Hofer, C. (1993): Venture capitalists' decision criteria in new venture evaluation, in: Journal of Business Venturing, 8 (1), pp. 25-42.

Hall, M. / Tideman, N. (1967): Measures of concentration, in: Journal of the American Statistical Association, 62 (317), pp. 162-168.

Hamilton, B.H. (2000): Does entrepreneurship pay? An empirical analysis of the returns of self-employment, in: Journal of Political Economy, 108 (3), pp. 604-631.

Han, X. (2009): The Specialization Choices and Performance of Venture Capital Funds, Working Paper, 01/2009, Tsinghua University.

Hansen, E.L. (1995): Entrepreneurial Networks and New Organization Growth, in: Entrepreneurship Theory and Practice, 19 (4), pp. 7-19.

Hardin, J.W. / Hilbe, J. (2007): Generalized linear models and extensions, Ed. 2, Stata press, College Station.

Harrison, R.T. / Cooper, S.Y. / Mason, C.M. (2004): Entrepreneurial activity and the dynamics of technology-based cluster development: the case of Ottawa, in: Urban Studies, 41 (5/6), pp. 1045-1070.

Hassebrauck, M. / Küpper, B. (2002): Theorien interpersonaler Attraktion, in: D. Frey / M. Irle (Ed.): Theorien der Sozialpsychologie – Band II Gruppen-, Interaktions- und Lerntheorien, Ed. 2, Hans Huber, Bern, pp. 156-177.

Hatfield, E. / Walster, G.W. / Berscheid, E. (1978): Equity theory and research, Allyn & Bacon, Boston.

Hauschildt, J. (1997): Innovationsmanagement, Ed. 2, Vahlen, Munich.

Heider, F. (1958): The psychology of interpersonal relations, Wiley, New York.

Heinen, E. (1991): Industriebetriebslehre als entscheidungsorientierte Unternehmensführung, in: E. Heinen (Ed.): Industriebetriebslehre – Entscheidungen im Industriebetrieb, Ed. 9, Gabler, Wiesbaden, pp. 1-71.

Hellmann, T. / Puri, M. (2000): The interaction between product market and financing strategy: the role of venture capital, in: Review of Financial Studies, 13 (4), pp. 959-984.

Hellmann, T. / Puri, M. (2002): Venture Capital and the Professionalization of Start-Up Firms: Empirical Evidence, in: Journal of Finance, 57 (1), pp. 169-197.

Hellmer, F. / Friese, C. / Kollros, H. / Krumbein, W. (1999): Mythos Netzwerke. Regionale Innovationsprozesse zwischen Kontinuität und Wandel, Sigma, Berlin.

Herfindahl, O.C. (1950): Concentration in the steel industry, Columbia University, New York.

Heyning, D. (1999): Due diligence, in: W. Bygrave / M. Hay / J. Peeters (Ed.): The venture capital handbook, Pearson Education, Harlow, pp. 143-161.

Hirschman, A.O. (1945): National power and the structure of foreign trade, University of California Press, Berkeley / Los Angeles.

Hochberg, Y.V. / Ljungqvist, A. / Lu, Y. (2007): Whom You Know Matters: Venture Capital Networks and Investment Performance, in: Journal of Finance, 62 (1), pp. 251-301.

Hoffman, H.M. / Blakey, J. (1987): You can negotiate with venture capitalists, in: Harvard Business Review, 65 (2), pp. 16-24.

Holler, M.J. / Illing, G. (2006): Einführung in die Spieltheorie, Springer, Berlin.

Hollingshead, A.B. (1950): Cultural Factors in the Selection of Marriage Mates, in: American Sociological Review, 15 (5), pp. 619-627.

Holmstrom, B. (1979): Moral hazard and observability, in: Bell Journal of Economics, 10 (1), pp. 74-91.

Holzer, B. (2006): Netzwerke, Transcript, Bielefeld.

Homans, G.C. (1958): Social Behavior as Exchange, in: American Journal of Sociology, 63 (6), pp. 597-606.

Homans, G.C. (1961): Social Behavior – Its Elementary Forms, Harcourt, Brace & World, New York.

Hosmer, L.T. (1995): Trust: the connecting link between organisational theory and philosophical ethics, in: Academy of Management Review, 20 (2), pp. 379-403.

Houben, E. (2002): Venture Capital, Double-sided Adverse Selection, and Double-sided Moral Hazard, Working Paper, 12/2002, University of Kiel.

Houben, E. / Nippel, P. (2005): Vertragsgestaltung bei Venture-Capital-Finanzierungen, in: C.J. Börner / D. Grichnik (Ed.): Entrepreneurial Finance: Kompendium der Gründungs- und Wachstumsfinanzierung, Physica, Heidelberg, pp. 325-346.

Hsu, D.H. (2004): What Do Entrepreneurs Pay for Venture Capital Affiliation?, in: Journal of Finance, 59 (4), pp. 1805-1844.

HTGF (2009): Finanzierung, http://www.htgf.de/htgf/index.php?id=137, High-Tech Gründerfonds, [Access: 11.09.09].

Imbens, G.W. (1992): An Efficient Method of Moments Estimator for Discrete Choice Models With Choice-Based Sampling, in: Econometrica, 60 (5), pp. 1187-1214.

Imbens, G.W. / Lancaster, T. (1996): Efficient estimation and stratified sampling, in: Journal of Econometrics, 74 (2), pp. 289-318.

Inside CRM (2009): The 20 Worst Venture Capital Investments of All Time, http://www.insidecrm.com/features/20-worst-vc-investments-111907/, Inside CRM, [Access: 25.06.2009].

Jääskeläinen, M. / Maula, M. / Seppä, T. (2006): Allocation of Attention to Portfolio Companies and the Performance of Venture Capital Firms, in: Entrepreneurship Theory and Practice, 30 (2), pp. 185-206.

Jaccard, J. / Turrisi, R. (1990): Interaction Effects in Multiple Regression – Quantitative Applications in the Social Sciences, Ed. 2, Sage University Papers Vol. 72.

Jackson, S.E. / Brett, J.F. / Sessa, V.I. / Cooper, D.M. / Julin, J.A. / Peyronnin, K. (1991): Some Differences Make a Difference: Individual Dissimilarity and Group Heterogeneity as Correlates of Recruitment, Promotions, and Turnover, in: Journal of Applied Psychology, 76 (5), pp. 675-689.

Jaffe, A.B. (1986): Technological Opportunity and Spillovers of R&D: Evidence from Firms' Patents, Profits, and Market Values, in: American Economic Review, 76 (5), pp. 984-1001.

Jansen, D. (2000): Netzwerke und soziales Kapital – Methoden zur Analyse struktureller Einbettung, in: J. Weyer (Ed.): Soziale Netzwerke, Oldenbourg, Munich, pp. 35-62.

Jansen, D. (2003): Einführung in die Netzwerkanalyse, Ed. 2, Leske + Budrich, Opladen.

Jarillo, J.C. (1988): On Strategic Networks, in: Strategic Management Journal, 9 (1), pp. 31-41.

Jarillo, J.C. (1989): Entrepreneurship and growth: the strategic use of external resources, in: Journal of Business Venturing, 4 (2), pp. 133-147.

Jegen, D.L. (1998): Community Development Venture Capital Creating a Viable Business Model for the Future, in: Nonprofit Management and Leadership, 9 (2), pp. 187-200.

Jensen, M. (1986): Agency costs of free cash flow, corporate finance, and takeovers, in: American Economic Review, 76 (2), pp. 323-329.

Jensen, M. / Meckling, W. (1976): Theory of the firm: managerial behavior, agency costs and ownership structure, in: Journal of Financial Economics, 3 (4), pp. 305-360.

Jost, P.-J. (2001): Die Prinzipal-Agenten-Theorie im Unternehmenskontext, in: P.-J. Jost (Ed.): Die Prinzipal-Agenten-Theorie in der Betriebswirtschaftslehre, Schäffer-Poeschel, Stuttgart, pp. 11-43.

Jugel, S. (2001): Der Leistungsstand deutscher Beteiligungsgesellschaften, Fachhochschule Wiesbaden, Baumgartner&Partner, RWB AG, VDI Nachrichten, Wiesbaden.

Kahneman, D. / Tversky, A. (1979): Prospect theory: An analysis of decision under risk, in: Econometrica, 47 (3), pp. 263–292.

Kang, J.-K. / Kim, J.-M. (2008): The Geography of Block Acquisitions, in: Journal of Finance, 62 (6), pp. 2817-2858.

Kanniainen, V. / Keuschnigg, C. (2004): Start-up investment with scarce venture capital support, in: Journal of Banking and Finance, 28 (8), pp. 1935-1959.

Kaplan, S.N. / Martel, F. / Strömberg, P. (2004): How Do Legal Differences and Learning Affect Financial Contracts?, Working Paper, 06/2004, University of Chicago Graduate School of Business, University of Lausanne IMD, UBS Global Asset Management.

Kaplan, S.N. / Sensoy, B.A. / Strömberg, P. (2002): How well do venture capital databases reflect actual investments?, Working Paper, 09/2002, University of Chicago Graduate School of Business.

Kaplan, S.N. / Strömberg, P. (2001): Venture Capitalists as Principals: Contracting, Screening, and Monitoring, in: The American Economic Review, 91 (2), pp. 426-430.

Kaplan, S.N. / Strömberg, P. (2003): Financial Contracting Theory Meets the Real World: An Empirical Analysis of Venture Capital Contracts, in: Review of Economic Studies, 70 (2), pp. 281-315.

Kaplan, S.N. / Strömberg, P. (2004): Characteristics, Contracts, and Actions: Evidence from Venture Capitalist Analyses, in: Journal of Finance, 59 (5), pp. 2177-2210.

Kaserer, C. / Achleitner, A.-K. / von Einem, C. / Schiereck, D. / Ampenberger, M. / Bender, M. / Buermeyer, I. / Geidner, A. / Lahr, H. / Mietzner, M. / Nathusius, E. (2007): Private Equity in Deutschland – Rahmenbedingungen, ökonomische Bedeutung und Handlungsempfehlungen, Books on Demand, Norderstedt.

Keren, G. / Raub, W. (1993): Resolving Social Conflicts Through Hostage Posting: Theoretical and Empirical Considerations, in: Journal of Experimental Psychology: General, 122 (4), pp. 429-448.

KfW Bankengruppe (2009): Unsere Geschichte - 60 Jahre KfW, http://www.kfw.de/DE_Home /Die_Bank/Unsere_Geschichte/index.jsp, KfW Bankengruppe, [Access: 09.09.2009].

King, G. / Zeng, L. (2001): Logistic Regression in Rare Events Data, in: Political Analysis, 9 (2), pp. 137-163.

Klöckner, O. (2008): Changes after Buyouts in Family Businesses, Technische Universität München, Wiesbaden.

Klonowski, D. (2007): The venture capital investment process in emerging markets: Evidence from Central and Eastern Europe, in: International Journal of Emerging Markets, 2 (4), pp. 361-382.

Knill, A.M. (2009): Should Venture Capitalists put all their Eggs in one Basket? Diversification versus pure play strategies in Venture Capital, in: Financial Management, 2009 (Autumn), pp. 441-486.

Knoben, J. / Oerlemans, L.A.G. (2006): Proximity and inter-organizational collaboration: A literature review, in: International Journal of Management Reviews, 8 (2), pp. 71-89.

Knockaert, M. / Lockett, A. / Clarysse, B. / Wright, M. (2006): Do human capital and fund characteristics drive follow-up behaviour of early stage high-tech VCs?, in: International Journal of Technology Management, 34 (1), pp. 7-27.

Knoke, D. / Kuklinski, J.H. (1993): Network analysis, Ed. 8, Sage, Newbury Park.

Kohn, K. / Spengler, H. (2008): KfW-Gründungsmonitor 2008 – Gründungen in Deutschland: weniger aber besser – Chancenmotiv rückt in den Vordergrund, KfW Bankengruppe, Frankfurt a.M.

Komorita, S.S. / Hilty, J.A. / Parks, C.D. (1991): Reciprocity and Cooperation in Social Dilemmas, in: Journal of Conflict Resolution, 35 (3), pp. 494-518.

Korte, C. / Milgram, S. (1970): Acquaintance networks between racial groups: Application of the small world method, in: Journal of Personality and Social Psychology, 15 (2), pp. 101-108.

Kortum, S. / Lerner, J. (2000): Assessing the Contribution of Venture Capital to Innovation, in: RAND Journal of Economics, 31 (4), pp. 674-692.

Krackhardt, D. (1988): Predicting with networks: Nonparametric multiple regression analysis of dyadic data, in: Social Networks, 10 (4), pp. 359-381.

Landström, H. (1992): The relationship between private investors and small firms: An agency theory approach, in: Entrepreneurship and Regional Development, 4 (3), pp. 199-223.

Larson, A. (1991): Partner networks: Leveraging external ties to improve entrepreneurial performance, in: Journal of Business Venturing, 6 (3), pp. 173-188.

Larson, A. (1992): Network Dyads in Entrepreneurial Settings: A Study of the Governance of Exchange Relationships, in: Administrative Science Quarterly, 37 (1), pp. 76-104.

Larson, A. / Starr, J.A. (1993): A Network Model of Organization Formation, in: Entrepreneurship Theory and Practice, 17 (2), pp. 5-15.

Lee, C. / Lee, K. / Pennings, J. (2001): Internal Capabilities, External Networks, and Performance: A Study on Technology-Based Ventures, in: Strategic Management Journal, 22 (6-7), pp. 615-640.

Lee, P.M. / O'Neill, H.M. (2003): Ownership structures and R&D investments of U.S. and Japanese firms: Agency and stewardship perspectives, in: Academy of Management Journal, 46 (2), pp. 212-225.

Leland, H.E. / Pyle, D.H. (1977): Informational Asymmetries, Financial Structure, and Financial Intermediation, in: Journal of Finance, 32 (2), pp. 371-387.

Leopold, G. (1993): Gewinnung von externem Eigenkapital für nicht börsennotierte Unternehmen, in: G. Gebhardt / W. Gerke / M. Steiner (Ed.): Handbuch des Finanzmanagements, C.H. Beck, Munich, pp. 346-364.

Leopold, G. / Frommann, H. (1998): Eigenkapital für den Mittelstand: Venture Capital im In- und Ausland, C.H. Beck, Munich.

Lerner, J. (1994a): The Syndication of Venture Capital Investments, in: Financial Management, 23 (3), pp. 16-27.

Lerner, J. (1994b): Venture capitalists and the decision to go public, in: Journal of Financial Economics, 35 (3), pp. 293-316.

Lerner, J. (1995): Venture capitalists and the oversight of private firms, in: Journal of Finance, 50 (1), pp. 301-318.

Lerner, J. / Schoar, A. (2003): Private equity in the developing world: The determinants of transaction structures, Working paper, 09/2003, MIT.

Lerner, J. / Schoar, A. (2004): The illiquidity puzzle: Theory and evidence from private equity, in: Journal of Financial Economics, 72 (1), pp. 3-40.

LexisNexis (2008): LexisNexis Wirtschaft, www.lexisnexis.com, [Access: 30/11/2008].

Lin, T. / Smith, R. (1998): Insider reputation and selling decisions: The unwinding of venture capital investments during equity IPOs, in: Journal of Corporate Finance, 4 (3), pp. 241-263.

Lincoln, J.R. (1984): Analyzing relations in dyads: Problems, models, and an application to interorganizational research, in: Sociological Methods and Research, 13 (1), pp. 45-76.

Lindskold, S. / Betz, B. / Walters, P.S. (1986): Transforming Competitive or Cooperative Climates, in: Journal of Conflict Resolution, 30 (1), pp. 99-114.

Loasby, B.J. (1999): Knowledge, Institutions and Evolution in Economics, Routledge, London.

Lockett, A. / Wright, M. (2001): The syndication of venture capital investments, in: Omega, 29 (5), pp. 375-390.

Long, J.S. / Freese, J. (2001): Regression models for categorical dependent variables using Stata, Ed. 2, Stata press, College Station.

Lorenzoni, G. / Ornati, O.A. (1988): Constellations of firms and new ventures, in: Journal of Business Venturing, 3 (1), pp. 41-57.

Lossen, U. (2007): Portfolio Strategies of Private Equity Firms – Theory and Evidence, Ludwig Maximilians Universität München, Munich.

Lothian, J.R. (2002): The internationalization of money and finance and the globalization of financial markets, in: Journal of International Money and Finance, 21 (6), pp. 699-724.

Lutz, E. / George, G. (2009): Giving Them Wings to Fly – The Influence of Venture Capitalists on Internationalization in New Ventures, Working Paper, 09/2009, Technische Universität München.

MacMillan, I. / Siegel, R. / Narasimha, P.N.S. (1985): Criteria used by venture capitalists to evaluate new venture proposals, in: Journal of Business Venturing, 1 (1), pp. 119-128.

MacMillan, I. / Zemann, L. / Subbanarasimha, P. (1987): Criteria distinguishing successful from unsuccessful ventures in the venture screening process, in: Journal of Business Venturing, 2 (2), pp. 123-137.

Mäkela, M.M. / Maula, M.V.J. (2008): Attracting cross-border venture capital: The role of a local investor, in: Entrepreneurship and Regional Development, 20 (3), pp. 237-257.

Mäkelä, M.M. / Maula, M.V.J. (2005): Cross-border venture capital and new venture internationalization: An isomorphism perspective, in: Venture Capital: An International Journal of Entrepreneurial Finance, 7 (3), pp. 227-257.

Mäkelä, M.M. / Maula, M.V.J. (2006): Interorganizational Commitment in Syndicated Cross-Border Venture Capital Investments, in: Entrepreneurship Theory and Practice, 30 (2), pp. 273-298.

Manigart, S. / Baeyens, K. / van Hyfte, W. (2002): The survival of venture capital backed companies, in: Venture Capital: An International Journal of Entrepreneurial Finance, 4 (2), pp. 103-124.

Manigart, S. / De Waele, K. / Wright, M. / Robbie, K. / Desbrières, P. / Sapienza, H. / Beekman, A. (2002a): Determinants of required return in venture capital investments: A five-country study, in: Journal of Business Venturing, 17 (4), pp. 291-312.

Manigart, S. / Korsgaard, A. / Folger, R. / Sapienza, H. / Baeyens, K. (2002b): The impact of trust on private equity contracts, Vlerick Working Papers No. 2002/1, 02/2002.

Manigart, S. / Lockett, A. / Meuleman, M. / Wright, M. / Landström, H. / Bruining, H. / Desbrières, P. / Hommel, U. (2002c): Why do European venture capital companies syndicate?, ERS-2002-98-ORG, 10/2002, Erasmus Research Institute of Management.

Manigart, S. / Sapienza, H.J. (1998): Venture-Capital and growth, in: D.L. Sexton (Ed.): The Blackwell handbook of entrepreneurship, Ed. 1, Blackwell, Oxford, pp. 240-258.

Manigart, S. / Wright, M. / Robbie, K. / Desbriéres, P. / De Waele, K. (1997): Venture Capitalists' Appraisal of Investment Projects: An Empirical European Study, in: Entrepreneurship Theory and Practice, 21 (4), pp. 29-43.

Mann, H.B. / Whitney, D.R. (1947): On a test whether one of two random variables is stochastically larger than the other, in: Annals of Mathematical Statistics, 18 (1), pp. 50-60.

Manski, C.F. / Lerman, S.R. (1977): The Estimation of Choice Probabilities from Choice Based Samples, in: Econometrica, 45 (8), pp. 1977-1988.

Marshall, A. ([1890] 1959): Principles of economics, Ed. 8, Macmillan, London.

Martin, R. / Berndt, C. / Klagge, B. / Sunley, P. (2005): Spatial proximity effects and regional equity gaps in the venture capital market: Evidence from Germany and the United Kingdom, in: Environment and Planning A, 37 (7), pp. 1207-1231.

Martin, R. / Sunley, P. / Turner, D. (2002): Taking risks in regions: the geographical anatomy of Europe's emerging venture capital market, in: Journal of Economic Geography, 2 (2), pp. 121-150.

Mason, C.M. (2007): Venture capital: A geographical perspective, in: H. Landström (Ed.): Handbook of Research on Venture Capital, Edward Elgar, Cheltenham, pp. 86-112.

Mason, C.M. / Harrison, R.T. (1992): The supply of equity finance in the UK a strategy for closing the equity gap, in: Entrepreneurship and Regional Development, 1992 (4), pp. 357-380.

Mason, C.M. / Harrison, R.T. (1995): Closing the regional equity capital gap: The role of informal venture capital, in: Small Business Economics, 7 (2), pp. 153-172.

Mason, C.M. / Harrison, R.T. (2002): The Geography of Venture Capital Investments in the UK, in: Transactions of the Institute of British Geographers, 27 (4), pp. 427-452.

Maula, M.V.J. / Autio, E. / Murray, G. (2003): Prerequisites for the creation of social capital and subsequent knowledge acquisition in corporate venture capital, in: Venture Capital, 5 (2), pp. 117.

Mayer, C. / Schoors, K.J. / Yafeh, Y. (2005): Sources of funds and investment activities of venture capital funds: evidence from Germany, Israel, Japan and the United Kingdom, in: Journal of Corporate Finance, 11 (3), pp. 586-608.

McPherson, J.M. (1982): Hypernetwork Sampling: Duality and Differentiation Among Voluntary Associations, in: Social Networks, 3 (4), pp. 225-249.

McPherson, M. / Smith-Lovin, L. / Cook, J.M. (2001): Birds of a Feather: Homophily in Social Networks, in: Annual Review of Sociology, 27 (1), pp. 415-444.

Megginson, W. / Weiss, K. (1991): Venture capitalist certification in initial public offerings, in: Journal of Finance, 46 (3), pp. 879-903.

Mellewigt, T. / Witt, P. (2002): Die Bedeutung des Vorgründungsprozesses für die Evolution von Unternehmen: Stand der empirischen Forschung, in: Zeitschrift für Betriebswirtschaft, 72 (1), pp. 81-110.

Metrick, A. (2006): Venture Capital and the Finance of Innovation, Wiley, New York.

Milgram, S. (1967): The small world problem, in: Psychology Today, 1 (1), pp. 60–67.

Milgrom, P.R. / Roberts, J. (1992): Economics, organization and management, Prentice-Hall, Englewood Cliffs, NJ.

Mitchell, J.C. (1971): The concept and use of social networks, in: J.C. Mitchell (Ed.): Social networks in urban situations, Manchester University Press, Manchester.

Mizruchi, M.S. (1989): Similarity of political behavior among large American corporations, in: American Journal of Sociology, 95 (2), pp. 401-424.

Modigliani, F. / Miller, M. (1958): The cost of capital, corporation finance and the theory of investment, in: American Economic Review, 48 (3), pp. 261-297.

Munich Network (2008): Mission Statement, http://www.munichnetwork.com/bfora/systems/xmlviewer/default.asp?arg=DS_MUN_ABOUTART_2/_page.xsl/5, [Access:24.08.2008].

Murray, G.C. / Lott, J. (1995): Have UK venture capitalists a bias against investment in new technology-based firms?, in: Research Policy, 24 (2), pp. 283-299.

Muth, M.M. / Donaldson, L. (1998): Stewardship Theory and Board Structure: A Contingency Approach, in: Corporate Governance: An International Review, 6 (1), pp. 5-28.

Muzyka, D. / Birley, S. / Leleux, B. (1996): Trade-offs in the investment decisions of European venture capitalists, in: Journal of Business Venturing, 11 (4), pp. 273-287.

Myers, S. (1977): Determinants of corporate borrowing, in: Journal of Financial Economics, 5 (2), pp. 147-175.

Nagtegaal, T. (1999): Post investment – venture management, in: W. Bygrave / M. Hay / J. Peeters (Ed.): The venture capital handbook, Pearson Education, Harlow, pp. 183-201.

Nahapiet, J. / Ghoshal, S. (1998): Social capital, intellectual capital, and the organizational advantage, in: Academy of Management Review, 23 (2), pp. 242-266.

Nalebuff, B.J. / Brandenburger, A.M. (1996): Coopetition – kooperativ konkurrieren, Campus Fachbuch, Frankfurt a.M.

Nash, J.F. (1950): Equilibrium Points in N-Person Games, in: Proceedings of the National Academy of Sciences of the United States of America, 36 (1), pp. 48-49.

Nathusius, E. (2005): Syndizierte Venture-Capital-Finanzierung, Technische Universität München, Sternenfels.

Nathusius, K. (2001): Grundlagen der Gründungsfinanzierung, Gabler, Wiesbaden.

Natusch, I. (2002): Due Diligence aus Sicht einer Beteiligungsgesellschaft, in: W. Berens / H. Brauner / J. Strauch (Ed.): Due Diligence bei Unternehmensakquisitionen, Ed. 3, Schäffer-Poeschel, Stuttgart, pp. 537-553.

Neuss, W. (2001): Einführung in die Betriebswirtschaftslehre aus institutionenökonomischer Sicht, Ed. 2, Mohr Siebeck, Tübingen.

Newcomb, T.M. (1961): The acquaintance process, Holt, Rinehart and Winston, New York.

Niederöcker, B. (2002): Finanzierungsalternativen in kleinen und mittleren Unternehmen, Technische Universität Ilmenau, Wiesbaden.

Niefert, M. / Metzger, G. / Heger, D. / Licht, G. (2006): Hichtech-Gründungen in Deutschland: Trends und Entwicklungsperspektiven, Zentrum für Europäische Wirtschaftsforschung, Mannheim.

North, D.C. / Thomas, R.P. (1973): The Rise of the Western World: A New Economic History, Cambridge University Press, Cambridge.

Norton, E. / Tenenbaum, B.H. (1993): Specialization versus diversification as a venture capital investment strategy, in: Journal of Business Venturing, 8 (5), pp. 431-442.

OECD (1996): Venture capital and innovation, Organisation for economic co-operation and development, Paris.

Ouchi, W.G. (1980): Markets, Bureaucracies, and Clans, in: Administrative Science Quarterly, 25 (1), pp. 129-141.

Pappi, F.U. (1987): Die Netzwerkanalyse aus soziologischer Perspektive, in: F.U. Pappi (Ed.): Methoden der Netzwerkanalyse, Oldenbourg, Munich, pp. 11-37.

Parkhe, A. (1993): Strategie alliance structuring: A game theoretic and transaction cost examination of interfirm cooperation, in: Academy of Management Journal, 36 (4), pp. 794-829.

Patton, D. / Kenney, M. (2005): The spatial configuration of the entrepreneurial support network for the semiconductor industry, in: R&D Management, 35 (1), pp. 1-16.

Pauly, M.V. (1968): The Economics of Moral Hazard: Comment, in: American Economic Review, 58 (3), pp. 531-537.

Perridon, L. / Steiner, M. (2004): Finanzwirtschaft der Unternehmung, Ed. 13, Vahlen, Munich.

Petersen, M.A. / Rajan, R.G. (2002): Does Distance Still Matter? The Information Revolution in Small Business Lending, in: Journal of Finance, 57 (6), pp. 2533-2570.

Picot, A. (1982): Transaktionskostenansatz in der Organisationstheorie: Stand der Diskussion und Aussagewert, in: Die Betriebswirtschaft, 42 (2), pp. 267-283.

Picot, A. (1991): Ökonomische Theorien der Organisation – Ein Überblick über neuere Ansätze und deren betriebswirtschaftliches Anwendungspotential, in: D. Ordelheide / B. Rudolph / E. Büsselmann (Ed.): Betriebswirtschaftslehre und Ökonomische Theorie, Schäffer-Poeschel, Stuttgart, pp. 143-170.

Picot, A. / Dietl, H. / Franck, E. (2005): Organisation – Eine ökonomische Perspektive, Ed. 4, Schäffer-Poeschel, Stuttgart.

Picot, A. / Reichwald, R. / Wigand, R. (2001): Die grenzenlose Unternehmung, Ed. 4, Gabler, Wiesbaden.

Poindexter, J.B. (1976): The Efficiency of Financial Markets: The Venture Capital Case, New York University, New York.

Polanyi, M. (1967): The tacit dimension, Routledge and Kegan Paul, London.

Popper, K. (1949): Naturgesetze und theoretische Systeme, in: S. Moser (Ed.): Gesetz und Wirklichkeit, Tyrolia, Innsbruck, pp. 43-60.

Popper, K. (1973): Kübelmodell und Scheinwerfermodell: zwei Theorien der Erkenntnis, in: K. Popper (Ed.): Objektive Erkenntnis, Hoffmann und Campe, Hamburg, pp. 369-390.

Porter, M.E. (1998): Clusters and the New Economics of Competition, in: Harvard Business Review, 76 (6), pp. 77-90.

Porter, M.E. (2000): Location, competition, and economic development: Local clusters in a global economy, in: Economic Development Quarterly, 14 (1), pp. 15-34.

Portes, A. (1998): Social Capital: Its Origins and Applications in Modern Sociology, in: Annual Review of Sociology, 24 (1), pp. 1-24.

Powell, W.W. (1990): Neither Market Nor Hierarchy: Network Forms of Organization, in: Research in Organizational Behavior, 12, pp. 295-336.

Powell, W.W. / Koput, K.W. / Bowie, J.I. / Smith-Doerrs, L. (2002): The Spatial Clustering of Science and Capital: Accounting for Biotech Firm-Venture Capital Relationships, in: Regional Studies, 36 (3), pp. 291-205.

Pratt, J.W. / Zeckhauser, R.J. (1985): Principals and Agents: An Overview, in: J.W. Pratt / R.J. Zeckhauser (Ed.): Principals and Agents: The Structure of Business, Harvard Business School, Boston, pp. 1-35.

Preston, L.E. (1998): Dialogue: Agents, Stewards, and Stakeholders, in: Academy of Management Review, 23 (1), pp. 9.

Pries, F. / Guild, P. (2002): Variability in the Importance Assigned to Investment Decision Criteria by Venture Capitalists, Working Paper, Department of Management Sciences, University of Waterloo, 04/2004.

Pruitt, D.G. (1967): Reward structure and cooperation: The decomposed Prisoner's Dilemma game, in: Journal of Personality and Social Psychology, 7 (1), pp. 21-27.

Puri, M. / Zarutskie, R. (2009): On the Lifecycle Dynamics of Venture-Capital- and Non-Venture-Capital-Financed Firms, EFA 2007 Ljubljana Meetings Paper, US Census Bureau Center for Economic Studies Paper No. CES-WP-08-13, 06/2009, Duke University - Fuqua School of Business.

Rammert, W. (1997): Innovation im Netz : Neue Zeiten für technische Innovationen: heterogen verteilt und interaktiv vernetzt, in: Soziale Welt, 48 (4), pp. 397-415.

Rees, R. (1985): The Theory of Principal and Agent: Part 1, in: Bulletin of Economic Research, 37 (1), pp. 3-26.

Richter, R. / Furubotn, E.G. (2003): Neue Institutionenökonomik, Ed. 3, Mohr Siebeck, Tübingen.

Riquelme, H. / Rickards, T. (1992): Hybrid conjoint analysis: An estimation probe in new venture decisions, in: Journal of Business Venturing, 7 (6), pp. 505-518.

Ritter, J.R. (2003): Behavioral finance, in: Pacific-Basin Finance Journal, 11 (4), pp. 429-437.

Robbie, K. / Wright, M. / Chiplin, B. (1997): The monitoring of venture capital firms, in: Entrepreneurship Theory and Practice, 21 (4), pp. 9-27.

Roberts, J. / McNulty, T. / Stiles, P. (2005): Beyond Agency Conceptions of the Work of the Non-Executive Director: Creating Accountability in the Boardroom, in: British Journal of Management, 16 (Supplement 1), pp. 5-26.

Robinson, R. (1987): Emerging strategies in the venture capital industry, in: Journal of Business Venturing, 2 (1), pp. 53-77.

Rosenstein, J. / Bruno, A. / Bygrave, W. / Taylor, N. (1993): The CEO, venture capitalists, and the board, in: Journal of Business Venturing, 8 (2), pp. 99-113.

Ross, S. (1973): The Economic Theory of Agency: The Principal's Problem, in: American Economic Review, 63 (2), pp. 134-139.

Ross, S. (1977): The Determination of Financial Structure: The Incentive Signalling Approach, in: Bell Journal of Economics, 8 (1), pp. 23-40.

Rousseeuw, P.J. / Leroy, A.M. (2003): Robust regression and outlier detection, Wiley, New York.

Rubin, J.S. (2001): Community development Venture Capital. A double bottom line approach to poverty alleviation, in: Proceedings of the Changing Financial Markets and Community Development conference, Washington, D.C.: Federal Reserve April 4-6, 2001, pp. 121-154.

Rusbult, C.E. (1980): Commitment and satisfaction in romantic associations: A test of the investment model, in: Journal of Experimental Social Psychology, 16 (2), pp. 172-186.

Sahlman, W.A. (1990): The structure and governance of venture-capital organizations, in: Journal of Financial Economics, 27 (2), pp. 473-521.

Samila, S. / Sorenson, O. (2008): Venture Capital, Entrepreneurship, and Regional Economic Growth, Working Paper, 08/2008, Brock University, University of Toronto.

Sandberg, W.R. / Schweiger, D.M. / Hofer, C.W. (1988): The Use of Verbal Protocols in Determining Venture Capitalists' Decision Process, in: Entrepreneurship Theory and Practice, 13 (2), pp. 8-20.

Sapienza, H.J. (1992): When do venture capitalists add value?, in: Journal of Business Venturing, 7 (1), pp. 9-27.

Sapienza, H.J. / Amason, A. (1993): Effects of innovativeness and venture stage on venture capitalist-entrepreneur relations, in: Interfaces, 23 (6), pp. 38-51.

Sapienza, H.J. / Amason, A. / Manigart, S. (1994): The level and nature of venture capitalist involvement in their portfolio companies: a study of three European countries, in: Managerial Finance, 20 (1), pp. 3-17.

Sapienza, H.J. / De Clercq, D. (2000): Venture Capitalist-Entrepreneur Relationships in Technology-Based Ventures, in: Enterprise and Innovation Management Studies, 1 (1), pp. 57-71.

Sapienza, H.J. / Gupta, A. (1994): Impact of agency risks and task uncertainty on venture capitalist-CEO interaction, in: Academy of Management Journal, 37 (6), pp. 1618-1632.

Sapienza, H.J. / Korsgaard, M.A. (1996): Procedural Justice in entrepreneur-investor relations, in: Academy of Management Journal, 39 (3), pp. 544-574.

Sapienza, H.J. / Manigart, S. / Vermeir, W. (1996): Venture capitalist governance and value added in four countries, in: Journal of Business Venturing, 11 (6), pp. 439-469.

Sapienza, H.J. / Timmons, J. (1989): The roles of venture capitalists in new ventures: What determines their importance?, in: Academy of Management Best Papers Proceedings, pp. 74-78.

Sapienza, H.J. / Villanueva, J. (2007): Conceptual and theoretical reflections on venture capital research, in: H. Landström (Ed.): Handbook of Research on Venture Capital, Edward Elgar, Cheltenham, pp. 66-85.

Saunders, M. / Lewis, P. / Thornhill, A. (2007a): The nature of business and management research and structure of this book, in: M. Saunders / P. Lewis / A. Thornhill (Ed.): Research Methods for Business Students, Ed. 4, Pearson Education, Harlow, pp. 2-17.

Saunders, M. / Lewis, P. / Thornhill, A. (2007b): Understanding research philosophies and approaches, in: M. Saunders / P. Lewis / A. Thornhill (Ed.): Research Methods for Business Students, Ed. 4, Pearson Education, Harlow, pp. 100-129.

Schefczyk, M. (1999): Erfolgsdeterminanten von Venture Capital-Investments in Deutschland, in: Zeitschrift für betriebswirtschaftliche Forschung, 51 (12), pp. 1123-1145.

Schefczyk, M. (2004): Erfolgsstrategien deutscher Venture Capital-Gesellschaften: Eine Analyse der Investitionsaktivitäten und des Beteiligungsmanagements von Venture Capital-Gesellschaften, Ed. 3, Schäffer-Poeschel, Stuttgart.

Scherer, A.G. (2006): Kritik der Organisation oder Organisation der Kritik? – Wissenschaftstheoretische Bemerkungen zum kritischen Umgang mit Organisationstheorien, in: A. Kieser / M. Ebers (Ed.): Organisationstheorien, Ed. 6, Kohlhammer, Stuttgart, pp. 19-61.

Schertler, A. (2001): Venture Capital in Europe´s common Market: A Quantative Description, Working Paper No. 01-4, 11/2001, Kiel Institute of World Economics.

Schmidt, K.M. (2003): Convertible Securities and Venture Capital Finance, in: Journal of Finance, 58 (3), pp. 1139-1166.

Schmidt, R.H. (1988): Neuere Property Rights-Analysen in der Finanzierungstheorie, in: D. Budäus / E. Gerum / G. Zimmermann (Ed.): Betriebswirtschaftslehre und Theorie der Verfügungsrechte, Gabler, Wiesbaden, pp. 239-268.

Schmidt, R.H. / Terberger, E. (1997): Grundzüge der Investitions- und Finanzierungstheorie, Ed. 4, Gabler, Wiesbaden.

Schüller, A. (1983): Einführung, in: A. Schüller (Ed.): Property Rights und ökonomische Theorie, Vahlen, Munich, pp. VII-XXI.

Schulz, E. (2000): Die Finanzierung von Existenzgründungen – Eine informationsökonomische Analyse, Westfälische Wilhelms-Universität Münster, Frankfurt a.M.

Schumpeter, J.A. (1942): Capitalism, Socialism and Democracy, Harper and Brothers, New York.

Schwartz, D. / Bar-El, R. (2007): Venture Investments in Israel – a Regional Perspective, in: European Planning Studies, 15 (5), pp. 623-644.

Scott, J. (1988): Social Network Analysis, in: Sociology, 22 (1), pp. 109-127.

Shane, S. / Cable, D. (2002): Network Ties, Reputation, and the Financing of New Ventures, in: Management Science, 48 (3), pp. 364-381.

Shane, S.A. (2004): Academic Entrepreneurship: University Spinoffs and Wealth Creation, Edward Elgar, Cheltenham.

Shefrin, H. (2000): Beyond Greed and Fear. Understanding Behavioral Finance and the Psychology of Investing, Oxford University Press, Boston.

Shepherd, D.A. (1999): Venture Capitalists' Introspection: A Comparison of "In Use" and "Espoused" Decision Policies, in: Journal of Small Business Management, 37 (2), pp. 76-87.

Shepherd, D.A. / Zacharakis, A. (1999): Conjoint analysis: a new methodological approach for researching the decision policies of venture capitalists, in: Venture Capital, 1 (3), pp. 197-217.

Shepherd, D.A. / Zacharakis, A. (2001): The venture capitalist-entrepreneur relationship: control, trust and confidence in co-operative behaviour, in: Venture Capital, 3 (2), pp. 129-149.

Sherling, C. (1999): Deal structuring and pricing, in: W.D. Bygrave / M. Hay / J.B. Peeters (Ed.): The venture capital handbook, Pearson Education, Harlow, pp. 163-182.

Shleifer, A. / Vishny, R.W. (1992): Liquidation Values and Debt Capacity: A Market Equilibrium Approach, in: Journal of Finance, 47 (4), pp. 1343-1366.

Söderblom, A. / Wiklund, J. (2006): Factors determining the performance of early stage high-technology venture capital funds – A review of the academic literature, 03/2006, Stockholm School of Economics.

Sorenson, O. / Stuart, T.E. (2001): Syndication Networks and the Spatial Distribution of Venture Capital Investments, in: American Journal of Sociology, 106 (6), pp. 1546-1588.

Spence, M. (1973): Job Market Signaling, in: Quarterly Journal of Economics, 87 (3), pp. 355-374.

Spremann, K. (1987): Agent and Principal, in: G. Bamberg / K. Spremann (Ed.): Agency theory, information, and incentives, Springer, Berlin, pp. 3-37.

Spremann, K. (1988): Reputation, Garantie, Information, in: Zeitschrift für Betriebswirtschaft, 58, pp. 613-629.

Spremann, K. (1990): Asymmetrische Information, in: Zeitschrift für Betriebswirtschaft, 60 (5/6), pp. 561-586.

Statistisches Bundesamt Deutschland (2009): GENESIS-Online, https://www-genesis.destatis.de/genesis/online/logon.

Steier, L. / Greenwood, R. (1995): Venture Capitalist relationship in the deal structuring and post-investment stages of new firm creation, in: Journal of Management Studies, 32 (3), pp. 337-357.

Sternberg, R. / Brixy, U. / Hundt, C. (2007): Global Entrepreneurship Monitor – Unternehmensgründungen im weltweiten Vergleich – Länderbericht Deutschland 2006, Ed. 1, Institut für Arbeitsmarkt- und Berufsforschung, Hannover.

Stuart, T.E. (1998): Network Positions and Propensities to Collaborate: An Investigation of Strategic Alliance Formation in a High-technology Industry, in: Administrative Science Quarterly, 43 (3), pp. 668-698.

Stuart, T.E. / Sorenson, O. (2003): The geography of opportunity: Spatial heterogeneity in founding rates and the performance of biotechnology firms, in: Research Policy, 32 (2), pp. 229-253.

Sunley, P. / Klagge, B. / Berndt, C. / Martin, R. (2005): Venture Capital Programmes in the UK and Germany: In what sense Regional Policies?, in: Regional Studies, 39 (2), pp. 255-273.

Svenson, O. (1979): Process descriptions of decision-making, in: Organizational Behavior and Human Decision Processes, 23 (1), pp. 86-112.

Sweeting, R. (1991): UK venture capital funds and the funding of new technology-based businesses: process and relationships, in: Journal of Management Studies, 28 (6), pp. 601-622.

Sweeting, R. / Wong, C. (1997): A UK 'hands-off' venture capital firm and the handling of post-investment investor-investee relationships, in: Journal of Management Studies, 34 (1), pp. 125-152.

Sydow, J. (1992a): Strategische Netzwerke – Evolution und Organisation, Gabler, Wiesbaden.

Sydow, J. (1992b): Strategische Netzwerke und Transaktionskosten. Über die Grenzen einer transaktionstheoretischen Erklärung der Evolution strategischer Netzwerke, in: W.H. Staehle / P. Conrad (Ed.): Managementforschung 2., Gabler, Wiesbaden, pp. 239-311.

The New York Times (2006): It's not the people you know. It's where you are, 10/22/2006.

Thibaut, J.W. / Kelley, H.H. (1959): The social psychology of groups, Wiley, New York.

Tian, X. (2009): Geography and the Structure of Venture Capital Financing, EFA 2007 Ljubljana Meetings Paper, 05/2009, Indiana University Bloomington.

Timmons, J. / Bygrave, W. (1986): Venture capital's role in financing innovation for economic growth, in: Journal of Business Venturing, 1 (2), pp. 161-176.

Tomz, M. / King, G. / Zeng, L. (1999): ReLogit: Rare Events Logistic Regression Software, http://gking.harvard.edu/stats.shtml#relogit, [Access: 30.10.2008].

Travers, J. / Milgram, S. (1969): An Experimental Study of the Small World Problem, in: Sociometry, 32 (4), pp. 425-443.

Trester, J.J. (1998): Venture Capital Contracting under Asymmetric Information, in: Journal of Banking and Finance, 22 (6-8), pp. 675-699.

Turner, J.H. (1978): Review: A Theory of Social Structure: An Assessment of Blau's Strategy, in: Contemporary Sociology, 7 (6), pp. 698-704.

Tyebjee, T. / Bruno, A. (1984a): A model of venture capitalist investment activity, in: Management Science, 30 (9), pp. 1051-1066.

Tyebjee, T. / Bruno, A. (1984b): Venture capital: Investor and investee perspectives, in: Technovation, 2 (3), pp. 185-208.

Tykvová, T. / Schertler, A. (2008): Syndication to Overcome Long Distances? Evidence from a Worldwide Private Equity Deals' Dataset, Conference paper, 11th Symposium on Finance, Banking, and Insurance, ZEW Mannheim, Kiel University.

Uysal, V.B. / Kedia, S. / Panchapagesan, V. (2008): Geography and acquirer returns, in: Journal of Financial Intermediation, 17 (2), pp. 256-275.

Uzzi, B. / Gillespie, J. (1999): Corporate social capital and the cost of financial capital: An embeddedness approach, in: R. Leenders / S. Gabbay (Ed.): Corporate Social Capital and Liability, Kluwer Academic Publishers, Boston.

van Slyke, D.M. (2007): Agents or Stewards: Using Theory to Understand the Government-Nonprofit Social Service Contracting Relationship in: Journal of Public Administration Research and Theory, 17 (2), pp. 157-187.

Vargas Sánchez, A. (2004): Development of Corporate Governance Systems: Agency Theory versus Stewardship Theory in Welsh Agrarian Cooperative Societies, Ponencia presentada en el 4º Congreso Anual de EURAM, 05/2004.

Vater, D. (2003): Die Qualität deutscher Private-Equity-Unternehmen – Optimierungsmöglichkeiten bei der Vergabe von Beteiligungskapital, DUV, Wiesbaden.

VentureSource (2007): Help, www.venturesource.com, DowJones VentureOne, [Access: 21/03/2007].

Vogel, B. (2001): Role of the venture capitalist, in: Der Schweizer Treuhänder, 11 (1), pp. 1049-1054.

von Neumann, J. / Morgenstern, O. (1944): Theory of Games and Economic Behavior, Princeton University Press, Princeton.

Wahl, S. (2004): Private Debt – Private Fremdkapital- und Mezzanine-Kapital-Platzierungen bei institutionellen Investoren, Technische Universität München, Sternenfels.

Wasserman, N. (2006): Stewards, agents, and the founder discount: Executive compensation in new ventures, in: Academy of Management Journal, 49 (5), pp. 960-976.

Wasserman, S. / Faust, K. (1994): Social Network Analysis: Methods and Applications, Cambridge University Press, Cambridge.

Weber, M. (1976): Wirtschaft und Gesellschaft, Ed. 5, Mohr, Tübingen.

Weitnauer, W. (2001): Handbuch Venture Capital – Von der Innovation zum Börsengang, Ed. 2, C.H. Beck, Munich.

Wells, W.A. (1974): Venture Capital Decision-Making, Carnegie-Mellon University.

Welpe, I.M. (2004): Venture-Capital-Geber und ihre Portfoliounternehmen – Erfolgsfaktoren der Kooperation, Universität Regensburg, Regensburg.

Welpe, I.M. (2008): Die Entstehung von Vertrauen im Kontext von Unsicherheit und Informationsasymmetrie, in: Zeitschrift für Betriebswirtschaft, 78 (12), pp. 1251-1284.

Welpe, I.M. / Dowling, M. (2005): Venture-Capital-Finanzierung aus Sicht der Portfoliounternehmen, in: C.J. Börner / D. Grichnik (Ed.): Entrepreneurial Finance: Kompendium der Gründungs- und Wachstumsfinanzierung, Physica, Heidelberg, pp. 277-299.

Weyer, J. (2000): Einleitung – Zum Stand der Netzwerkforschung in den Sozialwissenschaften, in: J. Weyer (Ed.): Soziale Netzwerke, Oldenbourg, Munich, pp. 1-34.

WGZ Bank (2009): Der FinanzVerbund, http://www.wgz-bank.de/de/wgzbank/unternehmen/ueber-uns/finanzverbund/index.html, [Access: 11.09.2009].

White, H. (1980): A heteroskedasticity-consistent covariance matrix estimator and a direct test for heteroskedasticity, in: Econometrica: Journal of the Econometric Society, 48 (4), pp. 817-838.

Wijbenga, F.H. / van Witteloostuijn, A. (2006): The Entrepreneur and the Venture Capitalist as a Team – A Game-theoretic and Upper-echelon Theory of Cooperation and Defection, in: J.E. Butler / A. Lockett / D. Ucbasaran (Ed.): Venture Capital in the Changing World of Entrepreneurship, IAP, Greenwich, pp. 91-114.

Wilcoxon, F. (1945): Individual comparisons by ranking methods, in: Biometrics Bulletin, 1 (6), pp. 80-83.

Williamson, O.E. (1975): Markets and hierarchies: analysis and antitrust implications, Ed. 4, Free Press, New York.

Williamson, O.E. (1979): Transaction-cost economies: the governance of contractual relations, in: Journal of Law and Economics, 22 (2), pp. 233-261.

Williamson, O.E. (1981): The Economics of Organization: The Transaction Cost Approach, in: American Journal of Sociology, 87 (3), pp. 548-577.

Williamson, O.E. (1985): The Economic Institutions of Capitalism. Firms, Market, Relational Contracting, Macmillan, New York.

Williamson, O.E. (1988): Corporate Finance and Corporate Governance, in: Journal of Finance, 43 (3), pp. 567-591.

Wilmerding, A. (2003): Term sheets & valuations – An inside look at the intricacies of term sheets & valuations, Aspatore Books, Boston.

Wöhe, G. / Bilstein, J. (2002): Grundzüge der Unternehmensfinanzierung, Ed. 9, Vahlen, Munich.

Wolf, J. (2005): Organisation, Management, Unternehmensführung – Theorien und Kritik, Ed. 2, Gabler, Wiesbaden.

Wooldridge, J.M. (2008): Introductory econometrics: A modern approach, Ed. 4, South-Western, Mason, OH.

Wright, M. / Lockett, A. (2002): Structure and management of syndicated venture capital investments, in: Journal of Private Equity, 5 (4), pp. 72-83.

Wright, M. / Lockett, A. (2003): The Structure and Management of Alliances: Syndication in Venture Capital Industry in: Journal of Management Studies, 40 (8), pp. 2073-2102.

Wright, M. / Lockett, A. / Pruthi, S. (2002): Internationalization of Western venture capitalists into emerging markets: risk assessment and information in India, in: Small Business Economics, 19 (1), pp. 13-29.

Wright, M. / Pruthi, S. / Lockett, A. (2005): International venture capital research: From cross-country comparisons to crossing borders, in: International Journal of Management Reviews, 7 (3), pp. 135-165.

Wright, M. / Robbie, K. (1998): Venture capital and private equity: A review and synthesis, in: Journal of Business Finance and Accounting, 25 (5/6), pp. 521-570.

Wright, M. / Thompson, S. / Robbie, K. / Wong, P. (1995): Management buy-outs in the short and long term, in: Journal of Business Finance and Accounting, 22 (4), pp. 461-482.

Zacharakis, A.L. (2007): Venture capitalists' decision policies across three countries: an institutional theory perspective, in: Journal of International Business Studies, 38 (5), pp. 691-708.

Zacharakis, A.L. / Meyer, D. (1998): A lack of insight: do venture capitalists really understand their own decision process?, in: Journal of Business Venturing, 13 (1), pp. 57-76.

Zacharakis, A.L. / Shepherd, D.A. (2001): The Nature of Information and Overconfidence on Venture Capitalists' Decision Making, in: Journal of Business Venturing, 16 (4), pp. 311.

Zemel, E. (1989): Small talk and cooperation: A note on bounded rationality, in: Journal of Economic Theory, 49 (1), pp. 1-9.

Zook, M.A. (2002): Grounded capital: venture financing and the geography of the internet industry, 1994-2000, in: Journal of Economic Geography, 2 (2), pp. 151-177.

Zook, M.A. (2004): The knowledge brokers: venture capitalists, tacit knowledge and regional development, in: International Journal of Urban & Regional Research, 28 (3), pp. 621-641.

Zook, M.A. (2005): The Geography of the Internet Industry, Ed. 1, Blackwell, Oxford.

Zutshi, R. / Tan, W. / Allampalli, D. / Gibbons, P. (1999): Singapore venture capitalists (VCs) investment evaluation criteria: A re-examination, in: Small Business Economics, 13 (1), pp. 9-26.

MIX
Papier aus verantwortungsvollen Quellen
Paper from responsible sources
FSC® C105338

If you have any concerns about our products,
you can contact us on
ProductSafety@springernature.com

In case Publisher is established outside the EU,
the EU authorized representative is:
Springer Nature Customer Service Center GmbH
Europaplatz 3, 69115 Heidelberg, Germany

Printed by Libri Plureos GmbH
in Hamburg, Germany